The Tomes of Delphi 3: Win32 Core API

by John Ayres, David Bowden, Larry Diehl, Phil Dorcas, Kenneth Harrison, Rod Mathes, Ovais Reza, and Mike Tobin

Wordware Publishing, Inc.

Library of Congress Cataloging-in-Publication Data

Ayres, John.
The tomes of Delphi 3 : Win32 core API / by John Ayres, David
Bowden, Larry Diehl.
p. cm.
Includes index.
ISBN 1-55622-556-3 (pbk)
1. Computer software—Development. 2. Delphi (Computer file)
3. Microsoft Win32. I. Bowden, David, 1966- . II. Diehl, Larry.
III. Title.
QA76.76.D47A923 1997 97-35969
005.26'8--dc21 CIP

2320 Los Rios Boulevard
Plano, Texas 75074

Printed in the United States of America

ISBN 1-55622-556-3
10 9 8 7 6 5 4 3 2
9711

All inquiries for volume purchases of this book should be addressed to Wordware Publishing, Inc., at the above address. Telephone inquiries may be made by calling:

(972) 423-0090

Dedication

John Ayres

I would like to dedicate this book to the following people and/or deities who have had a profound influence in my life: First, to God, whom I've been growing much closer to these last few years, for giving me the intelligence to wade through the confusing and sometimes maddening sea of Windows API documentation and make sense of it all; second, to my family, for putting up with my lack of participation in family activities during this project; and finally, but most of all, to my wife and soulmate, Marci, who made sure I had clothes to wear in the morning, food in the evening, fixed my lunches, and generally took up all of my housework responsibilities so I could concentrate on the book. She encouraged me and prodded me along when the weight of this project became unbearable, and because of this she is directly responsible for this work being completed. She is a very inspiring task master; cracking the whip to bring me in line when I would have rather been playing X-Wing Vs. Tie Fighter, she earned the nickname "Dragon Lady" from the guys on the writing staff when she used the same tactics to motivate them. I am unworthy of such a devoted and loving wife, and I thank God every day for providing me with such a perfect companion. Baby, this one's for you.

David Bowden

To Desireé and Ryan for their never-ending love and support; I could not ask for better children. It is not easy having a daddy who is driven. Thanks for being understanding and letting me be a dreamer for just a while. To my parents for their lifelong support and encouragement. Finally, to Don C. Allred for watching over me. I'm finally starting to fly low and slow, Papa; I wish you were here to see it.

Larry Diehl

I dedicate my work on this book to the past and to the future. From the bottom of my soul, I thank my wife, parents, and brother for their unwavering support through the years. That support has allowed me to reach a point in my life where I am as happy as any man could ever wish to be. In regards to the future, I only hope that our work here will in some way contribute to a better world, into which my first child shall soon be born. As for the present, it is what you make of it . . .

Phil Dorcas

To my daughters, Jennifer and Amanda, who are the joy of my life.

Kenneth Harrison

I would like to dedicate this book to my parents, Melvin and Judith Harrison, for all the sacrifices they made to provide myself and my siblings a safe, nurturing environment to grow up in, and the continuous belief that we could do anything we set our minds to. I would also like to thank Daniel Roberts and Stethman Grayson for all the fundamental knowledge of Windows and for being such good friends.

Rod Mathes

I would like to thank all of the co-authors for giving me this opportunity to be a part of such a great masterpiece. A very special thanks to John Ayres for allowing me to live even though some things were a little late at times. I would also like to give a really big thanks to my wife, Sherry, and three children, Keith, Kimberly, and Amber, who for nights on end had to live without me, but through it all we made it—we do have a life, wow!

Ovais Reza

This book is dedicated to my family and friends.

Mike Tobin

To my wife, Lisa, for putting up with my late hours on the book so close to our wedding and to my four cats for the company during those late hours.

Contents

About the Authors

John Ayres

John Ayres developed his love of programming using early home PC predecessors such as the Texas Instruments TI 99/4A and the Commodore 64. He got his start in the real world by taking classes in C and Pascal at the University of North Texas, where he participated in an advanced experimental course in computer game programming started by Dr. Ian Parberry. After college, he worked as a developer support technician at Stream International, where he authored numerous technical training manuals, and along with Kenneth Harrison produced his first professional application using Delphi 1, a call tracking database program. He moved on to become the lead developer for Puzzled Software, using Delphi 2, and also worked as a software engineer for 7th Level, where he worked on the Li'l Howie series of children's educational games. Currently, John works in Dallas at Ensemble, Inc., using Delphi 3 to create high-end client-server applications for Fortune 500 clients. He also serves on the board of directors for the Delphi Developers of Dallas users group as the director of vendor relations, contributing regularly to the group's newsletter. He has developed numerous Delphi components and shareware utilities, and has written articles for the *Delphi Informant*, including the cover article of the February 1997 issue.

David Bowden

Dave Bowden is the general manager of DemoShield Corporation (a division of InstallShield Corporation) where he is in charge of product design and development, domestic and international sales, and strategic business alliances. Bowden has over ten years of experience in programming, design, and graphics ranging from multimedia and photorealistic imagery to software interface design. Bowden began programming in 1982 on a Timex-Sinclair computer and moved on to the development of computer-aided drafting applications and multimedia/graphics programming.

Larry Diehl

Larry Diehl is a quality assurance engineer with InstallShield Corporation where he is responsible for not only testing software but also aids in communication and guidance issues necessary to bring to market award winning applications which meet the needs of users worldwide. Over the course of nearly 15 years, Diehl has used various programming languages but currently uses Borland's Delphi exclusively for work related utilities as well as shareware applications he produces in his spare time.

Phil Dorcas

Phil Dorcas received his degree in physics from Texas Tech in 1969, and has done graduate work in physics, electrical engineering, and computer science. He was co-owner and manager of the second computer store in Texas. He has worked as consultant and designer on numerous hardware and software projects. As an author he has contributed to computer coursework for junior colleges and trade schools and written computer columns for industry magazines. Phil has used Turbo Pascal since the first version for CP/M, and now enjoys Delphi as his development tool of choice.

Kenneth Harrison

Kenneth Harrison is a tools developer for Stream International. In his current position he is developing internal applications in Delphi, Visual Basic, and Access to automate and optimize the technical support call center environment. He has been working in the computer field for the last six years. Kenneth started in the computer field as a graphical imaging technician with Comedia Creative, a graphical imaging and presentation company in Richardson, Texas. Kenneth is also an officer of the Delphi Developers of Dallas in the position of Webmaster.

Rod Mathes

Rod Mathes has been programming for the past 12 years in several different languages including Cobol, RPGII, dBase, RBase, Pascal, and C++. He is currently a Delphi developer for Stream International, developing a wide range of software products for internal use. He has been a member of the Delphi Developers of Dallas for the past year, and has recently accepted a position on the board of directors.

Ovais Reza

Ovais Reza is a programmer/analyst working for First American. He is an experienced programmer in C/C++ and Delphi. He did his undergraduate work at Western Michigan University and is an active member of the Delphi Developers of Dallas users group. Ovais has seven years of PC- and UNIX-related experience. Currently, he is living in the Dallas area. Besides programming and pondering on the philosophies of the East, he likes to watch "The Simpsons" and old episodes of "Star Trek." His future goal is to receive his doctorate in neural networks.

Mike Tobin

Mike Tobin has been working with Delphi since version 1.0. Mike began his career in criminal justice but after realizing his purpose as a hacker, he left to join the software industry. He is currently a senior systems engineer for American General in Dallas and plays an active role in the Delphi Developers of Dallas users group as the director of communication. He enjoys spending time with his new bride, Lisa, and their four cats, Elisabeth, Alexander, Einstein, and Copernicus.

Acknowledgments

Teamwork. This abstract concept leads one to think of other abstract concepts such as victory, accomplishment, and conquest. Teamwork is the secret ingredient behind innumerable triumphs throughout history, and so it was with this book. The eight of us on the writing staff put in many long, hard hours, but this project would not have been completed without the help of so many generous, caring people. In an effort to give credit to those who deserve so much more, the writers would like to collectively thank the following people, in no particular order, for their contributions to the book:

Marian Broussard, who was our front-line proofreader. She ruthlessly pointed out all of our grammar mistakes and spelling errors, and helped correct a lot of inconsistencies in the book. She selflessly volunteered her time to help a group of new writers accurately and clearly transcribe their thoughts to paper.

Joe Hecht, our mentor and idol. Joe was always eager to answer any questions we had, looked at our code and pointed out our mistakes when we were having problems, and pointed us in the right direction when Microsoft's API documentation became a little confusing.

Jim Hill and all the good people down at Wordware Publishing, who took a chance on a bunch of eager, enthusiastic, greenhorn writers. He kept us in line, on track, and even took us all out for dinner once in a while.

DemoShield Consulting Services' Cuauhtemoc Chamorro, Henry Chung, and Dana Kovanic, for donating their time and efforts in creating the CD browser and the spectacular art for both the cover and the CD.

Our friends Jan and Jillian of Skyline tools for donating their entire evaluation line of image processing tools for the CD.

Marci Ayres, who performed a lot of code testing, grayscale image conversion, document formatting, and other support functions.

Lisa Tobin, for performing additional proofreading duties.

A very special thank you goes to Viresh Bhatia, president and CEO of InstallShield Corporation, for allowing the inclusion of both the retail version of PackageForTheWeb and the entire line of evaluation products from InstallShield.

Of course, no acknowledgment would be complete without thanking the Delphi development staff at Borland for giving all of us such an awesome development tool.

Additionally, John Ayres would like to thank all of the writing staff for pulling together, making the sacrifices, and helping produce a product that we can all be proud of; Rusty Cornet, for introducing me to this new development environment called Delphi; Debbie Vilbig and Darla Corley, for giving me the time to learn Delphi and write a call tracking application when I should have been doing real work; Sarah Miles, for providing me with a short-term loan that allowed me to buy the machine that this book was written on; and Suzy Weaver and Brian Donahoo for trusting a former employee and providing a nice, quiet place to work on the weekends.

Foreword

The Windows API is the foundation upon which most contemporary programs are built. It is the heart and soul of database applications, multimedia applications, even many network based applications. Every Windows application relies on the Windows API to perform everything from the most mundane to the most esoteric task.

All of the good programmers I know have a solid foundation in the Windows API. It is the language in which the architecture of the Windows operating system is most eloquently expressed, and it holds the secrets programmers need to know if they want to develop powerful, well tuned applications.

There are at least three reasons why most serious programmers need to know the Windows API:

1. It is occasionally possible to write strong, robust applications without having a good understanding of the Windows API. However, there comes a time in the course of most application development projects when you simply have to turn to the Windows API in order to solve a particular problem. Usually this happens because a tool you are using does not have a feature you need, or because the feature is not implemented properly. In such cases, you have to turn to the Windows API in order to implement the feature yourself.
2. Another reason to use the Windows API surfaces when you want to create a component or utility that others can use. If you want to build a component, ActiveX control, or simple utility that will perform a useful function needed by other developers or power users, then you probably will need to turn to the Windows API. Without recourse to the Windows API, such projects are usually not feasible.
3. The final and best reason for learning the Windows API is that it helps you see how you should architect your application. We have many high-level tools these days that let us build projects at a very remote, and powerful, level of abstraction. However, each of these tools is built on top of the Windows API, and it is difficult, if not impossible, to understand how to use them without understanding the architecture on which they are founded. If you understand the Windows API then you know what the operating system can do for you, and how it goes about providing that service. With this knowledge under your belt, you can use high-level tools in an intelligent and thoughtful manner.

I am particularly pleased to see the publication of Wordware's books on the Windows API because they are built around the world's greatest development tool: Delphi. Delphi gives you full access to the entire Windows API. It is a tool designed to let you plumb the depths of the operating system, to best utilize the features that have made Windows the preeminent operating system in the world today.

Armed with these books on the Windows API, and a copy of Delphi, you can build any type of application you desire, and can be sure that it is being constructed in the optimal possible manner. No other compiler can bring you closer to the operating system, nor can any other compiler let you take better advantage of the operating system's features. These books are the Rosetta stone which forms the link between Delphi and the Windows API. Readers will be able to use them to create the most powerful applications supported by the operating system. My hat is off to the authors for providing these books as a service to the programming community.

Charles Calvert
Borland Developer Relations Manager

Introduction

The Windows programming environment. No other operating system in history has caused so much controversy or confusion among the programming industry. Of course, no other operating system in history has made so many millionaires either. Like it or not, Windows is here to stay. It's hard to ignore such a large user base, and there are few job opportunities anymore that do not require the programmer to have knowledge of the Windows environment.

In the beginning, a programmer's only choice of tools for creating Windows applications was C/C++. The age of this language has resulted in a wealth of Windows API documentation, filled with abstract and incomplete information, and examples that are as esoteric and arcane as the C language itself. Then along came Delphi. A new era in Windows programming was born, with the ability to easily create complex and advanced Windows applications with a turnaround time unheard of previously. Although Delphi tries its best to insulate the programmer from the underlying Windows architecture, Delphi programmers have found that some programming obstacles simply cannot be overcome without using low-level Windows API functions. Although there have been a few books that touched on the subject of using Windows API functions in Delphi, none have ever tackled the issue in depth. There are numerous magazine articles that describe very specific subsets of the API, but unless the Delphi programmer has a background in C, and the time to convert a C example into Delphi, there was simply no recourse of action. Thus, this book was born.

This book is a reference manual for using Windows 32-bit API functions in the Delphi environment. As such, it is not a Windows or Delphi programming tutorial, nor is it a collection of Delphi tricks that solve specific problems. To date, this book is the most complete and accurate reference to the Windows API for the Delphi programmer. It is not a complete reference, as the Windows API includes thousands upon thousands of functions that would fill many volumes much larger than the one you are holding. However, this book covers the most common and important cross section of the Windows API. Additionally, every function in this book is available under both Windows 95 and Windows NT 4.0. Most of these functions will also work under Windows NT prior to the new version.

The Featured Chapters

Chapter 1: Delphi and the Windows API

This chapter introduces the reader to *The Tomes of Delphi 3: Win32 Core API*. It covers general Windows programming concerns and techniques, and explains various nuances of programming with the Win32 API in the Delphi environment.

Chapter 2: Windows 95 Logo Requirements and Delphi

This chapter covers Microsoft's application requirements for putting the "Made For Windows 95" logo on a product. It explores the different requirements for each product category, and outlines self tests that will help your application pass the VeriTest exam.

Chapter 3: Window Creation Functions

Creating a window is the most fundamental part of any Windows application. Chapter 3 covers the low-level window creation and class registration functions. Examples include techniques for creating windows and windowed controls using low-level API functions, and how to extend the functionality of existing Delphi windowed controls.

Chapter 4: Message Processing Functions

Windows allows applications to communicate with each other and with the system through the use of messages, and this chapter covers the functions used to manipulate and send them. Examples include interprocess communication using registered, user-defined Windows messages, and how to install Windows hooks.

Chapter 5: Window Information Functions

The developer may need to programmatically query a window for some piece of information. This chapter covers functions used to retrieve information on specific windows, such as a window's size, position, and attributes. Examples include subclassing a window and changing window attributes at runtime.

Chapter 6: Process and Thread Functions

Multitasking environments allow an application to spawn other applications, or even another thread of execution within itself. This chapter covers the functions used to create and manage threads and processes. Examples include creating and destroying a thread, launching an external process, creating a mutex, and using thread events.

Chapter 7: Dynamic Link Library Functions

Dynamic link libraries are at the core of the Windows operating system architecture, and Windows could not run without them. This chapter covers functions that allow an application to load and import functions from a DLL. Examples include explicitly loading a DLL and importing its functions at runtime, and providing a user-defined DLL entry point.

Chapter 8: Initialization File and Registry Functions

Well-designed and robust applications often need to save information about the last state of the program when it shuts down. This chapter covers functions used to manipulate and modify initialization files and the Windows registry. Examples including reading and writing values to initialization files, and modifying registry entries.

Chapter 9: Memory Management Functions

Only the most simplistic of programs will not need access to dynamically allocated memory. This chapter covers functions used to allocate and release system and virtual memory. Examples demonstrate heap management routines, virtual memory allocation, and retrieving information about allocated memory blocks.

Chapter 10: Clipboard Manipulation Functions

The ability to share information between applications through copy and paste is an expected requirement from Windows users. This chapter covers the functions used to manipulate and view the contents of the clipboard. Examples including enumerating clipboard formats, registering a new clipboard format, and viewing the clipboard contents.

Chapter 11: Input Functions

Without the functionality to interpret user input, most applications would be relatively useless. This chapter covers functions used to receive input from the user, such as keyboard and mouse input. Examples include receiving input from the joystick, retrieving information about the keyboard, and manipulating the cursor.

Chapter 12: File Input/Output Functions

Most applications need the ability to read and write information to an external storage device, and this chapter covers the functions used to manipulate disk-based files. Examples include creating files, manipulating file attributes, reading and writing to a file at the binary level, and performing a file search.

Chapter 13: String and Atom Functions

All applications need to display information to the user, which usually takes place in the form of a string. This chapter covers string manipulation functions and functions used to allocate and remove global atoms. Examples include formatting messages, atom manipulation, and string manipulation.

Chapter 14: System Information Functions

It may sometimes be useful to retrieve specific information about the system or hardware that is running an application. This chapter covers functions used to query the system for information. Examples include retrieving system hardware information, retrieving environment variables, and modifying system parameters.

Chapter 15: Timer Functions

Setting up a timer to repeatedly call a function is the only solution for some programming issues. This chapter covers essential functions used to create a low-level Windows timer. Examples include utilizing the high-resolution timer to measure code performance.

Chapter 16: Error Functions

Error management is always an issue with any programming project. This chapter covers functions used in debugging and error management. Examples include displaying system-defined error strings and user-defined error values.

Conventions

Certain writing conventions have been used throughout this book to convey specific meanings. All example code throughout each chapter appears in a monospace font, such as:

```
function HelloThere(Info: string): Integer;
begin
  ShowMessage(Info);
end;
```

In order to be consistent with other works on Delphi programming, the example code uses Borland's coding conventions, which includes using mixed case for variable names and identifiers, lowercase for reserved words, and nested code indented two spaces per level. Any constants used in the code will appear in all capitals, such as TRUE and FALSE. Also, notice that the name of the unit that contains an individual function is located on the same line as the function name. This unit must be included in the Uses clause of any unit in which this function is used. However, most of the functions covered in this series are located in the Windows.Pas file, which is automatically added to the Uses clause by Delphi. In addition, when the text refers to a window, as in a visual object on the screen, the word "window" will begin with a lowercase letter. When the text refers to Windows, as in the operating system, the word "Windows" will be capitalized.

Function Descriptions

The Windows API function descriptions have been laid out in a format that provides an increasing amount of detail to the reader. This should allow the reader to quickly glance at a function description for a simple reminder of required parameters, or to read further for a detailed explanation of the function, an example of its use, and any acceptable constant values used in a parameter.

Each function description includes the exact syntax found in the Delphi source code, a description of what the function does, a detailed list and description of the function's parameters, the value returned from the function, a list of related functions, and an example of its use. Any defined constants used in a function parameter are found in tables that follow the example, so that the descriptive text of the function is not broken by a distraction, and all of the constants are available in one place for easy perusal.

Sample Programs

Although every book reaches a point where the authors are frantically hacking away at the text trying to meet deadlines, the authors did not want the example code to suffer due to time restraints. Unlike some other books, we wanted to make sure that our example code worked in every case. Therefore, the writers have taken every effort to ensure that the source code on the CD works as expected and that the code in the book is the exact code on the CD. This should guarantee that code entered straight from the text will work as described. However, most of the code examples rely on buttons, edit boxes, or other components residing on the form, which may not be apparent from the code listing. When in doubt, always look at the source code included on the CD.

The CD-ROM

The companion CD-ROM that accompanies this book is a multimedia experience containing all of the source code from the book, a complete Delphi syntax-compliant help file, shareware, freeware, and an assortment of third-party development and evaluation tools. The third-party development and evaluation tools include:

PackageForTheWeb: FREE Retail version:

Rapidly deploy your applications and ActiveX controls on the Internet with PackageForTheWeb. Create self-extracting EXEs or CAB files to distribute your applications and components. PackageForTheWeb requests all the information needed in a simple wizard and immediately builds the file to your specifications. PackageForTheWeb will also digitally sign files so your customers know they are getting authentic software. This is a complete FREE version of this program courtesy of InstallShield Corporation.

DemoShield 5.1 Evaluation Edition:

DemoShield is a demo creation tool that lets even nontechnical Windows users design interactive software demos, tutorials, and CD browsers. Multimedia demos are a snap with DemoShield's SmartTemplates and wizards that automate demo creation, software simulation, and distribution by floppy disk, CD, intranet, or the Internet. Use our point-and-click designer and prebuilt templates to create fully interactive demonstrations easily. When you finish designing, our Setup Wizard walks you through the steps to create a custom installation that sets up your demo on any Windows PC.

InstallShield5 Professional Evaluation Edition:

InstallShield5 Professional Evaluation Edition will forever change the way commercial developers create world-class bulletproof installation systems for Windows applications. InstallShield5 features an installation integrated development environment (IDE) with integrated visual file layout and media-building tools. A Microsoft Visual C++-like IDE offers developers unprecedented levels of productivity for application installation design, development, and deployment. The new multiple-document interface eliminates multiple steps in the installation development process. A color syntax highlighted editor allows you to build and manage large-scale scripts.

InstallFromTheWeb Evaluation Edition:

InstallFromTheWeb allows you to web-enable existing installations for Windows applications so your end users can install applications from the web. A single click of a button will launch the installation for your end user directly from the web. InstallFromTheWeb works with your existing install to automatically build an HTML page that includes the code necessary to launch Web installations.

Skyline Tools Evaluation Software, Corporate Suite, GIF Shaker, and more:

The award-winning ImageLib DLL is a professional software programming tool that provides an inexpensive way to incorporate image and multimedia development into your applications, and is available in a convenient combo package that includes both 16-bit and 32-bit versions. A special VCL/DLL package is available for Delphi developers. GIF Shaker 1.0 Eval is Skyline Tools' first standalone application for Internet development that showcases Skyline Tools' imaging expertise with a feature-rich development environment that speeds the creation of animated GIFs for the web.

Who This Book is For

Due to the nature of reference manuals, and the lack of any involved explanations into general Windows or Delphi programming, this book is intended for use by experienced Delphi programmers with a working knowledge of Windows programming. This is not to say that intermediate or beginning Delphi programmers will not benefit from this book; in fact, there are quite a few example programs included that solve a number of everyday programming conundrums. The heavily documented examples should provide enough explanation for even the most neophyte Delphi programmer. As a reference manual, the book is not intended to be read sequentially. However, the chapters have been laid out in a logical order of progression, starting with the most fundamental Windows API functions and working towards the more specialized functions.

If you are looking for an introduction to Delphi programming, or a step-by-step Windows programming tutorial, there are plenty of other fine books out there to get you started. However, if you've got a nasty problem whose only hope of salvation is using the Windows API, if you want to extend the functionality of Delphi components and objects, or if you want a down-and-dirty, no-holds-barred collection of Delphi Win32 API programming examples, then this book is for you. You will not find a more complete and accurate guide to the Win32 API for the Delphi programmer.

Chapter 1

Delphi and the Windows API

Delphi has brought a new era to Windows programming. Never before has it been so easy to create robust, full-featured applications for the Windows environment with such short development times. Now in its third incarnation, Delphi is known worldwide as the de facto visual Windows programming environment. No other visual programming tool even comes close to matching Delphi's power, ease of use, or quality of executables.

One of Delphi's strengths is the Visual Component Library, Borland's new object model. This object model has allowed the Delphi development team to encapsulate the vast majority of Windows programming tedium into easy to use components. Earlier Windows programming languages required the developer to write large amounts of code just to squeeze a minimal amount of functionality out of Windows. The mere act of creating a window and accepting menu selections could take pages of code to create. Delphi's excellent encapsulation of this dreary requirement of Windows programming has turned what once was a chore into a fun, exciting experience.

The Windows API Versus the VCL

The Delphi development team did a world-class job of encapsulating that vast majority of important Windows API functionality into the VCL. However, due to the vastness of the Windows API, it would be impossible and impractical to wrap every API function in an Object Pascal object. To achieve certain goals or solve specific problems, a developer may be forced to use lower-level Windows API functions that are simply not encapsulated by a Delphi object. It may also be necessary to extend the functionality of a Delphi object, and if this object encapsulates some part of the Windows API, it will be the API that the developer will likely have to use to extend the functionality by any great amount.

Windows Data Types

Windows API functions use a number of data types that may be unfamiliar to the casual Delphi programmer. These data types are all taken from the original C header files that define the Windows API function syntax. For the most part, these new data types are simply Pascal data types that have been renamed to make them similar to the original data types used in legacy Windows programming languages. This was done so that experienced Windows programmers would understand the parameter types and function return values, and the function prototypes would match the syntax shown in existing Windows API documentation to avoid confusion. The following table outlines the most common Windows data types and their correlating Object Pascal data type.

Table 1-1: Windows Data Types

Windows Data Type	Object Pascal Data Type	Description
LPSTR	PAnsiChar;	String pointer
LPCSTR	PAnsiChar;	String pointer
DWORD	Integer;	Whole numbers
BOOL	LongBool;	Boolean values
PBOOL	^BOOL;	Pointer to a Boolean value
Pbyte	^Byte;	Pointer to a byte value
PINT	^Integer;	Pointer to an integer value
Psingle	^Single;	Pointer to a single (floating point) value
PWORD	^Word;	Pointer to a 16-bit value
PDWORD	^DWORD;	Pointer to a 32-bit value
LPDWORD	PDWORD;	Pointer to a 32-bit value
UCHAR	Byte;	8-bit values (can represent characters)
PUCHAR	^Byte;	Pointer to 8-bit values
SHORT	Smallint;	16-bit whole numbers
UINT	Integer;	32-bit whole numbers. Traditionally, this was used to represent unsigned integers, but Object Pascal does not have a true unsigned integer data type.
PUINT	^UINT;	Pointer to 32-bit whole numbers
ULONG	Longint;	32-bit whole numbers. Traditionally, this was used to represent unsigned integers, but Object Pascal does not have a true unsigned integer data type.
PULONG	^ULONG;	Pointer to 32-bit whole numbers
PLongint	^Longint;	Pointer to 32-bit values
PInteger	^Integer;	Pointer to 32-bit values
PSmallInt	^Smallint;	Pointer to 16-bit values
PDouble	^Double;	Pointer to double (floating point) values
LCID	DWORD;	A local identifier
LANGID	Word;	A language identifier
THandle	Integer;	An object handle. Many Windows API functions return a value of type THandle, which identifies that object within Windows' internal object tracking tables.
PHandle	^THandle;	A pointer to a handle

Windows Data Type	Object Pascal Data Type	Description
WPARAM	Longint;	A 32-bit message parameter. Under earlier versions of Windows, this was a 16-bit data type.
LPARAM	Longint;	A 32-bit message parameter
LRESULT	Longint;	A 32-bit function return value
HWND	Integer;	A handle to a window. All windowed controls, child windows, main windows, etc., have a corresponding window handle that identifies them within Windows' internal tracking tables.
HHOOK	Integer;	A handle to an installed Windows system hook
ATOM	Word;	An index into the local or global atom table for a string
HGLOBAL	THandle;	A handle identifying a globally allocated dynamic memory object. Under 32-bit Windows, there is no distinction between globally and locally allocated memory.
HLOCAL	THandle;	A handle identifying a locally allocated dynamic memory object. Under 32-bit Windows, there is no distinction between globally and locally allocated memory.
FARPROC	Pointer;	A pointer to a procedure, usually used as a parameter type in functions that require a callback function
HGDIOBJ	Integer;	A handle to a GDI object. Pens, device contexts, brushes, etc., all have a handle of this type that identifies them within Windows' internal tracking tables.
HBITMAP	Integer;	A handle to a Windows bitmap object
HBRUSH	Integer;	A handle to a Windows brush object
HDC	Integer;	A handle to a device context
HENHMETAFILE	Integer;	A handle to a Windows enhanced metafile object
HFONT	Integer;	A handle to a Windows logical font object
HICON	Integer;	A handle to a Windows icon object
HMENU	Integer;	A handle to a Windows menu object
HMETAFILE	Integer;	A handle to a Windows metafile object
HINST	Integer;	A handle to an instance object
HMODULE	HINST;	A handle to a module
HPALETTE	Integer;	A handle to a Windows color palette
HPEN	Integer;	A handle to a Windows pen object
HRGN	Integer;	A handle to a Windows region object
HRSRC	Integer;	A handle to a Windows resource object
HKL	Integer;	A handle to a keyboard layout
HFILE	Integer;	A handle to an open file
HCURSOR	HICON;	A handle to a Windows mouse cursor object
COLORREF	DWORD;	A Windows color reference value, containing values for the red, green, and blue components of a color

Handles

An important concept in Windows programming is the concept of an object handle. Many functions return a handle to an object that the function created or loaded from a resource. Functions like CreateWindow and CreateWindowEx return a window handle. Other functions return a handle to an open file, like CreateFile, or return a handle to a newly allocated heap, like HeapCreate. Internally, Windows keeps track of all of these handles, and the handle serves as the link through the operating system between the object and the application. It is this mechanism that allows an application to communicate so seamlessly with the operating system. Using these handles, an application can easily refer to any of these objects and the operating system instantly knows which object a piece of code wants to manipulate.

Constants

The Windows API functions declare literally thousands upon thousands of different constants to be used as parameter values. Constants for everything from color values to return values have been defined in the Windows.Pas file. The constants that are defined for each API function are listed with that function within the text. However, the Windows.Pas file may yield more information concerning the constants for any particular function, and it is a good rule of thumb to check this Delphi source code file when using complicated functions.

Strings

All Windows API functions that use strings require a pointer to a null-terminated string type. Windows is written in C, which does not have the Pascal string type. Earlier versions of Delphi required the application to allocate a string buffer and convert the String type to a PChar. However, Delphi 3's new string conversion mechanism allows a string to be used as a PChar by simply typecasting it (i.e., PChar(MyString), where MyString is declared as MyString: string). For the most part, this conversion will work with almost all Windows API functions that require a string parameter.

Importing Windows Functions

The Windows API is huge. It defines functions for almost every kind of utility or comparison or action that a programmer could think of. Due to the sheer volume of Windows API functions, some functions simply fell through the cracks and were not imported by the Delphi source code. Since all Windows API functions are simply functions exported from a DLL, importing a new Windows API function is a relatively simple process, if the function parameters are known.

Importing a new Windows API function is exactly like importing any other function from a DLL. For example, the BroadcastSystemMessage function described in the Message Processing Functions chapter is not imported by the Delphi source code. In order to import this function for use within an application, it is simply declared as a function from within a DLL as:

```
function BroadcastSystemMessage(Flags: DWORD; Recipients: PDWORD;
    uiMessage: UINT; wParam: WPARAM; lParam: LPARAM): Longint; stdcall;

implementation

function BroadcastSystemMessage; external user32 name 'BroadcastSystemMessage';
```

As long as the parameters required by the function and the DLL containing the function are known, any Windows API function can be imported and used by a Delphi application. It is important to note that the stdcall directive must be appended to the prototype for the function, as this defines the standard mechanism by which Windows passes parameters to a function on the stack.

Incorrectly Imported Functions

Some functions have been incorrectly imported by the Delphi source code. These exceptions are noted in the individual function descriptions. For the most part, the functions that have been imported incorrectly deal with the ability to pass NIL as a value to a pointer parameter, usually to retrieve the required size of a buffer so the buffer can be dynamically allocated to the exact length before calling the function to retrieve the real data. In Delphi, some of these functions have been imported with parameters defined as VAR or CONST. These types of parameters can accept a pointer to a buffer but can never be set to NIL, thus limiting the use of the function within the Delphi environment. As is the case with almost anything in Delphi, it is a simple matter to fix. Simply reimport the function as if it did not exist, as outlined above. Functions that have been imported incorrectly are identified in their individual function descriptions throughout the book.

Callback Functions

Another very important concept in Windows programming is that of a callback function. A callback function is a function within the developer's application that is never called directly by any other function or procedure within that application but is instead called by the Windows operating system. This allows Windows to communicate directly with the application, passing it various parameters as defined by the individual callback function. Most of the enumeration functions require some form of application-defined callback function that receives the enumerated information.

Individual callback functions have specific parameters that must be declared exactly by the application. This is required so that Windows passes the correct information to the application in the correct order. A good example of a function that uses a callback function is EnumWindows. The EnumWindows function parses through all top-level windows on the screen, passing the handle of each window to an application-defined callback function. This continues until all top-level windows have been enumerated or the callback function returns FALSE. The callback function used by EnumWindows is defined as:

```
EnumWindowsProc(
hWnd: HWND;            {a handle to a top-level window}
lParam: LPARAM         {the application-defined data}
): BOOL;               {returns TRUE or FALSE}
```

A function matching this function prototype is created within the application, and a pointer to the function is passed as one of the parameters to the EnumWindows function. The Windows operating system calls this callback function for each top-level window, passing the window's handle in one of the callback function's parameters. It is important to note that the stdcall directive must be appended to the prototype for the callback function, as this defines the standard mechanism by which Windows passes parameters to a function on the stack. For example, the above callback function would be prototyped as:

```
EnumWindowsProc(hWnd: HWND; lParam: LPARAM); stdcall;
```

Without the stdcall directive, Windows will not be able to access the callback function. This powerful software mechanism, in many cases, allows an application to retrieve information about the system that is only stored internally by Windows and would otherwise be unreachable. For a complete example of callback function usage, see the EnumWindows function, and many other functions throughout the book.

Function Parameters

The vast majority of Windows API functions simply take the static parameters handed to them and perform some function based on the value of the parameters. However, certain functions return values that must be stored in a buffer, and that buffer is passed to the function in the form of a pointer. In most cases, when the function description specifies that it returns some value in a buffer, null-terminated string buffer, or a pointer to a data structure, these buffers and data structures must be allocated by the application before the function is called.

In many cases, a parameter may state that it can contain one or more values from some table. These values are defined as constants, and they are combined using the Boolean OR operator. The actual value passed to the function usually identifies a bitmask, where the state of each bit has some significance to the function. This is why the constants can be combined using Boolean operations. For example, the CreateWindow function has a parameter called dwStyle which can accept a number of constants combined with the Boolean OR operator. To pass more than one constant to the function, the parameter would be set to something like "WS_CAPTION or WS_CHILD or WS_CLIPCHILDREN". This would create a child window that includes a caption bar and would clip around its child windows during painting.

Conversely, when a function states that it returns one or more values that are defined as specific constants, the return value can be combined with one of the constants using the Boolean AND operator to determine if that constant is contained within the return value. If the result of the combination is equal to the constant (i.e., if(Result and WS_CHILD)=WS_CHILD then …), the constant is included in the return value.

Unicode

Originally, software only needed a single byte to define a character within a character set. This allowed for up to 256 characters, which was more than plenty for the entire alphabet, numbers, punctuation symbols, and common mathematical symbols. However, due to the shrinking of the global community and the subsequent internationalization of Windows and Windows software, a new method of identifying characters was needed. Many languages have well over 256 characters used for writing, much more than a single byte can describe. Therefore, Unicode was invented. A Unicode character is 16 bits long, and can therefore identify 65,535 characters within a language's alphabet. To accommodate the new character set type, many Windows API functions come in two flavors: ANSI and Unicode. When browsing the Windows.Pas source code, many functions are defined with an A or W appended to the end of the function name, identifying them as an ANSI function or Wide character (Unicode) function. The functions within this book cover only the ANSI functions. However, the Unicode functions usually differ only in the type of string information passed to a function, and if the string is in Unicode format, the text within this book should adequately describe the Unicode function's behavior.

Chapter 2

Windows 95 Logo Requirements and Delphi

Software design and the human experience. These things didn't exist early on in the software industry. In the early days, programs interacted with the users via command lines and strange prompts. Data was presented in ambiguous ways that often confused the users and made using a computer a difficult and frustrating experience. This method of data representation and presentation changed in the late 1970s when the Xerox Systems Development Division at Palo Alto Research Center developed the Star System. This new operating environment marked the start of a new generation of software and interface design. With its innovation of windows, icons, and menus it paved the way for the operating systems used today.

Software design has often been described as being similar to that of architectural design, where the designer works within a defined environment to provide a solution that is pleasing, interesting, and usable to the people who interact with it. In 1991 *Dr. Dobb's Journal* printed "A Software Design Manifesto" by Mitchell Kapor, in which Kapor describes the biggest problem in the software industry as being the design of software and the manner in which people interact with it. By suggesting that there is more to creating software than just being a good programmer, Kapor set the stage for an entire new industry of software designers and describes the techniques and methodologies that should be taught and implemented for good software design.

A good example of applying this methodology was seen in the Apple Macintosh computers and operating system. The designers at Apple laid out a very solid foundation of requirements, tools, and development systems for creating software on the Macintosh. As a result, users found that if they learned one application, learning the others was easier. The user could count on experiencing things the same way in any application. These standards resulted in lower training costs and learning curves and truly pushed the computer to new levels of efficiency and productivity. In 1981 Microsoft (when it had the same goal in mind) began development of the Interface Manager, later renamed Microsoft Windows. This first rendition of the DOS operating system makeover included Multiplan- and Word-like menus at the bottom of the screen. After much debate, around 1982 the operating system add-on evolved into its pull-down menu and dialog system which emulated the look and feel implemented ten years earlier on the Xerox Star.

In November of 1985 Microsoft Windows Version 1.0 was available to the public as an add-on to its existing DOS-based system. Though Windows Version 1.0 was a far cry from Windows 95 and Windows NT, it set the stage for what was to come. As the complexity of the operating system increased, the need for more stringent development guidelines became apparent. It was then that Microsoft created the logo programs for the individual operating systems. These programs which began in 1994 were designed much like the architect in Mitchell Kapor's manifesto; they exist to guide developers as building codes guide architects and engineers in the creation of a building.

With this in mind it is important to consider that the Microsoft Logo Program is perceived in two very different ways, one from the developer's view and one from the consumer's view. In the developer's mind the "Designed for Windows NT and Windows 95 Logo Program" is supposed to help consumers identify products that have been created with the operating system and ease of use in mind. By promoting this type of development, Microsoft ensures the consumer a certain degree of functionality, tight integration with the operating system, easy access to all features, and the simple customization of interface elements for users who have physical or visual disabilities to those with just wild tastes.

In the mind of the consumer the Microsoft logo attached to a product is perceived much like a seal of approval or a confirmation of product quality. Underwriters Laboratories, *Consumers Digest*, *PC Magazine*, Ziff Davis, *Windows Magazine*, and others exist to give the consumer peace of mind in their computer and software purchases. When the consumer sees these seals affixed to a product they rightfully conclude that a professional organization has tested the product in question and verified that it performs as expected or designed. Such is the case with the "Designed for Windows NT and Windows 95 Logo Program." While consumers tend to think of the logo as an individual product endorsement, the truth is that both Microsoft and VeriTest openly claim that the logo is only intended to indicate that the program has passed the compliance test and has all of the features necessary to carry the logo. The test itself is not a quality assurance check nor a statement of individual product quality.

Before starting the development of any software product, a certain degree of advanced planning needs to happen. During this stage of schematic design, the development, marketing, and program management teams need to get together and decide exactly what benefits and drawbacks are associated with developing a Windows logo-compliant application. Some of the questions that need to be asked during this phase of development include:

1. Will the logo help us sell software?
2. Are the required features important to our users?
3. What is the cost both financially and in development time for adding the features necessary to carrying the logo?

4. Is it necessary to have the logo for the success of the product?
5. Does our competition have logo-compliant applications?

While in the process of answering these questions it may be noticed that some of the logo-compliant criteria does not apply to or enhance an individual product. Knowing this in advance, it is important to identify the product's potential market early in development and determine if the logo will benefit the sales and promotion of the product.

A good rule of thumb is that if the product is going to end up on a retail shelf or be heavily advertised it is a good thing to have the logo. This is based on consumer studies that indicate when given a choice between two equal products, more often the product with a logo will be chosen over the competitor. This, however, is not necessarily the case with products sold outside of the retail market.

It is easy to see that when considering these things the development, marketing, and management teams need to decide if the logo will have a monetary benefit that will justify the extra effort, time, and expense in creating an application that carries the Microsoft logo. The important thing to remember here is that this program is not something that everyone needs to take on. Developers need to make sure that marketing managers, program managers, and management in general understand what they are getting themselves into when they take on these additional features and requirements. There are several successful programs in the marketplace that have nothing to do with the "Designed for Windows NT and Windows 95 Logo Program." Before making any decisions, take a good hard look at the exceptions and exemption clauses in the handbook for creating logo-compliant applications to see first hand what these new requirements mean to the product's development.

To properly facilitate the Microsoft Logo Program, Microsoft enlisted the help of VeriTest, a longtime industry leader in impartial and objective software testing and evaluation. VeriTest, along with Microsoft's *Logo Handbook for Software Applications*, takes each submitted application and tests it based on the criteria for that particular product category. Once a product is tested the results are returned to the developer with either a successful test evaluation or a list of areas where the product failed and why so that the development team can make the necessary changes and resubmit the product for further testing.

This chapter is not a total regurgitated version of the Microsoft document for obtaining a Windows NT or Windows 95 logo. It is a simple guide designed to inform and enlighten developers about the requirements for logo compliance and point out some special considerations that need to be made before taking on the task of obtaining the Microsoft logo. This chapter will cover some of the requirements for the test as well as expand a great deal on those associated with operating system integration, product installation, user assistance, and application/user interface design considerations. While a great deal of this information is an expansion of the Microsoft document, it is not intended as a replacement. For more detailed information about VeriTest and the Microsoft "Designed for Windows NT and Windows 95 Logo Program," go to the VeriTest web site at:

http://www.veritest.com or http://www.veritest.com/microsoft.htm.

This site contains the official *Logo Handbook for Software Applications* as well as additional information in regards to the different kinds of logos and how to obtain them. Of special interest on this site are the top ten reasons applications fail the logo test. Take the time to review this portion of the site as it contains important items to look for when pretesting an application before formal submission. This chapter will focus on the "Designed for Windows NT and Windows 95 Logo Program" primarily for commercial desktop software applications.

Getting a Logo

There are several steps involved in getting a logo for a product. The first and most important is to review the criteria in the logo handbook before submitting an application for testing. This way, any potential problem areas can be identified before the formal submission. Once the development team is satisfied that the product is logo compliant, perform a pretest on the application with the Installation Analyzer provided by VeriTest. This program is located on VeriTest's web site at:

http://www.veritest.com/labs/logolab/Microsoft/microsoft(f).htm.

This test is designed to give the development team some help in identifying any potential problems with the Windows registry, software installation and uninstallation, and Windows and System INI files. Once the initial testing is complete there are three clerical steps remaining that conclude the submission process. They are:

1. Filing the License Agreements: Properly complete the Microsoft License Agreements and the VeriTest Testing Agreement. These documents must be completed and returned with the product being tested.

2. VeriTest Online Questionnaire: VeriTest has an online questionnaire that must be filled out completely prior to submitting the application.

Note: *This questionnaire is very important. It is within the questionnaire that exemptions must be noted for any submitted application. The more information provided, the better and faster the product will be tested.*

3. Product Submission: Submit the application and all supporting documentation to VeriTest for formal product testing. The submission pack must include the following:

1. Application to be tested.
2. Pretest results.
3. VeriTest Testing Agreement.
4. Windows NT and Windows 95 Logo Licensing Agreement.

5. A check to VeriTest for the initial test. This fee is (as of printing) $950 with an additional charge of $300 for retests on new product builds. There are different fee structures associated with each different logo program. For more up-to-date information on the fees associated with testing, refer to the VeriTest web site at:

http://www.veritest.com/labs/logolab/Microsoft/microsoft(f).htm.

To obtain a logo for a product there is a series of very stringent criteria that the application must meet. The criteria range from requiring that the overall application be a 32-bit executable to the inclusion of Object Linking and Embedding. It is important to note that not all applications have the same criteria for receiving a logo. The criteria is set based on the product category the application falls into. The various application product categories are listed below with a brief description.

Product Categories

File Based Applications	Applications of this type have file creation, manipulation, and saving as the core of their functionality. **Example:** **Microsoft Word**
Non-File Based Applications	Non-file based applications are those whose primary function is not to create, manipulate, or save files. These application types are exempt from OLE, Universal Naming Conventions, and Long File Name requirements. **Example:** **Internet Browser**
Utilities	Utilities are applications that perform very specific tasks and do not involve the general editing, creating, and saving of files. These applications must provide some useful functionality in both Windows 95 and Windows NT to qualify for a logo. **Example:** **Scandisk** or **WinSight**
Development Tools	Development tools are those applications that create executable files based on a compiled or interpreted language. Development tools must be able to create applications that are capable of passing logo compliance tests. **Example:** **Delphi** or **Visual Basic**
Add-on Applications	Add-on applications are those things which augment a regular application but are not executables. These product types must be used by a 32-bit application that carries the logo and must be tested both with the parent application and separately. **Example:** **Wizards**, **Templates**, and **Macros**

Note: *Add-on applications can be distributed as either part of the program they enhance or as a separate product. They do not have to be EXE files to qualify for this category.*

Application Suites	Application suites are a collection of applications that all perform together or when used together form a unified solution set. All the individual applications in the suite must be able to pass the logo requirements for that particular product category. **Example:** **Microsoft Office**
Games and Multimedia	Programs that involve interactive graphics or action and are graphically rich in their operation. These applications may range from video games to multimedia development tools. **Example:** **DemoShield** or **Innovous**

In certain instances Microsoft, via a waiver or through formal exemption request, can place the application into a different application category, thereby changing the criteria in which the application is tested. These changes depend on the circumstances surrounding the application in question, where it is failing in the test, and if that feature can be eliminated from the test because its required presence has no meaning to the application.

Taking the Test

After a product has been submitted to VeriTest for testing it will be subjected to one holistic test designed for that product category. In general the test covers three areas:

1. Product reliability
2. User experience
3. Application compatibility

Within each of these areas there are individual subcategories that will further test various elements of the application. Each of these subcategories has requirements or exceptions that pertain to the various product groups as listed above. It is important to verify what the requirements and exemptions are early on in development so that development time and effort is not used unwisely.

Note: *To help the developer prevent such product test failures, an in-depth look at some of the problem areas is covered. This information is not available in the logo handbook and should be considered during the project planning and development process.*

Product Reliability (Basic Requirements)

Product reliability and the basic requirements cover a variety of topics. In general the application being tested must be both functional and stable in Windows 95 and Windows NT 4.0. This means that when VeriTest runs the application it does not crash or cause exceptions or faults in the operating system. This portion of the testing also involves some basic application requirements that pertain to the compiled nature of the application and its dependent DLLs to product distribution.

32-Bit Requirement: The application must be a 32-bit executable compiled with a 32-bit compiler. It is to be a portable executable of type [PE_Win32]. There are some exceptions to this rule that are generally applicable to legacy systems and backward compatibility. All major EXE and DLL portions of the application must be 32 bit. Any support DLLs that are 16 are only allowed if no 32-bit equivalent exists, or if they do not constitute a major portion of the application or host the application's primary functions.

Note: *To properly test an application's ability to function under a congested operating system, it is recommended that the developer use the Stress Application located in the Win32 SDK. To determine if the application is running properly, execute the Stress Application and then perform all of the application's functions in the normal manner. Record any abnormal results and attempt to diagnose the problem after verifying that these functions work properly on a system that is not stressed.*

Other tests that are important to try before submitting an application for testing are:

1. *Video mode switching while the application is running.*
2. *Printing and all I/O functions.*
3. *Operation while 16-bit and 32-bit programs are running simultaneously.*
4. *In Windows 95 only, run the system informant located on the CD to verify the system resources before and after running the application. This will test to see if any persistent memory leaks exist in the application. In Windows NT use the system monitor to verify any memory anomalies.*

Product Distribution: The product distribution requirement pertains to what is included on the product installation media. These days it is very common to find that when purchasing a 32-bit application, a 16-bit version is also included on the same media. If this is the case, the requirement is that the installation program inform the user that there are two versions of the software on the media and further inform them which version they are attempting to install. If by chance they choose to install the 16-

bit version, it is further required that the installation indicate that the version they are installing is not logo compliant or that it will run in this environment but was not designed for it. Product installation will be discussed in much greater detail in the User Experience section.

In the event the installation media has a suite of applications on it, they must all meet logo requirements before the box containing the suite can carry the logo. This means that all of the applications within the package must be able to pass a logo test on their own in their respective product category. If one application does not pass, the logo application will be denied for the suite until the problems with that one program are resolved or it is eliminated from the suite. This includes product demos or limited versions of the applications.

User Experience

User experience is one larger group of tests that focuses on four subcategories that cover application installation, uninstallation, User Interface/Shell, and Universal Naming Conventions and Long File Names. The point to these tests is to ensure that the software is usable by any end user, and provide them with the necessary options and operational parameters that will make the user experience a pleasant one while using the product.

Software Installation: In the user experience category there is a great deal of information regarding software installation and the options and functionality that should be available to the user during the install. Even though several tools exist for the easy generation of logo-compliant installs, many developers do not take the time to research the installation requirements and subsequently fail this portion of the test. Therefore, software installation is covered in detail to ensure that all of the options are covered as well as point out some additional features and guidelines for better software installations.

One goal of a good software installation is to properly deliver the application to the user's machine while providing the user with the proper questions and feedback to ensure that the software is usable upon delivery. The other goal of a good install is to deliver the files in an organized manner such that the user is able to locate all the files easily and quickly. Finally, a good installation will properly configure and install all of the support files necessary for the application to run and reduce the redundancy of common files, thereby making the software easier to update and maintain.

Note: *There are several applications that are in the market to aid in the process of software delivery. Several examples of such programs have been provided on the companion CD located in the back of the book. All of the applications provided are capable of creating logo-compliant installations.*

Installation Requirements:

Interface: The installation program will provide the end user with a graphical interface for selecting the many options and file locations necessary for proper software installation.

Installation Guide: The installation must walk the user through the installation process or provide a mechanism for allowing the installation to operate in an unattended mode. Instructing the users to copy the files and then decompress them does not constitute compliance with this requirement.

To properly comply with this requirement the installation program should provide a default response to every setting in the installation so that the user can simply accept the defaults and deliver the application properly. Though not required, these are some special additional design issues that the developer should consider when creating a good software installation. When designing the installation there should be a choice for the setup type desired by the user. The normal setup types are:

Typical: This installation will deliver the common default files and settings for proper installation of the product. This installation type should deliver only the most common files for proper program operation and be the default choice during execution of the installation program.

Compact: The compact installation will only deliver the files absolutely necessary for the application to operate. This option is provided for users who have limited disk space or are using laptops.

Custom: The custom installation is designed for advanced users who want total control over what options and features of an application are installed. This option should include the ability to determine file locations, initial setting for the application, and what features to enable.

CD-ROM: The CD installation is designed much like the Compact install with the difference being that the user can install only the necessary runtime files while accessing the remaining files from the CD during program execution.

Other additional features that make for a more pleasant software installation include:

1. Reporting available system resources and need resources before the install.

2. Providing visual and audio cues during the installation to indicate any problems or the simple need to insert a new disk.

3. Support Universal Naming Convention paths.

4. Provide a mechanism for stopping the installation during the install.

When creating a proprietary installation program with Delphi, the following code snapshots will demonstrate how to obtain the free space on a drive.

Available Drive Space: To get the available drive information, use the Win32 API call GetDiskFreeSpace(). Typically the GetFreeDiskSpace API call returns the number of sectors per cluster, bytes per sector, and the number of free clusters. Free disk space must be calculated based on the information returned by this function. This code is based on a form with a button and two labels. The calculation is performed on the button click event.

```
procedure TForm1.Button1Click(Sender: TObject);
var
     Path: String;                  {Drive path}
     Sectors: Longint;              {Sectors}
     Bytes: LongInt;                {Bytes}
     FreeClusters: LongInt;         {Free clusters}
     Total: LongInt;                {Total clusters}
     Free: LongInt;                 {Free space}
     TotalSpace: LongInt;           {Total space}
begin
     Path:='C:\';
     GetDiskFreeSpace(PChar(Path),
     Sectors,Bytes,FreeClusters, Total);
     {--- Calculate available space ---}
     Free:= (Sectors*Bytes*FreeClusters)div @program = 1048576;
     {- 1048576 is the conversion factor for MB -}

     Label1.Caption := IntToStr(Free);

     {--- Calculate total disk space ---}
     Total := (Sectors*Bytes*Total) div 1048576;
     {- 1048576 is the conversion factor for MB -}
      Label2.Caption := IntToStr(Total);
end;
end.
```

Another method of obtaining the same information is to use the DiskFree function. This code assumes there is a form, button, and label. The calculation is performed on the button click event.

```
procedure TForm1.Button1Click(Sender: TObject);
var
     DriveSpace: Integer;
const
     DiskType =3;
{--- Where 0 is the current drive, 1 is drive
     A, 2 is drive  B and 3 is drive C ---}
begin
     DriveSpace:=(DiskFree(DiskType) div 1048576);
     {- 1048576 is the conversion factor for MB -}
     Label1.Caption:=IntToStr(DriveSpace);
end;
```

Note: *Due to a limitation in Delphi's implementation of the DiskFree function, it will only report the proper amount of free drive space up to two gigabytes.*

OS Detection: The installation application must automatically detect the version of the current operating system and install any and all files necessary for proper operation in that environment.

There are two methods for obtaining the operating system version in Delphi. One is to use the GetVersionEx() API call. This function only accepts one parameter of record type TOSVersionInfo by reference. The TOSVersionInfo record contains all of the operating system version information. The information returned includes major and minor operating system version numbers, build number, platform identifier, and description of the operating system in use. The TOSVersionInfo record is defined as:

```
TOSVersionInfo = record
    dwOSVersionInfoSize: DWORD            {size of the structure}
    dwMajorVersion: DWORD                 {major version number}
    dwMinorVersion: DWORD                 {minor version number}
    dwBuildNumber: DWORD                  {the build number}
    dwPlatformId: DWORD                   {system platform flags}
    szCSDVersion:array[0..127]of AnsiChar {additional info}
end;
```

To use this function, initialize dwOSVersionInfo to the SizeOf (TOSVersionInfo) as seen below.

```
procedure TForm1.Button1Click(Sender: TObject);
var
     VersionInfo: TOSVersionInfo;
begin
     VersionInfo.dwOSVersionInfoSize:=
     SizeOf(VersionInfo);
     GetVersionInfor(VersionInfo);
end;
```

From here, present the returned information to the user as visual feedback, or simply use this information to ensure the proper delivery of necessary application files that may be operating system specific.

There is another way to get the same information that involves less work. Since the logo program deals with 32-bit operating systems, the registry is present on both Windows 95 and Windows NT 4.0 platforms. Therefore, the operating system type can be read out of the system registry. This is accomplished by doing the following:

Note: *The Registry unit must be added to the Uses statement for this code to work properly.*

```
var
      Reg : TRegistry;
      Ver : string;
begin
      Reg := TRegistry.Create;
      Reg.RootKey := HKEY_LOCAL_MACHINE;

      Reg.OpenKey('\SOFTWARE\Microsoft\Windows\'+
      'CurrentVersion',FALSE);

      if Reg.ValueExists('VersionNumber') then
            Ver := Reg.ReadString('VersionNumber');
      Reg.Free;
end;
```

Shortcuts: All shortcuts created by the installation program must not return a "File not found" error or any other error when executed.

Shortcuts should be provided to allow easier access to the application. One good place for a shortcut is the Programs folder. To determine the location of this folder, access the registry with the Shell Folders subkey under: **HKEY_CURRENT_USERS**\ Software\Microsoft\Windows\CurrentVersion\Explorer. Path information can also be obtained for the Start Menu, Startup Group, and the Desktop from the Shell Folders subkey. All of these are good places to present an option for shortcut placement.

AutoPlay: Products that are distributed on CD-ROM are required to make use of the AutoPlay feature to begin the setup program, or another program that will guide the user to product installation. Along with this requirement, the installer should—for media types other than CD-ROM—allow the program to launch the installer via the Add/Remove applications selection in the Windows 95/NT Control Panel.

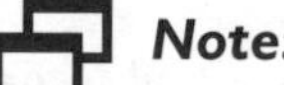

Note: *On the companion CD there is an evaluation version of DemoShield 5.1. This application is used by several development companies to create CD browsers. These browsers are graphical applications that allow users to navigate in a graphical manner to the software and additional content on the CD. The browser for the companion CD was created with DemoShield, and is an excellent example of such an interface for these applications. While this method of data presentation is not a requirement, it is an enhancement to the user experience and is quickly becoming the norm in software distribution.*

For proper operation this feature requires a file named **Autorun.inf** in the root directory of the CD. Inside this file is a single key that has the name of the program to run automatically. This is expressed as:

[autorun]
open = Filename

or

[autorun]
open = path\filename <switches if desired>

If a logical path is not supplied, the program will look for the file to run in the root directory of the CD. Each of these methods are simple forms of a command line to execute the program. In the second method, the path should be provided as relative to the root (meaning no drive letter), and can include switches if needed to execute the program.

The Autorun feature is intended to enhance the user experience by making the use of certain media easier. It is important when designing applications that will take advantage of this feature to provide feedback quickly, as the hardware the program is being operated on may be slower than that which it was tested on. A good testing procedure for this initial feedback is to design the Autorun application to respond and load quickly on a 2X CD-ROM. If the time for display is adequate on this older device then it will be acceptable on newer hardware.

Note: *Quick feedback is essential because of the time delay normally encountered when Autorun executes. If the application takes a long time to load, the user could be waiting for some time with no indication that the program is operating properly.*

Default Location: The installation program is required to offer a delivery directory of "drive:\Program Files" as the default location for the application's installation.

The easiest way to locate this directory is to once again read a value from the system registry. The key to look for is "ProgramFilesDir" and is located in the CurrentVersion key under:

HKEY_LOCAL_MACHINE\Software\Microsoft\Windows

A good installation strategy is to create more than one directory for the application and its support files. This directory is for files that the application must have to operate but are never accessed by the end user. Separating these files makes system maintenance easier for both the developer and the end user.

Any file that functions in a support role for multiple applications should be placed in the Windows system directory. A good example of such a component is the Visual Basic Run Time Library. Proper placement of such support files is crucial. To handle this process properly it is important to verify that the file does not exist in the system directory. If the file does exist, compare the date, time stamp, file size, and file version. Always prompt the user for replacing such files and give them the option not to install anything over the existing control. If the new file is not more recent than the file presently on the machine, DO NOT INSTALL over the existing file. If any new files are stored in the Windows 95/NT system directory, it is a good idea, though not required, to register these new files in the SharedDLL subkey of the system registry under HKEY_LOCAL_MACHINE.

Note: *If the application uses any of the Microsoft defined core components, the installation program must increment the shared count by one for each component used. The inverse is also true upon uninstallation. To get a list of the core components, go to the VeriTest web site at:*

http://www.veritest.com/labs/logolab/Microsoft/microsoft(f).htm

Enhancements/Suggestions: Software installation is the first impression the developer gets to make on the user. Therefore, it is important that the installation go smoothly while allowing the user to have total control of the additions being made to their machine. The following are some tips that are important when performing superior software installations.

1. If network installations are something the application will support, then remember to name files in the standard DOS 8+3 naming conventions so that they can be easily shared on networks that do not support long filenames.
2. Try to avoid using INI files in the applications being delivered. The Windows registry is a much better mechanism for storing the end user's settings. Furthermore, the registry is designed to be accessed via network connection, making software maintenance easier and avoiding hunting for INI files.
3. Prompt the user when creating shortcuts and allow them to decide if and where they should be created.
4. Installations should support the Universal Naming Conventions.

5. Make use of the registry rather than INI files to store information about the application and files it is dependent upon, and retrieve information about the system and its devices.

   Different uses for the system registry include:

   Program State Information:

   Place any information that used to be stored in INI files here. This would include the window state of the program, its screen location and product version information.

Primary Keys:	HKEY_LOCAL_MACHINE and HKEY_CURRENT_USER
SubKey:	Software

   Computer Specific Information:

   These subkeys are provided as a place to retrieve and store system configuration information like screen resolution, Windows version, and screen saver state.

Primary Keys:	HKEY_LOCAL_MACHINE
SubKey:	Hardware, Config, and Network

   User Specific Information:

   These subkeys are the place to retrieve system information and store any information about hardware for the application's easy reference.

Primary Keys:	HKEY_CURRENT_USER
SubKey:	Hardware, Config, and Network

   Application Path Information:

   By setting the application path information Windows will set the current path to the one that is registered when the application executes. This key is also used by Windows to locate the application if it cannot find it using the current path. The need for this functionality is apparent when users type in only the name of a program from the Task Bar's Run program.

Primary Keys:	HKEY_LOCAL_MACHINE
SubKey:	Software/Microsoft/Windows/ CurrentVersion/App Paths/ Application Executable Filename = path

   File Extensions:

   File-based applications should register any files which are available to users for editing and reference. At the same time the program registering the file's extension should verify that the extension has not already been registered.

Primary Keys:	HKEY_CLASSES_ROOT
SubKey:	The file extension
Identifier:	.ext = ApplicationID
	ApplicationID = Type Name

Note: *These are usually broken out by Default and then a content type if necessary.*

Uninstalling Software: Equally important to the end user experience is the removal of installed applications. During this portion of the test, the application's uninstallation routines are tested to verify and ensure that all portions of the application are totally removed. This includes shortcuts, GID files, ReadMe Files, registry settings, and any other files associated with the program. Like the installation application, the uninstallation program must be a 32-bit program capable of removing these files and making the necessary changes to the system registry seamlessly and without any end user intervention.

Note: *During an uninstallation, if the installer is removing what could be a shared DLL or support file, it is important to check the shared count for that DLL or file. If the shared count is zero then the program should prompt the user before removing the file. If the shared count is not zero, the program should decrement the shared count by one and continue.*

Uninstallation Requirements:

Add/Remove: The uninstallation program must be accessible from the Add/RemovePrograms section of the control panel. This requirement is designed to give users a consistent mechanism for removing their applications.

To allow the uninstallation program to run properly from the Add/Remove Programs application, the uninstallation program must be registered in the Windows 95/NT registry. The key for this registration is:

HKEY_LOCAL_MACHINE
Software/Microsoft/Windows/CurrentVersion
/Uninstall/ApplicationName

Inside this key are the values:

DisplayName = Application Name
UninstallString = path and switches to remove the application

Both DisplayName and UninstallString have to be provided and complete before the uninstallation program will be listed in the

Add/Remove Control Panel Program. UninstallString must be a complete command line to execute the uninstallation program.

Note: *Command line switches can be used in the UninstallString if desired.*

Software Removal: The uninstallation program is required to remove all files that were copied to the hard disk when the program was initially installed. Any data files that were created after the program was installed are to remain on the system. Included in this requirement are the removal of any shortcuts placed in the Start menu by the installer.

Registry: The uninstallation program must remove all registry keys that are associated with the product being removed. However, it must not remove any keys that are or could be associated with other applications.

Additional registry requirements include:

1. Disallowing the removal of Windows 95/NT core components. For the most up-to-date list of core components, refer to the Microsoft web site at:

   Http://www.microsoft.com/windows/thirdparty/winlogo

2. The adjustment and decrement of the count associated with all components that were shared by the application being removed.

3. If the reference count of a shared component is 0, then the program being removed must leave the count of that component at 0. This is to protect the reference count from installers incrementing this count if the shared component was on the system but not installed.

Note: *Additional requirements exist for products that are being removed from networks. If the application is being developed for Windows NT 5.0, please refer to section 6.3.4 for additional requirements pertaining to this operating system.*

User Interface/Shell: One of the most important aspects of the testing VeriTest does is to determine if the application is compliant with Microsoft's requirements for usability and interface integration. This section describes several requirements for system color, fonts, resolution, sound, keyboard access, and others. It is in this portion of the test where some applications fail due to poor support of application accessibility and interface customization. The basic idea of these tests is to measure an application's ability to deal with global interface changes as well as provide access to the functions and controls of the application. Rather than go through each requirement in this section, focus will be applied to certain elements of good accessibility design for software. These topics will expand on some of those discussed in the *Microsoft Logo Handbook*, and hopefully provide some insight to why these requirements are important. For more detailed information on making software more accessible, go the Microsoft web site for software accessibility at:

http://microsoft.com/enable/dev/apps.htm or
http://www.microsoft.com/win32dev/uiguide

Interface Colors: The User Interface portion of the logo test is very dependent on how the application responds to the GetSystemMetrics, SystemParameterInfo, and GetSysColors API functions. Through its object properties Delphi gives the developer automatic responses to these API calls by allowing the TForm, Tbutton, and other native VCL objects to automatically update themselves when the system variables are changed. If the objects have had their default color values changed at design time and the UI properties are edited from either a right-click on the desktop or the Display Control Panel applet, the objects will not update and will remain their hard coded or property set color.

A list of the native Delphi VCL objects and their default color settings is provided below. If the properties are set to the defaults then the user interface of any Delphi application will be updated automatically at runtime. By leaving these controls' Color or Brush properties set to the defaults there is no need to include code for the API calls listed above. If for some reason these defaults must be changed, the application should have a mechanism for adjusting the interface, or refer to the chapter on System Information Functions for detailed examples and API definitions for using these calls.

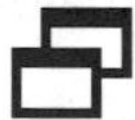

Note: *Only native VCL controls that have a color setting are listed. For custom controls, refer to the Color or Brush properties for the default setting.*

Default Color Setting	Native VCL Controls		
clBtnFace	TForm	TLabel	TButton
	TCheckBox	TRadioButton	TScrollBar
	TGroupBox	TRadioGroup	TPanel
	TBitBtn	TSpeedButton	TScrollBox
	TSplitter	TStaticText	TChart
	TTabControl	TPageControl	TProgressBar
	TUpDown	TAnimate	TStatusBar
	TToolBar	TCoolBar	TPaintBox
	TMediaPlayer	TDBNavigator	TDBText

Default Color Setting	Native VCL Controls		
	TDBCheckBox	TDBCtrlGrid	TDBRadioGroup
	TDBChart	TDecisionGrid	TDecisionGraph
	TQRPreview	TTabSet	TTabbedNotebook
	TNotebook	THeader	TGauge
	TSpinButton		
clWindow	TEdit	TMemo	TListBox
	TComboBox	TMaskEdit	TStringGrid
	TDrawGrid	TRichEdit	TCheckListBox
	THotKey	TTreeView	TDateTimePicker
	TListView	TOleContainer	TDBGrid
	TDBEdit	TDBMemo	TDBImage
	TDBListBox	TDBRichEdit	TDBComboBox
	TQRRichText	TOutline	TDBLookupListBox
	TFileListBox	TSpinEdit	TDBLookupComboBox
	TCalendar		TDBLookupList
	TQRDBRichText		TDriveComboBox
	TDBLookupCombo		TDirectoryListBox
	TFilterComboBox		TDirectoryOutline
clNone	TImageList		
clWhit	TShape	TQRSubDetail	TQRBand
	TQRGroup	TQRLabel	TQRDBText
	TQRExpr	TQRSysData	TQRMemo
	TQRShape		

Note: *For those components whose color is clWhite it may be necessary to provide some means of changing these elements' colors. clWhite is a property or hardcoded color and will not change as system properties are edited.*

At first glance these requirements may seem more trouble than they are worth. In fact such requirements may even seem trivial to the normal user or developer. However, to someone who suffers from a visual handicap, this requirement is very important, and can mean the difference in their keeping the software or returning it.

An excellent example of an application that has mass appeal but breaks this rule of interface compliance is CompuServe's 3.01 network access software. This program has a primary interface color of mixed blues. While this may have been appealing at design time, it is frustrating to a user who is not fond of that color or more seriously has a visual handicap. With no means of altering this color scheme the user is forced to use the product as is or resort to an older version of the software, thus losing the appeal of the upgrade.

Self Test: To verify if the application will meet the User Interface Color Requirements, perform the following self tests:

1. Run the application in its default mode of operation. While in this mode right-click on the desktop or bring up the control panel and select **Display**. When the dialog is visible, click on the button in the foreground and change its color to something obnoxious and bold. The result should be that all 3D objects in the application change color. If this does not happen, then the default clBtnFace settings for some of the controls have been altered and should be returned to its default setting. Refer to the color values previously listed.
2. For a more intense test of color compatibility bring up the Display Properties dialog again and select the High Contrast Black setting. This will dramatically affect the look of Windows and should provide an excellent means of testing the application. Use the application in this manner and test all functions. The potential problems to note are missing functions or user feedback, lost controls, or system messaging. If any of the program's normal functionality is not present, then the color properties need to be adjusted.
3. Verify that color is NOT the only means of communicating information to the end user. If the color of objects or text is the only means of communication, then allow for those elements to be edited for all potential users' needs.

Sound: Sound is a very important mechanism for communicating with end users. These sounds can be used to indicate system warnings, alert for program errors, or highlight successful completion of a task. While sound is a vital means of program and end user communication it cannot be the only means. Just as color could not be the only way to convey important application information, the same requirement applies to an application's use of sound.

There are several things that a developer can do along with or in place of sound to properly warn or get the attention of the user. All of these methods should be provided as a preference or in lieu of general sound alerts and prompts.

1. Use a highlighted font of end user preference to draw attention to areas on a program.

2. Flash the title of the application in the event of an error, or if data or a user response is required. This is accomplished in Delphi by doing the following:

   Note: *This code assumes a form with one button and one timer are present. The timer enabled property is set to true and the caption on the button is "Flashing" in its default state. This code will also cause the task bar to flash as well. This is a good means of gaining a user's attention if an application is minimized.*

```
procedure TForm1.Button1Click(Sender: TObject);
begin
     Timer1.Enabled := not(Timer1.Enabled);
     if Timer1.Enabled then
     Button1.Caption:='Flashing'
else
     Button1.Caption:='Not Flashing';
end;

procedure TForm1.Timer1Timer(Sender: TObject);
begin
     FlashWindow(Handle, TRUE);
     FlashWindow(Application.Handle, TRUE);
end;
end.
```

3. Provide the ability to customize the sounds played for warnings or alerts. Supply the user several options and make them easily available from a preferences or options dialog.

4. Avoid reinventing common graphical controls. Microsoft has provided 27 icons or graphics for buttons in both the standard 16 x 16 and 24 x 24 pixel sizes. Refer to: http://www.microsoft.com/win32dev/uiguide/uigui196.htm for actual button graphics in both formats.

5. Support Microsoft's SoundSentry functionality. This is a feature that will automatically present a visual cue to the user when a sound is played through the PC speaker only. While supporting this technology is not a formal requirement, it is a feature that is beneficial to both the developer and the user, and is appreciated by those users who need this functionality. For more information about SoundSentry and how to implement it, refer to the following web site:

   http://www.microsoft.com/msdn/sdk/platforms/doc/sdk/win32/struc/src/str20_31.htm

   Note: *For more information about sound support and software accessibility, see the Microsoft web site at:*

http://microsoft.com/enable/products/multimedia.htm

Microsoft does have a more comprehensive sound support technology known as ShowSounds. Please refer to

http://www.microsoft.com/win32dev/uiguide/uigui418.htm

General: There are several things developers can do to make software more accessible. While some of these things that have been discussed are not actual logo requirements, they are features and functionality that will make software a better experience for all users. Furthermore, since several of these features have been identified and addressed, it is safe to assume that some of these general usability features will become requirements for the logo programs. The following are some general tips for making software more accessible. For more detailed information about Microsoft's accessibility requirements and the Active Accessibility Software Development Kit, refer to the following web site:

http://www.microsoft.com/mscorp/enable/dev/msaa.htm

General Accessibility Requirements and Tips

1. Provide keyboard access to every control in the application. This should include pull-down menus and pop-up menus. *Requirement for logo compliance.*
2. Make sure tab orders make sense and are implemented for easy navigation on any application form or dialog.
3. Use text identifiers in situations where colors are used. This provides a secondary means of identifying the desired color.
4. Use standard Windows controls in application development where possible. These controls have been designed to work with other accessibility tools.
5. Support Large and Small Font Settings. This should allow the applications text on every control or object to be updated as the system parameters are changed. *Requirement for logo compliance.*
6. Fonts below 10 point should not be hard coded into an application.
7. When using icons or graphical elements in an application, provide a text description of the task or function that will be performed if selected.
8. When resizing the parent or primary form of an application, make sure that the controls reorganize or resize themselves such that they are still accessible. Try avoiding the use of application window scroll bars if possible.
9. Do not use general navigation techniques to initiate a function or procedure associated with a control. General navigation should only be used for accessing the controls and features on a project form.

10. Document all keyboard access functions for the application. This can be included in printed documentation, online documentation, or interactive help systems. *Requirement for logo compliance.*
11. Do not convey important program or system information by color or sound alone. Any message that involves direct attention of the user should rely on multiple methods of alerting the user.
12. Avoid a program's dependence on a particular hardware device for input. Users should be given the option to use a standard keyboard and mouse or have access to other means of input that better facilitate their individual needs.
13. Though not required, index the help files such that F1 will bring up a specific help function for the selected command, or have Context Sensitive Help implemented. This form of help is usually seen as a "?" associated with the mouse pointer and results in detailed flyover help for selected items.

Self Test: To verify if the application will meet the accessibility requirements, try these tests and record any problems that need to get resolved before formal submission.

1. While running the application in Windows 95 or NT, try resizing the primary window of the application. If commands are hidden from view make sure that there is a way to customize the interface such that in this particular view normal operation can occur. This is most commonly seen or accomplished with docking and resizable tool bars, fly-out commands, and extensive pop-up menus.
2. Run the application normally. Attempt using the program without the mouse. Can all of the commands be accessed via the keyboard? If not, then new menu items and hot keys need to be added to the program.
3. Verify that the application responds to color, font type, and size adjustments. If labels, button captions, and other interface elements are distorted or invisible, adjustments need to be made such that these controls function as would be expected. See the System Information Functions chapter for more information on responding to system parameter changes and events.
4. Refer to the Self Test for graphics and color for the testing of these elements.

For a complete list of accessibility issues and their solutions, refer to the Microsoft Accessibility web site at:

http://microsoft.com/enable/dev/guidelines.htm

Also of interest is Microsoft's "Above and Beyond the Windows 95 Logo." This site contains even more information for polishing up applications before they are submitted to VeriTest for formal testing. This site can be found at:

http://www.microsoft.com/win32dev/guidelns/modelap3.htm

Finally, Microsoft has a site specifically for Win32 development, containing a great deal of information pertaining to good software design and implementations along with SDKs and software specifications designed to make the development process easier. To access this information refer to:

http://www.microsoft.com/win32dev/default.htm

User Assistance: Help systems round out and complete the user experience of software. There comes a time when all users need help with an application. Interactive and immediate help systems are now common features in software applications. These systems should be designed to give the user the feedback they need to master the application or task at hand in a quick and efficient manner.

There are many different kinds of help systems users have come to expect in any Windows application. These systems range from providing immediate help on a selected function or control to those that involve searching a cross-referenced file. All logo-compliant applications have some form of help system implementation. In terms of effective help mechanisms, there is no formula for the use of one type over any other. The best applications use these different help types when and where appropriate to the individual products' interface and the perceived amount of information necessary to properly convey the use of the object in question. Therefore, a good mix of different help systems provides the best user experience and the most comprehensive coverage of all topics requiring help messaging.

Various Help Systems:

Tool Tips: Tool Tips are quick real-time help messages designed to provide simple information to users about the function, option, or control that has been or is about to be selected. These tips are added to an application or object by entering a text string in the object's Hint property and enabling the ShowHint property. Tool Tips are displayed when the pointer is left over an object for a short period of time. Tool Tips are hidden when the user moves the pointer or interacts with the control or the tip times out and hides itself due to inactivity.

Status Bar: A status bar is a constant interface element that text messages are displayed on as the user interacts with the program. Status bars can provide either a temporary stream of information or a constant one such as mouse coordinates or feedback concerning a program's progress.

Context Sensitive: Context Sensitive help answers the questions "What is this?" and "What does this thing do?" This form of help is an extension of the Tool Tip and a step under the formal search and research help system. Context help allows the user to select objects and functions within an application and get more detailed information as to the operation and use of the control being investigated. This help is not as verbose as formal help files but is a step up from the normal Tool Tip or status bar.

Reference Help: Reference Help files are a comprehensive mechanism for providing the user with detailed information on the control or process in question and the results of its use. Good integration of both Help files and Context Sensitive help depend on the Help file association found in the object's HelpFile property and the HelpContext value found in the individual object's properties as listed in the object inspector. Integrating the help files at this level allows the user to quickly click on objects and gain additional information that was not provided in the other forms of help. Help files will provide for the searching and linking of associated features and functionality based on keywords as determined by the help author.

Wizards: Wizards are a different help system that aid the user by walking them through several steps of a detailed process. Wizards are typically displayed as dialogs that question the user about the desired result, and then generate a final output based on the user's responses to the queries.

Interactive Help: Interactive help systems are those that provide information much like a Reference Help file but provide the user with the ability to interact with the help program. This type of help is very well suited to tutorials or "Show Me" help where the help system will interactively demonstrate to the user the proper method of using a function or control in a program.

Application Compatibility

The final section of the logo compliance test pertains to application compatibility. Application compatibility involves features that allow applications to work well together. The general areas of testing involve the implementations of Object Linking and Embedding (OLE), ActiveX controls, and some areas of communications for telephony applications. OLE is a software functionality that is required in many of the logo compliance application types. This technology allows users to ignore the source of data and simply integrate it into a compound document. Compound documents are those that are pieced together from several different source files to form one complete file in the end. For more information on OLE, its functionality, and its requirements for logo compliance, refer to Microsoft's Windows Interface Guidelines for Software Design web site at:

http://www.microsoft.com/win32dev/uiguide/uigui291.htm or
http://www.veritest.com/labs/logolab/Microsoft/microsoft(f).htm

While this chapter is a more in-depth look at some of the requirements for obtaining a Microsoft logo, it is not a replacement for the formal testing document. Please refer to the official *Logo Handbook for Software Applications (Version 3)* for more details on the requirements and exemptions associated with individual product categories.

Chapter 3

Window Creation Functions

Window creation is a fundamental part of any Windows program. Almost every user interface element is a window, such as the application window itself and controls that accept input from the mouse and keyboard. The window creation functions are also the most complex and error prone functions in the entire Windows API. Casual Delphi programmers will never have any need to know the information contained in this chapter, as Delphi does a very good job of hiding the details of creating a window. However, knowing the steps required to create a window the hard way can give the developer the knowledge needed to extend Delphi's basic functionality and accomplish things that are not encapsulated by the VCL.

Creating a window requires the developer to follow a complex and detailed sequence of steps. In general, creating a window involves registering a class with the operating system, followed by a complex function call to actually create the window based on this class. A window class is a set of attributes that define the basic look and behavior for a window. These attributes are used as a template from which any number of windows can be created. There are predefined classes for every common Windows user interface control, such as edit boxes, buttons, etc. However, to create a new type of window, such as the main window for an application, the developer must register a window class. Delphi's encapsulation of the Windows API makes all of this transparent to the developer. However, there may be certain instances when the developer needs to create a window the old-fashioned way.

Creating Windows: The Basic Steps

Creating a window using low-level Windows API functions is a detailed but straightforward task. There are three steps the developer generally must follow when creating a window:

1. A new window class must be registered. If the developer is creating a window based on one of the predefined Windows classes, this step is omitted.
2. The window is then created using one of the window creation functions.
3. Finally, this window is displayed on the screen. This step is omitted if the WS_VISIBLE style flag is used in the dwStyle parameter.

If a window is successfully created, it returns a handle. This window handle is used in a variety of API functions to perform tasks on the window associated with that handle. Any control that descends from TWinControl is a window created with one of the window creation functions and therefore has a window handle, accessible as the Handle property of that particular control. This handle can be used in any Windows API function that requires a window handle as a parameter.

The following example demonstrates how to create a window by following the above steps.

Listing 3-1: Creating a Window

```
{Register the Window Class}
function RegisterClass: Boolean;
var
  WindowClass: TWndClass;
begin
  {set up our new window class}
  WindowClass.Style := CS_HREDRAW or CS_VREDRAW;      {set the class styles}
  WindowClass.lpfnWndProc := @DefWindowProc;          {point to the default
                                                       window procedure}
  WindowClass.cbClsExtra := 0;                        {no extra class memory}
  WindowClass.cbWndExtra := 0;                        {no extra window memory}
  WindowClass.hInstance := hInstance;                 {the application instance}
  WindowClass.hIcon := 0;                             {no icon specified}
  WindowClass.hCursor := 0;                           {no cursor specified}
  WindowClass.hbrBackground := COLOR_WINDOW;          {use a predefined color}
  WindowClass.lpszMenuName := nil;                    {no menu}
  WindowClass.lpszClassName := 'TestClass';           {the registered class name}

  {now that we have our class set up, register it with the system}
  Result := Windows.RegisterClass(WindowClass) <> 0;
end;

procedure TForm1.Button1Click(Sender: TObject);
var
  hWindow: HWND;
begin
  {Step 1: Register our new window class}
  if not RegisterClass then
  begin
    ShowMessage('RegisterClass failed');
    Exit;
  end;

  {Step 2: Create a window based on our new class}
  hWindow := CreateWindow('TestClass',              {the registered class name}
                          'New Window',             {the title bar text}
                          WS_OVERLAPPEDWINDOW,      {a normal window style}
                          CW_USEDEFAULT,            {default horizontal position}
                          CW_USEDEFAULT,            {default vertical position}
                          CW_USEDEFAULT,            {default width}
                          CW_USEDEFAULT,            {default height}
                          0,                        {no owner window}
```

```
                        0,                      {no menu}
                        hInstance,              {the application instance}
                        nil                     {no additional information}
                        );

  {Step 3: If our window was created successfully, display it}
  if hWindow <> 0 then
  begin
    ShowWindow(hWindow, SW_SHOWNORMAL);
    UpdateWindow(hWindow);
  end
  else
  begin
    ShowMessage('CreateWindow failed');
    Exit;
  end;

end;
```

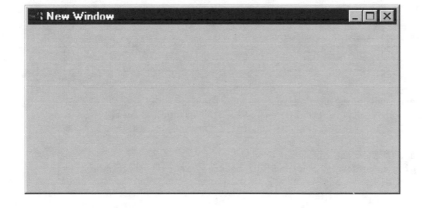

Figure 3-1: The new window.

The Window Procedure

Each window class has a function associated with it known as the window procedure. It is a callback function which Windows uses to communicate with the application. This function determines how the window interacts with the user and what is displayed in its client area. Windows created from a particular class will use the window procedure assigned to that class. See Listing 3-2 for an example of using a window procedure.

Delphi automatically creates window procedures that provide the appropriate functionality based on the window type. However, a developer may want to modify or extend this behavior. A window's functionality can be altered by subclassing the window procedure and providing a new one. This technique is covered in the chapter on Window Information Functions.

The window procedure is little more than a large Case statement, checking for specific messages that the developer wants to provide functionality for. Each message that will have an action associated with it has a line in the Case statement. In Delphi, this manifests itself as the events for any particular control, such as OnKeyPress or OnResize. Any messages that are not specifically handled must be passed to the DefWindowProc procedure. MDI child windows use the DefMDIChildProc procedure, and MDI frame windows use the DefFrameProc procedure. These procedures provide the basic behavior for any window, such as resizing, moving, etc.

Hardcore Windows Programming

Delphi is fully capable of bypassing the functionality provided by the VCL, allowing a developer to write an entire Windows program in nothing but Object Pascal. The following example demonstrates how such a program is written. Note that the main unit must be removed from the project, and the following code is typed directly into the project source file.

Listing 3-2: A Windows Application Written Entirely in Object Pascal

```
program HardCore;

uses
    Windows, Messages;

{$R *.RES}

{The window procedure for our hardcore API window}
function WindowProc(TheWindow: HWnd; TheMessage, WParam,
                    LParam: Longint): Longint; stdcall;
begin
  case TheMessage of
    {upon getting the WM_DESTROY message, we exit the application}
    WM_DESTROY: begin
                  PostQuitMessage(0);
                  Exit;
               end;
  end;

  {call the default window procedure for all unhandled messages}
  Result := DefWindowProc(TheWindow, TheMessage, WParam, LParam);
end;

{ Register the Window Class }
function RegisterClass: Boolean;
var
  WindowClass: TWndClass;
begin
  {set up our new window class}
  WindowClass.Style := CS_HREDRAW or CS_VREDRAW;      {set the class styles}
  WindowClass.lpfnWndProc := @WindowProc;             {our window procedure}
  WindowClass.cbClsExtra := 0;                        {no extra class memory}
  WindowClass.cbWndExtra := 0;                        {no extra window memory}
  WindowClass.hInstance := hInstance;                 {the application instance}
  WindowClass.hIcon := LoadIcon(0, IDI_APPLICATION); {load a predefined logo}
  WindowClass.hCursor := LoadCursor(0, IDC_UPARROW); {load a predefined cursor}
```

```
  WindowClass.hbrBackground := COLOR_WINDOW;          {use a predefined color}
  WindowClass.lpszMenuName := nil;                    {no menu}
  WindowClass.lpszClassName := 'TestClass';           {the registered class name}

  {now that we have our class set up, register it with the system}
  Result := Windows.RegisterClass(WindowClass) <> 0;
end;


var
  TheMessage: TMsg;
  OurWindow: HWND;
begin
  {register our new class first}
  if not RegisterClass then
  begin
    MessageBox(0,'RegisterClass failed',nil,MB_OK);
    Exit;
  end;

  {now, create a window based on our new class}
  OurWindow := CreateWindow('TestClass',           {the registered class name}
                            'HardCore Window',     {the title bar text}
                            WS_OVERLAPPEDWINDOW or {a normal window style}
                            WS_VISIBLE,            {initially visible}
                            CW_USEDEFAULT,         {default horizontal position}
                            CW_USEDEFAULT,         {default vertical position}
                            CW_USEDEFAULT,         {default width}
                            CW_USEDEFAULT,         {default height}
                            0,                     {no parent window}
                            0,                     {no menu}
                            hInstance,             {the application instance}
                            nil                    {no additional information}
                            );

  {if our window was not created successfully, exit the program}
  if OurWindow=0 then
  begin
    MessageBox(0,'CreateWindow failed',nil,MB_OK);
    Exit;
  end;

  {the standard message loop}
  while GetMessage(TheMessage,0,0,0) do
  begin
    TranslateMessage(TheMessage);
    DispatchMessage(TheMessage);
  end;

end.
```

Figure 3-2: The hardcore window.

Window Types

The style flags available for the dwStyle and dwExStyle parameters of the CreateWindow and CreateWindowEx functions provide an almost infinite variety of window types. In general, all windows can be classified under three categories:

Overlapped: This is the most common type of window, and is generally the style used by the main window of the application. This type of window includes the WS_OVERLAPPED style flag in the dwStyle parameter, can be resized by the user at runtime, and includes a caption bar, system menu, and minimize and maximize buttons. This type of window will appear on the task bar.

Child: This is the second most common style. All windowed controls and MDI child windows fit into this category. This window type includes the WS_CHILD style flag in the dwStyle parameter. MDI child windows will include the WS_EX_MDICHILD style flag in the dwExStyle parameter. The window whose handle is provided in the hWndParent parameter of the window creation function becomes the parent window to this child window. The parent window provides the surface upon which the child window displays itself. Conversely, a child window is completely contained within the parent. It is clipped to the edges of the parent window, and it is always shown on top of the parent window's client area. Child windows do not appear on the task bar. When the parent window of a child window is destroyed, the child windows are also destroyed.

Pop-up: Common dialog boxes and property sheets fall into this category. This type of window includes the WS_POPUP style flag in the dwStyle parameter. The parent window of a pop-up window is always the desktop window. The hWndParent parameter is used to specify an owner for pop-up windows. An unowned pop-up window will remain visible even when the main window of an application is minimized, and will appear on the task bar. If a window handle is provided in the hWndParent parameter, the window associated with that handle becomes the owner of the pop-up window. The owned pop-up window hides when the owner is minimized, reappears when the owner is restored, stays on top of the owner window even when the owner window is maximized or has focus, and does not appear on the task bar. This type of window is perfect for toolbar or palette windows.

Any window can have the WS_OVERLAPPED style flag, but the WS_CHILD and WS_POPUP flags are mutually exclusive. If the hWndParent parameter of an overlapped window contains the handle to another window, this window acts as the owner for the overlapped window, which takes on the characteristics of an owned pop-up. Since the parent window is responsible for providing a display area for its child windows, whenever the parent window of any window is destroyed, all related windows belonging to that parent are also destroyed. Figure 3-3 illustrates the various types of windows.

Figure 3-3: Window types.

Multiple Document Interface

Multiple Document Interface applications consist of a frame window, which acts as the main application window, a client window, the workspace where all of the child document windows are displayed, and one or more MDI child windows. The MDI child windows are where users perform their work. Delphi encapsulates most of this functionality through the FormStyle property of a form. Simply setting this property to fsMDIForm can create an MDI frame and client window; setting the property to fsMDIChild creates MDI child windows. However, there may be certain times when a developer needs to create an MDI application using conventional Windows API functions. Developers should follow these steps when creating an MDI application using the Windows API:

1. A new window class must be registered. This class is used to create the frame window, and cannot be one of the predefined Windows classes.
2. The frame window is then created using one of the window creation functions.
3. Display the frame window on the screen. This step is omitted if the WS_VISIBLE style flag is used in the dwStyle parameter.

4. Create a variable of type TClientCreateStruct, and fill in the members of the structure with the appropriate information.
5. The client window is created using one of the window creation functions. Use the predefined Window class name MDICLIENT, and pass the handle to the frame window in the hWndParent parameter. Use the WS_CLIPCHILDREN and WS_CHILD style flags in the dwStyle parameter, and pass a pointer to the TClientCreateStruct variable in the lpParam parameter.
6. Display the client window on the screen. This step is omitted if the WS_VISIBLE style flag is used in the dwStyle parameter.
7. Register the classes that will be used for the MDI child windows.
8. Create the MDI child window. This is done by creating a variable of type TMDICreateStruct, filling out the members of the structure, and sending a WM_MDICREATE message to the MDICLIENT window, passing a pointer to the TMDICreateStruct variable in the lParam member of the message, or by using the CreateMDIWindow API function.
9. Display the new MDI child window on the screen. This step is omitted if the WS_VISIBLE style flag is used in the dwStyle parameter.

The following example shows how to create an MDI application using hardcore Windows programming techniques. It must be created in the same fashion as the example under Hardcore Windows Programming, above.

Listing 3-3: Create an MDI Application in Object Pascal

```
program MDIApp;

uses
    Windows, Messages;

var
  TheMessage: TMsg;
  FrameWindow, ClientWindow, ChildWindow: HWND;

const
  {the ID for the first MDI child window}
  IDCHILDWND = 100;

{$R *.RES}

{this defines the window procedure for our frame window}
function FrameWindowProc(TheFrameWindow: HWnd; TheMessage, WParam,
                         LParam: Longint): Longint; stdcall;
var
  {this is used when creating an MDI client window}
  ClientStruct: TClientCreateStruct;
begin
  case TheMessage of
    {The frame window will be created first. Once it is created, the
     WM_CREATE message is sent to this function, where we create the
```

```
    MDI client window}
   WM_CREATE: begin
        {Step 4: Fill in the appropriate information about the client window}
        ClientStruct.hWindowMenu:=0;
        ClientStruct.idFirstChild:= IDCHILDWND;

        {Step 5: Create the MDI client window}
        ClientWindow := CreateWindow('MDICLIENT',       {registered class name}
                                     NIL,               {no window text}
                                     WS_CHILD or        {a child window}
                                     WS_CLIPCHILDREN or {clip its child
                                                         windows}
                                     WS_VISIBLE,        {initially visible}
                                     0,                 {horizontal position}
                                     0,                 {vertical position}
                                     0,                 {width}
                                     0,                 {height}
                                     TheFrameWindow,    {handle of the parent
                                                         window}
                                     0,                 {no menu}
                                     hInstance,         {application instance}
                                     @ClientStruct      {additional creation
                                                         information}
                                     );

        {Step 6 was taken care of by including the WS_VISIBLE flag in the
         dwStyle parameter. Now we check to see if it was created}
        if ClientWindow=0 then
             begin
                  MessageBox(0,'CreateClientWindow failed',nil,MB_OK);
                  Exit;
             end;
   end;
   {upon getting the WM_DESTROY message, we exit the application}
   WM_DESTROY: begin
                  PostQuitMessage(0);
                  Exit;
               end;
  end;

  {call the default frame window procedure for all unhandled messages}
  Result := DefFrameProc(TheFrameWindow, ClientWindow, TheMessage, WParam,
                         LParam);
end;

{ Register the frame window Class }
function RegisterFrameClass: Boolean;
var
  WindowClass: TWndClass;
begin
  {set up our frame window class}
  WindowClass.Style := CS_HREDRAW or CS_VREDRAW;      {set the class styles}
  WindowClass.lpfnWndProc := @FrameWindowProc;        {point to our frame window
                                                       procedure}
  WindowClass.cbClsExtra := 0;                        {no extra class memory}
```

3 Chapter

```
  WindowClass.cbWndExtra := 0;                        {no extra window memory}
  WindowClass.hInstance := hInstance;                 {the application instance}
  WindowClass.hIcon := LoadIcon(0, IDI_WINLOGO);      {load a predefined logo}
  WindowClass.hCursor := LoadCursor(0, IDC_ARROW);    {load a predefined cursor}
  WindowClass.hbrBackground := COLOR_WINDOW;          {use a predefined color}
  WindowClass.lpszMenuName := nil;                    {no menu}
  WindowClass.lpszClassName := 'FrameClass';          {the registered class name}

  {now that we have our class set up, register it with the system}
  Result := Windows.RegisterClass(WindowClass) <> 0;
end;

{ Register the child window Class }
function RegisterChildClass: Boolean;
var
  WindowClass: TWndClass;
begin
  {setup our child window class}
  WindowClass.Style := CS_HREDRAW or CS_VREDRAW;      {set the class styles}
  WindowClass.lpfnWndProc := @DefMDIChildProc;        {point to the default MDI
                                                       child window procedure}
  WindowClass.cbClsExtra := 0;                        {no extra class memory}
  WindowClass.cbWndExtra := 0;                        {no extra window memory}
  WindowClass.hInstance := hInstance;                 {the application instance}
  WindowClass.hIcon := LoadIcon(0, IDI_APPLICATION);  {load a predefined logo}
  WindowClass.hCursor := LoadCursor(0, IDC_ARROW);    {load a predefined cursor}
  WindowClass.hbrBackground := COLOR_WINDOW;          {use a predefined color}
  WindowClass.lpszMenuName := nil;                    {no menu}
  WindowClass.lpszClassName := 'ChildClass';          {the registered class name}

  {now that we have our class set up, register it with the system}
  Result := Windows.RegisterClass(WindowClass) <> 0;
end;

{this begins the main program}
begin
  {Step 1: Register our frame class first}
  if not RegisterFrameClass then
  begin
    MessageBox(0,'RegisterFrameClass failed',nil,MB_OK);
    Exit;
  end;

  {Step 2: Create the frame window based on our frame class}
  FrameWindow := CreateWindow('FrameClass',          {the registered class name}
                              'Frame Window',         {the title bar text}
                              WS_OVERLAPPEDWINDOW or {a normal window style}
                              WS_CLIPCHILDREN,        {clips all child windows}
                              CW_USEDEFAULT,          {default horizontal position}
                              CW_USEDEFAULT,          {default vertical position}
                              CW_USEDEFAULT,          {default width}
                              CW_USEDEFAULT,          {default height}
                              0,                      {handle of the parent window}
                              0,                      {no menu}
                              hInstance,              {the application instance}
```

```
                        nil                    {no additional information}
                        );

{Step 3: If our frame window was created successfully, show it}
if FrameWindow <> 0 then
begin
  ShowWindow(FrameWindow, SW_SHOWNORMAL);
  UpdateWindow(FrameWindow);
end
else
begin
  MessageBox(0,'CreateFrameWindow failed',nil,MB_OK);
  Exit;
end;

{For steps 4-6, see the FrameWindowProc procedure above}

{Step 7: Register the child window class}
if not RegisterChildClass then
begin
  MessageBox(0,'RegisterChildClass failed',nil,MB_OK);
  Exit;
end;

{Step 8: Create the MDI child window}
ChildWindow := CreateMDIWindow('ChildClass',     {the registered class name}
                               'Child Window',   {the title bar text}
                               WS_VISIBLE,       {initially visible}
                               CW_USEDEFAULT,    {default horizontal position}
                               CW_USEDEFAULT,    {default vertical position}
                               CW_USEDEFAULT,    {default width}
                               CW_USEDEFAULT,    {default height}
                               ClientWindow,     {handle of the parent window}
                               hInstance,        {the application instance}
                               0                 {no application defined value}
                               );

{Step 9 was taken care of by including the WS_VISIBLE flag in the
 dwStyle parameter. Now we check to see if it was created}
if ChildWindow <> 0 then
begin
  ShowWindow(ChildWindow, SW_SHOWNORMAL);
  UpdateWindow(ChildWindow);
end
else
begin
  MessageBox(0,'CreateChildWindow failed',nil,mb_ok);
  Exit;
end;

{the standard message loop}
while GetMessage(TheMessage,0,0,0) do
begin
  TranslateMessage(TheMessage);
  DispatchMessage(TheMessage);
```

```
  end;
end.
```

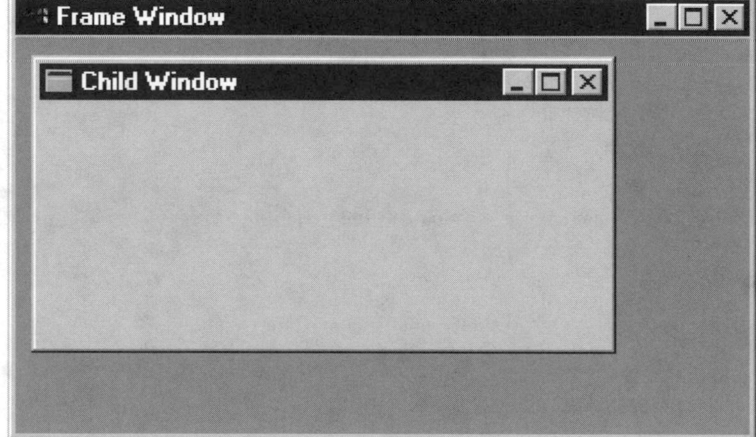

Figure 3-4: The Object Pascal MDI application.

The conventional way to create MDI child windows is to send the WM_MDICREATE message to the MDICLIENT window. However, this message cannot be used to create MDI child windows from a different thread. Use the CreateMDIWindow function to get around this limitation. A developer can use this function to allow each MDI child window to have its own thread.

It is possible to combine the functionality of the VCL with the power of low-level Windows API functions. The following example demonstrates how to use low-level Windows API functions to create MDI child windows with a Delphi form as the MDI frame window. Note that the main form must have the FormStyle set to fsMDIForm, and the ClientHandle property contains a handle to the MDICLIENT window.

Listing 3-4: Using the WM_MDICREATE Message with a Delphi Form

```
{ Register the MDI Child Window Class }
function RegisterClass: Boolean;
var
  WindowClass: TWndClass;
begin
  {set up our new window class}
  WindowClass.Style := CS_HREDRAW or CS_VREDRAW;      {set the class styles}
  WindowClass.lpfnWndProc := @DefMDIChildProc;        {point to the default MDI
                                                       child window procedure}
  WindowClass.cbClsExtra := 0;                        {no extra class memory}
  WindowClass.cbWndExtra := 0;                        {no extra window memory}
  WindowClass.hInstance := hInstance;                 {the application instance}
  WindowClass.hIcon := LoadIcon(0, IDI_WINLOGO);      {load a predefined logo}
  WindowClass.hCursor := LoadCursor(0, IDC_APPSTARTING); {load a predefined
                                                         cursor}
  WindowClass.hbrBackground := COLOR_WINDOW;          {use a predefined color}
  WindowClass.lpszMenuName := nil;                    {no menu}
```

```
  WindowClass.lpszClassName := 'TestClass';          {the registered class name}

  {now that we have our class set up, register it with the system}
  Result := Windows.RegisterClass(WindowClass) <> 0;
end;

procedure TForm1.FormCreate(Sender: TObject);
begin
  {register our child window class}
  if not RegisterClass then
  begin
    ShowMessage('RegisterClass failed');
    Exit;
  end;
end;

procedure TForm1.CreateChild1Click(Sender: TObject);
var
    ChildWnd: HWND;
    MDICreate: TMDICreateStruct;
begin
    {note that the main form has the FormStyle
     property set to fsMDIForm}

    {fill in the members of the MDICreate structure}
    with MDICreate do
    begin
      szClass:='TestClass';                       {our registered class name}
      szTitle:='MDI Child window';                {caption bar test}
      hOwner:=hInstance;                          {the application instance
                                                   handle}
      X:=CW_USEDEFAULT;                           {default horizontal position}
      Y:=CW_USEDEFAULT;                           {default vertical position}
      CX:=CW_USEDEFAULT;                          {default width}
      CY:=CW_USEDEFAULT;                          {default height}
      style:=WS_OVERLAPPEDWINDOW OR WS_VISIBLE;   {standard, visible window}
      lParam:=0;                                  {no extra information}
    end;

    {now, create the MDI child window using the WM_MDICREATE message}
    ChildWnd:=SendMessage(Form1.ClientHandle, WM_MDICREATE, 0,
                          Longint(@MDICreate));
end;
```

Extending Functionality

When Delphi creates a control that encapsulates one of the predefined Windows classes, such as an edit box or button, the code for that object calls the CreateWindowEx function to create the actual window. The CreateParams method is called prior to calling CreateWindowEx. In this method, a data structure of type TCreateParams is initialized with information that will eventually be used as the parameters in the CreateWindowEx call. The TCreateParams structure is defined as:

```
TCreateParams = record
    Caption: PChar;                      {the window text}
    Style: Longint;                      {the style flags}
    ExStyle: Longint;                    {the extended style flags}
    X: Integer;                          {the initial horizontal position}
    Y: Integer;                          {the initial vertical position}
    Width: Integer;                      {the initial width}
    Height: Integer;                     {the initial height}
    WndParent: HWND;                     {a handle to the parent window}
    Param: Pointer                       {additional creation data}
    WindowClass: TWndClass;              {window class information}
    WinClassName: array[0..63] of Char;  {the registered class name}
end;
```

The WindowClass member is of type TWndClass and contains information used in the parameters to the RegisterClass function. Please see the CreateWindow, CreateWindowEx, RegisterClass, and RegisterClassEx functions for a full description of what these parameters affect.

The developer can override the CreateParams method, specifying the appropriate information to be used when creating that control or window. In this way, a developer can extend the functionality of standard Delphi controls at the API level.

This example shows how a developer can create a multiple line, right aligned, numerical digit edit box from a TEdit control by modifying the flags in the Style member.

Listing 3-5: Overriding CreateParams to Extend the Functionality of a TEdit Control

```
unit NumEdit;

interface

uses
  Windows, Messages, SysUtils, Classes, Graphics, Controls, Forms, Dialogs,
  StdCtrls;

type
  TNumberEdit = class(TEdit)
  private
    { Private declarations }
  protected
    { Protected declarations }
  public
    { Public declarations }
    procedure CreateParams(var Params: TCreateParams); override;
    constructor Create(AOwner: TComponent); override;
  published
    { Published declarations }
  end;

procedure Register;
```

```
implementation

procedure TNumberEdit.CreateParams(var Params: TCreateParams);
begin
  {call the inherited procedure to fill in the default values}
  inherited CreateParams(Params);

  {create an edit box...}
  Params.Style:=Params.Style or      {that has default edit box properties plus}
                ES_MULTILINE or      {multiple lines,}
                ES_RIGHT or          {right edge alignment,}
                ES_NUMBER or         {accepts only numbers,}
                ES_WANTRETURN;       {and the enter key inserts a line return}
end;

constructor TNumberEdit.Create(AOwner: TComponent);
begin
  inherited Create(AOwner);

  {we reset the AutoSize property so the control can be enlarged.}
  AutoSize:=FALSE;
end;

procedure Register;
begin
  RegisterComponents('Samples', [TNumberEdit]);
end;

end.
```

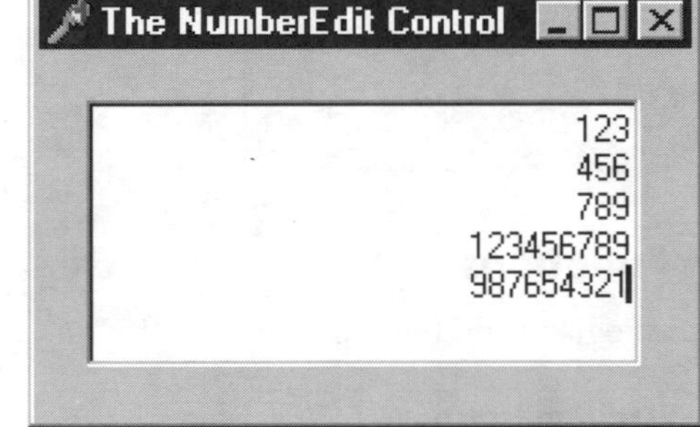

Figure 3-5: The right aligned, numerical digit edit box.

This technique can be used with forms as well. This example shows how to create a form with a raised edge.

Listing 3-6: Creating a Form with a Raised Edge

```
type
  TForm1 = class(TForm)
  private
    { Private declarations }
  public
```

```
    { Public declarations }
    procedure CreateParams(var Params: TCreateParams); override;
  end;

var
  Form1: TForm1;

implementation

{$R *.DFM}

procedure TForm1.CreateParams(var Params: TCreateParams);
begin
  {call the inherited function to create the default parameters}
  inherited CreateParams(Params);

  {this form will have an edge with a ridge}
  Params.ExStyle:=Params.ExStyle or WS_EX_OVERLAPPEDWINDOW;
end;
```

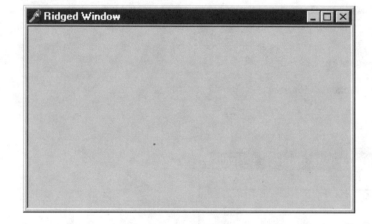

Figure 3-6: The raised edge form.

Window Creation and Registration Functions

The following window creation and registration functions are covered in this chapter:

Table 3-1: Window Creation and Registration Functions

Function	Description
CreateMDIWindow	Creates MDI child windows.
CreateWindow	The standard window creation function.
CreateWindowEx	Creates windows using extended style flags.
DestroyWindow	Destroys a window.
RegisterClass	Registers a new window class.
RegisterClassEx	Registers a new window class using extended style flags.
UnregisterClass	Unregisters a registered window class.

CreateMDIWindow Windows.Pas

Syntax

```
CreateMDIWindow(
lpClassName: PChar;          {a pointer to the child class name string}
lpWindowName: PChar;         {a pointer to the window name string}
dwStyle: DWORD;              {window style flags}
X: Integer;                  {initial horizontal position}
Y: Integer;                  {initial vertical position}
nWidth: Integer;             {initial width of the window}
nHeight: Integer;            {initial height of the window}
hWndParent: HWND;            {a handle to the parent MDI client window}
hInstance: HINST;            {a handle to the module instance}
lParam: LPARAM               {an application defined value}
): HWND;                     {returns a handle to the new window}
```


Description

This function creates Multiple Document Interface child windows, and is similar to sending a WM_MDICREATE message to an MDI client window. For more information on creating windows, see the CreateWindow function. This function is intended to be used for creating MDI child windows in a separate thread.

Note: Windows 95 can support a maximum of 16,364 window handles.

Parameters

lpClassName: A pointer to a null-terminated, case-sensitive string specifying the window class for the MDI child window. This class is registered by calling the RegisterClass function.

lpWindowName: A pointer to a null-terminated, case-sensitive string. This string is displayed in the title bar of the MDI child window.

dwStyle: A 32-bit number that specifies what styles this window uses. If the MDI client window is using the MDIS_ALLCHILDSTYLES window style flag, this parameter can be any combination of the styles from the window style table in the CreateWindow function. Otherwise, it can be any combination of styles from the following table. Two or more styles are specified by using the Boolean OR operator, i.e., WS_MINIMIZE OR WS_HSCROLL.

X: The initial horizontal position for the upper left corner of the MDI child window. This position is relative to the client area of the MDI client window. Using the CW_USEDEFAULT constant causes Windows to choose the default horizontal position for the window.

Y: The initial vertical position for the upper left corner of the MDI child window. This position is relative to the client area of the MDI client window. Using the CW_USEDEFAULT constant causes Windows to choose the default vertical position for the window.

nWidth: The initial width of the MDI child window. If the CW_USEDEFAULT constant is used, Windows gives the MDI child window an internally defined default width.

nHeight: The initial height of the MDI child window. If the CW_USEDEFAULT constant is used, Windows gives the MDI child window an internally defined default width.

hWndParent: A handle to the MDI client window that becomes the parent of the child window.

hInstance: The instance handle of the application or module creating this window.

lParam: A 32-bit application-defined value.

Return Value

If this function succeeds, it returns a handle to the newly created MDI child window; otherwise it returns zero.

See also

CreateWindow, CreateWindowEx, WM_MDICREATE

Example

Listing 3-7: Creating an MDI Child Window

```
{ Register the MDI Child Window Class }
function RegisterClass: Boolean;
var
  WindowClass: TWndClass;
begin
  {setup our new window class}
  WindowClass.Style := CS_HREDRAW or CS_VREDRAW;      {set the class styles}
  WindowClass.lpfnWndProc := @DefMDIChildProc;        {point to the default MDI
                                                       child window procedure}
  WindowClass.cbClsExtra := 0;                        {no extra class memory}
  WindowClass.cbWndExtra := 0;                        {no extra window memory}
  WindowClass.hInstance := hInstance;                 {the application instance}
  WindowClass.hIcon := LoadIcon(0, IDI_WINLOGO);      {load a predefined icon}
  WindowClass.hCursor := LoadCursor(0, IDC_APPSTARTING); {load a predefined
                                                          cursor}
  WindowClass.hbrBackground := COLOR_WINDOW;          {use a predefined color}
  WindowClass.lpszMenuName := nil;                    {no menu}
  WindowClass.lpszClassName := 'TestClass';           {the registered class name}
```

```
  {now that we have our class set up, register it with the system}
  Result := Windows.RegisterClass(WindowClass) <> 0;
end;

procedure TForm1.CreateChild1Click(Sender: TObject);
var
  hWindow: HWND;
begin
  {register our new class first. Note that the FormStyle property of the main
   form in this example is set to fsMDIForm.}
  if not RegisterClass then
  begin
    ShowMessage('RegisterClass failed');
    Exit;
  end;

  {now, create a window based on our new class}
  hWindow := CreateMDIWindow('TestClass',          {the registered class name}
                             'API Window',         {the title bar text}
                             WS_VISIBLE OR         {the MDI child window is
                                                    visible,}
                             WS_CAPTION OR         {has a caption bar,}
                             WS_SYSMENU OR         {a system menu,}
                             WS_MINIMIZEBOX OR     {and minimize and}
                             WS_MAXIMIZEBOX,       {maximize boxes}
                             CW_USEDEFAULT,        {default horizontal
                                                    position}
                             CW_USEDEFAULT,        {default vertical position}
                             CW_USEDEFAULT,        {default width}
                             CW_USEDEFAULT,        {default height}
                             Form1.ClientHandle,   {handle of the MDI client
                                                    window}
                             hInstance,            {the application instance}
                             0                     {no additional information}
                             );

  {if our window was created successfully, show it}
  if hWindow <> 0 then
  begin
    ShowWindow(hWindow, SW_SHOWNORMAL);
    UpdateWindow(hWindow);
  end
  else
  begin
    ShowMessage('CreateWindow failed');
    Exit;
  end;

end;
```

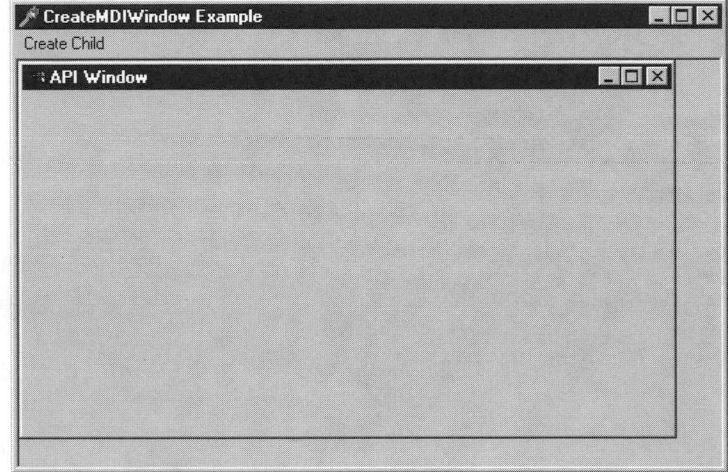

Figure 3-7: The MDI child window.

Table 3-2: CreateMDIWindow dwStyle Values

Value	Description
WS_MINIMIZE	The MDI child window is initially minimized.
WS_MAXIMIZE	The MDI child window is initially maximized.
WS_HSCROLL	The MDI child window has a horizontal scroll bar.
WS_VSCROLL	The MDI child window has a vertical scroll bar.

CreateWindow *Windows.Pas*

Syntax

```
CreateWindow(
lpClassName: PChar;           {a pointer to the class name string}
lpWindowName: PChar;          {a pointer to the window name string}
dwStyle: DWORD;               {window style flags}
X: Integer;                   {initial horizontal position}
Y: Integer;                   {initial vertical position}
nWidth: Integer;              {initial width of the window}
nHeight: Integer;             {initial height of the window}
hWndParent: HWND;             {a handle to the parent window}
hMenu: HMENU;                 {a handle to the menu, or a child window identifier}
hInstance: HINST;             {a handle to the module instance}
lpParam: Pointer              {a pointer to additional information}
): HWND;                      {returns a handle to the new window}
```

Description

The CreateWindow function creates an overlapped, pop-up, or child window based on either one of the predefined window classes or a new window class created with the RegisterClass function. This function is used when creating any type of window, including the main window of the application and any child windows or user interface controls that are used in the application. The initial size and position of the window may be set, and an owner, parent, or menu may be specified.

Before this function returns, it sends a WM_CREATE message to the window procedure. For overlapped, pop-up, and child windows, this function will also send the WM_GETMINMAXINFO and WM_NCCREATE messages. If the WS_VISIBLE style is specified, CreateWindow will send all of the messages necessary to activate and show the window.

Note: Windows 95 can support a maximum of 16,364 window handles.

Parameters

lpClassName: A pointer to a null-terminated, case-sensitive string, or an integer atom. It describes a valid, predefined class name or one created with the RegisterClass function. See Table 3-3 for valid predefined window classes. If this specifies an atom, the atom must have been created with a call to GlobalAddAtom. The atom, a 16-bit value less than $C000, must be in the low-order word of ClassName and the high-order word must be zero.

lpWindowName: A null-terminated string containing the name for this window. This is displayed on the title bar of the window. If this window is a control, this is the text displayed on the control.

dwStyle: A 32-bit number that describes what styles this window uses. Available style constants are listed in Table 3-4. Multiple styles are combined by using the Boolean OR operator; i.e., WS_HSCROLL OR WS_VSCROLL.

X: The initial horizontal position of the upper left corner of the window. For overlapped or pop-up windows, this coordinate is relative to the screen. For child windows, this coordinate is relative to the upper left corner of the parent window's client area. If the constant CW_USEDEFAULT is used, Windows selects the default position for the upper left corner, and the Y parameter is ignored. The CW_USEDEFAULT constant is only valid for overlapped windows. If it is specified for any other window type, the X and Y parameters are set to zero.

Y: The initial horizontal position of the upper left corner of the window. For overlapped or pop-up windows, this coordinate is relative to the screen. For child windows, this coordinate is relative to the upper left corner of the parent window's client area. If an overlapped window is created with the WS_VISIBLE style set and the X parameter is set to CW_USEDEFAULT, the Y parameter is ignored.

nWidth: The initial width of the window. Overlapped windows can use the CW_USEDEFAULT constant, in which case the nHeight parameter is ignored. If this constant is used, Windows selects a default width and height for the window. The default width will extend from the initial X coordinate to the right edge of the screen; the default height will extend from the initial Y coordinate to the top of the icon area. If CW_USEDEFAULT is specified for child or pop-up windows, the nWidth and nHeight parameters are set to zero.

nHeight: The initial height of the window. If the nWidth parameter is set to CW_USEDEFAULT, the nHeight parameter is ignored.

hWndParent: A handle to the window's parent or owner. A valid window handle must be specified if the window to be created is a child or owned window. Child windows are confined to the client area of the parent window. An owned window is an overlapped or pop-up window that is destroyed when its owner is destroyed and hidden when its owner is minimized; it is always displayed on top of its owner window. This can be set to NIL if the window does not have an owner. If no parent window is specified, the window will not automatically be destroyed when the application ends. The DestroyWindow function is used to remove the window in this instance. This parameter must have a valid window handle if the WS_CHILD style is used; it is optional if the WS_POPUP style is used.

hMenu: A handle to a menu object. For an overlapped or pop-up window, this parameter can be NIL if the class menu should be used. For controls, this is set to an integer value that is the ID of the control being created. All WM_COMMAND messages will reference this ID when an action has occurred with the control. The child window identifier must be unique among all child windows with the same parent window.

hInstance: The instance handle of the application or module creating the window.

lpParam: A pointer to application-defined data that is used during the window creation process. The window procedure receives a WM_CREATE message when the CreateWindow function is called. The lParam member of this message contains a pointer to a TCreateStruct data structure. The lpCreateParams member of the TCreateStruct structure contains the pointer to the application-defined data. For MDICLIENT windows, pass a pointer to a TClientCreateStruct structure in this parameter. If no extra creation information is needed, set this parameter to NIL.

The TClientCreateStruct structure contains additional information that is needed to create an MDICLIENT window. Delphi defines the TClientCreateStruct as:

```
TClientCreateStruct = packed record
    hWindowMenu: THandle;          {a handle to a menu}
    idFirstChild: UINT;            {the identifier of the first MDI child window}
end;
```

hWindowMenu: This is the handle to the MDI application's window menu.

idFirstChild: This specifies the identifier of the first MDI child window. Windows increments this identifier for every MDI child window created, and reassigns identifiers when child windows are destroyed so the range of identifiers are contiguous. These identifiers are used in the WM_COMMAND messages sent to the MDI frame window when a child window is chosen from the window menu, and should not conflict with other command identifiers.

The TCreateStruct structure contains all of the parameters that were passed to the CreateWindow function. The developer can use this information to perform any additional initialization at the time of window creation. The TCreateStruct data structure is defined as:

```
TCreateStruct = packed record
    lpCreateParams: Pointer;     {a pointer to application-defined data}
    hInstance: HINST;            {a handle to the module instance}
    hMenu: HMENU;                {a handle to the menu, or a child window identifier}
    hwndParent: HWND;            {a handle to the parent window}
    cy: Integer;                 {initial height of the window}
    cx: Integer;                 {initial width of the window}
    y: Integer;                  {initial vertical position}
    x: Integer;                  {initial horizontal position}
    style: Longint;              {window style flags}
    lpszName: PAnsiChar;         {a pointer to the window name string}
    lpszClass: PAnsiChar;        {a pointer to the class name string}
    dwExStyle: DWORD;            {extended window style flags}
end;
```

The lpCreateParams member is a pointer to application-defined data (see Listing 3-9 for an example of its use). The other members of this structure contain the information passed in the parameters to the CreateWindow or CreateWindowEx function.

Return Value

If this function succeeds, it returns a handle to the new window; otherwise it returns zero. To get extended error information, call the GetLastError function.

See also

CreateDialog, CreateWindowEx, DestroyWindow, DialogBox, MessageBox, RegisterClass, ShowWindow, WM_COMMAND, WM_CREATE, WM_GETMINMAXINFO, WM_NCCALCSIZE, WM_NCCREATE, WM_PAINT

Example

Listing 3-8: Creating a Multiline Edit Control on a Form Using CreateWindow

This code creates a multiline edit control. The text is centered horizontally within the control, and a vertical scroll bar is present.

```
procedure TForm1.Button1Click(Sender: TObject);
const
   MULTIEDIT1 = 1;
var
```

```
    WindowHandle: HWND;
begin
    WindowHandle:=CreateWindow(
                'EDIT',                 {registered class name}
                'Example Text',         {window name}
                WS_VISIBLE OR           {the window is initially visible}
                WS_CHILD OR             {it is a child window}
                WS_VSCROLL OR           {it has a vertical scroll bar}
                WS_BORDER OR            {it has a thin line border}
                ES_CENTER OR            {the text is centered in the control}
                ES_MULTILINE,           {this is a multiline edit control}
                50,50,                  {initial horizontal and vertical
                                         positions}
                300,200,                {initial width and height}
                Form1.Handle,           {handle to the parent window}
                MULTIEDIT1,             {child window identifier}
                hInstance,              {handle to the application instance}
                NIL);                   {pointer to window creation data}
end;
```

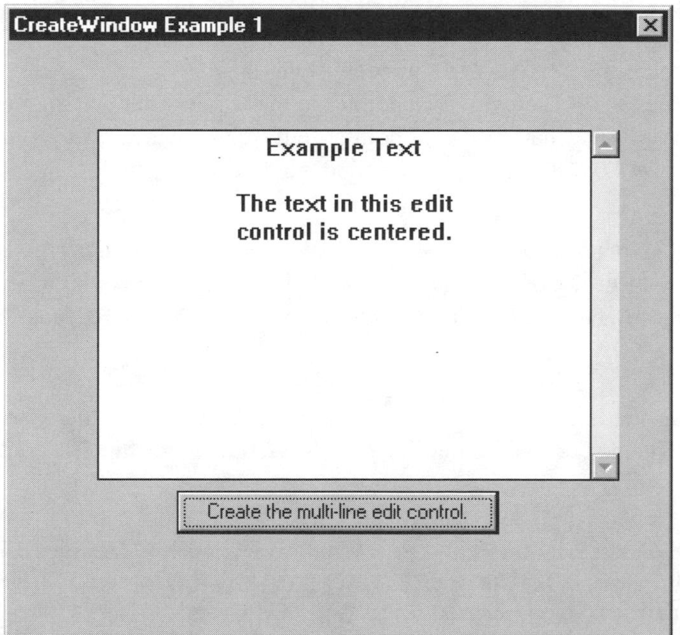

Figure 3-8: The multiple line edit control.

Listing 3-9: Creating a New Window Using CreateWindow

```
{this is used for extra window creation information}
  TMyData = record
    lpszInfo: PChar;
    dwNumber: DWORD;
  end;

  PMyData = ^TMyData;
```

```
var
  Form1: TForm1;

implementation

{$R *.DFM}

function WindowProc(TheWindow: HWnd; TheMessage, WParam,
                    LParam: Longint): Longint; stdcall;
var
  {these variables will be assigned the extra window creation information }
  lpszInfoString: PChar;
  dwInfoNumber: DWORD;
begin
  case TheMessage of
    {get our extra creation information when the window is created}
    WM_CREATE:
      begin
        {retrieve the extra creation data from the TCreateStruct data structure}
        lpszInfoString:=PMyData(PCreateStruct(LParam).lpCreateParams).lpszInfo;
        dwInfoNumber:=PMyData(PCreateStruct(LParam).lpCreateParams).dwNumber;

        {display this information. the developer could use this information
         for any initialization needed during the creation of the window}
        ShowMessage(Format('String: %s'+Chr(13)+'Number: %d',
                    [lpszInfoString,dwInfoNumber]));
      end;

    {upon getting the WM_DESTROY message, we exit the application}
    WM_DESTROY: begin
                  PostQuitMessage(0);
                  Exit;
                end;
  end;

  {call the default window procedure for all unhandled messages}
  Result := DefWindowProc(TheWindow, TheMessage, WParam, LParam);
end;

{ Register the Window Class }
function RegisterClass: Boolean;
var
  WindowClass: TWndClass;
begin
  {setup our new window class}
  WindowClass.Style := CS_HREDRAW or CS_VREDRAW;      {set the class styles}
  WindowClass.lpfnWndProc := @WindowProc;             {our window procedure}
  WindowClass.cbClsExtra := 0;                        {no extra class memory}
  WindowClass.cbWndExtra := 0;                        {no extra window memory}
  WindowClass.hInstance := hInstance;                 {the application instance}
  WindowClass.hIcon := LoadIcon(0, IDI_WINLOGO);      {load a predefined logo}
  WindowClass.hCursor := LoadCursor(0, IDC_APPSTARTING); {load a predefined
                                                          cursor}
  WindowClass.hbrBackground := COLOR_WINDOW;          {use a predefined color}
```

```
  WindowClass.lpszMenuName := nil;                 {no menu}
  WindowClass.lpszClassName := 'TestClass';        {the registered class name}

  {now that we have our class set up, register it with the system}
  Result := Windows.RegisterClass(WindowClass) <> 0;
end;

procedure TForm1.Button1Click(Sender: TObject);
var
  hWindow: HWND;
  ExtraCreationData: TMyData;
begin
  {register our new class first}
  if not RegisterClass then
  begin
    ShowMessage('RegisterClass failed');
    Exit;
  end;

  {fill in our extra creation data structure}
  ExtraCreationData.lpszInfo:='ExtraCreationData information string';
  ExtraCreationData.dwNumber:=12345;

  {now, create a window based on our new class}
  hWindow := CreateWindow('TestClass',         {the registered class name}
                          'API Window',        {the title bar text}
                          WS_OVERLAPPEDWINDOW, {a normal window style}
                          CW_USEDEFAULT,       {default horizontal position}
                          CW_USEDEFAULT,       {default vertical position}
                          CW_USEDEFAULT,       {default width}
                          CW_USEDEFAULT,       {default height}
                          Form1.Handle,        {handle of the parent window}
                          0,                   {no menu}
                          hInstance,           {the application instance}
                          @ExtraCreationData   {additional creation
                                                information}
                          );

  {if our window was created successfully, show it}
  if hWindow <> 0 then
  begin
    ShowWindow(hWindow, SW_SHOWNORMAL);
    UpdateWindow(hWindow);
  end
  else
  begin
    ShowMessage('CreateWindow failed');
    Exit;
  end;

end;
```

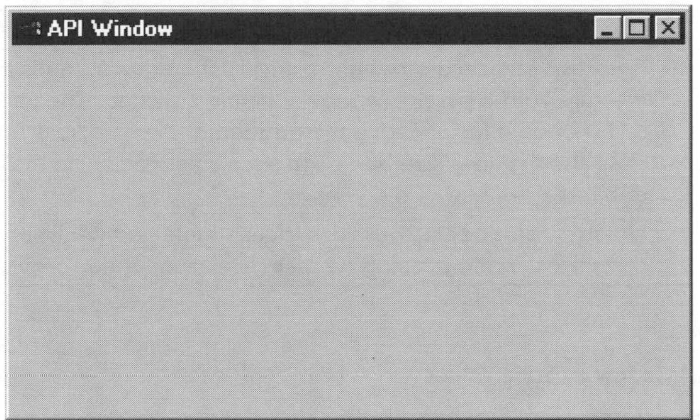

Figure 3-9: The new window.

Table 3-3: CreateWindow lpClassName Values

Value	Description
BUTTON	Used when creating buttons, group boxes, check boxes, radio buttons, or icon windows. The BS_OWNERDRAW style can be used to control its visual look in various states. Button controls can either be alone or in groups, with or without text, and typically change appearance when the user clicks on them.
COMBOBOX	Creates a list box with a selection area similar to an edit box. The list selection area can be displayed at all times or enabled as a drop-down. Depending on the style, the user can or cannot edit the contents of the selection area. If the list box is visible, typing characters in the selection area highlights the first entry in the list that matches the characters typed. Similarly, selecting an item from the list displays it in the selection area.
EDIT	Creates a standard edit control, either single or multiline. This control will receive focus by either clicking on it or moving to it using the Tab key. This allows a user to input text from the keyboard. The WM_SETFONT message can be sent to this control to change the default font. Tab characters are expanded into as many space characters as needed to fill it to the next tab stop. Tab stops are assumed to be at every eighth character position.
LISTBOX	Creates a standard list box, a control with a list of strings that can be selected. The user selects a string by simply clicking on it. The selected string is highlighted, and a notification message is sent to the parent window. Single or multiple selections are supported, and the styles LB_OWNERDRAWFIXED or LB_OWNERDRAWVARIABLE can be used to control how the strings are drawn.
MDICLIENT	Creates a Multiple Document Interface client window. An MDICLIENT window must exist before creating MDI child windows. The WS_CLIPCHILDREN and WS_CHILD styles should be specified when using this class.

Value	Description
SCROLLBAR	Creates a standard scroll bar control. This control sends a notification message to the parent window when it is clicked. The parent window is responsible for updating the position of the scroll bar thumb. This class also includes size box controls, a small rectangle the user can drag to change the size of the window.
STATIC	Creates a static text control, such as simple text fields, boxes, or rectangles. Static controls neither receive input nor provide output.

Table 3-4: CreateWindow dwStyle Values

Window Styles	Description
WS_BORDER	Gives the window a thin line border.
WS_CAPTION	Gives the window a title bar, and includes the WS_BORDER style.
WS_CHILD	Creates a child window. The WS_POPUP style cannot be used if this style is specified.
WS_CHILDWINDOW	The same as the WS_CHILD style.
WS_CLIPCHILDREN	Clips around child windows during painting, and is used when creating parent windows.
WS_CLIPSIBLINGS	Clips windows relative to each other during painting. Without this style, the entire area of the window will be included in the update region, even if overlapped by a sibling window, making it possible to draw in the client area of the overlapping child window. When this style is used, the sibling's overlapping area is left out of the update region.
WS_DISABLED	The window is initially disabled and cannot receive user input.
WS_DLGFRAME	Creates a window with the dialog box border style, and cannot have a title bar.
WS_GROUP	Marks the beginning of a group of controls. The next controls created will belong to this group, and when the WS_GROUP style is used again, it will end the grouping and create a new group. The user can change the focus from one control to the next in a group by using the cursor keys. This is commonly used when creating radio buttons.
WS_HSCROLL	Gives the window a horizontal scroll bar.
WS_ICONIC	This is the same as WS_MINIMIZE.
WS_MAXIMIZE	The window starts out maximized.
WS_MAXIMIZEBOX	Includes the maximize button in the title bar.
WS_MINIMIZE	The window starts out minimized.
WS_MINIMIZEBOX	Includes the minimize button in the title bar.

Window Styles	Description
WS_OVERLAPPED	Gives the window both a title bar and a border. This is the same as the WS_TILED style.
WS_OVERLAPPEDWINDOW	Combines the WS_OVERLAPPED, WS_CAPTION, WS_SYSMENU, WS_THICKFRAME, WS_MINIMIZEBOX, and WS_MAXIMIZEBOX styles. This is a standard window, and is the same as the WS_TILEDWINDOW style.
WS_POPUP	Creates a pop-up window. The WS_CHILD style cannot be used with this style.
WS_POPUPWINDOW	Combines the WS_BORDER, WS_POPUP, and WS_SYSMENU styles. The WS_CAPTION style must be specified before the system menu becomes visible.
WS_SIZEBOX	The window has a sizing border. This is the same as the WS_THICKFRAME style.
WS_SYSMENU	The system menu box is present in the title bar. The WS_CAPTION style must also be specified.
WS_TABSTOP	Indicates that the control can receive the keyboard focus when the user presses the Tab key. Pressing the Tab key again will change the focus to the next control with this style.
WS_THICKFRAME	Gives the window a sizing border.
WS_TILED	This is the same as the WS_OVERLAPPED style.
WS_TILEDWINDOW	This is the same as the WS_OVERLAPPEDWINDOW style.
WS_VISIBLE	The window is initially visible.
WS_VSCROLL	Gives the window a vertical scroll bar.

Button Styles	Description
BS_3STATE	Creates a check box with three states: unselected, selected, or grayed. The grayed state is used to show that the state of the check box is undetermined.
BS_AUTO3STATE	The same as BS_3STATE, but the check box will change its state when selected by a user. The cycle will go through checked, grayed, and unchecked.
BS_AUTOCHECKBOX	The same as BS_CHECKBOX, but it will change its state when selected by the user.
BS_AUTORADIOBUTTON	The same as BS_RADIOBUTTON, but the button is selected when the user clicks on it, and any other buttons in its group are unselected.
BS_BITMAP	The button will display a bitmap.
BS_BOTTOM	The title will be at the bottom of the button's rectangular area.
BS_CENTER	Centers the button title horizontally.

Button Styles	Description
BS_CHECKBOX	Creates a check box control with the title displayed to the right, unless the BS_LEFTTEXT or BS_RIGHTBUTTON style is specified.
BS_DEFPUSHBUTTON	If this button is in a dialog box, it is clicked if the user presses the Enter key, even if it doesn't have focus. This causes the button to have a thick, black border.
BS_FLAT	Creates a button with a flat border. When pressed, the text moves like a normal button, but the borders do not reflect any movement.
BS_GROUPBOX	Creates a group box control with a title displayed in the upper left corner.
BS_ICON	Creates a button that can display an icon.
BS_LEFT	Left justifies the title in a button. If the button is a radio button or check box and does not have the BS_RIGHTBUTTON style specified, the text will be left justified on the right side of the button.
BS_LEFTTEXT	Places the title on the left side of a check box or radio button. This is the same as the BS_RIGHTBUTTON style.
BS_MULTILINE	This button has multiple lines of text for its title. The text will wrap if the button is too narrow.
BS_NOTIFY	In addition to the BN_CLICKED message sent when a button is clicked, this style causes the BN_DBLCLK, BN_KILLFOCUS, and BN_SETFOCUS notification messages to be sent to the parent window.
BS_OWNERDRAW	Creates an owner-drawn button. The parent window receives a WM_MEASUREITEM message when the button is created, and a WM_DRAWITEM message when the button needs to be drawn. This style should not be used with any other styles.
BS_PUSHBUTTON	When the button is selected, it posts a WM_COMMAND message to the parent window.
BS_PUSHLIKE	Makes radio buttons and check boxes have a button-like look and feel. It will be sunken when it is checked, and raised when it is not checked.
BS_RADIOBUTTON	Creates a small circle with text to one side. The text is displayed to the right of the circle, unless the BS_LEFTTEXT or BS_RIGHTBUTTON styles are used. The circle can be clicked on or off, and this control usually groups a set of related but mutually exclusive choices.
BS_RIGHT	Right justifies the title in a button. If the button is a radio button or check box and does not have the BS_RIGHTBUTTON style specified, the text will be right justified on the right side of the button.

Button Styles	Description
BS_RIGHTBUTTON	Places the check box or radio button on the right side of the text. This is the same as the BS_LEFTTEXT style.
BS_TEXT	Causes a button to display text.
BS_TOP	Displays the title at the top of the button.
BS_USERBUTTON	This style is obsolete and provided only for 16-bit compatibility. Win32 applications should use the BS_OWNERDRAW style.
BS_VCENTER	Centers the text vertically in the button.

Combo Box Styles	Description
CBS_AUTOHSCROLL	Allows the edit control of the combo box to scroll horizontally when text reaches the box boundaries. Without this style, only text that fits in the boundaries is allowed.
CBS_DISABLENOSCROLL	Forces a vertical scroll bar to be visible even when all items in the list are displayed. It will be disabled unless needed to show additional items.
CBS_DROPDOWN	Creates a drop-down combo box, with the list visible only when the user clicks on a down arrow button next to the edit box.
CBS_DROPDOWNLIST	Creates a drop-list combo box. The user is unable to type in the edit control, and can only select items in the list.
CBS_HASSTRINGS	Used in conjunction with an owner-drawn list box. The combo box maintains the memory and address for all of the strings, and the application can use the CB_GETLBTEXT message to retrieve a particular string.
CBS_LOWERCASE	Only lowercase characters can be entered; uppercase characters are automatically converted to lowercase.
CBS_NOINTEGRALHEIGHT	Forces a combo box to the exact size specified. By default, Windows will resize the combo box so no item is partially displayed.
CBS_OEMCONVERT	Windows will convert any entered text to the OEM character set and then back to the Windows character set so that the CharToOem function, if used, converts characters properly. This style is useful when the combo box contains filenames, and is only valid with the CBS_SIMPLE or CBS_DROPDOWN styles.
CBS_OWNERDRAWFIXED	Creates an owner-drawn combo box control. The owner of this control is responsible for drawing the items, each of which will be the same height. The owner receives a WM_MEASUREITEM message when the control is created, and a WM_DRAWITEM message when an item needs to be redrawn.

Combo Box Styles	Description
CBS_OWNERDRAWVARIABLE	This is the same as the CBS_OWNERDRAWFIXED style, except that each item in the list can be different sizes. WM_MEASUREITEM is sent for each item in the combo box when it is created, and a WM_DRAWITEM message is sent when an item needs to be redrawn.
CBS_SIMPLE	Creates a combo box where the list of items is always visible, and the current selection is displayed in the edit control.
CBS_SORT	Sorts any string added to the list box when using the CB_ADDSTRING message.
CBS_UPPERCASE	Only uppercase characters can be entered; lowercase characters are automatically converted to uppercase.

Dialog Box Styles	Description
DS_3DLOOK	Gives dialog boxes a three-dimensional look by drawing three-dimensional borders around control windows in the dialog box. This style is included by default.
DS_ABSALIGN	Positions a dialog box relative to the upper left corner of the screen. Without this style, Windows assumes the coordinates are client coordinates.
DS_CENTER	Centers the dialog box in the screen area that is not obscured by the task bar.
DS_CENTERMOUSE	Causes the mouse cursor to be centered in the dialog box.
DS_CONTEXTHELP	Causes the WS_EX_CONTEXTHELP extended style to be defined for this dialog box. Please see the CreateWindowEx function for a description of the WS_EX_CONTEXTHELP style.
DS_CONTROL	Creates a dialog box that will work as a child window of another dialog box, like a page in a property sheet. This allows the user to tab among the child windows of this window, use its accelerator keys, etc.
DS_FIXEDSYS	The dialog box uses the SYSTEM_FIXED_FONT instead of the SYSTEM_FONT.
DS_MODALFRAME	The dialog box has a modal dialog box frame, and can be combined with the WS_CAPTION and WS_SYSMENU styles to give it a title bar and system menu.
DS_NOFAILCREATE	Creates the dialog box regardless of any errors encountered during creation.
DS_NOIDLEMSG	While the dialog box is displayed, no WM_ENTERIDLE messages are posted to the owner.

Dialog Box Styles	Description
DS_SETFONT	Indicates that the dialog box template contains information specifying a font name and point size. This font is used to display text information inside the dialog box client area and its controls. The font handle is passed to each control in the dialog box with the WM_SETFONT message.
DS_SETFOREGROUND	Calls the SetForegroundWindow function to force the dialog box into the foreground.
DS_SYSMODAL	Causes the dialog box to have the WS_EX_TOPMOST extended style. This has no other effect on any other windows in the system while the dialog box is displayed.

Edit Control Styles	Description
ES_AUTOHSCROLL	The control will scroll horizontally during editing by ten characters if the user reaches the end of the boundaries.
ES_AUTOVSCROLL	Scrolls text up one page when the user presses the Enter key on the last line.
ES_CENTER	Centers the text in a multiline control.
ES_LEFT	Left aligns text.
ES_LOWERCASE	Only lowercase characters can be entered; uppercase characters are automatically converted to lowercase.
ES_MULTILINE	Creates a multiple line edit control. The ES_WANTRETURN style must be specified to use the Enter key as a carriage return. If the ES_AUTOVSCROLL style is not specified, the system will beep when the user presses the Enter key and no more lines can be displayed. If the ES_AUTOHSCROLL style is specified, the user must press the Enter key to start a new line. Otherwise, the text will word wrap when it reaches the edge of the edit control box. If scroll bars are specified for edit controls, the control will automatically process all messages for them.
ES_NOHIDESEL	Selections in the edit control are shown after the control loses focus.
ES_NUMBER	This edit control only accepts numerical digits.
ES_OEMCONVERT	This style is the same as the CBS_OEMCONVERT combo box style.
ES_PASSWORD	Displays the password character, set using the EM_SETPASSWORDCHAR message, in place of any character typed. The default password character is an asterisk.
ES_READONLY	The edit control is read only, and users cannot edit the text therein.

Edit Control Styles	Description
ES_RIGHT	Causes text to be right aligned in multiple line edit controls.
ES_UPPERCASE	Only uppercase characters can be entered; lowercase characters are automatically converted to uppercase.
ES_WANTRETURN	The Enter key inserts carriage returns in a multiple line edit control. Ctrl+Enter is used to insert carriage returns when this style is not specified. This style has no effect on single line edit controls.

List Box Styles	Description
LBS_DISABLENOSCROLL	Displays a vertical scroll bar, even when all items are displayed. The scroll bar is disabled unless needed to display additional items.
LBS_EXTENDEDSEL	Allows a range of items to be selected using the Shift key and the mouse.
LBS_HASSTRINGS	Specifies that the list box has items consisting of strings. The list box maintains the memory and addresses for the strings, and the application can use the LB_GETTEXT message to retrieve a particular string. By default, all list boxes except owner-drawn list boxes have this style.
LBS_MULTICOLUMN	Creates a multiple column list box. The list box can be scrolled horizontally, and the LB_SETCOLUMNWIDTH message can be used to set the width of the columns.
LBS_MULTIPLESEL	Allows multiple items to be selected with the mouse.
LBS_NODATA	Indicates that no data is in the list box. The LBS_OWNERDRAWFIXED style must be used when this style is specified. This style is used when the number of items exceeds one thousand, and the LBS_SORT and LBS_HASSTRINGS styles cannot be used. Commands to add, insert, or delete an item are ignored, and requests to find a string always fail. Windows sends a WM_DRAWITEM message to the owner when an item needs to be drawn. The itemID member of the DRAWITEMSTRUCT structure passed with the WM_DRAWITEM message specifies the line number of the item to be drawn. A no-data list box does not send a WM_DELETEITEM message.
LBS_NOINTEGRALHEIGHT	Forces the list box to be displayed at the specified size. Without this style, Windows resizes the list box so that no item is partially displayed.
LBS_NOREDRAW	The list box does not receive the WM_PAINT message when this style is specified. Use the WM_SETREDRAW message to change this style at runtime.
LBS_NOSEL	The items in the list box can be viewed but not selected.

List Box Styles	Description
LBS_NOTIFY	Sends a notification message to the parent when a list box item is clicked or double-clicked.
LBS_OWNERDRAWFIXED	Indicates that the owner is responsible for drawing the contents of the list box, sending a WM_MEASUREITEM message to the owner when the list box is created, and a WM_DRAWITEM message when the list box has changed. All of the items will be the same height.
LBS_OWNERDRAWVARIABLE	This is the same as the LBS_OWNERDRAWFIXED style, except that each item in the list box can be different sizes. WM_MEASUREITEM is sent for each item in the list box when it is created, and a WM_DRAWITEM message is sent when an item needs to be redrawn.
LBS_SORT	Sorts alphabetically any string added to the list box when using the LB_ADDSTRING message.
LBS_STANDARD	Combines the LBS_SORT, LBS_NOTIFY, and WS_BORDER styles.
LBS_USETABSTOPS	Tabs are expanded when drawing strings, and the application can use the LB_SETTABSTOPS message to change tab positions.
LBS_WANTKEYBOARDINPUT	The list box parent receives WM_VKEYTOITEM messages when the user presses a key and the list box has focus, allowing the owner to perform any special processing on keyboard input.

MDI Client Styles	Description
MDIS_ ALLCHILDSTYLES	Allows MDI child windows to use any window style listed in this table. If this style flag is not specified, MDI child windows are limited to the styles available in Table 3-2.

Scroll Bar Styles	Description
SBS_BOTTOMALIGN	Aligns the bottom of the scroll bar with the bottom edge of the rectangle specified in the CreateWindow function. Use this style with the SBS_HORZ style.
SBS_HORZ	Creates a horizontal scroll bar. If the SBS_BOTTOMALIGN or SBS_TOPALIGN styles are not used, the scroll bar has the width, height, and position specified by the parameters of the CreateWindow function.
SBS_LEFTALIGN	Aligns the left edge of the scroll bar with the left edge of the rectangle specified in the CreateWindow function. Use this style with the SBS_VERT style.

Scroll Bar Styles	Description
SBS_RIGHTALIGN	Aligns the right edge of the scroll bar with the right edge of the rectangle specified in the CreateWindow function. Use this style with the SBS_VERT style.
SBS_SIZEBOX	Creates a scroll bar with a size box. If the SBS_SIZEBOXBOTTOMRIGHTALIGN or SBS_SIZEBOXTOPLEFTALIGN styles are not used, the scroll bar has the width, height, and position specified by the CreateWindow parameters.
SBS_SIZEBOXBOTTOMRIGHTALIGN	Aligns the size box with the lower right corner of the rectangle specified by the CreateWindow function. Use this style with the SBS_SIZEBOX style.
SBS_SIZEBOXTOPLEFTALIGN	Aligns the size box with the upper left corner of the rectangle specified by the CreateWindow function. Use this style with the SBS_SIZEBOX style.
SBS_SIZEGRIP	This is the same as the SBS_SIZEBOX style but with a raised edge.
SBS_TOPALIGN	Aligns the top of the scroll bar with the top edge of the rectangle specified in the CreateWindow function. Use this style with the SBS_HORZ style.
SBS_VERT	Creates a vertical scroll bar. If the SBS_RIGHTALIGN or SBS_LEFTALIGN styles are not used, the scroll bar has the width, height, and size as specified in the CreateWindow function.

Static Control Styles	Description
SS_BITMAP	Creates a static control that displays the bitmap specified by the lpWindowName parameter, ignoring the nWidth and nHeight parameters as these are calculated according to the bitmap's width and height. The lpWindowName parameter specifies a bitmap name as defined in the resource file; it is not a filename.
SS_BLACKFRAME	Creates a box that is drawn using the same color as window frames, usually black.
SS_BLACKRECT	Creates a filled rectangle using the same color as window frames, usually black.
SS_CENTER	Creates a static text control that is centered and wrapped as necessary.

Static Control Styles	Description
SS_CENTERIMAGE	Causes controls that have the SS_BITMAP or SS_ICON styles to keep the image centered vertically and horizontally when the control is resized. If the bitmap is smaller than the client area, the client area is filled with the color of the pixel in the bitmap's upper left corner. This does not happen when an icon is used.
SS_ENHMETAFILE	Displays an enhanced metafile. The metafile is scaled to fit the static control's client area. The lpWindowName parameter is the name of an enhanced metafile as defined in the resource file; it is not a filename.
SS_ETCHEDFRAME	Draws the frame of the static control using the EDGE_ETCHED style. See the DrawEdge function for more information.
SS_ETCHEDHORZ	Draws the top and bottom sides of the static control frame using the EDGE_ETCHED style. See the DrawEdge function for more information
SS_ETCHEDVERT	Draws the left and right sides of the static control frame using the EDGE_ETCHED style. See the DrawEdge function for more information
SS_GRAYFRAME	Creates a box that is drawn using the same color as the desktop, usually gray.
SS_GRAYRECT	Creates a filled rectangle using the same color as the desktop, usually gray.
SS_ICON	Creates a static control that displays the icon specified by the lpWindowName parameter, ignoring the nWidth and nHeight parameters as these are calculated according to the icon's width and height. The lpWindowName parameter is the name of an icon as defined in the resource file; it is not a filename.
SS_LEFT	Creates a static text control that is left aligned and wrapped as necessary.
SS_LEFTNOWORDWRAP	Creates a static text control that is left aligned. Tabs are expanded, but words are not wrapped and are clipped at the boundaries of the control.
SS_NOPREFIX	The ampersand (&) character in the control's text is not interpreted as an accelerator.
SS_NOTIFY	When the user clicks or double-clicks the control, STN_CLICKED, STN_DBLCLK, STN_ENABLE, and STN_DISABLE messages are sent to the parent.
SS_RIGHT	Creates a static text control that is right aligned and wrapped as necessary.

Static Control Styles	Description
SS_RIGHTJUST	With this style, the lower right corner of a static control with the SS_BITMAP or SS_ICON style flags set remains fixed when the control is resized. Only the top and left sides will be adjusted to accommodate a new icon or bitmap.
SS_SIMPLE	Creates a left aligned static text control. The parent window or dialog must not process the WM_CTLCOLORSTATIC message when using this style.
SS_SUNKEN	Creates a box that has a perimeter resembling a lowered bevel.
SS_WHITEFRAME	Creates a box that is drawn using the same color as the window background, usually white.
SS_WHITERECT	Creates a filled rectangle using the same color as the window background, usually white.

CreateWindowEx *Windows.Pas*

Syntax

```
CreateWindowEx(
dwExStyle: DWORD;              {extended window style flags}
lpClassName: PChar;            {a pointer to the class name string}
lpWindowName: PChar;           {a pointer to the window name string}
dwStyle: DWORD;                {window style flags}
X: Integer;                    {initial horizontal position}
Y: Integer;                    {initial vertical position}
nWidth: Integer;               {initial width of the window}
nHeight: Integer;              {initial height of the window}
hWndParent: HWND;              {a handle to the parent window}
hMenu: HMENU;                  {a handle to the menu, or a child window identifier}
hInstance: HINST;              {a handle to the module instance}
lpParam: Pointer               {a pointer to additional information}
): HWND;                       {returns a handle to the new window}
```

Description

This function is almost identical to the CreateWindow function, and gives the developer access to extended style types in addition to the styles listed in the previous tables. For more information concerning window styles, control styles, and messages sent when a window is created, see the CreateWindow function. In the Windows.Pas source code, the CreateWindow function is not imported from the User32.DLL. Instead, the function calls the CreateWindowEx function, passing a zero for the dwExStyle parameter.

Note: Windows 95 can support a maximum of 16,364 window handles.

Parameters

dwExStyle: A 32-bit number that specifies what extended styles this window uses. Available extended style constants are listed in the following table. Multiple styles are specified by using the Boolean OR operator, i.e., WS_EX_ABSPOSITION OR WS_EX_CONTROLPARENT. Using the WS_EX_RIGHT extended style for static or edit controls is equivalent to using the SS_RIGHT or ES_RIGHT styles, respectively. Using this style with button controls is the same as using BS_RIGHT and BS_RIGHTBUTTON styles.

lpClassName: A pointer to a null-terminated, case-sensitive string, or an integer atom. It describes either a valid, predefined class name or one created with the RegisterClass function. See Table 3-3 for valid predefined window classes. If this specifies an atom, the atom must have been created with a call to GlobalAddAtom. The atom, a 16-bit value less than $C000, must be in the low-order word of ClassName and the high-order word must be zero.

lpWindowName: A null-terminated string containing the name for this window. This string is displayed on the title bar of the window. If this window is a control, this is the text displayed within the control.

dwStyle: A 32-bit number that describes what styles this window uses. Available style constants are listed in the table under the CreateWindow function. Multiple styles can be combined by using the Boolean OR operator, i.e., WS_HSCROLL OR WS_VSCROLL.

X: The initial horizontal position of the upper left corner of the window. For overlapped or pop-up windows, this coordinate is relative to the screen. For child windows, this coordinate is relative to the upper left corner of the parent window's client area. If the constant CW_USEDEFAULT is used, Windows selects the default position for the upper left corner, and the Y parameter is ignored. The CW_USEDEFAULT constant is only valid for overlapped windows. If it is specified for any other window type, the X and Y parameters are set to zero.

Y: The initial horizontal position of the upper left corner of the window. For overlapped or pop-up windows, this coordinate is relative to the screen. For child windows, this coordinate is relative to the upper left corner of the parent window's client area. If an overlapped window is created with the WS_VISIBLE style set and the X parameter is set to CW_USEDEFAULT, the Y parameter is ignored.

nWidth: The initial width of the window. Overlapped windows can use the CW_USEDEFAULT constant, in which case the nHeight parameter will be ignored. If this constant is used, Windows selects a default width and height for the window. The default width will extend from the initial X coordinate to the right edge of the screen; the default height will extend from the initial Y coordinate to the top of the icon area. If

CW_USEDEFAULT is specified for child or pop-up windows, the nWidth and nHeight parameters are set to zero.

nHeight: The initial height of the window. If the nWidth parameter is set to CW_USEDEFAULT, the nHeight parameter is ignored.

hWndParent: A handle to the window's parent or owner. A valid window handle must be specified if the window to be created is a child or owned window. Child windows are confined to the client area of the parent window. An owned window is an overlapped or pop-up window that is destroyed when its owner is destroyed and hidden when its owner is minimized; it is always displayed on top of its owner window. This can be set to NIL if the window does not have an owner. If no parent window is specified, the window will not automatically be destroyed when the application ends. The DestroyWindow function is used to remove the window in this instance. This parameter must have a valid window handle if the WS_CHILD style is used; it is optional if the WS_POPUP style is used.

hMenu: A handle to a menu object. For an overlapped or pop-up window, this parameter can be NIL if the class menu should be used. For controls, this is set to an integer value that is the ID of the control being created. All WM_COMMAND messages will reference this ID when an action has occurred with the control. The application determines this child window identifier, which must be unique among all child windows with the same parent window.

hInstance: The instance handle of the application or module creating this window.

lpParam: A pointer to application-defined data that is used during the window creation process. The window procedure receives a WM_CREATE message when the CreateWindow function is called. The lParam member of this message contains a pointer to a TCreateStruct data structure. The lpCreateParams member of the TCreateStruct structure contains the pointer to the data. For MDICLIENT windows, use a pointer to a TClientCreateStruct structure. If no extra creation information is needed, set this parameter to NIL. See the CreateWindow function for more information.

Return Value

If this function succeeds, it returns a handle to the new window; otherwise it returns zero. To get extended error information, call the GetLastError function.

See also

CreateDialog, CreateWindow, CreateMDIWindow, DestroyWindow, DialogBox, MessageBox, RegisterClassEx, ShowWindow, WM_COMMAND, WM_CREATE, WM_GETMINMAXINFO, WM_NCCALCSIZE, WM_NCCREATE, WM_PAINT

Example

Listing 3-10: Creating a Window with Extended Window Styles

This example demonstrates how to create a window with a sunken edge and a context sensitive help button. The minimize and maximize buttons must be removed from the window so that they do not obscure the help button. This example also shows how to use the DestroyWindow, RegisterClassEx, and UnregisterClass functions.

```
var
  hWindow: HWND;

{ Register the extended Window class }
function RegisterClassEx: Boolean;
var
  WindowClassEx: TWndClassEx;
begin
  {setup our new window class}
  WindowClassEx.cbSize := SizeOf(TWndClassEx);      {the size of the structure}
  WindowClassEx.Style := CS_HREDRAW or CS_VREDRAW;  {set the class styles}
  WindowClassEx.lpfnWndProc := @DefWindowProc;      {point to the default window
                                                     procedure}
  WindowClassEx.cbClsExtra := 0;                    {no extra class memory}
  WindowClassEx.cbWndExtra := 0;                    {no extra window memory}
  WindowClassEx.hInstance := hInstance;             {the application instance}
  WindowClassEx.hIcon := LoadIcon(0, IDI_APPLICATION); {load a predefined logo}
  WindowClassEx.hCursor := LoadCursor(0, IDC_WAIT); {load a predefined cursor}
  WindowClassEx.hbrBackground := COLOR_WINDOW;      {use a predefined color}
  WindowClassEx.lpszMenuName := nil;                {no menu}
  WindowClassEx.lpszClassName := 'TestClass';       {the registered class name}
  WindowClassEx.hIconSm := 0;                       {no small icon}

  {now that we have our class set up, register it with the system}
  Result := Windows.RegisterClassEx(WindowClassEx) <> 0;
end;

procedure TForm1.Button1Click(Sender: TObject);
begin
  {register our new class first}
  if not RegisterClassEx then
  begin
    ShowMessage('RegisterClassEx failed');
    Exit;
  end;

  {now, create a window based on our new class}
  hWindow := CreateWindowEx(WS_EX_CLIENTEDGE OR      {this window has a sunken
                                                      edge}
                            WS_EX_CONTEXTHELP,       {and a context sensitive
                                                      help button}
                            'TestClass',             {the registered class name}
                            'API Window',            {the title bar text}
                            WS_OVERLAPPEDWINDOW AND  {a normal window}
                            NOT WS_MAXIMIZEBOX AND   {without a minimize or
```

3 Chapter

```
                                           maximize button}
                      NOT WS_MINIMIZEBOX,  {so the help button is not
                                           obscured}
                      CW_USEDEFAULT,       {default horizontal position}
                      CW_USEDEFAULT,       {default vertical position}
                      CW_USEDEFAULT,       {default width}
                      CW_USEDEFAULT,       {default height}
                      0,                   {no parent window}
                      0,                   {no menu}
                      hInstance,           {the application instance}
                      nil                  {no additional information}
                      );

  {if our window was created successfully, show it}
  if hWindow <> 0 then
  begin
    ShowWindow(hWindow, SW_SHOWNORMAL);
    UpdateWindow(hWindow);
  end
  else
  begin
    ShowMessage('CreateWindow failed');
    Exit;
  end;

end;

procedure TForm1.Button2Click(Sender: TObject);
begin
  {first, destroy our window}
  DestroyWindow(hWindow);

  {now we can unregister our new class}
  Windows.UnregisterClass('TestClass', hInstance);
end;
```

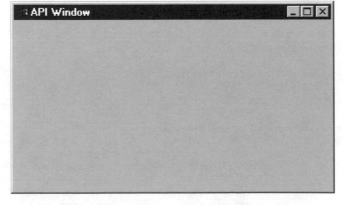

Figure 3-10: A window using extended styles.

Table 3-5: CreateWindowEx dwExStyle Values

Value	Description
WS_EX_ACCEPTFILES	Accepts files dragged and dropped from other applications, such as the Windows Explorer.
WS_EX_APPWINDOW	Forces a top-level window onto the task bar when the window is minimized.
WS_EX_CLIENTEDGE	The window border has a sunken edge.
WS_EX_CONTEXTHELP	Causes the context sensitive help button (a small button with a question mark) to appear in the title bar. When pressed, the mouse cursor changes to a pointer and a question mark. If the user clicks on a child window or control, it receives a WM_HELP message. The child should pass the message to the parent's window procedure, which should then call the WinHelp function using the HELP_WM_HELP command. The Help application displays a pop-up window that usually contains help information for the child window. The WS_MAXIMIZEBOX and WS_MINIMIZEBOX styles must not be included, or the context help button will be obscured by the minimize and maximize buttons.
WS_EX_CONTROLPARENT	Allows users to press the Tab key to move from child window to child window.
WS_EX_DLGMODALFRAME	This window has a double border. The WS_CAPTION style must be used to add a title to this style of window.
WS_EX_LEFT	Creates a window with left aligned properties. This is the default style.
WS_EX_LEFTSCROLLBAR	If the shell's language is Hebrew, Arabic, or any other language that supports reading order alignment, the vertical scroll bar, if any, will be placed to the left of the client area. For other languages, this style is simply ignored.
WS_EX_LTRREADING	Text displayed in this window is in a left-to-right reading order. This is the default style.
WS_EX_MDICHILD	Creates an MDI child window.
WS_EX_NOPARENTNOTIFY	A window with this style does not send WM_PARENTNOTIFY messages to its parent when it is created or destroyed.
WS_EX_OVERLAPPEDWINDOW	Combines the WS_EX_CLIENTEDGE and WS_EX_WINDOWEDGE styles.
WS_EX_PALETTEWINDOW	Combines the WS_EX_WINDOWEDGE, WS_EX_TOOLWINDOW, and WS_EX_TOPMOST styles.

Value	Description
WS_EX_RIGHT	If the shell's language is Hebrew, Arabic, or any other language that supports reading order alignment, this window has generic right aligned properties. For other languages, this style is simply ignored.
WS_EX_RIGHTSCROLLBAR	Places the vertical scroll bar, if present, on the right side of the client area. This is the default style.
WS_EX_RTLREADING	If the shell's language is Hebrew, Arabic, or any other language that supports reading order alignment, the window is displayed using right-to-left reading order properties. For other languages, this style is simply ignored.
WS_EX_STATICEDGE	Creates a window with a three-dimensional border style.
WS_EX_TOOLWINDOW	Creates a floating toolbar style window. The title bar is shorter than a normal title bar, and the window caption is drawn in a smaller font. This style of window will not show up on the task bar, or when the user presses Alt+Tab.
WS_EX_TOPMOST	This window stays above all other windows, even when deactivated. This style can be set using the SetWindowPos function.
WS_EX_TRANSPARENT	Any sibling windows that are beneath this window are not obscured by it, and will receive the WM_PAINT message first.
WS_EX_WINDOWEDGE	This window has a border with a raised edge.

DestroyWindow *Windows.Pas*

Syntax

```
DestroyWindow(
hWnd: HWND                    {a handle to a window}
): BOOL;                      {returns TRUE or FALSE}
```

Description

This function is used to destroy windows created with the CreateWindow or CreateWindowEx functions, or modeless dialogs created with the CreateDialog function. Child windows of the specified window are destroyed first, then the window's menu is destroyed, the thread message queue is emptied, any active timers are destroyed, clipboard ownership is removed, and the clipboard viewer chain is broken if the window is at the top of the viewer chain. Using this function to remove the parent window of an application will end that application. The messages WM_DESTROY and WM_NCDESTROY are sent to the window before it is deleted to deactivate it and remove its focus. This function cannot be used to destroy a window created by a different thread. If the window to be destroyed is a child window and does not have the WS_EX_NOPARENTNOTIFY style specified, a WM_PARENTNOTIFY is sent to its parent.

Parameters

hWnd: The handle to the window to be destroyed.

Return Value

If this function succeeds, it returns TRUE if the window is destroyed; otherwise it returns FALSE. To get extended error information, call the GetLastError function.

See also

CreateDialog, CreateWindow, CreateWindowEx, UnregisterClass, WM_DESTROY, WM_NCDESTROY, WM_PARENTNOTIFY

Example

Please see Listing 3-10 under CreateWindowEx.

RegisterClass Windows.Pas

Syntax

```
RegisterClass(
const lpWndClass: TWndClass          {a window class data structure}
): ATOM;                             {returns a unique atom}
```

Description

RegisterClass is used to create custom Windows controls and nonexisting classes for new windows. This same class can be used to create any number of windows in an application. All classes that an application registers are unregistered when the application terminates.

Parameters

lpWndClass: A variable of the type TWndClass data structure. The data structure is defined as:

```
TWndClass = packed record
    Style: UINT;                    {class style flags}
    lpfnWndProc: TFNWndProc;        {a pointer to the window procedure}
    cbClsExtra: Integer;            {extra class memory}
    cbWndExtra: Integer;            {extra window memory}
    hInstance: HINST;               {a handle to the module instance}
    hIcon: HICON;                   {a handle to an icon}
    hCursor: HCURSOR;               {a handle to a cursor}
    hbrBackground: HBRUSH;          {a handle to the background brush}
```

```
    lpszMenuName: PAnsiChar;        {the menu name}
    lpszClassName: PAnsiChar;       {the class name}
end;
```

Style: Defines some of the default behavior of the window. The style constants available are listed in Table 3-6, and can be combined using a Boolean OR operator, i.e., CS_DBLCLKS OR CS_NOCLOSE.

lpfnWndProc: The address of the application-defined callback function, known as the window procedure, that processes messages for this window. The syntax for this callback function is described below.

cbClsExtra: Specifies the number of extra bytes to allocate at the end of the window class structure. This space can be used to store any additional information required. Use the SetClassLong and GetClassLong functions to access this space. Windows initializes these bytes to zero. Windows 95 only: The RegisterClass function fails if this parameter specifies more than 40 bytes.

cbWndExtra: Specifies the number of extra bytes to allocate at the end of the window instance. Windows initializes these bytes to zero. This space can be used to store any additional information required. Use SetWindowLong and GetWindowLong to access this space. If an application uses the TWndClass structure to register a dialog box created by using the CLASS directive in a resource file, this member must be set to DLGWINDOWEXTRA. Windows 95 only: The RegisterClass function fails if this parameter specifies more than 40 bytes.

hInstance: The instance handle that contains the window procedure for this class.

hIcon: A handle to an icon resource that is used when a window of this class is minimized. If this member is set to zero, the window will use the Windows logo icon.

hCursor: A handle to a mouse cursor resource. If this member is set to zero, the application is responsible for setting the cursor when the mouse moves into the window. By default, the window uses the standard arrow cursor.

hbrBackground: A handle to a brush that will be used to paint the background of any window belonging to this window class. One of the system color values in Table 3-7 can be used in place of a brush handle. Background brushes are automatically deleted when the class is freed. If this member is set to zero, the application is responsible for painting its own background when requested to update its client area. To determine if the background must be painted, the application can either process the WM_ERASEBKGND message, or test the fErase member of the TPaintStruct structure filled by the BeginPaint function.

lpszMenuName: A pointer to a null-terminated string with the default menu resource name for this class, as it appears in the resource file. If an integer was used to identify the menu, use MakeIntResource to convert it to a string. Set this member to NIL if this class does not have a default menu.

lpszClassName: Either a pointer to a null-terminated string that describes the class name, or an atom. If this specifies an atom, the atom must have been created with a call to GlobalAddAtom. The atom, a 16-bit value, must be in the low-order word of ClassName and the high-order word must be zero. This value is used in the lpClassName parameter of the CreateWindow function.

Return Value

If this function succeeds, it returns an atom that uniquely identifies the new window class. Otherwise, the return value is zero. To get extended error information, call the GetLastError function.

Callback Syntax

```
WindowProc(
hWnd: HWND;              {a handle to a window}
uMsg: UINT;              {the message identifier}
wParam: WPARAM;          {32-bit message information}
lParam: LPARAM           {32-bit message information}
): Longint;              {returns a 32-bit value}
```


Description

This is an application-defined callback function that processes messages sent to a window, usually in the form of a Case statement. This function can perform any required task.

Parameters

hWnd: The handle to the window receiving the message.

uMsg: The message identifier.

wParam: A 32-bit value that is dependent on the type of message received.

lParam: A 32-bit value that is dependent on the type of message received.

Return Value

The return value of the window procedure is dependent on the message received and the result of processing the message.

See also

CreateWindow, CreateWindowEx, GetClassInfo, GetClassLong, GetClassName, RegisterClassEx, SetClassLong, UnregisterClass

Example

Please see Listing 3-9 under CreateWindow.

Table 3-6: RegisterClass lpWndClass.Style Values

Value	Description
CS_BYTEALIGNCLIENT	Aligns the window's client area to byte boundaries horizontally. This will improve drawing performance, but the width of the window and its horizontal positioning are affected.
CS_BYTEALIGNWINDOW	Aligns the entire window to horizontal byte boundaries. This will improve performance when moving or resizing a window, but the width of the window and its horizontal positioning are affected.
CS_CLASSDC	Allocates one device context (DC) to be shared by every window in this class. If multiple threads attempt to use this DC at the same time, only one thread is allowed to complete its drawing operations successfully.
CS_DBLCLKS	Sends the window procedure a double-click message when a double-click within the window occurs.
CS_GLOBALCLASS	Allows an application to create a window of this class regardless of the hInstance parameter passed to the CreateWindow or CreateWindowEx functions. If this style is not specified, the hInstance parameter passed to these functions must be the same hInstance parameter passed to the RegisterClass function. A global class is produced by creating a window class in a DLL. In Windows NT, the DLL must be listed in the registry under the key HKEY_LOCAL_MACHINE\Software\Microsoft\Windows NT\CurrentVersion\ Windows\APPINIT_DLLS. Whenever a process starts, Windows loads these DLLs in the context of the newly created process before calling the main function of that process. The DLL must register the class during its initialization procedure. Essentially, this will create a class that is available to every application while the application that created the class is running. A common example would be new custom controls implemented in a DLL.
CS_HREDRAW	Causes the entire window to be repainted when the width of the client area changes.
CS_NOCLOSE	Disables the Close command on the system menu.
CS_OWNDC	Allocates a unique device context for each window created with this class.
CS_PARENTDC	If a window created with this class is a child window, this style sets the clipping region of the window to that of its parent window, allowing the child window to draw on its parent. Although a window with this style will still receive a regular device context from those available, and does not receive its parent device context settings, specifying this style for child windows will improve performance.

Value	Description
CS_SAVEBITS	When a portion of this window is obscured by another window, this style causes the window to save this hidden area as a bitmap, which is used to repaint the window when the hidden area reappears. Windows will redisplay this image at its original location, and will not send a WM_PAINT message to a window that was previously obscured, assuming that the memory used by the bitmap has not been discarded and that other screen actions have not invalidated the image. This is useful for small windows that are displayed briefly but will decrease performance as Windows must allocate memory to store the bitmap before displaying the window.
CS_VREDRAW	Causes the entire window to be repainted when the height of the client area changes.

Table 3-7: RegisterClass lpWndClass.hbrBackground Values

Value	Description
COLOR_3DDKSHADOW	The dark shadow color for three-dimensional display elements.
COLOR_3DLIGHT	The lighted edge color for three-dimensional display elements.
COLOR_ACTIVEBORDER	The active window border color.
COLOR_ACTIVECAPTION	The active window caption color.
COLOR_APPWORKSPACE	The background color used in multiple document interface applications.
COLOR_BACKGROUND	The desktop color.
COLOR_BTNFACE	The color of pushbutton faces.
COLOR_BTNHIGHLIGHT	The color of a highlighted pushbutton.
COLOR_BTNSHADOW	The shaded edge color on pushbuttons.
COLOR_BTNTEXT	The text color on pushbuttons.
COLOR_CAPTIONTEXT	The text color used in caption, size box, and scroll bar arrow box controls.
COLOR_GRAYTEXT	The color of disabled text. This will be set to zero if the display driver cannot support solid gray.
COLOR_HIGHLIGHT	The color used for selected items in a control.
COLOR_HIGHLIGHTTEXT	The color used for the text of selected items in a control.
COLOR_INACTIVEBORDER	The inactive window border color.
COLOR_INACTIVECAPTION	The inactive window caption color.
COLOR_INACTIVECAPTIONTEXT	The text color in an inactive caption bar.
COLOR_INFOBK	The background color for tooltip controls.
COLOR_INFOTEXT	The text color for tooltip controls.

Value	Description
COLOR_MENU	The menu background color.
COLOR_MENUTEXT	The text color used in menus.
COLOR_SCROLLBAR	The scroll bar "gray" area color.
COLOR_WINDOW	The window background color.
COLOR_WINDOWFRAME	The window frame color.
COLOR_WINDOWTEXT	The color of text used in a window.

RegisterClassEx *Windows.Pas*

Syntax

```
RegisterClassEx(
const WndClass: TWndClassEx          {an extended window class data structure}
): ATOM;                             {returns a unique atom}
```

Description

This function is identical to the RegisterClass function, except that there are two extra members added to the TWndClass data type. One specifies the size of the TWndClassEx structure in bytes, and the other allows a small icon to be specified that is used in the title bar of windows created with this class.

Parameters

WndClass: A variable of the type TWndClassEx data structure. The data structure is defined as:

```
TWndClassEx = packed record
    cbSize: UINT;                       {the size of this structure}
    Style: UINT;                        {class style flags}
    lpfnWndProc: TFNWndProc;            {a pointer to the window procedure}
    cbClsExtra: Integer;                {extra class memory bytes}
    cbWndExtra: Integer;                {extra window memory bytes}
    hInstance: HINST;                   {a handle to the module instance}
    hIcon: HICON;                       {a handle to an icon}
    hCursor: HCURSOR;                   {a handle to a cursor}
    hbrBackground: HBRUSH;              {a handle to the background brush}
    lpszMenuName: PAnsiChar;            {the menu name}
    lpszClassName: PAnsiChar;           {the class name}
    hIconSm: HICON;                     {a handle to a small icon}
end;
```

Note that the TWndClassEx data structure is identical to the TWndClass structure, with the cbSize member added to the beginning and the hIconSm member added to the end. Refer to the RegisterClass function for a description of the other members of this data structure.

cbSize: Specifies the size of the TWndClassEx structure in bytes, and can be set with "SizeOf(TWndClassEx)." This is used when retrieving information about a class. See the GetClassInfoEx function for more information.

hIconSm: A handle to a small icon that will be displayed in the title bar of windows created with this class.

Return Value

If this function succeeds, an atom that uniquely identifies the new window class is returned; otherwise it returns zero. To get extended error information, call the GetLastError function.

See also

CreateWindow, CreateWindowEx, GetClassInfoEx, GetClassLong, GetClassName, RegisterClass, SetClassLong, UnregisterClass

Example

Please see Listing 3-10 under CreateWindowEx.

UnregisterClass Windows.Pas

Syntax

```
UnregisterClass(
lpClassName: PChar;          {a pointer to the class name string}
hInstance: HINST             {a handle to the module instance}
): BOOL;                     {returns TRUE or FALSE}
```

Description

This function removes a class that was previously registered with the RegisterClass or RegisterClassEx functions. The memory that was allocated by these functions is freed. This function is used while a program is still running. An application must destroy any windows that were created with the specified class before calling this function. Any classes that an application registers are automatically removed when the application terminates.

Parameters

lpClassName: Either a pointer to a null-terminated string that contains the name of the class, or an integer atom. If this specifies an atom, the atom must have been created with a call to GlobalAddAtom. The atom, a 16-bit value less than $C000, must be in the low-order word of ClassName and the high-order word must be zero. System global classes, such as dialog box controls, cannot be unregistered.

hInstance: The instance handle of the module that created the class.

Return Value

If the function succeeds, it returns TRUE; otherwise it returns FALSE. This function will fail if the class could not be found or if there are windows still open that are using this class. To get extended error information, call the GetLastError function.

See also

RegisterClass, RegisterClassEx.

Example

Please see Listing 3-10 under CreateWindowEx.

Chapter 4

Message Processing Functions

One of the things that sets Windows programming apart from DOS programming is the notion of an event-driven application. This event-driven architecture takes the form of messages that are sent between the operating system and the application. A message signals the application or the operating system that something has happened, and some sort of processing should take place as a result of this event.

The vast majority of messages are sent to an application as a direct result of user input, such as moving the mouse, clicking a button or scroll bar, or activating another application, but system events can also trigger a message, such as when hardware configuration has changed as a result of inserting or removing an expansion card. At the heart of every Windows program is a small loop that retrieves these messages and dispatches them to their destination window procedures. Fortunately, Delphi automatically takes care of this message management through the TApplication object.

The Message Queue and Message Loop

Each thread has its own message queue. This can be thought of as a first in, first out structure, where messages are processed in the order in which they were received. This takes place in the message loop, located in the WinMain function of a traditional Windows application. This message loop is implemented in Delphi as the ProcessMessages method of the TApplication object. This function spins in a tight loop, continually retrieving messages from the message queue and, after filtering out and handling specific message types, dispatching them to their destination window procedures. From the Forms unit, the message loop in every Delphi application is implemented as:

Listing 4-1: The Application Message Loop

```
procedure TApplication.ProcessMessages;
begin
  while ProcessMessage do {loop};
end;

function TApplication.ProcessMessage: Boolean;
var
  Handled: Boolean;
```

```
  Msg: TMsg;
begin
  Result := False;
  if PeekMessage(Msg, 0, 0, 0, PM_REMOVE) then
  begin
    Result := True;
    if Msg.Message <> WM_QUIT then
    begin
      Handled := False;
      if Assigned(FOnMessage) then FOnMessage(Msg, Handled);
      if not IsHintMsg(Msg) and not Handled and not IsMDIMsg(Msg) and
        not IsKeyMsg(Msg) and not IsDlgMsg(Msg) then
      begin
        TranslateMessage(Msg);
        DispatchMessage(Msg);
      end;
    end
    else
      FTerminate := True;
  end;
end;
```

An application could set up its own message loop by simply creating a loop that continually called GetMessage or PeekMessage, TranslateMessage if needed, and DispatchMessage, until a specific message was retrieved that signaled an end of the loop. This is, in fact, how Delphi implements modal dialog boxes.

Even though the main thread in an application automatically gets a message queue, each individual thread that an application creates can have its own message queue. A thread creates a message queue the first time it calls any of the functions in GDI32.DLL or USER32.DLL. Once a thread has created its own message queue, it must implement a message loop using GetMessage or PeekMessage, and will receive messages sent to it via the PostThreadMessage function.

Windows Hooks

An application can intercept messages going to itself or other applications through the use of hook functions. A hook function is installed using the SetWindowsHookEx function and uninstalled using the UnhookWindowsHookEx function. Multiple hook functions can be installed by the same or different applications, forming a chain of hook functions intercepting messages for their specific hook type. The last hook function installed becomes the first hook function in the hook chain, and will receive messages before the other hook functions in the chain.

The installed hook function receives the indicated messages for its hook type before the destination window procedure. If a hook function does not handle a message it has received, it should send it to the other hook functions in the chain by using CallNextHookEx. A hook that intercepts messages for only one application can reside in the source code for that application. However, a hook that intercepts messages for multiple applications or for the system must reside in a separate dynamic link library.

Interprocess Communication

Messages allow applications to communicate with each other through the use of PostMessage, SendMessage, and similar functions. Two applications can create a new message identifier simply by adding a constant value to WM_USER (i.e., WM_NEWMESSAGE = WM_USER+1), using this new message identifier to send custom messages back and forth. However, be aware that PostMessage, SendMessage, and other functions can broadcast a message to every window in the system. If this user-defined message identifier is broadcast to all applications, it is possible that other applications may contain a handler for the same user-defined message identifier as defined by the sending application, which could produce unexpected results. For this reason, it is best if the developer registered a unique message for interprocess communication using the RegisterWindowMessage function. Given a unique string, this will ensure that only the applications that registered the same string with RegisterWindowMessage will receive the message.

Message Processing Functions

The following message functions are covered in this chapter:

Table 4-1: Message Processing Functions

Function	Description
BroadcastSystemMessage	Sends a message to applications or drivers.
CallNextHookEx	Sends hook information to the next hook in the chain.
CallWindowProc	Passes a message to a window procedure.
DefFrameProc	Passes any unhandled messages to the default window procedure of a frame window for default processing.
DefMDIChildProc	Passes any unhandled messages to the default window procedure of an MDI child window for default processing.
DefWindowProc	Passes any unhandled messages to the default window procedure for default processing.
DispatchMessage	Dispatches a message to a window procedure.
GetMessage	Retrieves and removes a message from the message queue.
GetMessageExtraInfo	Retrieves extra message information.
GetMessagePos	Retrieves the coordinates of the mouse cursor when the last message was retrieved.
GetMessageTime	Retrieves the create time of the last message retrieved.
GetQueueStatus	Retrieves the types of messages found in the queue.
InSendMessage	Indicates if a message was sent via one of the SendMessage functions.
PeekMessage	Retrieves a message from the message queue, optionally removing it.

Function	Description
PostMessage	Posts a message to a message queue.
PostQuitMessage	Posts a WM_QUIT message to a message queue.
PostThreadMessage	Posts a message to the message queue of a thread.
RegisterWindowMessage	Retrieves a unique message identifier for an application defined message.
ReplyMessage	Sends a message processing return value back to a SendMessage function.
SendMessage	Sends a message to a window procedure.
SendMessageCallback	Sends a message to a window procedure, and provides a callback function that is called when the message is processed.
SendMessageTimeout	Sends a message to a window procedure, returning after a specified timeout period.
SendNotifyMessage	Sends a message to the window procedure in another thread and returns immediately.
SetMessageExtraInfo	Sets extra message information.
SetWindowsHookEx	Places a hook procedure into a hook procedure chain.
TranslateMessage	Translates virtual key messages into character messages.
UnhookWindowsHookEx	Removes a hook procedure from a hook chain.
WaitMessage	Yields control to other threads until the calling thread's message queue receives a message.

BroadcastSystemMessage *Windows.Pas*

Syntax

```
BroadcastSystemMessage(
Flags: DWORD;                {flags specifying message sending options}
Recipients: PDWORD;          {flags specifying message recipients}
uiMessage: UINT;             {the identifier of the message to send}
wParam: WPARAM;              {a 32-bit message specific value}
lParam: LPARAM               {a 32-bit message specific value}
): Longint;                  {returns a 32-bit value}
```

Description

This function sends the specified message to all indicated recipients. Unlike the SendMessage functions, this function can send messages to applications, drivers, and system components. If the BSF_QUERY flag is not specified in the Flags parameter, the function ignores message processing return values from recipients.

Parameters

Flags: Specifies message sending options. This parameter can be one or more values from Table 4-2.

Recipients: A pointer to a DWORD variable that contains flags indicating the recipients of the message. When the function returns, this variable will contain flags indicating the recipients that actually received the message. The variable can contain one or more values from Table 4-3. If this parameter is set to NIL, the message is sent to every component on the system.

uiMessage: The identifier of the message being sent.

wParam: A 32-bit value dependent on the message being sent.

lParam: A 32-bit value dependent on the message being sent.

Return Value

If the function succeeds, it returns a positive value; otherwise it returns –1. If the Flags parameter is set to BSF_QUERY and at least one recipient returns the BROADCAST_QUERY_DENY value upon receiving the message, the function returns zero.

See also

RegisterWindowMessage, SendMessage

Example

Please see Listing 4-2 under CallWindowProc.

Table 4-2: BroadcastSystemMessage Flags Values

Value	Description
BSF_FLUSHDISK	Process any pending disk read/write operations after each recipient returns from processing the message.
BSF_FORCEIFHUNG	Continue broadcasting the message even if the time-out period has expired or one of the recipients is hung.
BSF_IGNORECURRENTTASK	The message will not be sent to any windows belonging to the current task.
BSF_NOHANG	Hung applications are forced to time-out. If a recipient is hung and causes a time-out, message broadcasting is discontinued.
BSF_NOTIMEOUTIFNOTHUNG	The application waits for a response from a recipient as long as the recipient is not hung, and does not time-out.
BSF_POSTMESSAGE	Posts the message to the recipient's message queue and continues broadcasting. Do not use this value in combination with BSF_QUERY.

Value	Description
BSF_QUERY	The message is sent to one recipient at a time, and is sent to subsequent recipients only if the current recipient returns TRUE. Do not use this value in combination with BSF_POSTMESSAGE.

Table 4-3: BroadcastSystemMessage Recipients Values

Value	Description
BSM_ALLCOMPONENTS	The message is broadcast to all system components. This is the equivalent to setting the Recipients parameter to NIL.
BSM_ALLDESKTOPS	Windows NT only: The message is broadcast to all desktops. This flag requires the SE_TCB_NAME privilege.
BSM_APPLICATIONS	The message is broadcast to all running applications.
BSM_INSTALLABLEDRIVERS	Windows 95 only: The message is broadcast to all installable drivers.
BSM_NETDRIVER	Windows 95 only: The message is broadcast to all Windows-based network drivers.
BSM_VXDS	Windows 95 only: The message is broadcast to all system level device drivers.

CallNextHookEx *Windows.Pas*

Syntax

```
CallNextHookEx(
hhk: HHOOK;                 {a handle to the current hook}
nCode: Integer;             {the hook code}
wParam: WPARAM;             {a 32-bit hook specific value}
lParam: LPARAM              {a 32-bit hook specific value}
): LRESULT;                 {returns the return value of the next hook in the chain}
```

Description

This function passes the specified hook information to the next hook procedure in the current hook procedure chain. Unless otherwise specified, calling the CallNextHookEx function is optional. An application can call this function inside of the hook procedure either before or after processing the hook information. If CallNextHookEx is not called, Windows does not call any subsequent hook procedures in the chain (those that were installed before the current hook procedure was installed).

Parameters

hhk: A handle to the current hook. This is the value returned from the SetWindowsHookEx function.

nCode: Specifies the hook code passed to the current hook procedure. This code is used by the next hook procedure in the chain to determine how to process the hook information.

wParam: Specifies the wParam parameter value passed to the current hook procedure. The meaning of this value is dependent on the type of hook associated with the current hook procedure chain.

lParam: Specifies the lParam parameter value passed to the current hook procedure. The meaning of this value is dependent on the type of hook associated with the current hook procedure chain.

Return Value

If the function succeeds, it returns the value returned by the next hook procedure in the chain. This value must also be returned by the current hook procedure. The meaning of the return value is dependent on the type of hook associated with the current hook chain. If the function fails, it returns zero.

See also

SetWindowsHookEx, UnhookWindowsHookEx

Example

Please see Listing 4-15 under SetWindowsHookEx.

CallWindowProc ***Windows.Pas***

Syntax

```
CallWindowProc(
lpPrevWndFunc: TFNWndProc;    {a pointer to the previous window procedure}
hWnd: HWND;                   {a handle to a window}
Msg: UINT;                    {the identifier of the message to send}
wParam: WPARAM;               {a 32-bit message specific value}
lParam: LPARAM                {a 32-bit message specific value}
): LRESULT;                   {returns a message specific return value}
```

Description

This function passes the specified message and its associated parameters to the window procedure pointed to by the lpPrevWndFunc parameter. An application must use this function in the window procedure of a subclassed window to pass any unhandled messages to the previous window procedure.

Parameters

lpPrevWndFunc: A pointer to the previous window procedure of the subclassed window. This value is returned from the SetClassLong or SetWindowLong functions when a window is subclassed, or by calling the GetClassLong or GetWindowLong functions with the appropriate index value to retrieve a pointer to the window procedure.

hWnd: A handle to the window associated with the window procedure pointed to by the lpPrevWndFunc parameter.

Msg: The message identifier to send to the window procedure.

wParam: A 32-bit value dependent on the message being sent.

lParam: A 32-bit value dependent on the message being sent.

Return Value

The value returned from this function specifies the result of the message processing and is dependent on the message sent.

See also

GetClassLong, GetWindowLong, SetClassLong, SetWindowLong

Example

Listing 4-2: Calling the Previous Window Procedure in a Subclassed Window

This application sends a message:

```
{Whoops! The BroadcastSystemMessage function is linked in incorrectly, so
 we must explicitly link in the correct function}
function BroadcastSystemMessage; external user32 name 'BroadcastSystemMessage';

procedure TForm1.Button1Click(Sender: TObject);
var
  Recipients: DWORD;  // holds the recipient flags
begin
  {set the recipients to all applications}
  Recipients := BSM_APPLICATIONS;

  {send the user defined message to all applications on the system by
   posting it to their message queues}
  BroadcastSystemMessage(BSF_IGNORECURRENTTASK or BSF_POSTMESSAGE, @Recipients,
                         UserMessage, 0, 0);
end;

procedure TForm1.FormCreate(Sender: TObject);
begin
  {register a user defined message}
  UserMessage := RegisterWindowMessage('CallWindowProc Test Message');
end;
```

and this application receives the message:

```
{the prototype for the new window procedure}
  function NewWindowProc(TheWindow: HWND; Msg: Integer; wParam: WPARAM;
                         lParam: LPARAM): Longint; stdcall;

var
  Form1: TForm1;
  UserMessage: UINT;          // holds a user defined message identifier
  OldWindowProc: TFNWndProc; // holds a pointer to the previous window procedure

implementation

function NewWindowProc(TheWindow: HWND; Msg: Integer; wParam: WPARAM; lParam:
LPARAM): Longint;
var
  iLoop: Integer;         // a general loop counter
begin
  {if the user defined message has been received...}
  if Msg=UserMessage then
  begin
    {...turn on some user interface elements}
    Form1.ProgressBar1.Visible := TRUE;
    Form1.Label2.Visible := TRUE;
    Form1.Repaint;

    {animate the progress bar for a short period of time}
    for iLoop := 0 to 100 do
    begin
      Form1.ProgressBar1.Position := iLoop;
      Sleep(10);
    end;

    {turn off the user interface elements}
    Form1.ProgressBar1.Visible := FALSE;
    Form1.Label2.Visible := FALSE;

    {the message was handled, so return a one}
    Result := 1;
  end
  else
    {any other message must be passed to the previous window procedure}
    Result := CallWindowProc(OldWindowProc, TheWindow, Msg, wParam, lParam);
end;

procedure TForm1.FormCreate(Sender: TObject);
begin
  {register a user defined message}
  UserMessage := RegisterWindowMessage('CallWindowProc Test Message');

  {subclass this window.  Replace the window procedure with one of
   ours.  This window procedure will receive messages before the
   previous one, allowing us to intercept and process any message
   before the rest of the application ever sees it.}
  OldWindowProc := TFNWndProc(SetWindowLong(Form1.Handle, GWL_WNDPROC,
                              Longint(@NewWindowProc)));
end;
```

```
procedure TForm1.FormDestroy(Sender: TObject);
begin
  {reset the window procedure to the previous one}
  SetWindowLong(Form1.Handle, GWL_WNDPROC, Longint(OldWindowProc));
end;
```

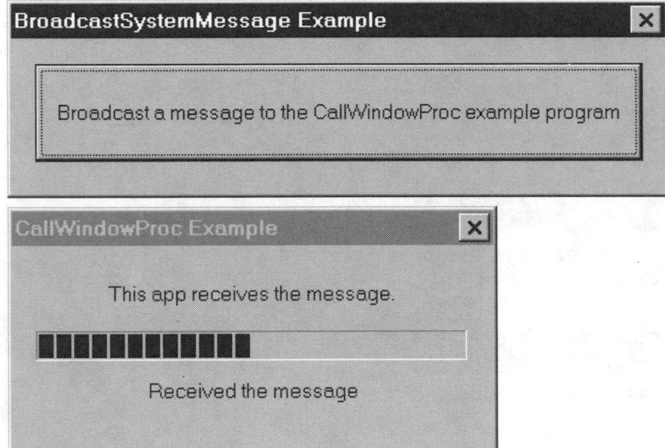

Figure 4-1: The New Window procedure received the message.

DefFrameProc Windows.Pas

Syntax

DefFrameProc(	
hWnd: HWND;	{a handle to the MDI frame window}
hWndMDIClient: HWND;	{a handle to the MDI client window}
uMsg: UINT;	{the identifier of the message to send}
wParam: WPARAM;	{a 32-bit message specific value}
lParam: LPARAM	{a 32-bit message specific value}
): LRESULT;	{returns a message specific return value}

Description

This function provides default message processing for any message not handled in the window procedure of a multiple document interface frame window. Any messages not explicitly handled by the MDI frame window procedure must be passed to the DefFrameProc function.

Parameters

hWnd: A handle to the MDI frame window.

hWndMDIClient: A handle to the MDI client window.

uMsg: The identifier of the message to send.

wParam: A 32-bit value dependent on the message being sent.

lParam: A 32-bit value dependent on the message being sent.

Return Value

The value returned from this function specifies the result of the message processing and is dependent on the message sent.

See also

CallWindowProc, DefMDIChildProc, DefWindowProc

Example

Listing 4-3: Providing Default Message Handling in an MDI Frame Window

```
program DefFrameProcExample;

uses
  Windows, Messages, SysUtils;

var
  TheMessage: TMsg;
  FrameWindow, ClientWindow, ChildWindow: HWND;

const
  {the ID for the first MDI child window}
  IDCHILDWND = 100;

{$R *.RES}

{this defines the window procedure for our frame window}
function FrameWindowProc(TheFrameWindow: HWnd; TheMessage, WParam,
                         LParam: Longint): Longint; stdcall;
var
    {this is used when creating an MDI client window}
    ClientStruct: TClientCreateStruct;
begin
  case TheMessage of
    {The frame window will be created first. Once it is created, the
     WM_CREATE message is sent to this function, where we create the
     MDI client window}
    WM_CREATE: begin
         {Fill in the appropriate information about the client window}
         ClientStruct.hWindowMenu:=0;
         ClientStruct.idFirstChild:=IDCHILDWND;

         {Create the MDI client window}
         ClientWindow := CreateWindow(
                          'MDICLIENT',          {the registered class name}
                          NIL,                  {no window text}
                          WS_CHILD or           {this is a child window}
                          WS_CLIPCHILDREN or    {clip its child windows}
                          WS_VISIBLE,           {initially visible}
                          0,                    {horizontal position}
                          0,                    {vertical position}
```

Chapter 4

```
                             0,                  {width}
                             0,                  {height}
                             TheFrameWindow,     {handle of the parent window}
                             0,                  {no menu}
                             hInstance,          {the application instance}
                             @ClientStruct       {additional creation information}
                             );

          {check to see if it was created}
          if ClientWindow=0 then
            begin
              MessageBox(0,'CreateClientWindow failed',nil,MB_OK);
              Exit;
            end;

          {indicate that the message was handled}
          Result := 1;
    end;
    {upon getting the WM_DESTROY message, we exit the application}
    WM_DESTROY: begin
                  PostQuitMessage(0);
                  Exit;
                end;
  else
    {call the default frame window procedure for all unhandled messages}
    Result := DefFrameProc(TheFrameWindow, ClientWindow, TheMessage,
                           WParam, LParam);
  end;
end;

{this defines the window procedure for our MDI child window}
function MDIChildWindowProc(TheMDIChildWindow: HWnd; TheMessage, WParam,
                            LParam: Longint): Longint; stdcall;
begin
  case TheMessage of
    {upon getting the WM_DESTROY message, we exit the application}
    WM_LBUTTONDOWN: begin
                      SetWindowText(TheMDIChildWindow,PChar('Mouse Button '+
                                    'Clicked at '+IntToStr(LoWord(GetMessagePos
                                    ))+', '+IntToStr(HiWord(GetMessagePos))));

                      {indicate that the message was handled}
                      Result := 1;
                    end;
  else
    {call the default MDI child window procedure for all unhandled messages}
    Result := DefMDIChildProc(TheMDIChildWindow, TheMessage, WParam, LParam);
  end;
end;

{ Register the frame window Class }
function RegisterFrameClass: Boolean;
var
  WindowClass: TWndClass;
begin
```

```
  {setup our frame window class}
  WindowClass.Style := CS_HREDRAW or CS_VREDRAW;      {set the class styles}
  WindowClass.lpfnWndProc := @FrameWindowProc;        {point to our frame
                                                       window procedure}
  WindowClass.cbClsExtra := 0;                        {no extra class memory}
  WindowClass.cbWndExtra := 0;                        {no extra window memory}
  WindowClass.hInstance := hInstance;                 {the application instance}
  WindowClass.hIcon := LoadIcon(0, IDI_WINLOGO);      {load a predefined logo}
  WindowClass.hCursor := LoadCursor(0, IDC_ARROW);    {load a predefined cursor}
  WindowClass.hbrBackground := COLOR_WINDOW;          {use a predefined color}
  WindowClass.lpszMenuName := nil;                    {no menu}
  WindowClass.lpszClassName := 'FrameClass';          {the registered class name}

  {now that we have our class set up, register it with the system}
  Result := Windows.RegisterClass(WindowClass) <> 0;
end;

{ Register the child window Class }
function RegisterChildClass: Boolean;
var
  WindowClass: TWndClass;
begin
  {setup our child window class}
  WindowClass.Style := CS_HREDRAW or CS_VREDRAW;      {set the class styles}
  WindowClass.lpfnWndProc := @MDIChildWindowProc;     {point to the default MDI
                                                       child window procedure}
  WindowClass.cbClsExtra := 0;                        {no extra class memory}
  WindowClass.cbWndExtra := 0;                        {no extra window memory}
  WindowClass.hInstance := hInstance;                 {the application instance}
  WindowClass.hIcon := LoadIcon(0, IDI_APPLICATION); {load a predefined logo}
  WindowClass.hCursor := LoadCursor(0, IDC_ARROW);    {load a predefined cursor}
  WindowClass.hbrBackground := COLOR_WINDOW;          {use a predefined color}
  WindowClass.lpszMenuName := nil;                    {no menu}
  WindowClass.lpszClassName := 'ChildClass';          {the registered class name}

  {now that we have our class set up, register it with the system}
  Result := Windows.RegisterClass(WindowClass) <> 0;
end;

{this begins the main program}
begin
  {Register our frame class first}
  if not RegisterFrameClass then
  begin
    MessageBox(0,'RegisterFrameClass failed',nil,MB_OK);
    Exit;
  end;

  {Create the frame window based on our frame class}
  FrameWindow := CreateWindow('FrameClass',           {the registered class name}
                              'DefFrameProc Example',{the title bar text}
                               WS_OVERLAPPEDWINDOW {a normal window style}
                               or WS_CLIPCHILDREN, {clips all child windows}
                               CW_USEDEFAULT,      {default horizontal position}
                               CW_USEDEFAULT,      {default vertical position}
```

```
                                 CW_USEDEFAULT,      {default width}
                                 CW_USEDEFAULT,      {default height}
                                 0,                  {handle of the parent window}
                                 0,                  {no menu}
                                 hInstance,          {the application instance}
                                 nil                 {no additional information}
                                 );

{If our frame window was created successfully, show it}
if FrameWindow <> 0 then
begin
  ShowWindow(FrameWindow, SW_SHOWNORMAL);
  UpdateWindow(FrameWindow);
end
else
begin
  MessageBox(0,'CreateFrameWindow failed',nil,MB_OK);
  Exit;
end;

{Register the child window class}
if not RegisterChildClass then
begin
  MessageBox(0,'RegisterChildClass failed',nil,MB_OK);
  Exit;
end;

{Create the MDI child window}
ChildWindow := CreateMDIWindow('ChildClass',    {the registered class name}
                               'Child Window',  {the title bar text}
                               WS_VISIBLE,      {initially visible}
                               CW_USEDEFAULT,   {default horizontal position}
                               CW_USEDEFAULT,   {default vertical position}
                               CW_USEDEFAULT,   {default width}
                               CW_USEDEFAULT,   {default height}
                               ClientWindow,    {handle of the parent window}
                               hInstance,       {the application instance}
                               0                {no application defined value}
                               );

{check to see if it was created}
if ChildWindow <> 0 then
begin
  ShowWindow(ChildWindow, SW_SHOWNORMAL);
  UpdateWindow(ChildWindow);
end
else
begin
  MessageBox(0,'CreateChildWindow failed',nil,mb_ok);
  Exit;
end;

{the standard message loop}
while GetMessage(TheMessage,0,0,0) do
begin
```

```
      TranslateMessage(TheMessage);
      DispatchMessage(TheMessage);
    end;
  end.
```

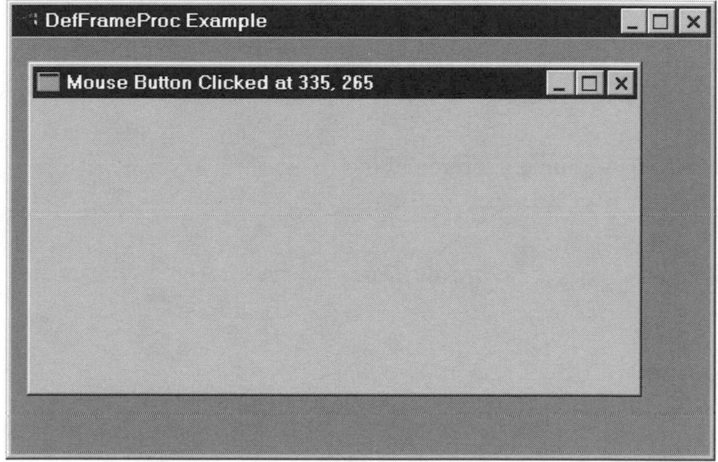

Figure 4-2: The MDI frame and child windows.

DefMDIChildProc Windows.Pas

Syntax

```
DefMDIChildProc(
hWnd: HWND;             {a handle to the MDI child window}
uMsg: UINT;             {the identifier of the message to send}
wParam: WPARAM;         {a 32-bit message specific value}
lParam: LPARAM          {a 32-bit message specific value}
): LRESULT;             {returns a message specific return value}
```


Description

This function provides default message processing for any message not handled in the window procedure of a multiple document interface child window. Any messages not explicitly handled by the MDI child window procedure must be passed to the DefMDIChildProc function. This function assumes that the parent window of the window identified by the hWnd parameter was created using the MDICLIENT class.

Parameters

hWnd: A handle to the child window.

uMsg: The identifier of the message to send.

wParam: A 32-bit value dependent on the message being sent.

lParam: A 32-bit value dependent on the message being sent.

Return Value

The value returned from this function specifies the result of the message processing and is dependent on the message sent.

See also

CallWindowProc, DefFrameProc, DefWindowProc

Example

Please see Listing 4-3 under DefFrameProc.

DefWindowProc Windows.Pas

Syntax

```
DefWindowProc(
hWnd: HWND;                {a handle to a window}
Msg: UINT;                 {the identifier of the message to send}
wParam: WPARAM;            {a 32-bit message specific value}
lParam: LPARAM             {a 32-bit message specific value}
): LRESULT;                {returns a message specific return value}
```

Description

This function provides default message processing for any message not handled in the window procedure of an application. Any messages not explicitly handled by the application's window procedure must be passed to the DefWindowProc function. This function ensures that all incoming Windows messages are processed.

Parameters

hWnd: A handle to the window.

Msg: The identifier of the message to send.

wParam: A 32-bit value dependent on the message being sent.

lParam: A 32-bit value dependent on the message being sent.

Return Value

The value returned from this function specifies the result of the message processing and is dependent on the message sent.

See also

CallWindowProc, DefFrameProc, DefMDIChildProc

Example

Please see Listing 4-4 under GetMessage.

DispatchMessage   Windows.Pas

Syntax

```
DispatchMessage(
const lpMsg: TMsg              {a pointer to a TMsg message structure}
): Longint;                    {returns a message specific return value}
```

Description

This function dispatches the specified message to a window procedure. The value specified by the lpMsg parameter is typically provided by the GetMessage function. The DispatchMessage function is used in the message loop of a Windows program.

Parameters

lpMsg: A pointer to a message information structure. This structure is typically passed as a parameter to the GetMessage or PeekMessage functions before the DispatchMessage function is called. The TMsg function is defined as:

```
TMsg = packed record
      hwnd: HWND;            {a handle to the window receiving the message}
      message: UINT;         {the message identifier}
      wParam: WPARAM;        {a 32-bit message specific value}
      lParam: LPARAM;        {a 32-bit message specific value}
      time: DWORD;           {the time when the message was posted}
      pt: TPoint;            {the position of the mouse cursor}
end;
```

hwnd: A handle to the window whose window procedure receives the message.

message: The message identifier.

wParam: A 32-bit message specific value.

lParam: A 32-bit message specific value. If the message member contains WM_TIMER and the lParam parameter of the WM_TIMER message is not zero, lParam will contain a pointer to a function that is called instead of the window procedure.

time: The time at which the message was posted.

pt: A TPoint structure containing the position of the mouse cursor at the time the message was posted, in screen coordinates.

Return Value

This function returns the value returned from the window procedure, and its meaning is dependent on the message being processed.

See also

GetMessage, PeekMessage, PostMessage, TranslateMessage

Example

Please see Listing 4-4 under GetMessage.

GetMessage Windows.Pas

Syntax

```
GetMessage(
var lpMsg: TMsg;            {a pointer to a TMsg message structure}
hWnd: HWND;                 {a handle to the window whose messages are retrieved}
wMsgFilterMin: UINT;        {the lowest message value to retrieve}
wMsgFilterMax: UINT         {the highest message value to retrieve}
): BOOL;                    {returns TRUE or FALSE}
```

Description

This function retrieves information about the next waiting message in a thread's message queue. The message information is stored in a TMsg structure pointed to by the lpMsg parameter. The retrieved message is removed from the queue unless it is a WM_PAINT message, which is removed after processing the message with the BeginPaint and EndPaint functions. GetMessage can be instructed to retrieve messages that lie only within a specified range, but if the wMsgFilterMin and wMsgFilterMax parameters are both set to zero, GetMessage will retrieve all available messages. The WM_KEYFIRST and WM_KEYLAST constants can be used to retrieve only keyboard input messages, and the WM_MOUSEFIRST and WM_MOUSELAST constants can be used to retrieve only mouse input messages. This function cannot retrieve messages for windows owned by other threads or applications, or for any thread other than the calling thread. This function will not return until a message has been placed in the message queue.

Parameters

lpMsg: A pointer to a message information structure. This structure receives the message information retrieved from the calling thread's message queue. The TMsg function is defined as:

```
TMsg = packed record
    hwnd: HWND;             {a handle to the window receiving the message}
    message: UINT;          {the message identifier}
    wParam: WPARAM;         {a 32-bit message specific value}
    lParam: LPARAM;         {a 32-bit message specific value}
    time: DWORD;            {the time when the message was posted}
    pt: TPoint;             {the position of the mouse cursor}
end;
```

Note that the hwnd member of messages posted to the calling thread by the PostThreadMessage function will be set to zero. Please see the DispatchMessage function for a description of this data structure.

hWnd: A handle to the window whose messages are to be retrieved. If this value is zero, GetMessage retrieves message information for any window owned by the calling thread, including thread messages sent to the calling thread by the PostThreadMessage function.

wMsgFilterMin: The message identifier of the lowest message value to be retrieved.

wMsgFilterMax: The message identifier of the highest message value to be retrieved.

Return Value

If the function succeeds and does not retrieve the WM_QUIT message, it returns TRUE. If the function fails, or it retrieves the WM_QUIT message, it returns FALSE.

See also

PeekMessage, PostMessage, PostThreadMessage, WaitMessage

Example

Listing 4-4: A Windows API Window with a Normal Message Loop

```
program GetMessageExample;

uses
    Windows, Messages, SysUtils;

{$R *.RES}

{The window procedure for our API window}
function WindowProc(TheWindow: HWnd; TheMessage, WParam,
                    LParam: Longint): Longint; stdcall;
begin
  case TheMessage of
    {upon getting the WM_DESTROY message, we exit the application}
    WM_DESTROY: begin
                  PostQuitMessage(0);
                  Exit;
                end;
    WM_LBUTTONDOWN: begin
                      {show the message time and the mouse coordinates}
                      SetWindowText(TheWindow, PChar('Message Time: '+IntToStr(
                                   GetMessageTime)+'   Mouse Coordinates: '+
                                   IntToStr(LoWord(GetMessagePos))+', '+
                                   IntToStr(HiWord(GetMessagePos))));

                      {indicate that the message was handled}
                      Result := 1;
                    end;
    else
      {call the default window procedure for all unhandled messages}
```

```
      Result := DefWindowProc(TheWindow, TheMessage, WParam, LParam);
    end;
end;

{ Register the Window Class }
function RegisterClass: Boolean;
var
  WindowClass: TWndClass;
begin
  {setup our new window class}
  WindowClass.Style := CS_HREDRAW or CS_VREDRAW;     {set the class styles}
  WindowClass.lpfnWndProc := @WindowProc;            {point to our window procedure}
  WindowClass.cbClsExtra := 0;                       {no extra class memory}
  WindowClass.cbWndExtra := 0;                       {no extra window memory}
  WindowClass.hInstance := hInstance;                {the application instance}
  WindowClass.hIcon := LoadIcon(0, IDI_APPLICATION); {load a predefined logo}
  WindowClass.hCursor := LoadCursor(0, IDC_ARROW);   {load a predefined cursor}
  WindowClass.hbrBackground := COLOR_WINDOW;          {use a predefined color}
  WindowClass.lpszMenuName := nil;                    {no menu}
  WindowClass.lpszClassName := 'TestClass';           {the registered class name}

  {now that we have our class set up, register it with the system}
  Result := Windows.RegisterClass(WindowClass) <> 0;
end;

var
  TheMessage: TMsg;   // holds a message
  OurWindow: HWND;    // the handle to our window
begin
  {register our new class first}
  if not RegisterClass then
  begin
    MessageBox(0,'RegisterClass failed',nil,MB_OK);
    Exit;
  end;

  {now, create a window based on our new class}
  OurWindow := CreateWindow('TestClass',           {the registered class name}
                            'GetMessage Example',  {the title bar text}
                            WS_OVERLAPPEDWINDOW or {a normal window style}
                            WS_VISIBLE,            {initially visible}
                            CW_USEDEFAULT,         {default horizontal position}
                            CW_USEDEFAULT,         {default vertical position}
                            CW_USEDEFAULT,         {default width}
                            CW_USEDEFAULT,         {default height}
                            0,                     {handle of the parent window}
                            0,                     {no menu}
                            hInstance,             {the application instance}
                            nil                    {no additional information}
                            );

  {if our window was not created successfully, exit the program}
  if OurWindow=0 then
  begin
    MessageBox(0,'CreateWindow failed',nil,MB_OK);
```

```
    Exit;
  end;

  {the standard message loop}
  while GetMessage(TheMessage,0,0,0) do
  begin
    TranslateMessage(TheMessage);
    DispatchMessage(TheMessage);
  end;

end.
```

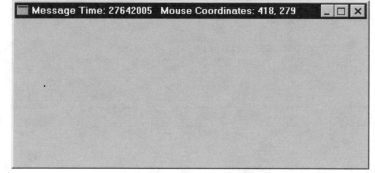

Figure 4-3: The time and position of the WM_LBUTTONDOWN message.

GetMessageExtraInfo Windows.Pas

Syntax

GetMessageExtraInfo: Longint; {returns an application-defined value}

Description

This function retrieves the 32-bit application-defined value associated with the last message retrieved by the GetMessage or PeekMessage functions. This value is specified by using the SetMessageExtraInfo function.

Return Value

If the function succeeds, it returns the 32-bit application-defined value associated with the last message retrieved by the GetMessage or PeekMessage functions that was set using the SetMessageExtraInfo function. If the function fails, it returns zero.

See also

GetMessage, PeekMessage, SetMessageExtraInfo

Example

Listing 4-5: Retrieving Extra Message Information

```
{define an application specific user message}
const
  UserMessage = WM_USER+1;

type
  TForm1 = class(TForm)
    Button1: TButton;
    procedure Button1Click(Sender: TObject);
  private
    { Private declarations }
  public
    {the handler for our user message}
    procedure DoMessage(var Msg: TMessage); message UserMessage;
  end;

var
  Form1: TForm1;

implementation

{$R *.DFM}

procedure TForm1.Button1Click(Sender: TObject);
begin
  {set the message extra information}
  SetMessageExtraInfo(12345);

  {send the user message to the window}
  Perform(UserMessage, 0, 0);
end;

procedure TForm1.DoMessage(var Msg: TMessage);
begin
  {the user message was retrieved, show the message extra info}
  Button1.Caption := 'User Message Received. Info: '+
                     IntToStr(GetMessageExtraInfo);
end;
```

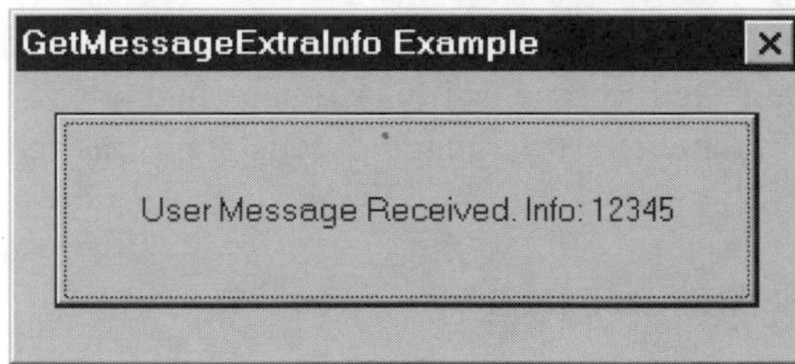

Figure 4-4: The extra message information was retrieved.

GetMessagePos Windows.Pas

Syntax

GetMessagePos: DWORD; {returns the mouse position in screen coordinates}

Description

This function returns the horizontal and vertical position, in screen coordinates, of the mouse cursor at the moment when the last message retrieved by the GetMessage function occurred. The horizontal position of the mouse cursor is in the low-order word of the return value, and the vertical position is in the high-order word.

Return Value

If the function succeeds, it returns the horizontal and vertical position, in screen coordinates, of the mouse cursor at the moment when the last message retrieved by the GetMessage function occurred. If the function fails, it returns zero.

See also

GetCursorPos, GetMessage, GetMessageTime, PeekMessage

Example

Please see Listing 4-4 under GetMessage.

GetMessageTime Windows.Pas

Syntax

GetMessageTime: Longint; {returns the time that the message was created}

Description

This function retrieves the elapsed time, in milliseconds, from the time that the system was started to the time that the last message that was retrieved by the GetMessage function was put into the thread's message queue.

Return Value

If the function succeeds, it retrieves the elapsed time, in milliseconds, from the time that the system was started to the time that the last message that was retrieved by the GetMessage function was put into the thread's message queue. If the function fails, it returns zero.

See also

GetMessage, GetMessagePos, PeekMessage

Example

Please see Listing 4-4 under GetMessage.

GetQueueStatus Windows.Pas

Syntax

GetQueueStatus(
flags: UINT {message queue status flags}
): DWORD {returns message queue status flags}

Description

This function returns a series of flags indicating the types of messages found in the calling thread's message queue at the time the function was called. However, if the return value indicates that a message is currently in the queue, it does not guarantee that the GetMessage or PeekMessage functions will return a message as these functions perform some filtering that may process some messages internally.

Parameters

flags: Specifies the types of messages to check for in the calling thread's message queue. This parameter can be a combination of one or more values from Table 4-4.

Return Value

If this function succeeds, it returns a DWORD value. The high-order word of this return value contains a combination of the flag's values that indicate the types of messages currently in the message queue. The low-order word contains a combination of the flag's values that indicate the types of messages that have been added to the queue since the last call to the GetQueueStatus, GetMessage, or PeekMessage functions. If the function fails, or there are no messages in the queue, it returns zero.

See also

GetInputState, GetMessage, PeekMessage

Example

Listing 4-6: Retrieving the Current Message Queue Status

```
procedure TForm1.Button1Click(Sender: TObject);
var
  CurrentMessage: DWORD;      // holds the current message information
begin
  {look for any message}
  CurrentMessage := GetQueueStatus(QS_ALLINPUT);

  {display the queue status}
  PrintStatus(HiWord(CurrentMessage), ListBox1);
  PrintStatus(LoWord(CurrentMessage), ListBox2);
  Label3.Caption := 'GetQueueStatus value: '+IntToHex(CurrentMessage, 8);
end;

{this simply converts the GetQueueStatus return value into a string}
function PrintStatus(Index: Integer; ListBox: TListBox): string;
```

```
begin
  ListBox.Items.Clear;

  if (Index and QS_KEY)=QS_KEY
    then ListBox.Items.Add('QS_KEY');
  if (Index and QS_MOUSEMOVE)=QS_MOUSEMOVE
    then ListBox.Items.Add('QS_MOUSEMOVE');
  if (Index and QS_MOUSEBUTTON)=QS_MOUSEBUTTON
    then ListBox.Items.Add('QS_MOUSEBUTTON');
  if (Index and QS_POSTMESSAGE)=QS_POSTMESSAGE
    then ListBox.Items.Add('QS_POSTMESSAGE');
  if (Index and QS_TIMER)=QS_TIMER
    then ListBox.Items.Add('QS_TIMER');
  if (Index and QS_PAINT)=QS_PAINT
    then ListBox.Items.Add('QS_PAINT');
  if (Index and QS_SENDMESSAGE)=QS_SENDMESSAGE
    then ListBox.Items.Add('QS_SENDMESSAGE');
  if (Index and QS_HOTKEY)=QS_HOTKEY
    then ListBox.Items.Add('QS_HOTKEY');
  if (Index and QS_ALLPOSTMESSAGE)=QS_ALLPOSTMESSAGE
    then ListBox.Items.Add('QS_ALLPOSTMESSAGE');
end;
```

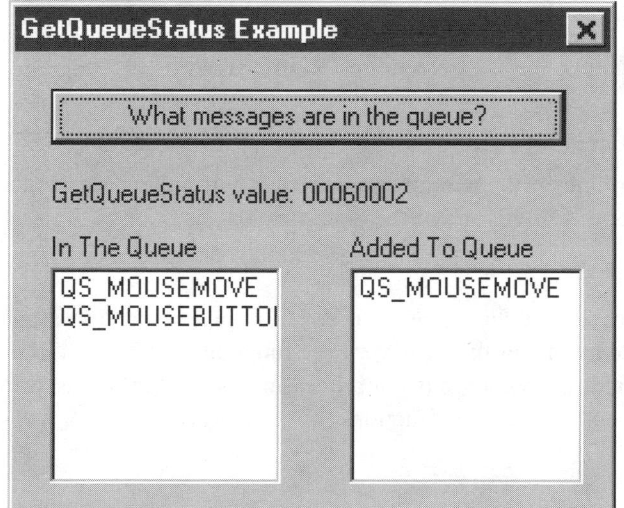

Figure 4-5: The current queue status.

Table 4-4: GetQueueStatus flags Values

Value	Description
QS_ALLEVENTS	A user input message, the WM_TIMER, WM_PAINT, and WM_HOTKEY messages, or a posted message is in the queue
QS_ALLINPUT	Any Windows message is in the queue.
QS_HOTKEY	A WM_HOTKEY message is in the queue.

Value	Description
QS_INPUT	Any user input message is in the queue.
QS_KEY	A WM_KEYUP, WM_KEYDOWN, WM_SYSKEYUP, or WM_SYSKEYDOWN message is in the queue
QS_MOUSE	A WM_MOUSEMOVE message or mouse-button message (such as WM_LBUTTONDOWN) is in the queue.
QS_MOUSEBUTTON	A mouse-button message (such as WM_LBUTTONUP) is in the queue.
QS_MOUSEMOVE	A WM_MOUSEMOVE message is in the queue.
QS_PAINT	A WM_PAINT message is in the queue.
QS_POSTMESSAGE	A posted message (excluding all messages listed in this table) is in the queue.
QS_SENDMESSAGE	A message sent by another thread or application via one of the SendMessage functions is in the queue.
QS_TIMER	A WM_TIMER message is in the queue.

InSendMessage *Windows.Pas*

Syntax

InSendMessage: BOOL; {returns TRUE or FALSE}

Description

This function determines if the window procedure is currently processing a message sent to it by another thread via one of the SendMessage functions.

Return Value

If the function succeeds and the window procedure is processing a message sent to it from another thread by one of the SendMessage functions, it returns TRUE. If the function fails, or the window procedure is not processing a message sent to it from another thread by one of the SendMessage functions, it returns FALSE.

See also

PostThreadMessage, PostMessage, ReplyMessage, SendMessage, SendMessageCallback, SendMessageTimeout

Example

Please see Listing 4-11 under RegisterWindowMessage and Listing 4-8 under PostMessage.

PeekMessage Windows.Pas

Syntax

```
PeekMessage(
var lpMsg: TMsg;            {a pointer to a TMsg message structure}
hWnd: HWND;                 {a handle to the window whose messages are retrieved}
wMsgFilterMin: UINT;        {the lowest message value to retrieve}
wMsgFilterMax: UINT         {the highest message value to retrieve}
wRemoveMsg: UINT            {message removal flags}
): BOOL;                    {returns TRUE or FALSE}
```

Description

This function retrieves information about the next waiting message in a thread's message queue. The message information is stored in a TMsg structure pointed to by the lpMsg parameter. Messages can optionally be removed from the queue. PeekMessage can be instructed to retrieve messages that lie only within a specified range, but if the wMsgFilterMin and wMsgFilterMax parameters are both set to zero, PeekMessage will retrieve all available messages. The WM_KEYFIRST and WM_KEYLAST constants can be used to retrieve only keyboard input messages, and the WM_MOUSEFIRST and WM_MOUSELAST constants can be used to retrieve only mouse input messages. This function cannot retrieve messages for windows owned by other threads or applications, or for any thread other than the calling thread. Unlike GetMessage, this function returns immediately and does not wait until a message has been placed into the message queue.

Parameters

lpMsg: A pointer to a message information structure. This structure receives the message information retrieved from the calling thread's message queue. The TMsg function is defined as:

```
TMsg = packed record
      hwnd: HWND;              {a handle to the window receiving the message}
      message: UINT;           {the message identifier}
      wParam: WPARAM;          {a 32-bit message specific value}
      lParam: LPARAM;          {a 32-bit message specific value}
      time: DWORD;             {the time when the message was posted}
      pt: TPoint;              {the position of the mouse cursor}
end;
```

Note that the hwnd member of messages posted to the calling thread by the PostThreadMessage function will be set to zero. Please see the DispatchMessage function for a description of this data structure.

hWnd: A handle to the window whose messages are to be retrieved. If this parameter is set to zero, PeekMessage retrieves message information for any window owned by the calling thread, including thread messages sent to the calling thread by the PostThreadMessage function. If this parameter is set to –1, PeekMessage retrieves messages posted to the thread only by the PostThreadMessage function.

wMsgFilterMin: The message identifier of the lowest message value to be retrieved.

wMsgFilterMax: The message identifier of the highest message value to be retrieved.

wRemoveMsg: A flag indicating if the message is to be removed from the message queue. If this parameter is set to PM_NOREMOVE, the message is not removed from the queue. If this parameter is set to PM_REMOVE, the message is removed. WM_PAINT messages cannot normally be removed, but if a WM_PAINT message indicates a null update region, PeekMessage can remove it from the queue.

Return Value

If the function succeeds and there is a message available in the queue, it returns TRUE. If the function fails, or there are no messages waiting in the queue, it returns FALSE.

See also

GetMessage, PostMessage, PostThreadMessage, WaitMessage

Example

Listing 4-7: Retrieving Messages Using PeekMessage

```
procedure TForm1.FormMouseDown(Sender: TObject; Button: TMouseButton;
  Shift: TShiftState; X, Y: Integer);
var
  CurMouse: TPoint;       // identifies the mouse position in client coordinates
  TheMessage: TMSG;       // the message information structure
begin
  {if the left button was not clicked, don't start tracking the mouse}
  if Button<>mbLeft then Exit;

  {indicate that the mouse is being tracked}
  Caption := 'PeekMessage Example  -  Mouse is being tracked';

  {this causes the program to go into a tight loop that will exit
   only when the right mouse button is clicked}
  while not PeekMessage(TheMessage, Handle, WM_RBUTTONDOWN,
                        WM_RBUTTONDOWN, PM_NOREMOVE) do
  begin
    {get the current mouse cursor position in screen coordinates}
    GetCursorPos(CurMouse);

    {translate this into client coordinates}
    CurMouse := Form1.ScreenToClient(CurMouse);

    {draw a line to the new mouse position}
    Canvas.LineTo(CurMouse.X, CurMouse.Y);
  end;
```

```
  {the loop has ended, indicate that the mouse is no longer being tracked}
  Caption := 'PeekMessage Example  -  Mouse not tracked';
end;
```

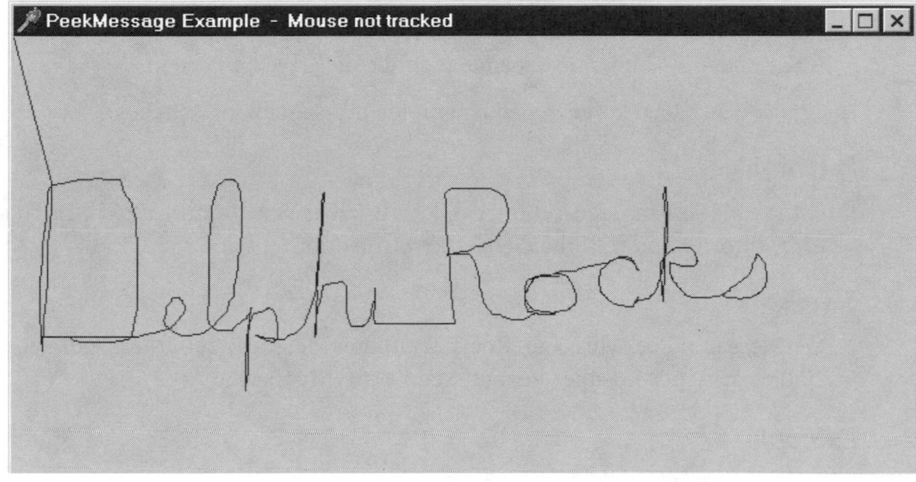

Figure 4-6: A crude drawing example.

PostMessage Windows.Pas

Syntax

PostMessage(
hWnd: HWND; {a handle to a window}
Msg: UINT; {the identifier of the message to send}
wParam: WPARAM; {a 32-bit message specific value}
lParam: LPARAM {a 32-bit message specific value}
): BOOL; {returns TRUE or FALSE}

Description

This function places the indicated message in the message queue of the thread that owns the specified window, returning immediately without waiting for the message to be processed. Caution is advised when sending a message whose parameters contain pointers, as the function will return before the thread associated with the specified window has a chance to process the message and the pointers could be freed before they are used.

Parameters

hWnd: A handle to the window whose window procedure is to receive the specified message. If this parameter is set to zero, PostMessage functions exactly like a call to the PostThreadMessage function with the idThread parameter set to the identifier of the calling thread. If this parameter is set to HWND_BROADCAST, the message is sent to all top-level windows in the system, including disabled and invisible windows. The message is not sent to child windows. Applications that need to send a user-defined message to other applications using HWND_BROADCAST should use the Register-WindowMessage to obtain a unique message identifier.

Msg: The identifier of the message to send.

wParam: A 32-bit value dependent on the message being sent.

lParam: A 32-bit value dependent on the message being sent.

Return Value

If the function succeeds, it returns TRUE; otherwise it returns FALSE. To get extended error information, call the GetLastError function.

See also

GetMessage, PeekMessage, RegisterWindowMessage, SendMessage, SendMessage-Callback, SendMessageTimeout, SendNotifyMessage

Example

Listing 4-8: Posting a Message to a Window's Message Queue

This application posts the message:

```
procedure TForm1.FormCreate(Sender: TObject);
begin
  {register a user defined message}
  UserMessage := RegisterWindowMessage('PostMessage Test Message');
end;

procedure TForm1.Button1Click(Sender: TObject);
begin
  {post the user defined message to the specified window's
   message queue}
  PostMessage(FindWindow('TForm1','PostMessage Get Example'), UserMessage, 0,0);

  {this message box will pop up immediately, as PostMessage
   does not wait for the message to be processed.}
  ShowMessage('Returned');
end;
```

and this application receives it:

```
procedure TForm1.DefaultHandler(var Msg);
var
  iLoop: Integer;      // a general loop control variable
begin
  {allow default message handling to occur}
  inherited DefaultHandler(Msg);

  {if the message was our user defined message...}
  if TMessage(Msg).Msg=UserMessage then
  begin
```

```
    {...turn on some user interface components}
    ProgressBar1.Visible := TRUE;
    Label2.Visible := TRUE;

    {indicate if the message was sent via one of the SendMessage functions}
    if InSendMessage then Label3.Visible := TRUE;

    {repaint the form}
    Form1.Repaint;

    {animate the progress bar for a short amount of time}
    for iLoop := 0 to 100 do
    begin
      ProgressBar1.Position := iLoop;
      Sleep(10);
    end;

    {turn off the user interface elements}
    ProgressBar1.Visible := FALSE;
    Label2.Visible := FALSE;
    Label3.Visible := FALSE;

    {indicate the message was handled}
    TMessage(Msg).Result := 1;
  end;
end;

procedure TForm1.FormCreate(Sender: TObject);
begin
  {register a user defined message}
  UserMessage := RegisterWindowMessage('PostMessage Test Message');
end;
```


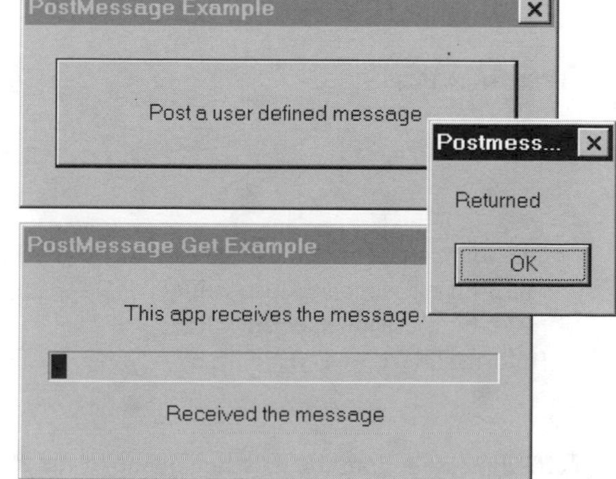

Figure 4-7: The PostMessage function posts the message and returns immediately.

PostQuitMessage Windows.Pas

Syntax

```
PostQuitMessage(
nExitCode: Integer          {the application-defined exit code}
);                          {this procedure does not return a value}
```

Description

This function posts a WM_QUIT message to the calling thread's message queue, causing the application to terminate.

Parameters

nExitCode: An application-defined value that is passed to the wParam parameter of the WM_QUIT message. This value is returned to Windows when the application terminates.

See also

GetMessage, PeekMessage, PostMessage

Example

Listing 4-9: Terminating an Application

```
procedure TForm1.Button1Click(Sender: TObject);
begin
  {indicate to Windows that the application should terminate}
  PostQuitMessage(0);
end;
```

PostThreadMessage Windows.Pas

Syntax

```
PostThreadMessage(
idThread: DWORD;
Msg: UINT;                  {the identifier of the message to send}
wParam: WPARAM;             {a 32-bit message specific value}
lParam: LPARAM              {a 32-bit message specific value}
): BOOL;                    {returns TRUE or FALSE}
```

Description

This function places the specified message into the message queue of the thread identified by the idThread parameter. The function returns immediately, without waiting for the thread to process the message. A thread creates a message queue the first time it makes a call to any Win32 user or GDI functions. When the thread retrieves messages by using the GetMessage or PeekMessage functions, the hWnd member of the returned message structure will be set to zero.

Parameters

idThread: The identifier of the thread to which the message is posted.

Msg: The identifier of the message to send.

wParam: A 32-bit value dependent on the message being sent.

lParam: A 32-bit value dependent on the message being sent.

Return Value

If the function succeeds, it returns TRUE; otherwise it returns FALSE. To get extended error information, call the GetLastError function. GetLastError will return ERROR_INVALID_THREAD_ID if the idThread parameter does not contain a valid thread identifier, or if the thread it identifies does not have a message queue.

See also

CreateThread, GetCurrentThreadID, GetMessage, GetWindowThreadProcessID, PeekMessage, PostMessage, SendMessage

Example

Listing 4-10: Posting a Message to a Thread

```
const
  NewMessage = WM_USER+1;     // a new user defined message

implementation

function ThreadFunction(Parameter: Pointer): Integer; stdcall;
var
  DC: HDC;      // holds a device context
  Msg: TMsg;    // a message information structure
begin
  {create a message loop}
  while (GetMessage(Msg, 0, 0, 0)) do
  begin
    {if the retrieved message is our user defined message...}
    if Msg.Message = NewMessage then
    begin
      {...retrieve a handle to the device context}
      DC := GetDC(Form1.Handle);

      {set the background mode to be transparent}
      SetBkMode(DC, TRANSPARENT);

      {display text indicating that the message was received}
      TextOut(DC, 10, 10, 'User message seen by thread', 27);

      {release the device context}
```

```
      ReleaseDC(Form1.Handle, DC);
    end;
  end;
end;

procedure TForm1.Button1Click(Sender: TObject);
var
  ThreadId: Integer;    // holds the new thread ID
begin
  {create a new thread}
  ThreadHandle := CreateThread(nil, 0, @ThreadFunction, nil, 0, ThreadId);

  {make sure that the thread was created correctly}
  if ThreadHandle = 0 then
  begin
    ShowMessage('New thread not started');
    Halt;
  end;

  {pause for 100 milliseconds}
  Sleep(100);

  {post the user defined message to the thread}
  PostThreadMessage(ThreadId, NewMessage, 0, 0);
end;
```

RegisterWindowMessage Windows.Pas

Syntax

RegisterWindowMessage(
lpString: PChar {a pointer to a message string}
): UINT; {returns a unique message identifier}

Description

This function generates a new message identifier that is unique throughout the system. This new message identifier can be used by any of the PostMessage or SendMessage functions, and is typically used to provide a means of communication between two applications. If two different applications register the same message string, each application will receive an identical unique message identifier. This identifier remains valid until the current Windows session terminates.

Parameters

lpString: A pointer to a null-terminated string containing the message to be registered.

Return Value

If the function succeeds, it returns a unique message identifier in the range of $C000 through $FFFF. If the function fails, it returns zero.

See also

PostMessage, PostThreadMessage, SendMessage, SendMessageCallback, SendMessageTimeout, SendNotifyMessage

Example

Listing 4-11: Communicating Using a Unique Message Identifier

This application sends the message:

```
procedure TForm1.FormCreate(Sender: TObject);
begin
  {register the user defined message}
  UserMessage := RegisterWindowMessage('System Wide User Defined Message');
end;

procedure TForm1.Button1Click(Sender: TObject);
var
  ReturnValue: LRESULT;    // holds the result returned by SendMessage
begin
  {send the user defined message to the specified window}
  ReturnValue := SendMessage(FindWindow('TForm1','RegisterMessage Get Example'),
                             UserMessage, 0, 0);

  {display the result of the message processing}
  Button1.Caption := 'SendMessage Result: '+IntToStr(ReturnValue);
end;
```

and this application receives it:

```
procedure TForm1.DefaultHandler(var Msg);
begin
  {allow default message handling to occur}
  inherited DefaultHandler(Msg);

  {if the user defined message was received...}
  if (TMessage(Msg).Msg=UserMessage) then
  begin
    {...send a reply. this causes the message to return
     immediately if sent by one of the SendMessage functions}
    ReplyMessage(5);

    {enable the timer and turn on a user interface object}
    Timer1.Enabled := TRUE;
    Label2.Visible := TRUE;

    {indicate if the message was sent via one of the SendMessage functions}
    if InSendMessage then Label3.Visible := TRUE;
  end;
end;

procedure TForm1.FormCreate(Sender: TObject);
begin
  {register the system wide user defined message}
```

```
  UserMessage := RegisterWindowMessage('System Wide User Defined Message');
end;

procedure TForm1.Timer1Timer(Sender: TObject);
begin
  {turn off the user interface elements after one second}
  Timer1.Enabled := FALSE;
  Label2.Visible := FALSE;
  Label3.Visible := FALSE;
end;
```

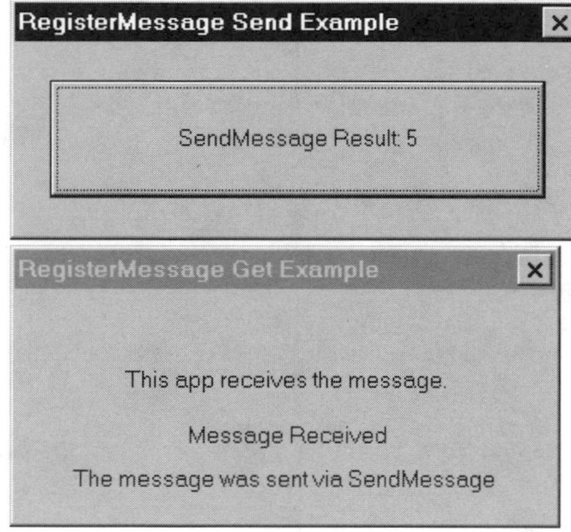

Figure 4-8: Using the unique message identifier.

ReplyMessage Windows.Pas

Syntax

ReplyMessage(
lResult: LRESULT {a message processing result value}
): BOOL; {returns TRUE or FALSE}

Description

This function is used to reply to a message sent to the calling thread by another thread or process through one of the SendMessage functions. This causes the thread sending the message to return from the SendMessage function immediately as if the thread receiving the message had completed the message processing. If the message was not sent through one of the SendMessage functions, or was sent by the same thread, this function has no effect.

Parameters

lResult: A value specifying the result of the message processing. This is used as the return value from the SendMessage function for which this function is replying, and can specify an application-defined value.

Return Value

If the function succeeds and the calling thread was processing a message sent to it from another thread or process via one of the SendMessage functions, then it returns TRUE. If the function fails, or the calling thread was not processing a message sent to it from another thread or process via one of the SendMessage functions, then it returns FALSE.

See also

InSendMessage, SendMessage, SendMessageCallback, SendMessageTimeout

Example

Please see Listing 4-11 under RegisterWindowMessage.

SendMessage Windows.Pas

Syntax

```
SendMessage(
hWnd: HWND;                {a handle to a window}
Msg: UINT;                 {the identifier of the message to send}
wParam: WPARAM;            {a 32-bit message specific value}
lParam: LPARAM             {a 32-bit message specific value}
): LRESULT;                {returns a message specific result}
```


Description

This function sends the specified message to the window procedure of the indicated window, and does not return until the called window procedure has processed the message. If the specified window belongs to the calling thread, that window's window procedure is called immediately as a subroutine. However, if the window belongs to a different thread, Windows switches to that thread, sending the message to the appropriate window procedure, and the thread sending the message is blocked until the receiving thread processes the message.

Parameters

hWnd: A handle to the window whose window procedure is to receive the specified message. If this parameter is set to HWND_BROADCAST, the message is sent to all top-level windows in the system, including disabled and invisible windows. The message is not sent to child windows. Applications that need to send a user-defined message to other applications using HWND_BROADCAST should use the RegisterWindowMessage function to obtain a unique message identifier.

Msg: The identifier of the message to send.

wParam: A 32-bit value dependent on the message being sent.

lParam: A 32-bit value dependent on the message being sent.

Return Value

If the function succeeds, it returns a message specific value indicating the result of the message processing. If the function fails, it returns zero.

See also

InSendMessage, PostMessage, RegisterWindowMessage, ReplyMessage, SendMessageCallback, SendMessageTimeout, SendNotifyMessage

Example

Please see Listing 4-11 under RegisterWindowMessage.

SendMessageCallback   Windows.Pas

Syntax

```
SendMessageCallback(
hWnd: HWND;                        {a handle to a window}
Msg: UINT;                         {the identifier of the message to send}
wParam: WPARAM;                    {a 32-bit message specific value}
lParam: LPARAM                     {a 32-bit message specific value}
lpResultCallBack: TFNSendAsyncProc;    {a pointer to an application-defined
                                       callback procedure}
dwData: DWORD                      {an application-defined value}
): BOOL;                           {returns TRUE or FALSE}
```

Description

This function sends the specified message to the window procedure of the window indicated by the hWnd parameter. Unlike SendMessage, this function returns immediately. After the window procedure in the receiving thread has finished processing the message, the system calls the application-defined callback procedure specified by the lpResultCallBack parameter, passing the message sent, the result of the message processing, and an application-defined value. The callback procedure will only be called when the receiving thread calls the GetMessage, PeekMessage, or WaitMessage functions. Caution is advised when sending a message whose parameters contain pointers, as the function will return before the thread associated with the specified window has a chance to process the message and the pointers could be freed before they are used.

Parameters

hWnd: A handle to the window whose window procedure is to receive the specified message. If this parameter is set to HWND_BROADCAST, the message is sent to all top-level windows in the system, including disabled and invisible windows. The message is not sent to child windows. Applications that need to send a user-defined message to other applications using HWND_BROADCAST should use the RegisterWindowMessage function to obtain a unique message identifier.

Msg: The identifier of the message to send.

wParam: A 32-bit value dependent on the message being sent.

lParam: A 32-bit value dependent on the message being sent.

lpResultCallBack: A pointer to the application-defined callback procedure. If the hWnd parameter is set to HWND_BROADCAST, this procedure is called once for every top-level window receiving the message.

dwData: An application-defined value sent to the callback function pointed to by the lpResultCallBack parameter.

Return Value

If the function succeeds, it returns TRUE; otherwise it returns FALSE. To get extended error information, call the GetLastError function.

Callback Syntax

```
SendMessageCallbackProc(
hWnd: HWND;              {a handle to the receiving window}
Msg: UINT;               {the identifier of the received message}
dwData: DWORD;           {an application-defined value}
lResult: LRESULT         {the result of the message processing}
);                       {this procedure does not return a value}
```

Description

This callback procedure is called once for every window receiving the sent message, and may perform any desired task.

Parameters

hWnd: A handle to the window whose window procedure received the message.

Msg: The identifier of the message that was sent to the window procedure associated with the window identified by the hWnd parameter.

dwData: An application-defined value. This is the value specified by the dwData parameter of the SendMessageCallback function.

lResult: The result of the message processing as returned by the receiving window's window procedure. This value is dependent on the type of message processed.

See also

PostMessage, RegisterWindowMessage, SendMessage, SendMessageTimeout, SendNotifyMessage

Example

Listing 4-12: Sending a Message with a Callback Function

```
{the callback function}
  procedure MessageCallback(Window: HWND; Msg: UINT; Data: DWORD;
                            LResult: LRESULT); stdcall;

var
  Form1: TForm1;

implementation

procedure TForm1.Button1Click(Sender: TObject);
begin
  {send the message, specifying a callback function}
  SendMessageCallback(Form1.Handle, WM_SYSCOMMAND, SC_MAXIMIZE, 0,
                      @MessageCallback, 12345);
end;

procedure MessageCallback(Window:HWND; Msg:UINT; Data:DWORD; LResult:LRESULT);
begin
  {when the message is received, this function is called}
  ShowMessage('The message callback function was called: '+IntToStr(Data));
end;
```

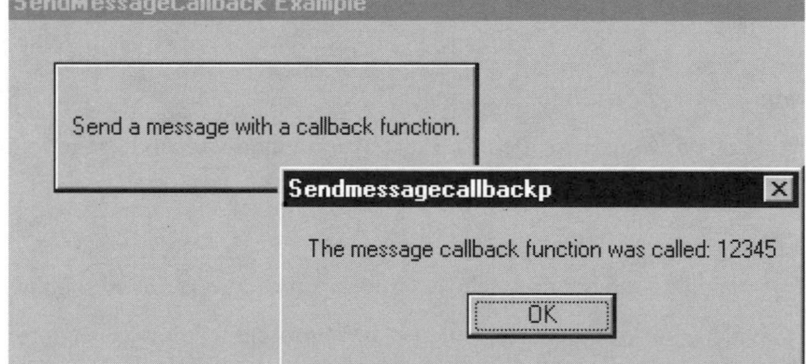

Figure 4-9: The callback function was called.

SendMessageTimeout   *Windows.Pas*

Syntax

```
SendMessageTimeout(
hWnd: HWND;                {a handle to a window}
Msg: UINT;                 {the identifier of the message to send}
wParam: WPARAM;            {a 32-bit message specific value}
lParam: LPARAM             {a 32-bit message specific value}
fuFlags: UINT;             {send message behavior flags}
```

```
uTimeout: UINT;            {the timeout period in milliseconds}
var lpdwResult: DWORD      {a variable to receive the result of message processing}
): BOOL;                   {returns TRUE or FALSE}
```

Description

This function sends the specified message to the window procedure associated with the window indicated by the hWnd parameter. If this window belongs to another thread, the function does not return until the message has been processed or the specified time-out period has elapsed. If the window specified by the hWnd parameter belongs to the calling thread, this function behaves exactly like SendMessage, calling the window procedure directly and ignoring the uTimeout parameter.

Parameters

hWnd: A handle to the window whose window procedure is to receive the specified message. If this parameter is set to HWND_TOPMOST, the message is sent to all top-level windows in the system, including disabled and invisible windows. The message is not sent to child windows. Applications that need to send a user-defined message to other applications using HWND_TOPMOST should use the RegisterWindowMessage to obtain a unique message identifier.

Msg: The identifier of the message to send.

wParam: A 32-bit value dependent on the message being sent.

lParam: A 32-bit value dependent on the message being sent.

fuFlags: A series of flags indicating how the message is to be sent. This parameter can be set to one value from Table 4-5.

uTimeout: Specifies, in milliseconds, the amount of time to wait before the function returns.

var lpdwResult: A pointer to a variable receiving the result of the message processing. This value is dependent on the type of message processed.

Return Value

If the function succeeds, it returns TRUE; otherwise it returns FALSE. To get extended error information, call the GetLastError function.

See also

InSendMessage, PostMessage, SendMessage, SendMessageCallback, SendNotifyMessage

Example

Listing 4-13: Sending a Message and Returning Before it is Processed

This application sends the message:

```
{Whoops! This function is imported in the Delphi source code incorrectly; the
 return value should be BOOL, not LRESULT}
function SendMessageTimeout(hWnd: HWND; Msg: UINT; wParam: WPARAM;
  lParam: LPARAM; fuFlags, uTimeout: UINT; var lpdwResult: DWORD):BOOL; stdcall;

var
  Form1: TForm1;
  UserMessage: UINT;  // holds our user defined message identifier

implementation

{re-link the external function}
function SendMessageTimeout; external user32 name 'SendMessageTimeoutA';

procedure TForm1.FormCreate(Sender: TObject);
begin
  {register the user defined Windows message}
  UserMessage := RegisterWindowMessage('SendMessageTimout Test Message');
end;

procedure TForm1.Button1Click(Sender: TObject);
var
  MsgResult: DWORD;
begin
  {send the message, and time out after 300 milliseconds}
  SendMessageTimeout(HWND_TOPMOST, UserMessage, 0, 0,
                     SMTO_NORMAL, 300, MsgResult);

  {indicate that the SendMessageTimeout function has returned}
  ShowMessage('Returned');
end;
```

and this application receives it:

```
var
  Form1: TForm1;
  UserMessage: UINT;  // holds our user defined message identifier

implementation

procedure TForm1.DefaultHandler(var Msg);
var
  iLoop: Integer;  // general loop counter
begin
  {process message normally}
  inherited DefaultHandler(Msg);

  {if this is our user defined message...}
  if TMessage(Msg).Msg=UserMessage then
  begin
    {...display some user interface objects}
    ProgressBar1.Visible := TRUE;
    Label2.Visible := TRUE;
    Form1.Repaint;
```

```
    {animate the progress bar for a short time}
    for iLoop := 0 to 100 do
    begin
      ProgressBar1.Position := iLoop;
      Sleep(10);
    end;

    {turn off the user interface objects}
    ProgressBar1.Visible := FALSE;
    Label2.Visible := FALSE;

    {indicate that the message was handled}
    TMessage(Msg).Result := 1;
  end;
end;

procedure TForm1.FormCreate(Sender: TObject);
begin
  {register the user defined Windows message}
  UserMessage := RegisterWindowMessage('SendMessageTimout Test Message');
end;
```

Figure 4-10: The function timed out.

Table 4-5: SendMessageTimeout fuFlags Values

Value	Description
SMTO_ABORTIFHUNG	The function will return before the timeout period has elapsed if the receiving process is hung.
SMTO_BLOCK	The calling thread is blocked and stops execution until the function returns.
SMTO_NORMAL	The calling thread is not blocked while waiting for the function to return.

SendNotifyMessage Windows.Pas

Syntax

```
SendNotifyMessage(
hWnd: HWND;                {a handle to a window}
Msg: UINT;                 {the identifier of the message to send}
wParam: WPARAM;            {a 32-bit message specific value}
lParam: LPARAM             {a 32-bit message specific value}
): BOOL;                   {returns TRUE or FALSE}
```

Description

This function sends the specified message to the window procedure of the window indicated by the hWnd parameter. If this window belongs to another thread, the function returns immediately without waiting for the message to be processed. If the window specified by the hWnd parameter belongs to the calling thread, this function behaves exactly like SendMessage. Caution is advised when sending a message whose parameters contain pointers to a window in another thread, as the function will return before the thread associated with the specified window has a chance to process the message and the pointers could be freed before they are used.

Parameters

hWnd: A handle to the window whose window procedure is to receive the specified message. If this parameter is set to HWND_BROADCAST, the message is sent to all top-level windows in the system, including disabled and invisible windows. The message is not sent to child windows. Applications that need to send a user-defined message to other applications using HWND_BROADCAST should use the RegisterWindowMessage function to obtain a unique message identifier.

Msg: The identifier of the message to send.

wParam: A 32-bit value dependent on the message being sent.

lParam: A 32-bit value dependent on the message being sent.

Return Value

If the function succeeds, it returns TRUE; otherwise it returns FALSE. To get extended error information, call the GetLastError function.

See also

PostMessage, PostThreadMessage, RegisterWindowMessage, SendMessage, SendMessageCallback, SendMessageTimeout

Example

Listing 4-14: Sending a Message Via SendNotifyMessage

This application sends the message:

```
procedure TForm1.Button1Click(Sender: TObject);
begin
  {send a message. this function will return immediately}
  SendNotifyMessage(HWND_BROADCAST, WM_CLEAR, 0, 0);

  {indicate that the function has returned}
  ShowMessage('Returned');
end;
```

and this application receives it:

```
{we override the WM_CLEAR message handler to do
 something special when received}
procedure TForm1.WMClear(var Msg: TWMClear);
var
  iLoop: Integer;   // general loop control variable
begin
    {turn on some user interface objects}
    ProgressBar1.Visible := TRUE;
    Label2.Visible := TRUE;
    Form1.Repaint;

    {animate the progress bar for a short time}
    for iLoop := 0 to 100 do
    begin
      ProgressBar1.Position := iLoop;
      Sleep(10);
    end;

    {turn off the user interface objects}
    ProgressBar1.Visible := FALSE;
    Label2.Visible := FALSE;

    {indicate that the message was processed}
    Msg.Result := 1;
end;
```

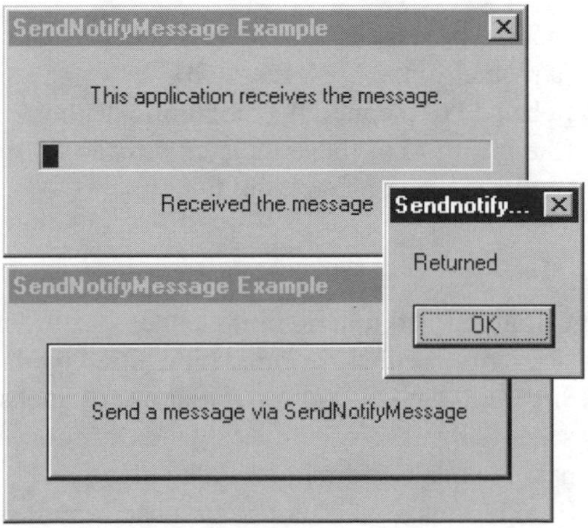

Figure 4-11: The SendNotify-Message function returned immediately.

SetMessageExtraInfo Windows.Pas

Syntax

```
SetMessageExtraInfo(
lParam: LPARAM                {a 32-bit application-defined value}
): LPARAM;                    {returns the previous 32-bit application-defined value}
```

Description

This function sets the 32-bit application-defined value associated with the calling thread's message queue. This 32-bit value can be retrieved by calling the GetMessage-ExtraInfo function.

Parameters

lParam: A 32-bit application-defined value.

Return Value

If the function succeeds, it returns the previous 32-bit application-defined value associated with the calling thread's message queue; otherwise it returns zero.

See also

GetMessageExtraInfo

Example

Please see Listing 4-5 under GetMessageExtraInfo.

SetWindowsHookEx Windows.Pas

Syntax

```
SetWindowsHookEx(
idHook: Integer;              {hook type flag}
lpfn: TFNHookProc;            {a pointer to the hook function}
hmod: HINST;                  {a handle to the module containing the hook function}
dwThreadId: DWORD             {the identifier of the associated thread}
): HHOOK;                     {returns a handle to a hook function}
```

Description

This function installs an application-defined function into a hook chain. This hook function can be used to monitor events in either the thread identified by the dwThreadId parameter or all threads in the system. A popular use of hooks is to intercept and process specific messages before the system or a window procedure ever sees them. The hook function can pass the hook information to the next function in the hook chain by calling the CallNextHookEx function. This function can be called before or after any processing occurs in the called hook function. Calling the next hook in the chain is completely optional; however, if the next hook function in the chain is not called, other applications that have installed hooks will not receive hook notifications and could behave erratically. Hooks can be scoped to either a single thread or to the system, depending on the hook type. For a specific hook type, thread hooks are called first, then system hooks. A system hook is a shared resource, affecting all applications when installed. All system hooks must be located in a dynamic link library. Before an application terminates, it must call UnhookWindowsHookEx for every hook function it installed to free system resources associated with installing a hook.

Parameters

idHook: A flag indicating the type of hook function to install. This parameter can be set to one value from the following table.

lpfn: A pointer to the hook function. If the dwThreadId parameter is set to zero or specifies the identifier of a thread created by another process, this parameter must point to a function located in a dynamic link library; otherwise, this parameter can point to a function in the code associated with the current process. The idHook parameter identifies the type of hook function to which this parameter should point. See below for a detailed description of each type of hook function.

hmod: A handle to the module (a dynamic link library) containing the hook function pointed to by the lpfn parameter. This parameter must be set to zero if the dwThreadId identifies a thread created by the current process and lpfn points to a hook function located in the code associated with the current process.

dwThreadId: The identifier of the thread to which the installed hook function will be associated. If this parameter is set to zero, the hook will be a systemwide hook that is associated with all existing threads.

Return Value

If the function succeeds, it returns a handle to the newly installed hook function; otherwise it returns zero.

Table 4-6: SetWindowsHookEx idHook Values

Value	Description
WH_CALLWNDPROC	Installs a hook function that intercepts messages before they are sent to the destination window procedure. This hook can be either a system or thread level hook.
WH_CALLWNDPROCRET	Installs a hook function that receives messages after they have been processed by the destination window procedure. This hook can be either a system or thread level hook.
WH_CBT	Installs a hook function that receives hook notifications useful in providing computer based training functionality. This hook can be a system level hook only.

Value	Description
WH_DEBUG	Installs a hook function that is used to debug other hook functions. This hook can be either a system or thread level hook.
WH_GETMESSAGE	Installs a hook function that intercepts messages posted to a message queue. This hook can be either a system or thread level hook.
WH_JOURNALPLAYBACK	Installs a hook function that replays messages previously recorded by a WH_JOURNALRECORD hook. This hook can be a system level hook only.
WH_JOURNALRECORD	Installs a hook function that records all input messages sent to the system message queue, and is useful in providing macro functionality. This hook can be a system level hook only.
WH_KEYBOARD	Installs a hook function that intercepts keystroke messages. This hook can be either a system or thread level hook.
WH_MOUSE	Installs a hook function that intercepts mouse messages. This hook can be either a system or thread level hook.
WH_MSGFILTER	Installs a hook function that intercepts messages generated as result of user interaction in a dialog box, message box, menu, or scroll bar. This hook can be a thread level hook only.
WH_SHELL	Installs a hook function that receives notifications as a result of shell interaction. This hook can be either a system or thread level hook.
WH_SYSMSGFILTER	Installs a hook function that intercepts messages generated as a result of user interaction in a dialog box, message box, menu, or scroll bar throughout the entire system. This hook can be a system level hook only.

WH_CALLWNDPROC Hook Function

Syntax

```
CallWndProcProc(
nCode: Integer;              {the hook code}
wParam: WPARAM;              {message sent by current process flag}
lParam: LPARAM               {a pointer to a TCWPStruct structure}
): LRESULT;                  {this function should always return zero}
```

Description

This hook function is called when a message is sent via one of the SendMessage functions. Before the message is sent to the destination window procedure, it is passed through this hook function. The hook function can examine the message but cannot modify it. Otherwise, this function can perform any desired task. This hook function must be associated with the thread calling the SendMessage function, not the thread receiving the message.

Parameters

nCode: Indicates if the hook function should process the message or pass it to the next hook in the chain. If this parameter is set to HC_ACTION, the hook function must process the message. If it is less than zero, this hook function should pass the message to the next hook by calling the CallNextHookEx function without further processing, and should return the value returned by CallNextHookEx.

wParam: Indicates if the message was sent by the current process or a different process. If this parameter is set to zero, the message was sent by another process; a nonzero value indicates that the message was sent by the current process.

lParam: A pointer to a TCWPStruct data structure that contains information about the message. The TCWPStruct data structure is defined as:

```
TCWPStruct = packed record
    lParam: LPARAM;         {a 32-bit message specific value}
    wParam: WPARAM;         {a 32-bit message specific value}
    message: UINT;          {the identifier of the message}
    hwnd: HWND;             {a handle to the window receiving the message}
end;
```

lParam: A 32-bit value dependent on the message being sent.

wParam: A 32-bit value dependent on the message being sent.

message: The identifier of the intercepted message.

hwnd: The handle of the window whose window procedure will receive the message.

Return Value

This hook function should always return zero.

WH_CALLWNDPROCRET Hook Function

Syntax

```
CallWndProcRetProc(
nCode: Integer;             {the hook code}
wParam: WPARAM;             {message sent by current process flag}
lParam: LPARAM              {a pointer to a TCWPRetStruct structure}
): LRESULT;                 {this function should always return zero}
```

Description

This hook function is called after a message is sent via one of the SendMessage functions. After the message is sent to the destination window procedure, it is passed through this hook function. The hook function can examine the message, but cannot modify it. Otherwise, this function can perform any desired task. This hook function must be associated with the thread calling the SendMessage function, not the thread receiving the message.

Parameters

nCode: Indicates if the hook function should process the message or pass it to the next hook in the chain. If this parameter is set to HC_ACTION, the hook function must process the message. If it is less than zero, this hook function should pass the message to the next hook by calling the CallNextHookEx function without further processing, and should return the value returned by CallNextHookEx.

wParam: Indicates if the message was sent by the current process or a different process. If this parameter is set to zero, the message was sent by another process; a nonzero value indicates that the message was sent by the current process.

lParam: A pointer to a TCWPRetStruct data structure that contains information about the message. The TCWPRetStruct data structure is defined as:

```
TCWPRetStruct = packed record
    lResult: LRESULT;
    lParam: LPARAM;           {a 32-bit message specific value}
    wParam: WPARAM;           {a 32-bit message specific value}
    message: UINT;            {the identifier of the message}
    hwnd: HWND;               {a handle to the window receiving the message}
end;
```

lResult: The result of the message processing as returned by the window procedure that processed the message.

lParam: A 32-bit value dependent on the message that was sent.

wParam: A 32-bit value dependent on the message that was sent.

message: The identifier of the intercepted message.

hwnd: The handle of the window whose window procedure processed the message.

Return Value

This hook function should always return zero.

WH_CBT Hook Function

Syntax

```
CBTProc(
nCode: Integer;               {a hook code}
wParam: WPARAM;               {a value dependent on hook code}
lParam: LPARAM                {a value dependent on hook code}
): LRESULT;                   {returns 1 or 0}
```

Description

This hook function is used to provide computer based training functionality for an application. It is called by the system before activating, creating, destroying, minimizing, maximizing, moving, or sizing a window, before completing a system command, before setting the keyboard input focus to a window, before removing a mouse or keyboard message from the system message queue, or before synchronizing with the system message queue. The return value from this hook function indicates if Windows prevents one of these events from taking place. This hook must not install a WH_JOURNALPLAYBACK hook except as described in Table 4-7, but otherwise can perform any desired task. This is a system level hook only and as such must reside in a dynamic link library.

Parameters

nCode: Indicates how the hook function should process the message. If it is less than zero, this hook function should pass the message to the next hook by calling the CallNextHookEx function without further processing, and should return the value returned by CallNextHookEx. Otherwise, this parameter will contain one value from the following table.

wParam: A 32-bit value dependent on the value of the nCode parameter. See the following table for possible values.

lParam: A 32-bit value dependent on the value of the nCode parameter. See the following table for possible values.

Return Value

For the following nCode values, the hook function should return zero to allow the operation to continue; it should return one to prevent it: HCBT_ACTIVATE, HCBT_CREATEWND, HCBT_DESTROYWND, HCBT_MINMAX, HCBT_MOVESIZE, HCBT_SETFOCUS, HCBT_SYSCOMMAND. For the HCBT_CLICKSKIPPED, HCBT_KEYSKIPPED, and HCBT_QS nCode values, the return value is ignored.

Table 4-7: CBTProc nCode Values

Value	Description
HCBT_ACTIVATE	A window is about to be activated. wParam: Specifies the handle of the window being activated. lParam: Contains a pointer to a TCBTActivateStruct structure containing information about the window being activated.
HCBT_CLICKSKIPPED	A mouse message has been removed from the system message queue. When this hook code is received, the CBTProc function must install a WH_JOURNALPLAYBACK hook function in response to the mouse message. This value is sent to the CBTProc only if a WH_MOUSE hook function is installed.

Value	Description
	wParam: The identifier of the mouse message removed from the message queue. lParam: Contains a pointer to a TMouseHookStruct structure containing information about the mouse message.
HCBT_CREATEWND	A window has been created, but the hook function is called before the window receives the WM_CREATE or WM_NCCREATE messages, and before its final size and position have been established. If the hook function returns zero, the window will be destroyed, but it will not receive a WM_DESTROY message. wParam: Contains a handle to the newly created window. lParam: Contains a pointer to a TCBTCreateWnd structure containing information about the newly created window.
HCBT_DESTROYWND	A window is about to be destroyed. wParam: Contains a handle to the window being destroyed. lParam: This value is undefined and will contain zero.
HCBT_KEYSKIPPED	A keyboard message has been removed from the system message queue. When this hook code is received, the hook function must install a WH_JOURNALPLAYBACK hook function in response to the keyboard message. This value is sent to the CBTProc only if a WH_KEYBOARD hook function is installed. wParam: The virtual key code of the keyboard message removed from the message queue. lParam: Contains a value indicating the repeat count, scan code, key transition code, previous key state, and context code of the keyboard message removed from the message queue.
HCBT_MINMAX	A window is about to be minimized or maximized. wParam: Contains a handle to the window being minimized or maximized. lParam: A 32-bit value whose low-order word specifies the show window value used for the operation. The high-order word is undefined. See the ShowWindow function for a list of possible values.
HCBT_MOVESIZE	A window is about to be repositioned or sized. wParam: Contains a handle to the window being repositioned or sized. lParam: Contains a pointer to a TRect structure containing the new coordinates of the window.
HCBT_QS	A WS_QUEUESYNC message has been retrieved from the message queue. wParam: This value is undefined and will contain zero. lParam: This value is undefined and will contain zero.

Value	Description
HCBT_SETFOCUS	A window is about to receive input focus. wParam: Contains a handle to the window receiving the keyboard input focus. lParam: Contains a handle to the window losing the keyboard input focus.
HCBT_SYSCOMMAND	A system command message has been retrieved from the message queue. wParam: Contains a system command value indicating the system command. Set the WM_SYSCOMMAND message for a list of possible values. lParam: Contains the value of the lParam parameter of the WM_SYSCOMMAND message.

The TCBTActivateStruct data structure is defined as:

```
TCBTActivateStruct = packed record
      fMouse: BOOL;                {mouse click activate flag}
      hWndActive: HWND;            {a handle to the active window}
end;
```

fMouse: A Boolean value indicating if the window was activated by a mouse click. A value of TRUE indicates that a mouse click activated the window.

hWndActive: A handle to the active window.

The TMouseHookStruct data structure is defined as:

```
TMouseHookStruct = packed record
      pt: TPoint;                  {the screen coordinates of the mouse cursor}
      hwnd: HWND;                  {a handle to the window receiving the message}
      wHitTestCode: UINT;          {a hit test value}
      dwExtraInfo: DWORD;          {message-defined information}
end;
```

pt: A TPoint structure containing the horizontal and vertical coordinates of the mouse cursor, in screen coordinates.

hwnd: A handle to the window receiving the mouse message.

wHitTestCode: A value indicating the part of the window where the mouse cursor was at the time of the event. See the WM_NCHITTEST message for a list of possible values.

dwExtraInfo: A value containing extra information associated with the mouse message.

The TCBTCreateWnd data structure is defined as:

```
TCBTCreateWnd = packed record
     lpcs: PCreateStruct;              {a pointer to a TCreateStruct structure}
     hwndInsertAfter: HWND;            {a handle to the preceding window in the Z-order}
end;
```

lpcs: A pointer to a TCreateStruct data structure containing information about the window being created. See the CreateWindow function for a description of this data structure.

hwndInsertAfter: A handle to the window preceding the newly created window in the Z-order.

WH_DEBUG Hook Function

Syntax

```
DebugProc(
nCode: Integer;                    {the hook code}
wParam: WPARAM;                    {the type of hook being called}
lParam: LPARAM                     {a pointer to a TDebugHookInfo structure}
): LRESULT;                        {returns a nonzero value to block the hook}
```

Description

This hook function is used to debug other hook functions. The system calls this hook function before calling the hook functions for any other hook, passing it information about the hook to be called. This function can instruct Windows to call the destination hook function or to skip it, and can perform any desired task.

Parameters

nCode: Indicates if the hook function should process the message or pass it to the next hook in the chain. If this parameter is set to HC_ACTION, the hook function must process the message. If it is less than zero, this hook function should pass the message to the next hook by calling the CallNextHookEx function without further processing, and should return the value returned by CallNextHookEx.

wParam: Specifies the type of hook being called. This parameter can contain one value from Table 4-6.

lParam: A pointer to a TDebugHookInfo data structure containing the parameters being passed to the hook function about to be called. The TDebugHookInfo data structure is defined as:

```
TDebugHookInfo = packed record
     idThread: DWORD;              {a thread identifier}
     idThreadInstaller: DWORD;     {a thread identifier}
     lParam: LPARAM;               {the lParam parameter being passed to the hook}
```

```
    wParam: WPARAM;          {the wParam parameter being passed to the hook}
    code: Integer;           {the nCode parameter being passed to the hook}
end;
```

idThread: The identifier of the thread containing the hook procedure to be called.

idThreadInstaller: The identifier of the thread containing the debug hook function.

lParam: The lParam parameter that will be passed to the hook procedure being called.

wParam: The wParam parameter that will be passed to the hook procedure being called.

code: The nCode parameter that will be passed to the hook procedure being called.

Return Value

To prevent the destination hook from being called, the hook function should return a nonzero value. Otherwise, the hook procedure must pass the hook information to the CallNextHookEx function, returning the value returned from CallNextHookEx.

WH_GETMESSAGE Hook Function

Syntax

```
GetMsgProc(
nCode: Integer;              {the hook code}
wParam: WPARAM;              {message removal flag}
lParam: LPARAM               {a pointer to a TMsg structure}
): LRESULT;                  {this function should always return zero}
```


Description

This hook function is called when the GetMessage or PeekMessage functions are called to retrieve a message from the message queue. The retrieved message is passed through this hook function before being passed to the destination window procedure. This hook function can modify the message parameters, sending the modified message to the destination window procedure when the hook function returns, and can perform any desired task.

Parameters

nCode: Indicates if the hook function should process the message or pass it to the next hook in the chain. If this parameter is set to HC_ACTION, the hook function must process the message. If it is less than zero, this hook function should pass the message to the next hook by calling the CallNextHookEx function without further processing, and should return the value returned by CallNextHookEx.

wParam: Indicates if the message has been removed from the queue. A value of PM_REMOVE indicates that the message has been removed from the queue; a value of PM_NOREMOVE indicates that the message has not been removed from the queue.

lParam: A pointer to a TMsg data structure containing information about the message. The TMsg data structure is defined as:

```
TMsg = packed record
    hwnd: HWND;              {a handle to the window receiving the message}
    message: UINT;           {the message identifier}
    wParam: WPARAM;          {a 32-bit message specific value}
    lParam: LPARAM;          {a 32-bit message specific value}
    time: DWORD;             {the time when the message was posted}
    pt: TPoint;              {the position of the mouse cursor}
end;
```

Please see the DispatchMessage function for a detailed description of this data structure.

Return Value

This hook function should always return zero.

WH_JOURNALPLAYBACK Hook Function

Syntax

```
JournalPlaybackProc(
nCode: Integer;              {a hook code}
wParam: WPARAM;              {this parameter is not used}
lParam: LPARAM               {a pointer to a TEventMsg structure}
): LRESULT;                  {returns a wait time in clock ticks}
```

Description

This hook procedure is used to insert a mouse or keyboard message into the system message queue by copying the message information to the TEventMsg structure pointed to by the lParam parameter. Its most common use is playing back a series of mouse and keyboard messages recorded by a previous use of the WH_JOURNALRECORD hook function. While this hook function is installed, mouse and keyboard input are disabled. The JournalPlaybackProc function is always called in the context of the thread that initially set the WH_JOURNALPLAYBACK hook. If the user presses the Ctrl+Esc or Ctrl+Alt+Del key combinations while a WH_JOURNALPLAYBACK hook is installed, the system stops the message playback, unhooks the hook function, and posts a WM_CANCELJOURNAL message to the application. Otherwise, this function can perform any desired task.

Parameters

nCode: A code specifying how the hook function should process the message. This parameter can contain one value from the following table. If it is less than zero, this hook function should pass the message to the next hook by calling the

CallNextHookEx function without further processing, and should return the value returned by CallNextHookEx.

wParam: This parameter is not used and is set to zero.

lParam: A pointer to a TEventMsg structure containing information about the message being processed. This parameter is only used when the nCode parameter is set to HC_GETNEXT. The TEventMsg data structure is defined as:

```
TEventMsg = packed record
    message: UINT;          {a message identifier}
    paramL: UINT;           {additional message specific information}
    paramH: UINT;           {additional message specific information}
    time: DWORD;            {the time the message was posted}
    hwnd: HWND;             {a handle to the window receiving the message}
end;
```

message: The identifier of the message.

paramL: Additional message specific information. If the message is between WM_KEYFIRST and WM_KEYLAST, this member contains the virtual key code of the key that was pressed.

paramH: Additional message specific information. If the message is between WM_KEYFIRST and WM_KEYLAST, this member contains the scan code of the key that was pressed.

time: The time at which the message was posted to the message queue of the window identified by the hwnd member.

hwnd: A handle to the window whose window procedure received the message.

Return Value

The hook function should return the amount of time, in clock ticks, that the system should wait before processing the next message, if a pause is desired. When the application continues, the hook function will be called again with an nCode value of HC_GETNEXT. The hook function should return a zero after this second call or this loop will continue and the application will appear to be hung. If the next message should be processed immediately, the function should return zero. If the nCode parameter is not set to HC_GETNEXT, the return value is ignored.

Table 4-8: JournalPlaybackProc nCode Values

Value	Description
HC_GETNEXT	The hook function must copy the current mouse or keyboard message to the TEventMsg data structure pointed to by the lParam parameter. The same message can be retrieved repeatedly by continuing to specify HC_GETNEXT without specifying HC_SKIP.

Value	Description
HC_NOREMOVE	An application called the PeekMessage function using a PM_NOREMOVE flag.
HC_SKIP	The hook function should prepare to copy the next mouse or keyboard message to the TEventMsg data structure.
HC_SYSMODALOFF	A system modal dialog box has been destroyed, indicating that the hook function must resume message playback.
HC_SYSMODALON	A system modal dialog box has been displayed, indicating that the hook function must suspend message playback.

WH_JOURNALRECORD Hook Function

Syntax

```
JournalRecordProc(
nCode: Integer;                 {a hook code}
wParam: WPARAM;                 {this parameter is not used}
lParam: LPARAM                  {a pointer to a TEventMsg structure}
): LRESULT;                     {the return value is ignored}
```

Description

This hook procedure is used to record messages that have been removed from the system message queue. The hook function must not modify the messages being copied. These messages can be replayed later by using the WH_JOURNALPLAYBACK hook function. The hook function should watch for a VK_CANCEL message to be recorded, which is sent to the system when the user presses the Ctrl+Break key combination. This indicates that the user wishes to stop message recording, and the record sequence should be halted and the WH_JOURNALRECORD hook should be removed. If the user presses the Ctrl+Esc or Ctrl+Alt+Del key combinations while a WH_JOURNALRECORD hook is installed, the system stops the message playback, unhooks the hook function, and posts a WM_CANCELJOURNAL message to the application. The JournalRecordProc function is always called in the context of the thread that initially set the WH_JOURNALRECORD hook. Otherwise, this function can perform any desired task.

Parameters

nCode: A code specifying how the hook function should process the message. This parameter can contain one value from the following table. If it is less than zero, this hook function should pass the message to the next hook by calling the CallNextHookEx function without further processing, and should return the value returned by CallNextHookEx.

wParam: This parameter is not used and is set to zero.

lParam: A pointer to a TEventMsg structure containing information about the message being processed. This parameter is only used when the nCode parameter is set to HC_GETNEXT. The TEventMsg data structure is defined as:

```
TEventMsg = packed record
    message: UINT;          {a message identifier}
    paramL: UINT;           {additional message specific information}
    paramH: UINT;           {additional message specific information}
    time: DWORD;            {the time the message was posted}
    hwnd: HWND;             {a handle to the window receiving the message}
end;
```

Please see the WH_JOURNALPLAYBACK hook function for a description of this data structure.

Return Value

The return value from this hook function is ignored.

Table 4-9: JournalRecordProc nCode Values

Value	Description
HC_ACTION	The lParam parameter contains a pointer to a TEventMsg structure containing information on the message removed from the system message queue. This structure should be copied to a buffer or file for later playback by the WH_JOURNALPLAYBACK hook.
HC_SYSMODALOFF	A system modal dialog box has been destroyed, indicating that the hook function must resume message recording.
HC_SYSMODALON	A system modal dialog box has been displayed, indicating that the hook function must suspend message recording.

WH_KEYBOARD Hook Function

Syntax

```
KeyboardProc(
nCode: Integer;           {the hook code}
wParam: WPARAM;           {a virtual key code}
lParam: LPARAM            {a bitmask containing keystroke information}
): LRESULT;               {indicates if the message is to be discarded}
```

Description

This hook function is called when the application calls the GetMessage or PeekMessage function and a keyboard message is retrieved. This function can perform any desired task.

Parameters

nCode: A code specifying how the hook function should process the message. This parameter can contain one value from Table 4-10. If it is less than zero, this hook function should pass the message to the next hook by calling the CallNextHookEx function without further processing, and should return the value returned by CallNextHookEx.

wParam: Contains the virtual key code of the key generating the message.

lParam: A 32-bit bitmask that indicates the repeat count, scan code, extended key flag, context code, previous key flag, and transition flag for the keyboard message. The values represented by the bits in this parameter are described in Table 4-11.

Return Value

To prevent the keyboard message from being passed to the destination window procedure, the hook function should return a nonzero value. To pass the message to the destination window procedure, the hook function should return zero.

Table 4-10: KeyboardProc nCode Values

Value	Description
HC_ACTION	The wParam and lParam parameters contain information about a keyboard message.
HC_NOREMOVE	The wParam and lParam parameters contain information about a keyboard message. This message has not been removed from the message queue.

Table 4-11: KeyboardProc lParam Bitmask Values

Bits	Description
0-15	Specifies the number of times the keyboard message has been repeated due to the user holding down the key.
16-23	Identifies the original equipment manufacturer scan code.
24	A value of 1 in this bit indicates that the key is an extended key, such as a function or a numeric keypad key.
25-28	These bits are reserved and their value is undefined.
29	A value of 1 in this bit indicates that the Alt key is down.
30	A value of 1 in this bit indicates that the key was down before the message was sent; 0 indicates that the key was up.
31	A value of 1 in this bit indicates that the key is being released; 0 indicates that the key is being pressed.

WH_MOUSE Hook Function

Syntax

```
MouseProc(
nCode: Integer;              {the hook code}
wParam: WPARAM;              {a mouse message identifier}
lParam: LPARAM               {a pointer to a TMouseHookStruct structure}
): LRESULT;                  {indicates if the message is to be discarded}
```

Description

This hook function is called when the application calls the GetMessage or PeekMessage function and a mouse message is retrieved. It must not install a WH_JOURNALPLAYBACK hook. Otherwise, this function can perform any desired task.

Parameters

nCode: A code specifying how the hook function should process the message. This parameter can contain one value from Table 4-12. If it is less than zero, this hook function should pass the message to the next hook by calling the CallNextHookEx function without further processing, and should return the value returned by CallNextHookEx.

wParam: Contains the identifier of the mouse message.

lParam: A pointer to a TMouseHookStruct structure containing information about the mouse message. The TMouseHookStruct is defined as:

```
TMouseHookStruct = packed record
      pt: TPoint;                 {the screen coordinates of the mouse cursor}
      hwnd: HWND;                 {a handle to the window receiving the message}
      wHitTestCode: UINT;         {a hit test value}
      dwExtraInfo: DWORD;         {message defined information}
end;
```

Please see the HC_CBT hook function for a description of this data structure.

Return Value

To prevent the mouse message from being passed to the destination window procedure, the hook function should return a nonzero value. To pass the message to the destination window procedure, the hook function should return zero.

Table 4-12: MouseProc nCode Values

Value	Description
HC_ACTION	The wParam and lParam parameters contain information about a mouse message.
HC_NOREMOVE	The wParam and lParam parameters contain information about a mouse message. This message has not been removed from the message queue.

WH_MSGFILTER Hook Function

Syntax

```
MsgFilterProc(
nCode: Integer;                 {a hook code}
wParam: WPARAM;                 {this parameter is not used}
lParam: LPARAM                  {a pointer to a TMsg structure}
): LRESULT;                     {indicates if the message was processed}
```

Description

This hook event is used to monitor messages generated from user interaction with a dialog box, message box, menu, or scroll bar. The system calls this hook function when an input event has occurred in one of these objects, but before the message generated by such an event has been dispatched to the destination window procedure. This hook function must reside in the code of the thread that installed the hook, and can perform any desired task.

Parameters

nCode: A code specifying how the hook function should process the message. This parameter can contain one value from Table 4-13. If it is less than zero, this hook function should pass the message to the next hook by calling the CallNextHookEx function without further processing, and should return the value returned by CallNextHookEx.

wParam: This parameter is not used and is set to zero.

lParam: A pointer to a TMsg data structure containing information about the message. The TMsg data structure is defined as:

```
TMsg = packed record
    hwnd: HWND;                 {a handle to the window receiving the message}
    message: UINT;              {the message identifier}
    wParam: WPARAM;             {a 32-bit message specific value}
    lParam: LPARAM;             {a 32-bit message specific value}
    time: DWORD;                {the time when the message was posted}
    pt: TPoint;                 {the position of the mouse cursor}
end;
```

Please see the DispatchMessage function for a detailed description of this data structure.

Return Value

If the hook function processed the message, it should return a nonzero value. If the hook function did not process the message, it should return zero.

Table 4-13: MsgFilterProc nCode Values

Value	Description
MSGF_DDEMGR	The input event happened while the dynamic data exchange management library was waiting for a synchronous transaction to be completed.
MSGF_DIALOGBOX	The input event happened in a dialog or message box.
MSGF_MENU	The input event happened in a menu.
MSGF_NEXTWINDOW	The input event was generated by the user pressing the Alt+Tab key combination to switch to a different window.
MSGF_SCROLLBAR	The input event happened in a scroll bar.

WH_SHELL Hook Function

Syntax

```
ShellProc(
nCode: Integer;              {a hook code}
wParam: WPARAM;              {additional hook specific information}
lParam: LPARAM               {additional hook specific information}
): LRESULT;                  {this function should always return zero}
```

Description

This hook function is used by shell applications to receive notification about system events. It is used to monitor window activation and creation, and may perform any desired task.

Parameters

nCode: A code specifying how the hook function should process the message. This parameter can contain one value from Table 4-14. If it is less than zero, this hook function should pass the message to the next hook by calling the CallNextHookEx function without further processing, and should return the value returned by CallNextHookEx.

wParam: Specifies information dependent on the nCode parameter. See Table 4-14 for a list of possible values. Unless otherwise specified, this parameter is ignored.

lParam: Specifies information dependent on the nCode parameter. See Table 4-14 for a list of possible values. Unless otherwise specified, this parameter is ignored.

Return Value

This function should always return zero.

Table 4-14: ShellProc nCode Values

Value	Description
HSHELL_ACTIVATESHELLWINDOW	Indicates that the shell application should activate its main window.
HSHELL_GETMINRECT	Indicates that a window is being minimized or maximized and the system needs the new window position coordinates. The wParam parameter contains a handle to the window being resized, and the lParam parameter contains a pointer to a TRect structure that receives the new coordinates.
HSHELL_LANGUAGE	Indicates that the keyboard language has changed or that a new keyboard layout was loaded.
HSHELL_REDRAW	Indicates that the title of a window in the task bar has been redrawn. The wParam parameter contains a handle to this window.
HSHELL_TASKMAN	Indicates that the user has activated the system task list.
HSHELL_WINDOWACTIVATED	Indicates that focus has changed to a different top-level, unowned window. The wParam parameter contains a handle to the newly activated window.
HSHELL_WINDOWCREATED	Indicates that a top-level, unowned window has been created. The window will already exist when the ShellProc hook function is called. The wParam parameter contains a handle to the newly created window.
HSHELL_WINDOWDESTROYED	Indicates that a top-level, unowned window has been destroyed. This window still exists when the ShellProc hook function is called. The wParam parameter contains a handle to the window about to be destroyed.

WH_SYSMSGFILTER Hook Function

Syntax

```
SysMsgFilterProc(
nCode: Integer;              {a hook code}
wParam: WPARAM;              {this parameter is not used}
lParam: LPARAM               {a pointer to a TMsg structure}
): LRESULT;                  {indicates if the message was processed.}
```

Description

This hook event is used to monitor messages generated from user interaction with a dialog box, message box, menu, or scroll bar throughout the entire system. The system calls this hook function when an input event has occurred in one of these objects, but before the message generated by such an event has been dispatched to the destination window procedure. This hook function must reside in a dynamic link library, and can perform any desired task.

Parameters

nCode: A code specifying how the hook function should process the message. This parameter can contain one value from Table 4-15. If it is less than zero, this hook function should pass the message to the next hook by calling the CallNextHookEx function without further processing, and should return the value returned by CallNextHookEx.

wParam: This parameter is not used and is set to zero.

lParam: A pointer to a TMsg data structure containing information about the message. The TMsg data structure is defined as:

```
TMsg = packed record
    hwnd: HWND;            {a handle to the window receiving the message}
    message: UINT;         {the message identifier}
    wParam: WPARAM;        {a 32-bit message specific value}
    lParam: LPARAM;        {a 32-bit message specific value}
    time: DWORD;           {the time when the message was posted}
    pt: TPoint;            {the position of the mouse cursor}
end;
```

Please see the DispatchMessage function for a detailed description of this data structure.

Return Value

If the hook function processed the message, it should return a nonzero value. If the hook function did not process the message, it should return zero.

Table 4-15: SysMsgFilterProc nCode Values

Value	Description
MSGF_DIALOGBOX	The input event happened in a dialog or message box.
MSGF_MENU	The input event happened in a menu.
MSGF_NEXTWINDOW	The input event was generated by the user pressing the Alt+Tab key combination to switch to a different window.
MSGF_SCROLLBAR	The input event happened in a scroll bar.

See also

CallNextHookEx, UnhookWindowsHookEx

Example

Listing 4-15: Intercepting the Tab and Enter Keys

```
{the prototype for the new keyboard hook function}
  function KeyboardHook(nCode: Integer; wParam: WPARAM;
                        lParam: LPARAM): LResult; stdcall;

var
  Form1: TForm1;
  WinHook: HHOOK;     // a handle to the keyboard hook function

implementation

{$R *.DFM}

procedure TForm1.FormCreate(Sender: TObject);
begin
  {install the keyboard hook function into the keyboard hook chain}
  WinHook:=SetWindowsHookEx(WH_KEYBOARD, @KeyboardHook, 0, GetCurrentThreadID);
end;

procedure TForm1.FormDestroy(Sender: TObject);
begin
  {remove the keyboard hook function from the keyboard hook chain}
  UnhookWindowsHookEx(WinHook);
end;

function KeyboardHook(nCode: Integer; wParam: WPARAM; lParam: LPARAM): LResult;
begin
  {if we can process the hook information...}
  if (nCode>-1) then
    {...was the TAB key pressed?}
    if (wParam=VK_TAB) then
    begin
      {if so, output a beep sound}
      MessageBeep(0);

      {indicate that the message was processed}
      Result := 1;
    end
    else
    {...was the RETURN key pressed?}
    if (wParam=VK_RETURN) then
    begin
      {if so, and if the key is on the up stroke, cause
       the focus to move to the next control}
      if ((lParam shr 31)=1) then
         Form1.Perform(WM_NEXTDLGCTL, 0, 0);

      {indicate that the message was processed}
      Result := 1;
    end
    else
      {otherwise, indicate that the message was not processed.}
```

```
      Result := 0
  else
    {we must pass the hook information to the next hook in the chain}
    Result := CallNextHookEx(WinHook, nCode, wParam, lParam);
end;
```

TranslateMessage   Windows.Pas

Syntax

TranslateMessage(
const lpMsg: TMsg   {a structure containing the message to be translated}
): BOOL;   {returns TRUE or FALSE}

Description

This function translates virtual key messages into character messages, posting the resulting message back into the calling thread's message queue. WM_CHAR messages are created only for those keys that are directly mapped to an ASCII character by the keyboard driver. Applications that process virtual key messages for special purposes should not call TranslateMessage.

Parameters

lpMsg: A pointer to a TMsg data structure containing information about the message to be translated. This data structure is retrieved by the GetMessage and PeekMessage functions, and is not modified by TranslateMessage. The TMsg data structure is defined as:

TMsg = packed record
    hwnd: HWND;   {a handle to the window receiving the message}
    message: UINT;   {the message identifier}
    wParam: WPARAM;   {a 32-bit message specific value}
    lParam: LPARAM;   {a 32-bit message specific value}
    time: DWORD;   {the time when the message was posted}
    pt: TPoint;   {the position of the mouse cursor}
end;

Please see the GetMessage function for a description of this data structure.

Return Value

If the function succeeds and a virtual key message was translated into a character message and posted to the calling thread's queue, this function returns TRUE. If the function fails, or a virtual key message was not translated into a character message, it returns FALSE. Note that under Windows NT, this function will return TRUE if the message is a function key or arrow key message.

See also

GetMessage, PeekMessage

Example

Please see Listing 4-4 under GetMessage.

UnhookWindowsHookEx Windows.Pas

Syntax

```
UnhookWindowsHookEx(
hhk: HHOOK                  {a handle to the hook being removed}
): BOOL;                    {returns TRUE or FALSE}
```

Description

This function removes the specified hook that was installed into a hook chain by the SetWindowsHookEx function. The hook is not removed until all threads have finished their current call to the hook procedure. If no thread is calling the hook procedure at the time UnhookWindowsHookEx is called, the hook is removed immediately.

Parameters

hhk: A handle to the hook being removed.

Return Value

If this function succeeds, it returns TRUE; otherwise it returns FALSE.

See also

SetWindowsHookEx

Example

Please see Listing 4-15 under SetWindowsHookEx.

WaitMessage Windows.Pas

Syntax

```
WaitMessage: BOOL;          {returns TRUE or FALSE}
```

Description

This function suspends the calling thread, yielding control to other threads. This function will not return until a message is placed into the calling thread's message queue, at which time execution will resume.

Return Value

If the function succeeds, it returns TRUE; otherwise it returns FALSE. To get extended error information, call the GetLastError function.

See also

GetMessage, PeekMessage

Example

Listing 4-16: Waiting for a Message

```
{this function places the application into a message loop
 that will break only when the left mouse button is clicked
 on the client area of the form.  the user will be unable to
 resize or move the form until then.}
procedure TForm1.Button1Click(Sender: TObject);
var
  TheMessage: TMSG;       // holds message info
  MouseClicked: boolean;  // general loop control variable
begin
  {initialize the loop control variable}
  MouseClicked := FALSE;

  {place the application into a loop until a mouse button is clicked}
  while not MouseClicked do
  begin
    {empty the message queue}
    while PeekMessage(TheMessage, Handle, 0, 0, PM_REMOVE) do;

    {suspend the thread until a new message is placed in the queue}
    WaitMessage();

    {a new message has just dropped into the queue. retrieve it.}
    PeekMessage(TheMessage, Handle, 0, 0, PM_REMOVE);

    {if the new message was a mouse click, break out of the loop}
    if TheMessage.Message=WM_LBUTTONDOWN then
    begin
      MouseClicked := TRUE;
      {indicate that the message was a mouse click}
      ShowMessage('A message was received, resume execution');
    end;
  end;
end;
```

Chapter 5

Window Information Functions

A window, by its very nature, has a lot of specific information associated with it. Details such as a window's dimensions, position, its parent, or even its style flags may need to be retrieved by an application, or even modified. The class that the window itself is based on may contain information that an application needs to retrieve on the fly. Fortunately, the Win32 API has a collection of functions that allows the application to retrieve, and sometimes modify, almost any detail concerning a window or its class.

Information Storage

Every window has an information storage mechanism known as a property list. This property list is intended solely for user required data, and is not used directly by the Windows operating system. Every window has one, including forms and any controls descending from TWinControl. The property list is stored in a memory area associated with each specific window that Windows manages automatically.

A property list works in a manner similar to INI files, in that a string is associated with a specific value. The SetProp function takes a string and a 32-bit integer number. If the string does not already exist in the property list, the specified string and data are added. If the string does exist, then the data for that string is changed to the specified number. The GetProp function provides the method to extract these properties, and the RemoveProp function deletes them from the property list. An application should not remove properties that another application assigned to the list, but it should remove its own properties before halting execution.

Property lists give the developer a good alternative to global variables, which can sometimes cause problems such as scoping issues or name collisions. It allows the developer to store any amount of information for any purpose, while giving Windows the job of managing the memory required for the storage. It is also a very flexible way to communicate information, as a calling function does not need to know the number of properties in the list or even a specific offset, only the string associated with the desired data. See the EnumProps function description for an example of using window property lists.

Window Specific Information

In addition to the property list, each window automatically has a storage area for a single 32-bit number. This is also intended for user-defined data requirements, and is not used by the Windows operating system. A developer could use this to store a 32-bit pointer to a data structure, an object, etc. The 32-bit user data area is accessed through the GetWindowLong and SetWindowLong functions. The following example demonstrates setting and retrieving this value for Delphi components descended from TWinControl.

Listing 5-1: Setting and Retrieving the 32-Bit User Data Value

```
{the enumeration callback function}
procedure EnumerateChildWindows(hWnd: HWND; lParam: LPARAM); stdcall;

var
  Form1: TForm1;

implementation

{this is called for every existing child window on the form}
procedure EnumerateChildWindows(hWnd: HWND; lParam: LPARAM);
var
  TheClassName: Array[0..255] of char;
begin
  {retrieve the window text of the child window...}
  GetClassName(hWnd, TheClassName, 255);

  {...and display it}
  Form1.ListBox1.Items.AddObject(TheClassName,TObject(hWnd));
end;

procedure TForm1.FormActivate(Sender: TObject);
begin
  {display the class names of all child windows upon activation}
  EnumChildWindows(Form1.Handle,@EnumerateChildWindows,0);
end;

procedure TForm1.ListBox1Click(Sender: TObject);
begin
  {empty the edit box when another control is clicked on}
  Edit1.Clear;
end;

{notice in these two procedures that the window handle for the control
 is stored in the Objects array. Since the Objects array holds pointers,
 and a pointer is just a 32-bit number, we can cast the window handle
 as a TObject, and cast the TObject back into a 32-bit integer (which is
 what an HWND is defined as) to store window handles with their
 associated window text.}

procedure TForm1.Button1Click(Sender: TObject);
begin
```

```
  {retrieve the 32-bit user-defined value}
  Edit1.Text := IntToStr(GetWindowLong(Longint(ListBox1.Items.Objects[ListBox1.
                                    ItemIndex]), GWL_USERDATA));
end;

procedure TForm1.Button2Click(Sender: TObject);
begin
  {set the 32-bit user-defined value for the selected window}
  SetWindowLong(Longint(ListBox1.Items.Objects[ListBox1.ItemIndex]),
             GWL_USERDATA, StrToInt(Edit1.Text));

  {empty the edit box to indicate the function completed}
  Edit1.Clear;
end;
```

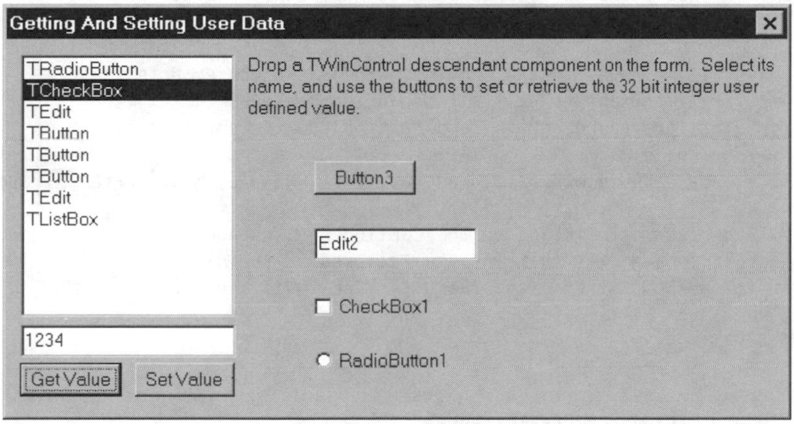

Getting And Setting User Data

TRadioButton
TCheckBox
TEdit
TButton
TButton
TButton
TEdit
TListBox

Drop a TWinControl descendant component on the form. Select its name, and use the buttons to set or retrieve the 32 bit integer user defined value.

Button3

Edit2

CheckBox1

RadioButton1

1234

Get Value | Set Value

Figure 5-1: The 32-bit user data value.

Subclassing a Window

The GetWindowLong and SetWindowLong functions (and their sister functions for classes) provide the developer with a method to change other window properties programmatically. One of the most powerful tricks a developer can perform with these functions is to replace the window procedure for a window, creating what is known as a subclass. All windows of a specific class share the window procedure defined for that class when the window was registered. The window procedure for a class can be replaced with a new window procedure by using the SetClassLong function, affecting all windows created using that class; to replace the window procedure for one specific window, use the SetWindowLong function. Messages for the subclassed window go to the new window procedure first, allowing the developer to drastically change the behavior of a window on the fly. The following example demonstrates how to use the SetWindowLong function to replace the window procedure of the main form at runtime. The new window procedure intercepts the WM_NCHITTEST message. If the user is trying to move the form by clicking on the caption bar and dragging, the new window procedure replaces the result of the message with a result which indicates the user clicked on the client area. This prevents the user from moving the window with the mouse.

Listing 5-2: Replacing the Window Procedure at Runtime

```
{the prototype for the subclassed window procedure}
  function SubclassedWndProc(hWnd: HWND; Msg: UINT; wParam: WPARAM;
                             lParam: LPARAM): LResult; stdcall;
var
  Form1: TForm1;
  OldWndProc: Pointer;  // a pointer to the old window procedure

implementation

function SubclassedWndProc(hWnd: HWND; Msg: UINT; wParam: WPARAM;
                           lParam: LPARAM): LResult;
begin
  {pass all messages to the previous window procedure. Note that it
   is very important to pass all unhandled messages back to the
   original procedure, or the application and the entire system
   may crash.}
  Result := CallWindowProc(OldWndProc, Form1.Handle, Msg, wParam, lParam);

  {if the user is clicking on the caption bar, change the
   result to indicate that the user clicked on the client area}
  if ((Msg=WM_NCHITTEST) and (Result=HTCAPTION)) then
    Result := HTCLIENT;

end;

procedure TForm1.FormCreate(Sender: TObject);
begin
  {subclass the form upon creation}
  OldWndProc := Pointer(SetWindowLong(Form1.Handle, GWL_WNDPROC,
                        longint(@SubclassedWndProc)));
end;
```

Knowing It All

The Win32 API includes a number of enumeration functions. These functions allow the developer to retrieve information on every window without knowing how many windows currently exist. These functions, coupled with the other window information functions, give the application the ability to change dynamically as the system environment changes.

The ClassInfo example on the CD demonstrates the use of the EnumChildWindows and GetClassInfo functions to display runtime class information on standard Delphi components. This example iterates through every TWinControl component on the form to retrieve its class name. When a specific class name is selected from a list box, its class information is displayed.

Listing 5-3: Displaying Class Information for Delphi Components

```
{the enumeration callback function}
procedure EnumerateChildWindows(hWnd: HWND; lParam: LPARAM); stdcall;
var
  Form1: TForm1;

implementation

{this is called once for each child window}
procedure EnumerateChildWindows(hWnd: HWND; lParam: LPARAM);
var
   TheClassName: Array[0..255] of char;   // holds the child window class name
begin
   {retrieve the name of the child window class...}
   GetClassName(hWnd, TheClassName, 255);

   {...and display it}
   Form1.ListBox1.Items.Add(TheClassName);
end;

procedure TForm1.FormActivate(Sender: TObject);
begin
   {retrieve the class names when the form becomes active}
   EnumChildWindows(Form1.Handle,@EnumerateChildWindows,0);
end;

procedure TForm1.ListBox1Click(Sender: TObject);
var
   ClassInfo: TWndClass;                 // a class information structure
   ClassName: array[0..255] of char;     // holds the class name
begin
   {get the class information for the selected class}
   StrPCopy(ClassName,ListBox1.Items[ListBox1.ItemIndex]);
   GetClassInfo(hInstance,ClassName,ClassInfo);

   {display the information in the TWndClass structure
    retrieved from the specified class}
   ListBox2.Items.Clear;

   ListBox2.Items.Add(Format('Style: %d',[ClassInfo.style]));
   ListBox2.Items.Add(Format('WndProc: %d',[integer(ClassInfo.lpfnWndProc)]));
   ListBox2.Items.Add(Format('ClsExtra: %d',[ClassInfo.cbClsExtra]));
   ListBox2.Items.Add(Format('WndExtra: %d',[ClassInfo.cbWndExtra]));
   ListBox2.Items.Add(Format('Instance: %d',[integer(ClassInfo.hInstance)]));
   ListBox2.Items.Add(Format('Icon: %d',[integer(ClassInfo.hIcon)]));
   ListBox2.Items.Add(Format('Cursor: %d',[integer(ClassInfo.hCursor)]));
   ListBox2.Items.Add(Format('Background: %d',[integer(ClassInfo.hbrBackground)]));
   if (ClassInfo.lpszMenuName<>nil) then
      ListBox2.Items.Add('Menu Name: '+ClassInfo.lpszMenuName)
   else
      ListBox2.Items.Add('No class menu name');
   if (ClassInfo.lpszClassName<>nil) then
      ListBox2.Items.Add('Class Name: '+ClassInfo.lpszClassName);
end;
```

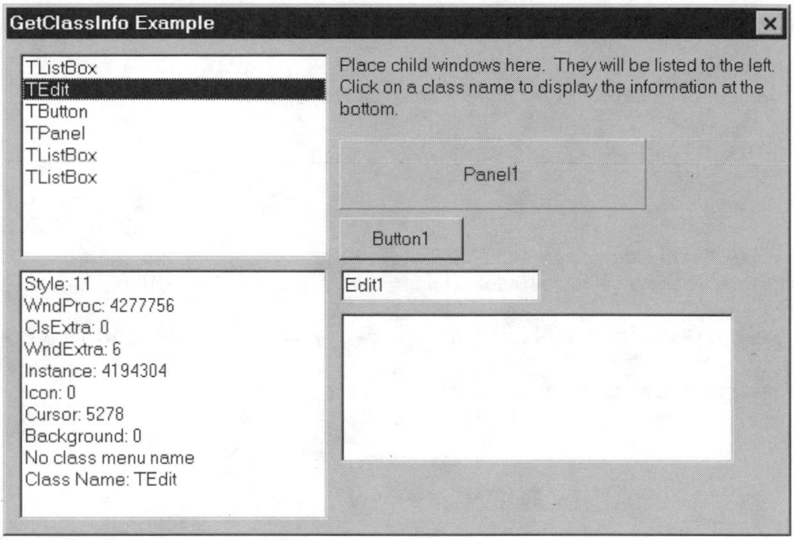

Figure 5-2: Delphi object class information.

These functions can be combined with other enumeration functions to provide almost any detail about any window in the system. The following example is from the WindowInfo application included on the CD. It demonstrates multiple enumeration and window information functions. This application can be used as a complement to the WinSight32 application that ships with Delphi to provide a complete source of information for every window in the system.

Listing 5-4: Displaying Window and Class Information

```
{prototypes for enumeration functions. These must all have the stdcall
 keyword at the end.}
function EnumerateWindows(hWnd: HWND; lParam: LPARAM): BOOL; stdcall;
function EnumerateChildWindows(hWnd: HWND;lParam: LPARAM):BOOL; stdcall;
function EnumProperties(hWnd: HWND; lpszString: PChar;
                        hData: THandle): BOOL; stdcall;

var
  Form1: TForm1;

implementation

function EnumerateChildWindows(hWnd: HWND; lParam: LPARAM): BOOL;
var
   WindowText: array[0..255] of char;
begin
   {get the text displayed in the child window}
   GetWindowText(hWnd, WindowText, 255);

   {indicate if the child window does not have any text}
   if (WindowText='') then WindowText:='[No Child Window Text]';

   {add an item to the treeview object for a child window}
```

```
   Form1.Treeview1.Items.AddChild(Form1.Treeview1.Items[lParam],IntToStr(hWnd)+
                                 ' - '+WindowText);

   {continue enumeration}
   Result:=TRUE;
end;

function EnumerateWindows(hWnd: HWND; lParam: LPARAM): BOOL;
var
   WindowText: array[0..255] of char;
begin
   {get the text displayed in the window}
   GetWindowText(hWnd, WindowText, 255);

   {indicate if the window does not have any text}
   if (WindowText='') then WindowText:='[No Window Text]';

   {add an item to the treeview object for a top level window}
   Form1.TreeView1.Items.Add(nil,IntToStr(hWnd)+' - '+WindowText);

   {now, enumerate all of the child windows of this top-level window}
   EnumChildWindows(hWnd, @EnumerateChildWindows,
                    Form1.TreeView1.Items.Count-1);

   {continue enumeration of top-level windows}
   Result:=TRUE;
end;

function EnumProperties(hWnd: HWND; lpszString: PChar; hData: THandle): BOOL;
begin
   {add the property and its value to the listbox}
   Form1.ListBox1.Items.Add(Format('%s=%d',[lpszString,hData]));

   {continue property enumeration}
   Result:=TRUE;
end;

procedure TForm1.FormActivate(Sender: TObject);
begin
   {clear the treeview object...}
   TreeView1.Items.Clear;

   {...and fill it with information about every window in the system}
   EnumWindows(@EnumerateWindows,0);
end;

procedure TForm1.TreeView1Click(Sender: TObject);
var
   TheWindow: HWND;                       // holds a window handle
   ParentWindow: HWND;                    // holds a parent window handle
   TheInstance: Longint;                  // holds an instance handle
   TheClassName: array[0..255] of char;   // holds the name of the class of a
                                             window
   TheClassInfo: TWndClass;               // holds information about a window
                                             class
```

```
   ErrorCode: Integer;                      // general error code variable
   BoolError: Boolean;                      // boolean error code variable
begin
   {get the window handle of the window selected in the treeview object}
   TheWindow:=HWND(StrToInt(Copy(TreeView1.Selected.Text,0,Pos
                       ('-',TreeView1.Selected.Text)-2)));

   {if this window is a child window, retrieve a handle to its parent}
   if (TreeView1.Selected.Parent<>nil) then
      ParentWindow:=HWND(StrToInt(Copy(TreeView1.Selected.Parent.Text,0,
                       Pos('-',TreeView1.Selected.Parent.Text)-2)))
   else
      ParentWindow:=0;

   {indicate if this window is a child window}
   if IsChild(ParentWindow,TheWindow) then
      Shape1.Brush.Color:=clRed
   else
      Shape1.Brush.Color:=clWhite;

   {indicate if this window is minimized}
   if IsIconic(TheWindow) then
      Shape2.Brush.Color:=clRed
   else
      Shape2.Brush.Color:=clWhite;

   {indicate if the TheWindow variable contains a valid window handle}
   if IsWindow(TheWindow) then
      Shape3.Brush.Color:=clRed
   else
      Shape3.Brush.Color:=clWhite;

   {indicate if this window is enabled}
   if IsWindowEnabled(TheWindow) then
      Shape4.Brush.Color:=clRed
   else
      Shape4.Brush.Color:=clWhite;

   {indicate if this window is a Unicode window}
   if IsWindowUnicode(TheWindow) then
      Shape5.Brush.Color:=clRed
   else
      Shape5.Brush.Color:=clWhite;

   {indicate if this window is visible}
   if IsWindowVisible(TheWindow) then
      Shape6.Brush.Color:=clRed
   else
      Shape6.Brush.Color:=clWhite;

   {indicate if this window is maximized}
   if IsZoomed(TheWindow) then
      Shape7.Brush.Color:=clRed
   else
      Shape7.Brush.Color:=clWhite;
```

```
{clear the property display list box...}
ListBox1.Items.Clear;

{...and display all of the property entries for the selected window}
EnumProps(TheWindow, @EnumProperties);

{clear the class information list box...}
ListBox2.Items.Clear;

{...and retrieve the class name of the selected window}
ErrorCode:=GetClassName(TheWindow,TheClassName,255);

{if there was an error retrieving the class name...}
if (ErrorCode=0) then
begin
  {...display an error message...}
  ShowMessage('GetClassName failed.  No class name available.');
  Exit;
end
else
  {...or display the class name of the selected window}
  ListBox2.Items.Add('This window is a '+string(TheClassName)+' class.');

{retrieve the instance handle associated with the selected window}
TheInstance:=GetWindowLong(TheWindow,GWL_HINSTANCE);

{if there was an error retrieving the instance handle...}
if (TheInstance=0) then
begin
  {...display an error message...}
  ShowMessage('GetWindowLong failed.  No application instance available.');
  Exit;
end
else
  {...or display the instance handle}
  ListBox2.Items.Add('Instance Handle: '+IntToStr(TheInstance));

{indicate if the retrieved instance handle is the same as the current instance}
if (TheInstance=hInstance) then
   ListBox2.Items.Add('This window belongs to the application instance');

{retrieve the class information for the class that the selected window
              belongs to}
BoolError:=GetClassInfo(TheInstance,TheClassName,TheClassInfo);

{if there was an error retrieving the class info...}
if (not BoolError) then
begin
     {...display an error message...}
     ListBox2.Items.Add('GetClassInfo failed.  No class information
                       available.');
     Exit;
end;
```

```
    {...otherwise, display the information on this class}
    ListBox2.Items.Add('This class is defined as -');
    ListBox2.Items.Add(Format('    Style: %d',[TheClassInfo.style]));
    ListBox2.Items.Add(Format('    WndProc: %d',
                       [integer(TheClassInfo.lpfnWndProc)]));
    ListBox2.Items.Add(Format('    ClsExtra: %d',[TheClassInfo.cbClsExtra]));
    ListBox2.Items.Add(Format('    WndExtra: %d',[TheClassInfo.cbWndExtra]));
    ListBox2.Items.Add(Format('    Instance: %d',
                       [integer(TheClassInfo.hInstance)]));
    ListBox2.Items.Add(Format('    Icon: %d',[integer(TheClassInfo.hIcon)]));
    ListBox2.Items.Add(Format('    Cursor: %d',[integer(TheClassInfo.hCursor)]));
    ListBox2.Items.Add(Format('    Background: %d',
                       [integer(TheClassInfo.hbrBackground)]));
    if (TheClassInfo.lpszMenuName<>nil) then
      ListBox2.Items.Add('    Menu Name: '+TheClassInfo.lpszMenuName)
    else
      ListBox2.Items.Add('    No class menu name');
    if (TheClassInfo.lpszClassName<>nil) then
      ListBox2.Items.Add('    Class Name: '+TheClassInfo.lpszClassName);

end;
```

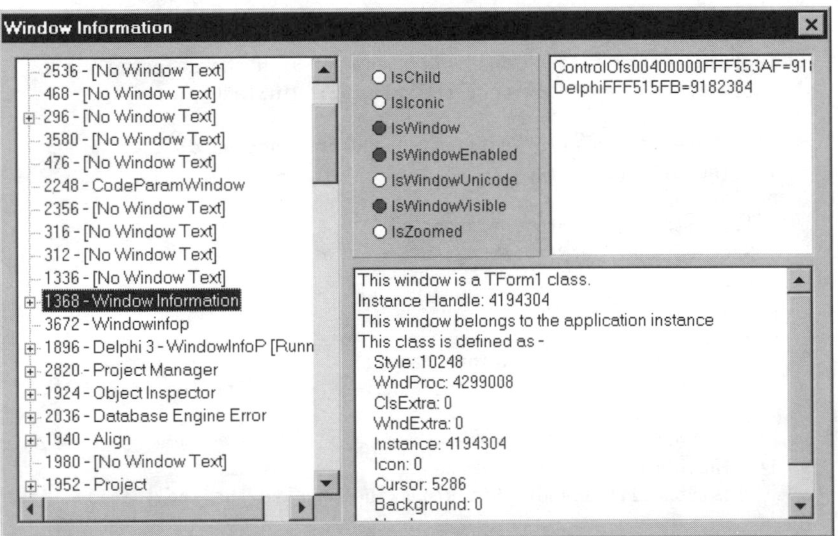

Figure 5-3: Information on every window in the system.

Window Information Functions

The following window information functions are covered in this chapter.

Table 5-1: Window Information Functions

Function	Description
AnyPopup	Indicates if any pop-up windows exist anywhere on the screen.
ChildWindowFromPoint	Determines if a specific coordinate lies within any child windows.
ChildWindowFromPointEx	Determines if a specific coordinate lies within any child windows. This function can ignore invisible, disabled, or transparent child windows.
EnableWindow	Toggles the enable state of a window.
EnumChildWindows	Passes the handle of every child window belonging to the specified window to an application-defined callback function.
EnumProps	Passes the entries in a window property list to an application-defined callback function.
EnumPropsEx	Passes the entries in a window property list to an application-defined callback function. A user-defined value can be passed along with the property entry.
EnumThreadWindows	Passes the handle to every nonchild window associated with a thread to an application-defined callback function.
EnumWindows	Passes the handle to every top-level window on the screen to an application-defined callback function.
FindWindow	Retrieves the handle to a top-level window.
FindWindowEx	Retrieves the handle to a child window.
FlashWindow	Toggles the caption bar color of a window.
GetActiveWindow	Retrieves the handle of the currently active window.
GetClassInfo	Retrieves information about the specified window's class.
GetClassInfoEx	Retrieves information about the specified window's class. This function can retrieve extended window styles and small cursor handles.
GetClassLong	Retrieves a value of the specified window's class.
GetClassName	Retrieves the name of the specified window's class.
GetClientRect	Retrieves the rectangular coordinates of the specified window's client area.
GetDesktopWindow	Retrieves a handle to the desktop window.
GetFocus	Retrieves the handle of the window with the keyboard focus.
GetForegroundWindow	Retrieves the handle of the current foreground window.
GetNextWindow	Retrieves the handle of the next or previous window in its relative Z-order.

Function	Description
GetParent	Retrieves the handle of the specified window's parent window.
GetProp	Retrieves a property from the specified window's property list.
GetTopWindow	Retrieves the handle of the child window at the top of its relative Z-order.
GetWindow	Retrieves the handle of the window with the specified relationship to the given window.
GetWindowLong	Retrieves a value of the window.
GetWindowRect	Retrieves the overall rectangular coordinates of the specified window.
GetWindowText	Retrieves the text displayed in the window.
GetWindowTextLength	Retrieves the length of the text displayed in the window.
IsChild	Determines if the specified window is a child window.
IsIconic	Determines if the specified window is minimized.
IsWindow	Determines if the specified handle is a valid window handle.
IsWindowEnabled	Determines if the specified window is enabled.
IsWindowUnicode	Determines if the specified window is a Unicode window.
IsWindowVisible	Determines if the specified window is visible.
IsZoomed	Determines if the specified window is maximized.
RemoveProp	Removes a property entry from the specified window's property list.
SetActiveWindow	Activates a window.
SetClassLong	Sets a value in the specified window's class.
SetFocus	Gives the specified window the keyboard input focus.
SetForegroundWindow	Activates a window and puts its thread into the foreground.
SetParent	Sets the parent window of the specified window.
SetProp	Adds a property entry into the specified window's property list.
SetWindowLong	Sets a specified value in the window.
SetWindowText	Sets the specified windows text to the given string.
WindowFromPoint	Retrieves the handle of the window containing the specified coordinates.

AnyPopup Windows.Pas

Syntax

AnyPopup: BOOL; {returns TRUE or FALSE}

Description

This will indicate whether an owned, visible, top-level pop-up or overlapped window exists anywhere on the entire screen. However, it will not detect unowned pop-up windows or windows that do not have the WS_VISIBLE style specified. This is a function used mainly in earlier Windows applications and is retained for compatibility purposes.

Return Value

If this function succeeds and a pop-up window is found, this function returns TRUE even if the popup is completely covered by other windows. If the function fails, or it does not find a pop-up window, it returns FALSE.

See also

EnumWindows, FindWindow, FindWindowEx, GetWindow, GetTopWindow, ShowOwnedPopups

Example

Listing 5-5: Finding any Pop-up Window

```
procedure TForm1.Button1Click(Sender: TObject);
begin
   if (AnyPopup) then
      Label1.Caption:='Pop-ups found: TRUE'
   else
      Label1.Caption:='Pop-ups found: FALSE';
end;
```

ChildWindowFromPoint Windows.Pas

Syntax

ChildWindowFromPoint(
hWndParent: HWND; {the handle of the parent window}
Point: TPoint {a data structure containing coordinates to check}
): HWND; {returns a handle to a child window}

Description

This function determines if the specified point, containing coordinates relative to the parent window, falls inside the boundaries of any child window. It returns the handle to this child window even if it is disabled or hidden.

Parameters

hWndParent: A handle to the parent window.

Point: A variable of type TPoint defining the coordinates to be checked. These coordinates are relative to the parent window's client area.

Return Value

If this function succeeds, a handle to the child window containing the point is returned. If the point is within the boundaries of the parent window but not a child window, the return value is the handle to the parent window. If more than one child window contains the point, the return value is the first child window in the Z-order. If the function fails or the point is outside of the parent window boundaries, the return value is zero.

See also

ChildWindowFromPointEx, WindowFromPoint, WM_MOUSEMOVE, WM_LBUTTONDOWN, WM_RBUTTONDOWN

Example

Listing 5-6: Finding a Child Window at a Specific Coordinate

The form for this example has a panel whose Align property is set to alTop. It is this panel that the following code will find.

```
procedure TForm1.Button1Click(Sender: TObject);
var
   WindowText: array[0..255] of char;  // holds the text of the child window
   TheChildWnd: HWND;                  // holds the handle to the child window
   ThePoint: TPoint;                   // our coordinate structure
begin
   {we want to find the child window at coordinates 5,5 relative to the main
    form}
   ThePoint.X:=5;
   ThePoint.Y:=5;

   {retrieve the child window handle at these coordinates, if any}
   TheChildWnd:=ChildWindowFromPoint(Form1.Handle,ThePoint);

   {if we found a child window...}
   if (TheChildWnd<>0) then
   begin
      {...display its text...}
      GetWindowText(TheChildWnd, WindowText, 255);
      Button1.Caption:=WindowText;
   end
   else
      {...or display a message}
      Button1.Caption:='No Child Window Found.';
end;
```

ChildWindowFromPointEx Windows.Pas

Syntax

```
ChildWindowFromPointEx(
hWnd: HWND;              {the handle of the parent window}
Point: TPoint;           {a data structure with coordinates to be checked}
Flags: UINT              {disregard flags}
): HWND;                 {returns a handle to a child window}
```

Description

This function determines if the specified point, containing coordinates relative to the parent window, falls inside the boundaries of any child window. Functionally equivalent to ChildWindowFromPoint, this function can skip invisible, disabled, or transparent child windows.

Parameters

hWndParent: A handle to the parent window.

Point: A variable of type TPoint defining the coordinates to be checked. These coordinates are relative to the parent window's client area.

Flags: A 32-bit number specifying which child windows to skip. The values from Table 5-2 are used in this parameter, and two or more can be combined using the Boolean OR operator (i.e., CWP_SKIPINVISIBLE OR CWP_SKIPDISABLED).

Return Value

If this function succeeds, a handle to the child window containing the point and meeting the criteria in Flags is returned. If the point is within the boundaries of the parent window but not any child window meeting the criteria in Flags, the return value is the handle to the parent window. If more than one child window contains the point, the return value is the first child window in the Z-order. If the function fails, or the point is outside of the parent window boundaries, the return value is zero.

See also

ChildWindowFromPoint, WindowFromPoint, WM_MOUSEMOVE, WM_LBUTTONDOWN, WM_RBUTTONDOWN

Example

Listing 5-7: Finding a Child Window at Specific Coordinates

The form for this example has a panel whose Align property is set to alTop. It is this panel that the following code will find.

```
procedure TForm1.Button1Click(Sender: TObject);
var
  WindowText: array[0..255] of char;  // holds the text of the child window
  TheChildWnd: HWND;                  // holds the handle to the child window
```

```
   ThePoint: TPoint;                     // our coordinate structure
begin
   {we want to find the child window at coordinates 5,5 relative to the
                                  main form}
   ThePoint.X:=5;
   ThePoint.Y:=5;

   {retrieve the child window handle at these coordinates, if any}
   TheChildWnd:=ChildWindowFromPointEx(Form1.Handle,ThePoint,CWP_ALL);

   {if we found a child window...}
   if (TheChildWnd<>0) then
   begin
      {...display its text...}
      GetWindowText(TheChildWnd, WindowText, 255);
      Button1.Caption:=WindowText;
   end
   else
      {...or display a message}
      Button1.Caption:='No Child Window Found.';
end;
```

Table 5-2: ChildWindowFromPointEx Flags Values

Value	Description
CWP_ALL	Do not skip any child windows.
CWP_SKIPINVISIBLE	Skip invisible child windows.
CWP_SKIPDISABLED	Skip disabled child windows.
CWP_SKIPTRANSPARENT	Skip transparent child windows.

EnableWindow *Windows.Pas*

Syntax

```
EnableWindow(
hWnd: HWND;          {a handle to a window}
bEnable: BOOL        {enable/disable flag}
): BOOL;             {returns TRUE or FALSE}
```

Description

This function enables or disables mouse and keyboard input to the specified window or control. When disabled, a window or control will not receive any input such as mouse clicks or key presses, and generally cannot be accessed by the user. If the enabled state of a window or control is changing, the WM_ENABLE message is sent before this function returns. If a disabled window contains child windows, all of those child windows are disabled, but they are not sent the WM_ENABLE message. A disabled window must be enabled before it can be activated.

Parameters

hWnd: A handle to the window to be enabled or disabled.

bEnable: If this parameter is TRUE, the window is enabled; if it is FALSE, the window will be disabled.

Return Value

This function returns TRUE if the window was already disabled; otherwise it returns FALSE. To get extended error information, call the GetLastError function.

See also

GetActiveWindow, GetFocus, IsWindowEnabled, SetActiveWindow, SetFocus, WM_ENABLE

Example

Listing 5-8: Enabling and Disabling a Window

```
procedure TForm1.Button1Click(Sender: TObject);
begin
   {if the edit box is currently enabled...}
   if (IsWindowEnabled(Edit1.Handle)) then
   begin
      {...disable it and modify the appropriate captions...}
      EnableWindow(Edit1.Handle,FALSE);
      Button1.Caption:='Enable Window';
      Edit1.Text:='This window is disabled';
   end
   else
   begin
      {...otherwise enable it and modify the appropriate captions}
      EnableWindow(Edit1.Handle,TRUE);
      Button1.Caption:='Disable Window';
      Edit1.Text:='This window is enabled';
   end;
end;
```

Enabled

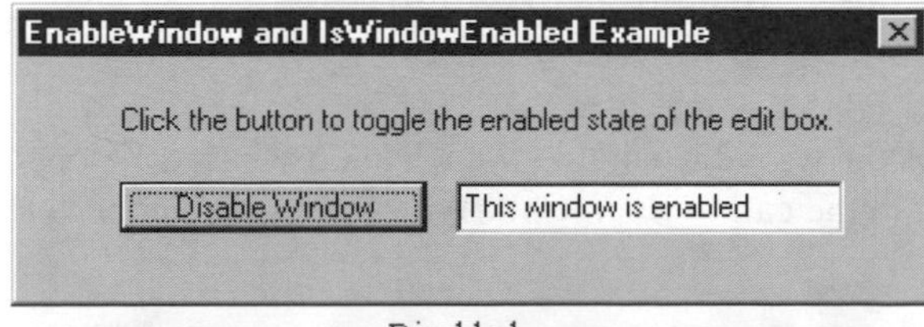

Disabled

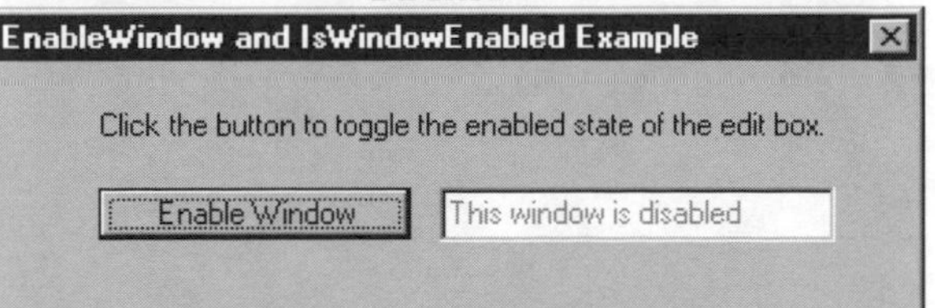

Figure 5-4: Enabled/Disabled window states.

EnumChildWindows Windows.Pas

Syntax

```
EnumChildWindows(
hWndParent: HWND;                  {the handle of the parent window}
lpEnumFunc: TFNWndEnumProc;        {a pointer to the callback function}
lParam: LPARAM                     {an application-defined 32-bit value}
): BOOL;                           {returns TRUE or FALSE}
```

Description

EnumChildWindows parses through all of the child windows belonging to the parent window, sending the handle of each child window to an application-defined callback function. This function continues until all child windows have been enumerated or the callback function returns FALSE. If a child window has created child windows of its own, these child windows are enumerated as well. This function will ignore child windows that have been destroyed and those which have been created during the enumeration process.

Parameters

hWndParent: The handle of the parent window whose child windows are to be enumerated.

lpEnumFunc: The address of the application-defined callback function.

lParam: A 32-bit application-defined value that will be passed to the callback function.

Return Value

If this function succeeds, it returns TRUE; otherwise it returns FALSE.

Callback Syntax

```
EnumChildProc(
hWnd: HWND;            {a handle to a child window}
lParam: LPARAM         {an application-defined 32-bit value}
): BOOL;               {returns TRUE or FALSE}
```

Description

This function receives the window handle for each child window belonging to the parent window specified in the call to EnumChildWindows, and may perform any desired task.

Parameters

hWnd: The handle of a child window.

lParam: A 32-bit application-defined number. This value is intended for application specific use inside of the callback function, and is the value of the lParam parameter passed to the EnumChildWindows function.

Return Value

The callback function should return TRUE to continue enumeration; otherwise it should return FALSE.

See also

EnumThreadWindows, EnumWindows, GetWindow, GetParent, FindWindow, FindWindowEx, IsChild

Example

Listing 5-9: Enumerating Child Windows

```
{our callback function prototype}
function EnumerateChildWindows(hWnd:HWND; lParam:LPARAM): BOOL; stdcall;

var
  Form1: TForm1;

implementation

procedure TForm1.EnumerateChildWindows1Click(Sender: TObject);
begin
   {empty our list box}
   ListBox1.Items.Clear;

   {enumerate all child windows belonging to Form1}
   EnumChildWindows(Form1.Handle,@EnumerateChildWindows,0);
end;

{these steps execute for every child window belonging to the parent}
function EnumerateChildWindows(hWnd: HWND; lParam: LPARAM): BOOL;
var
   ClassName: Array[0..255] of char;  // holds the class name of child windows
begin
   {get the class name of the given child window}
   GetClassName(hWnd,ClassName,255);

   {display it in the list box}
   Form1.ListBox1.Items.Add(ClassName);

   {continue enumeration}
   Result:=TRUE;
end;
```

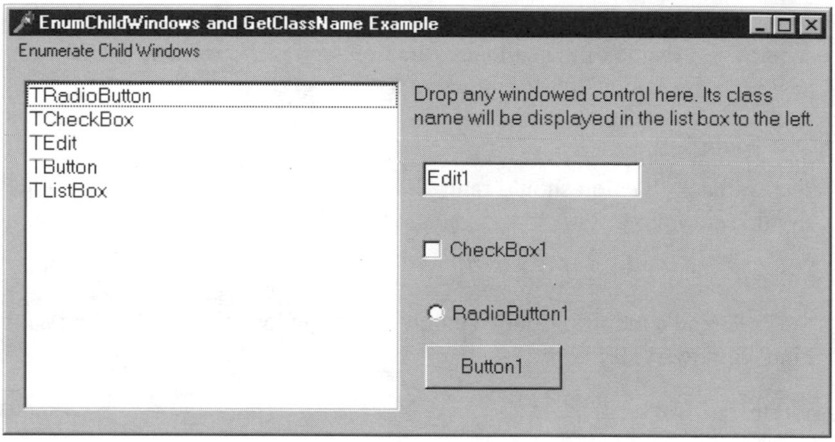

Figure 5-5: Child window class names.

EnumProps Windows.Pas

Syntax

```
EnumProps(
hWnd: HWND;                        {a handle to a window}
lpEnumFunc: TFNPropEnumProc        {the address of the enumeration callback function}
): Integer;                        {returns the value returned from the callback
                                   function}
```

Description

This function passes each entry in the property list of the specified window to an application-defined callback function. This continues until all properties have been enumerated or the callback function returns FALSE. This function is intended to be used to find the data associated with a window without knowing how many property entries exist.

Parameters

hWnd: The handle of the window whose property list is to be enumerated.

lpEnumFunc: The address of the application-defined callback function that receives the property list entries.

Return Value

This function returns the last value returned by the callback function. If the function fails, or the callback function did not find a property for the specified window, the value is –1. Note that the callback function returns a value of type BOOL, which the Windows.Pas file defines as a LongBool. This type exists for compatibility reasons and holds a Longint value, where a value of 0 is assumed to mean FALSE and nonzero values are assumed to mean TRUE.

Callback Syntax

EnumPropProc(	
hWnd: HWND;	{the handle to the window with properties}
lpszPropString: PChar;	{a pointer to a null-terminated string}
hData: THandle	{the data component of a property list entry}
): BOOL;	{returns TRUE or FALSE}

Description

This function receives property entry information for each property in the property list of the specified window. While this function is running, it should not yield control to any other process or attempt to add a property entry. It can call RemoveProp to remove a property entry, but it can only remove the current entry passed to the function.

Parameters

hWnd: The handle of the window whose property list is being enumerated.

lpszPropString: A pointer to a null-terminated string. This is the string component of the property list entry that was added by a call to the SetProp function.

hData: The 32-bit value that is the data component of the property list entry that was added by a call to the SetProp function.

Return Value

The callback function should return TRUE to continue enumeration; otherwise it should return FALSE.

See also

EnumPropsEx, GetProp, RemoveProp, SetProp

Example

Listing 5-10: Enumerating the Property Entries in a Window Property List

```
{our callback function prototype}
function EnumWinProps(hWnd: HWND; pString: PChar; Data: THandle): BOOL; stdcall;

var
  Form1: TForm1;

implementation

{these steps will be executed for each property entry in the window's property list}

function EnumWinProps(hWnd: HWND; pString: PChar; Data: THandle): BOOL;
begin
   {add the string and associated value to the list box}
   Form1.ListBox1.Items.Add(Format('%s=%d',[pString,Data]));

   {continue enumeration}
```

```
   Result:=TRUE;
end;

procedure TForm1.Button1Click(Sender: TObject);
begin
   {add a new property to the window's property list}
   SetProp(Form1.Handle,PChar(Edit1.Text),StrToInt(Edit2.Text));

   {clear the edit boxes}
   Edit1.Text:='';
   Edit2.Text:='';

   {clear the list box}
   Form1.ListBox1.Items.Clear;

   {list all of the properties associated with the window}
   EnumProps(Form1.Handle, @EnumWinProps);
end;

procedure TForm1.Button2Click(Sender: TObject);
begin
   {clear the list box}
   Form1.ListBox1.Items.Clear;

   {list all of the properties associated with the window}
   EnumProps(Form1.Handle, @EnumWinProps);
end;

procedure TForm1.Button3Click(Sender: TObject);
begin
   {remove the selected property from the property list}
   RemoveProp(Form1.Handle,PChar(Copy(ListBox1.Items[ListBox1.ItemIndex],
              0,Pos('=',ListBox1.Items[ListBox1.ItemIndex])-1)));

   {clear the list box}
   Form1.ListBox1.Items.Clear;
   {list all of the properties associated with the window}
   EnumProps(Form1.Handle, @EnumWinProps);
end;

procedure TForm1.Button4Click(Sender: TObject);
var
   Data: THandle;  // this stores the property entry data
begin
   {get property entry data associated with the given string}
   Data:=GetProp(Form1.Handle,PChar(Edit1.Text));

   {if there was a property value returned...}
   if (Data<>0) then
      {...display it...}
      Edit2.Text:=IntToStr(Data)
   else
      {...otherwise display an error message}
      Edit2.Text:='No property found.';
end;
```

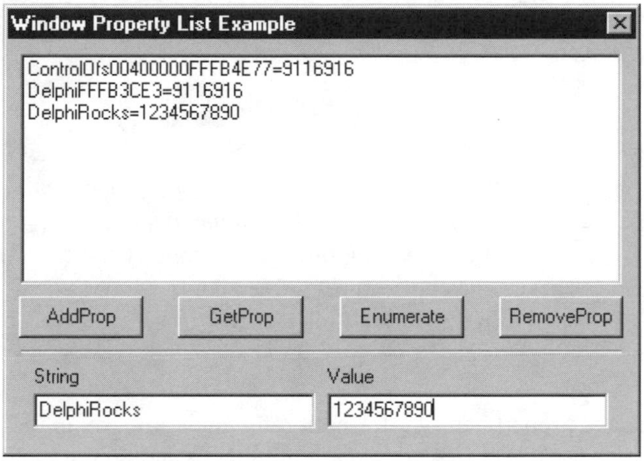

Figure 5-6: Window property list.

EnumPropsEx Windows.Pas

Syntax

```
EnumPropsEx(
hWnd: HWND;                          {a handle to a window}
lpEnumFunc: TFNPropEnumProcEx;       {the enumeration callback function address}
lParam: LPARAM                       {a 32-bit application-defined value}
): Integer;                          {returns value returned from the callback function}
```

Description

This function passes each entry in the property list of the specified window to an application-defined callback function. This continues until all properties have been enumerated or the callback function returns FALSE. This function is intended to be used to find the data associated with a window without knowing how many property entries exist. This is functionally equivalent to EnumProps, except there is an extra parameter for user-defined values that are passed to the callback function.

Parameters

hWnd: The handle of the window whose property list is to be enumerated.

lpEnumFunc: The address of the application-defined callback function that receives the property list entries.

lParam: A 32-bit application-defined value that is passed to the callback function.

Return Value

This function returns the last value returned by the callback function. If the function fails or the callback function did not find a property for the specified window, the value is –1. Note that the callback function returns a value of type BOOL, which the Windows.Pas file defines as a LongBool. This type exists for compatibility reasons and holds a Longint value, where a value of 0 is assumed to mean FALSE and nonzero values are assumed to mean TRUE.

Callback Syntax

EnumPropProcEx(
hWnd: HWND; {the handle to the window with properties}
lpszPropString: PChar; {a pointer to a null-terminated string}
hData: Handle; {the data component of a property list entry}
dwData: DWORD {the application-defined data}
): BOOL; {returns TRUE or FALSE}

Description

This function receives property entry information for each property in the property list of the specified window. While this function is running, it should not yield control to any other process or attempt to add a property entry. It can call RemoveProp to remove a property entry, but it can only remove the current entry passed to the function.

Parameters

hWnd: The handle of the window whose property list is being enumerated.

lpszPropString: A pointer to a null-terminated string. This is the string component of the property list entry that was added by a call to the SetProp function.

hData: The 32-bit value that is the data component of the property list entry that was added by a call to the SetProp function.

dwData: A 32-bit application-defined value. This value is intended for application specific use inside of the callback function, and is the value of the lParam parameter passed to the EnumPropsEx function.

Return Value

The callback function should return TRUE to continue enumeration; otherwise it should return FALSE.

See also

EnumProps, GetProp, RemoveProp, SetProp

Example

Listing 5-11: Enumerating Window Property Entries With User Data

```
{our callback function prototype}
function EnumWinPropsEx(hWnd: HWND; pString: PChar; Data: THandle;
                        dwData: DWORD): BOOL; stdcall;

var
  Form1: TForm1;

implementation
```

```
{these steps will be executed for each property
 entry in the window's property list}
function EnumWinPropsEx(hWnd: HWND; pString: PChar; Data: THandle;
                        dwData: DWORD): BOOL;
begin
   {add the string and associated value to the list box}
   Form1.ListBox1.Items.Add(Format('%s=%d, User Data: %d',
                               [pString,Data,dwData]));

   {continue enumeration}
   Result:=TRUE;
end;

procedure TForm1.Button1Click(Sender: TObject);
begin
   {add a new property to the window's property list}
   SetProp(Form1.Handle,PChar(Edit1.Text),StrToInt(Edit2.Text));

   {clear the edit boxes}
   Edit1.Text:='';
   Edit2.Text:='';

   {clear the list box}
   Form1.ListBox1.Items.Clear;

   {list all of the properties associated with the window}
   EnumPropsEx(Form1.Handle, @EnumWinPropsEx, 1);
end;

procedure TForm1.Button2Click(Sender: TObject);
begin
   {clear the list box}
   Form1.ListBox1.Items.Clear;

   {list all of the properties associated with the window}
   EnumPropsEx(Form1.Handle, @EnumWinPropsEx, 2);
end;

procedure TForm1.Button3Click(Sender: TObject);
begin
   {remove the selected property from the property list}
   RemoveProp(Form1.Handle,PChar(Copy(ListBox1.Items[ListBox1.ItemIndex],
            0,Pos('=',ListBox1.Items[ListBox1.ItemIndex])-1)));

   {clear the list box}
   Form1.ListBox1.Items.Clear;

   {list all of the properties associated with the window}
   EnumPropsEx(Form1.Handle, @EnumWinPropsEx, 3);
end;

procedure TForm1.Button4Click(Sender: TObject);
var
   Data: THandle;  // this stores the property entry data
```

```
begin
   {get property entry data associated with the given string}
   Data:=GetProp(Form1.Handle,PChar(Edit1.Text));

   {if there was a property value returned...}
   if (Data<>0) then
      {...display it...}
      Edit2.Text:=IntToStr(Data)
   else
      {...otherwise display an error message}
      Edit2.Text:='No property found.';
end;
```

EnumThreadWindows Windows.Pas

Syntax

EnumThreadWindows(	
dwThreadId: DWORD;	{the thread identification number}
lpfn: TFNWndEnumProc;	{the address of the enumeration callback function}
lParam: LPARAM	{a 32-bit application-defined value}
): BOOL;	{returns TRUE or FALSE}

Description

This function enumerates all of the nonchild windows associated with the specified thread. Each window handle associated with the specified thread is passed to an application-defined callback function. This function will continue until all of the windows are enumerated or the callback function returns FALSE.

Parameters

dwThreadId: The thread whose windows are to be enumerated.

lpfn: The address of the application-defined callback function.

lParam: A 32-bit application-defined value that is passed to the callback function.

Return Value

If this function succeeds, it returns TRUE; otherwise it returns FALSE.

Callback Syntax

EnumThreadWndProc(	
hWnd: HWND;	{a handle to a window}
lParam: LPARAM	{the application-defined data}
): BOOL;	{returns TRUE or FALSE}

Description

This function receives a window handle for every window associated with the given thread, and can perform any desired task.

Parameters

hWnd: The handle of a window associated with the specified thread.

lParam: A 32-bit application-defined value. This value is intended for application specific use inside of the callback function, and is the value of the lParam parameter of the EnumThreadWindows function.

Return Value

The callback function should return TRUE to continue enumeration; otherwise it should return FALSE.

See also

EnumChildWindows, EnumWindows, GetWindowThreadProcessId, GetCurrentThreadID

Example

Listing 5-12: Finding All Windows Belonging to a Thread

```
{our callback function prototype}
function EnumerateThreadWindows(Wnd: HWND; Data: LPARAM): BOOL; stdcall;

var
  Form1: TForm1;

implementation

procedure TForm1.Button1Click(Sender: TObject);
begin
   {clear the listbox}
   ListBox1.Items.Clear;

   {enumerate all windows that belong to the current thread}
   EnumThreadWindows(GetCurrentThreadID, @EnumerateThreadWindows, 0);
end;

{these steps are performed for every window belonging to the current thread}
function EnumerateThreadWindows(Wnd: HWND; Data: LPARAM): BOOL;
var
   WindowText: array[0..255] of char; // holds the text of the window
begin
   {get the text from the window...}
   GetWindowText(Wnd, WindowText, 255);

   {...and display it in the listbox}
   Form1.ListBox1.Items.Add(WindowText);

   {continue enumeration}
   Result:=TRUE;
end;
```

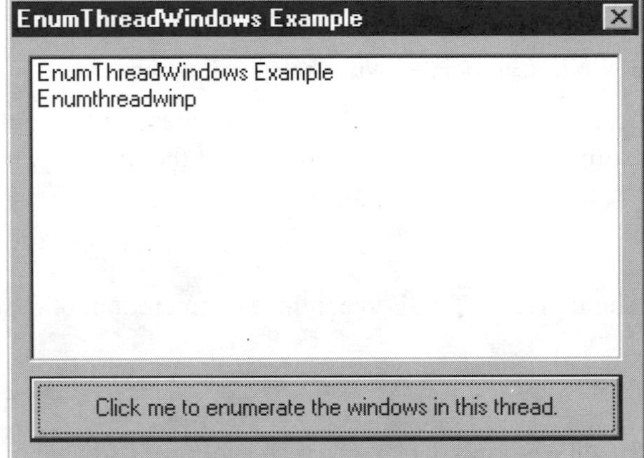

Figure 5-7: Windows belonging to the current thread.

EnumWindows   Windows.Pas

Syntax

```
EnumWindows(
lpEnumFunc: TFNWndEnumProc; {the address of the enumeration callback function}
lParam: LPARAM              {a 32-bit application-defined value}
): BOOL;                    {returns TRUE or FALSE}
```

Description

This function parses through all top-level windows on the screen, passing the handle of each window to an application-defined callback function. This continues until all top-level windows have been enumerated or the callback function returns FALSE. The EnumWindows function does not enumerate child windows.

Parameters

lpEnumFunc: The address of the application-defined callback function.

lParam: A 32-bit application-defined value that will be passed to the callback function.

Return Value

If this function succeeds, it returns TRUE; otherwise it returns FALSE.

Callback Syntax

```
EnumWindowsProc(
hWnd: HWND;       {a handle to a top-level window}
lParam: LPARAM    {the application-defined data}
): BOOL;          {returns TRUE or FALSE}
```

Description

This function receives the window handle for each top-level window in the system, and may perform any desired task.

Parameters

hWnd: The handle of a top-level window being enumerated.

lParam: A 32-bit application-defined value. This value is intended for application specific use inside of the callback function, and is the value of the lParam parameter passed to the EnumWindows function.

Return Value

The callback function should return TRUE to continue enumeration; otherwise it should return FALSE.

See also

EnumChildWindows, EnumThreadWindows, FindWindow, FindWindowEx, GetWindow, GetTopWindow

Example

Listing 5-13: List The Window Text for Every Top-Level Window in the System

```
{our callback function prototype}
function EnumerateWindows(hWnd: HWND; lParam: LPARAM): BOOL; stdcall;

var
  Form1: TForm1;

implementation

procedure TForm1.Button1Click(Sender: TObject);
begin
   {empty the listbox that will hold the window names}
   ListBox1.Items.Clear;

   {enumerate all the top-level windows in the system}
   EnumWindows(@EnumerateWindows,0);
end;

{these steps execute for every top-level window in the system}
function EnumerateWindows(hWnd: HWND; lParam: LPARAM): BOOL;
var
   TheText: Array[0..255] of char;  // this holds the window text
begin
   {if the window does not have any text...}
   if (GetWindowText(hWnd, TheText, 255)=0) then
      {...display the window handle and a note...}
      Form1.ListBox1.Items.Add(Format('%d = {This window has no text}',[hWnd]))
   else
      {otherwise display the window handle and the window text}
```

5 Chapter

```
        Form1.ListBox1.Items.Add(Format('%d = %s',[hWnd,TheText]));

     {continue enumeration}
     Result:=TRUE;
  end;
```

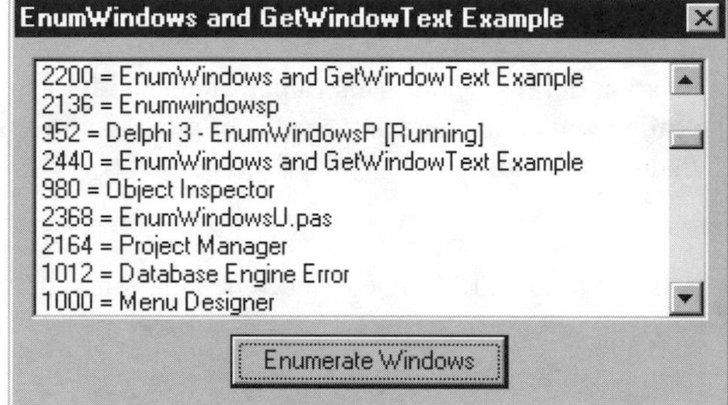

Figure 5-8: All top-level windows.

FindWindow ***Windows.Pas***

Syntax

FindWindow(	
lpClassName: PChar;	{a pointer to a null-terminated class name string}
lpWindowName: PChar	{a pointer to a null-terminated window name string}
): HWND;	{returns a handle to a window}

Description

FindWindow retrieves the handle of the top-level window with the specified class name and window name. Child windows are not searched.

Parameters

lpClassName: A pointer to a case-sensitive, null-terminated string that specifies the class name, or an integer atom identifying the class name string. If this specifies an atom, the atom must be created with a call to GlobalAddAtom. The atom, a 16-bit value, must be in the low-order word of ClassName and the high-order word must be zero.

lpWindowName: A pointer to a case-sensitive, null-terminated string that specifies the window name, which is the title in the caption bar. If this parameter is NIL, all window names match.

Return Value

If this function succeeds, the return value is the handle of the window with the specified class name and window name; otherwise it returns zero. To get extended error information, call the GetLastError function.

See also

EnumWindows, FindWindowEx, GetClassName, GetWindow

Example

Listing 5-14: Finding a Window

For this example, start the Windows Explorer, but do not minimize it. When the example is run and the button is pressed, Windows Explorer is brought into the foreground.

```
procedure TForm1.Button1Click(Sender: TObject);
var
   TheWindow: HWND;                    // holds the window handle found
   WindowText: array[0..255] of char; // holds the window's text
begin
   {find a handle to the Delphi IDE window}
   TheWindow:=FindWindow('TAppBuilder',nil);

   {retrieve its text}
   GetWindowText(TheWindow, @WindowText[0], 255);

   {display the text}
   Button1.Caption := WindowText;
end;
```

FindWindowEx Windows.Pas

Syntax

```
FindWindowEx(
Parent: HWND;            {a handle to a parent window}
Child: HWND;             {a handle to a child window}
ClassName: PChar;        {a pointer to a null-terminated class name string}
WindowName: PChar        {a pointer to a null-terminated window name string}
): HWND;                 {returns a handle to a window}
```

Description

This function retrieves the handle of the window with the specified class name and window name. Unlike FindWindow, this function searches child windows, starting with the one following the given child window.

Parameters

Parent: The handle of the parent window whose child windows are to be searched. If this parameter is zero, the desktop window is used as the parent and the child windows of the desktop are searched.

Child: The handle of a child window. The search will begin with the next child window in the Z-order of the specified child window. The specified child window must be a direct child window of the window defined by the Parent parameter. If this parameter is zero, the search will start with the first child window in the parent window. Note that if this parameter and the Parent parameter are both zero, this function searches all top-level windows.

ClassName: A pointer to a case-sensitive, null-terminated string that specifies the class name, or an integer atom identifying the class name string. If this specifies an atom, the atom must be created with a call to GlobalAddAtom. The atom, a 16-bit value, must be in the low-order word of ClassName and the high-order word must be zero.

WindowName: A pointer to a case-sensitive, null-terminated string that specifies the window's name (the window text). If this parameter is NIL, all window names match.

Return Value

If this function succeeds, the return value is the handle of the window with the specified class name and window name; otherwise it returns zero. To get extended error information, call the GetLastError function.

See also

EnumChildWindows, EnumWindows, FindWindow, GetClassName, GetWindow

Example

Listing 5-15: Using FindWindowEx to Find a Child Window

```
procedure TForm1.Button1Click(Sender: TObject);
var
   FoundWindow: HWND;
   WindowText: array[0..255] of char;
begin
   {find a TEdit child window}
   FoundWindow:=FindWindowEx(Form1.Handle, 0, 'TEdit',nil);

   {get its text...}
   GetWindowText(FoundWindow, WindowText, 255);

   {...and display it}
   Label1.Caption:='FindWindowEx found window handle '+IntToStr(FoundWindow)+
                   ': '+WindowText;
end;
```

FlashWindow   Windows.Pas

Syntax

```
FlashWindow(
hWnd: HWND;                {the handle to the window to flash}
bInvert: BOOL              {flash flag}
): BOOL;                   {returns TRUE or FALSE}
```

Description

This function will flash the window from an inactive to active state, or vice versa. It is flashed only once, and the window can be opened or minimized.

Parameters

hWnd: The handle of the window to be flashed.

bInvert: A Boolean value specifying how the window is to be flashed. A value of TRUE will cause the window to be flashed from one state to the other (i.e., inactive to active). A value of FALSE causes the window to flash back to its original state.

Return Value

If the function succeeds and the window was active before the call to this function, the return value is TRUE. If the function fails, or if the function succeeds and the window was inactive before calling this function, it returns FALSE.

See also

GetActiveWindow, GetFocus, SetActiveWindow, SetFocus

Example

Listing 5-16: Flashing a Window

Note that this code is put into an OnTimer event of a TTimer set to fire once every 1000 milliseconds.

```
procedure TForm1.Timer1Timer(Sender: TObject);
begin
   {flash the main form}
   FlashWindow(Form1.Handle, TRUE);

   {this is necessary under Delphi to get the
    icon on the task bar to flash}
   FlashWindow(Application.handle, TRUE);
end;
```

GetActiveWindow Windows.Pas

Syntax

GetActiveWindow: HWND; {returns a handle to the active window}

Description

This function returns a handle to the active window associated with the thread that calls the function.

Return Value

If this function succeeds, the return value is a handle to the active window associated with the thread that called the function. If the function fails, or if the thread does not have an active window, the return value is zero.

See also

SetActiveWindow, GetFocus, GetForegroundWindow, GetTopWindow, SetFocus, SetForegroundWindow

Example

Listing 5-17: Retrieving a Handle to the Currently Active Window

```
procedure TForm1.Button1Click(Sender: TObject);
var
   TheWindow: HWND;                     // this will hold the active window handle
   WindowText: array[0..255] of char; // this will hold the text of that window
begin
   {get the handle to the active window associated with this thread}
   TheWindow:=GetActiveWindow;

   {get the text of that window}
   GetWindowText(TheWindow,WindowText,255);

   {display the text}
   Label1.Caption:='Active Window Text: '+string(WindowText);
end;
```

GetClassInfo   Windows.Pas

Syntax

```
GetClassInfo(
hInstance: HINST;                {a handle to an application instance}
lpClassName: PChar;              {a pointer to a null-terminated class name string}
var lpWndClass: TWndClass        {a pointer to a TWndClass structure}
): BOOL;                         {returns TRUE or FALSE}
```

Description

This function returns information about the given window class. This information is stored in the members of the WndClass variable, a TWndClass data structure, and is the same information passed to the RegisterClass function that created the class.

Parameters

hInstance: The instance handle of the application that created the class. To get information about classes defined by Windows, such as buttons or list boxes, set this parameter to zero.

lpClassName: A pointer to a null-terminated string that contains the name of the class, either an application-defined name used in the RegisterClass function or the name of a preregistered window class. This can also be an integer atom, created with a call to GlobalAddAtom. The atom, a 16-bit value less than $C000, must be in the low-order word and the high-order word must be zero.

lpWndClass: A pointer to a TWndClass structure that will receive the information about the specified class. The TWndClass structure is defined by Delphi as:

```
TWndClass = packed record
    Style: UINT;                      {class style flags}
    lpfnWndProc: TFNWndProc;          {a pointer to the window procedure}
    cbClsExtra: Integer;              {extra class memory bytes}
    cbWndExtra: Integer;              {extra window memory bytes}
    hInstance: HINST;                 {a handle to the module instance}
    hIcon: HICON;                     {a handle to an icon}
    hCursor: HCURSOR;                 {a handle to a cursor}
    hbrBackground: HBRUSH;            {a handle to the background brush}
    lpszMenuName: PAnsiChar;          {the menu name}
    lpszClassName: PAnsiChar;         {the class name}
end;
```

The members of this data structure are described under the RegisterClass function.

Return Value

If this function succeeds, it returns TRUE; otherwise it returns FALSE. To get extended error information, call the GetLastError function.

See also

GetClassInfoEx, GetClassLong, GetClassName, RegisterClass

Example

Listing 5-18: Retrieving Information about the Main Form's Class

```
procedure TForm1.FormActivate(Sender: TObject);
var
   ClassInfo: TWndClass;  // this will hold our class information
begin
   {get the information for our main form's class}
   GetClassInfo(hInstance,'TForm1',ClassInfo);

   {empty the list box}
   ListBox1.Items.Clear;

   {display all of the information about the main form's class}
   ListBox1.Items.Add(Format('Style: %d',[ClassInfo.style]));
   ListBox1.Items.Add(Format('WndProc: %d',[integer(ClassInfo.lpfnWndProc)]));
   ListBox1.Items.Add(Format('ClsExtra: %d',[ClassInfo.cbClsExtra]));
```

```
    ListBox1.Items.Add(Format('WndExtra: %d',[ClassInfo.cbWndExtra]));
    ListBox1.Items.Add(Format('Instance: %d',[integer(ClassInfo.hInstance)]));
    ListBox1.Items.Add(Format('Icon: %d',[integer(ClassInfo.hIcon)]));
    ListBox1.Items.Add(Format('Cursor: %d',[integer(ClassInfo.hCursor)]));
    ListBox1.Items.Add(Format('Background: %d',[integer(ClassInfo.hbrBackground)]));
    if (ClassInfo.lpszMenuName<>nil) then
       ListBox1.Items.Add('Menu Name: '+ClassInfo.lpszMenuName)
    else
       ListBox1.Items.Add('No class menu name');
    if (ClassInfo.lpszClassName<>nil) then
       ListBox1.Items.Add('Class Name: '+ClassInfo.lpszClassName);
end;
```

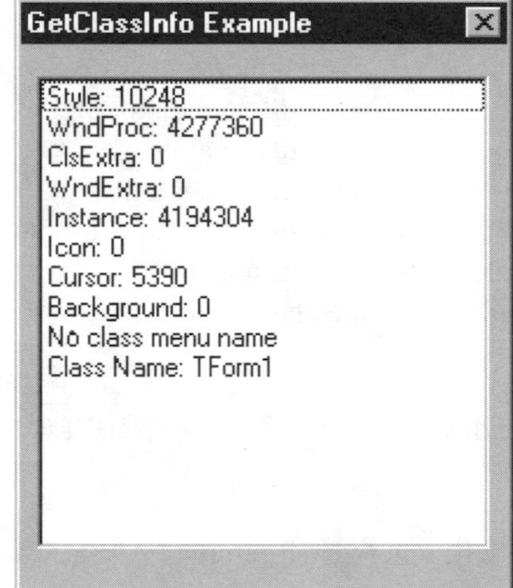

Figure 5-9: The Main form's class information.

GetClassInfoEx Windows.Pas

Syntax

GetClassInfoEx(
Instance: HINST; {a handle to an application instance}
ClassName: PChar; {a pointer to a null-terminated class name string}
var WndClass: TWndClassEx {a pointer to a TWndClassEx structure}
): BOOL; {returns TRUE or FALSE}

Description

This function returns information about the given window class. This information is stored in the members of the WndClass variable, a TWndClassEx data structure, and is the same information passed to the RegisterClassEx function that created the class. This function is equivalent to GetClassInfo, except it returns a handle to the small icon associated with the given class.

Parameters

Instance: The instance handle of the application that created the class. To get information about classes defined by Windows, such as buttons or list boxes, set this parameter to zero.

ClassName: A pointer to a null-terminated string that contains the name of the class, either an application-defined name used in the RegisterClass function or the name of a preregistered window class. This can also be an integer atom, created with a call to GlobalAddAtom. The atom, a 16-bit value less than $C000, must be in the low-order word and the high-order word must be zero.

WndClass: A pointer to a TWndClassEx structure that will receive the information about the specified class. The TWndClassEx structure is defined by Delphi as:

```
TWndClassEx = packed record
    cbSize: UINT;                    {the size of this structure}
    Style: UINT;                     {class style flags}
    lpfnWndProc: TFNWndProc;         {a pointer to the window procedure}
    cbClsExtra: Integer;             {extra class memory bytes}
    cbWndExtra: Integer;             {extra window memory bytes}
    hInstance: HINST;                {a handle to the module instance}
    hIcon: HICON;                    {a handle to an icon}
    hCursor: HCURSOR;                {a handle to a cursor}
    hbrBackground: HBRUSH;           {a handle to the background brush}
    lpszMenuName: PAnsiChar;         {the menu name}
    lpszClassName: PAnsiChar;        {the class name}
    hIconSm: HICON;                  {a handle to a small icon}
end;
```

The members of this data structure are described under the RegisterClassEx description. Before calling the GetClassInfoEx function, the cbSize member of this structure must be set to SizeOf(TWndClassEx).

Return Value

If this function succeeds, it returns TRUE; otherwise it returns FALSE. To get extended error information, call the GetLastError function.

See also

GetClassInfo, GetClassLong, GetClassName, RegisterClassEx

Example

Listing 5-19: Retrieving Class Information for All Child Windows

This example enumerates through all child windows present on the form. It displays the class name for each in a list box, and when a class name is selected, it displays the information for that class in a separate list box.

```
{function prototype for enumerating child windows}
function EnumerateChildWindows(hWnd:HWND; lParam:LPARAM): BOOL; stdcall;

var
  Form1: TForm1;

implementation

function EnumerateChildWindows(hWnd: HWND; lParam: LPARAM): BOOL;
var
   TheClassName: Array[0..255] of char;
begin
   {get the class name of this child window}
   GetClassName(hWnd, TheClassName, 255);

   {display it in the list box}
   Form1.ListBox1.Items.Add(TheClassName);

   {continue enumeration}
   Result:=TRUE;
end;

procedure TForm1.FormActivate(Sender: TObject);
begin
   {populate the list box with the class names of all child windows}
   EnumChildWindows(Form1.Handle,@EnumerateChildWindows,0);
end;

procedure TForm1.ListBox1Click(Sender: TObject);
var
   ClassInfo: TWndClassEx;             // this holds our class info
   ClassName: array[0..255] of char;   // this holds the class name
begin
   {copy the class name to a PChar string that is passed to the GetClassInfoEx
    function. the classname parameter must be a PChar, or the memory pointed
    to by ClassInfo becomes corrupted when accessing certain members of the
    data structure.}
   StrPCopy(ClassName,ListBox1.Items[ListBox1.ItemIndex]);

   {set the size of the data structure}
   ClassInfo.cbSize:=SizeOf(TWndClassEx);

   {get the class information for the selected class}
   GetClassInfoEx(hInstance,ClassName,ClassInfo);

   {clear the list box}
   ListBox2.Items.Clear;

   {display the class information}
   ListBox2.Items.Add(Format('Size: %d',[ClassInfo.cbSize]));
   ListBox2.Items.Add(Format('Style: %d',[ClassInfo.Style]));
   ListBox2.Items.Add(Format('WndProc: %d',[integer(ClassInfo.lpfnWndProc)]));
   ListBox2.Items.Add(Format('ClsExtra: %d',[ClassInfo.cbClsExtra]));
   ListBox2.Items.Add(Format('WndExtra: %d',[ClassInfo.cbWndExtra]));
```

```
    ListBox2.Items.Add(Format('Instance: %d',[integer(ClassInfo.hInstance)]));
    ListBox2.Items.Add(Format('Icon: %d',[integer(ClassInfo.hIcon)]));
    ListBox2.Items.Add(Format('Cursor: %d',[integer(ClassInfo.hCursor)]));
    ListBox2.Items.Add(Format('Background: %d',
                       [integer(ClassInfo.hbrBackground)]));
    if (ClassInfo.lpszMenuName<>nil) then
       ListBox2.Items.Add('Menu Name: '+ClassInfo.lpszMenuName)
    else
       ListBox2.Items.Add('No class menu name');
    if (ClassInfo.lpszClassName<>nil) then
       ListBox2.Items.Add('Class Name: '+ClassInfo.lpszClassName);
    ListBox2.Items.Add(Format('Small Icon: %d',[ClassInfo.hIconSm]));

end;
```

GetClassLong Windows.Pas

Syntax

GetClassLong(
hWnd: HWND; {a handle to a window}
nIndex: Integer {the offset of the value to retrieve}
): DWORD; {returns a 32-bit value}

Description

This function returns the 32-bit value at the specified offset into the extra memory for the window class that the given window belongs to. This extra memory is reserved by specifying a value in the ClsExtra member of the TWndClass structure used when the RegisterClass function is called. In addition, this function can return information about the window class by using one of the values in Table 5-3 for the nIndex parameter.

Parameters

hWnd: The handle to the window with the class memory to be accessed.

nIndex: Specifies the zero-based byte offset for the 32-bit value to be retrieved. This can be a value between zero and the number of bytes of extra class memory minus four (i.e., if 16 bytes of extra class memory are allocated, a value of 8 would index into the third 32-bit value). In addition, one of the values in Table 5-3 can be used to access specific information about the class.

Return Value

If this function succeeds, it returns the 32-bit value at the specified index into the class memory area; otherwise it returns a zero. To get extended error information, call the GetLastError function.

See also

GetClassInfo, GetClassInfoEx, GetClassName, RegisterClass, RegisterClassEx, SetClassLong

Example

Listing 5-20: Modifying Class Settings

This example cycles through the default cursors available through Delphi. Note that the array elements of the Cursors property of the TScreen object are numbered backwards for the standard cursors.

```
procedure TForm1.Button1Click(Sender: TObject);
var
   HandleCursor: HCURSOR;          // holds the handle to a cursor
const
   CursorIndex: Integer = 0;       // we will start with the first screen cursor
begin
   {get a handle to the current cursor for this class}
   HandleCursor:=GetClassLong(Form1.Handle, GCL_HCURSOR);

   {display the cursor handle}
   Label1.Caption:='The previous cursor handle was: '+IntToStr(HandleCursor);

   {set a new cursor for this class from the list of built in Delphi cursors}
   SetClassLong(Form1.Handle, GCL_HCURSOR, Screen.Cursors[CursorIndex]);

   {display what this new cursor handle is}
   Label2.Caption:='The new cursor handle is: '+
                   IntToStr(Screen.Cursors[CursorIndex]);

   {go to the next cursor in the screen cursor list}
   Dec(CursorIndex);
end;
```

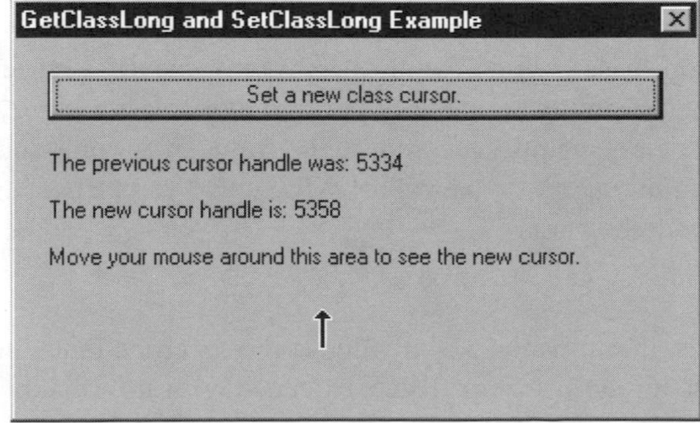

Figure 5-10: A new default cursor.

Table 5-3: GetClassLong nIndex Values

Value	Description
GCL_CBCLSEXTRA	The size of the extra memory associated with this class, in bytes. Setting this value will not change the amount of memory already allocated.
GCL_CBWNDEXTRA	The size of the extra memory associated with each window of this class, in bytes. Setting this value will not change the amount of memory already allocated.
GCL_HBRBACKGROUND	The handle to the default background brush.
GCL_HCURSOR	The handle to the window class cursor.
GCL_HICON	The handle to the window class icon.
GCL_HICONSM	The handle to the window class small icon.
GCL_HMODULE	The handle of the module that registered the class.
GCL_MENUNAME	A pointer to the menu name string.
GCL_STYLE	The 32-bit style bits for this class.
GCL_WNDPROC	A pointer to the window procedure for this class. If a developer replaces the window procedure using this index, it must conform to the window procedure callback definition as outlined in the RegisterClass function. This subclass will affect all windows subsequently created with this class. An application should not subclass a window created by another process.
GCW_ATOM	An atom that uniquely identifies this class. This is the same atom returned by the RegisterClass and RegisterClassEx functions.

GetClassName Windows.Pas

Syntax

```
GetClassName(
hWnd: HWND;                {a handle to a window}
lpClassName: PChar;        {a pointer to a buffer to receive the string}
nMaxCount: Integer         {the size of the buffer in characters}
): Integer;                {returns the number of characters copied}
```

Description

This function simply copies the class name of the specified window to the buffer pointed to by the ClassName parameter.

Parameters

hWnd: A handle to the window to get the class name from.

lpClassName: A pointer to a buffer that will receive the null-terminated class name string.

nMaxCount: Specifies the length of the buffer pointed to by the ClassName parameter. The class name string will be truncated if it is larger than the buffer.

Return Value

If this function succeeds it returns the length of the class name string in bytes, excluding the null-terminating character; otherwise it returns zero. To get extended error information, call the GetLastError function.

See also

GetClassInfo, GetClassInfoEx, GetClassLong, RegisterClass, SetClassLong

Example

This function is used in a number of examples throughout this chapter. Please see Listing 5-9 under EnumChildWindows, and the window Information application on the CD.

GetClientRect Windows.Pas

Syntax

```
GetClientRect(
hWnd: HWND;                 {a handle to a window}
var lpRect: TRect           {a pointer to a rectangle data structure}
): BOOL;                    {returns TRUE or FALSE}
```

Description

This function returns the coordinates of the client area of the given window in the TRect structure pointed to by the Rect variable.

Parameters

hWnd: The handle of the window to get the client coordinates from.

lpRect: A pointer to a TRect structure that will receive the coordinates. These coordinates are in terms of the client area of the specified window. Thus, the Left and Top members will be zero, and the Right and Bottom members will contain the width and height of the client area.

Return Value

If this function succeeds, it returns TRUE; otherwise it returns FALSE. To get extended error information, call the GetLastError function.

See also

GetWindowPlacement, GetWindowRect, SetWindowPlacement

Example

Listing 5-21: Displaying the Client and Window Rectangle Coordinates

Note that this code has been placed in the OnResize event of the form. The displayed coordinates will change whenever the window is resized.

```
procedure TForm1.FormResize(Sender: TObject);
var
   WinRect, ClientRect: TRect;  // these hold the appropriate rectangle coordinates
begin
   {get the window rectangle coordinates}
   Windows.GetWindowRect(Form1.Handle, WinRect);

   {get the client rectangle coordinates}
   Windows.GetClientRect(Form1.Handle, ClientRect);

   {display the coordinates}
   Label1.Caption:=Format('Window Rectangle - Left: %d, Top: %d, Right: %d,
                          Bottom: %d', [WinRect.Left, WinRect.Top,
                          WinRect.Right, WinRect.Bottom]);
   Label2.Caption:=Format('Client Rectangle - Left: %d, Top: %d, Right: %d,
                          Bottom: %d', [ClientRect.Left, ClientRect.Top,
                          ClientRect.Right,ClientRect.Bottom]);
end;
```

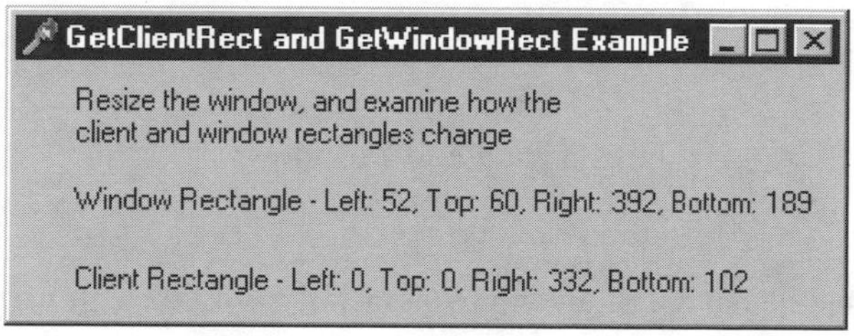

GetClientRect and GetWindowRect Example

Resize the window, and examine how the client and window rectangles change

Window Rectangle - Left: 52, Top: 60, Right: 392, Bottom: 189

Client Rectangle - Left: 0, Top: 0, Right: 332, Bottom: 102

Figure 5-11: Client and window rectangle coordinates.

GetDesktopWindow   Windows.Pas

Syntax

GetDesktopWindow: HWND;   {returns a handle to the desktop window}

Description

This function returns a handle to the desktop window. This window encompasses the entire screen, and is the area on which all other windows and icons are painted. A developer can pass the handle returned from this function to the GetDC function to get a device context for drawing directly on the desktop surface.

Return Value

If this function succeeds, it returns the handle to the desktop window; otherwise it returns zero.

See also

EnumWindows, GetWindow

Example

Listing 5-22: Retrieving a Handle to the Desktop Window

```
procedure TForm1.Button1Click(Sender: TObject);
var
   ClassName: array[0..255] of char;
   DesktopWindow: HWND;
begin
   {get the desktop window handle}
   DesktopWindow:=GetDesktopWindow;

   {get the class name of the desktop window}
   GetClassName(DesktopWindow, ClassName, 255);

   {display the class name on the button}
   Button1.Caption:=ClassName;
end;
```

GetFocus Windows.Pas

Syntax

GetFocus: HWND; {returns a handle to a window}

Description

This function retrieves the handle of a window associated with the calling thread that has the input focus.

Return Value

If this function succeeds, it returns the handle to the window associated with the calling thread that has the input focus. If the function fails, or there is no window associated with the calling thread that has the input focus, it returns zero. If the return value is zero, another thread may have a window with the input focus.

See also

GetActiveWindow, GetCapture, GetForegroundWindow, GetTopWindow, IsWindowEnabled, SetActiveWindow, SetFocus, WM_KILLFOCUS, WM_SETFOCUS

Example

Listing 5-23: Getting the Window with the Input Focus

This code is put in the OnEnter event of multiple controls.

```
procedure TForm1.Button1Enter(Sender: TObject);
var
   FocusWnd: HWND;                      // this will hold the window handle
   ClassName: array[0..255] of char;  // this will hold the class name
begin
   {get the handle of the window that currently has input focus}
   FocusWnd:=GetFocus;

   {get the class name of this window}
   GetClassName(FocusWnd,ClassName,255);

   {display the class name of the window with input focus}
   Label2.Caption:=string(ClassName)+' has input focus.'
end;
```

GetForegroundWindow   Windows.Pas

Syntax

GetForegroundWindow: HWND;   {returns a handle to a window}

Description

This function returns the handle of the window with which the user is currently working.

Return Value

If the function succeeds, it returns a handle to the foreground window; otherwise it returns zero.

See also

GetTopWindow, GetFocus, SetForegroundWindow

Example

Listing 5-24: Retrieving a Handle to the Foreground Window

The form for this project has its FormStyle property set to fsStayOnTop so it is visible when other applications have the focus. This code is fired from a timer set at 250 milliseconds.

```
procedure TForm1.Timer1Timer(Sender: TObject);
var
   TheWindowText: array[0..255] of char;
   TheForegroundWindow: HWND;
begin
```

```
   {get a handle to the foreground window}
   TheForegroundWindow:=GetForegroundWindow;

   {get its caption text}
   GetWindowText(TheForegroundWindow, TheWindowText, 255);

   {display the foreground window's caption}
   Label2.Caption:='Foreground Window Text: '+TheWindowText;
end;
```

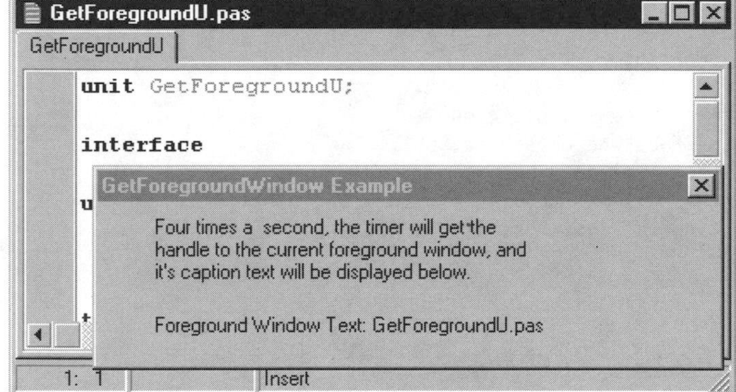

Figure 5-12: The foreground window.

GetNextWindow Windows.Pas

Syntax

GetNextWindow(
hWnd: HWND; {a handle to the current window}
uCmd: UINT {direction flags}
): HWND; {returns a handle to a window}

Description

This function returns the handle to the next or previous window in the relative Z-order of the specified window. The next window is below the specified window in the Z-order, and the previous window is above it. Windows maintains a separate Z-order for topmost windows, top-level windows, and child windows, and this function returns a handle to a window relative to the specified window in the appropriate Z-order list.

Parameters

hWnd: A handle to the current window.

uCmd: Specifies whether the handle to the next window or previous window, relative to the current window, should be returned. It can be either value from Table 5-4.

Return Value

If this function is successful, it returns the handle to the next or previous window in the relative Z-order. If the function fails, or there is no next or previous window relative to the given window, it returns zero. To get extended error information, call the GetLastError function.

See also

BringWindowToTop, GetTopWindow, GetWindow, FindWindow, FindWindowEx, EnumWindows

Example

Listing 5-25: Finding the Top Sibling Window and its Nearest Neighbor in the Z-Order

This example contains five panels arranged on top of each other. The button and all five panels are siblings. When the button is pressed, the text of the window at the top of the Z-order relative to its siblings and the text of the window just underneath it are displayed.

```
procedure TForm1.Button1Click(Sender: TObject);
var
   WindowText: array[0..255] of char;
   TheWindow: HWND;
   ThePreviousWindow: HWND;
begin
     {get the handle to the Form1 child window at the
      top of the Z order relative to its siblings}
     TheWindow:=GetTopWindow(Form1.Handle);

     {get the text displayed on this window...}
     GetWindowText(TheWindow,WindowText,255);

     {...and display it in the label}
     Label2.Caption:='Top Window: '+WindowText;

     {now get the window just under it in the Z order}
     ThePreviousWindow:=GetNextWindow(TheWindow,GW_HWNDNEXT);

     {get the text displayed on this window...}
     GetWindowText(ThePreviousWindow,WindowText,255);

     {...and display it in the label}
     Label3.Caption:='Next To Top: '+WindowText;
end;
```

Table 5-4: GetNextWindow uCmd Values

Value	Description
GW_HWNDNEXT	Returns a handle to the window below the specified window in the relative Z-order.
GW_HWNDPREV	Returns a handle to the window above the specified window in the relative Z-order.

GetParent Windows.Pas

Syntax

```
GetParent(
hWnd: HWND                    {a handle of a child window}
): HWND;                      {returns a handle to a parent window}
```

Description

This function returns a handle to the given window's parent window, if any.

Parameters

hWnd: A handle to the window whose parent window handle is to be retrieved.

Return Value

If this function succeeds, it returns the handle to the parent window of the given window. If this function fails, or the specified window does not have a parent window, it returns zero. To get extended error information, call the GetLastError function.

See also

EnumWindows, FindWindow, FindWindowEx, GetWindow, SetParent

Example

Listing 5-26: Finding a Control's Parent Window

```
procedure TForm1.Button1Click(Sender: TObject);
var
   TheText: array[0..255] of char;
   TheParent: HWND;
begin
   {get the button's parent window handle}
   TheParent:=GetParent(Button1.Handle);

   {get the parent window's text}
   GetWindowText(TheParent, TheText, 255);

   {display this text on the button}
   Button1.Caption:=TheText;
end;
```

GetProp Windows.Pas

Syntax

```
GetProp(
hWnd: HWND;                {a handle to a window}
lpString: PChar            {a pointer to a string}
): THandle;                {returns a 32-bit value}
```

Description

This function retrieves the 32-bit value associated with the given string from the property list of the specified window.

Parameters

hWnd: The handle of the window whose property list is to be searched.

lpString: A pointer to a null-terminated string or an atom identifying a string. If this parameter is an atom, the atom must have been created with a call to GlobalAddAtom. The atom, a 16-bit value, must be in the low-order word and the high-order word must be zero.

Return Value

If this function succeeds and it contains the specified string, it returns the data value associated with that string in the property list of the given window. If the function fails, or the specified string is not in the property list of the window, it returns zero.

See also

EnumProps, EnumPropsEx, RemoveProp, SetProp

Example

Please see either Listing 5-10 under EnumProps or Listing 5-11 under EnumPropsEx.

GetTopWindow Windows.Pas

Syntax

```
GetTopWindow(
hWnd: HWND                 {a handle of a parent window}
): HWND;                   {returns a handle to a child window}
```

Description

This function examines the child windows of the specified parent window, and returns a handle to the child window at the top of the Z-order relative to its siblings. Only the siblings of child windows belonging to the parent window are searched. If the child windows have child windows themselves, they are excluded.

Parameters

hWnd: A handle to the parent window whose child windows are to be searched. If this value is zero, this function will return the first child window belonging to the desktop window.

Return Value

If this function succeeds, it returns a handle to the child window at the top of the Z-order relative to its siblings. If the function fails, or the parent window has no child windows, it returns zero. To get extended error information, call the GetLastError function.

See also

BringWindowToTop, EnumChildWindows, EnumWindows, GetActiveWindow, GetForegroundWindow, GetWindow, GetNextWindow, SetActiveWindow, SetForegroundWindow, ShowWindow

Example

Please see Listing 5-25 under GetNextWindow.

GetWindow Windows.Pas

Syntax

```
GetWindow(
hWnd: HWND;                {a handle to a window}
uCmd: UINT                 {relationship flags}
): HWND;                   {returns a handle to a window}
```

Description

This function returns a handle to a window that has the specified relationship to the window in the hWnd parameter.

Parameters

hWnd: A handle to a window. The search starts from the window associated with this window handle.

uCmd: Specifies the relationship of the returned window to the specified window, and can be one value from Table 5-5.

Return Value

If this function is successful, it returns the handle of the related window. If the function fails, or there is no window with the specified relationship to the given window, it returns zero. To get extended error information, call the GetLastError function.

See also

GetActiveWindow, GetNextWindow, GetTopWindow, EnumWindows, FindWindow

Example

Listing 5-27: Get the Child Window at the Top of the Z-Order

```
procedure TForm1.Button1Click(Sender: TObject);
var
   TheWindow: HWND;                    // identifies a window
   TheText: array[0..255] of char;     // holds the window text
begin
   {get the child window at the top of the Z order on our main form}
   TheWindow:=GetWindow(Form1.Handle, GW_CHILD);

   {get its text...}
   GetWindowText(TheWindow, TheText, 255);

   {...and display it}
   Button1.Caption:=TheText;
end;
```

Table 5-5: GetWindow uCmd Values

Value	Description
GW_CHILD	Returns a handle to the child window at the top of the Z-order if the specified window has child windows; otherwise the function returns zero.
GW_HWNDFIRST	Returns a handle to the window at the top of the Z-order of the Z-order group containing the specified window (i.e., if the specified window is a child window, the window at the top of the child window Z-order is returned; if the specified window is a top-level window, the window at the top of the top-level window Z-order is returned).
GW_HWNDLAST	Returns a handle to the window at the bottom of the Z-order of the Z-order group containing the specified window (i.e., if the specified window is a child window, the window at the bottom of the child window Z-order is returned; if the specified window is a top-level window, the window at the bottom of the top-level window Z-order is returned).
GW_HWNDNEXT	Returns a handle to the window below the specified window in the relative Z-order.
GW_HWNDPREV	Returns a handle to the window above the specified window in the relative Z-order.
GW_OWNER	Returns a handle to the specified window's owner.

GetWindowLong Windows.Pas

Syntax

GetWindowLong(
hWnd: HWND; {a handle to a window}
nIndex: Integer {the offset of the value to retrieve}
): Longint; {returns a 32-bit value}

Description

This function returns the 32-bit value at the specified offset into the extra window memory for the specified window. This extra memory is reserved by specifying a value in the WndExtra member of the TWndClass structure used when the RegisterClass function is called. In addition, this function can return information about the window by using one of the values in Table 5-6 for the nIndex parameter.

Parameters

hWnd: A handle to the window with the extra window memory to be accessed.

nIndex: Specifies the zero-based byte offset for the value to be retrieved. This can be a value between zero and the number of bytes of extra window memory minus four (i.e., if 16 bytes of extra window memory are allocated, a value of 8 would index into the third 32-bit value). In addition, one of the values in Table 5-6 can be used to access specific information about the window.

Return Value

If this function succeeds, it returns the 32-bit value at the specified index into the window memory area; otherwise it returns zero. To get extended error information, call the GetLastError function.

See also

GetClassInfo, GetClassInfoEx, GetClassName, RegisterClass, RegisterClassEx, SetClassLong, SetWindowLong

Example

Listing 5-28: Modifying Window Styles at Runtime

```
procedure TForm1.CheckBox1Click(Sender: TObject);
var
   WindowStyle: Longint;   // holds the window style
begin
   {get the current styles used by this window}
   WindowStyle:=GetWindowLong(Form1.Handle, GWL_STYLE);

   {toggle the WS_CAPTION style}
   if (CheckBox1.Checked) then
      WindowStyle:=WindowStyle OR WS_CAPTION
   else
```

```
      WindowStyle:=WindowStyle AND NOT WS_CAPTION;

   {toggle the WS_BORDER style}
   if (CheckBox2.Checked) then
      WindowStyle:=WindowStyle OR WS_BORDER
   else
      WindowStyle:=WindowStyle AND NOT WS_BORDER;

   {toggle the WS_SYSMENU style}
   if (CheckBox3.Checked) then
      WindowStyle:=WindowStyle OR WS_SYSMENU
   else
      WindowStyle:=WindowStyle AND NOT WS_SYSMENU;

   {toggle the WS_MAXIMIZEBOX style}
   if (CheckBox4.Checked) then
      WindowStyle:=WindowStyle OR WS_MAXIMIZEBOX
   else
      WindowStyle:=WindowStyle AND NOT WS_MAXIMIZEBOX;

   {toggle the WS_MINIMIZEBOX style}
   if (CheckBox5.Checked) then
      WindowStyle:=WindowStyle OR WS_MINIMIZEBOX
   else
      WindowStyle:=WindowStyle AND NOT WS_MINIMIZEBOX;


   {make the window use the new styles}
   SetWindowLong(Form1.Handle, GWL_STYLE, WindowStyle);

   {this little trick forces the entire window to redraw,
    including nonclient areas}
   SetWindowPos(Handle, 0, 0, 0, 0, 0, SWP_DRAWFRAME or SWP_NOACTIVATE or
                SWP_NOMOVE or SWP_NOSIZE or SWP_NOZORDER);

   {display the current styles used by this window}
   Label1.Caption:='Current Style: '+IntToStr(WindowStyle);
end;

procedure TForm1.FormCreate(Sender: TObject);
var
   WindowStyle: Longint;   // holds the window style information
begin
   {get the current styles used by this window}
   WindowStyle:=GetWindowLong(Form1.Handle, GWL_STYLE);

   {initialize the check boxes according to the styles that are present}
   if (WindowStyle AND WS_CAPTION)>0 then CheckBox1.Checked:=TRUE;
   if (WindowStyle AND WS_BORDER)>0 then CheckBox2.Checked:=TRUE;
   if (WindowStyle AND WS_SYSMENU)>0 then CheckBox3.Checked:=TRUE;
   if (WindowStyle AND WS_MAXIMIZEBOX)>0 then CheckBox4.Checked:=TRUE;
   if (WindowStyle AND WS_MINIMIZEBOX)>0 then CheckBox5.Checked:=TRUE;

   {hook up the OnClick events for the checkboxes. this step is necessary
    because the OnClick event is automatically fired when the Checked
```

```
      property is accessed.}
    CheckBox1.OnClick:=CheckBox1Click;
    CheckBox2.OnClick:=CheckBox1Click;
    CheckBox3.OnClick:=CheckBox1Click;
    CheckBox4.OnClick:=CheckBox1Click;
    CheckBox5.OnClick:=CheckBox1Click;
end;
```

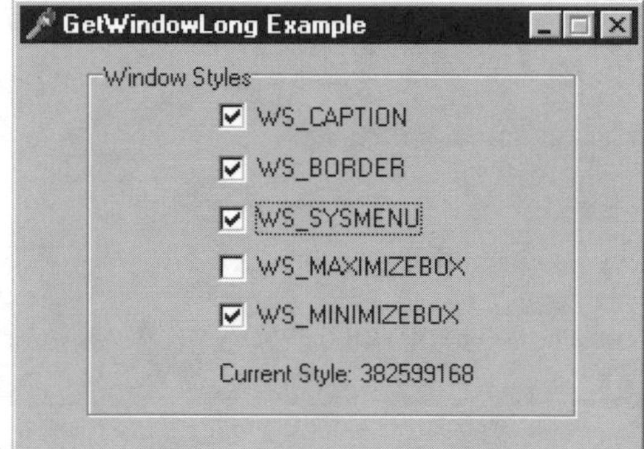

Figure 5-13: The window styles.

Table 5-6: GetWindowLong nIndex Values

Value	Description
GWL_EXSTYLE	The extended styles used by this window.
GWL_STYLE	The styles used by this window.
GWL_WNDPROC	A pointer to the window procedure for this window. If a developer replaces the window procedure using this index, it must conform to the window procedure callback definition as outlined in the RegisterClass function. The process of replacing a window procedure with a new one is called subclassing. An application should not subclass a window created by another process. A developer must pass any unhandled messages back to the original window procedure. This is accomplished by using the return value from this function with the CallWindowProc function to access the original window procedure.
GWL_HINSTANCE	The handle of the application instance.
GWL_HWNDPARENT	The handle to the parent window, if any.
GWL_ID	The identifier of the window.
GWL_USERDATA	The 32-bit user data value of this window. Every window has a 32-bit user data value that is intended for application-defined data associated with the window.

These values are available if the Wnd parameter specifies a dialog box:

Value	Description
DWL_DLGPROC	A pointer to the dialog box procedure for this dialog box. If a developer replaces the dialog box procedure using this index, it must conform to the dialog box procedure callback function as defined in the CreateDialog function. The process of replacing a dialog box procedure with a new one is called subclassing. An application should not subclass a dialog box created by another process. A developer must pass any unhandled messages back to the original window procedure. This is accomplished by using the return value from this function with the CallWindowProc function to access the dialog box procedure.
DWL_MSGRESULT	The return value of a message processed in the dialog box procedure.
DWL_USER	The 32-bit extra dialog box information.

GetWindowRect Windows.Pas

Syntax

```
GetWindowRect(
hWnd: HWND;                {a handle of a window}
var lpRect: TRect          {a pointer to a rectangle coordinate structure}
): BOOL;                   {returns TRUE or FALSE}
```

Description

This function stores the coordinates of the bounding rectangle for the given window in the structure pointed at by the Rect variable. The coordinates are relative to the upper left corner of the screen, and include the title bar, scroll bars, border, etc., of the specified window.

Parameters

hWnd: A handle to the window whose bounding rectangle is to be retrieved.

lpRect: A pointer to a TRect structure, whose members contain the coordinates for the upper left and lower right corners of the specified window.

Return Value

If this function succeeds, it returns TRUE; otherwise it returns FALSE. To get extended error information, call the GetLastError function.

See also

GetWindowPlacement, GetClientRect, SetWindowPlacement

Example

Please see Listing 5-21 under GetClientRect.

GetWindowText   Windows.Pas

Syntax

GetWindowText(	
hWnd: HWND;	{a handle to a window}
lpString: PChar;	{a pointer to a buffer to receive the string}
nMaxCount: Integer	{the maximum number of characters to copy}
): Integer;	{returns the length of the copied string}

Description

This function copies the specified window's title bar text into the given buffer. If the window is a control, the text within the control is copied to the buffer. This function sends a WM_GETTEXT message to the specified window.

Parameters

hWnd: A handle to the window containing the text to be copied to the buffer.

lpString: A pointer to the buffer that will receive the window text.

nMaxCount: Specifies the number of characters to be copied to the buffer. This number includes the terminating null character (i.e., if 21 is specified, 20 characters will be copied to the buffer, and the last character will be set to the null terminator). The window text is truncated if it contains more characters than what is specified in this parameter.

Return Value

If this function succeeds, it returns the length of the copied string, in bytes, excluding the terminating null character. If the function fails, or if there was no text in the specified window, it returns zero. To get extended error information, call the GetLastError function.

See also

GetWindowTextLength, SetWindowText, WM_GETTEXT

Example

Listing 5-29: Getting and Setting the Window Text

```
procedure TForm1.Button1Click(Sender: TObject);
var
   TheText: PChar;     // this will hold the window text
   TextLen: Integer;   // the length of the window text
begin
```

```
   {get the length of the window text}
   TextLen:=GetWindowTextLength(Form1.Handle);

   {dynamically allocate space based on the window text length}
   GetMem(TheText,TextLen);

   {get the window text. we must add 1 to account for the terminating null
    character}
   GetWindowText(Form1.Handle,TheText,TextLen+1);

   {display this text in the edit box}
   Edit1.Text:=string(TheText);

   {free the memory for the new string}
   FreeMem(TheText);

end;

procedure TForm1.Button2Click(Sender: TObject);
begin
   {set the text of the window to the string in the edit box}
   SetWindowText(Form1.Handle, PChar(Edit1.Text));
end;
```

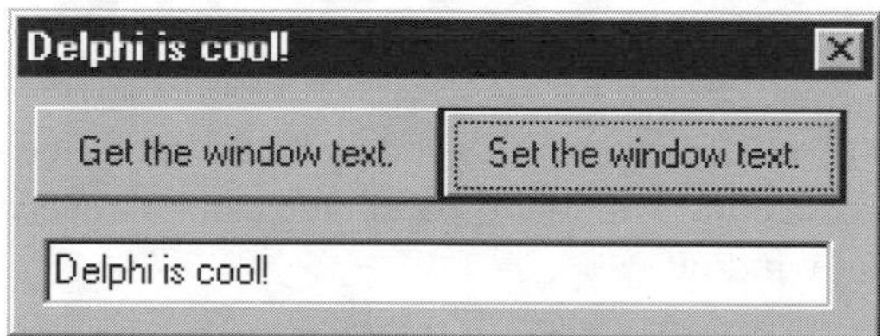

Figure 5-14: The window text has changed.

GetWindowTextLength Windows.Pas

Syntax

GetWindowTextLength(
hWnd: HWND {a handle to a window}
): Integer; {returns the length of the window text}

Description

This function retrieves the length of the text in the given window's title bar, in bytes. If the window is a control, the length of the text within the control is returned. This function sends a WM_GETTEXTLENGTH message to the given window. It is possible that this function will return a result larger than the actual size of the text when using a mixture of ANSI and Unicode functions within an application.

Parameters

hWnd: A handle to the window from which to extract the text length.

Return Value

If this function succeeds, it returns the length of the text in the given window, in bytes, excluding the terminating null character; otherwise it returns zero. To get extended error information, call the GetLastError function.

See also

GetWindowText, SetWindowText, WM_GETTEXT, WM_GETTEXTLENGTH

Example

Please see Listing 5-29 under GetWindowText.

IsChild Windows.Pas

Syntax

```
IsChild(
hWndParent: HWND;        {a handle to a parent window}
hWnd: HWND               {a handle to the window to test}
): BOOL;                 {returns TRUE or FALSE}
```

Description

This function tests a window to see if it is a child window of the specified parent window. The window is considered a child window if parentage can be traced from the window to the specified parent window.

Parameters

hWndParent: A handle to the parent window.

hWnd: A handle to the child window to be tested.

Return Value

If this function succeeds, and the window in the Wnd parameter is a child window of the window in the WndParent parameter, it returns TRUE. If the function fails, or the given window is not a child window of the specified parent window, it returns FALSE.

See also

EnumChildWindows, GetParent, IsWindow, SetParent

Example

Listing 5-30: Testing Child Window Status

See the Window Information application on the CD for a more practical example of the use of this function.

```
procedure TForm1.Button1Click(Sender: TObject);
```

```
begin
   {is this button a child of the main form?}
   if (IsChild(Form1.Handle,Button1.Handle)) then
      Button1.Caption:='TRUE'
   else
      Button1.Caption:='FALSE'
end;

procedure TForm1.Button2Click(Sender: TObject);
begin
   {is this button a child of the main form?
    (this button is in a panel, so it is the
    child of a child window)}
   if (IsChild(Form1.Handle,Button2.Handle)) then
      Button2.Caption:='TRUE'
   else
      Button2.Caption:='FALSE'
end;

procedure TForm1.Button3Click(Sender: TObject);
begin
   {is this button a child of the panel?
    (this button is outside of the panel)}
   if (IsChild(Panel1.Handle,Button3.Handle)) then
      Button3.Caption:='TRUE'
   else
      Button3.Caption:='FALSE'
end;
```

IsIconic Windows.Pas

Syntax

```
IsIconic(
hWnd: HWND              {a handle to a window}
): BOOL;                {returns TRUE or FALSE}
```

Description

This function tests the specified window to see if it is minimized.

Parameters

hWnd: A handle to the window being tested.

Return Value

If this function succeeds and the specified window is minimized, it returns TRUE. If the function fails, or the specified window is not minimized, it returns FALSE.

See also

ArrangeIconicWindows, CloseWindow, DestroyWindow, IsWindowVisible, IsZoomed, OpenIcon, ShowWindow, WM_SIZE

Example

Please see the CloseWindow function in the Window Movement Functions chapter in *The Tomes of Delphi 3: Win32 Graphical API.*

IsWindow Windows.Pas

Syntax

```
IsWindow(
hWnd: HWND                    {a potential handle to a window}
): BOOL;                      {returns TRUE or FALSE}
```

Description

This function will test the given window handle to determine if it identifies a valid, existing window.

Parameters

hWnd: The window handle being tested.

Return Value

If this function succeeds and the handle identifies an existing window, it returns TRUE. If this function fails, or the given window handle does not identify an existing window, it returns FALSE.

See also

EnumWindows, EnumChildWindows, GetWindow, FindWindow, FindWindowEx, IsWindowEnabled, IsWindowVisible

Example

Listing 5-31: Testing for a Valid Window Handle

See the Window Information application on the CD for a more practical example of the use of this function.

```
procedure TForm1.Button1Click(Sender: TObject);
begin
   {see if the button has a valid window handle}
   if (IsWindow(Button1.Handle)) then
      Button1.Caption:='TRUE'
   else
      Button1.Caption:='FALSE';
end;
```

IsWindowEnabled Windows.Pas

Syntax

```
IsWindowEnabled(
hWnd: HWND                    {a handle to a window to test}
): BOOL;                      {returns TRUE or FALSE}
```

Description

This function tests the specified window to see if it is enabled for mouse or keyboard input. A child window can receive input only if it is enabled and visible.

Parameters

hWnd: A handle to the window being tested.

Return Value

If this function succeeds and the specified window is enabled, it returns TRUE. If this function fails, or the specified window is disabled, it returns FALSE.

See also

EnableWindow, GetActiveWindow, GetFocus, IsWindowVisible, SetActiveWindow, SetFocus, WM_ENABLE

Example

Please see Listing 5-8 under EnableWindow.

IsWindowUnicode Windows.Pas

Syntax

```
IsWindowUnicode(
hWnd: HWND                    {a handle to a window to test}
): BOOL;                      {returns TRUE or FALSE}
```

Description

This function determines if the given window is a native Unicode window.

Parameters

hWnd: A handle to the window being tested.

Return Value

If the function succeeds and the specified window is a native Unicode window, it returns TRUE. If the function fails, or the specified window is not a native Unicode window, it returns FALSE.

See also

IsWindow

Example

Listing 5-32: Determining if a Window is a Unicode Window

See the Window Information application on the CD for a more practical example of the use of this function.

```
procedure TForm1.Button1Click(Sender: TObject);
begin
   {determine if the window is a Unicode window}
   if (IsWindowUnicode(Form1.Handle)) then
      Button1.Caption:='This window is a Unicode window'
   else
      Button1.Caption:='This window is not a Unicode window'
end;
```

IsWindowVisible   *Windows.Pas*

Syntax

IsWindowVisible(
hWnd: HWND {a handle to a window to test}
): BOOL; {returns TRUE or FALSE}

Description

This function determines if the specified window has the WS_VISIBLE style flag set. This function will return TRUE as long as the WS_VISIBLE style flag is set, even if the window is completely obscured by other windows or is not visible because it has been clipped by its parent window.

Parameters

hWnd: A handle to the window being tested.

Return Value

If this function succeeds and the specified window has the WS_VISIBLE style flag set, it returns TRUE. If the function fails, or the specified window does not have the WS_VISIBLE style set, it returns FALSE.

See also

BringWindowToTop, CloseWindow, FindWindow, GetWindowPlacement, SetWindow-Placement, ShowWindow

Example

Listing 5-33: Testing the Visibility of a Window

Two edit boxes have been placed on a form. One is visible, the other is not. See the Window Information application on the CD for a more practical example of the use of this function.

```
procedure TForm1.Button1Click(Sender: TObject);
begin
   {test Edit1 for visibility}
   if (IsWindowVisible(Edit1.Handle)) then
      Button1.Caption:='Edit1 is visible'
   else
      Button1.Caption:='Edit1 is not visible';
end;

procedure TForm1.Button2Click(Sender: TObject);
begin
   {test Edit2 for visibility}
   if (IsWindowVisible(Edit2.Handle)) then
      Button2.Caption:='Edit2 is visible'
   else
      Button2.Caption:='Edit2 is not visible';
end;
```

IsZoomed Windows.Pas

Syntax

IsZoomed(
hWnd: HWND {a handle to a window to test}
): BOOL; {returns TRUE or FALSE}

Description

This function tests the specified window to see if it is maximized.

Parameters

hWnd: A handle to the window to be tested.

Return Value

If the function succeeds and the window is maximized, it returns TRUE. If the function fails, or the window is not maximized, it returns FALSE.

See also

GetWindowPlacement, GetWindowRect, IsIconic, ShowWindow

Example

Listing 5-34: Testing for a Maximized State

See the Window Information application on the CD for a more practical example of the use of this function.

```
procedure TForm1.FormResize(Sender: TObject);
begin
   {indicate if the window is maximized or not}
   if (IsZoomed(Form1.Handle)) then
      Label1.Caption:='This window is zoomed'
   else
      Label1.Caption:='This window is not zoomed';
end;
```

RemoveProp Windows.Pas

Syntax

RemoveProp(
hWnd: HWND; {a handle to a window}
lpString: PChar {a pointer to a string}
): THandle; {returns a 32-bit value}

Description

This function removes the property associated with the specified string from the property list of the specified window. Before a window is destroyed, the application must remove all properties it has added to that window's property list. An application can only remove properties it has added, and should never remove properties added by other applications or by Windows.

Parameters

hWnd: A handle to a window whose property list is to be modified.

lpString: A pointer to a null-terminated string, or an atom identifying a string, that identifies the property entry to remove. If this parameter is an atom, the atom must have been created with a call to GlobalAddAtom. The atom, a 16-bit value, must be in the low-order word and the high-order word must be zero.

Return Value

If the function succeeds, it returns the 32-bit value associated with the specified string. If the function fails, or the string does not exist in the property list, it returns zero.

See also

EnumProps, EnumPropsEx, GetProp, SetProp

Example

Please see either Listing 5-10 under EnumProps or Listing 5-11 under EnumPropsEx.

SetActiveWindow Windows.Pas

Syntax

```
SetActiveWindow(
hWnd: HWND                    {a handle to a window to activate}
): HWND;                      {returns a handle to the previously active window}
```

Description

This function activates the specified window, giving it input focus. The window will only be brought to the foreground if the specified window is owned by the thread calling this function. Use the SetForegroundWindow to activate a window and force its associated thread into the foreground.

Parameters

hWnd: A handle to the top-level window to be activated.

Return Value

If this function succeeds, it returns a handle to the previously active window; otherwise it returns zero.

See also

GetActiveWindow, SetForegroundWindow, WM_ACTIVATE

Example

Listing 5-35: Toggling Active Windows

This code is put into the OnTimer event of a timer set to fire every 1000 milliseconds.

```
procedure TForm1.Timer1Timer(Sender: TObject);
var
   ActiveWindow: HWND;  // holds the currently active form handle
begin
   {get the current active form}
   ActiveWindow:=GetActiveWindow;

   {toggle the active form}
   if (ActiveWindow=Form1.Handle) then
      SetActiveWindow(Form2.Handle)
   else
      SetActiveWindow(Form1.Handle);
end;

procedure TForm1.FormShow(Sender: TObject);
```

```
begin
  {display form2}
  Form2.Show;
end;
```

SetClassLong Windows.Pas

Syntax

```
SetClassLong(
hWnd: HWND;                 {a handle to a window}
nIndex: Integer;            {the index of the value to change}
dwNewLong: Longint          {the new value}
): DWORD;                   {returns the previous value at the specified index}
```

Description

This function replaces the 32-bit value at the specified offset into the extra memory for the window class associated with the given window. This extra memory is reserved by specifying a value in the ClsExtra member of the TWndClass structure used when the RegisterClass function is called. In addition, this function can modify information about the window class by using one of the values in the following table for the nIndex parameter.

Parameters

hWnd: The handle to the window with the class memory to be modified.

nIndex: Specifies the zero-based byte offset for the 32-bit value to be set. This can be a value between zero and the number of bytes of extra class memory minus four (i.e., if 16 bytes of extra class memory are allocated, a value of 8 would index into the third 32-bit value). In addition, one of the values in Table 5-7 can be used to modify specific information about the class.

dwNewLong: The new 32-bit value to be used at the specified index.

Return Value

If this function succeeds, it returns the previous 32-bit value at the specified offset; otherwise it returns zero. To get extended error information, call the GetLastError function.

See also

GetClassInfo, GetClassInfoEx, GetClassLong, GetClassName, RegisterClass, RegisterClassEx, SetWindowLong

Example

Please see Listing 5-20 under GetClassLong.

Table 5-7: SetClassLong nIndex Values

Value	Description
GCL_CBCLSEXTRA	The size of the extra memory associated with this class, in bytes. Setting this value will not change the amount of memory already allocated.
GCL_CBWNDEXTRA	The size of the extra memory associated with each window of this class, in bytes. Setting this value will not change the amount of memory already allocated.
GCL_HBRBACKGROUND	The handle to the default background brush.
GCL_HCURSOR	The handle to the window class cursor.
GCL_HICON	The handle to the window class icon.
GCL_HICONSM	The handle to the window class small icon.
GCL_HMODULE	The handle of the module that registered the class.
GCL_MENUNAME	A pointer to the menu name string.
GCL_STYLE	The 32-bit style bits for this class.
GCL_WNDPROC	A pointer to the window procedure for this class. If a developer replaces the window procedure using this index, it must conform to the window procedure callback definition as outlined in the RegisterClass function. This subclass will affect all windows subsequently created with this class. An application should not subclass a window created by another process.

SetFocus Windows.Pas

Syntax

```
SetFocus(
hWnd: HWND                {a handle to a window}
): HWND;                  {returns a handle to the previous focus window}
```

Description

This function gives the specified window the keyboard input focus, activating the window or the parent of the window. It sends a WM_KILLFOCUS message to the window losing the keyboard input focus, and a WM_SETFOCUS message to the window receiving the keyboard input focus. If a window is active but no window has the keyboard input focus (the hWnd parameter was set to zero), any keys pressed will send a WM_SYSCHAR, WM_SYSKEYDOWN, or WM_SYSKEYUP message, as appropriate, to the active window's window procedure. In the event that the VK_MENU key is also pressed, the lParam of the messages will have bit 30 set. If the calling thread created the window associated with the window handle in the hWnd parameter, its keyboard focus status is set to this window.

Parameters

hWnd: A handle to the window that will receive keyboard focus. If this parameter is zero, keyboard input is ignored. (see above)

Return Value

If this function succeeds, it returns the handle of the window that previously had the keyboard input focus. If the function fails, the hWnd parameter has a handle to an invalid window, or there was no window that previously had keyboard focus, it returns zero.

See also

GetActiveWindow, GetFocus, SetActiveWindow, SetForegroundWindow, WM_KILLFOCUS, WM_SETFOCUS, WM_SYSCHAR, WM_SYSKEYDOWN, WM_SYSKEYUP

Example

Listing 5-36: Changing the Keyboard Input Focus

Note that this code is placed in the OnTimer event of a timer set to fire every 1000 milliseconds.

```
procedure TForm1.Timer1Timer(Sender: TObject);
var
   HasFocus: HWND;  // identifies a window
begin
   {determine which edit box has the keyboard focus}
   HasFocus:=GetFocus;

   {switch focus to the other edit box}
   if (HasFocus=Edit1.Handle) then
      Windows.SetFocus(Edit2.Handle)
   else
      Windows.SetFocus(Edit1.Handle);
end;
```

SetForegroundWindow   *Windows.Pas*

Syntax

```
SetForegroundWindow(
hWnd: HWND               {a handle to a window}
): BOOL;                 {returns TRUE or FALSE}
```

Description

This function activates the specified window, brings it to the top of the window Z-order, gives it keyboard input focus, and forces the thread that created the window into the foreground. Applications should use this function to force themselves into the foreground.

Parameters

hWnd: A handle to the window to be activated and brought to the foreground.

Return Value

If the function succeeds, it returns TRUE; otherwise it returns FALSE. To get extended error information, call the GetLastError function.

See also

GetForegroundWindow, SetActiveWindow, WM_ACTIVATE

Example

Listing 5-37: Bringing the Windows Explorer into the Foreground

```
{note that the Windows Explorer must be running for this example to work}
procedure TForm1.Button1Click(Sender: TObject);
var
   TheWindow: HWND;
begin
   {find a handle to the Windows Explorer window}
   TheWindow:=FindWindow('ExploreWClass',nil);

   {bring it into the foreground}
   SetForegroundWindow(TheWindow);
end;
```

SetParent Windows.Pas

Syntax

SetParent(	
hWndChild: HWND;	{a handle to a window whose parent is changing}
hWndNewParent: HWND	{a handle to the new parent window}
): HWND;	{returns a handle to the previous parent window}

Description

This function sets the parent window of the hWndChild window to the hWndNewParent window. Both windows must belong to the same application. If the child window is visible, Windows performs any necessary redrawing.

Parameters

hWndChild: A handle to a child window.

hWndNewParent: A handle to the new parent window. If this parameter is zero, the desktop window is assumed to be the new parent window.

Return Value

If the function succeeds, it returns a handle to the previous parent window; otherwise it returns zero. To get extended error information, call the GetLastError function.

See also

GetParent

Example

Listing 5-38: Changing a Button's Parent

This example has a button placed underneath a panel. The button and panel begin as siblings, but when the parent of the button is set to the panel, the button appears inside of the panel and is clipped to its boundaries.

```
procedure TForm1.Button1Click(Sender: TObject);
begin
   {the parent of button1 is currently the main form. this
    will set it to panel1, and the button will be displayed
    and clipped by the panel.}
   Windows.SetParent(Button2.Handle,Panel1.Handle);
end;
```

Before

After

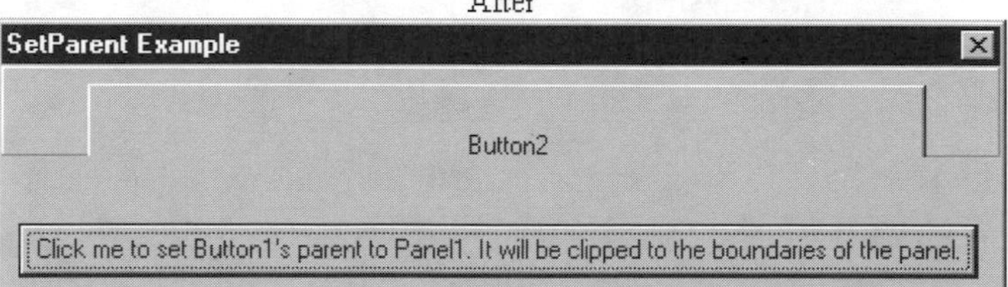

Figure 5-15: The button's parent has changed.

SetProp Windows.Pas

Syntax

SetProp(
hWnd: HWND; {a handle to a window}
lpString: PChar; {a pointer to a string}
hData: THandle {a 32-bit value}
): BOOL; {returns TRUE or FALSE}

Description

This function will add or modify a property list entry of the specified window. If the specified string does not exist in the property list, a new property entry is created. If the string does exist, the data value associated with the specified string is replaced by the new data value. Before a window is destroyed, an application must remove all property entries it has added by using the RemoveProp function.

Parameters

hWnd: A handle to the window whose property list is to be modified.

lpString: A pointer to a null-terminated string or an atom identifying a string. This string will be associated with the data value once it is added to the property list of the window. If this parameter is an atom, the atom must have been created with a call to GlobalAddAtom. The atom, a 16-bit value, must be in the low-order word and the high-order word must be zero.

hData: A 32-bit value that will be associated with the given string in the property list, and can be any value of use to the application.

Return Value

If the function succeeds, it returns TRUE; otherwise it returns FALSE.

See also

EnumProps, EnumPropsEx, GetProp, RemoveProp

Example

Please see either Listing 5-10 under EnumProps or Listing 5-11 under EnumPropsEx.

SetWindowLong   Windows.Pas

Syntax

```
SetWindowLong(
hWnd: HWND;                {a handle to a window}
nIndex: Integer;           {the index of the value to change}
dwNewLong: Longint         {the new value}
): Longint;                {returns the previous value at the specified index}
```

Description

This function replaces the 32-bit value at the specified offset into the extra memory for the window. This extra memory is reserved by specifying a value in the cbWndExtra member of the TWndClass structure used when the RegisterClass function is called. In addition, this function can modify information about the window by using one of the values in the following table for the nIndex parameter.

Parameters

hWnd: A handle to the window with the extra window memory to be modified.

nIndex: Specifies the zero-based byte offset for the value to be modified. This can be a value between zero and the number of bytes of extra window memory minus four (i.e., if 16 bytes of extra window memory are allocated, a value of 8 would index into the third 32-bit value). In addition, one of the values in Table 5-8 can be used to modify specific information about the window.

dwNewLong: The new 32-bit value to be used at the specified index.

Return Value

If the function succeeds, it returns the previous 32-bit value at the specified index; otherwise it returns zero. To get extended error information, call the GetLastError function.

If the function succeeds and the previous value at the specified index is zero, the return value will be zero. However, the last error information will not be cleared, making it difficult to determine if the function succeeded or failed. Developers should clear the last error information by calling the SetLastError function, passing it a value of 0, before calling the SetWindowLong function. If this is done, SetWindowLong failure will be indicated by a return value of zero and a nonzero return value from GetLastError.

See also

CallWindowProc, GetClassLong, GetWindowLong, RegisterClass, SetClassLong, SetParent

Example

Please see Listing 5-28 under GetWindowLong.

Table 5-8: SetWindowLong nIndex Values

Value	Description
GWL_EXSTYLE	The extended styles used by this window.
GWL_STYLE	The styles used by this window.
GWL_WNDPROC	A pointer to the window procedure for this window. If a developer replaces the window procedure using this index, it must conform to the window procedure callback definition as outlined in the RegisterClass function. The process of replacing a window procedure with a new one is called subclassing. An application should not subclass a window created by another process. A developer must pass any unhandled messages back to the original window procedure. This is accomplished by using the return value from this function with the CallWindowProc function to access the original window procedure.
GWL_HINSTANCE	The handle of the application instance.
GWL_HWNDPARENT	The handle to the parent window, if any.

Value	Description
GWL_ID	The identifier of the window.
GWL_USERDATA	The 32-bit user data value of this window. Every window has a 32-bit user data value that is intended for application-defined data associated with the window.

These values are available if the Wnd parameter specifies a dialog box:

Value	Description
DWL_DLGPROC	A pointer to the dialog box procedure for this dialog box. If a developer replaces the dialog box procedure using this index, it must conform to the dialog box procedure callback function as defined in the CreateDialog function. The process of replacing a dialog box procedure with a new one is called subclassing. An application should not subclass a dialog box created by another process. A developer must pass any unhandled messages back to the original window procedure. This is accomplished by using the return value from this function with the CallWindowProc function to access the dialog box procedure.
DWL_MSGRESULT	The return value of a message processed in the dialog box procedure.
DWL_USER	The 32-bit extra dialog box information.

SetWindowText *Windows.Pas*

Syntax

```
SetWindowText(
hWnd: HWND;                  {a handle to a window}
lpString: PChar              {a pointer to a string}
): BOOL;                     {returns TRUE or FALSE}
```

Description

This function changes the text in the title bar of the specified window. If the window is a control, the text in the control is changed. This function sends a WM_SETTEXT message to the specified window. Tab characters are not expanded, and will appear as a vertical bar.

Note that if the specified window is a list box control with the WS_CAPTION style specified, this function sets the text for the control, not for the list box entries.

Parameters

hWnd: A handle to a window whose text is to be changed.

lpString: A pointer to a null-terminated string. This string will become the text in the specified window or control.

Return Value

If the function succeeds, it returns TRUE; otherwise it returns FALSE. To get extended error information, call the GetLastError function.

See also

GetWindowText, GetWindowTextLength, WM_SETTEXT

Example

Please see Listing 5-29 under GetWindowText.

WindowFromPoint Windows.Pas

Syntax

```
WindowFromPoint(
Point: TPoint                  {coordinate information}
): HWND;                       {returns a handle to a window}
```

Description

This function returns the handle of the window containing the specified point. This function does not work with hidden or disabled windows.

Parameters

Point: Specifies a TPoint structure containing the coordinates to check. These coordinates are relative to the screen.

Return Value

If this function succeeds, it returns a handle to the window containing the specified point. If it fails, or there is not a window containing the specified point, it returns zero.

See also

ChildWindowFromPoint, ChildWindowFromPointEx, WindowFromDC

Example

Listing 5-39: Finding a Window at a Specific Coordinate

```
procedure TForm1.Button1Click(Sender: TObject);
var
   WindowText: array[0..255] of char;  // holds the text of the window
   TheWindow: HWND;                    // holds the window handle
   ThePoint: TPoint;                   // holds the coordinates to check
begin
```

```
    {fill in the coordinates}
    ThePoint.X:=5;
    ThePoint.Y:=5;

    {retrieve the window}
    TheWindow:=WindowFromPoint(ThePoint);

    {get the window text...}
    GetWindowText(TheWindow, WindowText, 255);

    {...and display it}
    Button1.Caption:=WindowText;
end;
```

Chapter 6

Process and Thread Functions

Multithreaded applications allow the developer to divide an executable into many smaller tasks that will execute independently of one another. The Windows API provides a number of functions concerned with the creation and synchronization of threads. Delphi includes a very efficient encapsulation of some of these API functions through its TThread object. This object allows an application to create threads that can interact with other elements of the VCL in a threadsafe manner, and allows the thread to take advantage of Delphi's exception handling mechanism.

It is important to note that multiple threads accessing GDI objects simultaneously will result in general protection faults. In order for multiple threads to access GDI objects, they must be synchronized using various methods found throughout this chapter.

Processes

A *process* consists of memory and resources. The memory in a process consists of three parts: stack, data, and code. The stack consists of all local variables and the call stack. Each new thread will have its own stack. Data consists of all variables that are not local and memory that is dynamically allocated. The code consists of the executable part of a program that is read only. These three parts are available to all threads in a single process. The process cannot do anything except hold a thread and memory. The process has an identifier that can be retrieved by calling the GetCurrentProcessId function. This process identifier is unique throughout the system.

Threads

A *thread* of execution is started when the processor begins executing code. The thread is owned by a process, and a process can own one or more threads. Each thread has its own stack and message queue. In addition, a thread can use thread local storage to allocate a memory block that all threads can use for storage. The TlsAlloc function allocates the storage area, and the TlsGetValue and TlsSetValue functions are used to manipulate the stored value. When one thread allocates local storage, the memory area is available to all threads, but each thread will see its own unique value when accessing the memory.

Critical Section

A *critical section* is a fast form of synchronization. It is used to protect a resource within a thread from manipulation by any other thread until the current thread has terminated. The application must declare a global variable of type TCriticalSection and initialize it using the InitializeCriticalSection function. When the thread function begins, it calls EnterCriticalSection. Once the critical section is entered, no other thread has access to the resource until the current thread calls the LeaveCriticalSection function.

Semaphores

A *semaphore* object is used as another form of thread synchronization. A semaphore object can be locked by multiple threads up to a set threshold. This threshold is determined when the semaphore object is created by calling the CreateSemaphore function. A semaphore can be used to synchronize multiple threads across process boundaries and may be locked by the same thread multiple times.

Mutexes

A *mutex* is a form of synchronization that will only allow one thread to access a resource at a time, across process boundaries. Mutex stands for MUTual EXclusion and it is akin to what is called a binary semaphore. A binary semaphore is a semaphore where only one thread can lock the object.

Events

An *event* object is a synchronization object that is under the direct control of the programmer. Instead of changing state as a result of calling one of the wait functions (such as WaitForSingleObject), the programmer can use three different functions to control the state of the object. The SetEvent function sets the state of the event object to signaled, the ResetEvent function sets the state of the event object to nonsignaled, and the PulseEvent function quickly sets the state of the event object to signaled and then nonsignaled. A deadlock can occur when a thread is suspended in a permanent wait state as a result of a lost event object. If PulseEvent or SetEvent is used with an auto reset event and no threads are waiting, the event object is lost and a deadlock will occur. When the event object is created, the application can determine if it will be a manual or automatic reset event. Manual reset events remain signaled until explicitly reset to nonsignaled by a call to the ResetEvent function. Auto reset events remain signaled until a single waiting thread is released, at which point the system automatically sets the state to nonsignaled.

Interlocked Variables

An *interlocked variable* is a 32-bit variable that is accessed sequentially by any number of threads in a threadsafe manner. The InterlockedIncrement and Interlocked-Decrement functions allow the application to increment or decrement the variable and compare its return value with zero all in one function. The InterlockedExchange function exchanges the current value of the variable with a new one, returning the old value.

Priority Levels

The system determines when a thread gets a quantum of CPU time based on its priority level. Each process has a priority class, which determines that process' thread's base priority level. Each thread in turn has its own priority level. Processes and threads with high priority levels take precedence over those with lower priorities. Low priority levels are used for threads that monitor system activity, such as screen savers. High priority threads should only be used for time critical events or for threads that must communicate directly with hardware and cannot tolerate interruptions.

Processes and Thread Functions

The following process and thread functions are covered in this chapter:

Table 6-1: Process and Thread Functions

Function	Description
CreateEvent	Creates an event object.
CreateMutex	Creates a mutex object.
CreateProcess	Launches another application.
CreateSemaphore	Creates a semaphore object.
CreateThread	Creates and executes a thread.
DeleteCriticalSection	Deletes a critical section.
DuplicateHandle	Duplicates a handle.
EnterCriticalSection	Enters a critical section.
ExitProcess	Terminates a process
ExitThread	Terminates a thread.
GetCurrentProcess	Retrieves a handle to the current process.
GetCurrentProcessId	Retrieves the current process' identifier.
GetCurrentThread	Retrieves a handle to the current thread.
GetCurrentThreadId	Retrieves the current thread's identifier.
GetExitCodeProcess	Retrieves the exit code from a terminated process.
GetExitCodeThread	Retrieves the exit code from a terminated thread.
GetPriorityClass	Retrieves the priority class of the process.

Function	Description
GetThreadPriority	Retrieves the priority level of a thread.
GetWindowThreadProcessId	Retrieves the specified window's process and thread identifiers.
InitializeCriticalSection	Initializes a critical section for use.
InterlockedDecrement	Decrements an interlocked variable.
InterlockedExchange	Exchanges the value of an interlocked variable.
InterlockedIncrement	Increments an interlocked variable.
LeaveCriticalSection	Leaves the critical section.
OpenEvent	Opens a handle to an existing event object.
OpenMutex	Opens a handle to an existing mutex object.
OpenProcess	Opens a handle to an existing process.
OpenSemaphore	Opens a handle to an existing semaphore object.
PulseEvent	Rapidly sets the state of an event object to signaled and unsignaled.
ReleaseMutex	Releases ownership of a mutex object.
ReleaseSemaphore	Releases ownership of a semaphore object.
ResetEvent	Resets an event object to an unsignaled state.
ResumeThread	Allows a previously suspended thread to resume execution.
SetEvent	Sets.the state of an event object to signaled.
SetPriorityClass	Sets the priority class of the process.
SetThreadPriority	Sets the priority level of a thread.
Sleep	Suspends a thread for a specific period of time.
SuspendThread	Suspends a thread indefinitely.
TerminateProcess	Terminates the specified process and all of its threads.
TerminateThread	Terminates a thread without allowing it to perform cleanup routines.
TlsAlloc	Allocates a thread local storage index.
TlsFree	Frees an allocated thread local storage index.
TlsGetValue	Retrieves a value from a thread local storage index.
TlsSetValue	Sets a value into a thread local storage index.
WaitForInputIdle	Suspends the calling thread until the specified process is waiting for user input.
WaitForSingleObject	Suspends the calling thread until the specified object becomes signaled.

CreateEvent Windows.Pas

Syntax

```
CreateEvent(
lpEventAttributes: PSecurityAttributes;    {pointer to security attributes}
bManualReset: BOOL;                        {flag for manual reset event}
bInitialState: BOOL;                       {flag for initial state}
lpName: PChar                              {name of the event object}
): THandle;                                {returns a handle of the event object}
```

Description

Creates an event object that is signaled or nonsignaled. The handle returned by CreateEvent has EVENT_ALL_ACCESS access to the new event object and can be used in any function that requires a handle of an event object. An event object is under the direct control of the programmer, with the functions SetEvent, ResetEvent, and PulseEvent. A deadlock occurs when two threads wait on each other indefinitely.

Parameters

lpEventAttributes: A pointer to a record that holds the security attributes information. If this parameter is set to NIL, the event object will have default security attributes. Please see the CreateFile function for a description of the TSecurityAttributes structure.

bManualReset: Specifies whether a manual-reset or auto-reset event object is created. If TRUE, the ResetEvent function must be used to reset the state to nonsignaled. If FALSE, Windows automatically resets the state to nonsignaled after a single waiting thread has been released.

bInitialState: Specifies the initial state of the event object. If TRUE, the initial state is signaled; otherwise it is nonsignaled.

lpName: A pointer to a null-terminated string specifying the name of the event. The name is limited to a maximum size of MAX_PATH characters and can contain any characters except the backslash ("\").

Note: Name comparison is case sensitive.

If this parameter matches the name of any existing event object, the function requests EVENT_ALL_ACCESS access to the existing event object. If this occurs, the previous parameters of bInitialState and bManualReset are ignored because they have already been set by the creating process. The lpName parameter can be set to NIL, in which case the event is created without a name. If the name matches an existing semaphore, mutex, or file mapping object, then the function fails. In this instance, a call to GetLastError() will return ERROR_INVALID_HANDLE.

Return Value

If the function succeeds, it returns a handle to the event object. If the function fails, it returns zero. To get extended error information, call the GetLastError function.

See also

CloseHandle, CreateProcess, DuplicateHandle, OpenEvent, ResetEvent, SetEvent, WaitForSingleObject

Example

Listing 6-1: Creating an Event and Waiting for it

```
var
  Form1: TForm1;
  EventHandle: THandle;     // holds the event handle
  ThreadHandle: THandle;    // holds the thread handle

implementation

{$R *.DFM}

function ThreadFunction(Info: Pointer): Integer; stdcall;
var
  FormDC: HDC;          // holds a handle to the form device context
  Counter: Integer;     // general loop counter
  CounterStr: string;   // a string representation of the loop counter
  ObjRtn: Integer;      // wait function return value
begin
  {WaitForSingleObject will wait for the event to
   become signaled (ready to do something)}
  ObjRtn := WaitForSingleObject(EventHandle, INFINITE);

  {retrieve a handle to the form's device context}
  FormDC := GetDC(Form1.Handle);

  {begin a large loop}
  for Counter := 1 to 100000 do
  begin
    {display the counter value}
    CounterStr := IntToStr(Counter);
    TextOut(FormDC, 10, 10, PChar(CounterStr), Length(CounterStr));

    {process any pending messages}
    Application.ProcessMessages;

    {this causes the loop to pause, as the PulseEvent function
     rapidly sets the event's signaled state to signaled and
     then unsignaled}
    ObjRtn := WaitForSingleObject(EventHandle, INFINITE);
  end;
```

```
  {release the form's device context and exit the thread}
  ReleaseDC(Form1.Handle, FormDC);
  ExitThread(4);
end;

procedure TForm1.Button1Click(Sender: TObject);
var
  ThreadID: Integer;    // holds the thread identifier
begin
  {create a new thread}
  ThreadHandle := CreateThread(nil, 0, @ThreadFunction, nil, 0, ThreadId);
end;

procedure TForm1.Button2Click(Sender: TObject);
begin
  {indicate that the event is signaled.  This will cause the waiting
   thread to get past the WaitForSingleObject function, thus starting
   the loop}
  SetEvent(EventHandle);
  Label1.Caption := 'Event is signaled';
end;

procedure TForm1.Button3Click(Sender: TObject);
begin
  {reset the event object to a nonsignaled state.  this will
   cause the thread loop to pause at the WaitForSingleObject
   function inside the loop}
  ResetEvent(EventHandle);
  Label1.Caption := 'Event is nonsignaled';
end;

procedure TForm1.Button4Click(Sender: TObject);
begin
  {if the event has been reset (above), the thread's loop will be
   paused at the internal WaitForSingleObject function. PulseEvent
   will toggle the event's state from nonsignaled to signaled and back,
   causing the thread's loop to fire once.}
  PulseEvent(EventHandle); //Set to signaled and then nonsignaled
  Label1.Caption := 'signaled/nonsignaled';
end;

procedure TForm1.Button5Click(Sender: TObject);
begin
  {create the event}
  EventHandle := CreateEvent(Nil, True, False, 'MyEvent');
end;
```

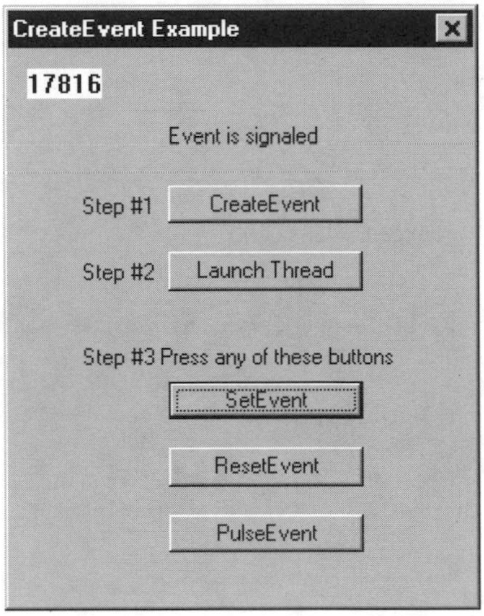

Figure 6-1: The event was created.

CreateMutex Windows.Pas

Syntax

```
CreateMutex(
lpMutexAttributes: PSecurityAttributes; {a pointer to security attributes}
bInitialOwner: BOOL;                    {flag for the initial ownership}
lpName: PChar                           {mutex object name}
): THandle;                             {returns a handle of the mutex object}
```

Description

This function creates a named or unnamed mutex object. Mutex is an acronym for MUTual EXclusion. A mutex is like a semaphore but is optimized by the operating system. It will act like a binary semaphore that will only allow one thread to own it at any given time. The mutex can be specified in any of the wait functions (i.e., WaitForSingleObject) across processes or within the same process. When a thread uses a wait function with a mutex, it owns the mutex until it calls ReleaseMutex. The thread that has ownership of the mutex can call wait functions with the same mutex specified more than once without fear of blocking its own execution. However, for each call to a wait function within the same thread and using the same mutex, the ReleaseMutex function must be called. Multiple processes can call CreateMutex with the same name specified. This action will cause the second call to only open a handle to the existing mutex, not create a new one. Set bInitialOwner to FALSE in this situation. CloseHandle will close the handle to a mutex. The handle is automatically closed when the process that opened the handle is closed. When the last handle to the mutex is closed, the mutex is destroyed.

Parameters

lpMutexAttributes: A pointer to a TSecurityAttributes record that describes the security attributes of the mutex object. Please see the CreateFile function for a description of this data structure. If this parameter is set to NIL, the mutex will have the default security attributes and the handle is not inheritable.

bInitialOwner: Specifies mutex ownership. If this parameter is set to TRUE, the calling thread requests immediate ownership of the mutex; otherwise the mutex is not owned.

lpName: A pointer to a null-terminating string specifying the name of the created mutex.

Return Value

If the function succeeds, it returns the handle of the mutex that is created. The handle will have MUTEX_ALL_ACCESS access to the mutex. If the function fails, it returns zero. To get extended error information, call the GetLastError function. If the lpName parameter contains a mutex name that already exists, then GetLastError will return ERROR_ALREADY_EXISTS.

See also

CloseHandle, CreateProcess, DuplicateHandle, OpenMutex, ReleaseMutex, WaitForSingleObject

Example

Listing 6-2: Using a Mutex to Synchronize Thread Execution

```
function ThreadFunc0(Info: Pointer): Integer; stdcall
var
  ICount: Integer;        // general loop counter
  CountStr: string;       // holds a string representation of the counter
begin
  {wait for the mutex to become signaled. the mutex is created signaled so
  this thread gets ownership of the mutex and starts immediately}
  WaitForSingleObject(Form1.MutexHandle, INFINITE);

  {start a counter to display something}
  for ICount := 1 to 10000 do
  begin
    CountStr := IntToStr(ICount);
    Form1.Canvas.TextOut(10, 10, 'Thread 1 '+CountStr);
  end;

  {Release ownership of the mutex so the other threads can fire}
  ReleaseMutex(Form1.MutexHandle);
  ExitThread(1);
end;

function ThreadFunc1(Info: Pointer): Integer; stdcall
var
  ICount: Integer;        // general loop counter
```

```
  CountStr: string;       // holds a string representation of the counter
begin
  {wait for the mutex to become signaled. The mutex is created signaled so
  this thread gets ownership of the mutex and starts immediately}
  WaitForSingleObject(Form1.MutexHandle, INFINITE);

  {start a counter to display something}
  for ICount := 1 to 10000 do
  begin
    CountStr := IntToStr(ICount);
    Form1.Canvas.TextOut(110, 10, 'Thread 2 '+CountStr);
  end;

  {Release ownership of the mutex so the other threads can fire}
  ReleaseMutex(Form1.MutexHandle);
  ExitThread(2);
end;

function ThreadFunc2(Info: Pointer): Integer; stdcall
var
  ICount: Integer;            // general loop counter
  CountStr: string;           // holds a string representation of the counter
  LocalMutexHandle: THandle; // holds a handle to the mutex
begin
  {open a Handle to the mutex from this thread}
  LocalMutexHandle := OpenMutex(MUTEX_ALL_ACCESS, FALSE, 'MyMutex');

  {take ownership of the mutex. This will wait until the mutex is signaled}
  WaitForSingleObject(LocalMutexHandle, INFINITE);

  {start a counter to display something}
  for ICount := 1 to 10000 do
  begin
    CountStr := IntToStr(ICount);
    Form1.canvas.TextOut(210, 10, 'Thread 3 '+CountStr);
  end;

  {Release ownership of the mutex}
  ReleaseMutex(LocalMutexHandle);

  {close the mutex handle}
  CloseHandle(LocalMutexHandle);
  ExitThread(3);
end;

procedure TForm1.CreateThreadClick(Sender: TObject);
var
  ThreadId0, ThreadId1, ThreadId2: Integer; // holds thread identifiers
begin
  {Create the mutex with the name MyMutex. The mutex is signaled
   so the first thread will start immediately}
  MutexHandle := CreateMutex(nil, False, 'MyMutex');

  {Create the first thread, and start it immediately}
  ThreadHandle := Windows.CreateThread(nil, 0, @ThreadFunc0, nil, 0, ThreadId0);
```

```
  {Create the second thread, and start it immediately}
  ThreadHandle1 := Windows.CreateThread(nil,0, @ThreadFunc1, nil, 0, ThreadId1);

  {Create the third thread, and start it immediately}
  ThreadHandle2 := Windows.CreateThread(nil,0, @ThreadFunc2, nil, 0, ThreadId2);

  {Stop the main thread for a short time so that the other threads get
   a chance to take ownership of the mutex before the main thread
   calls WaitForSingleObject}
  Sleep(1000);

  {Take ownership of the mutex; this will wait until the mutex is signaled}
  WaitForSingleObject(MutexHandle, INFINITE);

  {Close the mutexHandle so that this will work again}
  CloseHandle(MutexHandle);
end;
```

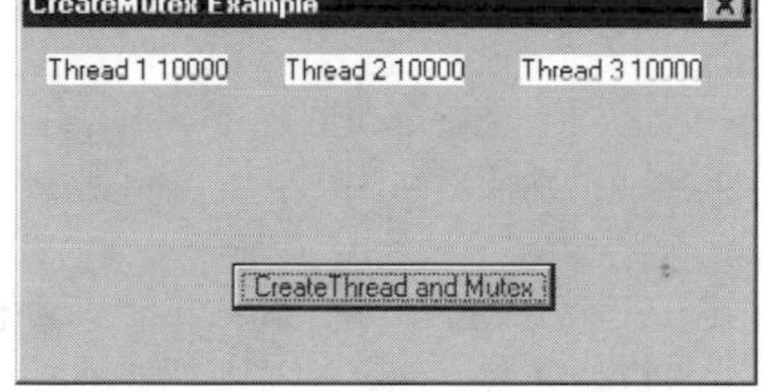

Figure 6-2: The threads fire one at a time.

CreateProcess Windows.Pas

Syntax

```
CreateProcess(
lpApplicationName: PChar;                    {pointer to name of application}
lpCommandLine: PChar;                        {pointer to command line of application}
lpProcessAttributes,                         {pointer to process security attributes}
lpThreadAttributes: PSecurityAttributes;     {pointer to the thread security attributes}
bInheritHandles: BOOL;                       {inheritance flag}
dwCreationFlags: DWORD;                      {creation flag}
lpEnvironment: Pointer;                      {pointer to environment block}
lpCurrentDirectory: PChar;                   {pointer to the current directory}
const lpStartupInfo: TStartupInfo;           {pointer to a TStartupInfo data structure}
var lpProcessInformation:                    {pointer to a TProcessInformation
      TProcessInformation                          data structure}
): BOOL;                                     {returns TRUE or FALSE}
```

Description

This function will create a new process and its primary thread. The primary thread created will have an initial stack size that is specified in the header of the executable, and the thread will begin execution at the executable image's entry point. The entry point of a Delphi executable is set by choosing Project|Options, clicking on the Linker page, and modifying the image base setting. The default value for the image base should never need to be modified.

Parameters

lpApplicationName: A pointer to a null-terminated string that specifies the name of the executable. If this parameter is set to NIL, the lpCommandLine parameter must contain the path and executable name (i.e., C:\Windows\Wordpad.exe Readme.txt). Under Windows NT, this parameter should be set to NIL and the lpCommandLine parameter should be used to specify the executable name.

lpCommandLine: A null-terminated string that specifies the command line for the executable. If this parameter is set to NIL, the lpApplicationName parameter can be used for the command line of the application. If neither of these parameters are set to NIL, the lpApplicationName parameter will indicate the path and name of the application, and the lpCommandLine parameter will indicate the command line of the application. If the lpApplicationName parameter is set to NIL, the first space delimited portion of the lpCommandLine parameter will be the application name. If the EXE extension is not given, it will be appended unless there is a (.) in the filename or the filename contains the path.

lpProcessAttributes: A pointer to a TSecurityAttributes structure that specifies the security descriptor for the process. If this parameter is set to NIL, the process will have the default security descriptor and is not inheritable. See the CreateFile function for a description of this parameter.

lpThreadAttributes: A pointer to a TSecurityAttributes structure that specifies the security descriptor for the thread of the process. If this parameter is set to NIL, the thread will have the default security descriptor and is not inheritable. See the CreateFile function for a description of this parameter.

bInheritHandles: Indicates if the new process will inherit handles opened by the calling process. If this parameter is set to TRUE, the created process will inherit all the open handles of the calling process. The inherited handles will have the same value and access privileges as the original handles.

dwCreationFlags: Specifies the creation of the process and control of the priority class. Priority class defaults to NORMAL_PRIORITY_CLASS. If the creating process has a priority class of IDLE_PRIORITY_CLASS, the child default priority class will be IDLE_PRIORITY_CLASS. This parameter can contain any combination of values from the following Creation Flags table, and one value from the following Priority Class table.

lpEnvironment: A pointer to an environment block for the new process. If this parameter is set to NIL, the new process will use the environment of the calling process. Please see the GetEnvironmentStrings function for more information.

lpCurrentDirectory: A null-terminated string specifying the current drive and directory for the new process. If this parameter is set to NIL, the new process will have the same current directory as the calling process.

lpStartupInfo: A pointer to a TStartupInfo structure that specifies how the main window of the new process should appear. Please see the GetStartupInfo function for more information.

lpProcessInformation: A variable of type TProcessInformation that receives information about the new process. The TProcessInformation data structure is defined as:

```
TProcessInformation = record
    hProcess: THandle;          {the process handle}
    hThread: THandle;           {a handle to the primary thread}
    dwProcessId: DWORD;         {a global process identifier}
    dwThreadId: DWORD;          {a global thread identifier}
end;
```

hProcess: A handle to the newly created process.
hThread: A handle to the primary thread of the newly created process.
dwProcessId: A global process identifier used to identify a process.
dwThreadId: A global thread identifier used to identify a thread.

Return Value

If the function succeeds, it returns TRUE; otherwise it returns FALSE. To get extended error information, call the GetLastError function.

See also

CloseHandle, CreateThread, ExitProcess, ExitThread, GetCommandLine, GetEnvironmentStrings, GetExitCodeProcess, GetFullPathName, GetStartupInfo, GetSystemDirectory, GetWindowsDirectory, OpenProcess, ResumeThread, TerminateProcess, WaitForInputIdle

Example

Please see Listing 6-3 under CreateSemaphore.

Table 6-2: CreateProcess dwCreationFlags Creation Flags Values

Value	Description
CREATE_DEFAULT_ERROR_MODE	The new process will get the current default error mode instead of the error mode of the calling process.
CREATE_NEW_CONSOLE	The new process will not inherit the parent's console; it will have its own. This flag cannot be used with the DETACHED_PROCESS flag.

Value	Description
CREATE_NEW_PROCESS_GROUP	The new process will be the root process of a new process group. A process group consist of the root process and all the descendants.
CREATE_SEPARATE_WOW_VDM	Windows NT only: This flag is only valid when starting a 16-bit application. The resulting process will run in its own private Virtual DOS Machine (VDM). By default, 16-bit Windows applications run in a shared VDM. Running a 16-bit application in a separate VDM has the advantage of letting one 16-bit application continue when another 16-bit application hangs during input.
CREATE_SHARED_WOW_VDM	Windows NT only: This flag is only valid when starting a 16-bit application. This flag will cause the function to override the setting in the Win.ini for the DefaultSeparateVDM=TRUE and run the new process in the shared Virtual DOS Machine.
CREATE_SUSPENDED	The primary thread of the new process is created and suspended, and will not begin executing until the ResumeThread function is called.
CREATE_UNICODE_ENVIRONMENT	The block pointed to by lpEnvironment uses Unicode characters; otherwise the environment uses ANSI characters.
DEBUG_PROCESS	The calling process will be treated as a debugger and the called process as a process being debugged. When this flag is used, only the calling process can call the WaitForDebugEvent function.
DEBUG_ONLY_THIS_PROCESS	If this flag is not set and the calling process is being debugged, the new process becomes another process being debugged by the debugger. If the calling process is not being debugged, no debugging occurs.
DETACHED_PROCESS	The new process will not have access to the console of the calling process. This flag cannot be used with the CREATE_NEW_CONSOLE flag.

Table 6-3: CreateProcess dwCreationFlags Priority Class Values

Value	Description
HIGH_PRIORITY_CLASS	Indicates time-critical tasks that must be executed immediately to run smoothly. The threads of a high-priority class process preempt the threads of normal or idle priority class processes. An example is the Windows Task List, which must be responsive to the user. HIGH_PRIORITY_CLASS can use nearly all cycles of a CPU, so use care when specifying this priority.
IDLE_PRIORITY_CLASS	A process with this priority will be preempted by all higher priority classes. A screen saver is a good example. This priority class is inherited by child processes.
NORMAL_PRIORITY_CLASS	This priority class has no special scheduling needs, and is the default priority.
REALTIME_PRIORITY_CLASS	This is the highest possible priority class. The threads of this priority class will preempt any other threads of a lower priority class, including operating system processes performing important tasks. A real-time process that executes for a long interval (for a computer) can cause the mouse to be unresponsive or disk caches not to function. Be very careful when using this priority class.

CreateSemaphore Windows.Pas

Syntax

```
CreateSemaphore(
lpSemaphoreAttributes:            {pointer to a TSecurityAttributes
      PSecurityAttributes;              structure}
lInitialCount: Longint;           {initial count}
lMaximumCount: Longint;           {maximum count}
lpName: PChar                     {pointer to the name of the semaphore object}
): THandle;                       {returns handle of semaphore object returned}
```

Description

This function creates a named or unnamed semaphore object. The handle returned by CreateSemaphore has SEMAPHORE_ALL_ACCESS access to the new semaphore object and can be used in any function that requires a handle to a semaphore object, such as the wait functions or DuplicateHandle. Single-object wait functions return when the state of the specified object is signaled. Multiple-object wait functions can be instructed to return either when only one or all of the specified objects are signaled. When a wait function returns, the waiting thread is released to continue its execution.

The state of a semaphore object is signaled when its count is greater than zero, and nonsignaled when its count is equal to zero. The lInitialCount parameter specifies the initial count. Each time a waiting thread is released because of the semaphore's signaled state, the count of the semaphore is decreased by one. The ReleaseSemaphore function will increment a semaphore's count by a specified amount. The count can never be less than zero or greater than the value specified in the lMaximumCount parameter. Multiple processes can have access to the same semaphore object, enabling use of the object, enabling synchronization across process boundaries. If the lpSemaphoreAttributes parameter of CreateSemaphore is set to enable inheritance, the handle returned by CreateSemaphore may be inherited by a child process created with CreateProcess. The handle returned by the CreateSemaphore function can be duplicated with a call to DuplicateHandle.

Parameters

lpSemaphoreAttributes: A pointer to a TSecurityAttributes structure that specifies the security descriptor for the semaphore. If this parameter is set to NIL, the semaphore will have the default security descriptor and is not inheritable. See the CreateFile function for a description of this parameter.

lInitialCount: Sets the initial count for the semaphore, and must be greater than or equal to zero. If this parameter is zero, the state of the semaphore is nonsignaled. Whenever a wait function releases a thread that was waiting for the semaphore, the count is decreased by one.

lMaximumCount: Sets the maximum count of the semaphore, and must be greater than zero.

lpName: A null-terminated string containing the name of the semaphore. The name is limited to a maximum size of MAX_PATH characters. The name contained in this parameter is case sensitive. The name may contain any character except the backslash character. If this parameter is set to NIL, the semaphore object is created without a name. If the name matches another semaphore object, the function will request SEMAPHORE_ALL_ACCESS access to the object. Semaphore, mutex, event, and file mapping objects all share the same address space, so the function will fail if the name matches any other semaphore. In this situation, a call to GetLastError will return ERROR_INVALID_HANDLE.

Return Value

If the function succeeds, it returns a handle to the semaphore object. If there is an existing semaphore with the same name before the call to CreateSemaphore, a call to GetLastError will return ERROR_ALREADY_EXISTS. If the function fails, it returns zero.

See also

CloseHandle, CreateProcess, DuplicateHandle, OpenSemaphore, ReleaseSemaphore, WaitForSingleObject

Example

Listing 6-3: Creating a Semaphore to Synchronize Multiple Processes

```
procedure TForm1.ShowProgress;
var
  ICount: Integer;    // general loop counter
begin
  {wait for the semaphore, and get ownership}
  WaitForSingleObject(SemaphoreHandle, INFINITE);

  {display a visual indicator}
  for ICount := 1 to 1000 do
  begin
    Gauge1.Progress := ICount;
  end;

  {release the semaphore}
  ReleaseSemaphore(Form1.SemaphoreHandle, 1, nil);
end;

procedure TForm1.Button1Click(Sender: TObject);
var
  StartUpInfo: TStartUpInfo;         // holds startup information
  ProcessInfo: TProcessInformation; // holds process information
  CurDir: string;                    // holds the current directory
begin
  {create the semaphore, nonsignaled}
  SemaphoreHandle := CreateSemaphore(nil, 0, 2, 'MikesSemaphore');

  {initialize the startup info structure}
  FillChar(StartupInfo, SizeOf(TStartupInfo), 0);
  with StartupInfo do
  begin
    cb := SizeOf(TStartupInfo);
    dwFlags := STARTF_USESHOWWINDOW;
    wShowWindow := SW_SHOWNORMAL;
  end;

  {launch the semaphore sibling program for the example}
  CurDir := ExtractFilePath(ParamStr(0))+'ProjectOpenSemaphore.exe';
  CreateProcess(PChar(CurDir), nil, nil, nil, False,
      NORMAL_PRIORITY_CLASS, nil, nil, StartupInfo, ProcessInfo);
end;

procedure TForm1.Button2Click(Sender: TObject);
var
  OldValue: DWORD;  // holds the previous semaphore count
begin
  {release the semaphore}
  ReleaseSemaphore(SemaphoreHandle, 2, @OldValue);

  {start the visual indication}
  ShowProgress;
end;
```

Listing 6-4: The Semaphore Sibling Program

```
procedure TForm1.Button1Click(Sender: TObject);
var
  ICount: Integer;              // general loop counter
  SemaphoreHandle: THandle;     // holds the semaphore handle
  PrevCount: DWORD;             // holds the previous semaphore counter
begin
  {Open a handle to the semaphore}
  SemaphoreHandle := OpenSemaphore($00f0000 or $00100000 or $3, FALSE,
                                   'MikesSemaphore');

  {wait to achieve ownership of the semaphore}
  WaitForSingleObject(SemaphoreHandle, INFINITE);

  {display a visual indication}
  for ICount := 1 to 100000 do
  begin
    Gauge1.Progress := ICount;
  end;

  {release the semaphore}
  ReleaseSemaphore(SemaphoreHandle, 1, @PrevCount);
end;
```

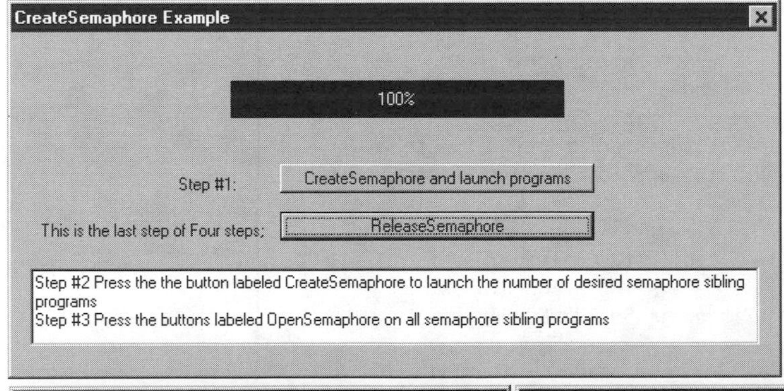

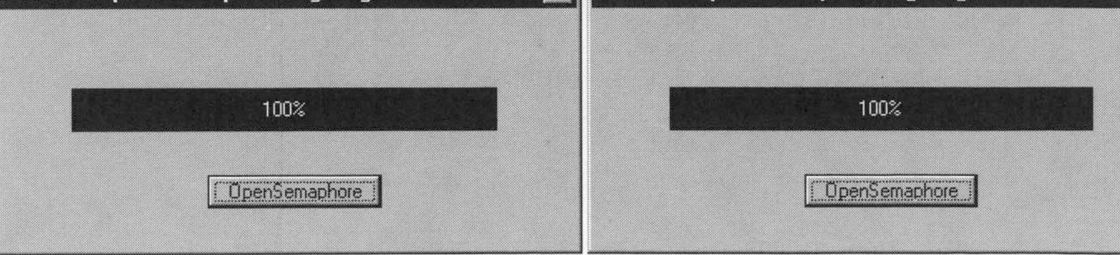

Figure 6-3: The processes were synchronized.

CreateThread Windows.Pas

Syntax

```
CreateThread(
lpThreadAttributes: Pointer;              {a pointer to a TSecurityAttributes structure}
dwStackSize: DWORD;                       {initial stack size of the thread in bytes}
lpStartAddress: TFNThreadStartRoutine;    {address of the thread routine}
lpParameter: Pointer;                     {argument of the new thread}
dwCreationFlags: DWORD;                   {creation flags}
var lpThreadId: DWORD                     {address of the thread ID}
): THandle;                               {returns the handle of the new thread}
```

Description

This function creates and executes a new thread. The resulting thread will occupy the same address space as the calling process. The thread execution begins at the address of the lpStartAddress parameter. The GetExitCodeThread function will return the exit code of the thread. The thread created has a THREAD_PRIORITY_NORMAL priority. To set the priority of the thread, call the SetThreadPriority function.

Parameters

lpThreadAttributes: A pointer to a TSecurityAttributes structure that specifies the security descriptor for the thread. If this parameter is set to NIL, the thread will have the default security descriptor and is not inheritable. See the CreateFile function for a description of this parameter.

dwStackSize: Specifies the initial stack size for the thread. If this parameter is set to zero, the thread will have the same stack size as the main thread of the process. The stack size of the thread may grow if necessary.

lpStartAddress: A pointer to a thread function. The function must use the stdcall calling convention. It must take a pointer parameter and return a LongInt.

lpParameter: A pointer to the parameter that is passed to the function.

dwCreationFlags: Controls the creation of the thread. If CREATE_SUSPENDED is specified, the thread will not run until the ResumeThread function is called. If this parameter is set to zero, the thread will run immediately.

lpThreadId: A variable that receives the identifier of the new thread. This value is unique for the entire system.

Return Value

If the function succeeds, it returns the handle of the created thread. If the function fails, it returns zero. To get extended error information, call the GetLastError function.

See also

CloseHandle, CreateProcess, ExitProcess, ExitThread, GetExitCodeThread, GetThreadPriority, ResumeThread, SetThreadPriority

Example

Please see Listing 6-12 under InitializeCriticalSection, and other examples throughout the chapter.

DeleteCriticalSection Windows.Pas

Syntax

```
DeleteCriticalSection(
var lpCriticalSection: TRTLCriticalSection    {pointer to the critical section object}
);                                            {this procedure does not return a value}
```

Description

This function will delete the specified critical section object and free the resources associated with the object. Once the object is deleted, it cannot be used with EnterCriticalSection or LeaveCriticalSection.

Parameters

lpCriticalSection: A variable of type TRTLCriticalSection containing the critical section to delete. The TRTLCriticalSection structure should be treated by the application as a totally encapsulated object, and the members of the structure should never be directly manipulated.

See also

EnterCriticalSection, InitializeCriticalSection, LeaveCriticalSection

Example

Please see Listing 6-12 under InitializeCriticalSection.

DuplicateHandle Windows.Pas

Syntax

```
DuplicateHandle(
hSourceProcessHandle: THandle;   {handle of the process with the handle to duplicate}
hSourceHandle: THandle;          {handle to duplicate}
hTargetProcessHandle: THandle;   {handle of the process to duplicate to}
lpTargetHandle: PHandle;         {pointer to the duplicate handle}
dwDesiredAccess: DWORD;          {access flags for duplicate handle}
```

```
bInheritHandle: BOOL;          {handle inheritance flag}
dwOptions: DWORD               {special action options}
): BOOL;                       {returns TRUE or FALSE}
```

Description

This function is used to duplicate a handle with different access than the original handle or a handle that is noninheritable where the original handle was inheritable. The source and target process can be the same for this function. The duplicating process uses GetCurrentProcess to get the handle of itself. To get a handle outside of the current process, it may be necessary to use a named pipe or shared memory to communicate the process identifier to the duplicating process, then use the identifier in the OpenProcess function to open a handle. Duplicated handles can have more access rights than the original handle, in most cases. For example, if the original handle provided GENERIC_READ access the duplicated handle could not give GENERIC_READ and GENERIC_WRITE access.

Parameters

hSourceProcessHandle: Specifies the handle of the process that contains the handle to duplicate. Please note the handle must have PROCESS_DUP_HANDLE access.

hSourceHandle: The handle to duplicate. This handle can be the handle returned from one of the functions listed in Table 6-4.

hTargetProcessHandle: Specifies the handle of the process that is to receive the duplicate handle. Note that the handle must have PROCESS_DUP_HANDLE access.

lpTargetHandle: A variable that receives the duplicated handle.

dwDesiredAccess: Specifies access options for the new handle. If the dwOptions parameter specifies the DUPLICATE_SAME_ACCESS flag, this parameter is ignored. If this flag is not set, the access specification will depend on the type of object handle being duplicated. See the descriptions for the individual functions that created the object handle for more information about access options.

bInheritHandle: Specifies handle inheritance. If this parameter is set to TRUE, the duplicate handle can be inherited by new processes created by the target process. A value of FALSE indicates that the new handle cannot be inherited.

dwOptions: Specifies optional actions. This parameter can be set to zero or any combination of values from Table 6-5.

Return Value

If the function succeeds, it returns TRUE; otherwise it returns FALSE. To get extended error information, call the GetLastError function.

See Also

CloseHandle, CreateEvent, CreateFile, CreateFileMapping, CreateMutex, CreateProcess, CreateSemaphore, CreateThread, GetCurrentProcess,

GetExitCodeProcess, GetExitCodeThread, GetPriorityClass, GetThreadPriority, OpenEvent, OpenMutex, OpenProcess, OpenSemaphore, RegCreateKeyEx, RegOpenKeyEx, ReleaseMutex, ReleaseSemaphore, ResetEvent, ResumeThread, SetEvent, SetPriorityClass, SetThreadPriority, SuspendThread, TerminateProcess, TerminateThread

Example

Listing 6-5: Use a Duplicated Thread Handle to Resume a Thread

```
var
  Form1: TForm1;
  ThreadHandle: THandle;         // holds a handle to the current thread
  TargetHandle: THandle;         // holds a duplicated thread handle

implementation

{$R *.DFM}

function ThreadFunc(Info: Pointer): Integer;
var
  ICount: Integer;     // general loop counter
  FormDC: HDC;         // holds the form device context
begin
  {get a handle to the form's device context}
  FormDC := GetDC(Form1.Handle);

  {display something visual}
  for ICount := 1 to 10000 do
    TextOut(FormDC, 10, 50, PChar(IntToStr(ICount)), Length(IntToStr(ICount)));

  {pause the thread until ResumeThread is called. Note SuspendThread
   is called with the duplicated handle}
  SuspendThread(TargetHandle);

  {display something visual}
  for ICount := 1 to 10000 do
    TextOut(FormDC, 110, 50, PChar(IntToStr(ICount)), Length(IntToStr(ICount)));

  {release the form's device context}
  ReleaseDC(Form1.Handle, FormDC);

  {end the thread}
  ExitThread(5);
end;

procedure TForm1.Button1Click(Sender: TObject);
var
  Duplicated: Bool;          // holds the result of handle duplication
  CurrentProcess: THandle;   // holds the current process handle
  CurrentThread: THandle;    // holds the current thread identifier
  ThreadId: DWORD;           // holds the created thread identifier
begin
  {Create the thread and start it immediately}
```

```
  ThreadHandle := CreateThread(nil, 0, @ThreadFunc, nil, 0, ThreadId);

  {retrieve the current process and thread}
  CurrentProcess := GetCurrentProcess;
  CurrentThread := GetCurrentThread;

  {duplicate the handle of the created thread into TargetHandle}
  Duplicated := DuplicateHandle(CurrentProcess, ThreadHandle, CurrentProcess,
                                @TargetHandle, 0, FALSE, DUPLICATE_SAME_ACCESS);

  {indicate if there was an error}
  if not(Duplicated) then
  begin
    ShowMessage('The duplication did not work');
  end;
end;

procedure TForm1.Button2Click(Sender: TObject);
begin
  {Start the thread again after the pause, note ResumeThread is called with the
  duplicated handle}
  ResumeThread(TargetHandle);
end;
```

Table 6-4: DuplicateHandle hSourceHandle Values

Handle Type	Function
Console input	CreateFile function will return the handle only when CONIN$ is specified.
Console screen buffer	The CreateFile function returns the handle when CONOUT$ is specified. A handle of a console can only be duplicated in the same process.
Event	The CreateEvent or OpenEvent function will return this handle.
File or communications device	The CreateFile function will return this handle.
File mapping	The CreateFileMapping function will return this handle.
Mutex	The CreateMutex or OpenMutex function will return this handle.
Pipe	The CreateNamedPipe or CreateFile function will return a named pipe handle. The CreatePipe function will return an anonymous pipe handle.
Process	The CreateProcess or OpenProcess function will return this handle.
Registry key	The RegCreateKey, RegCreateKeyEx, RegOpenKey, or RegOpenKeyEx function will return this handle. The DuplicateHandle function cannot use handles returned by the RegConnectRegistry function.
Semaphore	The CreateSemaphore or OpenSemaphore function will return this handle.

Handle Type	Function
Thread	The CreateProcess, CreateThread, or CreateRemoteThread function will return this handle.

Table 6-5: DuplicateHandle dwOptions Values

Value	Description
DUPLICATE_CLOSE_SOURCE	Closes the source handle. This will occur regardless of error status returned.
DUPLICATE_SAME_ACCESS	The duplicate handle has the same access as the source. Setting this will ignore the dwDesiredAccess parameter.

EnterCriticalSection Windows.Pas

Syntax

```
EnterCriticalSection(
var lpCriticalSection: TRTLCriticalSection    {pointer to the critical section object}
);                                            {this procedure does not return a value}
```

Description

The critical section object can be used to provide mutually exclusive access to a section of code within a single process. The object must be initialized before it can be used. EnterCriticalSection will be called by each thread to request ownership of the protected resource. No more than one thread may gain access to the resource at a time and the current thread using the resource must call LeaveCriticalSection to release the code for the next thread. A thread may call EnterCriticalSection more than once after it has initial ownership of the critical section. This can help smooth the access to a critical section, as a thread may stop itself from gaining access to code it already owns. The thread must call LeaveCriticalSection for each time that it called EnterCriticalSection.

Parameters

lpCriticalSection: A variable of type TRTLCriticalSection containing the critical section to enter. The TRTLCriticalSection structure should be treated by the application as a totally encapsulated object, and the members of the structure should never be directly manipulated.

See also

CreateMutex, DeleteCriticalSection, InitializeCriticalSection, LeaveCriticalSection

Example

Please see Listing 6-12 under InitializeCriticalSection.

ExitProcess Windows.Pas

Syntax

```
ExitProcess(
uExitCode: UINT          {exit code for all threads}
);                       {this procedure does not return a value}
```

Description

This procedure will end a process and all of its threads, returning a common exit code. After a process is exited, its state and the state of all its threads become signaled.

A successful call to this procedure causes the following:

1. All object handles opened by the process are closed.

2. All threads in the process terminate.

3. The state of the process becomes signaled, satisfying any threads that have been waiting for the process.

4. The states of all threads within the process become signaled, satisfying any threads that have been waiting for the threads.

5. The termination status is changed from STILL_ACTIVE to the exit code specified by the uExitCode parameter.

Terminating the process might not remove it or any of its child processes from the system. Only when all the open handles of the process are closed is the process removed from the system.

Parameters

uExitCode: Specifies the exit code for the process and for all threads that are terminated as a result of this call. Use the GetExitCodeProcess function to retrieve the process's exit value and the GetExitCodeThread function to retrieve a thread's exit value.

See also

CreateProcess, CreateThread, ExitThread, GetExitCodeProcess, GetExitCodeThread, OpenProcess, TerminateProcess

Example

Listing 6-6: Exiting a Process

```
procedure TForm1.Button1Click(Sender: TObject);
begin
  {exit the application}
  Windows.ExitProcess(10);
end;
```

ExitThread Windows.Pas

Syntax

```
ExitThread(
dwExitCode: DWORD          {exit code for the thread}
);                         {this procedure does not return a value}
```

Description

This procedure will end a thread and clean up any associated DLLs. If this is the last thread of the process, the process will also end. Any threads that have been waiting for the thread in question to terminate will be released, and the thread in question will become signaled.

A successful call to this procedure causes the following:

1. All object handles opened by the thread are closed.

2. All threads started by the specified thread terminate.

3. The state of the thread becomes signaled, satisfying any threads that have been waiting for the thread.

4. The states of all threads within the thread become signaled, satisfying any threads that have been waiting for the threads.

5. The termination status is changed from STILL_ACTIVE to the exit code specified by the uExitCode parameter.

Parameters

dwExitCode: Specifies the exit code for the process, and for all threads that are terminated as a result of this call. Use the GetExitCodeThread function to retrieve this value.

See also

CreateProcess, CreateThread, ExitProcess, FreeLibraryAndExitThread, GetExitCode-Thread, TerminateThread

Example

Please see Listing 6-5 under DuplicateHandle, and various other examples throughout this chapter.

GetCurrentProcess Windows.Pas

Syntax

GetCurrentProcess: THandle; {returns a handle to the current process}

Description

This function returns a pseudohandle of the currently executing process. This handle is valid only in the context of the calling process. To use the handle in another process, create a duplicate of it using the DuplicateHandle function. This handle can also be used in the OpenProcess function to create a real handle. The returned handle is not inherited by child processes.

Return Value

If this function succeeds, it returns a handle to the current process; otherwise it returns zero.

See also

CloseHandle, DuplicateHandle, GetCurrentProcessId, GetCurrentThread, OpenProcess

Example

Please see Listing 6-5 under DuplicateHandle.

GetCurrentProcessId Windows.Pas

Syntax

GetCurrentProcessId: DWORD; {returns the identifier of the current process}

Description

This function retrieves the identifier of the current process. This value is unique for the entire system.

Return Value

If this function succeeds, it returns the identifier of the current process; otherwise it returns zero.

See also

GetCurrentProcess, OpenProcess

Example

Listing 6-7: Retrieving the Current Process and Thread Identifiers

```
procedure TForm1.Button1Click(Sender: TObject);
begin
  Label1.Caption := 'Process Id: '+IntToStr(GetCurrentProcessId);
```

```
  Label2.Caption := 'Thread Id:  '+IntToStr(GetCurrentThreadId);
end;
```

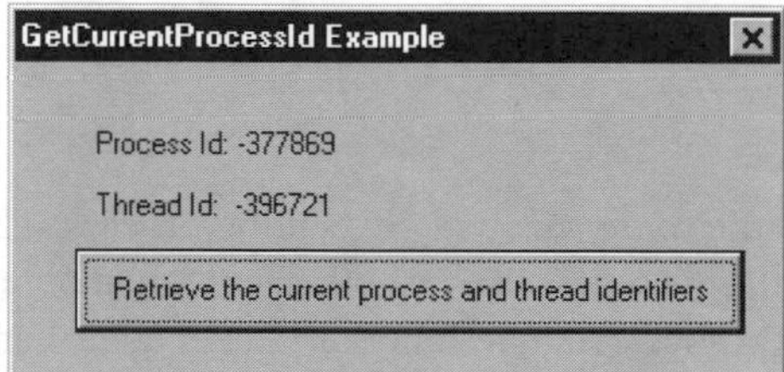

Figure 6-4: The process and thread identifiers.

GetCurrentThread Windows.Pas

Syntax

GetCurrentThread: THandle; {returns a handle for the current thread}

Description

This function returns a pseudohandle of the currently executing thread. This handle is valid only in the context of the calling process. To use the handle in another process, create a duplicate of it using the DuplicateHandle function. The returned handle is not inherited by child processes.

Return Value

If this function succeeds, it returns a handle to the current thread; otherwise it returns zero.

See also

CloseHandle, DuplicateHandle, GetCurrentProcess, GetCurrentThreadId

Example

Please see Listing 6-5 under DuplicateHandle.

GetCurrentThreadId Windows.Pas

Syntax

GetCurrentThreadId: DWORD {the return value is the ID of the current thread}

Description

This function returns the identifier for the current thread. This value will be unique for the entire system.

Return Value

If this function succeeds, it returns the identifier of the current thread; otherwise it returns zero.

See also

GetCurrentThread

Example

Please see Listing 6-7 under GetCurrentProcessId.

GetExitCodeProcess Windows.Pas

Syntax

```
GetExitCodeProcess(
hProcess: THandle;              {handle to the process}
var lpExitCode: DWORD           {receives the termination status}
): BOOL;                        {returns TRUE or FALSE}
```

Description

This function is used to retrieve the value of the process exit code. If the process has not terminated, the function will return STILL_ACTIVE. If the process has terminated, the exit code can be one of the following:

1. The exit value specified in the ExitProcess or TerminateProcess function.

2. The return value from the main application function, known as WinMain in traditional Windows programming.

3. The exception value for an unhandled exception.

If the TerminateProcess function is called after the process code has run its course, GetExitCodeProcess may not return the correct exit code specified in TerminateProcess.

Parameters

hProcess: Specifies the handle for the process. Under Windows NT, the handle must have PROCESS_QUERY_INFORMATION access.

lpExitCode: A variable that will receive the status of the process. This value is specified when the ExitProcess or TerminateProcess functions are called.

Return Value

If the function succeeds, it returns TRUE; otherwise it returns FALSE. To get extended error information, call the GetLastError function.

See also

ExitProcess, ExitThread, TerminateProcess

Example

Please see Listing 6-16 under TerminateProcess.

GetExitCodeThread Windows.Pas

Syntax

```
GetExitCodeThread(
hThread: THandle;               {handle of the thread}
var lpExitCode: DWORD           {receives the termination status}
): BOOL;                        {returns TRUE or FALSE}
```

Description

This function is used to retrieve the value of the thread exit code. If the thread has not terminated, the function will return STILL_ACTIVE. If the thread has terminated, the exit code can be one of the following:

1. The exit value specified in the ExitThread or TerminateThread function.
2. The return value from the thread function.
3. The exit value of the thread's process.

If the TerminateThread function is called after the thread code has run its course, GetExitCodeThread may not return the correct exit code specified in TerminateThread.

Parameters

hThread: A handle identifying the thread. Under Windows NT, the handle must have THREAD_QUERY_INFORMATION access to the thread.

lpExitCode: A variable that receives the value of the exit code.

Return Value

If the function succeeds, it returns TRUE; otherwise it returns FALSE. To get extended error information, call the GetLastError function.

See also

ExitThread, GetExitCodeProcess, TerminateThread

Example

Listing 6-8: Retrieving a Thread's Exit Code

```
function ThreadFunction(Info: Pointer): Integer; stdcall
var
```

```
  Count: Integer;        // general loop counter
  FormDC: HDC;           // holds the form device context
  CountStr: string;      // holds a string representation of the counter
begin
  {retrieve the form device context}
  FormDC := GetDC(Form1.Handle);

  {display something visual}
  for Count := 1 to 1000 do
  begin
    CountStr := IntToStr(Count);
    TextOut(FormDC, 10, 10, PChar(CountStr), Length(CountStr));
  end;

  {release the device context and exit the thread}
  ReleaseDC(Form1.Handle, FormDC);
  ExitThread(4);
end;

procedure TForm1.Button_CreateThreadClick(Sender: TObject);
var
  ThreadId: Integer;        // holds the thread identifier
begin
  {create and execute a thread}
  ThreadHandle := CreateThread(nil, 0, @ThreadFunction, nil, 0, ThreadId);
  if (ThreadHandle = 0) then
  begin
    MessageBox(Handle, 'No Thread Created', nil, MB_OK);
  end;
end;

procedure TForm1.Button_GetExitCodeClick(Sender: TObject);
var
  ExitCode: Integer;       // holds the thread exit code
begin
  {retrieve and display the thread's exit code}
  GetExitCodeThread(ThreadHandle, ExitCode);
  ShowMessage('The exit code is ' + IntToStr(ExitCode));
end;
```

GetPriorityClass Windows.Pas

Syntax

```
GetPriorityClass(
hProcess: THandle           {a handle of the process}
): DWORD;                   {returns the priority class of the object}
```

Description

This function retrieves the priority class for the specified process. Every thread has a priority level based on a combination of the thread priority and the process's priority.

Chapter 6

The system will determine when the thread gets a quantum of time on the CPU based on its priority.

Parameters

hProcess: The handle of the process in question. Under Windows NT, the handle must have THREAD_QUERY_INFORMATION access to the process.

Return Value

If the function succeeds, it returns a priority class for the specified process, and can be one value from Table 6-6. If the function fails, it returns zero. To get extended error information, call the GetLastError function.

See also

GetThreadPriority, SetPriorityClass, SetThreadPriority

Example

Listing 6-9: Setting and Retrieving the Priority Class

```
procedure TForm1.Button1Click(Sender: TObject);
var
  Process: THandle;       // holds a handle to the process
  PriorityClass: DWORD;   // holds the priority class
begin
  {retrieve the current process handle}
  Process := Windows.GetCurrentProcess;

  {retrieve the priority class}
  PriorityClass := GetPriorityClass(Process);

  {display the priority class}
  case PriorityClass of
    NORMAL_PRIORITY_CLASS:   Edit1.Text := 'NORMAL_PRIORITY_CLASS';
    IDLE_PRIORITY_CLASS:     Edit1.Text := 'IDLE_PRIORITY_CLASS';
    HIGH_PRIORITY_CLASS:     Edit1.Text := 'HIGH_PRIORITY_CLASS';
    REALTIME_PRIORITY_CLASS: Edit1.Text := 'REALTIME_PRIORITY_CLASS';
  end;
end;

procedure TForm1.Button2Click(Sender: TObject);
begin
  {set the selected priority class}
  case RadioGroup1.ItemIndex of
    0: SetPriorityClass(Windows.GetCurrentProcess, NORMAL_PRIORITY_CLASS);
    1: SetPriorityClass(Windows.GetCurrentProcess, IDLE_PRIORITY_CLASS);
    2: SetPriorityClass(Windows.GetCurrentProcess, HIGH_PRIORITY_CLASS);
    3: SetPriorityClass(Windows.GetCurrentProcess, REALTIME_PRIORITY_CLASS);
  end;
end;
```

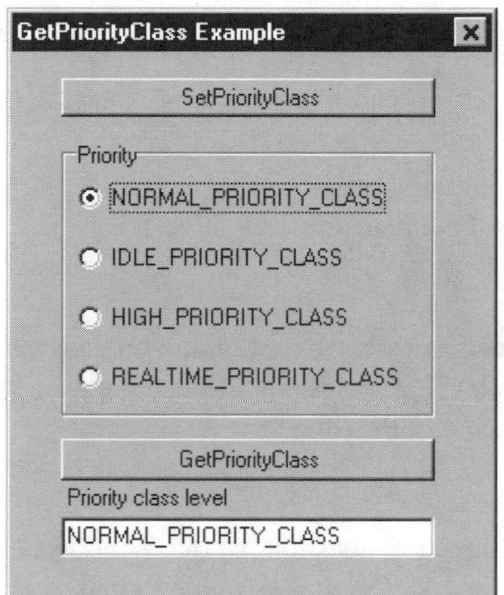

Figure 6-5: The priority class.

Table 6-6: GetPriorityClass Return Values

Value	Description
HIGH_PRIORITY_CLASS	Indicates time-critical tasks that must be executed immediately for it to run smoothly. The threads of a high-priority class process preempt the threads of normal or idle priority class processes. An example is the Windows Task List, which must be responsive to the user. HIGH_PRIORITY_CLASS can use nearly all cycles of a CPU, so use care when specifying this priority.
IDLE_PRIORITY_CLASS	A process with this priority will be preempted by all higher priority class processes. A screen saver is a good example. This priority class is inherited by child processes.
NORMAL_PRIORITY_CLASS	This priority class has no special scheduling needs, and is the default priority.
REALTIME_PRIORITY_CLASS	This is the highest possible priority class. The threads of this priority class will preempt any other threads of a lower priority class, including operating system processes performing important tasks. A real-time process that executes for a long interval (for a computer) can cause the mouse to be unresponsive or disk caches not to function. Be very careful when using this priority class.

GetThreadPriority Windows.Pas

Syntax

GetThreadPriority(
hThread: THandle {handle of the thread}
): Integer; {returns the thread's priority level}

Description

GetThreadPriority will return the thread's priority based on the process's base priority class and the current thread's priority level. The system will use the priority level in scheduling the next thread to get a slice of CPU time.

Parameters

hThread: Specifies the handle of the thread in question. Under Windows NT, the handle must have THREAD_QUERY_INFORMATION access to the thread.

Return Value

If the function succeeds, it returns an integer value indicating the thread's priority level, and may be one value from Table 6-7. If the function fails, it returns THREAD_PRIORITY_ERROR_RETURN. To get extended error information, call the GetLastError function.

See also

GetPriorityClass, SetPriorityClass, SetThreadPriority

Example

Listing 6-10: Setting and Retrieving the Thread Priority

```
procedure TForm1.Button1Click(Sender: TObject);
var
  ThreadPriority: Integer;   // holds the thread priority level
begin
  {retrieve the thread priority}
  ThreadPriority := GetThreadPriority(GetCurrentThread);

  {display the thread priority}
  case (ThreadPriority) of
    THREAD_PRIORITY_LOWEST        : Edit1.Text :=
                                    'THREAD_PRIORITY_LOWEST (-2 to base)';
    THREAD_PRIORITY_BELOW_NORMAL  : Edit1.Text :=
                                    'THREAD_PRIORITY_BELOW_NORMAL (-1 to base)';
    THREAD_PRIORITY_NORMAL        : Edit1.Text :=
                                    'THREAD_PRIORITY_NORMAL (0 to base)';
    THREAD_PRIORITY_HIGHEST       : Edit1.Text :=
                                    'THREAD_PRIORITY_HIGHEST (+2 to base)';
    THREAD_PRIORITY_ABOVE_NORMAL  : Edit1.Text :=
                                    'THREAD_PRIORITY_ABOVE_NORMAL (+1 to base)';
    THREAD_PRIORITY_ERROR_RETURN  : Edit1.Text :=
```

```
                                     'THREAD_PRIORITY_ERROR_RETURN';
    THREAD_PRIORITY_TIME_CRITICAL : Edit1.Text :=
                                     'THREAD_PRIORITY_TIME_CRITICAL (base 15)';
    THREAD_PRIORITY_IDLE          : Edit1.Text :=
                                     'THREAD_PRIORITY_IDLE (base set to one)';
  end;
end;

procedure TForm1.Button2Click(Sender: TObject);
var
  ThreadHandle: THandle;   // holds the current thread handle
begin
  {retrieve the current thread}
  ThreadHandle := GetCurrentThread;

  {set the selected priority}
  case RadioGroup1.ItemIndex of
    0: SetThreadPriority(ThreadHandle, THREAD_PRIORITY_LOWEST);
    1: SetThreadPriority(ThreadHandle, THREAD_PRIORITY_BELOW_NORMAL);
    2: SetThreadPriority(ThreadHandle, THREAD_PRIORITY_NORMAL);
    3: SetThreadPriority(ThreadHandle, THREAD_PRIORITY_ABOVE_NORMAL);
    4: SetThreadPriority(ThreadHandle, THREAD_PRIORITY_HIGHEST);
    5: SetThreadPriority(ThreadHandle, THREAD_PRIORITY_TIME_CRITICAL);
    6: SetThreadPriority(ThreadHandle, THREAD_PRIORITY_IDLE);
  end;
end;
```

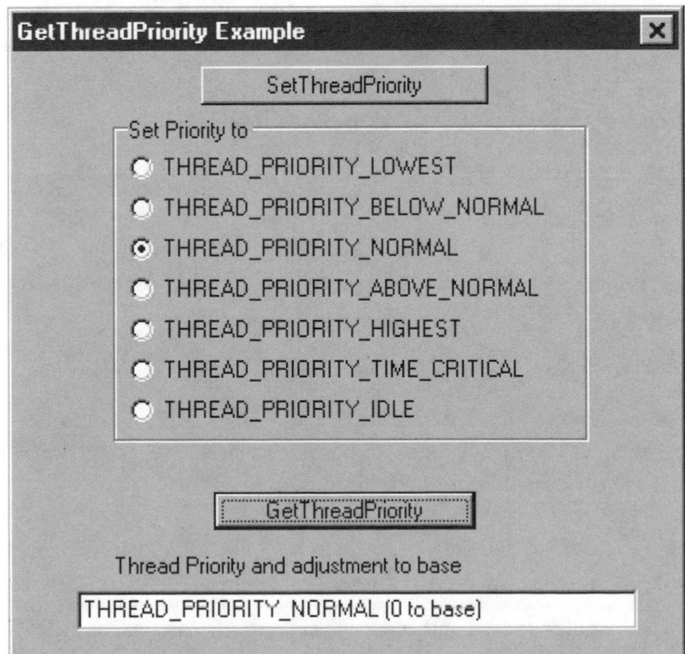

Figure 6-6: Displaying the thread's priority.

Table 6-7: GetThreadPriority Return Values

Value	Description
THREAD_PRIORITY_ABOVE_NORMAL	One point above normal priority for the priority class.
THREAD_PRIORITY_BELOW_NORMAL	One point below normal priority for the priority class.
THREAD_PRIORITY_HIGHEST	Two points above normal priority for the priority class.
THREAD_PRIORITY_IDLE	Indicates a base priority level of one for IDLE_PRIORITY_CLASS, NORMAL_PRIORITY_CLASS, or HIGH_PRIORITY_CLASS processes, and a base priority level of 16 for REALTIME_PRIORITY_CLASS processes.
THREAD_PRIORITY_LOWEST	Two points below normal priority for the priority class.
THREAD_PRIORITY_NORMAL	Normal priority for the priority class.
THREAD_PRIORITY_TIME_CRITICAL	Indicates a base priority level of 15 for IDLE_PRIORITY_CLASS, NORMAL_PRIORITY_CLASS, or HIGH_PRIORITY_CLASS processes, and a base priority level of 31 for REALTIME_PRIORITY_CLASS processes.

GetWindowThreadProcessId   *Windows.Pas*

Syntax

```
GetWindowThreadProcessId(
hWnd: HWND;                 {a handle to a window}
lpdwProcessId: Pointer      {a pointer to a buffer receiving the process identifier}
): DWORD;                   {returns the thread identifier}
```

Description

This function retrieves the identifier of the thread that created the window identified by the hWnd parameter. If the lpdwProcessId parameter is not set to NIL, it also returns the identifier of the process that created the window.

Parameters

hWnd: A handle to the window whose thread and process identifiers are to be retrieved.

lpdwProcessId: A pointer to a 32-bit buffer that receives the process identifier. This parameter can be set to NIL if the process identifier is not needed.

Return Value

If the function succeeds, it returns the identifier of the thread that created the specifier window; otherwise it returns zero.

See also

GetCurrentProcessId, GetCurrentThreadId

Example

Listing 6-11: Retrieving the Window's Thread and Process Identifiers

```
procedure TForm1.Button1Click(Sender: TObject);
var
  ProcessId: LongInt;   // holds the process identifier
begin
  {display the thread identifier}
  Label1.Caption:='Thread Id: '+IntToStr(GetWindowThreadProcessId(Form1.Handle,
                                                                   @ProcessId));

  {display the process identifier}
  Label2.Caption:='Process Id: '+IntToStr(ProcessId);
end;
```

InitializeCriticalSection *Windows.Pas*

Syntax

InitializeCriticalSection(
var lpCriticalSection: TRTLCriticalSection {pointer to the critical section}
); {this procedure does not return a value}

Description

This function will initialize a critical section object. This object will be used for synchronization of the threads within a single process. A critical section can only be used within a single process and will ensure that no thread will use the same section of code at the same time. After the initialization of the critical section object, the other threads of the process will use EnterCriticalSection and LeaveCriticalSection to provide mutually exclusive access to the same area of code.

Parameters

lpCriticalSection: A variable of type TRTLCriticalSection containing the critical section to initialize. The TRTLCriticalSection structure should be treated by the application as a totally encapsulated object, and the members of the structure should never be directly manipulated.

See also

CreateMutex, DeleteCriticalSection, EnterCriticalSection, LeaveCriticalSection

Example

Listing 6-12: Using Critical Sections to Synchronize a Thread Within the Process

```
var
  Form1: TForm1;
  ThreadHandle: THandle;                // holds the handles the the threads
  ThreadHandle2: THandle;
  CriticalSection: TRTLCriticalSection;  // holds the critical section info

implementation

{$R *.DFM}

function ThreadFunc(Info: Pointer): Integer; stdcall;
var
  Count : Integer;    // general loop control variable
begin
  {performing the EnterCriticalSection function prevents the second thread
   from executing until this thread leaves the critical section}
  EnterCriticalSection(CriticalSection);

  {show a visual display}
  for Count := 0 to 100 do
  begin
    Form1.Edit1.Text := IntToStr(Count);
  end;

  {display a message}
  Form1.Edit1.Text := 'Hello from the thread!';

  {pause for a second}
  Sleep(1000);

  {leave the critical section and exit the thread}
  LeaveCriticalSection(CriticalSection);
  ExitThread(4);
end;

procedure TForm1.Button1Click(Sender: TObject);
var
  ThreadId1, ThreadId2: DWORD;   // holds the created thread identifiers
begin
  {initialize the critical section information}
  InitializeCriticalSection(CriticalSection);

  {create and execute the first thread}
  ThreadHandle := CreateThread(nil, 0, @ThreadFunc, nil, 0, ThreadId1);

  {create and execute the second thread}
  ThreadHandle2 := CreateThread(nil, 0, @ThreadFunc, nil, 0, ThreadId2);
end;

procedure TForm1.FormDestroy(Sender: TObject);
begin
```

```
  {we are done, so destroy the critical section information}
  DeleteCriticalSection(CriticalSection);
end;
```

InterlockedDecrement Windows.Pas

Syntax

InterlockedDecrement(
var Addend: Integer {pointer to a 32-bit variable to decrement}
): Integer; {returns a code indicating the resulting value's sign}

Description

This function will decrement a given 32-bit value. It will not allow more than one thread using any of the interlocked functions to access the same 32-bit value at the same time, thus resulting in a threadsafe mechanism for modifying an integer variable. If the variable pointed to by the Addend parameter is not aligned on a 32-bit boundary, the function will fail on a multiprocessor x86 machine. Delphi will automatically align variables on a 32-bit boundary.

Parameters

Addend: A variable containing a 32-bit value that will be decremented by the function.

Return Value

If the resulting decremented value is zero, the function returns zero. The function returns a positive number if the result is positive, or a negative number if the result is negative. This function does not indicate an error upon failure.

See also

InterlockedExchange, InterlockedIncrement

Example

Listing 6-13: Modifying a Variable in a Threadsafe Manner

```
var
  Form1: TForm1;
  ThreadHandle: THandle;   // holds a thread handle
  ThreadHandle1: THandle;  // holds a thread handle
  MultiVar: Integer;       // the incrementing variable

implementation

{$R *.DFM}

function ThreadFunc(Info: Pointer): Integer; stdcall;
var
  Count: Integer;          // general loop variable
```

```
begin
  {increment the variable by 10}
  for Count := 1 to 10 do
  begin
    InterlockedIncrement(MultiVar);
  end;

  {exit the thread}
  ExitThread(4);
end;

procedure TForm1.Button1Click(Sender: TObject);
var
  ThreadId, ThreadId1: DWORD;   // holds the thread identifiers
begin
  {launch a thread, incrementing the variable by 10}
  ThreadHandle := CreateThread(nil, 0, @ThreadFunc, Nil, 0, ThreadId);

  {increment the variable again by 1}
  InterlockedIncrement(MultiVar);

  {increment the variable by 10 again.  thanks to the InterlockedIncrement
   function, the variable will be exactly equal to 21, even though
   multiple threads have been incrementing it simultaneously}
  ThreadHandle1 := CreateThread(nil, 0, @ThreadFunc, Nil, 0, ThreadId1);
end;

procedure TForm1.Button2Click(Sender: TObject);
begin
  {show the variable}
  ShowMessage(IntToStr(MultiVar));
end;

procedure TForm1.Button3Click(Sender: TObject);
var
  RtnValue: Integer;     // holds the return value from InterlockedDecrement
begin
  {increment the variable}
  RtnValue := InterlockedDecrement(MultiVar);

  {display the return value}
  Label2.Caption := IntToStr(RtnValue);
end;

procedure TForm1.Button4Click(Sender: TObject);
var
  RtnValue: Integer;    // holds the return value from InterlockedExchange
begin
  {exchange the current variable's value with 50}
  RtnValue := InterlockedExchange(MultiVar, 50);

  {display the return value}
  Label2.Caption := IntToStr(RtnValue);
end;
```

```
procedure TForm1.Button5Click(Sender: TObject);
var
  RtnValue: Integer;    // holds the return value from InterlockedIncrement
begin
  {increment the variable}
  RtnValue := InterlockedIncrement(MultiVar);

  {display the return value}
  Label2.Caption := IntToStr(RtnValue);
end;

procedure TForm1.FormCreate(Sender: TObject);
begin
  {initialize the variable}
  Multivar := 0;
end;
```

InterlockedExchange   Windows.Pas

Syntax

InterlockedExchange(	
var Target: Integer;	{the 32-bit value to exchange}
Value: Integer	{new value for target}
): Integer;	{returns the prior value}

Description

This function will exchange the interlocked 32-bit value of the variable pointed to by the Target parameter with the 32-bit value identified by the Value parameter. This function will work across process boundaries as long as the variable to exchange is in shared memory. If the variable pointed to by the Target parameter is not aligned on a 32-bit boundary, the function will fail on a multiprocessor x86 machine. Delphi will automatically align variables on a 32-bit boundary.

Parameters

Target: A variable containing a 32-bit value that will be exchanged with the Value parameter.

Value: Specifies the new 32-bit value.

Return Value

The function returns the prior value of the variable identified by the Target parameter. This function does not indicate an error upon failure.

See also

InterlockedDecrement, InterlockedIncrement

Example

Please see Listing 6-13 under InterlockedDecrement.

InterlockedIncrement   Windows.Pas

Syntax

```
InterlockedIncrement(
var Addend: Integer              {pointer to a 32-bit variable to increment}
): Integer;                      {returns a code indicating the resulting value's sign}
```

Description

This function will increment a given 32-bit value. It will not allow more than one thread using any of the interlocked functions to access the same 32-bit value at the same time, thus resulting in a threadsafe mechanism for modifying an integer variable. If the variable pointed to by the Addend parameter is not aligned on a 32-bit boundary, the function will fail on a multiprocessor x86 machine. Delphi will automatically align variables on a 32-bit boundary.

Parameters

Addend: A variable containing a 32-bit value that will be incremented by the function.

Return Value

If the resulting incremented value is zero, the function returns zero. The function returns a positive number if the result is positive, or a negative number if the result is negative. This function does not indicate an error upon failure.

See also

InterlockedDecrement, InterlockedExchange

Example

Please see Listing 6-13 under InterlockedDecrement.

LeaveCriticalSection   Windows.Pas

Syntax

```
LeaveCriticalSection(
var lpCriticalSection: TRTLCriticalSection   {pointer to the critical section}
);                                           {this procedure does not return a value}
```

Description

This function will release the critical section object for the next thread that needs access. If the same thread has called EnterCriticalSection more than once, it must call LeaveCriticalSection the same number of times. If a thread calls LeaveCriticalSection and the thread has not previously called EnterCriticalSection, it could lock the current thread of the section in question.

Parameters

lpCriticalSection: A variable of type TRTLCriticalSection containing the critical section to be released. The TRTLCriticalSection structure should be treated by the application as a totally encapsulated object, and the members of the structure should never be directly manipulated.

See also

CreateMutex, DeleteCriticalSection, EnterCriticalSection, InitializeCriticalSection

Example

Please see Listing 6-12 under InitializeCriticalSection.

OpenEvent Windows.Pas

Syntax

```
OpenEvent(
dwDesiredAccess: DWORD;        {access flags}
bInheritHandle: BOOL;          {inheritance flag}
lpName: PChar                  {a pointer to the event object name}
): THandle;                    {returns the handle to the event object}
```

Description

This function will allow multiple processes to open a handle to an event object that has already been created. Use the DuplicateHandle function to make a duplicate of the handle, and the CloseHandle function to close it. After all handles to the event object are closed, the event object is destroyed and all memory associated with the object will be freed. When a process terminates, any handles it may have had to the event object are automatically closed.

Parameters

dwDesiredAccess: Specifies the requested access to the event object. If the system supports object security and the security descriptor does not support the requested access, the function will fail. This parameter can contain one or more values from Table 6-8.

bInheritHandle: Specifies handle inheritance. If this parameter is set to TRUE, a process created by CreateProcess can inherit the handle. If it is FALSE the handle cannot be inherited.

lpName: A null-terminated string containing the name of the event object to be opened. Name comparisons are case sensitive.

Return Value

If the function succeeds, it returns the handle to the event object that was opened. If the function fails, it returns zero.

See also

CloseHandle, CreateEvent, CreateProcess, DuplicateHandle, PulseEvent, ResetEvent, SetEvent, WaitForSingleObject

Example

Listing 6-14: Opening an Event Created in Another Process

```
procedure TForm1.Button1Click(Sender: TObject);
begin
  {open the previously existing event}
  EventHandle := OpenEvent(EVENT_ALL_ACCESS, FALSE, 'MyEvent');
end;

procedure TForm1.Button2Click(Sender: TObject);
begin
  {set the event, which was opened from the other application}
  SetEvent(EventHandle);
end;
```

Table 6-8: OpenEvent dwDesiredAccess Values

Value	Description
EVENT_ALL_ACCESS	Specifies all access flags for the event.
EVENT_MODIFY_STATE	Enables use of the SetEvent and ResetEvent functions with the given handle.
SYNCHRONIZE	Windows NT only: Enables any of the wait functions to specify the handle returned by OpenEvent.

OpenMutex Windows.Pas

Syntax

```
OpenMutex(
dwDesiredAccess: DWORD;        {access flags}
bInheritHandle: BOOL;          {inheritance flag}
lpName: PChar                  {a pointer to the name of the mutex object}
): THandle;                    {returns a handle of the mutex object}
```

Description

This function opens a previously created mutex, allowing a mutex to be opened across process boundaries. Use the DuplicateHandle function to make a duplicate of the handle, and the CloseHandle function to close it. The handle is automatically closed when the calling process is closed. The mutex is destroyed when the last handle is closed.

Parameters

dwDesiredAccess: Specifies the desired access to the mutex object. This function will fail if the security descriptor does not permit the requested access for the calling process. This parameter can contain one or more values from Table 6-9.

bInheritHandle: Specifies handle inheritance. If this parameter is set to TRUE, a process created by CreateProcess can inherit the handle. If it is FALSE the handle cannot be inherited.

lpName: A null-terminated string containing the name of the mutex object to be opened. Name comparisons are case sensitive.

Return Value

If the function succeeds, it returns the handle to the opened mutex object. If the function fails, it returns zero. To get extended error information, call the GetLastError function.

See also

CloseHandle, CreateMutex, CreateProcess, DuplicateHandle, ReleaseMutex, WaitForSingleObject

Example

Please see Listing 6-2 under CreateMutex.

Table 6-9: OpenMutex dwDesiredAccess Values

Value	Description
MUTEX_ALL_ACCESS	All access for the mutex object.
SYNCHRONIZE	Windows NT only: Enables the use of any of the wait functions to acquire ownership of the mutex with the given handle, or the ReleaseMutex function to release ownership.

OpenProcess Windows.Pas

Syntax

```
OpenProcess(
dwDesiredAccess: DWORD;        {access flags}
bInheritHandle: BOOL;          {handle inheritance flag}
dwProcessId: DWORD             {the process identifier}
): THandle;                    {returns the handle of the open process}
```

Description

OpenProcess will return the handle of an existing process object. This handle can be used in any function that requires a handle to a process where the appropriate rights were requested.

Parameters

dwDesiredAccess: Indicates the desired access privilege to the process. For a system that supports security checking, this parameter is checked against any security descriptor for the process. This parameter may contain one or more values from Table 6-10.

bInheritHandle: Specifies if the returned handle may be inherited by a process created by the current process. If this parameter is set to TRUE, the handle may be inherited.

dwProcessId: Specifies the identifier of the process to open.

Return Value

If the function succeeds, it returns the handle of the specified process; otherwise it returns zero. To get extended error information, call the GetLastError function.

See also

CreateProcess, DuplicateHandle, GetCurrentProcess, GetCurrentProcessId, GetExitCodeProcess, GetPriorityClass, SetPriorityClass, TerminateProcess

Example

Listing 6-15: Launching and Terminating a Process

```
procedure TForm1.Button1Click(Sender: TObject);
const
  PROCESS_TERMINATE = $0001;    // OpenProcess constant
var
  ProcessHandle: THandle;       // a handle to the process
  ProcessId: Integer;           // the process identifier
  TheWindow: HWND;              // a handle to a window
begin
  {retrieve a handle to the window whose process is to be closed}
  TheWindow := FindWindow('TForm1', 'OpenProcess Example Window');

  {retrieve the window's process identifier}
  GetWindowThreadProcessId(TheWindow, @ProcessId);

  {retrieve a handle to the window's process}
  ProcessHandle := OpenProcess(PROCESS_TERMINATE, FALSE, ProcessId);

  {display a message}
  ShowMessage('goodbye');

  {terminate the spawned process}
  TerminateProcess(ProcessHandle, 4);
end;
```

```
procedure TForm1.Button2Click(Sender: TObject);
var
  StartUpInfo: TStartUpInfo;        // holds startup information
  ProcessInfo: TProcessInformation; // holds process information
  CurDir: string;                   // holds the current directory
begin
  {initialize the startup info structure}
  FillChar(StartupInfo, SizeOf(TStartupInfo), 0);
  with StartupInfo do
  begin
    cb := SizeOf(TStartupInfo);
    dwFlags := STARTF_USESHOWWINDOW;
    wShowWindow := SW_SHOWNORMAL;
  end;

  {launch the spawned process}
  CurDir := ExtractFilePath(ParamStr(0))+'ProjectOpenProcess.exe';
  CreateProcess(PChar(CurDir), nil, nil, nil, False,
      NORMAL_PRIORITY_CLASS, nil, nil, StartupInfo, ProcessInfo);
end;
```

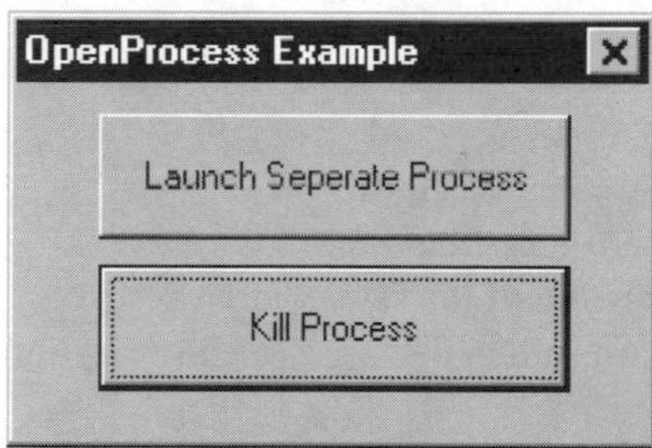

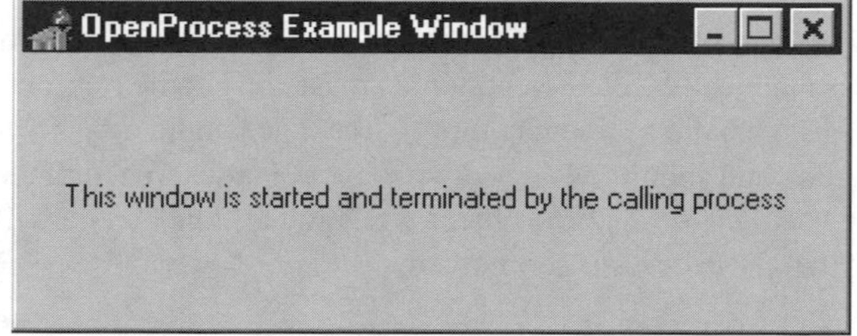

Figure 6-7: The opened process.

Table 6-10: OpenProcess dwDesiredAccess Values

Value	Description
PROCESS_ALL_ACCESS	All possible access flags for the given process.
PROCESS_CREATE_THREAD	Enables using the CreateRemoteThread function with the given handle to create a thread in the process.
PROCESS_DUP_HANDLE	Enables using the process handle as either the source or target process in the DuplicateHandle function to duplicate a handle.

Value	Description
PROCESS_QUERY_INFORMATION	Enables using the GetExitCodeProcess and GetPriorityClass functions to read information from the process object, using the given handle.
PROCESS_SET_INFORMATION	Enables using the SetPriorityClass function to set the priority class of the process with the given handle.
PROCESS_TERMINATE	Enables using the TerminateProcess function to terminate the process with the given handle.
PROCESS_VM_OPERATION	Enables using the VirtualProtectEx function to modify the virtual memory of the process with the given handle.
SYNCHRONIZE	Windows NT only: Enables using any of the wait functions with the given handle.

OpenSemaphore *Windows.Pas*

Syntax

```
OpenSemaphore(
dwDesiredAccess: DWORD;          {desired access rights}
bInheritHandle: BOOL;            {inheritance flag}
lpName: PChar                    {the name of the semaphore object}
): THandle;                      {returns a handle of the open semaphore}
```

Description

This function will open multiple handles to the same semaphore object from a different process. The process that calls OpenSemaphore can use the handle returned for any function that requires a handle to a semaphore object. The handle may be duplicated with DuplicateHandle, and should be closed with CloseHandle. When the last handle to the semaphore is closed, the semaphore object is destroyed. The handle will be automatically closed when the process is terminated.

Parameters

dwDesiredAccess: Indicates the desired access to the semaphore object. If the system supports object security, this function will fail if the security descriptor does not grant the requested access to the specified object from the calling process. This parameter may contain one or more values from Table 6-11.

bInheritHandle: Specifies if the returned handle may be inherited by a process created by the current process. If this parameter is set to TRUE, the handle may be inherited.

lpName: A null-terminated string containing the name of the semaphore to be opened. Name comparisons are case sensitive.

Return Value

If the function succeeds, it returns the handle of the existing semaphore object. If the function fails it returns zero. To get extended error information, call the GetLastError function.

See also

CloseHandle, CreateSemaphore, DuplicateHandle, ReleaseSemaphore, WaitForSingleObject

Example

Please see Listing 6-4 under CreateSemaphore.

Table 6-11: OpenSemaphore dwDesiredAccess Values

Value	Description
SEMAPHORE_ALL_ACCESS	All possible access for the semaphore object.
SEMAPHORE_MODIFY_STATE	Enables use of the ReleaseSemaphore function to modify the semaphore's count with the given handle.
SYNCHRONIZE	Windows NT only: Enables use of any of the wait functions to wait for the semaphore's state to be signaled with the given handle.

PulseEvent Windows.Pas

Syntax

```
PulseEvent(
hEvent: THandle                {handle of the event object}
): BOOL;                       {returns TRUE or FALSE}
```

Description

The PulseEvent function will set the event object to a signaled state, then resets it to a nonsignaled state after releasing the appropriate number of waiting threads. For manual reset objects, all waiting threads that can be released are immediately released. The event object is then reset to a nonsignaled state and the function returns. For an auto event object, the function will reset the event to a nonsignaled state and release only one waiting thread, even if multiple threads are waiting. If no threads can be released or if none are waiting, the function will set the event object to a nonsignaled state and return.

Parameters

hEvent: Specifies the handle of the event object. Under Windows NT, the handle must have EVENT_MODIFY_STATE access.

Return Value

If the function succeeds, it returns TRUE; otherwise it returns FALSE. To get extended error information, call the GetLastError function.

See also

CreateEvent, OpenEvent, ResetEvent, SetEvent, WaitForSingleObject

Example

Please see Listing 6-1 under CreateEvent.

ReleaseMutex Windows.Pas

Syntax

```
ReleaseMutex(
hMutex: THandle              {handle of the mutex object}
): BOOL;                     {returns TRUE or FALSE}
```

Description

The ReleaseMutex function will release ownership of the specified mutex object. The calling thread must own the mutex object or the function will fail. A thread gets ownership of the mutex object by using it in one of the wait functions or by calling the CreateMutex function. ReleaseMutex will release the mutex for other threads to use. A thread can specify a mutex in more than one wait function if the thread owns the mutex in question, without blocking its execution. This will prevent a deadlock situation in a thread that already owns a mutex. The thread must call ReleaseMutex for each wait function in which the mutex object is specified.

Parameters

hMutex: Specifies the handle of the mutex object to be released.

Return Value

If the function succeeds, it returns TRUE; otherwise it returns FALSE. To get extended error information, call the GetLastError function.

See also

CreateMutex, WaitForSingleObject

Example

Please see Listing 6-2 under CreateMutex.

ReleaseSemaphore Windows.Pas

Syntax

```
ReleaseSemaphore(
hSemaphore: THandle;            {handle to the semaphore}
lReleaseCount: Longint;         {amount to add to the current count}
lpPreviousCount: Pointer        {pointer to the previous count}
): BOOL;                        {returns TRUE or FALSE}
```

Description

This function increases the count of the given semaphore object by the specified amount. The state of the semaphore is signaled when the count is greater than zero, and nonsignaled when the count is zero. The count of the semaphore is decreased by one when a waiting thread is released due to the semaphore's signaled state.

Parameters

hSemaphore: Specifies the handle of the semaphore object. This will be returned by the CreateSemaphore or OpenSemaphore functions. Under Windows NT, this handle must have SEMAPHORE_MODIFY_STATE access.

lReleaseCount: Specifies the amount that the count of the semaphore object will be increased. This value must be greater than zero. The function will return FALSE if the specified count exceeds the maximum count of the semaphore after the increase.

lpPreviousCount: A pointer to a 32-bit value that receives the previous count of the semaphore. This parameter can be set to NIL if the previous count is not needed.

Return Value

If the function succeeds, it returns TRUE; otherwise it returns FALSE. To get extended error information, call the GetLastError function.

See also

CreateSemaphore, OpenSemaphore, WaitForSingleObject

Example

Please see Listing 6-3 under CreateSemaphore.

ResetEvent Windows.Pas

Syntax

```
ResetEvent(
hEvent: THandle                 {the handle of the event object}
): BOOL;                        {returns TRUE or FALSE}
```

Description

This function is used to set the state of an event object to nonsignaled. The nonsignaled state of the event object will block the execution of any threads that have specified the object in a call to a wait function. The event object will remain in the nonsignaled state until set by the SetEvent or PulseEvent functions. This function is used for manual reset event objects as opposed to automatic reset event objects.

Parameters

hEvent: Specifies the handle of the event object. Under Windows NT, the handle must have EVENT_MODIFY_STATE access.

Return Value

If the function succeeds, it returns TRUE; otherwise it returns FALSE. To get extended error information, call the GetLastError function.

See also

CreateEvent, OpenEvent, PulseEvent, SetEvent

Example

Please see Listing 6-1 under CreateEvent.

ResumeThread Windows.Pas

Syntax

```
ResumeThread(
hThread: THandle            {the handle of the thread to start}
): DWORD;                   {returns the previous suspend count}
```

Description

This function will decrement the thread's suspend count by one. When the count is zero, the thread will resume execution. If the count is greater than one after the call to this function, the thread will still be suspended.

Parameters

hThread: A handle to the thread whose execution is being resumed.

Return Value

If the function succeeds, it returns the thread's previous suspend count; otherwise it returns $FFFFFFFF. To get extended error information, call the GetLastError function.

See also

SuspendThread

Example

Please see Listing 6-5 under DuplicateHandle.

SetEvent Windows.Pas

Syntax

```
SetEvent(
hEvent: THandle                {the handle of the event object to set}
): BOOL;                       {returns TRUE or FALSE}
```

Description

This function will set the state of the specified event object to signaled. Any number of waiting threads, or threads that subsequently begin wait operations, are released while the object state is signaled.

Parameters

hEvent: Specifies the handle of the event object to set. The CreateEvent or OpenEvent functions will return this handle. Under Windows NT, the handle must have EVENT_MODIFY_STATE access.

Return Value

If the function succeeds, it returns TRUE; otherwise it returns FALSE. To get extended error information, call the GetLastError function.

See also

CreateEvent, OpenEvent, PulseEvent, ResetEvent, WaitForSingleObject

Example

Please see Listing 6-1 under CreateEvent.

SetPriorityClass Windows.Pas

Syntax

```
SetPriorityClass(
hProcess: THandle;             {the handle of the process}
dwPriorityClass: DWORD         {the priority class value}
): BOOL;                       {returns TRUE or FALSE}
```

Description

The SetPriorityClass function is used to set the priority class of a process, together with the priority value of any threads owned by the process. The priority class of a process is used to set the base priority of a thread. The threads will be scheduled in a round robin fashion based on their base priority level. Only when no other threads with a higher priority level are next in line will the threads of the next level get a slice of CPU time.

Parameters

hProcess: Specifies the handle of the process. Under Windows NT, the handle must have PROCESS_SET_INFORMATION access.

dwPriorityClass: Specifies the priority class for the process. This parameter can be one value from Table 6-12.

Return Value

If the function succeeds, it returns TRUE; otherwise it returns FALSE. To get extended error information, call the GetLastError function.

See also

CreateProcess, CreateThread, GetPriorityClass, GetThreadPriority, SetThreadPriority

Example

Please see Listing 6-9 under GetPriorityClass.

Table 6-12: SetPriorityClass dwPriorityClass Values

Value	Description
HIGH_PRIORITY_CLASS	Indicates time-critical tasks that must be executed immediately for it to run smoothly. The threads of a high-priority class process preempt the threads of normal or idle priority class processes. An example is the Windows Task List, which must be responsive to the user. HIGH_PRIORITY_CLASS can use nearly all cycles of a CPU, so use care when specifying this priority.
IDLE_PRIORITY_CLASS	A process with this priority will be preempted by all higher priority classes. A screen saver is a good example. This priority class is inherited by child processes.
NORMAL_PRIORITY_CLASS	This priority class has no special scheduling needs, and is the default priority.
REALTIME_PRIORITY_CLASS	This is the highest possible priority class. The threads of this priority class will preempt any other threads of a lower priority class, including operating system processes performing important tasks. A real-time process that executes for a long interval (for a computer) can cause the mouse to be unresponsive or disk caches not to function. Be very careful when using this priority class.

SetThreadPriority Windows.Pas

Syntax

```
SetThreadPriority(
hThread: THandle;          {the handle of the thread}
nPriority: Integer         {the priority level}
): BOOL;                   {returns TRUE or FALSE}
```

Description

This function will set the thread's priority level. This value, along with the value of the process' priority, determines the thread's base priority level.

Parameters

hThread: Specifies the handle of the thread. Under Windows NT, the handle must have THREAD_SET_INFORMATION access.

nPriority: Specifies the priority level for the thread. This parameter can be one value from Table 6-13.

Return Value

If the function succeeds, it returns TRUE; otherwise it returns FALSE. To get extended error information, call the GetLastError function.

See also

GetPriorityClass, GetThreadPriority, SetPriorityClass

Example

Please see Listing 6-10 under GetThreadPriority.

Table 6-13: SetThreadPriority nPriority Values

Value	Description
THREAD_PRIORITY_ABOVE_NORMAL	One point above normal priority for the priority class.
THREAD_PRIORITY_BELOW_NORMAL	One point below normal priority for the priority class.
THREAD_PRIORITY_HIGHEST	Two points above normal priority for the priority class.
THREAD_PRIORITY_IDLE	Indicates a base priority level of one for IDLE_PRIORITY_CLASS, NORMAL_PRIORITY_CLASS, or HIGH_PRIORITY_CLASS processes, and a base priority level of 16 for REALTIME_PRIORITY_CLASS processes.
THREAD_PRIORITY_LOWEST	Two points below normal priority for the priority class.

Value	Description
THREAD_PRIORITY_NORMAL	Normal priority for the priority class.
THREAD_PRIORITY_TIME_CRITICAL	Indicates a base priority level of 15 for IDLE_PRIORITY_CLASS, NORMAL_PRIORITY_CLASS, or HIGH_PRIORITY_CLASS processes, and a base priority level of 31 for REALTIME_PRIORITY_CLASS processes.

Sleep Windows.Pas

Syntax

```
Sleep(
dwMilliseconds: DWORD        {specifies the number of milliseconds to pause}
);                           {this procedure does not return a value}
```

Description

This function will pause a thread for a specified number of milliseconds.

Parameters

dwMilliseconds: This is the time in milliseconds to pause the thread. If this parameter is set to zero, the thread will relinquish the rest of its time to another thread of the same priority. If there is no other thread with the same priority, the function will return immediately and continue execution.

See also

SuspendThread

Example

Please see Listing 6-2 under CreateMutex.

SuspendThread Windows.Pas

Syntax

```
SuspendThread(
hThread: THandle             {the handle of a thread}
): DWORD;                    {returns the previous suspend count}
```

Description

This function will suspend a thread and increment the thread's suspend count. If the suspend count is zero, the thread is eligible for execution. If the count is greater than zero, the thread is suspended. A thread's suspend count may be no larger than 127.

Parameters

hThread: Specifies the handle of the thread in question.

Return Value

If the function succeeds, it returns the previous suspend count of the thread. If the function fails, it returns $FFFFFFFF.

See also

ResumeThread

Example

Please see Listing 6-5 under DuplicateHandle.

TerminateProcess Windows.Pas

Syntax

```
TerminateProcess(
hProcess: THandle;          {the process handle}
uExitCode: UINT             {the exit code}
): BOOL;                    {returns TRUE or FALSE}
```

Description

TerminateProcess will end a process and all of its threads. This function will not check for or unload DLLs, so calling this function can cause memory leaks.

Parameters

hProcess: The handle to the process to terminate. Under Windows NT, the handle must have PROCESS_TERMINATE access.

uExitCode: Specifies the process exit code. This value may be retrieved from the GetExitCodeProcess function.

Return Value

If the function succeeds, it returns TRUE; otherwise it returns FALSE. To get extended error information, call the GetLastError function.

See also

ExitProcess, OpenProcess, GetExitCodeProcess, GetExitCodeThread

Example

Listing 6-16: Terminating a Launched Process

```
var
  Form1: TForm1;
```

```
  ProcessInfo: TProcessInformation;   // holds process information

implementation

{$R *.DFM}

procedure TForm1.Button1Click(Sender: TObject);
var
  StartUpInfo: TStartUpInfo;   // holds startup information
begin
  {initialize the startup information}
  FillChar(StartupInfo, SizeOf(TStartupInfo), 0);
  with StartupInfo do
  begin
    cb := SizeOf(TStartupInfo);
    dwFlags := STARTF_USESHOWWINDOW;
    wShowWindow := SW_SHOWNORMAL;
  end;

  {launch a process}
  CreateProcess('c:\Windows\calc.exe', nil, nil, nil, False,
      NORMAL_PRIORITY_CLASS, nil, nil, StartupInfo, ProcessInfo);
end;

procedure TForm1.Button2Click(Sender: TObject);
var
  ExitCode: DWORD;             // holds the process exit code
begin
  {terminate the process and retrieve the exit code}
  TerminateProcess(ProcessInfo.HProcess, 10);
  GetExitCodeProcess(ProcessInfo.HProcess, ExitCode);

  {display the exit code}
  Label1.Caption := 'The exit code is '+Inttostr(ExitCode);
end;
```

TerminateThread Windows.Pas

Syntax

TerminateThread(
hThread: THandle; {handle of the thread to terminate}
dwExitCode: DWORD {exit code for the thread}
): BOOL; {returns TRUE or FALSE}

Description

This function terminates a thread without allowing any normal cleanup code to fire. If the target thread owns a critical section, the critical section will not be released. The KERNAL32 state for the thread's process could be inconsistent if the target thread is executing certain KERNAL32 calls when it is terminated. If the target thread is manipulating a shared DLL and changing its global state, its global state could be destroyed, affecting other users of the DLL. Threads cannot be protected against a call to TerminateThread, except by controlling access to its handle.

Parameters

hThread: Specifies the handle of the thread to terminate.

dwExitCode: Specifies the exit code of the thread. To retrieve this value, call the GetExitCodeThread function.

Return Value

If the function succeeds, it returns TRUE; otherwise it returns FALSE. To get extended error information, call the GetLastError function.

See also

CreateProcess, CreateThread, ExitThread, GetExitCodeThread

Example

Listing 6-17: Terminating a Thread Prematurely

```
var
  Form1: TForm1;
  ThreadHandle: THandle;   // holds a handle to the thread

implementation

{$R *.DFM}

function ThreadFunction(Info: Pointer): Integer; stdcall
var
  Count: Integer;       // general loop counter
  FormDC: HDC;          // holds a handle to the form device context
  CountStr: string;     // holds a string representation of Count
begin
  {retrieve a handle to the form's device context}
  FormDC := GetDC(Form1.Handle);

  {show something visual}
  for Count := 1 to 10000 do begin
    CountStr := IntToStr(Count);
    TextOut(FormDC, 10, 10, PChar(CountStr), Length(CountStr));
  end;

  {release the device context}
  ReleaseDC(Form1.Handle, FormDC);
end;

procedure TForm1.Button1Click(Sender: TObject);
var
  ThreadId: Integer;    // holds the thread identifier
  ExitCode: Integer;    // holds the thread exit code
begin
```

```
  {create and execute a thread}
  ThreadHandle := CreateThread(nil, 0, @ThreadFunction, nil, 0, ThreadId);
  if ThreadHandle = 0 then
    ShowMessage('Thread not Started');

  {pause for a very short period}
  Sleep(100);

  {discontinue the thread prematurely}
  TerminateThread(ThreadHandle, 4);

  {retrieve and display the thread's exit code}
  GetExitCodeThread(ThreadHandle, ExitCode);
  Label1.Caption := 'The Thread is Terminated with '+ IntToStr(ExitCode)+
                    ' as the Exit Code';
end;
```

TlsAlloc *Windows.Pas*

Syntax

TlsAlloc: DWORD; {returns a thread local storage index slot}

Description

This function will allocate a thread local storage index. Any thread belonging to the calling process may use the created index to store and retrieve values local to that thread. Each thread of the process will use a thread local storage index to access its own storage slot. Use the TlsSetValue and TlsGetValue functions to set and get values from the index. Indexes cannot be seen across processes. The minimum number of indexes available on most systems is 64.

Return Value

If the function succeeds, it returns a thread local storage index. If the function fails, it returns $FFFFFFFF. To get extended error information, call the GetLastError function.

See also

TlsFree, TlsGetValue, TlsSetValue

Example

Listing 6-18: Using Thread Local Storage to Store String Information

```
var
  Form1: TForm1;
  ThreadHandle: THandle;    // holds a handle to a thread
  NDX: DWORD;               // holds the thread local storage index

implementation

{$R *.DFM}
```

```
function ThreadFunc(Info: Pointer): Integer; stdcall;
Var
  FormDC: HDC;         // holds the forms device context
  AString: PChar;      // points to a string
begin
  {retrieve a handle to the form's device context}
  FormDC := GetDC(Form1.Handle);

  {initialize the string}
  AString := 'Second thread';

  {place this value into the specified index of the thread local storage}
  if not(TlsSetValue(NDX, AString)) then
    ShowMessage('value not set');

  {display the value retrieved from the index of the thread local storage}
  TextOut(FormDC, 10, 50, TlsGetValue(NDX), 13);

  {display the thread local storage index}
  Form1.Label4.Caption := IntToStr(NDX);

  {release the form device context and exit the thread}
  ReleaseDC(Form1.Handle, FormDC);
  ExitThread(4);
end;

procedure TForm1.Button1Click(Sender: TObject);
var
  ThreadId: DWORD;      // holds a thread identifier
  Value: PChar;         // points to a string
  FormDC: HDC;          // holds the form device context
begin
  {allocate a thread local storage index slot}
  NDX := TlsAlloc;

  {retrieve a handle to the form's device context}
  FormDC := GetDC(Form1.Handle);

  {create a thread}
  ThreadHandle := CreateThread(nil, 0, @ThreadFunc, nil, 0, ThreadId);

  {initialize the string}
  Value := 'Main Thread';

  {place this value into the same index of the same thread local
   storage allocated slot.  This value will be different than the
   one in the thread, although they are using the same index}
  if not(TlsSetValue(NDX, Value)) then
    ShowMessage('value not set');

  {display the value at the specified thread local storage slot}
  TextOut(FormDC, 300, 50, TlsGetValue(NDX), 11);

  {display the thread local storage index.  Note that it is the
```

```
     same as reported by the thread}
    Label3.Caption := IntToStr(NDX);

    {release the form's device context}
    ReleaseDC(Form1.Handle, FormDC);
  end;

  procedure TForm1.Button2Click(Sender: TObject);
  begin
    {free the thread local storage slot}
    if not(TlsFree(NDX)) then
      ShowMessage('the TLS index was not freed')
    else
      ShowMessage('the TLS index was freed');
  end;
```

TlsFree Windows.Pas

Syntax

TlsFree(	
dwTlsIndex: DWORD	{the thread local storage index to free}
): BOOL;	{returns TRUE or FALSE}

Description

The TlsFree function will release a thread local storage index. If the index contains a pointer to allocated memory, this memory should be freed before calling TlsFree.

Parameters

dwTlsIndex: A thread local storage index as returned by a previous call to the TlsAlloc function.

Return Value

If the function succeeds, it returns TRUE; otherwise it returns FALSE. To get extended error information, call the GetLastError function.

See also

TlsAlloc, TlsGetValue, TlsSetValue

Example

Please see Listing 6-18 under TlsAlloc.

TlsGetValue Windows.Pas

Syntax

```
TlsGetValue(
dwTlsIndex: DWORD        {thread local storage index containing information}
): Pointer;              {returns the value in the specified index of the calling
                            thread}
```

Description

This function will retrieve the value stored in the specified thread local storage index of the calling thread.

Parameters

dwTlsIndex: The index to the thread local storage as returned by a previous call to the TlsAlloc function.

Return Value

If the function succeeds, it returns a pointer to the value stored at the specified index of thread local storage, and calls the SetLastError function to clear the last error value. If the function fails, it returns NIL.

See also

GetLastError, SetLastError, TlsAlloc, TlsFree, TlsSetValue

Example

Please see Listing 6-18 under TlsAlloc.

TlsSetValue Windows.Pas

Syntax

```
TlsSetValue(
dwTlsIndex: DWORD;       {the thread local storage index}
lpTlsValue: Pointer      {the value to be stored}
): BOOL;                 {returns TRUE or FALSE}
```

Description

This function stores a value in the calling thread's local storage at the specified index. The value stored is unique for each thread, even though the index may be the same.

Parameters

dwTlsIndex: Specifies the thread local storage index at which to store the value, as returned by a previous call to the TlsAlloc function.

lpTlsValue: A pointer to the value to be stored in the thread local storage index specified by the dwTlsIndex parameter.

Return Value

If the function succeeds, it returns TRUE; otherwise it returns FALSE. To get extended error information, call the GetLastError function.

See also

TlsAlloc, TlsFree, TlsGetValue

Example

Please see Listing 6-18 under TlsAlloc.

WaitForInputIdle   Windows.Pas

Syntax

```
WaitForInputIdle(
hProcess: THandle;              {a handle to the process}
dwMilliseconds: DWORD           {the timeout interval in milliseconds}
): DWORD;                       {returns a wait code}
```

Description

This function will wait until the given process has no more input pending and is waiting for user input, or until the timeout period specified by the dwMilliseconds parameter has elapsed. WaitForInputIdle can be used to suspend the execution of a thread that has created a process until that process is finished with all initialization and is ready for input. This function can be used at any time.

Parameters

hProcess: Specifies the handle of the process upon which to wait until it is ready for input.

dwMilliseconds: Specifies the timeout period in milliseconds. If this parameter is set to INFINITE, the function will not return until the specified process is idle.

Return Value

If the function succeeds, it returns one value from Table 6-14. If the function fails, it returns $FFFFFFFF. To get extended error information, call the GetLastError function.

See also

CreateProcess

Example

Listing 6-19: Waiting for a Process to Load

```
procedure TForm1.Button1Click(Sender: TObject);
var
  StartUpInfo: TStartUpInfo;           // holds startup information
  ProcessInfo: TProcessInformation;    // holds process information
begin
  {initialize the startup info structure}
  FillChar(StartupInfo, SizeOf(TStartupInfo), 0);
  with StartupInfo do
  begin
    cb := SizeOf(TStartupInfo);
    dwFlags := STARTF_USESHOWWINDOW;
    wShowWindow := SW_SHOWNORMAL;
  end;

  {launch another copy of Delphi}
  CreateProcess('c:\Program Files\Borland\Delphi 3\Bin\Delphi32.exe', nil, nil,
                nil, False, NORMAL_PRIORITY_CLASS, nil, nil,
                StartupInfo, ProcessInfo);

  {this will cause the application to become unresponsive until Delphi
   has completely finished loading.  the application will not even
   accept focus}
  WaitForInputIdle(ProcessInfo.HProcess, infinite);

  {indicates that Delphi has finished loading}
  ShowMessage('responsiveness restored');
end;
```

Table 6-14: WaitForInputIdle Return Values

Value	Description
0	The wait was satisfied.
WAIT_TIMEOUT	The timeout interval elapsed and the wait was terminated.

WaitForSingleObject Windows.Pas

Syntax

```
WaitForSingleObject(
hHandle: THandle;              {the handle of the object to wait for}
dwMilliseconds: DWORD          {the timeout interval in milliseconds}
): DWORD;                      {returns an event code}
```

Description

This function will check the current state of the specified object. The current thread will enter an efficient wait state if the object is nonsignaled. After the wait condition is satisfied (i.e., the object becomes signaled), the thread resumes execution. In some circumstances, a wait function can specify a handle of a file, named pipe, or communications device as an object to wait for.

Parameters

hHandle: Specifies the handle of the object for which to wait. The object type can be any one value from Table 6-15.

dwMilliseconds: Specifies the timeout period in milliseconds. The function will return after the specified time-out even if the object is nonsignaled. If the parameter is set to zero, the function will test the object and return immediately. If this parameter is set to INFINITE, the timeout interval will never elapse.

Return Value

If the function succeeds, it returns one value from Table 6-16. If the function fails, it returns WAIT_FAILED. To get extended error information, call the GetLastError function.

See also

CreateEvent, CreateFile, CreateMutex, CreateProcess, CreateSemaphore, CreateThread, FindFirstChangeNotification, OpenEvent, OpenMutex, OpenProcess, OpenSemaphore, PulseEvent, ResetEvent, SetEvent, Sleep

Example

Please see Listing 6-1 under CreateEvent.

Table 6-15: WaitForSingleObject hHandle Values

Value	Description
Change notification	The FindFirstChangeNotification function will return this handle. The state of an object is signaled when a specified type of change occurs within a specified directory or directory tree.
Console input	The CreateFile function with CONIN$ specified will return this handle. When there is unread input in the console's input buffer the state is signaled, and it is nonsignaled when the input buffer is empty.
Event	The CreateEvent or OpenEvent function will return this handle. The SetEvent or PulseEvent function will explicitly set the event object to signaled. A manual-reset event object's state must be reset explicitly to nonsignaled by the ResetEvent function. For an auto-reset event object, the wait function resets the object's state to nonsignaled before returning. Event objects are also used in overlapped operations, in which the state is set by the system.

Value	Description
Mutex	The CreateMutex or OpenMutex function will return this handle. When a mutex object is not owned by any thread it is said to be signaled. One of the wait functions will request ownership of the mutex for the calling thread. The state of the mutex is said to be nonsignaled when ownership is granted to a thread.
Process	The CreateProcess or OpenProcess function will return this handle. A process object is said to be signaled when it is terminated.
Thread	The CreateProcess or CreateThread functions will return this handle. The state of the thread is said to be signaled when the thread terminates.
Semaphore	The CreateSemaphore or OpenSemaphore function will return this handle. A semaphore object will maintain a count between zero and some maximum value. The state is signaled when the count is greater than zero and nonsignaled when the count is zero. The wait function will decrease the count by one, if the object is signaled.

Table 6-16: WaitForSingleObject Return Values

Value	Description
WAIT_ABANDONED	The specified object is a mutex whose owning thread was terminated before the mutex was released. Ownership of the mutex object is granted to the calling thread, and the mutex is set to nonsignaled.
WAIT_OBJECT_0	The state of the specified object is signaled.
WAIT_TIMEOUT	The state of the object is nonsignaled, because the timeout interval elapsed.

Chapter 7

Dynamic Link Library Functions

A dynamic link library is a compiled executable file containing functions that can be linked to an application on the fly at runtime. The concept of DLLs is the core of the Windows architectural design; for the most part Windows is simply a collection of DLLs. The core DLLs containing the majority of Win32 API functions are KERNAL32.DLL, USER32.DLL, and GDI32.DLL.

Using a DLL is a powerful way to implement code reusability and code sharing, and can result in smaller executables and better memory management. Bear in mind that DLLs do not have a message queue, and must rely on the calling application to process messages and events. A DLL also shares the calling application's stack.

Importing/Exporting Functions

In order to use a function located within a DLL, it must be exported. This is accomplished in the Exports section of the dynamic link library project code. A function can be exported in four formats:

```
exports
  ShowAboutBox;
```

or

```
exports
  ShowAboutBox name 'ShowAboutBox';
```

or

```
exports
  ShowAboutBox index 1;
```

or

```
exports
  ShowAboutBox index 1 name 'ShowAboutBox';
```

An application can import a function from a dynamic link library at runtime or compile time. At compile time, the application can import a function from a dynamic link library in three formats:

```
function ShowAboutBox(ExampleName, Comments: ShortString): Boolean;
  external 'EXAMPLE.DLL';
```

or

```
function ShowAboutBox(ExampleName, Comments: ShortString): Boolean;
  external 'EXAMPLE.DLL' name 'ShowAboutBox';
```

or

```
function ShowAboutBox(ExampleName, Comments: ShortString): Boolean;
  external 'EXAMPLE.DLL' index 1;
```

To import a function at load time, an application uses the LoadLibrary or LoadLibraryEx functions in conjunction with the GetProcAddress function. This allows a DLL to be loaded and unloaded at will, and can help an application manage resources in a more efficient manner.

Calling Conventions

The nature of Windows and the dynamic link library architecture allow an application written in one language to call a DLL written in another language. However, the developer must pay attention to the method by which the different languages pass parameters on the stack when calling a function, as this will vary from language to language and will come into play when calling a function in a DLL written in a language other than Delphi. There are four different standard methods by which parameters are passed on the stack: pascal, cdecl, fastcall or register, and stdcall. In exporting or importing functions, the calling conventions must match in both the exported and the imported code.

Table 7-1: Function Calling Conventions

Object Pascal	C ++	Description
pascal	PASCAL or _pascal	Parameters are passed from left to right.
cdecl	_cdecl	Parameters are passed from right to left.
stdcall	_stdcall	Parameters are pushed on stack from right to left and retrieved from left to right. This is the Windows standard calling convention.
register	_fastcall	Places the first three parameters into CPU registers, and passes any other parameters on the stack from left to right.

The Dynamic Link Library Entry Point Function

Dynamic link libraries have the option of defining an entry point function that is called whenever the DLL is attached to a process or thread. When the DLL is linked in, either dynamically or explicitly, the entry point function receives a DLL_PROCESS_ATTACH notification. When the DLL is unloaded, the entry point receives a DLL_PROCESS_DETACH notification. If a thread is created by the calling process, it will automatically attach itself to the DLL, and the DLL entry point function receives a DLL_THREAD_ATTACH notification. When the thread terminates, the DLL receives a DLL_THREAD_DETACH notification.

Dynamic Link Library Functions

The following dynamic link library functions are covered in this chapter:

Table 7-2: Dynamic Link Library Functions

Function	Description
DLLEntrypoint	A DLL-defined callback function that receives DLL notification messages.
DisableThreadLibraryCalls	Disables the DLL_THREAD_ATTACH and DLL_THREAD_DETACH DLL entry point notifications.
FreeLibrary	Decrements the reference count of a loaded module by one.
FreeLibraryAndExitThread	Decrements the reference count of a loaded module by one and terminates the calling thread.
GetModuleFileName	Retrieves the module path and filename from a module handle.
GetModuleHandle	Retrieves a module handle from a module name.
GetProcAddress	Retrieves the address of a function within a dynamic link library.
LoadLibrary	Maps a dynamic link library into the address space of the calling process.
LoadLibraryEx	Maps a dynamic link library or an executable into the address space of the calling process.

DLLEntrypoint

Syntax

```
DLLEntrypoint(
hinstDLL HINSTANCE;          {the handle of the DLL module}
dwReason: DWORD;             {the DLL notification message}
lpvReserved: LPVOID;         {initialization indication}
):BOOL;                      {returns TRUE or FALSE}
```

Description

This function is a callback function defined in a dynamic link library for the specific purpose of receiving DLL notification messages. These messages are received when an application or thread loads the DLL into memory. It allows the DLL to initialize any dynamic memory allocations or data structures according to the type of attachment occurring, or to clean up such objects upon detachment.

Parameters

hinstDLL: Specifies the handle to the DLL module.

dwReason: Specifies the DLL notification message. This parameter will contain one value from Table 7-3.

lpvReserved: Specifies more information concerning initialization and cleanup. If the dwReason parameter contains DLL_PROCESS_ATTACH, lpvReserved is set to NIL for dynamic loads and non-NIL for static loads. If dwReason contains DLL_PROCESS_DETACH, lpvReserved is NIL if the DLLEntrypoint function has been called by using FreeLibrary, and non-NIL if the DLLEntrypoint function has been called during process termination.

Return Value

The callback function should return TRUE to indicate that initialization has succeeded, or FALSE to indicate initialization failure. The return value is ignored by the system when sending any notification message other than DLL_PROCESS_ATTACH.

Example

Please see Listing 7-1 under FreeLibraryAndExitThread and Listing 7-3 under LoadLibrary.

Table 7-3: DLLEntrypoint dwReason Values

Value	Description
DLL_PROCESS_ATTACH	Sent when the DLL is attaching to the process's address space.
DLL_PROCESS_DETACH	Sent when the DLL is detaching or being unmapped from process's address space.
DLL_THREAD_ATTACH	Sent when the current process creates a thread.
DLL_THREAD_DETACH	Sent when the current process terminates a thread.

DisableThreadLibraryCalls Windows.Pas

Syntax

```
DisableThreadLibraryCalls(
hLibModule: HMODULE          {the handle to the module}
): BOOL;                     {returns TRUE or FALSE}
```

Description

This function disables the DLL_THREAD_ATTACH and DLL_THREAD_DETACH DLL entry point notifications for the DLL identified by the hLibModule parameter. This is useful in multithreaded applications where threads are created and destroyed frequently and the DLLs they call do not need the thread attachment notification. By disabling the thread attachment notifications, the DLL initialization code is not paged in when a thread is created or deleted, thus reducing the size of the application's working code set. This function should be implemented in the code servicing the DLL_PROCESS_ATTACH notification.

Parameters

hLibModule: Specifies the handle of the dynamic link library.

Return Value

If the function succeeds, it returns TRUE; otherwise it returns FALSE. To get extended error information, call the GetLastError function.

See also

FreeLibraryAndExitThread

Example

Please see Listing 7-1 under FreeLibraryAndExitThread.

FreeLibrary Windows.Pas

Syntax

```
FreeLibrary(
hLibModule: HMODULE     {specifies a handle to the module being freed}
): BOOL;                {returns TRUE or FALSE}
```

Description

The FreeLibrary function decrements the reference count of the loaded dynamic link library. When the reference count reaches zero, the module is unmapped from the address space of the calling process and the handle is no longer valid. Before unmapping a library module, the system enables the DLL to detach from the process by calling the DLL entry point function, if it has one, with the DLL_PROCESS_DETACH notification. Doing so gives the DLL an opportunity to clean up resources allocated on behalf of the current process. After the entry point function returns, the library module is removed from the address space of the current process. Calling FreeLibrary does not affect other processes using the same DLL.

Parameters

hLibModule: A handle to the dynamic link library whose reference count is to be decremented.

Return Value

If the function succeeds, it returns TRUE; otherwise it returns FALSE. To get extended error information, call the GetLastError function.

See also

FreeLibrary, GetModuleHandle, LoadLibrary

Example

Please see Listing 7-4 under LoadLibrary.

FreeLibraryAndExitThread Windows.Pas

Syntax

FreeLibraryAndExitThread(	
hLibModule: HMODULE;	{a handle to the module being freed}
dwExitCode: DWORD	{the exit code for the calling thread}
);	{this procedure does not return a value}

Description

This function frees the dynamic link library identified by the hLibModule parameter and terminates the calling thread. Internally, the function calls the FreeLibrary function to unload the DLL, passing it the value in the hLibModule parameter, then calls the ExitThread function to exit the calling thread, passing it the value in the dwExitCode parameter.

Parameters

hLibModule: Specifies the dynamic link library module whose reference count is to be decremented.

dwExitCode: Specifies the exit code to pass to the calling thread.

See also

FreeLibrary, ExitThread, DisableThreadLibraryCalls

Example

Listing 7-1: The Example Dynamic Link Library

```
library Example;

uses
  SysUtils,
  Classes,
  Windows,
  Dialogs,
  DLLAboutForm in 'DLLAboutForm.pas' {AboutBox};

{the exported functions}
exports
  ShowAboutBox name 'ShowAboutBox';
```

```
{the DLL entry point function.  This fires whenever a process or thread
 attaches to the DLL.  If a process has already loaded the DLL, any new
 threads created by the process will automatically attach themselves}
procedure DLLMain(AttachFlag: DWORD);
 begin
   {indicate attachment type}
   case AttachFlag of
     DLL_PROCESS_ATTACH: begin
                           MessageBox(0, 'Process: Attaching' , 'Alert', MB_OK);

                           {this function disables the DLL_THREAD_ATTACH and
                            DLL_THREAD_DETACH notifications. If the following
                            line is commented out, the DLL will receive
                            the thread attach/detach notification}
                           DisableThreadLibraryCalls(hInstance)
                         end;
     DLL_PROCESS_DETACH: MessageBox(0, 'Process: Dettaching', 'Alert', MB_OK);
     DLL_THREAD_ATTACH:  MessageBox(0, 'Thread: Attaching'  , 'Alert', MB_OK);
     DLL_THREAD_DETACH:  MessageBox(0, 'Thread: Dettaching' , 'Alert', MB_OK);
   end;
end;

begin
  {initialize the DLL entry point function}
  DLLProc := @DLLMain;

  {call the entry point function on DLL initialization}
  DLLMain(DLL_PROCESS_ATTACH);
end.
```

Unit 2

```
{the exported prototype for displaying the about box}
  function ShowAboutBox(DLLHandle: THandle; ExampleName,
                        Comments: ShortString): Boolean; export;

var
  AboutBox: TAboutBox;

implementation

{$R *.DFM}

function ShowAboutBox(DLLHandle: THandle; ExampleName,
                        Comments: ShortString): Boolean;
begin
  {initialize the result value}
  Result := FALSE;

  {create the about box form}
  AboutBox := TAboutBox.Create(Application);

  {initialize the labels with the strings passed in}
  AboutBox.ProductName.Caption := ExampleName;
  AboutBox.Comments.Caption := Comments;
```

```
  {display a modal about box}
  AboutBox.ShowModal;

  {release the form}
  AboutBox.Release;

  {free the DLL and exit the thread from which it was called}
  FreeLibraryAndExitThread(DLLHandle, 12345);

  {indicate that the function completed}
  Result := TRUE;
end;
```

Listing 7-2: Calling the DLL from Within a Thread

```
{the thread function prototype}
  function ThreadFunc(Info: Pointer): Longint; stdcall;

var
  Form1: TForm1;
  hMod: THandle;            // holds the DLL module handle

  {the prototype for the imported DLL function}
  MyFunction: function(DllHandle: THandle; ExampleName,
                       Comments: ShortString): Boolean;

implementation

{$R *.DFM}

function ThreadFunc(Info: Pointer): Longint; stdcall;
begin
  {retrieve the address of the desired function}
  @MyFunction := GetProcAddress(hMod, 'ShowAboutBox' );

  {if an address to the desired function was retrieved...}
  if (@MyFunction<>nil) then
    {display the about box from the DLL}
    MyFunction(hMod, 'FreeLibraryAndExitThread Example',
          'This example demonstrates how to free a dynamic link library '+
          'from within a thread via the FreeLibraryAndExitThread function.');
end;

procedure TForm1.Button1Click(Sender: TObject);
var
  TheThread: DWORD;         // holds the thread identifier
  ThreadHandle: THandle;    // holds a handle to the thread
  ExitCode: integer;        // holds the DLL exit code
begin
  {explicitly load the DLL}
  hMod := LoadLibrary('EXAMPLE.DLL');

  {create a thread that uses the function inside the DLL}
  ThreadHandle := CreateThread(nil, 0, @ThreadFunc, nil, 0, TheThread);
```

```
  if ThreadHandle=0 then
    ShowMessage('Thread not started');

  {wait until the thread has finished execution}
  WaitForSingleObject(ThreadHandle, INFINITE);

  {retrieve the exit code of the thread (returned from the DLL)}
  GetExitCodeThread(ThreadHandle, ExitCode);

  {display the exit code}
  ShowMessage(IntToStr(ExitCode));
end;
```

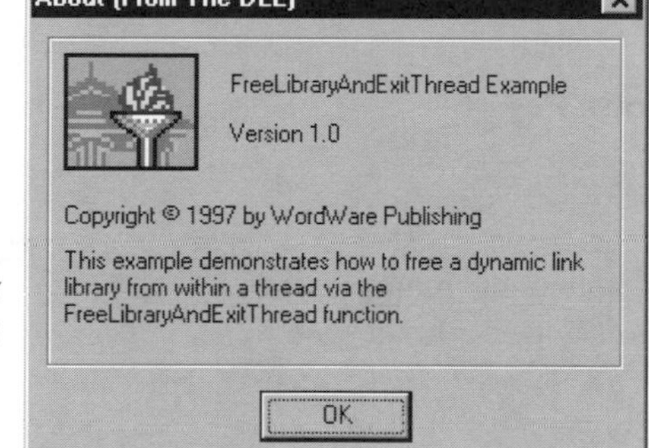

Figure 7-1: The About box displayed from a DLL called inside a thread.

GetModuleFileName   Windows.Pas

Syntax

GetModuleFileName(	
hModule: HINST;	{a handle to the module}
lpFilename: PChar;	{pointer to a null-terminated string buffer}
nSize: DWORD	{the size of the lpFilename buffer}
): DWORD;	{returns the number of characters copied to the buffer}

Description

This function retrieves the full path and filename of the module identified by the handle in the hModule parameter.

Parameters

hModule: A handle to the module whose full path and filename are to be retrieved. If this parameter is set to zero, the function returns the full path and filename of the calling process.

lpFilename: A pointer to a null-terminated string buffer that receives the path and filename.

nSize: Specifies the size of the buffer pointed to by the lpFilename parameter, in characters. If the returned path and filename is larger than this value, the string is truncated.

Return Value

If the function succeeds, it returns the number of characters copied to the buffer pointed to by the lpFilename parameter; otherwise it returns zero. To get extended error information, call the GetLastError function.

See also

GetModuleHandle, LoadLibrary

Example

Please see Listing 7-4 under LoadLibrary.

GetModuleHandle Windows.Pas

Syntax

```
GetModuleHandle(
lpModuleName: PChar          {the name of the module}
): HMODULE;                  {returns a handle to the module}
```

Description

This function returns a handle to the module specified by the lpModuleName parameter if the module has been mapped into the calling process's address space. The returned handle cannot be duplicated, used by another process, or inherited by child processes. GetModuleHandle does not map a module into memory, and will not increment the reference count of a mapped module. Therefore, using a handle returned by this function in a call to the FreeLibrary function can cause a module to be prematurely removed from the process's address space.

Parameters

lpModuleName: A pointer to a null-terminated string containing the name of the loaded module whose handle is to be retrieved. This module can identify either a dynamic link library or an executable. If the file extension is omitted, a default file extension of .DLL is assumed. Name comparison is not case sensitive. If this parameter is set to NIL, the function returns a handle to the calling process.

Return Value

If the function succeeds, it returns a handle to the specified module; otherwise it returns zero. To get extended error information, call the GetLastError function.

See also

FreeLibrary, GetModuleFileName, GetProcAddress, LoadLibrary

Example

Please see Listing 7-4 under LoadLibrary.

GetProcAddress Windows.Pas

Syntax

```
GetProcAddress(
hModule: HMODULE;          {a handle to a module}
ProcName: LPCSTR           {a string identifying the name of the function}
): FARPROC;                {returns the function's address}
```

Description

The GetProcAddress function returns the address of the specified exported dynamic link library function. The returned function can then be called like any other function within the application.

Parameters

hModule: A handle to a dynamic link library. This handle can be retrieved by the LoadLibrary or GetModuleHandle functions.

ProcName: A null-terminated string specifying either the name of the function whose address is to be retrieved, or its ordinal value. If this parameter identifies a function's ordinal value, the value must be in the low-order word, and the high-order word must be zero. The spelling and case of the function name pointed to by the ProcName parameter must be identical to that in the EXPORTS clause of the DLL.

Return Value

If the function succeeds, it returns the address of the exported function within the dynamic link library. If the function fails, it returns NIL.

See also

FreeLibrary, GetModuleHandle, LoadLibrary

Example

Please see Listing 7-4 under LoadLibrary.

LoadLibrary Windows.Pas

Syntax

```
LoadLibrary(
lpLibFileName: PChar       {a string containing the name of the module}
): HMODULE;                {returns a handle to the loaded module}
```

Description

This function maps the module identified by the lpLibFileName parameter into the address space of the calling process. In the case of mapping an executable into the address space, this function returns a handle that can be used with the FindResource or

LoadResource functions. Module handles are not global or inheritable, and cannot be used by another process. If the module specifies a DLL that is not already mapped into the calling process, the system calls the DLL's entry point function with the DLL_PROCESS_ATTACH notification.

Parameters

lpLibFileName: A pointer to a null-terminated string containing the name of the module to load. This module can identify either a dynamic link library or an executable. If the file extension is omitted, a default file extension of .DLL is assumed. If a module of the same name from within the same directory has already been mapped in to the calling process's address space (name comparison is not case sensitive), the reference count for that module is incremented by one, and the function returns a handle to the previously loaded module. If the string specifies a path but the file does not exist, the function fails. If no path is specified, the function searches for the file in the following sequence:

1. The directory from which the calling application was loaded.
2. The current directory.
3. The Windows system directory.
4. The Windows directory.
5. The directories as listed in the PATH environment variable.

Return Value

If the function succeeds, it returns a handle to the loaded module. If the function fails, it returns NIL. To get extended error information, call the GetLastError function.

See also

FindResource, FreeLibrary, GetProcAddress, GetSystemDirectory, GetWindowsDirectory, LoadResource, LoadLibraryEx

Example

Listing 7-3: The Example Dynamic Link Library

```
library Example;

uses
  SysUtils,
  Classes,
  Windows,
  Dialogs,
  DLLAboutForm in 'DLLAboutForm.pas' {AboutBox};

{the exported functions}
exports
  ShowAboutBox name 'ShowAboutBox';

{the DLL entry point procedure.  This procedure will fire every time a
 process or thread attaches to the DLL.  If a process has attached to a DLL,
```

```
 any newly created threads will automatically attach themselves}
procedure DLLMain(AttachFlag: DWORD);
 begin
  {display attachment type}
  case AttachFlag of
    DLL_PROCESS_ATTACH: MessageBox(0, 'Process: Attaching', 'Alert', MB_OK);
    DLL_PROCESS_DETACH: MessageBox(0, 'Process: Detaching', 'Alert', MB_OK);
    DLL_THREAD_ATTACH:  MessageBox(0, 'Thread: Attaching' , 'Alert', MB_OK);
    DLL_THREAD_DETACH:  MessageBox(0, 'Thread: Detaching' , 'Alert', MB_OK);
  end;
end;

begin
  {initialize the DLL entry function}
  DLLProc := @DLLMain;

  {call the entry function upon DLL initialization}
  DLLMain(DLL_PROCESS_ATTACH);
end.
```

Unit 2

```
{the prototype for the exported function}
  function ShowAboutBox(ExampleName, Comments: ShortString): Boolean; export;

var
  AboutBox: TAboutBox;

implementation

{$R *.DFM}

function ShowAboutBox(ExampleName, Comments: ShortString): Boolean;
begin
  {initialize the function results}
  Result := FALSE;

  {create the about box form}
  AboutBox := TAboutBox.Create(Application);

  {initialize labels from the supplied strings}
  AboutBox.ProductName.Caption := ExampleName;
  AboutBox.Comments.Caption := Comments;

  {show a modal about box}
  AboutBox.ShowModal;

  {release the form}
  AboutBox.Release;

  {indicate that the function completed}
  Result := TRUE;
end;
```

Listing 7-4: Loading the Example Dynamic Link Library

```
procedure TForm1.Button1Click(Sender: TObject);
var
   hMod: THandle;                            // holds the DLL handle
   ModuleFileName: array[0..255] of char;    // holds the DLL name

   {this is the prototype for the function imported from the DLL}
   MyFunction: function(ExampleName, Comments: ShortString): Boolean;
begin
   {explicitly load the DLL}
   hMod := LoadLibrary('EXAMPLE.DLL');
   if (hMod=0) then Exit;

   {retrieve the address of the desired function}
   @MyFunction := GetProcAddress(hMod, 'ShowAboutBox' );

   {if the address was returned...}
   if (@MyFunction<>nil) then
   begin
     {call the function to display an about box}
     MyFunction('LoadLibrary Example','This example demonstrates loading '+
                'a dynamic link library via the LoadLibrary function.');

     {retrieve the module filename}
     GetModuleFileName(GetModuleHandle('EXAMPLE.DLL'), @ModuleFileName[0],
                       SizeOf(ModuleFileName));

     {display the DLL's name}
     ShowMessage('The loaded DLL was: '+ModuleFileName);
   end
   else
     {indicate an error}
     ShowMessage('GetProcAddress Failed');

   {free the DLL}
   FreeLibrary(hMod);
end;
```

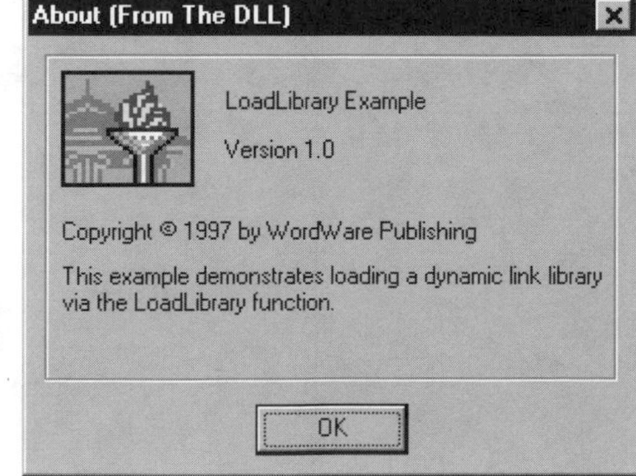

Figure 7-2: The function called from the dynamic link library.

LoadLibraryEx Windows.Pas

Syntax

```
LoadLibraryEx(
lpLibFileName: PChar;          {a string containing the name of the module}
hFile: THandle;                {reserved for future use}
dwFlags: DWORD                 {extended optional behavior flag}
): HMODULE;                    {returns a handle to the loaded module}
```

Description

The LoadLibraryEx function is equivalent to the LoadLibrary function, in that it maps the module identified by the lpLibFileName parameter into the address space of the calling process. However, LoadLibraryEx can map the DLL without calling the DLL entry point function, it can use either of two file search strategies to find the specified module, and it can load a module in a way that is optimized for the case where the module will never be executed, loading the module as if it were a data file. These extended behaviors can be accomplished by setting the dwFlags parameter to a value listed in Table 7-4. Module handles are not global or inheritable, and cannot be used by another process.

Parameters

lpLibFileName: A pointer to a null-terminated string containing the name of the module to load. This module can identify either a dynamic link library or an executable. If the file extension is omitted, a default file extension of .DLL is assumed. If a module of the same name from within the same directory has already been mapped into the calling process's address space (name comparison is not case sensitive), the reference count for that module is incremented by one, and the function returns a handle to the previously loaded module. If the string specifies a path but the file does not exist, the function fails. If no path is specified, the function searches for the file in the following sequence:

1. The directory from which the calling application was loaded.
2. The current directory.
3. The Windows system directory.
4. The Windows directory.
5. The directories as listed in the PATH environment variable.

hFile: Reserved for future use. Set this parameter to zero.

dwFlags: Specifies optional behavior when loading the module. This parameter can contain one value from Table 7-4.

Return Value

If the function succeeds, it returns a handle to the loaded module. If the function fails, it returns NIL. To get extended error information, call the GetLastError function.

See also

FindResource, FreeLibrary, GetProcAddress, GetSystemDirectory, GetWindowsDirectory, LoadResource, LoadLibraryEx

Example

Listing 7-5: The Example DLL

```
library BitmapDLL;

{all this DLL does is provide a storage mechanism for a bitmap}

uses
  SysUtils,
  Classes;

  {link in the bitmap resource}
  {$R BitmapResources.res}
begin
end.
```

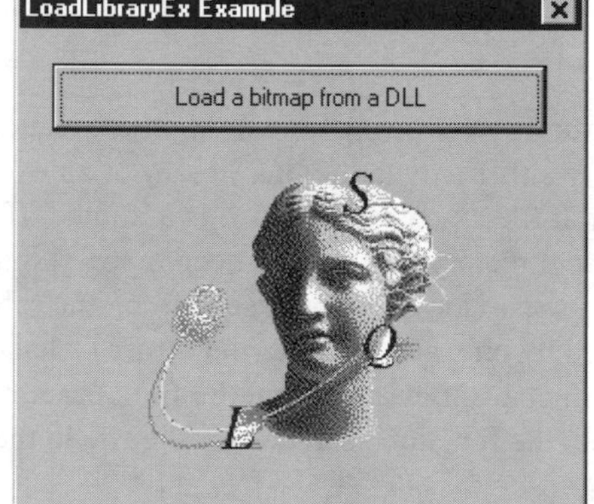

Figure 7-3: The retrieved bitmap resource.

Listing 7-6: Retrieving Resources from a Loaded Dynamic Link Library

```
procedure TForm1.Button1Click(Sender: TObject);
var
   hMod: THandle;            // a handle to the DLL
   BitmapHandle: HBitmap;    // a handle to a bitmap
begin
   {explicitly load the DLL}
   hMod := LoadLibraryEx('BitmapDll.DLL', 0, 0);
   if (hMod = 0) then Exit;

   {retrieve a handle to the bitmap stored in the DLL}
   BitmapHandle := LoadBitmap(hMod, 'BITMAPEXAMPLE');
   If (Bitmaphandle = 0)then Exit;
```

```
   {assign the bitmap to the TImage component}
   Image1.Picture.Bitmap.Handle := BitmapHandle;

   {unload the DLL}
   FreeLibrary(hMod);
end;
```

Table 7-4: LoadLibraryEx dwFlags values

Value	Description
DONT_RESOLVE_DLL_REFERENCES	Windows NT only: The operating system does not call the DLL entry point function for DLL initialization and termination.
LOAD_LIBRARY_AS_DATAFILE	Windows NT only: Maps the specified module into memory as if it were a data file. Functions within a DLL are not available, but the returned handle can be used to retrieve resources.
LOAD_WITH_ALTERED_SEARCH_PATH	Changes the search strategy It is identical to the normal search strategy, except that the function will start its search in the directory of the module being loaded, as opposed to the directory of the calling application.

Chapter 8

Initialization File and Registry Functions

When an application needs to store information that will be persistent from instance to instance, it can either use the file creation functions to store the information in a proprietary format, or it can store it in an initialization file or the Windows registry. Storing information in an initialization file or the registry allows the user to modify the information as needed, which could include enabling or disabling specific functionality. The initialization file and registry functions also give the developer a quick and easy way to store information without having to go through the trouble of writing low-level file output logic or designing a file format.

Initialization Files

Although Microsoft suggests that applications written for Windows 95 or NT write information to the registry, initialization files are still commonly used. Initialization files are somewhat easier to use, and can have much less drastic side effects on the system if they are corrupted or damaged, as opposed to the registry.

An initialization file can store information in a number of formats. The WritePrivateProfileSection and WritePrivateProfileString functions allow the application to write string information to a user-defined initialization file. The WriteProfileSection and WriteProfileString functions perform the same duties, but write information only to the Win.ini file. Although information can only be written in string form, if the string being written consists of a numeric value, it can be retrieved directly as an integer through the GetPrivateProfileInt or GetProfileInt functions. Additionally, the WritePrivateProfileStruct allows the application to write a structured information block to an initialization file key, such as the contents of a data structure. It can subsequently be retrieved by calling the GetPrivateProfileStruct function. The information is stored in the registry in a hexadecimal format. There are no equivalent functions for the Win.ini file.

Windows 95 retains a copy of the Win.ini file in memory. When an application writes information to the Win.ini file, it is actually writing to this cached memory file, and the values will not be immediately written to disk. To force Windows to flush the cached Win.ini file and write all values to disk, call the WriteProfileString function, passing a NIL to all three parameters. Under Windows NT, when an application attempts to read from or write to specific Win.ini key names, the system redirects the action to the registry, reading or writing to registry keys instead of the Win.ini file. This is automatic and completely transparent to the application. To retrieve the remapping settings for Windows NT, look under the key HKEY_LOCAL_MACHINE \ Software \ Microsoft \ Windows NT \ CurrentVersion \ IniFileMapping.

The Registry

Some of the registry functions allow the application to save out a registry key and its subkeys and values to a hive file. Under the FAT file system, this file may not have an extension. These files simply contain the registry information in a format that can be reloaded into the same or another registry. Information in hive files may only be loaded under certain registry keys; see the individual function descriptions concerning hive files for more information.

All example code for the registry functions in this chapter is excerpted from the RegSampApp project under the RegistryEditor directory on the CD.

Initialization File and Registry Functions

The following initialization file and registry functions are covered in this chapter:

Table 8-1: Initialization File and Registry Functions

Function	Description
GetPrivateProfileInt	Retrieves an integer value from a private initialization file.
GetPrivateProfileSection	Retrieves an entire section of values from a private initialization file.
GetPrivateProfileSectionNames	Retrieves all section names from a private initialization file.
GetPrivateProfileString	Retrieves a string value from a private initialization file.
GetPrivateProfileStruct	Retrieves information in the form of a structure from a private initialization file.
GetProfileInt	Retrieves an integer value from the Win.ini file.
GetProfileSection	Retrieves an entire section of values from the Win.ini file.
GetProfileString	Retrieves a string value from the Win.ini file.
RegCloseKey	Closes an opened registry key.
RegCreateKeyEx	Creates a new registry key.
RegDeleteKey	Deletes a registry key.

Function	Description
RegDeleteValue	Deletes a key value for a registry key.
RegEnumKeyEx	Enumerates subkeys of an open registry key.
RegEnumValue	Enumerates the values of an open registry key.
RegFlushKey	Forces new attributes of the key to be written to the registry.
RegLoadKey	Loads registry information into a root key.
RegOpenKeyEx	Opens a registry key.
RegQueryInfoKey	Retrieves information about an open registry key.
RegQueryValueEx	Retrieves the type and data of a value name for a registry key.
RegReplaceKey	Replaces a subkey value in an open key.
RegSaveKey	Saves registry key information to a hive file.
RegSetValueEx	Sets the data of a value name for a registry key.
RegUnLoadKey	Unloads a registry key previously loaded by a call to RegLoadKey.
WritePrivateProfileSection	Writes an entire section of values to a private initialization file.
WritePrivateProfileString	Writes a string value to a private initialization file.
WritePrivateProfileStruct	Writes information in the form of a structure to a private initialization file.
WriteProfileSection	Writes an entire section of values to the Win.ini file.
WriteProfileString	Writes a string value to the Win.ini file.

GetPrivateProfileInt Windows.Pas

Syntax

```
GetPrivateProfileInt(
lpAppName: PChar;          {pointer to section name}
lpKeyName: PChar;          {pointer to key name}
nDefault: Integer;         {default value }
lpFileName: PChar          {pointer to the initialization filename string}
): UINT;                   {returns the integer value}
```

Description

This function retrieves the integer value from the specified key under the specified section in the user-defined private initialization file identified by the lpFileName parameter.

Parameters

lpAppName: A null-terminated string containing the section name from the initialization file.

lpKeyName: A null-terminated string containing the key name from the initialization file.

nDefault: Specifies the default value that is returned if the section and key name is not found.

lpFileName: A null-terminated string containing the name of the initialization file. If the filename does not contain the full path, the system looks for the file in the Windows directory.

Return Value

If the function succeeds, it returns the integer value of the specified key. If the key value is less then zero, the function will return zero. If the function fails, or the key or the section is not found, it returns the default value.

See also

GetProfileInt, WritePrivateProfileString

Example

Listing 8-1: Retrieving an Integer Value from a Private Initialization File

```
procedure TForm1.Button1Click(Sender: Tobject);
var
  IniFile: array[0..255] of char;     //variable to hold filename
begin
  {retrieve the current directory and assemble the ini file name}
  GetCurrentDirectory(254,IniFile);
  StrCat(IniFile,'\MyFile.Ini');

  {retrieve an integer from the ini file}
  Panel1.Caption := IntToStr(GetPrivateProfileInt('transfer','nextnum',0,
                             IniFile))+' is the value of the nextnum entry';
end;
```

GetPrivateProfileSection Windows.Pas

Syntax

GetPrivateProfileSection(	
lpAppName: PChar;	{pointer to section name}
lpReturnedString: PChar;	{buffer to receive section values}
nSize: DWORD;	{size of lpReturnedString buffer}
lpFileName: PChar	{pointer to initialization filename}
): DWORD;	{returns number of bytes copied to the buffer}

Description

This function retrieves all of the key names and key values for the specified section of a private user-defined initialization file. These values are returned as an array of strings.

Parameters

lpAppName: A null-terminated string containing the section name from the initialization file.

lpReturnedString: A null-terminated string buffer that will receive the section key names and values. The function returns key names and key values in the form of a string. Each string is separated by a null character. The last string is followed by two null characters.

nSize: Specifies the maximum size of the lpReturnedString buffer. Under Windows 95, this cannot exceed 32,767 bytes.

lpFileName: A null-terminated string that contains the name of the initialization file. If the filename does not contain the full path, the system will look for the file in the Windows directory.

Return Value

If the function is successful, it returns the number of bytes written to the buffer. If the buffer is too small to receive all of the strings, the function will return a value of nSize-2. If the function fails, it returns zero.

See also

GetProfileSection, WritePrivateProfileSection

Example

Please see Listing 8-18 under WritePrivateProfileSection.

GetPrivateProfileSectionNames Windows.Pas

Syntax

```
GetPrivateProfileSectionNames(
lpszReturnBuffer: PChar;        {buffer to receive strings}
nSize: DWORD;                   {size of lpszReturnBuffer buffer}
lpFileName: PChar               {pointer to initialization filename}
): DWORD;                       {returns number of bytes copied to the buffer}
```

Description

This function retrieves all of the section names contained in a private user-defined initialization file. The names are returned as a series of strings.

Parameters

lpszReturnBuffer: A null-terminated string buffer that will receive the section names. The function returns section names in the form of a string. Each string is separated by a null character. The last string is followed by two null characters.

nSize: Specifies the maximum size of the lpszReturnBuffer buffer.

lpFileName: A null-terminated string that contains the name of the initialization file. If the filename does not contain the full path, the system will look for the file in the Windows directory.

Return Value

If the function is successful, it returns the number of bytes written to the buffer. If the buffer is too small to receive all of the strings, the function will return a value of nSize-2. If the function fails, it returns zero.

See also

GetPrivateProfileSection, WritePrivateProfileSection

Example

Listing 8-2: Retrieving Section Names from a Private Initialization File

```
procedure TForm1.Button1Click(Sender: Tobject);
var
  Buffer: array[0..1024] of char;     // holds the ini section names
  IniFile: array[0..255] of char;     // holds the name of the ini file
  CurString: PChar;                   // a pointer to a section name string
  Return: integer;                    // value for error checking
begin
  {delete any items in the list view}
  ListView1.Items.Clear;

  {retrieve the current directory and assemble the ini file name}
  GetCurrentDirectory(254,IniFile);
  StrCat(IniFile,'\myfile.ini');

  {read in all section names from the users ini file}
  Return := GetPrivateProfileSectionNames(Buffer, SizeOf(Buffer), IniFile);

  {set the pointer to the first string in the buffer}
  CurString := Buffer;

  {if the section ini names were retrieved...}
  if (Return < SizeOf(Buffer)) and (Return > 0) then
    repeat
      {add the name of the section to the list view}
      with ListView1.Items.Add do
      begin
        Caption := StrPas(CurString);
      end;
```

```
      {each string in the buffer is seperated by a null-terminating character.
       increment the string pointer past the null terminator, setting it
       to the first character in the next string}
      Inc(CurString,StrLen(CurString)+1);
    until CurString[0] = Char(0)
  else
    {indicate an error if section names were not retrieved}
    ShowMessage('Error : No Section Names Found');
end;
```


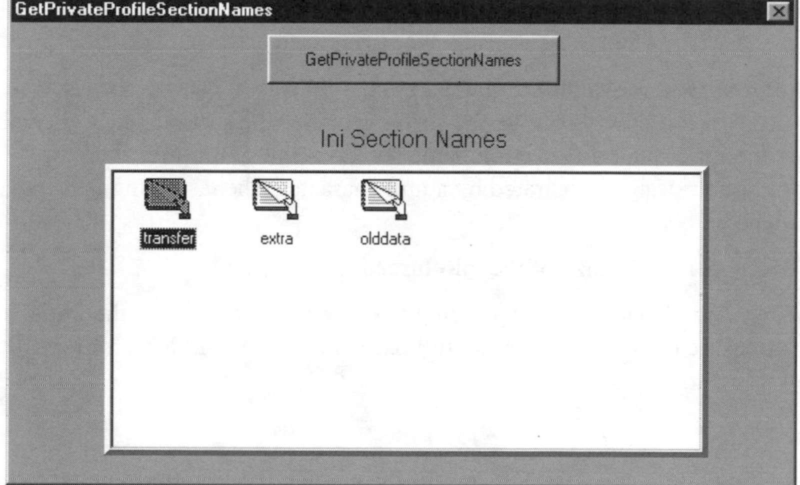

Figure 8-1: The section names from the private initialization file.

GetPrivateProfileString Windows.Pas

Syntax

```
GetPrivateProfileString(
lpAppName:PChar;              {pointer to section name}
lpKeyName:PChar;              {pointer to key name}
lpDefault: PChar;             {default string if key not found}
lpReturnedString: PChar;      {buffer to receive string}
nSize: DWORD;                 {size of lpReturnedString buffer}
lpFileName: PChar             {pointer to initialization filename}
): DWORD;                     {returns number of bytes copied}
```

Description

This function retrieves the string value for the specified registry key in the specified section of a private user-defined initialization file. The function also can retrieve all of the section names for an initialization file or all of the key names for a section.

Parameters

lpAppName: A null-terminated string that contains the section name from the initialization file. If this parameter is set to NIL, the function will return all of the section names in the file.

lpKeyName: A null-terminated string that contains the key name from the initialization file. If this parameter is set to NIL, the function will return all of the key names in the file.

lpDefault: A null-terminated string containing the default value to return if the section or the key is not found.

lpReturnedString: A null-terminated string buffer that receives the retrieved string value. This buffer will receive the string value for the section and key combination. If the function is returning section names or key names, it returns them in the form of a string. Each string is separated by a null character. The last string is followed by two null characters.

nSize: Specifies the size of the lpReturnedString buffer.

lpFileName: A null-terminated string that contains the name of the initialization file. If the filename does not contain the full path, the system will look for the file in the Windows directory.

Return Value

If the function is successful, it returns the number of characters copied to the buffer. If the lpReturnedString buffer is too small, the function returns the value of nSize-1, or nSize-2 if returning key or section names. If the function fails, it returns zero.

See also

GetProfileString, WritePrivateProfileString

Example

Listing 8-3: Retrieving a String from a Private Initialization File

```
procedure TForm1.Button1Click(Sender: TObject);
var
  Buffer:  array[0..255] of char;     // holds the string from the ini file
  IniFile: array[0..255] of char;     // holds the name of the ini file
  KeyName: array[0..255] of char;     // holds the ini key name
  Count: integer;                     // a loop counter
begin
  {initialize the string grid}
  StringGrid1.Cells[0,0] := 'Keyname';
  StringGrid1.Cells[1,0] := 'Value';

  {set the current directory and assemble the ini filename}
  GetCurrentDirectory(254, IniFile);
  StrCat(IniFile, '\myfile.ini');
```

```
  {initialize the counter}
  Count := 1;

  {begin reading a number of strings from the ini file}
  While Count < (GetPrivateProfileInt('transfer', 'nextnum', 0, IniFile)-1) do
  begin
    {assemble the ini key name}
    StrFmt(Keyname,'name%d',[Count]);//Add a number to the name string

    {read in the specified string from the ini file}
    GetPrivateProfileString('Transfer', KeyName, '', Buffer,
                            SizeOf(Buffer), IniFile);

    {display the string}
    StringGrid1.Cells[0,Count] := KeyName; //set to keyname name
    StringGrid1.Cells[1,Count] := Buffer;  //Set to return string

    {continue the loop}
    Inc(Count);
  end;
end;
```


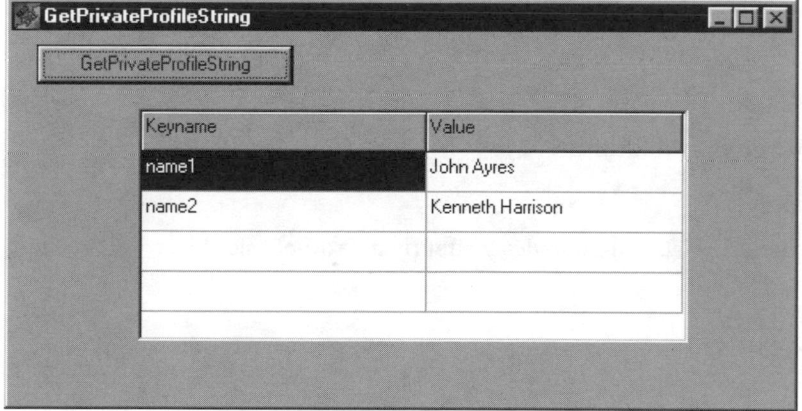

Figure 8-2: The retrieved strings.

GetPrivateProfileStruct *Windows.Pas*

Syntax

GetPrivateProfileStruct(	
lpAppName:PChar;	{pointer to section name}
lpKeyName:PChar;	{pointer to key name}
lpStruct: Pointer;	{buffer to receive structured information}
nSize: UINT;	{size of lpStruct buffer}
lpFileName: PChar	{pointer to initialization filename}
): BOOL;	{returns TRUE or FALSE}

Description

This function retrieves a block of data from the specified key in a section of a private user-defined initialization file. Typically, this is used to retrieve information in the form of a specific data structure.

Parameters

lpAppName: A null-terminated string that contains the section name from the initialization file.

lpKeyName: A null-terminated string that contains the key name from the initialization file.

lpStruct: A pointer to a buffer or data structure that receives the data.

nSize: Specifies the size of the buffer pointed to by the lpStruct parameter.

lpFileName: A null-terminated string that contains the name of the initialization file. If the filename does not contain the full path, the system will look for the file in the Windows directory.

Return Value

If the function succeeds, it returns TRUE; otherwise it returns FALSE.

See also

WritePrivateProfileStruct

Example

Please see Listing 8-20 under WritePrivateProfileStruct.

GetProfileInt Windows.Pas

Syntax

```
GetProfileInt(
lpAppName: PChar;               {pointer to section name}
lpKeyName: PChar;               {pointer to key name}
nDefault: Integer               {default value}
): UINT;                        {returns the integer value}
```

Description

This function retrieves the integer value from a key under a section in the Win.ini initialization file.

Parameters

lpAppName: A null-terminated string that contains the section name from the Win.ini file.

lpKeyName: A null-terminated string that contains the key name from the Win.ini file.

nDefault: Specifies the default value that is returned if the section and key name is not found.

Return Value

If the function succeeds, it returns the integer value of the specified key. If the key value is less then zero the function will return zero. If the function fails, or the key or the section is not found, it returns the default value.

See also

GetPrivateProfileInt, WriteProfileString

Example

Listing 8-4: Retrieving an Integer from the Win.ini File

```
procedure TForm1.Button1Click(Sender: TObject);
begin
  {retrieve a value from the Win.INI file, specifically the value
   for tiling wallpaper}
  if GetProfileInt('Desktop','TileWallpaper',0) > 0 then
    CheckBox1.Checked := True
  else
    CheckBox1.Checked := False;
end;
```

GetProfileSection Windows.Pas

Syntax

GetProfileSection(
lpAppName: PChar; {pointer to section name}
lpReturnedString: PChar; {buffer to receive section values}
nSize: DWORD; {size of lpReturnedString buffer}
): DWORD; {returns number of bytes copied to the buffer}

Description

This function retrieves all of the key names and key values for the specified section in the Win.ini file. These values are returned as a series of strings.

Parameters

lpAppName: A null-terminated string containing the section name from the initialization file.

lpReturnedString: A null-terminated string buffer that will receive the section key names and values. The function returns key names and key values in the form of a string. Each string is separated by a null character. The last string is followed by two null characters.

nSize: Specifies the maximum size of the lpReturnedString buffer. Under Windows 95, this cannot exceed 32,767 bytes

Return Value

If the function is successful, it returns the number of bytes written to the buffer. If the buffer is too small to receive all of the strings, the function will return a value of nSize-2. If the function fails, it returns zero.

See also

GetPrivateProfileSection, WriteProfileSection

Example

Please see Listing 8-21 under WriteProfileSection.

GetProfileString Windows.Pas

Syntax

```
GetProfileString(
lpAppName:PChar;              {pointer to section name}
lpKeyName:PChar;              {pointer to key name}
lpDefault: PChar;             {default string if key not found}
lpReturnedString: PChar;      {buffer to receive string}
nSize: DWORD;                 {size of lpReturnedString buffer}
): DWORD;                     {returns number of bytes copied}
```

Description

This function retrieves the string value for the specified registry key in the specified section of the Win.ini file. The function also can retrieve all of the section names for an initialization file or all of the key names for a section.

Parameters

lpAppName: A null-terminated string that contains the section name from the initialization file. If this parameter is set to NIL, the function will return all of the section names in the file.

lpKeyName: A null-terminated string that contains the key name from the initialization file. If this parameter is set to NIL, the function will return all of the key names in the file.

lpDefault: A null-terminated string containing the default value to return if the section or the key is not found.

lpReturnedString: A null-terminated string buffer that receives the retrieved string value. This buffer will receive the string value for the section and key combination. If the function is returning section names or key names, it does so in the form of a string. Each string is separated by a null character. The last is followed by two null characters.

nSize: Specifies the size of the lpReturnedString buffer.

Return Value

If the function is successful, it returns the number of characters copied to the buffer. If the lpReturnedString buffer is too small, the function returns the value of nSize-1, or nSize-2 if returning key or section names. If the function fails, it returns zero.

See also

GetPrivateProfileString, WriteProfileString

Example

Please see Listing 8-22 under WriteProfileString.

RegCloseKey Windows.Pas

Syntax

```
RegCloseKey(
hKey: HKEY                  {handle of the key to close}
): Longint;                 {returns an error code}
```

Description

This function releases the open registry key handle retrieved from a prior call to the RegCreateKeyEx or RegOpenKeyEx functions. Calling RegClose key does not guarantee that a new value is written to the registry. The system can take up to several seconds to write the new values. To guarantee that all values are written to the registry, call the RegFlushKey function.

Parameters

hKey: Specifies the handle of the registry key to close.

Return Value

If the function succeeds, it returns ERROR_SUCCESS. If it fails, it returns an error code that can be used with the FormatMessage function to retrieve an error message.

See also

RegCreateKeyEx, RegDeleteKey, RegFlushKey, RegOpenKeyEx, RegSetValueEx

Example

Please see Listing 8-5 under RegCreateKeyEx.

RegCreateKeyEx Windows.Pas

Syntax

```
RegCreateKeyEx(
hKey: HKEY;                                   {parent key of subkey to create}
lpSubKey: PChar;                              {string that contains the name of the subkey}
Reserved: DWORD;                              {reserved}
lpClass: PChar;                               {points to a class string}
dwOptions: DWORD;                             {storage option flags}
samDesired: REGSAM;                           {security option flags}
lpSecurityAttributes: PSecurityAttributes;    {requested security attributes}
var phkResult: HKEY;                          {buffer for the handle of the new key}
lpdwDisposition: PDWORD                       {existence flags}
): Longint;                                   {returns an error code}
```

Description

This function is used to create or open a subkey of a parent key. The newly created key does not contain any values.

Parameters

hKey: Specifies the handle of the parent key of the subkey to open or create. This can be any open key or one of the following root key values:

HKEY_CLASSES_ROOT
HKEY_CURRENT_USER
HKEY_LOCAL_MACHINE
HKEY_USERS

lpSubKey: A null-terminated string containing the name of the subkey to create. If the key already exists, the function will simply open the existing key.

Reserved: Reserved for future use; must be set to zero.

lpClass: A null-terminated string containing the class type of the subkey to create.

dwOptions: Specifies storage options for the key. This parameter may contain one value from Table 8-2.

samDesired: Specifies access security options for the key. This parameter may contain one value from Table 8-3.

lpSecurityAttributes: A pointer to a TSecurityAttributes structure that determines if the open key handle can be inherited by child processes. If this parameter is set to NIL, the handle cannot be inherited. The TSecurityAttributes data structure is defined as:

```
TSecurityAttributes = record
    nLength: DWORD;                       {the size of the TSecurityAttributes structure}
    lpSecurityDescriptor: Pointer;        {the security descriptor}
    bInheritHandle: BOOL;                 {handle inheritance flags}
```

end;

Please see the CreateFile function for a description of this data structure.

phkResult: A pointer to a buffer that receives the newly created registry key handle.

lpdwDisposition: A pointer to a buffer that receives a flag indicating the key's previous existence. This parameter can contain one value from Table 8-4.

Return Value

If the function succeeds, it returns ERROR_SUCCESS. If the function fails, it returns an error code that can be used with the FormatMessage function to retrieve an error message.

See also

RegCloseKey, RegDeleteKey, RegOpenKeyEx, RegSaveKey

Example

Listing 8-5: Creating a New Registry Key

```
procedure TForm1.Key1Click(Sender: TObject);
var
  KeyName: string;          // holds a registry key name
  NewName: string;          // holds the new registry key name
  nKey,                     // holds handles of the opened and new keys
  pKey: hKey;
  KeyResult: DWORD;         // holds the disposition value
begin
  {retrieve the name for the new key}
  NewName := InputBox('Enter new Key ','Enter New Key Name','');

  {if a name was specified, open the parent key from the selected treenode}
  pKey:=0;
  if NewName <> '' then
    pKey := OpenNodeKey(TreeView1.Selected, KeyName);

  {if the parent key was opened...}
  if pKey = 0 then
    ShowMessage('Error opening parent key')
  else
  begin
    {...create a new child key with the specified name}
    RegCreateKeyEx(pKey, PChar(NewName), 0, nil, 0, Key_All_Access,
                   nil, nKey, @KeyResult);

    {if the key did not already exist, add it to the treeview}
    if KeyResult = REG_OPENED_EXISTING_KEY then
      ShowMessage('Key Already Exists')
    else
    begin
      TreeView1.Selected:=TreeView1.Items.AddChild(TreeView1.Selected,NewName);
      TreeView1.Selected.ImageIndex := 0;
```

```
      TreeView1.Selected.SelectedIndex := 1;
    end;

    {close both the parent key and the child key}
    RegCloseKey(nKey);
    RegCloseKey(pKey);
  end;
end;
```

Table 8-2: RegCreateKeyEx dwOptions

Value	Description
REG_OPTION_NON_VOLATILE	Saves the key when the system is restarted. This is the default value.
REG_OPTION_VOLATILE	Windows NT only: The key is created but will only be in memory. When the system is restarted the values will be gone. RegSaveKey will not save a key with this option set.
REG_OPTION_BACKUP_RESTORE	Windows NT only: Creates a key with access to the system security to backup and restore values to the registry.

Table 8-3: RegCreateKeyEx samDesired Values

Value	Description
KEY_ALL_ACCESS	Total access.
KEY_CREATE_LINK	Allowed to create links.
KEY_CREATE_SUB_KEY	Allowed to create subkeys.
KEY_ENUMERATE_SUB_KEYS	Allowed to enumerate all subkeys.
KEY_EXECUTE	Allowed to read data.
KEY_NOTIFY	Allowed to set a notification value.
KEY_QUERY_VALUE	Allowed to read subkey data.
KEY_READ	Combination of KEY_ENUMERATE_SUB_KEYS, KEY_NOTIFY, and KEY_QUERY_VALUE flags.
KEY_SET_VALUE	Allowed to set subkey values.
KEY_WRITE	Allowed to set values and create subkeys.

Table 8-4: RegCreateKeyEx lpdwDisposition Values

Value	Description
REG_CREATED_NEW_KEY	A key was created.
REG_OPENED_EXISTING_KEY	A currently existing key was opened.

RegDeleteKey Windows.Pas

Syntax

RegDeleteKey(
hKey: HKEY; {handle to the parent key of the subkey to delete}
lpSubKey: PChar {specifies the name of the key to delete}
): Longint; {returns an error code}

Description

This function is used to delete a subkey from inside of a parent key. The function deletes the subkey and all of its associated values from the registry.

Parameters

hKey: Specifies the handle of the parent key of the subkey to delete. This can be any open key or one of the following root key values:

HKEY_CLASSES_ROOT
HKEY_CURRENT_USER
HKEY_LOCAL_MACHINE
HKEY_USERS

lpSubKey: A pointer to a null-terminated string that contains the name of the subkey to delete.

Return Value

If the function succeeds, it returns ERROR_SUCCESS. If the function fails, it returns an error code that can be used with the FormatMessage function to retrieve an error message.

See also

RegCloseKey, RegDeleteKey, RegOpenKeyEx, RegSaveKey

Example

Listing 8-6: Deleting a Registry Key

```
procedure TForm1.DeleteKey2Click(Sender: TObject);
var
  KeyName: string;                      // holds the name of the key to be deleted
  pValueName: array[0..100] of char;  // holds the value name
  pKey: hKey;                           // the handle of the key to be deleted
begin
  {ensure that the user has not elected to delete a base key}
  if TreeView1.Selected.Level <= 1 then
    ShowMessage('Cannot Delete base Keys')
  else
    {confirm that the selected key is to be deleted}
    if MessageBox(Form1.Handle, 'Are you sure you want to delete this registry'+
                  ' key?', 'Confirmation Box', MB_OKCANCEL) = IDOK then
```

Chapter 8

```
    begin
      {open the selected key's parent}
      pKey := OpenNodeKey(TreeView1.Selected.Parent, KeyName);

      if pKey = 0 then
        ShowMessage('Cannot open parent key')
      else
      begin
        StrPCopy(pValueName, TreeView1.Selected.Text);
        {if the parent key was opened, delete the selected key}
        if RegDeleteKey(pKey, pValueName)= 0 then
          TreeView1.Items.Delete(TreeView1.Selected)
        else
          ShowMessage('Could not delete key');
      end;
    end;
end;
```

RegDeleteValue Windows.Pas

Syntax

RegDeleteValue(	
hKey: HKEY;	{handle of key from which to delete a value}
lpValueName: PChar	{string that identifies the value}
): Longint;	{returns an error code}

Description

This function is used to delete the value specified by the lpValueName parameter from inside the open key identified by the hKey parameter.

Parameters

hKey: Specifies the handle of the key from which the specified value is to be deleted. This can be any open key or one of the following root key values:

HKEY_CLASSES_ROOT
HKEY_CURRENT_USER
HKEY_LOCAL_MACHINE
HKEY_USERS

lpValueName: A null-terminated string identifying the name of the value to delete.

Return Value

If the function succeeds, it returns ERROR_SUCCESS. If the function fails, it returns an error code that can be used with the FormatMessage function to retrieve an error message.

See also

RegSetValueEx

Example

Listing 8-7: Deleting a Registry Value

```
procedure TForm1.ListView1DblClick(Sender: TObject);
var
  phKey: hKey;                         // holds the open key handle
  KeyName: string;                     // holds the name of the open key
  NewValue: string;                    // holds the new key value
  pNewValue: array[0..255] of char;    // a PChar holding the new key value
  pValueName: array[0..255] of char;  // a PChar holding the new value name
  ValueSize: DWORD;                    // holds the size of the new value buffer
begin
  if ListView1.Selected.ImageIndex = 0 then
  begin
    {retrieve the size of the new value buffer}
    ValueSize := SizeOf(pNewValue);

    {open the selected key}
    phKey := OpenNodeKey(TreeView1.Selected,KeyName);

    {retrieve the name of the selected value}
    StrPCopy(pValueName, ListView1.Selected.Caption);
    if pValueName = '[Default]' then
      pValueName := '';

    {retrieve the current value setting}
    RegQueryValueEx(phKey, @pValueName, nil, nil, @pNewValue, @ValueSize);

    {query the user for a new value}
    NewValue := InputBox('Edit value','Enter New string value', pNewValue);

    if (NewValue <> '') and not (NewValue = ListView1.Selected.Subitems[0])then
    begin
      {set the value to the new user supplied value and update the screen}
      StrPCopy(pNewValue, NewValue);
      RegSetValueEx(phKey, pValueName,0, Reg_sz, @pNewValue, StrLen(pNewValue));
      TreeView1Change(TreeView1,TreeView1.Selected)
    end;

    {if no value was specified, attempt to delete the value}
    if NewValue = '' then
     if MessageBox(Form1.Handle,'Do you want to delete this value from the '+
                 'registry', 'Confirmation Box', MB_OKCANCEL) = IDOK then
     begin
       {delete the selected value and update the screen}
       StrPCopy(pValueName, ListView1.Selected.Caption);
       if pValueName = '[Default]' then pValueName := '';
       RegDeleteValue(phKey, pValueName);
       TreeView1Change(TreeView1,TreeView1.Selected)
     end;
```

```
  {close the registry key}
  RegCloseKey(phKey);
  end;
end;
```

RegEnumKeyEx Windows.Pas

Syntax

```
RegEnumKeyEx(
hKey: HKEY;                        {handle to key to be enumerated}
dwIndex: DWORD;                    {index of subkey to retrieve}
lpName: PChar;                     {buffer to receive name of subkey}
var lpcbName: DWORD;               {size of the name buffer}
lpReserved: Pointer;               {reserved for future use}
lpClass: PChar;                    {buffer to receive the class name}
lpcbClass: PDWORD;                 {size of the class name buffer}
lpftLastWriteTime: PFileTime       {time of the last edit to the subkey}
): Longint;                        {returns an error code}
```

Description

This function is used to retrieve all of the subkeys for key specified by the hKey parameter. On the first call to the function, the dwIndex parameter should be set to zero. The value of the parameter is increased by one for each subsequential call until the function returns ERROR_NO_MORE_ITEMS.

Parameters

hKey: Specifies the handle of the key whose subkeys are to be enumerated. This can be any open key or one of the following root key values.

HKEY_CLASSES_ROOT
HKEY_CURRENT_USER
HKEY_LOCAL_MACHINE
HKEY_USERS

dwIndex: Specifies the index of the item to be retrieved. This parameter should initially be set to 0 and increased by 1 for each subsequential call until all subkeys are retrieved.

lpName: A pointer to a null-terminated string buffer that receives the name of the subkey for the current index.

var lpcbName: Specifies the maximum size of the subkey name buffer.

lpReserved: Reserved for future use.

lpClass: A pointer to a null-terminated string buffer that will receive the name of the class of the subkey retrieved by the function.

lpcbClass: Specifies the maximum size of the class name buffer.

lpftLastWriteTime: A pointer to a buffer that will receive the time stamp of the last time this subkey was changed.

Return Value

If the function succeeds, it returns ERROR_SUCCESS. The function will return ERROR_NO_MORE_ITEMS when the dwIndex parameter exceeds the number of subkeys for the key. If the function fails, it returns an error code that can be used with the FormatMessage function to retrieve an error message.

See also

RegCreateKeyEx, RegDeleteKey, RegOpenKeyEx, RegQueryInfoKey

Example

Listing 8-8: Retrieving All Subkeys for a Specific Key

```
procedure AddChildren(pString: string; pKey: hKey; pNode: TTreeNode);
var
  ChildKey: hKey;                       // holds a registry key
  ICounter: integer;                    // holds a subkey index
  ID: TTreeNode;                        // points to a treenode
  BufferSize: DWORD;                    // holds the size of a key name
  ElementName: array[0..100] of char; // holds a key name
begin
  {initialize index and key name buffer length variables}
  ICounter := 0;
  BufferSize := 100;

  {add a new node to the treeview}
  ID := TreeView1.Items.AddChild(pNode, pString);
  ID.ImageIndex := 0;
  ID.SelectedIndex := 1;

  {begin enumerating sub keys}
  while RegEnumKeyEx(pKey, ICounter, ElementName, BufferSize,
                     nil, nil, nil, nil) = 0 do
  begin
    {open this sub key...}
    if RegOpenKeyEx(pKey, ElementName, 0, KEY_ENUMERATE_SUB_KEYS,
                    ChildKey) = 0 then
    begin
      {...and enumerate its children}
      AddChildren(ElementName, ChildKey, ID);

      {close the key}
      RegCloseKey(ChildKey);
    end;
```

```
    {reset the key name length buffer}
    BufferSize := 100;

    {increment the sub key index counter}
    Inc(ICounter);
  end;
end;
```

RegEnumValue *Windows.Pas*

Syntax

```
RegEnumValue(
hKey: HKEY;                     {handle to key to be enumerated}
dwIndex: DWORD;                 {index of item to retrieve}
lpValueName: PChar;             {buffer to receive value name}
var lpcbValueName: DWORD;       {size of name buffer}
lpReserved: Pointer;            {reserved for future use}
lpType: PDWORD;                 {type of value retrieved}
lpData: PByte;                  {buffer to receive value}
lpcbData: PDWORD                {size of value buffer}
): Longint;                     {returns an error code}
```

Description

This function is used to retrieve all of the values for an open key. On the first call to the function, the dwIndex parameter should be set to zero. The value of the parameter is increased by one for each subsequent call until the function returns ERROR_NO_MORE_ITEMS.

Parameters

hKey: Specifies the handle of the key whose values are to be enumerated. This can be any open key or one of the following root key values:

HKEY_CLASSES_ROOT
HKEY_CURRENT_USER
HKEY_LOCAL_MACHINE
HKEY_USERS

dwIndex: Specifies the index of the item to be retrieved. This parameter should initially be set to 0 and increased by 1 for each subsequent call until all values are retrieved.

lpValueName: A pointer to a null-terminated string buffer that will receive the name of the value that is retrieved.

var lpcbValueName: Specifies the size of the value name buffer.

lpReserved: Reserved for future use.

lpType: A pointer to a buffer that receives a flag indicating the type of value retrieved, and may contain one value from Table 8-5. This parameter can be set to NIL if the type value is not needed.

lpData: A pointer to a buffer that receives the data.

lpcbData: Specifies the size of the data buffer.

Return Value

If the function succeeds, it returns ERROR_SUCCESS. The function will return ERROR_NO_MORE_ITEMS when the dwIndex parameter exceeds the number of value names for the key. If the function fails, it returns an error code that can be used with the FormatMessage function to retrieve an error message.

See also

RegCreateKeyEx, RegEnumKeyEx, RegOpenKeyEx, RegQueryInfoKey

Example

Listing 8-9: Enumerating Key Values

```
procedure TForm1.TreeView1Change(Sender: TObject; Node: TTreeNode);
var
  KeyName: string;                      // holds the key name
  ICount: integer;                      // value index
  dType,dLength: DWORD;                 // holds the type and length of key value
  IData: array[0..255] of char;         // holds the retrieved key value
  BufferSize: DWORD;                    // holds the size of a key name
  ElementName: array[0..100] of char; // holds a key name
begin
  {if there is a key currently open, close it}
  if SelKey <> 0 then RegCloseKey(SelKey);

  {open a key for the selected treenode}
  SelKey := 0;
  SelKey := OpenNodeKey(Node, KeyName);

  {clear out the list view}
  ListView1.Items.Clear;

  {initialize the required variables}
  ICount := 0;
  BufferSize:=100 ;
  dLength:=254;

  {begin enumerating key values}
  while RegEnumValue(SelKey, ICount, ElementName, BufferSize, nil,
                     @dType, @iData, @dLength) = 0 do
  begin
    {reset length variables for the next pass}
    BufferSize:= 100;
    dLength:=254;
```

Chapter 8

```
    {create a new item in the listview}
    with ListView1.Items.Add do
    begin
      {display the value name}
      if ElementName = '' then
        Caption := '[Default]'
      else
        Caption := ElementName;

      {display the value's data}
      case dType of
        REG_SZ: SubItems.Add(iData);
        REG_DWORD: begin
                     SubItems.Add(FloatToStr(DWORD(iData[0])));
                     ImageIndex:=1;
                   end
      else
        SubItems.Add('');
      end;
    end;

    {increment the counter for the next enumeration pass}
    Inc(ICount);
  end;

  {display the selected registry key's name}
  StatusBar1.SimpleText := KeyName;

  {turn on specific UI elements according to the level of the selected node}
  if Node.Level > 0 then
    New1.Enabled := TRUE
  else
    New1.Enabled := FALSE;
  New2.Enabled := New1.Enabled;
  if Node.Level > 1 then
    DeleteKey1.Enabled := TRUE
  else
    DeleteKey1.Enabled := FALSE;
  DeleteKey2.Enabled := DeleteKey1.Enabled;
end;
```

Table 8-5: RegEnumValue lpType Values

Value	Description
REG_BINARY	Binary data.
REG_DWORD	Double word value.
REG_DWORD_LITTLE_ENDIAN	Double word value in little endian format. This format has the most significant byte in the high-order byte of each word. This is the same as REG_DWORD.
REG_DWORD_BIG_ENDIAN	Double word value in big endian format. This format has the most significant byte in the low-order byte of each word.

Value	Description
REG_EXPAND_SZ	A string that contains an unexpanded reference to a system environment variable.
REG_LINK	A link to another subkey.
REG_MULTI_SZ	An array of null-terminated strings followed by a double null character.
REG_NONE	Undefined type.
REG_RESOURCE_LIST	A device-driver resource list.
REG_SZ	A null-terminated string.

RegFlushKey *Windows.Pas*

Syntax

```
RegFlushKey(
hKey: HKEY                    {handle of key to be written to disk}
): Longint;                   {returns an error code}
```

Description

This function is used to immediately write all of the values and subkeys contained within the key identified by the hKey parameter to disk. The system normally will write to the disk only after the key is closed. This normal process can take several seconds at which time an incorrect value could be retrieved from the registry. This function will write the information before any other action is taken. This will cause a performance hit to the system. This function should only be used when the values have to be immediately written.

Parameters

hKey: Specifies the handle of the key whose values and subkeys are to be immediately written to disk. This can be any open key or one of the following root key values:

HKEY_CLASSES_ROOT
HKEY_CURRENT_USER
HKEY_LOCAL_MACHINE
HKEY_USERS

Return Value

If the function succeeds, it returns ERROR_SUCCESS. If the function fails, it returns an error code that can be used with the FormatMessage function to retrieve an error message.

See also

RegCloseKey, RegDeleteKey

Example

Listing 8-10: Forcing a Registry Key to be Written to Disk

```
procedure TForm1.NewStringValue1Click(Sender: TObject);
var
  phKey: hKey;                          // a handle to the key
  KeyName: string;                      // holds the opened key name
  pNewValue: array[0..255] of char;     // holds the new string value
  pValueName: array[0..255] of char;    // holds the new value name
begin
  {prompt the user for a new string value}
  if Form2.ShowModal = IDOK then
  begin
    {open the selected key}
    phKey := OpenNodeKey(TreeView1.Selected, KeyName);

    {copy the value name and value to the null terminated strings}
    StrPCopy(pNewValue,Form2.Edit2.Text);
    StrPCopy(pValueName,Form2.Edit1.Text);

    {create the new value in the selected key}
    RegSetValueEx(phKey, pValueName, 0, REG_SZ, @pNewValue, StrLen(pNewValue));

    {force the key to be written to the registry}
    RegFlushKey(phKey);

    {update UI elements to reflect the new value}
    TreeView1Change(TreeView1,TreeView1.Selected);
    Form2.Edit1.Text := '';
    Form2.Edit2.Text := '';
  end;
end;
```

RegLoadKey Windows.Pas

Syntax

```
RegLoadKey(
hKey: HKEY;                 {handle of parent key to be loaded}
lpSubKey: PChar;            {name of subkey where values are to be loaded}
lpFile: PChar               {filename of hive file}
): Longint;                 {returns an error code}
```

Description

This function is used to create a subkey and load a series of subkeys and values under the new subkey from a hive file. A hive file is a file created with the RegSaveKey function, and contains subkeys and values.

Parameters

hKey: Specifies the key into which a new key is to be created and subkey values are loaded. This has to be set to either HKEY_USER or HKEY_LOCAL_MACHINE.

lpSubKey: A pointer to a null-terminated string that contains the name of the new key to create.

lpFile: A pointer to a null-terminated string that contains the name of the hive file which holds the subkeys and values to be loaded. Under the FAT file system, this filename cannot have an extension.

Return Value

If the function succeeds, it returns ERROR_SUCCESS. If the function fails, it returns an error code that can be used with the FormatMessage function to retrieve an error message.

See also

RegDeleteKey, RegReplaceKey, RegRestoreKey, RegSaveKey, RegUnloadKey

Example

Listing 8-11: Loading a Registry Hive File

```
procedure TForm1.ImportRegistryFile1Click(Sender: TObject);
var
  phKey: hKey;                         // holds the open key handle
  FileName: array[0..255] of char;     // holds the registry filename to import
  NewKeyName: array[0..255] of char;   // holds the new key name
  KeyName: string;                     // holds the opened key name
  InputName: string;                   // holds the registry filename to import
begin
  {open the selected key}
  phKey := OpenNodeKey(TreeView1.Selected, KeyName);

  {retrieve the name of the registry file to import}
  InputName := InputBox('Enter file name','Enter a file name without extension',
                        '');

  {retrieve the name for the new key}
  KeyName := InputBox('Enter key name','Enter the new key name','');

  {copy the keyname and filename to null terminated string buffers}
  StrPCopy(FileName,InputName);
  StrPCopy(NewKeyName,KeyName);

  {load the registry key file}
  if RegLoadKey(phKey, NewKeyName, FileName)= 0 then
    ShowMessage('Registry file was loaded')
  else
    ShowMessage('Registry file was not loaded');

  {close the key and update the screen}
```

```
  RegCloseKey(phKey);
  Refresh1Click(Form1);
end;
```

RegOpenKeyEx Windows.Pas

Syntax

```
RegOpenKeyEx(
hKey: HKEY;                    {handle of the parent key to open}
lpSubKey: PChar;               {the subkey name}
ulOptions: DWORD;              {reserved}
samDesired: REGSAM;            {key security requested}
var phkResult: HKEY            {handle of new open key}
): Longint;                    {returns an error code}
```

Description

This function is used to open an existing subkey in the registry or to open another handle to an open key.

Parameters

hKey: This can be any open key or one of the following root key values:

HKEY_CLASSES_ROOT
HKEY_CURRENT_USER
HKEY_LOCAL_MACHINE
HKEY_USERS

lpSubKey: A pointer to a null-terminated string that contains the name of the subkey to open. If this parameter points to an empty string, the function will open another handle to the key identified by the hKey parameter.

ulOptions: Reserved for future use. Set this parameter to zero.

samDesired: Specifies the security access option requested. This parameter can contain one or more values from Table 8-6.

phkResult: A variable that will receive the new handle to the opened key.

Return Value

If the function succeeds, it returns ERROR_SUCCESS. If the function fails, it returns an error code that can be used with the FormatMessage function to retrieve an error message.

See also

RegCreateKeyEx, RegDeleteKey

Example

Listing 8-12: Opening a Registry Key

```
function OpenNodeKey(sNode: TTreeNode; var KeyName: string): hKey;
var
  iNode: TTreeNode;             // a treenode pointer
  RootKey: hKey;                // a handle to the root key of the specific node
begin
  {initialize the temporary pointer to the specified treenode}
  iNode := sNode;

  {initialize the root key handle}
  RootKey := 0;

  {begin working our way up the tree until we hit the root,
   building a comprehensive registry key name from the treenode strings.}
  if sNode.Level > 1 then
  begin
    KeyName := sNode.Text;
    iNode := sNode.Parent;
    while iNode.Level > 1 do
    begin
      KeyName := iNode.Text+'\'+KeyName;
      iNode := iNode.Parent;
    end;
  end;

  {retrieve the root key for the specified node}
  case iNode.Index of
    0: RootKey := HKEY_CLASSES_ROOT;
    1: RootKey := HKEY_CURRENT_USER;
    2: RootKey := HKEY_LOCAL_MACHINE;
    3: RootKey := HKEY_USERS;
    4: RootKey := HKEY_PERFORMANCE_DATA;
    5: RootKey := HKEY_CURRENT_CONFIG;
    6: RootKey := HKEY_DYN_DATA;
  end;

  {open the specified key}
  if KeyName = '' then
    Result := RootKey
  else
    RegOpenKeyEx(RootKey, PChar(KeyName), 0, KEY_ALL_ACCESS, Result);
end;
```

Table 8-6: RegOpenKeyEx samDesired Values

Value	Description
KEY_ALL_ACCESS	Total access.
KEY_CREATE_LINK	Allowed to create links.
KEY_CREATE_SUB_KEY	Allowed to create subkeys.
KEY_ENUMERATE_SUB_KEYS	Allowed to enumerate all subkeys.

8 Chapter

Value	Description
KEY_EXECUTE	Allowed to read data.
KEY_NOTIFY	Allowed to set a notification value.
KEY_QUERY_VALUE	Allowed to read subkey data.
KEY_READ	Combination of KEY_ENUMERATE_SUB_KEYS, KEY_NOTIFY, and KEY_QUERY_VALUE flags.
KEY_SET_VALUE	Allowed to set subkey values.
KEY_WRITE	Allowed to set values and create subkeys.

RegQueryInfoKey *Windows.Pas*

Syntax

```
RegQueryInfoKey(
hKey: HKEY;                          {handle of key to query}
lpClass: PChar;                      {buffer to receive class name of key}
lpcbClass: PDWORD;                   {size of class name buffer}
lpReserved: Pointer;                 {reserved}
lpcSubKeys: PDWORD;                  {buffer to receive count of subkeys}
lpcbMaxSubKeyLen: PDWORD;            {buffer to receive max size of subkey name}
lpcbMaxClassLen: PDWORD;     {buffer to receive max size of subkey class name}
lpcValues: PDWORD;                   {buffer to receive count of values}
lpcbMaxValueNameLen: PDWORD;         {buffer to receive max size of value name}
lpcbMaxValueLen: PDWORD;             {buffer to receive max size of value}
lpcbSecurityDescriptor: PDWORD;      {buffer to rcv. size of key security desc.}
lpftLastWriteTime: PFileTime         {buffer to receive time stamp of last mod.}
): Longint;                          {returns an error code}
```

Description

This function is used to retrieve information about an open key. This function will retrieve the number of subkeys, values, class name, security descriptor, and the maximum lengths for the subkey names, class names, and value names.

Parameters

hKey: Specifies the handle of the key whose information is to be retrieved. This can be any open key or one of the following root key values:

HKEY_CLASSES_ROOT
HKEY_CURRENT_USER
HKEY_LOCAL_MACHINE
HKEY_USERS

lpClass: A pointer to a null-terminated string buffer that will receive the name of the key's class.

lpcbClass: Specifies the maximum size of the class name buffer, not including the terminating null character.

lpReserved: Reserved for future use.

lpcSubKeys: A pointer to a buffer that will receive the number of subkeys that the key contains.

lpcbMaxSubKeyLen: A pointer to a buffer that will receive the length of the longest subkey name, not including the terminating null character.

lpcbMaxClassLen: A pointer to a buffer that will receive the length of the longest subkey class name, not including the terminating null character.

lpcValues: A pointer to a buffer that will receive the number of values that the key contains.

lpcbMaxValueNameLen: A pointer to a buffer that will receive the length of the longest value name, not including the terminating null character.

lpcbMaxValueLen: A pointer to a buffer that will receive the size of the largest value.

lpcbSecurityDescriptor: A pointer to a buffer that will receive the security descriptor for the key.

lpftLastWriteTime: A pointer to a buffer that will receive the time stamp of the last modification to the key.

Return Value

If the function succeeds, it returns ERROR_SUCCESS. If the function fails, it returns an error code that can be used with the FormatMessage function to retrieve an error message.

See also

RegDeleteKey, RegEnumKeyEx, RegEnumValue, RegQueryValueEx

Example

Listing 8-13: Retrieving Key Information

```
procedure TForm1.GetKeyInfo1Click(Sender: TObject);
var
  phKey: hKey;                          // holds a handle to a registry key
  KeyName: string;                      // holds the key name
  ClassName: array[0..255] of char;     // holds a key class name
  CNLen, SubLen, MaxSubLen,             // holds various length values
  MaxClassLen, NumValues, MaxVNLen,
  MaxVLen: DWORD;
begin
  {initialize the classname string and length variables}
  CNLen := 255;
  ClassName := '';
```

```
  {open the selected key}
  phKey := OpenNodeKey(TreeView1.Selected, KeyName);

  {retrieve information about the selected key}
  RegQueryInfoKey(phKey, @ClassName, @CNLen, nil, @SubLen, @MaxSubLen,
                  @MaxClassLen, @NumValues, @MaxVNLen, @MaxVLen, nil, nil);

  {display the retrieved information}
  Form3.Panel2.Caption :=StrPas(ClassName);
  Form3.Panel3.Caption :=IntToStr(SubLen);
  Form3.Panel4.Caption :=IntToStr(MaxSubLen);
  Form3.Panel5.Caption :=IntToStr(MaxClassLen);
  Form3.Panel6.Caption :=IntToStr(NumValues);
  Form3.Panel7.Caption :=IntToStr(MaxVNLen);
  Form3.Panel8.Caption :=IntToStr(MaxVLen);
  Form3.label1.Caption :=KeyName;
  Form3.ShowModal;

  {close the selected key}
  RegCloseKey(phKey);
end;
```

RegQueryValueEx Windows.Pas

Syntax

```
RegQueryValueEx(
hKey: HKEY;                    {handle to key to retrieve value}
lpValueName: PChar;            {name of value to retrieve}
lpReserved: Pointer;           {reserved}
lpType: PDWORD;                {buffer to receive value type}
lpData: PByte;                 {buffer to receive data}
lpcbData: PDWORD               {maximum value size}
): Longint;                    {returns an error code}
```

Description

This function retrieves the value and the value type from the specified value name under an open register key.

Parameters

hKey: Specifies the key from which to retrieve the value. This can be any open key or one of the following root key values:

HKEY_CLASSES_ROOT
HKEY_CURRENT_USER
HKEY_LOCAL_MACHINE
HKEY_USERS

lpValueName: A null-terminated string containing the name of the value to retrieve.

lpReserved: Reserved for future use. Set this parameter to NIL.

lpType: A pointer to a buffer that will receive the type of the value that is retrieved. This buffer will contain one value from Table 8-7.

lpData: A pointer to a buffer that receives the value of the specified value name.

lpcbData: Specifies the maximum size of the buffer pointed to by the lpData parameter.

Return Value

If the function succeeds, it returns ERROR_SUCCESS. If the function fails, it returns an error code that can be used with the FormatMessage function to retrieve an error message.

See also

RegCreateKeyEx, RegEnumKeyEx, RegEnumValue, RegOpenKeyEx, RegQueryInfoKey

Example

Listing 8-14: Retrieving Value Information

```
procedure TForm1.Button1Click(Sender: TObject);
var
  MyKey: HKey;                       // holds a registry key handle
  ValueType: DWORD;                  // holds the key value type
  MyData: array[0..255] of char;     // holds the string from the registry
  dLength: DWORD;                    // holds the length of the returned string
begin
  {open the registry key}
  if RegOpenKeyEx(HKEY_LOCAL_MACHINE, 'SOFTWARE\Borland\Delphi\3.0',
                  0, 0, MyKey) = 0 then
  begin
    {retrieve and display directory information}
    dLength := SizeOf(MyData);
    RegQueryValueEx(MyKey, 'RootDir', nil, @ValueType, @MyData[0], @dLength);
    StaticText1.Caption := MyData;

    {retrieve and display version information}
    dLength := SizeOf(MyData);
    RegQueryValueEx(MyKey, 'Version', nil, @ValueType, @MyData[0], @dLength);
    StaticText2.Caption := MyData;

    {retrieve and display program file information}
    dLength := SizeOf(MyData);
    RegQueryValueEx(MyKey, 'Delphi 3', nil, @ValueType, @MyData[0], @dLength);
    StaticText3.Caption := MyData;

    {close the registry key}
    RegCloseKey(MyKey);
   end
  else
    {indicate if there was an error opening the registry key}
```

```
    ShowMessage('Key not Opened');
end;
```

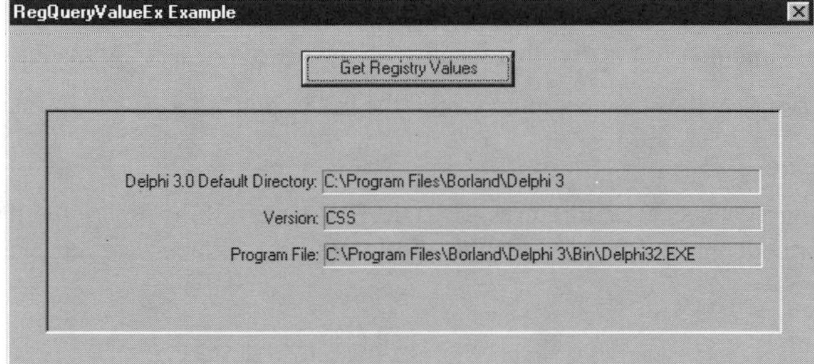

Figure 8-3: The registry key value information.

Table 8-7: RegQueryValueEx lpType Values

Value	Description
REG_BINARY	Binary data.
REG_DWORD	Double word value.
REG_DWORD_LITTLE_ENDIAN	Double word value in little endian format. This format has the most significant byte in the high-order byte of each word. This is the same as REG_DWORD.
REG_DWORD_BIG_ENDIAN	Double word value in big endian format. This format has the most significant byte in the low-order byte of each word.
REG_EXPAND_SZ	A string that contains an unexpanded reference to a system environment variable.
REG_LINK	A link to another subkey.
REG_MULTI_SZ	An array of null-terminated strings followed by a double null character.
REG_NONE	Undefined type.
REG_RESOURCE_LIST	A device-driver resource list.
REG_SZ	A null-terminated string.

RegReplaceKey   Windows.Pas

Syntax

```
RegReplaceKey(
hKey: HKEY;            {handle to open parent key}
lpSubKey: PChar;       {name of subkey}
lpNewFile: PChar;      {filename for imported key information}
```

lpOldFile: PChar {filename for saving key information}
): Longint; {returns an error code}

Description

This function is used to replace a subkey value in an open key, saving a backup of the old subkey values. The key values are imported from and saved to a hive file. This function will only work on keys that were previously loaded with the RegLoadKey function.

Parameters

hKey: Specifies the key into which the new key is to be created. This has to be set to either HKEY_USER or HKEY_LOCAL_MACHINE.

lpSubKey: A pointer to a null-terminated string that contains the name of the key to replace.

lpNewFile: A pointer to a null-terminated string that contains the name of the hive file which contains the subkeys and values to be loaded. Under the FAT file system, this filename cannot have an extension.

lpOldFile: A pointer to a null-terminated string that contains the name of the hive file which will receive the original subkeys and values. Under the FAT file system, this filename cannot have an extension.

Return Value

If the function succeeds, it returns ERROR_SUCCESS. If the function fails, it returns an error code that can be used with the FormatMessage function to retrieve an error message.

See also

RegDeleteKey, RegLoadKey, RegRestoreKey

Example

Listing 8-15: Replacing a Registry Key

```
procedure TForm1.RegistryReplaceKey1Click(Sender: TObject);
var
  phKey: hKey;                          // holds the open key handle
  FileName: array[0..255] of char;      // holds the imported filename
  OldFileName: array[0..255] of char;   // holds the saved filename
  NewKeyName: array[0..255] of char;    // holds the selected key name
  KeyName: string;                      // holds the selected key name
  InputName: string;                    // holds the imported filename
  OutPutName: string;                   // holds the saved filename
begin
  {open the selected key}
  phKey := OpenNodeKey(TreeView1.Selected.Parent, KeyName);

  {retrieve the filename for the key to load}
```

```
  InputName := InputBox('Enter file name','Enter file name to load','');

  {retrieve a filename to save the selected key to}
  OutputName:= InputBox('Enter file name','Enter file name to save to','');

  {copy the filenames and the selected key name to null terminated string buffers
  StrPCopy(FileName, InputName);
  StrPCopy(OldFileName, OutputName);
  StrPCopy(NewKeyName, TreeView1.Selected.Text);

  {save the current key to a file and replace it with the
   key information from the specified file}
  if RegReplaceKey(phKey, NewKeyName, FileName, OldFileName)= 0 then
  begin
    ShowMessage('Key Replaced');
    Refresh1Click(Form1);
  end
  else
    ShowMessage('Key Not Replaced');

  {close the selected key}
  RegCloseKey(phKey);
end;
```

RegSaveKey *Windows.Pas*

Syntax

```
RegSaveKey(
hKey: HKEY;                                     {handle of parent key}
lpFile: PChar;                                  {name of hive file to create}
lpSecurityAttributes: PSecurityAttributes       {points to a security descriptor }
): Longint;                                     {returns an error code}
```

Description

This function is used to export a registry key and all of its subkeys and their values to a hive file. This hive file then can be reloaded using RegReplaceKey or RegLoadKey.

Parameters

hKey: Specifies the handle of the key to save. This can be any open key or one of the following root key values:

HKEY_CLASSES_ROOT
HKEY_CURRENT_USER
HKEY_LOCAL_MACHINE
HKEY_USERS

lpFile: A null-terminated string containing the filename of the hive file to create. Under the FAT file system, this filename cannot have an extension.

lpSecurityAttributes: A pointer to a TSecurityAttributes structure that determines if the open key handle can be inherited by child processes. If this parameter is set to NIL, the handle cannot be inherited.

Return Value

If the function succeeds, it returns ERROR_SUCCESS. If the function fails, it returns an error code that can be used with the FormatMessage function to retrieve an error message.

See also

RegCreateKeyEx, RegDeleteKey, RegLoadKey, RegReplaceKey

Example

Listing 8-16: Saving Registry Information

```
procedure TForm1.ExportRegistryFile1Click(Sender: TObject);
var
  phKey: hKey;                          // holds the open key handle
  FileName: array[0..255] of char;  // holds an exported registry filename
  KeyName: string;                      // holds the opened key name
  InputName: string;                    // holds the exported registry filename
begin
  {open the selected key}
  phKey := OpenNodeKey(TreeView1.Selected, KeyName);

  {retrieve a filename for the exported registry keys}
  InputName := InputBox('Enter filename','Enter a filename without extension.',
                        '');
  StrPCopy(FileName,InputName);

  {save the selected key's information to disk}
  if RegSaveKey(phKey, FileName, nil)= 0 then
    ShowMessage('Key information exported.')
  else
    ShowMessage('Key information not exported.');

  {close the open key}
  RegCloseKey(phKey);
end;
```

RegSetValueEx   Windows.Pas

Syntax

```
RegSetValueEx(
hKey: HKEY;                   {handle to parent key}
lpValueName: PChar;           {name of value to save}
Reserved: DWORD;              {reserved}
dwType: DWORD;                {type of value to save}
```

```
lpData: Pointer;              {value to save}
cbData: DWORD                 {size of data}
): Longint;                   {returns an error code}
```

Description

This function is used to create a value name and set a value under an open registry key.

Parameters

hKey: Specifies the handle of the parent key that is receiving a new value. This can be any open key or one of the following root key values:

HKEY_CLASSES_ROOT
HKEY_CURRENT_USER
HKEY_LOCAL_MACHINE
HKEY_USERS

lpValueName: A null-terminated string that contains the name of the value to set. If this value is not present under the specified key, it is created.

Reserved: Reserved for future use. Set this parameter to zero.

dwType: Specifies the type of data to be set. This parameter can be set to one value from Table 8-8.

lpData: A pointer to a buffer that holds the value to be set.

cbData: Specifies the size of the data buffer pointed to by the lpData parameter. If the data is a string value, the size must include the null-terminating character.

Return Value

If the function succeeds, it returns ERROR_SUCCESS. If the function fails, it returns an error code that can be used with the FormatMessage function to retrieve an error message.

See also

RegCreateKeyEx, RegFlushKey, RegOpenKeyEx, RegQueryValueEx

Example

Please see Listing 8-10 under RegFlushKey.

Table 8-8: RegSetValueEx dwType Values

Value	Description
REG_BINARY	Binary data.
REG_DWORD	Double word value.
REG_DWORD_LITTLE_ENDIAN	Double word value in little endian format. This format has the most significant byte in the high-order byte of each word. This is the same as REG_DWORD.

Value	Description
REG_DWORD_BIG_ENDIAN	Double word value in big endian format. This format has the most significant byte in the low-order byte of each word.
REG_EXPAND_SZ	A string that contains an unexpanded reference to a system environment variable.
REG_LINK	A link to another subkey.
REG_MULTI_SZ	An array of null-terminated strings followed by a double null character.
REG_NONE	Undefined type.
REG_RESOURCE_LIST	A device-driver resource list.
REG_SZ	A null-terminated string.

RegUnLoadKey Windows.Pas

Syntax

```
RegUnLoadKey(
hKey: HKEY;               {handle of parent key}
lpSubKey: PChar           {name of subkey to unload}
): Longint;               {returns an error code}
```

Description

This function is used to unload a subkey from the registry. This subkey must have been loaded from a hive file using the RegLoadKey function.

Parameters

hKey: Specifies the parent key of the subkey to be unloaded. This must be set to either HKEY_USER or HKEY_LOCAL_MACHINE.

lpSubKey: A null-terminated string that contains the name of the subkey to unload. This subkey must have been created from a previous call to the RegLoadKey function.

Return Value

If the function succeeds, it returns ERROR_SUCCESS. If the function fails, it returns an error code that can be used with the FormatMessage function to retrieve an error message.

See also

RegDeleteKey, RegLoadKey

Example

Listing 8-17: Unloading a Previously Loaded Registry Key

```
procedure TForm1.RegistryUnloadKey1Click(Sender: TObject);
```

```
var
  phKey: hKey;                          // holds the open key handle
  NewKeyName: array[0..255] of char;  // holds the key name
  KeyName: string;                      // holds the key name
begin
  {open the selected key}
  phKey := OpenNodeKey(TreeView1.Selected.Parent, KeyName);

  {retrieve the keyname and store it in the null-terminated string buffer}
  KeyName := TreeView1.Selected.Text;
  StrPCopy(NewKeyName,KeyName);

  {unload the selected key.  Note that this key must have previously
   been loaded with the RegLoadKey function}
  RegUnloadKey(phKey,NewKeyName);

  {close the opened key and update the screen}
  RegCloseKey(phKey);
  ShowMessage('key unloaded');
  Refresh1Click(form1)
end;
```

WritePrivateProfileSection *Windows.Pas*

Syntax

```
WritePrivateProfileSection(
lpAppName: PChar;             {pointer to section name}
lpString: PChar;              {pointer to section value strings}
lpFileName: PChar             {pointer to initialization filename}
): BOOL;                      {returns TRUE or FALSE}
```

Description

This function deletes all key names and values from the specified section of a private user-defined initialization file and replaces them with the key names and values pointed to by the lpString parameter. If the section identified by the lpAppName parameter does not exist, a new section is created at the end of the initialization file.

Parameters

lpAppName: A null-terminated string containing the section name from the initialization file.

lpString: A pointer to a buffer that contains a string or a series of strings. Each string is formatted as

"Key = Value"

If the buffer contains more than one string, each string is separated by a null character. The last string is followed by two null characters.

lpFileName: A null-terminated string that contains the name of the initialization file. If the filename does not contain the full path, the system will look for the file in the Windows directory. If the file does not exist, a new initialization file will be created.

Return Value

If the function succeeds, it returns TRUE; otherwise it returns FALSE.

See also

GetPrivateProfileSection, WriteProfileSection

Example

Listing 8-18: Writing a Section of a Private Initialization File

```
procedure TForm1.Button1Click(Sender: TObject);
var
  Buffer: array[0..1024] of char;     // holds returned ini section strings
  IniFile: array[0..255] of char;     // holds the name of the ini file
  CurString: PChar;                   // a pointer to a section string
  Return: integer;                    // value for error checking
begin
  {clear the memo}
  Memo1.Lines.Clear;

  {get the current directory and assemble the ini file name}
  GetCurrentDirectory(254,IniFile);
  StrCat(IniFile,'\myfile.ini');

  {read in a section from the private ini file}
  Return := GetPrivateProfileSection('transfer', Buffer,  SizeOf(Buffer), IniFile);

  {set the string pointer to the beginning of the ini file section}
  CurString := Buffer;

  {if the ini section was retrieved...}
  if (Return < SizeOf(Buffer)) and (Return > 0) then
    repeat
      {add the ini section line to the memo component}
      Memo1.Lines.Add(StrPas(CurString));

      {the ini section strings are seperated with a null-terminated
       character, so increment the string pointer to the next character
       after the null terminator, which starts the next string}
      Inc(CurString,StrLen(CurString)+1);
    until CurString[0] = Char(0)
 else
   {indicate an error if the section was not retrieved}
   ShowMessage('Error: No Strings found');
end;

procedure TForm1.Button2Click(Sender: TObject);
var
  Buffer: array[0..1024] of char;     // holds returned ini section strings
```

```
  IniFile: array[0..255] of char;       // holds the name of the ini file
  CurString: PChar;                     // a pointer to a section string
  Counter: integer;                     // general loop counter
begin
  {set the string pointer to the beginning of the buffer, and clear the buffer}
  CurString := Buffer;
  FillChar(Buffer,SizeOf(Buffer),Char(0));

  {copy each line in the memo to the buffer}
  for Counter := 0 to Memo1.Lines.Count-1 do
  begin
    {copy the string as a PChar}
    StrPCopy(CurString,Memo1.Lines[Counter]);

    {since each line in the buffer must be separated by a null terminator
     character, we must increment the string pointer past this last
     null terminating character so that the next line is copied after
     the previous line and the separating null terminators are preserved}
    Inc(CurString,StrLen(CurString)+1);
  end;

  {assemble the ini file name}
  GetCurrentDirectory(254,IniFile);
  StrCat(IniFile,'\myfile.ini');

  {write the collection of strings to the ini file section}
  WritePrivateProfileSection('transfer', Buffer, IniFile);
end;
```

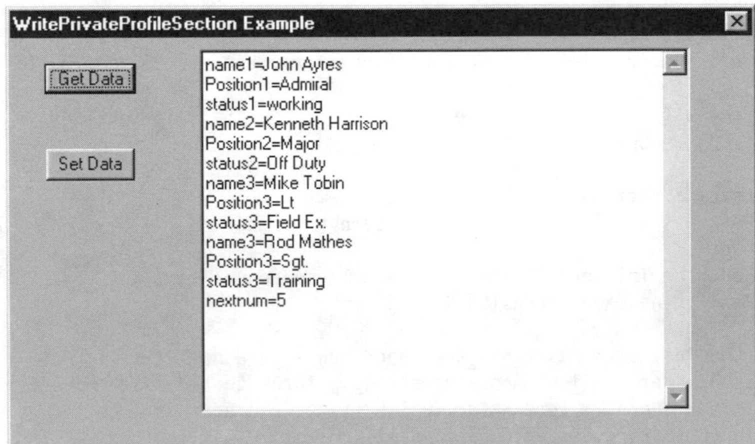

Figure 8-4: The initialization file section.

WritePrivateProfileString Windows.Pas

Syntax

```
WritePrivateProfileString(
lpAppName:PChar;            {pointer to section name}
lpKeyName:PChar;            {pointer to key name}
lpString: PChar;            {pointer to a string}
lpFileName: PChar           {pointer to initialization filename}
): BOOL;                    {returns TRUE or FALSE}
```


Description

This function sets the string value for the specified registry key in the specified section of a private user-defined initialization file. The function can also create sections inside of the initialization file.

Parameters

lpAppName: A null-terminated string that contains the section name from the initialization file. If the section does not exist, the function will create it.

lpKeyName: A null-terminated string that contains the key name from the initialization file. If the key does not exist, the function will create it. If this parameter is set to NIL, the function will delete the entire section.

lpString: A pointer to a buffer that contains a string or a series of strings. Each string is formatted as

"Key = Value"

If the buffer contains more than one string, each string is separated by a null character. The last string is followed by two null characters.

lpFileName: A null-terminated string that contains the name of the initialization file. If the filename does not contain the full path, the system will look for the file in the Windows directory. If the file does not exist, a new initialization file will be created.

Return Value

If the function succeeds, it returns TRUE; otherwise it returns FALSE.

See also

GetPrivateProfileString, WriteProfileString

Example

Listing 8-19: Writing a String Value to an Initialization File

```
procedure TForm1.Button1Click(Sender: TObject);
var
  Buffer:  array[0..255] of char;     // holds the string from the ini file
  IniFile: array[0..255] of char;     // holds the name of the ini file
```

```
begin
  {set the current directory and assemble the ini filename}
  GetCurrentDirectory(254, IniFile);
  StrCat(IniFile, '\myfile.ini');

  {retrieve a string from the ini file}
  GetPrivateProfileString('Transfer', 'Position1', '', Buffer,
                          SizeOf(Buffer), IniFile);

  {display the retrieved string}
  Edit1.Text := Buffer;
end;

procedure TForm1.Button2Click(Sender: TObject);
var
  IniFile: array[0..255] of char;     // holds the name of the ini file
begin
  {set the current directory and assemble the ini filename}
  GetCurrentDirectory(254,IniFile);
  StrCat(IniFile,'\myfile.ini');

  {write the string to the ini file}
  WritePrivateProfileString('Transfer', 'Position1', PChar(Edit1.Text), IniFile);
end;
```

WritePrivateProfileStruct ***Windows.Pas***

Syntax

WritePrivateProfileStruct(	
lpAppName:PChar;	{pointer to section name}
lpKeyName:PChar;	{pointer to key name}
lpStruct: Pointer;	{buffer to receive structured information}
nSize: UINT;	{size of lpStruct buffer}
lpFileName: PChar	{pointer to initialization file name}
): BOOL;	{returns TRUE or FALSE}

Description

This function writes a block of data to the specified key in a section of a private user-defined initialization file. Typically, this is used to write information in the form of a specific data structure.

Parameters

lpAppName: A null-terminated string that contains the section name from the initialization file.

lpKeyName: A null-terminated string that contains the key name from the initialization file.

lpStruct: A pointer to a buffer or data structure that contains the data to be written to the initialization file.

nSize: Specifies the size of the buffer pointed to by the lpStruct parameter.

lpFileName: A null-terminated string that contains the name of the initialization file. If the filename does not contain the full path, the system will look for the file in the Windows directory.

Return Value

If the function succeeds, it returns TRUE; otherwise it returns FALSE.

See also

GetPrivateProfileStruct

Example

Listing 8-20: Writing Structured Information to an Initialization File

```
{declare the record structure for our data}
  MyRecord = packed record
    Name: string[20];
    Position: string[20];
    Status: string[20];
  end;

{Whoops!  Delphi incorrectly imports the GetPrivateProfileStruct and
 WritePrivateProfileStruct functions, so we must import them manually}
function GetPrivateProfileStruct(lpszSection, lpszKey: PChar;
  lpStruct: Pointer; uSizeStruct: UINT; szFile: PChar): BOOL; stdcall;
function WritePrivateProfileStruct(lpszSection, lpszKey: PChar;
  lpStruct: Pointer; uSizeStruct: UINT; szFile: PChar): BOOL; stdcall;

var
  Form1: TForm1;
  MyData: MyRecord;  // holds information in our data structure

implementation

{link in the imported function}
function GetPrivateProfileStruct;    external 'Kernel32.dll' name
                                'GetPrivateProfileStructA';
function WritePrivateProfileStruct; external 'Kernel32.dll' name
                                'WritePrivateProfileStructA';

procedure TForm1.Button1Click(Sender: TObject);
var
  IniFile: array[0..255] of char;     // holds the ini file name
begin
  {get the current directory and assemble the ini filename}
  GetCurrentDirectory(254, IniFile);
  StrCat(IniFile, '\myfile.ini');
```

```
  {retrieve the data from the member1 key.  in the ini file, this data
   is represented in hexadecimal form, but when retrieved it will be in
   the form of our data structure}
  if GetPrivateProfileStruct('Transfer', 'member1', @MyData,
                             SizeOf(MyData), IniFile) then
  begin
    {display the retrieved data}
    Panel1.caption := MyData.Name;
    Panel2.caption := MyData.Position;
    Panel3.caption := MyData.Status;
  end;
end;

procedure TForm1.Button2Click(Sender: TObject);
var
  IniFile: array[0..255] of char;     // holds the ini file name
begin
  {assemble the user supplied information}
  MyData.Name     := Edit1.Text;
  MyData.Position := Edit2.Text;
  MyData.Status   := Edit3.Text;

  {get the current directory and assemble the ini filename}
  GetCurrentDirectory(254,IniFile);
  StrCat(IniFile,'\myfile.ini');

  {write the information out to the ini file}
  WritePrivateProfileStruct('Transfer', 'member1', @MyData,SizeOf(MyData),IniFile);
                            SizeOf(MyData),IniFile);
end;
```

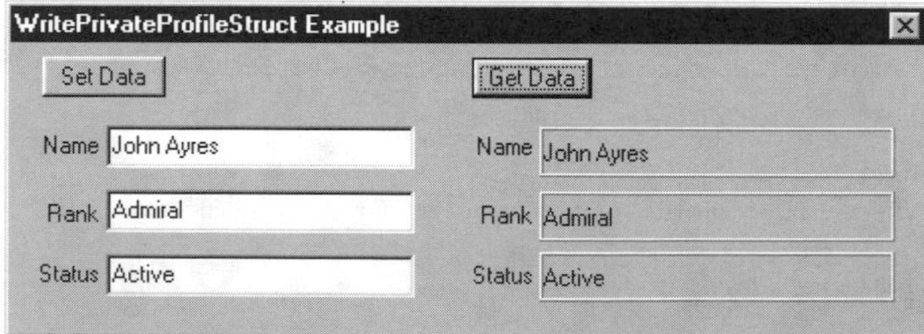

Figure 8-5: The structured initialization file information.

```
myfile.ini - Notepad
File  Edit  Search  Help
[transfer]
name1=John Ayres
Position1=Captain
status1=working
name2=Kenneth Harrison
Position2=LT.
status2=Off Duty
name3=Mike Tobin
Position3=Lt
status3=Field Ex.
nextnum=4
member1=0A4A6F686E2041797265734D6974657300000000000741646D6972616C68616
```

Figure 8-6: The structured information inside the initialization file.

WriteProfileSection Windows.Pas

Syntax

WriteProfileSection(
lpAppName: PChar; {pointer to section name}
lpString: PChar {pointer to a buffer that holds section strings}
): BOOL; {returns TRUE or FALSE}

Description

This function writes all of the key names and key values in the buffer pointed to by the lpString parameter to the specified section in the Win.ini file

Parameters

lpAppName: A null-terminated string containing the section name from the initialization file. If the section does not exist, the function will create it.

lpString: A pointer to a buffer that contains a string or a series of strings. Each string is formatted as

"Key = Value"

If the buffer contains more than one string, each string is separated by a null character. The last string is followed by two null characters.

Return Value

If the function succeeds, it returns TRUE; otherwise it returns FALSE.

See also

GetProfileSection, WritePrivateProfileSection

Example

Listing 8-21: Writing an Entire Section to the Win.ini File

```
procedure TForm1.Button1Click(Sender: TObject);
var
  Buffer: array[0..1024] of char;     // holds the section strings
  CurString: PChar;                   // a pointer to a string
  Return: integer;                    // value for error checking
begin
  {clear out the memo}
  Memo1.Lines.Clear;

  {retrieve the Desktop section from the Win.ini file}
  Return := GetProfileSection('Desktop', Buffer, SizeOf(Buffer));

  {set the pointer to the first string in the buffer}
  CurString := Buffer;

  {if the ini section was retrieved...}
```

```
    if (Return < SizeOf(Buffer)) and (Return > 0) then
      repeat
        {add the ini section line to the memo component}
        Memo1.Lines.Add(StrPas(CurString));

        {the ini section strings are separated with a null-terminated
         character, so increment the string pointer to the next character
         after the null terminator, which starts the next string}
        Inc(CurString,StrLen(CurString)+1);
      until CurString[0] = Char(0)
   else
     {indicate an error if the section was not retrieved}
     ShowMessage('Error: No Strings found');
  end;

  procedure TForm1.Button2Click(Sender: TObject);
  var
    Buffer: array[0..1024] of char;     // holds the section strings
    CurString: PChar;                   // a pointer to a string
    Counter: integer;                   // general loop counter
  begin
    {set the string pointer to the beginning of the buffer}
    CurString := Buffer;

    {erase anything currently in the buffer}
    FillChar(Buffer, SizeOf(Buffer), Char(0));

    {begin moving the memo text into the buffer}
    for Counter := 0 to Memo1.Lines.Count-1 do
    begin
      {copy one line of the memo into the buffer}
      StrPCopy(CurString,Memo1.Lines[Counter]);

      {increment the string pointer by one to leave room
       for the null terminator character}
      Inc(CurString,StrLen(CurString)+1);
    end;

    {write the buffer out to the ini file}
    WriteProfileSection('Desktop', Buffer);
  end;
```

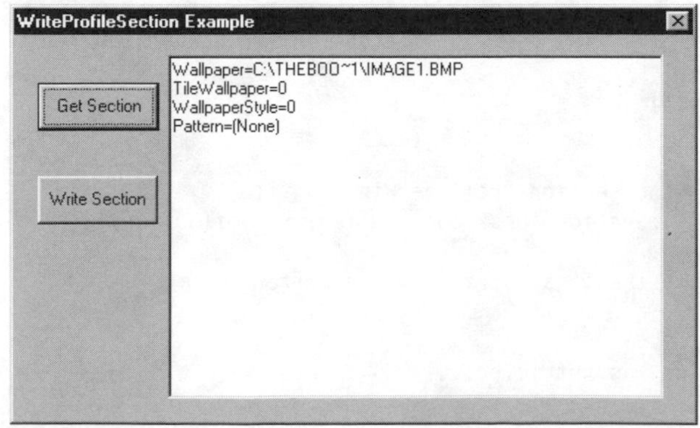

Figure 8-7: The desktop section of the Win.ini file.

WriteProfileString Windows.Pas

Syntax

```
WriteProfileString(
lpAppName:PChar;                {pointer to section name}
lpKeyName:PChar;                {pointer to key name}
lpString: PChar                 {pointer to a buffer containing the string}
): BOOL;                        {returns TRUE or FALSE}
```


Description

This function writes or deletes string values from the specified registry key in the specified section of the Win.ini file

Parameters

lpAppName: A null-terminated string that contains the section name from the initialization file. If the section does not exist the function will create it.

lpKeyName: A null-terminated string that contains the key name from the initialization file. If this parameter is set to NIL, the section identified by the lpAppName parameter and all values within it will be deleted.

lpString: A pointer to a buffer that contains a string or a series of strings. Each string is formatted as

"Key = Value"

If the buffer contains more than one string, each string is separated by a null character. The last string is followed by two null characters. If this parameter is set to NIL, the key identified by the lpKeyName parameter and its value will be deleted.

Return Value

If the function succeeds, it returns TRUE; otherwise it returns FALSE.

See also

GetProfileString, WritePrivateProfileString

Example

Listing 8-22: Writing a String to the Win.ini File

```
procedure TForm1.Button1Click(Sender: TObject);
var
  Buffer: array[0..1024] of char;     // holds the returned ini string
  Return: integer;                    // value for error checking
begin
  {retrieve a string from the ini file}
  Return := GetProfileString('Desktop', 'Wallpaper','', Buffer, SizeOf(Buffer));

  {if a string was returned, then display it}
  if (Return < SizeOf(Buffer)) and (Return > 0) then
```

```
    Edit1.Text := Buffer
  else
    ShowMessage('Error: No Strings found');
end;

procedure TForm1.Button2Click(Sender: TObject);
begin
  {write the string to the ini file}
  WriteProfileString('Desktop', 'Wallpaper', PChar(Edit1.Text))
end;
```

Chapter 9

Memory Management Functions

The Win32 API functions for memory management give the Delphi programmer effective tools for monitoring and managing memory resources. The 32-bit API is designed to have a reasonable compatibility with 16-bit applications even though there are dramatic changes in the memory structure of the 32-bit operating systems. Knowing how to use memory resources effectively allows the developer to write code that is stable and efficient. Writing code for DLLs and threads places even more importance on the functions which are discussed in this chapter.

API Versus Delphi

In a strict sense it is not necessary to use any of the API memory allocation calls listed here. A program can use the Pascal New or GetMem functions, which allocate memory from the default memory space. However, using these functions prevents the developer from controlling the allocation of additional heaps, selecting error trapping for Windows to use, or designing large buffers effectively. Windows provides a number of heap management functions for creating heaps and allocating memory from them, as well as the virtual memory functions. Delphi does not use any of the heap functions internally for allocating memory. Instead, Delphi uses the virtual memory functions. Although the Windows memory functions give the developer greater control over memory allocation and management, benchmarks have shown that Delphi's internal memory management functions are faster that using most of the Windows memory functions directly.

The Win32 Virtual Memory Architecture

Windows 95 and Windows NT introduce a new memory design which differs remarkably from the memory model design of 16-bit Windows and DOS. The programmer is provided with a flat memory model that extends beyond the limits of physical memory. This "virtual" memory model contains a memory manager which maps a program's virtual memory reference to a physical address at runtime. The swap file on a hard drive is used to swap pages of memory to disk when the system uses more virtual memory than is available in the physical RAM address space.

This memory design affords the Windows programmer room to operate. Data structures can be built in sizes under the virtual memory model that were previously impossible. Regardless of how much physical memory is installed in a target computer, the 2-gigabyte memory model is there for the developer to allocate as desired while the operating system performs mapping to disk. However, be aware that available disk space can limit the size of virtual memory availability.

Each program has its own 4-gigabyte virtual address space, with the lower 2 gigabytes available to the programmer for general use. The upper 2 gigabytes is reserved for system use. The API memory functions will allocate the requested amounts of memory from the lower 2 gigabytes of virtual address space.

Categories of Memory Allocation Functions

There are four types of memory allocation API calls. Virtual functions are for reserving and managing large memory buffers. Heap functions are for smaller memory allocations. Global and Local functions are for smaller memory allocations, and are provided for 16-bit compatibility.

There are only private address spaces in a Win32 environment. 16-bit Windows had both local (private) and global (shared) address spaces. The Win32 API still maintains global and local versions of heap functions for compatibility, but they both allocate memory from the same local 2-gigabyte address space. All of the heap is local to a process and cannot be accessed by any other process.

Heaps

When a program needs buffer allocations of at least several kilobytes in size, then it would be appropriate to use VirtualAlloc to get the memory block. VirtualAlloc gets memory in multiples of 4K in size, with the exact amount rounded up to the nearest 4K boundary. When the memory that the program allocates is to be used for small objects, arrays, or structures, then calls to HeapAlloc would be most efficient. To use VirtualAlloc for a very small structure would be a waste of resources for typical memory fetches used in linked lists or construction of binary trees. This waste would also slow down the system due to disk swap file activity if all the memory allocation cannot fit into physical memory at once.

Each process has a default heap, but an application can allocate additional heaps for efficiency and management. Each heap has its own handle. An application can get the handle for the default heap with the GetProcessHeap API function.

Performance note: Threads within a process have access to the default heap of the process. Access to the heap is serialized by the Win32 memory manager. When a thread performs a heap function, other threads which want memory are held waiting until the function is finished. This results in a small delay that the application experiences. If a thread wants to have some heap space and will not be sharing that heap with other threads, then it would be much faster for the thread to allocate its own heap and not use the default heap. When a thread uses its own heap there is optionally no serialization during heap allocations. The other threads which might also want heap space from other heaps are not delayed. The programmer has a choice when designing memory usage in threads: Use the default heap for convenience and slightly smaller code size, or use heaps which are private to threads for speed.

DLLs do not contain their own heap by default. A DLL shares heap space with the calling application. However, a DLL can allocate its own heap space and use it, just like the main thread of a process can allocate a heap in addition to the default heap.

It is very important to release heap memory when an application is through using it. Programs which do not do this are said to contain "memory leaks," and will produce errors if allowed to run indefinitely. The rule of thumb is, if an application allocated it, then it is responsible for freeing it.

The 16-Bit Memory Functions

16-bit Windows maintained a global heap which was common to the entire system and a local heap which was private to a process. The local heap was limited to a 64K segment and was usually set by the programmer to be much less. Of the function calls in this chapter, only the Global and Local functions were available in the 16-bit Windows API.

The Global and Local memory calls in Win32 perform the same function. The Global functions are not "global" as they are in 16-bit Windows. There is no shared memory except for the use of memory mapped files. All the available memory in the lower 2 gigabytes of virtual address space is designed to be private to the application and is not seen by any other application, and the Global and Local memory allocation functions both allocate memory from this address space.

Virtual Memory

Memory allocations using VirtualAlloc are straightforward, with few options to confuse the issue. The main consideration is to request the correct amount of memory. Keep in mind that VirtualAlloc will grant memory in 4K sizes. If this is too much memory, then consider using HeapAlloc instead. Although it is true that the application might not run out of virtual memory by using VirtualAlloc, it would create unnecessary work for the disk swapping routines if too much memory is wasted. If the application commits the block to physical memory, then it will be swapped to disk when necessary because Windows thinks that committed memory is being used. An application should reserve memory to keep it from being used by other applications, then commit it when the memory is actually used. This will reduce disk swap file access drastically, resulting in performance improvements. Always release memory when the application is finished with it. It is easier and faster for the Windows virtual memory manager to keep the current memory pages mapped to physical memory when there are fewer of them to manage.

Three States of Memory

Memory can exist in three separate states. The state of a memory object will change as it is allocated, reallocated, and freed. These three states are:

Free: The page is neither committed nor reserved. It is not accessible to the process, but is available for allocation by one of the memory allocation functions.

Reserved: The memory has been reserved for use by the calling process, and cannot be used by other processes or threads. It is not being used, and is not committed to physical storage.

Committed: The memory object is committed to physical storage. It is marked as being used, and may contain volatile information. If the physical RAM memory needs to use the space for other virtual memory blocks, this page will be saved to the disk swap file. This memory can be used only by the process that allocated it.

How Much Memory is Really There?

Theoretically there are 2 gigabytes of memory for the application to use in the virtual memory model. However, committing the memory to physical storage requires the support of the swap file on disk. Windows will use all of the available disk space on the system disk for swap file space as the default configuration, or will use less if configured to do so. As VirtualAlloc or other functions are used to commit virtual memory, the virtual memory manager will begin to consume available system (RAM) memory. When that physical memory comes close to being exhausted, it will begin to map memory pages to disk. When the available disk space is also exhausted, the allocation functions will report allocation failures. Therefore, the design limit is not really the 2-gigabyte limit of the theoretical design, but is, in fact, the size of available physical RAM memory plus swap file space (less some reserve and overhead).

When making a request for memory allocation, it is wise to check the amount of memory available before making the request. Do not use all of the memory resources on the system because Windows or other software will need some of it. The 2 gigabytes of virtual memory is private to the process, but the swap file is a resource that is shared by the operating system and all running tasks. Check this margin by calling the GlobalMemoryStatus function and checking the dwMemoryLoad or the dwAvailPageFile members that are provided in the returned structure. Leave several megabytes of virtual memory to provide elbow room for the operating system and other applications. The dwMemoryLoad value will reach 100 percent well before the limit is reached. For a detailed example of virtual memory allocation, see the SwapTest.exe program on the accompanying CD.

Multiple Heaps

A program can perform all heap allocations from the default heap, getting the handle to the heap with the GetProcessHeap function call. However, this forces the program to deal with all the performance hits and issues that come with all the default error trapping and threads waiting in line for memory allocations.

Creating multiple heaps allows the developer to fine-tune the system performance. Multiple heaps can be organized for separate purposes. If the application has several large linked lists and/or binary trees, then it might be more efficient to allocate a separate heap for each one. Separate heaps allow multiple threads to perform memory allocations from them while avoiding the conflicts that would be inherent with using only one heap. Separate heaps also allow certain ones to have additional exception handling turned on. There are no disadvantages in creating multiple heaps.

Error Trapping

A solid software design would have tests after each memory allocation to be sure that the returned pointer was valid. In addition to the common pointer tests, there are the API options for turning Windows error trapping on or off. It is easiest and safest to leave all the error trapping options turned on. However, if the design is well tested, and if the application might be making thousands or perhaps even millions of calls for heap allocation, then the developer can avoid the performance hits by removing the Windows error trapping that involves exception handling. Windows will still, of course, return NIL pointer values so that the application can detect a failed API call.

The developer can fine-tune the exception handling by specifying exactly which heap API calls will use the better (and somewhat slower) error trapping. By specifying the HEAP_GENERATE_EXCEPTIONS flag for the HeapCreate call, that error trapping will be in effect for every subsequent API call made to that heap without being further specified. By omitting that flag on HeapCreate, the developer can individually select which API calls will use the exception handling. However, keep in mind that the application can always detect the error by simply checking the return value of the function regardless of whether or not the HEAP_GENERATE_EXCEPTIONS flag was in effect.

Thread Access

Heap allocations might conflict with one another when more than one thread makes a request for memory from a shared heap. To prevent allocation conflicts in simultaneous requests, omit the flag HEAP_NO_SERIALIZE. This is indeed the default condition for heaps. When a thread performs a HeapAlloc request and another similar request is already in progress by another thread, one thread will be put to sleep until the heap system is available for another request. The heap allocation is said to be serialized. This involves a performance hit for the thread that is put to sleep. This performance hit can be significant when there are many threads making requests or when there are thousands or perhaps even millions of requests.

To eliminate this bottleneck on common heaps, create heaps that are private to the thread. Use a call to CreateHeap to establish a heap for each thread (or several heaps per thread if appropriate). Keep the heap handle, and then use that heap everywhere in that thread. This guarantees there will be no conflicts in memory allocation for the thread on that heap, and the developer can specify the HEAP_NO_SERIALIZE option for the allocation calls. This means that Windows will not even check to see if there are heap access conflicts since the programmer has claimed responsibility and risk for that issue. This speeds up the allocation, with performance gains that can be significant and measurable.

Speed

When an application has several heaps, or even several different uses for the same heap, try to get all of the memory for one purpose allocated as contiguous memory. Do this by performing all the HeapAlloc requests for each purpose together rather than interspersed with other code that might be making heap requests.

Consider the case of loading some huge databases into memory, perhaps into a linked list or binary tree. For several megabytes of data, the heap requests could exceed the physical memory available. This means that there will be much disk activity as the virtual memory manager tries to keep the currently addressed memory loaded into physical RAM. An application can reduce this disk activity by keeping all the memory being accessed clustered together rather than fragmented.

There are design tradeoffs here that can make or break a system. Suppose the application needs to read a large file that will exceed physical RAM, and the application needs two allocated structures for two purposes from the same file. It would be wise to use two heaps to keep the small memory allocations for each purpose clustered together. The heaps will be managed in chunks of 4K pages by the virtual memory manager, so that when one set of data is active, those pages will be resident in physical memory. The inactive structure in the other heap will have its pages swapped off to disk. This will minimize disk thrashing while the application performs work on the individual heaps. Since each HeapAlloc request takes the heap handle as its first parameter, it requires no extra effort on the programmer's part to specify the correct heap. The application only has to create the necessary heaps at the beginning of the process and destroy them at the end.

Note that it does not matter in which order allocations are made from the heaps created. If the allocations are intermingled among several heaps, the system will still work effectively. Each heap will use its separate virtual memory pages for its own allocations. The application does not need to make all the allocations for one heap before beginning the allocations for another one. The only tuning the programmer needs to do to optimize heap usage is to provide a separate heap for each purpose or structure and to set the flags appropriately.

Memory Management Functions

The following memory management functions are covered in this chapter:

Table 9-1: Memory Management Functions

Function	Description
CopyMemory	Copies the values stored in one memory location to another memory location.
FillMemory	Fills a memory location with a value.
GetProcessHeap	Retrieves a handle to the process heap.
GlobalAlloc	Allocates memory from the process address space.
GlobalDiscard	Discards allocated memory.
GlobalFlags	Retrieves information about a memory object.
GlobalFree	Frees allocated memory.
GlobalHandle	Converts a pointer to memory into a handle.
GlobalLock	Converts a memory object handle into a pointer.
GlobalMemoryStatus	Retrieves information about available memory.
GlobalReAlloc	Reallocates an allocated memory object.
GlobalSize	Retrieves the size of a memory object.
GlobalUnlock	Unlocks a locked memory object
HeapAlloc	Allocates memory from a heap.
HeapCreate	Creates a heap.
HeapDestroy	Destroys a heap.
HeapFree	Frees memory allocated from a heap.
HeapReAlloc	Reallocates memory allocated from a heap.
HeapSize	Retrieves the size of a memory object allocated from a heap.
IsBadCodePtr	Determines if a process has read access to a specific memory address.
IsBadReadPtr	Determines if a process has read access to a range of memory.
IsBadStringPtr	Determines if a process has read access to a range of memory stored as a string.
IsBadWritePtr	Determines if a process has write access to a range of memory.
LocalAlloc	Allocates memory from the process address space.
LocalDiscard	Discards allocated memory.
LocalFlags	Retrieves information about a memory object.
LocalFree	Frees allocated memory.
LocalHandle	Converts a pointer to memory into a handle.
LocalLock	Converts a memory object handle into a pointer.
LocalReAlloc	Reallocates an allocated memory object.
LocalSize	Retrieves the size of a memory object.
LocalUnlock	Unlocks a locked memory object

Function	Description
MoveMemory	Moves the values stored in one memory location to another memory location. The memory locations may overlap.
VirtualAlloc	Allocates memory from the virtual address space.
VirtualFree	Frees allocated virtual memory.
VirtualProtect	Sets access protection on a range of virtual memory.
VirtualQuery	Retrieves information about a range of virtual memory.
ZeroMemory	Fills the values at a memory location with zero.

CopyMemory Windows.Pas

Syntax

```
CopyMemory(
Destination: Pointer;        {address of the target memory block}
Source: Pointer;             {address of memory block to copy}
Length: DWORD                {size of memory block in bytes}
);                           {this procedure does not return a value}
```

Description

CopyMemory copies the requested number of bytes from one memory address to another memory address. This is similar to Delphi's Move procedure except that the source and destination parameters are in the reverse order. The memory blocks do not have to begin or end on any specific boundary or address, but all of the referenced addresses must be within the memory range assigned to the process by the memory manager. The range of memory pointed to by Source and Destination must not overlap. If there is a possible overlap in addresses of the memory blocks, then use the MoveMemory function. Overlapping blocks used with CopyMemory may produce unpredictable results.

Parameters

Destination: The target address to which the requested amount of memory will be copied.

Source: The source address from which the requested amount of memory will be copied.

Length: The number of bytes to copy.

See also

FillMemory, MoveMemory, ZeroMemory

Example

Listing 9-1: Copying Memory from One Array to Another

```
var
  Form1: TForm1;
  Info1, Info2: array[0..99] of byte;      // the copy from and copy to buffers

implementation

procedure TForm1.FormCreate(Sender: TObject);
var
  iLoop: Integer;
begin
  {fill the source buffer with information, and display this in the string grid}
  for iLoop := 1 to 100 do
  begin
    Info1[iLoop-1] := iLoop;
    StringGrid1.Cells[iLoop-1,0] := IntToStr(Info1[iLoop-1]);
  end;
end;

procedure TForm1.Button1Click(Sender: TObject);
var
  iLoop: integer;
begin
  {copy the source buffer into the destination buffer}
  CopyMemory(@Info2,@Info1,SizeOf(Info1));

  {display the result in the second string grid}
  for iLoop := 1 to 100 do
    StringGrid2.Cells[iLoop-1,0] := IntToStr(Info2[iLoop]);
end;
```


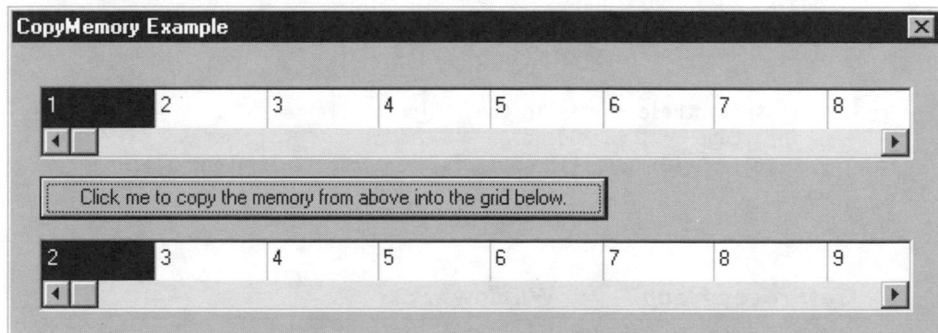

Figure 9-1: The array was copied.

FillMemory *Windows.Pas*

Syntax

FillMemory(
Destination: Pointer; {address of memory block to initialize}
Length: DWORD; {size of memory block in bytes}
Fill: Byte {data to use for initialization}

);   {this procedure does not return a value}

Description

FillMemory initializes the requested block of memory to the given byte value. FillMemory is useful if every byte in a memory block needs to be initialized to the same value. The memory block does not have to begin or end on any specific boundary or address, but all of the referenced addresses must be within the memory range assigned to the process by the memory manager.

Parameters

Destination: The address of the block of memory to be initialized.

Length: The number of bytes of memory to be initialized.

Fill: The byte value used to initialize each byte of the memory block.

See also

CopyMemory, MoveMemory, ZeroMemory

Example

Listing 9-2: Initializing Buffer Values

```
procedure TForm1.Button1Click(Sender: TObject);
var
  Info: array[0..199] of byte;     // the information buffer
  iLoop: integer;
begin
  {initialize the information buffer with a value}
  FillMemory(@Info,SizeOf(Info),123);

  {display these values in the string grid}
  for iLoop := 1 to 200 do
    StringGrid1.Cells[iLoop-1,0] := IntToStr(Info[iLoop-1]);
end;
```

GetProcessHeap   Windows.Pas

Syntax

GetProcessHeap: THandle;   {returns the handle of the default heap}

Description

This function gets the handle of the heap for the calling process. The function can be used with HeapAlloc, HeapReAlloc, HeapFree, and HeapSize to allocate memory from the process heap without having to first create a heap using the HeapCreate function.

Return Value

If the function succeeds, it returns a handle to the default heap for the current process; otherwise it returns zero.

See also

HeapAlloc, HeapCreate, HeapDestroy, HeapFree, HeapReAlloc, HeapSize

Example

Listing 9-3: Allocating Memory from the Process Heap

```
procedure TForm1.Button1Click(Sender: TObject);
type
  BufferType = array[0..63] of byte;    // defines the buffer type
var
  Buffer: ^BufferType;                  // the buffer variable
  iLoop: Integer;                       // general loop control variable
begin
  {allocate memory from the heap of the calling process}
  Buffer := HeapAlloc(GetProcessHeap, HEAP_ZERO_MEMORY,sizeof(BufferType));

  {display the default values from the new buffer (should be all zeros)}
  for iLoop := 0 to 63 do
    StringGrid1.Cells[iLoop, 0] := IntToStr(Buffer^[iLoop]);

  {return the memory}
  HeapFree(GetProcessHeap,0,Buffer);
end;
```


GlobalAlloc Windows.Pas

Syntax

```
GlobalAlloc(
uFlags: UINT;            {object allocation attributes}
dwBytes: DWORD           {number of bytes to allocate}
): HGLOBAL;              {returns a handle to a global memory object}
```

Description

The GlobalAlloc function allocates the requested number of bytes from the Windows heap. Memory allocated with this function will be double word aligned, and may allocate a greater amount than specified to facilitate the alignment.

Parameters

uFlags: Specifies how the memory is to be allocated. GMEM_FIXED is the default value and is used if this parameter is set to zero. Except where noted, this parameter can be set to one or more values from Table 9-2.

dwBytes: The number of bytes to be allocated.

Return Value

If the function succeeds, it returns a handle to the global memory block; otherwise it returns zero. To get extended error information, call the GetLastError function.

See also

GlobalFree, GlobalLock, GlobalReAlloc, GlobalSize, LocalAlloc

Example

Listing 9-4: Allocating Global Memory

```
procedure TForm1.Button1Click(Sender: TObject);
type
  Arrayspace = array[0..199] of integer;
var
  Arrayptr: ^Arrayspace;  // pointer to a dynamic array
  Arrayhandle: HGLOBAL;   // handle to the array object
  iLoop: Integer;         // loop counter
begin
  {allocate memory from the global heap}
  Arrayhandle := GlobalAlloc(GPTR,SizeOf(Arrayspace));
  if Arrayhandle = 0 then
    begin
      ShowMessage('Error getting memory block!');
      exit;
    end;

  {retrieve a pointer to the allocated memory}
  Arrayptr := GlobalLock(Arrayhandle);
  if Arrayptr = nil then
    begin
      ShowMessage('Error getting pointer to memory!');
      exit;
    end;

  {initialize the allocated memory block with values, and display it}
  for iLoop := 0 to 199 do
  begin
    Arrayptr^[iLoop] := iLoop;
    StringGrid1.Cells[iLoop,0] := IntToStr(Arrayptr^[iLoop]);
  end;

  {unlock the global memory...}
  GlobalUnlock(Arrayhandle);

  {...and free it}
  GlobalFree(Arrayhandle);
end;
```

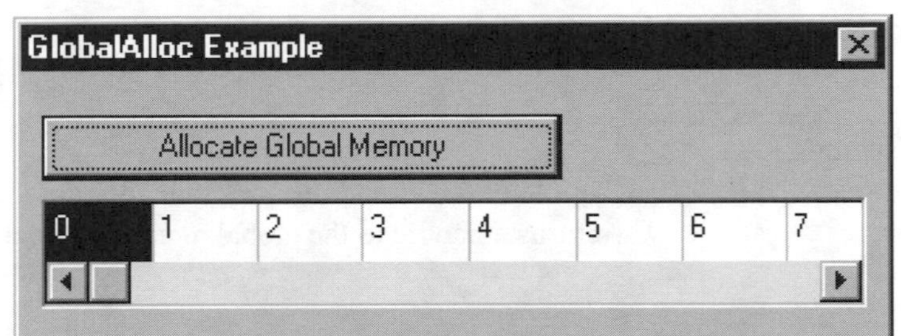

Figure 9-2: The memory was allocated and initialized.

Table 9-2: GlobalAlloc uFlags Values

Value	Description
GHND	Combination of the GMEM_MOVEABLE and GMEM_ZEROINIT flags.
GMEM_DDESHARE	Allocates memory to be used by DDE functions for a DDE conversation. This memory is not shared globally like it was in 16-bit Windows. This flag is available for compatibility purposes, and may be used by applications to enhance DDE operations when the memory will be used for dynamic data exchange in clipboard access or interprocess communications.
GMEM_DISCARDABLE	Allocates memory that can be discarded if it has not been used recently. This flag cannot be combined with GMEM_FIXED.
GMEM_FIXED	Allocates a fixed memory block. Do not combine this flag with either the GMEM_MOVEABLE or GMEM_DISCARDABLE flags. The return value can be typecast as a pointer to access the memory block. GlobalLock can also be used to acquire the pointer though no lock will be set.
GMEM_MOVEABLE	Allocates a moveable memory block. Do not combine this with the GMEM_FIXED flag.
GMEM_NOCOMPACT	Memory will not be compacted nor discarded to satisfy the allocation request.
GMEM_NODISCARD	Memory will not be discarded to satisfy the allocation request.
GMEM_ZEROINIT	Initializes the contents of the allocated memory to zero.
GPTR	Combination of the GMEM_FIXED and GMEM_ZEROINIT flags.

GlobalDiscard Windows.Pas

Syntax

```
GlobalDiscard(
h: THandle                    {handle of the global memory to be discarded}
): THandle;                   {returns a handle to the global memory object}
```

Description

The GlobalDiscard function discards the memory block specified by the h parameter. A memory block can be discarded only if it was created using the GMEM_DISCARDABLE flag. The lock count for this memory object must be zero for this function to succeed. Once a global memory object has been discarded, its handle remains valid and can be used in subsequent calls to GlobalReAlloc.

Parameters

h: The handle to the memory object to be discarded.

Return Value

If the function succeeds, it returns a handle to the discarded global memory object; otherwise it returns zero. To get extended error information, call the GetLastError function.

See also

GlobalAlloc, GlobalReAlloc

Example

Please see Listing 9-6 under GlobalReAlloc.

GlobalFlags Windows.Pas

Syntax

```
GlobalFlags(
hMem: HGLOBAL                 {a handle to the memory object}
): UINT;                      {returns information flags and lock count}
```

Description

GlobalFlags provides information about the allocation flags and lock count for the specified memory object.

Parameters

hMem: A handle to the memory object for which information is to be retrieved.

Return Value

If the function succeeds, it returns a 32-bit value indicating the lock count and allocation flags of the specified memory object. The low-order byte of the low-order word contains the lock count of the specified memory object, and can be retrieved by combining the return value with the constant GMEM_LOCKCOUNT using the Boolean AND operator. The high-order byte of the low-order word contains the allocation flags for the specified memory object, and can be zero or any combination of values from Table 9-3. If the function fails, it returns zero. To get extended error information, call the GetLastError function.

See also

GlobalAlloc, GlobalDiscard, GlobalLock, GlobalReAlloc, GlobalUnlock, LocalFlags

Example

Please see Listing 9-6 under GlobalReAlloc.

Table 9-3: GlobalFlags Return Values

Value	Description
GMEM_DDESHARE	Memory was allocated for DDE purposes. This memory is not shared globally like it was in 16-bit Windows. This flag is available for compatibility purposes, and may be used by applications to enhance DDE operations when the memory will be used for dynamic data exchange in clipboard access or interprocess communications.
GMEM_DISCARDABLE	The memory block can be discarded.
GMEM_DISCARDED	The memory block has been discarded.

GlobalFree Windows.Pas

Syntax

```
GlobalFree(
hMem: HGLOBAL          {handle to the memory object to be deallocated}
): HGLOBAL;            {returns zero or the handle to the memory object}
```

Description

GlobalFree deallocates the memory block. It returns the memory to the heap and renders the handle invalid. This function will free a memory object regardless of its lock count.

Parameters

hMem: The pointer to the memory block to be returned to the system.

Return Value

If the function succeeds, it returns zero; otherwise it returns a handle to the global memory object. To get extended error information, call the GetLastError function.

See also

GlobalAlloc, GlobalFlags, GlobalLock, GlobalReAlloc, GlobalUnlock, LocalFree

Example

Please see Listing 9-4 under GlobalAlloc and Listing 9-6 under GlobalReAlloc.

GlobalHandle Windows.Pas

Syntax

```
GlobalHandle(
Mem: Pointer               {a pointer to the start of the memory block}
): HGLOBAL;                {returns zero or the handle to the memory object}
```

Description

GlobalHandle converts the pointer to a memory block specified by the Mem parameter into a global memory object handle. For memory objects allocated with the GMEM_FIXED flag set, the GlobalHandle and GlobalLock functions are not needed, because the handle and the pointer to memory are the same value. When GMEM_FIXED is used, the developer is responsible for being sure that all routines are finished with the memory object when it is freed.

Parameters

Mem: A pointer to the first byte of the memory block whose global memory handle is to be retrieved.

Return Value

If the function succeeds, it returns a handle to the global memory object; otherwise it returns zero. To get extended error information, call the GetLastError function.

See also

GlobalAlloc, GlobalFree, GlobalLock

Example

Please see Listing 9-6 under GlobalReAlloc.

GlobalLock Windows.Pas

Syntax

```
GlobalLock(
hMem: HGLOBAL                {a handle to a memory object}
): Pointer;                  {returns a pointer to the memory block}
```

Description

GlobalLock increments the lock counter for the given memory object by one, and forces the memory object to be maintained at a specific memory address. A memory object that is locked will not be moved to another address by the memory manager except for calls to the GlobalReAlloc function. The address that is returned will be a valid address for the memory object as long as the object has a lock count of at least one. Multiple routines can place lock counts on the object, so that the object cannot be moved as long as any routine is using the memory. The lock count can be decremented by calling the GlobalUnlock function. When a memory object is allocated with the GMEM_FIXED flag, it will always have a lock count of zero and will never be moved.

Parameters

hMem: A handle of the memory object whose pointer is to be retrieved.

Return Value

If the function succeeds, it returns a pointer to the first byte of the global memory block; otherwise it returns zero. To get extended error information, call the GetLastError function.

See also

GlobalAlloc, GlobalFlags, GlobalReAlloc, GlobalUnlock

Example

Please see Listing 9-4 under GlobalAlloc and Listing 9-6 under GlobalReAlloc.

GlobalMemoryStatus Windows.Pas

Syntax

```
GlobalMemoryStatus(
var lpBuffer: TMemoryStatus      {a pointer to a TMemoryStatus structure}
);                               {this procedure does not return a value}
```

Description

This procedure fills a TMemoryStatus structure with information regarding physical and virtual memory. However, due to the nature of Window's memory management, two sequential calls to this function may yield different results.

Parameters

lpBuffer: A pointer to a TMemoryStatus structure that receives the information about physical and virtual memory status. The TMemoryStatus data structure is defined as:

```
TMemoryStatus = record
    dwLength: DWORD;           {the size of the structure in bytes}
    dwMemoryLoad: DWORD;       {estimated memory usage}
    dwTotalPhys: DWORD;        {the total amount of physical memory}
    dwAvailPhys: DWORD;        {the available amount of physical memory}
    dwTotalPageFile: DWORD;    {the total amount of swap file storage}
    dwAvailPageFile: DWORD;    {the available amount of swap file storage}
    dwTotalVirtual: DWORD;     {the total amount of virtual memory}
    dwAvailVirtual: DWORD;     {the available amount of virtual memory}
end;
```

dwLength: This member contains the size of the structure in bytes, and must be set to SizeOf(TMemoryStatus) before the call to GlobalMemoryStatus is made.

dwMemoryLoad: Contains a value between 0 and 100 indicating the approximate percentage of memory in use.

dwTotalPhys: Indicates the total amount of physical RAM in bytes.

dwAvailPhys: Indicates the total amount of available physical RAM in bytes.

dwTotalPageFile: Indicates the maximum amount of storage space in the swap file in bytes, including both used space and available space. This number does not represent the actual physical size of the swap file.

dwAvailPageFile: Indicates the total amount of available space in the swap file in bytes.

dwTotalVirtual: Indicates the total amount of virtual address space for the calling process in bytes.

dwAvailVirtual: Indicates the total amount of unreserved and uncommitted space in the virtual address space of the calling process in bytes.

See also

GlobalFree, LocalFree

Example

Listing 9-5: Retrieving the Memory Status

```
procedure TGlobalMemoryStatusForm.ButtonGlobalMemoryStatusClick(
  Sender: TObject);
var
  GlobalMemoryInfo : TMemoryStatus;  // holds the global memory status information
begin
  {set the size of the structure before the call.}
  GlobalMemoryInfo.dwLength := SizeOf(GlobalMemoryInfo);
```

```
  {retrieve the global memory status...}
  GlobalMemoryStatus(GlobalMemoryInfo);

  {and display the information}
  Label1.caption := 'Results of GlobalMemoryStatus:';
  Label2.caption := 'Record structure size: '+IntToStr(
                    GlobalMemoryInfo.dwLength)+' bytes';
  Label3.caption := 'Current memory load: '+IntToStr(
                    GlobalMemoryInfo.dwMemoryLoad)+'%';
  Label4.caption := 'Total physical memory: '+Format('%.0n',[
                    GlobalMemoryInfo.dwTotalPhys/1])+' bytes';
  Label5.caption := 'Total available physical memory: '+Format('%.0n',[
                    GlobalMemoryInfo.dwAvailPhys/1])+' bytes';
  Label6.caption := 'Total paging file size: '+Format('%.0n',[
                    GlobalMemoryInfo.dwTotalPageFile/1])+' bytes';
  Label7.Caption := 'Total available paging file memory: '+Format('%.0n',[
                    GlobalMemoryInfo.dwAvailPageFile/1])+' bytes';
  Label8.caption := 'Total virtual memory: '+Format('%.0n',[
                    GlobalMemoryInfo.dwTotalVirtual/1])+' bytes';
  Label9.caption := 'Total available virtual memory: '+Format('%.0n',[
                    GlobalMemoryInfo.dwAvailVirtual/1])+' bytes';
end;
```

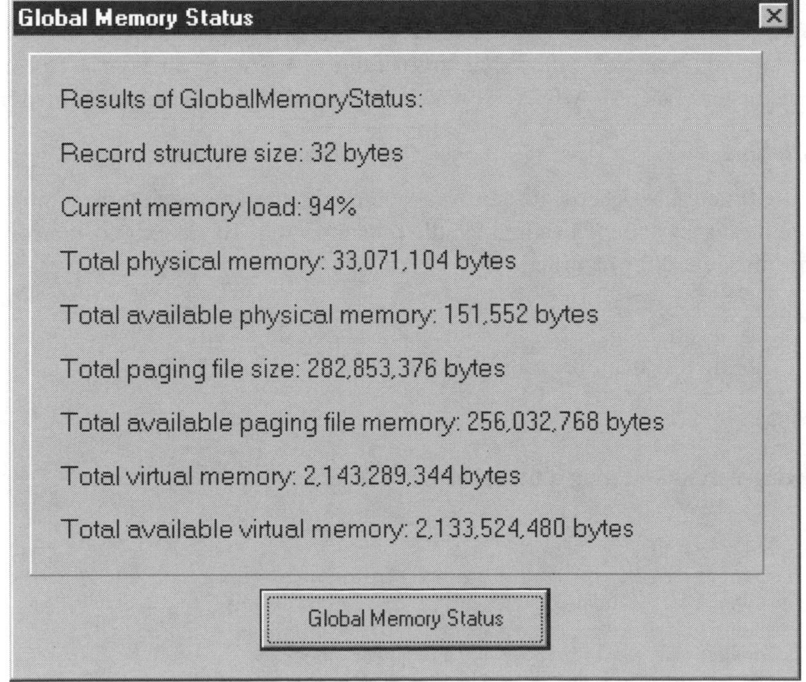

Figure 9-3: Displaying the memory status.

GlobalReAlloc Windows.Pas

Syntax

GlobalReAlloc(
hMem: HGLOBAL; {a handle to a global memory object}
dwBytes: DWORD; {the size of the memory object}
uFlags: UINT {reallocation flags}
): HGLOBAL; {returns a handle to a global memory object}

Description

This function is used to change the size or attributes of the specified global memory object. If this function reallocates a fixed memory object, the returned global memory handle can be used as a pointer to this memory block.

Parameters

hMem: A handle to the global memory object whose size or attributes are to be modified.

dwBytes: The new size of the global memory object in bytes. If the uFlags parameter contains the GMEM_MODIFY flag, this parameter is ignored.

uFlags: Specifies how the global memory object is to be modified. This parameter may contain one or more of the values from Table 9-4. These values may be combined with the constant GMEM_MODIFY, which changes their behavior as outlined in the table.

Return Value

If the function succeeds, it returns a handle to the reallocated memory object; otherwise it returns zero and the original handle remains valid. To get extended error information, call the GetLastError function.

See also

GlobalAlloc, GlobalFree, GlobalLock

Example

Listing 9-6: Reallocating a Global Memory Object

```
var
  Form1: TForm1;
  Arrayptr: ^Byte;          // pointer to a dynamic array
  Arrayhandle: HGLOBAL;     // handle to the array object
  PtrHandle: HGLOBAL;       // handle from GlobalHandle
  UnlockResult: Boolean;    // Unlock error checking
  ArrayFlags: integer;      // result of GlobalFlags call
  FreeResult: Hglobal;      // Free error checking
  FlagCount: integer;       // number of lock flags set
  Arraysize : integer;      // size of the memory object
```

```
implementation

procedure TForm1.Button1Click(Sender: TObject);
var
  iLoop: Byte;              // loop counter
  Baseptr: Pointer;         // temporary pointer
begin
  {allocate global memory}
  Arrayhandle := GlobalAlloc(GHND,200);

  {retrieve a pointer to the global memory}
  Arrayptr := GlobalLock(Arrayhandle);

  {do something with the global memory block}
  Baseptr := Arrayptr;
  for iLoop := 0 to 199 do
  begin
    Byte(Baseptr^) := iLoop;
    StringGrid1.Cells[iLoop,0] := IntToStr(Byte(Baseptr^));
    BasePtr := Pointer(Longint(BasePtr)+1);
  end;

  {retrieve a pointer from the global memory handle}
  PtrHandle := GlobalHandle(Arrayptr);
  if PtrHandle <> Arrayhandle then
    ShowMessage('Memory Object Handle Error');

  {retrieve information on the global memory block}
  ArrayFlags := GlobalFlags(PtrHandle);
  Flagcount := ArrayFlags and GMEM_LOCKCOUNT;
  Showmessage('# of global locks on Arrayhandle is ' +IntToStr(Flagcount));

  {get the size of the global memory block}
  ArraySize := GlobalSize(PtrHandle);
  Showmessage('Initial object size is ' + IntToStr(Arraysize));

  Button2.Enabled := TRUE;
  Button1.Enabled := FALSE;
end;

procedure TForm1.Button2Click(Sender: TObject);
var
  iLoop: Integer;
  Baseptr: Pointer;
begin
  {unlock the global memory block. This is not required
   if GMEM_FIXED was set on allocation.}
  if Flagcount > 0 then GlobalUnlock(Arrayhandle);

  {discard the memory block}
  Arrayhandle := GlobalDiscard(Arrayhandle);
  if Arrayhandle = 0 then
  begin
    ShowMessage('GlobalDiscard failed');
    exit;
```

```
  end;

  {our global memory handle is still valid}
  Arraysize := GlobalSize(Arrayhandle);
  Showmessage('Discarded object size is ' + IntToStr(Arraysize));

  {reallocate global memory}
  Arrayhandle := GlobalReAlloc(Arrayhandle,400,GMEM_ZEROINIT);
  if Arrayhandle = 0 then
  begin
    ShowMessage('Error in GlobalAlloc');
    exit;
  end;

  {retrieve the new size of the global memory block}
  ArraySize := GlobalSize(Arrayhandle);
  Showmessage('ReAlloc''ed object size is ' + IntToStr(ArraySize));

  {do something with the new memory block}
  StringGrid1.ColCount := ArraySize;
  Baseptr := Arrayptr;
  for iLoop := 0 to 399 do
  begin
    StringGrid1.Cells[iLoop,0] := IntToStr(Byte(Baseptr^));
    BasePtr := Pointer(Longint(BasePtr)+1);
  end;

  {unlock the global memory block}
  SetLastError(NO_ERROR);           //Reset error trapping
  UnlockResult := GlobalUnlock(Arrayhandle);
  if UnlockResult then ShowMessage('Lock count is nonzero');
  if (not UnlockResult) and (GetLastError <> NO_ERROR) then
    ShowMessage('Error unlocking memory');

  {Free the global memory and invalidate its handle. Note
   that GlobalFree will free a locked memory block, and calling
   GlobalUnlock will not affect the behavior of GlobalFree.}
  FreeResult := GlobalFree(Arrayhandle);
  if (FreeResult <> 0)
    then ShowMessage('Error Freeing Memory');
end;
```

Table 9-4: GlobalReAlloc uFlags Values

Value	Description
GMEM_DISCARDABLE	Allocates discardable memory. The memory object must have been created as moveable or the GMEM_MOVEABLE flag must be specified, or this flag is ignored. This flag can be used only if the GMEM_MODIFY flag is also specified.
GMEM_MOVEABLE	If dwBytes is zero, this discards a previously moveable and discardable memory object. The function will fail if the lock count for the specified memory block is nonzero or if the block is neither moveable nor discardable.

Value	Description
	If dwBytes is nonzero, the block is moved to a new location (if necessary) to alter the size without changing the moveable or fixed status. For fixed memory objects the handle that is returned might be different than the hMem parameter. For moveable objects, the memory can be moved without the handle being changed even if the memory was locked with GlobalLock. This functionality is available only if the GMEM_MODIFY flag is not specified. Windows NT only: Changes fixed memory to moveable memory only if the GMEM_MODIFY flag is also specified.
GMEM_NOCOMPACT	The memory object will neither be compacted nor destroyed. This functionality is available only if the GMEM_MODIFY flag is not specified.
GMEM_ZEROINIT	If the memory object is set to a larger size, this specifies that the new memory contents are initialized to zero. This functionality is available only if the GMEM_MODIFY flag is not specified.

GlobalSize Windows.Pas

Syntax

```
GlobalSize(
hMem: HGLOBAL              {a handle to the memory object}
): DWORD;                  {returns the size of the memory object in bytes}
```

Description

This function returns the size of the specified memory object in bytes.

Parameters

hMem: The handle of the memory object whose size is to be retrieved.

Return Value

If the function succeeds, it returns the size of the specified global memory object in bytes; otherwise it returns zero. To get extended error information, call the GetLastError function.

See also

GlobalAlloc, GlobalFlags, GlobalReAlloc

Example

Please see Listing 9-6 under GlobalReAlloc.

GlobalUnlock Windows.Pas

Syntax

```
GlobalUnlock(
hMem: HGLOBAL               {a handle to the memory object}
): BOOL;                    {returns TRUE or FALSE}
```

Description

GlobalUnlock decrements the lock count on moveable memory objects allocated with the GMEM_MOVEABLE flag, and has no effect on fixed memory objects allocated with the GMEM_FIXED flag.

Parameters

hMem: A handle to the memory object being unlocked.

Return Value

If the function succeeds and the object is still locked after decrementing the lock count, it returns TRUE; otherwise it returns FALSE. To get extended error information, call the GetLastError function. If GetLastError returns ERROR_SUCCESS, then the memory object is not locked.

See also

GlobalAlloc, GlobalFlags, GlobalLock, GlobalReAlloc

Example

Please see Listing 9-4 under GlobalAlloc and Listing 9-6 under GlobalReAlloc.

HeapAlloc Windows.Pas

Syntax

```
HeapAlloc(
hHeap: THandle;             {a handle to a heap}
dwFlags: DWORD;             {allocation flags}
dwBytes: DWORD              {the requested size of allocation in bytes}
): Pointer;                 {returns a pointer to allocated memory}
```

Description

HeapAlloc allocates the requested number of bytes from the specified heap.

Parameters

hHeap: A handle to the heap from which memory is allocated. This can be either a heap created with the HeapCreate function or the system heap as retrieved by the GetProcessHeap function.

dwFlags: Specifies how the allocation is made from the heap. If this parameter is set to zero, then the corresponding flags given as parameters to HeapCreate will be in effect; otherwise they will override the settings made in HeapCreate. If the hHeap parameter contains a handle to the system heap as returned by the GetProcessHeap function, this parameter is ignored. This parameter may be set to one or more of the values from Table 9-5.

dwBytes: Specifies the size of the requested memory block in bytes. If the heap is a nongrowable heap, then the requested size must be less than 524,280 bytes ($7FFF8).

Return Value

If the function succeeds, it returns a pointer to the newly allocated memory block. If the function fails and the HEAP_GENERATE_EXCEPTIONS flag was not specified, the function returns NIL. If the function fails and the HEAP_GENERATE_EXCEPTIONS flag was specified, the function returns one of the values from Table 9-6.

See also

GetProcessHeap, HeapCreate, HeapDestroy, HeapFree, HeapReAlloc, HeapSize

Example

Listing 9-7: Allocating Memory from the Heap

```
var
  Form1: TForm1;
  Arrayptr: ^Byte;           // pointer to byte array
  Baseptr: Pointer;          // a pointer to access the byte array
  MyHeap: THandle;           // private heap handle
  MySize: integer;           // heap size

implementation

procedure TForm1.Button1Click(Sender: TObject);
var
  iLoop: integer;            // loop counter
begin
  {Create a new private heap and test for errors}
  MyHeap := HeapCreate(HEAP_NO_SERIALIZE, $FFFF,0);
  if MyHeap = 0 then
  begin
    ShowMessage('Error creating private heap.');
    Exit;
  end;

  {Allocate memory for the array and test for errors}
  Arrayptr := HeapAlloc(MyHeap,HEAP_ZERO_MEMORY,200);
  if Arrayptr = nil then
  begin
    ShowMessage('Error Allocating memory');
    {release the heap if there was an error}
    if not HeapDestroy(MyHeap)
      then ShowMessage('Error destroying private heap');
```

```
  end;

  {fill memory}
  Baseptr := Arrayptr;
  for iLoop := 0 to 199 do
  begin
    Byte(Baseptr^) := iLoop;
    StringGrid1.Cells[iLoop,0] := IntToStr(Byte(Baseptr^));
    BasePtr := Pointer(Longint(BasePtr)+1);
  end;

  {How big is the heap?}
  MySize := HeapSize(MyHeap, 0, Arrayptr);
  Label1.Caption := 'HeapSize is ' + IntToStr(MySize);

  Button2.Enabled := TRUE;
  Button1.Enabled := FALSE;
end;

procedure TForm1.Button2Click(Sender: TObject);
begin
  {Extend the Array size}
  Arrayptr := HeapReAlloc(MyHeap, HEAP_ZERO_MEMORY, Arrayptr, 600);
  StringGrid1.ColCount := 600;
  if Arrayptr = nil then ShowMessage('Error expanding array.');

  {check the current (expanded) size}
  MySize := HeapSize(MyHeap, 0, Arrayptr);
  Label1.Caption := 'HeapSize is ' + IntToStr(MySize);

  {We're done, release the memory}
  if not HeapFree(MyHeap,0,Arrayptr)
    then ShowMessage('Error returning memory to heap.');

  {Destroy the heap}
  if not HeapDestroy(MyHeap)
    then ShowMessage('Error destroying heap.');
end;
```

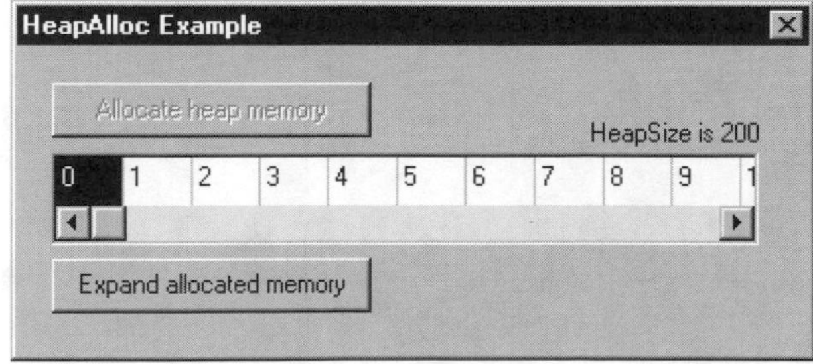

Figure 9-4: Memory was allocated.

Table 9-5: HeapAlloc dwFlags Values

Value	Description
HEAP_GENERATE_EXCEPTIONS	Indicates that Windows will generate an exception for an exception handler instead of returning a NIL.
HEAP_NO_SERIALIZE	Specifies that requests for heap will not be serialized. This should only be used for heaps that are created and used by a single thread. This flag removes the serialized locking feature which enables multiple threads to access the same heap.
HEAP_ZERO_MEMORY	The allocated memory will be initialized to zero.

Table 9-6: HeapAlloc Return Values

Value	Description
STATUS_ACCESS_VIOLATION	Indicates that the heap was corrupt or the function parameters were not accepted.
STATUS_NO_MEMORY	Indicates that the heap was corrupt or there was not enough memory to satisfy the request.

HeapCreate *Windows.Pas*

Syntax

```
HeapCreate(
flOptions: DWORD;            {allocation option flags}
dwInitialSize: DWORD;        {the starting heap size}
dwMaximumSize: DWORD         {the maximum heap size}
): THandle;                  {returns a handle to the new heap}
```

Description

This function reserves a block of memory from the virtual address space to be used as a heap by the calling processes. The initial size of the heap is allocated from available physical storage in the virtual address space.

Parameters

flOptions: Specifies heap attributes affecting all subsequent access to the new heap. This parameter can be one or more values from Table 9-7.

dwInitialSize: The initial size of the heap in bytes that is committed to physical memory. This value is rounded up to the nearest page boundary used by the virtual memory manager. The size of a page boundary can be determined by calling the GetSystemInfo function.

dwMaximumSize: The maximum size of the heap in bytes, rounded up to the nearest page boundary used by the virtual memory manager. This space will be marked as reserved in the virtual address space of the process. If this parameter is set to a nonzero value, the heap is nongrowable, and memory can only be allocated up to the maximum size of the heap. If this parameter is zero, the heap is growable and the system will continue to grant memory allocations from the heap up to the available size of the virtual memory space.

Return Value

If the function is successful, it returns a handle to the newly created heap; otherwise it returns zero. To get extended error information, call the GetLastError function.

See also

GetProcessHeap, GetSystemInfo, HeapAlloc, HeapReAlloc, HeapDestroy, HeapFree, HeapSize, HeapValidate, VirtualAlloc.

Example

Please see Listing 9-7 under HeapAlloc.

Table 9-7: HeapCreate flOptions Values

Value	Description
HEAP_GENERATE_EXCEPTIONS	Indicates that Windows will generate an exception for an exception handler instead of returning a NIL.
HEAP_NO_SERIALIZE	Specifies that requests for access to the heap will be not be serialized. This should only be used for heaps that are created and used by a single thread. This flag removes the serialized locking feature which enables multiple threads to access the same heap.
HEAP_ZERO_MEMORY	The allocated memory will be initialized to zero.

HeapDestroy *Windows.Pas*

Syntax

```
HeapDestroy(
hHeap: THandle          {a handle of the heap being destroyed}
): BOOL;                {returns TRUE or FALSE}
```

Description

This function decommits and releases all pages from a heap created with the HeapCreate function, destroys the heap object, and invalidates the specified heap handle. A heap can be destroyed without first calling the HeapFree function to deallocate its memory.

Parameters

hHeap: The handle of the heap that is to be destroyed. This parameter must not be set to the value returned by the GetProcessHeap function.

Return Value

If the function succeeds, it returns TRUE; otherwise it returns FALSE. To get extended error information, call the GetLastError function.

See also

GetProcessHeap, HeapAlloc, HeapCreate, HeapFree, HeapReAlloc, HeapSize

Example

Please see Listing 9-7 under HeapAlloc.

HeapFree Windows.Pas

Syntax

```
HeapFree(
hHeap: THandle;          {a handlc to thc hcap}
dwFlags: DWORD;          {option flags}
lpMem: Pointer           {a pointer to the memory to be freed}
): BOOL;                 {returns TRUE or FALSE}
```

Description

This function frees memory previously allocated from the heap by the HeapAlloc or HeapReAlloc functions. The freed memory will be available in the heap for the next heap allocation.

Parameters

hHeap: The handle of the heap from which the memory was originally allocated.

dwFlags: Specifies heap access behavior. This parameter can be either zero or HEAP_NO_SERIALIZE. See the HeapCreate function for a description of the HEAP_NO_SERIALIZE flag.

lpMem: A pointer to the memory block to be freed.

Return Value

If the function succeeds, it returns TRUE; otherwise it returns FALSE. To get extended error information, call the GetLastError function.

See also

GetProcessHeap, HeapAlloc, HeapCreate, HeapDestroy, HeapReAlloc, HeapSize

Example

Please see Listing 9-7 under HeapAlloc.

HeapReAlloc   Windows.Pas

Syntax

```
HeapReAlloc(
hHeap: THandle;          {a handle to the heap}
dwFlags: DWORD;          {allocation option flags}
lpMem: Pointer;          {a pointer to the memory block being reallocated}
dwBytes: DWORD           {the requested size of reallocation in bytes}
): Pointer;              {returns a pointer to the memory block}
```

Description

This function resizes the memory allocated from a heap, and changes the memory block's attributes.

Parameters

hHeap: A handle to the heap from which memory is allocated. This can be either a heap created with the HeapCreate function or the system heap as retrieved by the GetProcessHeap function.

dwFlags: Specifies how the allocation is made from the heap. If this parameter is set to zero, then the corresponding flags given as parameters to HeapCreate will be in effect; otherwise they will override the settings made in HeapCreate. If the hHeap parameter contains a handle to the system heap as returned by the GetProcessHeap function, this parameter is ignored. This parameter may be set to one or more of the values from Table 9-8.

lpMem: A pointer to the memory block being reallocated.

dwBytes: Specifies the new size of the requested memory block in bytes. If the heap is a nongrowable heap, then the requested size must be less than 524,280 bytes ($7FFF8).

Return Value

If the function succeeds, it returns a pointer to the reallocated memory block. If the function fails and the HEAP_GENERATE_EXCEPTIONS flag was not specified, the function returns NIL. If the function fails and the HEAP_GENERATE_EXCEPTIONS flag was specified, the function returns one of the values from Table 9-9.

See also

GetProcessHeap, HeapAlloc, HeapCreate, HeapDestroy, HeapFree, HeapSize

Example

Please see Listing 9-7 under HeapAlloc.

Table 9-8: HeapReAlloc dwFlags Values

Value	Description
HEAP_GENERATE_EXCEPTIONS	Indicates that Windows will generate an exception for an exception handler instead of returning a NIL.
HEAP_NO_SERIALIZE	Specifies that requests for heap will be not be serialized. This should only be used for heaps that are created and used by a single thread. This flag removes the serialized locking feature which enables multiple threads to access the same heap.
HEAP_REALLOC_IN_PLACE_ONLY	Forces the memory manager to make any desired changes at the same location in virtual memory. If the request cannot be granted in place, the function fails and the original memory block is not modified.
HEAP_ZERO_MEMORY	The allocated memory will be initialized to zero.

Table 9-9: HeapReAlloc Return Values

Value	Description
STATUS_ACCESS_VIOLATION	Indicates that the heap was corrupt or the function parameters were not accepted.
STATUS_NO_MEMORY	Indicates that the heap was corrupt or there was not enough memory to satisfy the request.

HeapSize Windows.Pas

Syntax

```
HeapSize(
hHeap: THandle;           {a handle to the heap}
dwFlags: DWORD;           {option flags}
lpMem: Pointer            {a pointer to the memory block}
): DWORD;                 {returns the size of the memory block in bytes}
```

Description

This function returns the size of a block of memory allocated from the specified heap in bytes.

Parameters

hHeap: A handle to the heap from which the memory was allocated. This can be either a heap created with the HeapCreate function or the system heap as retrieved by the GetProcessHeap function.

dwFlags: Specifies heap access behavior. This parameter can be either zero or HEAP_NO_SERIALIZE. See the HeapCreate function for a description of the HEAP_NO_SERIALIZE flag.

lpMem: A pointer to the memory block whose size is to be retrieved.

Return Value

If the function succeeds, it returns the size in bytes of the allocated memory block. If the function fails, it returns $FFFFFFFF.

See also

GetProcessHeap, HeapAlloc, HeapCreate, HeapDestroy, HeapFree, HeapReAlloc

Example

Please see Listing 9-7 under HeapAlloc.

IsBadCodePtr Windows.Pas

Syntax

```
IsBadCodePtr(
lpfn: FARPROC                {pointer to possible code memory area}
): BOOL;                     {returns TRUE or FALSE}
```

Description

This function determines if the address pointed to by the lpfn parameter contains code to which the current process has read access. Even if IsBadCodePtr is used before accessing memory at a given address, it is wise to use structured exception handling while accessing the memory. Rights can change by other processes in a preemptive multitasking environment. This function tests read access only at the specified memory address. For testing access to a memory block, use IsBadReadPtr instead.

Parameters

lpfn: A pointer to the memory address being checked.

Return Value

If the function succeeds and the process does not have read access to the specified memory address, the function returns TRUE. If the function fails, or the process has read access to the specified memory address, it returns FALSE. To get extended error information, call the GetLastError function.

See also

IsBadReadPtr, IsBadStringPtr, IsBadWritePtr

Example

Listing 9-8: Testing for Read Access at a Specific Memory Address

```
procedure TForm1.Button1Click(Sender: TObject);
var
  TestPtr: Pointer;   // an untyped pointer of questionable access
begin
  {try for a valid read address}
  Testptr := @TForm1.Button1Click;
  if IsBadCodePtr(Testptr)
    then ShowMessage('no read access')
    else ShowMessage('valid read access');
end;

procedure TForm1.Button2Click(Sender: TObject);
var
  TestPtr: Pointer;   // an untyped pointer of questionable access
begin
  {try for an invalid read address}
  TestPtr := Pointer($7FFFFFFF);
  if IsBadCodePtr(Testptr)
    then ShowMessage('no read access')
    else ShowMessage('valid read access');
end;
```


IsBadReadPtr   ***Windows.Pas***

Syntax

IsBadReadPtr(	
lp: Pointer;	{a pointer to a memory block}
ucb: UINT	{the size of the memory block in bytes}
): BOOL;	{returns TRUE or FALSE}

Description

IsBadReadPtr tests the specified memory block for read access rights. Even if IsBad-ReadPtr is used before accessing memory, always use structured exception handling to trap errors resulting from dynamically changing memory rights in preemptive multi-tasking systems.

Parameters

lp: A pointer to the memory block whose read access rights are being checked.

ucb: The size of the memory block in bytes.

Return Value

If the function succeeds and the process does not have read access to every byte in the specified memory block, the function returns TRUE. If the function fails, or the process has read access to every byte in the specified memory block, it returns FALSE. To get extended error information, call the GetLastError function.

See also

IsBadCodePtr, IsBadStringPtr, IsBadWritePtr

Example

Listing 9-9: Testing for Read Access to a Range of Memory

```
procedure TForm1.Button1Click(Sender: TObject);
var
  Testptr: Pointer;   // pointer to memory block of unknown access
  TestArray: array[1..64] of Integer;
begin
  {try for valid read access}
  Testptr := @TestArray;
  if IsBadReadPtr(Testptr, SizeOf(TestArray))
    then ShowMessage('no read access')
    else ShowMessage('valid read access');
end;

procedure TForm1.Button2Click(Sender: TObject);
var
  Testptr: Pointer;   // pointer to memory block of unknown access
begin
  {try for invalid read access}
  Testptr := nil;
  if IsBadReadPtr(Testptr, 9)
    then ShowMessage('no read access')
    else ShowMessage('valid read access');
end;
```

IsBadStringPtr　　Windows.Pas

Syntax

```
IsBadStringPtr(
lpsz: PChar;          {a pointer to a string}
ucchMax: UINT         {the maximum size of the string in bytes}
): BOOL;              {returns TRUE or FALSE}
```

Description

IsBadStringPtr tests for read access to the entire range of memory occupied by the string pointed to by the lpsz parameter. The test will check the actual string area up to the null-terminating character, or up to the specified maximum size if no null terminator is found. This function can report a valid access if the memory block contains a null character near the beginning of the address range.

Parameters

lpsz: A pointer to a string whose read access is being checked.

ucchMax: The maximum size of the string, and the number of bytes to test for read access. Read access is tested for every byte up to the size specified by this parameter or until the null terminating character is found.

Return Value

If the function succeeds and the process does not have read access to every byte up to the null terminating character, or to the size specified by the ucchMax parameter, the function returns TRUE. If the function fails, or the process has read access to every byte up to the null terminating character or to the size specified by the ucchMax parameter, it returns FALSE. To get extended error information, call the GetLastError function.

See also

IsBadCodePtr, IsBadReadPtr, IsBadWritePtr

Example

Listing 9-10: Testing for Read Access to a String

```
procedure TForm1.Button1Click(Sender: TObject);
var
  Stringptr : PChar;          // a pointer to a string
begin
  {initialize the string pointer}
  Stringptr := 'Delphi Rocks';

  {Try for valid string access}
  if IsBadStringPtr(Stringptr, 20)
    then ShowMessage('no read access to string')
    else ShowMessage('Valid read access to string');
end;

procedure TForm1.Button2Click(Sender: TObject);
var
  Stringptr: PChar;           // a pointer to a string
begin
  {try for invalid access}
  Stringptr := nil;
  if IsBadStringPtr(Stringptr,10000)
    then ShowMessage('no read access to string')
    else ShowMessage('Valid read access to string');
end;
```

IsBadWritePtr *Windows.Pas*

Syntax

IsBadWritePtr(
lp: Pointer; {a pointer to a memory block}
ucb: UINT {the size of the memory block in bytes}
): BOOL; {returns TRUE or FALSE}

Description

IsBadWritePtr tests to see if the current process would be granted write access to all locations in the specified memory block.

Parameters

lp: A pointer to the memory block whose write access rights are being checked.

ucb: The size of the memory block in bytes.

Return Value

If the function succeeds and the process does not have write access to every byte in the specified memory block, the function returns TRUE. If the function fails, or the process has write access to every byte in the specified memory block, it returns FALSE. To get extended error information, call the GetLastError function.

See also

IsBadCodePtr, IsBadReadPtr, IsBadStringPtr

Example

Listing 9-11: Testing for Write Access to a Range of Memory

```
procedure TForm1.Button1Click(Sender: TObject);
var
  Testptr: pointer;                        // a pointer of unknown access
  AnArray: array[1..100] of integer;       // test data
begin
  {test for valid write access}
  Testptr := @AnArray;
  if IsBadWritePtr(Testptr,SizeOf(AnArray))
    then ShowMessage('no write access')
    else ShowMessage('valid write access');
end;

procedure TForm1.Button2Click(Sender: TObject);
var
  Testptr: Pointer;                        // a pointer of unknown access
begin
  {test for invalid write access}
  Testptr := Pointer($3FFFFFFF);           // points to a random memory address
  if IsBadWritePtr(Testptr, 1000)
    then ShowMessage('no write access')
```

```
    else ShowMessage('valid write access');
end;
```

LocalAlloc Windows.Pas

Syntax

LocalAlloc(
uFlags: UINT; {object allocation attributes}
uBytes: UINT {number of bytes to allocate}
): HLOCAL; {returns a handle to a local memory object}

Description

The LocalAlloc function allocates the requested number of bytes from the Windows heap. Memory allocated with this function will be double word aligned, and may allocate a greater amount than specified to facilitate the alignment.

Parameters

uFlags: Specifies how the memory is to be allocated. LMEM_FIXED is the default value and is used if this parameter is set to zero. Except where noted, this parameter can be set to one or more values from Table 9-10.

uBytes: The number of bytes to be allocated.

Return Value

If the function succeeds, it returns a handle to the local memory block; otherwise it returns zero. To get extended error information, call the GetLastError function.

See also

GlobalAlloc, LocalFree, LocalLock, LocalReAlloc, LocalSize

Example

Listing 9-12: Allocating Local Memory

```
procedure TForm1.Button1Click(Sender: TObject);
type
  Arrayspace = array[0..199] of integer;
var
  Arrayptr: ^Arrayspace;  // pointer to a dynamic array
  Arrayhandle: HLOCAL;    // handle to the array object
  iLoop: Integer;         // loop counter
  UnlockResult: Boolean;  // Unlock error checking
  FreeResult: HLOCAL;     // Free error checking
begin
  {allocate local memory}
  Arrayhandle := LocalAlloc(GPTR,SizeOf(Arrayspace));
  if Arrayhandle = 0 then
  begin
```

Chapter 9

```
    ShowMessage('Error getting memory block!');
    Exit;
  end;

  {lock the new memory block}
  Arrayptr := LocalLock(Arrayhandle);
  if Arrayptr = nil then
  begin
    ShowMessage('Error getting pointer to memory!');
    Exit;
  end;

  {do something with the memory}
  for iLoop := 0 to 199 do
  begin
    Arrayptr^[iLoop] := iLoop;
    StringGrid1.Cells[iLoop,0] := IntToStr(Arrayptr^[iLoop]);
  end;

  {unlock the memory block}
  SetLastError(NO_ERROR);     // Reset error trapping
  UnlockResult := LocalUnlock(Arrayhandle);
  if UnlockResult then ShowMessage('Lock count is nonzero');
  if (not UnlockResult) and (GetLastError <> NO_ERROR) then
  begin
    ShowMessage('Error unlocking memory');
    Exit;
  end;

  {we are done with the memory, so free it}
  FreeResult := LocalFree(Arrayhandle);
  if (FreeResult <> 0)
    then ShowMessage('Error Freeing Memory');
end;
```

Table 9-10: LocalAlloc uFlags Values

Value	Description
LHND	Combination of the LMEM_MOVEABLE and LMEM_ZEROINIT flags.
LMEM_DISCARDABLE	Allocates memory that can be discarded if it has not been used recently. This flag cannot be combined with LMEM_FIXED.
LMEM_FIXED	Allocates a fixed memory block. Do not combine this flag with either the LMEM_MOVEABLE or LMEM_DISCARDABLE flag. The return value can be typecast as a pointer to access the memory block. LocalLock can also be used to acquire the pointer though no lock will be set.
LMEM_MOVEABLE	Allocates a moveable memory block. Do not combine this with the LMEM_FIXED flag.

Value	Description
LMEM_NOCOMPACT	Memory will not be compacted nor discarded to satisfy the allocation request.
LMEM_NODISCARD	Memory will not be discarded to satisfy the allocation request.
LMEM_ZEROINIT	Initializes the contents of the allocated memory to zero.
LPTR	Combination of the LMEM_FIXED and LMEM_ZEROINIT flags.

LocalDiscard Windows.Pas

Syntax

```
LocalDiscard(
h: THandle              {handle of the local memory to be discarded}
): THandle              {returns a handle to the local memory object}
```


Description

The LocalDiscard function discards the memory block specified by the h parameter. A memory block can be discarded only if it was created using the LMEM_DISCARDABLE flag. The lock count for this memory object must be zero for this function to succeed. Once a local memory object has been discarded, its handle remains valid and can be used in subsequent calls to LocalReAlloc.

Parameters

h: The handle to the memory object to be discarded.

Return Value

If the function succeeds, it returns a handle to the discarded local memory object; otherwise it returns zero. To get extended error information, call the GetLastError function.

See also

LocalAlloc, LocalReAlloc

Example

Please see Listing 9-13 under LocalReAlloc.

LocalFlags Windows.Pas

Syntax

```
LocalFlags(
hMem: HLOCAL                {a handle to the memory object}
): UINT;                    {returns information flags and lock count}
```

Description

LocalFlags provides information about the allocation flags and lock count for the specified memory object.

Parameters

hMem: A handle to the memory object for which information is to be retrieved.

Return Value

If the function succeeds, it returns a 32-bit value indicating the lock count and allocation flags of the specified memory object. The low-order byte of the low-order word contains the lock count of the specified memory object, and can be retrieved by combining the return value with the constant LMEM_LOCKCOUNT using the Boolean AND operator. The high-order byte of the low-order word contains the allocation flags for the specified memory object, and can be zero or any combination of values from Table 9-11. If the function fails, it returns zero. To get extended error information, call the GetLastError function.

See also

GlobalFlags, LocalAlloc, LocalDiscard, LocalLock, LocalReAlloc, LocalUnlock

Example

Please see Listing 9-13 under LocalReAlloc.

Table 9-11: LocalFlags Return Values

Value	Description
LMEM_DISCARDABLE	The memory block can be discarded.
LMEM_DISCARDED	The memory block has been discarded.

LocalFree Windows.Pas

Syntax

```
LocalFree(
hMem: HLOCAL                {handle to the memory object to be deallocated}
): HLOCAL;                  {returns zero or the handle to the memory object}
```

Description

LocalFree deallocates the memory block. It returns the memory to the heap and renders the handle invalid. This function will free a memory object regardless of its lock count.

Parameters

hMem: The pointer to the memory block to be returned to the system.

Return Value

If the function succeeds, it returns zero; otherwise it returns a handle to the local memory object. To get extended error information, call the GetLastError function.

See also

GlobalFree, LocalAlloc, LocalFlags, LocalLock, LocalReAlloc, LocalUnlock

Example

Please see Listing 9-12 under LocalAlloc and Listing 9-13 under LocalReAlloc.

LocalHandle Windows.Pas

Syntax

```
LocalHandle(
Mem: Pointer                {a pointer to the start of the memory block}
): HGLOBAL;                 {returns zero or the handle to the memory object}
```

Description

LocalHandle converts the pointer to a memory block specified by the Mem parameter into a local memory object handle. For memory objects allocated with the LMEM_FIXED flag set, the LocalHandle and LocalLock functions are not needed, because the handle and the pointer to memory are the same value. When LMEM_FIXED is used, the developer is responsible for being sure that all routines are finished with the memory object when it is freed.

Parameters

Mem: A pointer to the first byte of the memory block whose local memory handle is to be retrieved.

Return Value

If the function succeeds, it returns a handle to the local memory object; otherwise it returns zero. To get extended error information, call the GetLastError function.

See also

LocalAlloc, LocalLock, LocalFree

Example

Please see Listing 9-13 under LocalReAlloc.

LocalLock Windows.Pas

Syntax

```
LocalLock(
hMem: HLOCAL              {a handle to the memory object}
): Pointer;               {returns a pointer to the memory block}
```

Description

LocalLock increments the lock counter for the given memory object by one, and forces the memory object to be maintained at a specific memory address. A memory object that is locked will not be moved to another address by the memory manager except for calls to the LocalReAlloc function. The address that is returned will be a valid address for the memory object as long as the object has a lock count of at least one. Multiple routines can place lock counts on the object, so that the object cannot be moved as long as any routine is using the memory. The lock count can be decremented by calling the LocalUnlock function. When a memory object is allocated with the LMEM_FIXED flag, it will always have a lock count of zero and will never be moved.

Parameters

hMem: A handle of the memory object whose pointer is to be retrieved.

Return Value

If the function succeeds, it returns a pointer to the first byte of the local memory block; otherwise it returns zero. To get extended error information, call the GetLastError function.

See also

LocalAlloc, LocalFlags, LocalReAlloc, LocalUnlock

Example

Please see Listing 9-12 under LocalAlloc and Listing 9-13 under LocalReAlloc.

LocalReAlloc Windows.Pas

Syntax

```
LocalReAlloc(
hMem: HLOCAL;             {a handle to a local memory object}
uBytes: UINT;             {the size of the memory object}
```

```
uFlags: UINT                {reallocation flags}
): HLOCAL;                  {returns a handle to a local memory object}
```

Description

This function is used to change the size or attributes of the specified local memory object. If this function reallocates a fixed memory object, the returned local memory handle can be used as a pointer to this memory block.

Parameters

hMem: A handle to the local memory object whose size or attributes are to be modified.

uBytes: The new size of the local memory object in bytes. If the uFlags parameter contains the LMEM_MODIFY flag, this parameter is ignored.

uFlags: Specifies how the local memory object is to be modified. This parameter may contain one or more of the values from Table 9-12. These values may be combined with the constant LMEM_MODIFY, which changes their behavior as outlined in the table.

Return Value

If the function succeeds, it returns a handle to the reallocated memory object; otherwise it returns zero and the original handle remains valid. To get extended error information, call the GetLastError function.

See also

LocalAlloc, LocalFree, LocalLock

Example

Listing 9-13: Reallocating a Local Memory Object

```
{Whoops!  Delphi does not have an imported function for the LocalHandle
   function, so we must explicitly import it ourselves}
  function LocalHandle(Mem: Pointer): HLOCAL; stdcall;

var
  Form1: TForm1;
  Arrayptr: ^Byte;         // pointer to a dynamic array
  Arrayhandle: HLOCAL;     // handle to the array object
  PtrHandle: HLOCAL;       // handle from LocalHandle
  UnlockResult: Boolean;   // Unlock error checking
  ArrayFlags: Integer;     // result of LocalFlags call
  FreeResult: HLOCAL;      // Free error checking
  FlagCount: Integer;      // number of lock flags set
  Arraysize : Integer;     // size of the memory object

implementation

{$R *.DFM}
```

```
{link in the LocalHandle function}
function LocalHandle; external kernel32 name 'LocalHandle';

procedure TForm1.Button1Click(Sender: TObject);
var
  iLoop: Byte;              // loop counter
  Baseptr: Pointer;         // temporary pointer
begin
  {allocate Local memory}
  Arrayhandle := LocalAlloc(GHND,200);

  {retrieve a pointer to the Local memory}
  Arrayptr := LocalLock(Arrayhandle);

  {do something with the Local memory block}
  Baseptr := Arrayptr;
  for iLoop := 0 to 199 do
  begin
    Byte(Baseptr^) := iLoop;
    StringGrid1.Cells[iLoop,0] := IntToStr(Byte(Baseptr^));
    BasePtr := Pointer(Longint(BasePtr)+1);
  end;

  {retrieve a pointer from the Local memory handle}
  PtrHandle := LocalHandle(Arrayptr);
  if PtrHandle <> Arrayhandle then
    ShowMessage('Memory Object Handle Error');

  {retrieve information on the Local memory block}
  ArrayFlags := LocalFlags(PtrHandle);
  Flagcount := ArrayFlags and GMEM_LOCKCOUNT;
  Showmessage('# of Local locks on Arrayhandle is ' +IntToStr(Flagcount));

  {get the size of the Local memory block}
  ArraySize := LocalSize(PtrHandle);
  Showmessage('Initial object size is ' + IntToStr(Arraysize));

  Button2.Enabled := TRUE;
  Button1.Enabled := FALSE;
end;

procedure TForm1.Button2Click(Sender: TObject);
var
  iLoop: Integer;
  Baseptr: Pointer;
begin
  {unlock the Local memory block. this is not required
   if GMEM_FIXED was set on allocation.}
  if Flagcount > 0 then LocalUnlock(Arrayhandle);

  {discard the memory block}
  Arrayhandle := LocalDiscard(Arrayhandle);
  if Arrayhandle = 0 then
  begin
    ShowMessage('LocalDiscard failed');
```

```
    exit;
  end;

  {our Local memory handle is still valid}
  Arraysize := LocalSize(Arrayhandle);
  Showmessage('Discarded object size is ' + IntToStr(Arraysize));

  {reallocate Local memory}
  Arrayhandle := LocalReAlloc(Arrayhandle,400,GMEM_ZEROINIT);
  if Arrayhandle = 0 then
  begin
    ShowMessage('Error in LocalAlloc');
    exit;
  end;

  {retrieve the new size of the Local memory block}
  ArraySize := LocalSize(Arrayhandle);
  Showmessage('ReAlloc''ed object size is ' + IntToStr(ArraySize));

  {do something with the new memory block}
  StringGrid1.ColCount := ArraySize;
  Baseptr := Arrayptr;
  for iLoop := 0 to 399 do
  begin
    StringGrid1.Cells[iLoop,0] := IntToStr(Byte(Baseptr^));
    BasePtr := Pointer(Longint(BasePtr)+1);
  end;

  {unlock the Local memory block}
  SetLastError(NO_ERROR);            //Reset error trapping
  UnlockResult := LocalUnlock(Arrayhandle);
  if UnlockResult then ShowMessage('Lock count is nonzero');
  if (not UnlockResult) and (GetLastError <> NO_ERROR) then
    ShowMessage('Error unlocking memory');

  {Free the Local memory and invalidate its handle. Note
   that LocalFree will free a locked memory block, and calling
   LocalUnlock will not affect the behavior of LocalFree.}
  FreeResult := LocalFree(Arrayhandle);
  if (FreeResult <> 0)
    then ShowMessage('Error Freeing Memory');
end;
```

Table 9-12: LocalReAlloc uFlags Values

Value	Description
LMEM_DISCARDABLE	Allocates discardable memory. The memory object must have been created as moveable or the LMEM_MOVEABLE flag must be specified, or this flag is ignored. This flag can be used only if the LMEM_MODIFY flag is also specified.
LMEM_MOVEABLE	If dwBytes is zero, this discards a previously moveable and discardable memory object. The function will fail if the lock

Value	Description
	count for the specified memory block is nonzero or if the block is neither moveable nor discardable. If dwBytes is nonzero, the block is moved to a new location (if necessary) to alter the size without changing the moveable or fixed status. For fixed memory objects the handle that is returned might be different than the hMem parameter. For moveable objects, the memory can be moved without the handle being changed even if the memory was locked with LocalLock. This functionality is available only if the LMEM_MODIFY flag is not specified. Windows NT only: Changes fixed memory to moveable memory only if the LMEM_MODIFY flag is also specified.
LMEM_NOCOMPACT	The memory object will neither be compacted nor destroyed. This functionality is available only if the LMEM_MODIFY flag is not specified.
LMEM_ZEROINIT	If the memory object is set to a larger size, this specifies that the new memory contents are initialized to zero. This functionality is available only if the LMEM_MODIFY flag is not specified.

LocalSize *Windows.Pas*

Syntax

```
LocalSize(
hMem: HLOCAL                {a handle to the memory object}
): UINT;                    {returns the size of the memory object in bytes}
```

Description

This function returns the size of the specified memory object in bytes.

Parameters

hMem: The handle of the memory object whose size is to be retrieved.

Return Value

If the function succeeds, it returns the size of the specified local memory object in bytes; otherwise it returns zero. To get extended error information, call the GetLastError function.

See also

LocalAlloc, LocalFlags, LocalReAlloc

Example

Please see Listing 9-13 under LocalReAlloc.

LocalUnlock Windows.Pas

Syntax

```
LocalUnlock(
hMem: HLOCAL                {a handle to the memory object}
): BOOL;                    {returns TRUE or FALSE}
```

Description

LocalUnlock decrements the lock count on moveable memory objects allocated with the LMEM_MOVEABLE flag, and has no effect on fixed memory objects allocated with the LMEM_FIXED flag.

Parameters

hMem: A handle to the memory object being unlocked.

Return Value

If the function succeeds and the object is still locked after decrementing the lock count, it returns TRUE; otherwise it returns FALSE. To get extended error information, call the GetLastError function. If GetLastError returns ERROR_SUCCESS, then the memory object is not locked.

See also

LocalAlloc, LocalFlags, LocalLock, LocalReAlloc

Example

Please see Listing 9-12 under LocalAlloc and Listing 9-13 under LocalReAlloc.

MoveMemory Windows.Pas

Syntax

```
MoveMemory(
Destination: Pointer;       {a pointer to the target memory block}
Source: Pointer;            {a pointer to the destination memory block}
Length: DWORD               {the size of the memory block in bytes}
);                          {this procedure does not return a value}
```

Description

MoveMemory copies the requested number of bytes from one memory address to another memory address. This is similar to Delphi's Move procedure except that the source and destination parameters are in the reverse order. The memory blocks do not have to begin or end on any specific boundary or address, but all of the referenced addresses must be within the memory range assigned to the process by the memory manager. The address ranges identified by the Source and Destination parameters may overlap.

Parameters

Destination: The target address to which the requested amount of memory will be moved.

Source: The source address from which the requested amount of memory will be moved.

Length: The number of bytes to move.

See also

CopyMemory, FillMemory, ZeroMemory

Example

Listing 9-14: Moving Memory from One Array to Another

```
var
  Form1: TForm1;
  Array1,Array2: array[0..400] of Integer;  // holds the information to be moved

implementation

procedure TForm1.Button1Click(Sender: TObject);
var
  iLoop: Integer;   // general loop counter
begin
  {move the information from one array to the other}
  MoveMemory(@Array2,@Array1,SizeOf(Array1));

  {display the information}
  for iLoop := 0 to 400 do
  begin
    StringGrid1.Cells[iLoop,0] := IntToStr(Array1[iLoop]);
    StringGrid2.Cells[iLoop,0] := IntToStr(Array2[iLoop]);
  end;
end;

procedure TForm1.FormCreate(Sender: TObject);
var
  iLoop: Integer;    // general loop counter
begin
  {initialize the arrays}
  for iLoop := 0 to 400 do
  begin
    {set the values in this array to equal the loop counter}
    Array1[iLoop] := iLoop;
    StringGrid1.Cells[iLoop,0] := IntToStr(Array1[iLoop]);

    {set all values in this array to zero}
    Array2[iLoop] := 0;
```

```
    StringGrid2.Cells[iLoop,0] := IntToStr(Array2[iLoop]);
  end;
end;
```

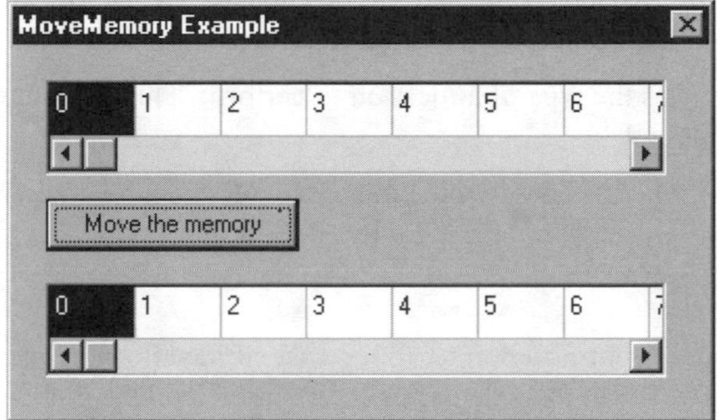

Figure 9-5: The memory was moved.

VirtualAlloc Windows.Pas

Syntax

VirtualAlloc(	
lpvAddress: Pointer;	{pointer to memory region to reserve or commit}
dwSize: DWORD;	{the size of the memory region in bytes}
flAllocationType: DWORD;	{the type of allocation}
flProtect: DWORD	{the type of access protection}
): Pointer;	{returns a pointer to newly allocated memory}

Description

VirtualAlloc is used for reserving or committing a region of pages in the virtual address space of the process. The memory committed by VirtualAlloc is initialized to zero. The region will be reserved or committed according to which flags are set in the flAllocationType parameter. To commit a region of memory to physical storage using the MEM_COMMIT flag, the application must first reserve it with the MEM_RESERVE flag. This can be done on two successive calls to VirtualAlloc for the same memory region. VirtualAlloc can be used to reserve a large block of pages, and then later commit smaller portions from the reserved block, allowing an application to reserve memory in its virtual address space without consuming physical memory until needed.

Parameters

lpvAddress: A pointer to the desired starting address of the virtual memory region to allocate. This parameter must be set to the return value from a previous call to VirtualAlloc if the virtual memory region has been reserved and is now being committed. A value of NIL allows Windows to determine the starting location of the region, which is the preferred method. If an address is specified, it will be rounded down to the next 64k page boundary.

dwSize: Specifies the number of bytes to reserve or commit. The actual region of pages allocated includes all pages containing one or more bytes in the memory range of lpvAddress through lpvAddress+dwSize. Thus, a two-byte range of memory crossing a 64k page boundary will cause both 64k pages to be allocated. If the lpvAddress parameter is set to NIL, this value is rounded up to the next 64k page boundary.

flAllocationType: Specifies the type of allocation to perform. This parameter can be one or more values from Table 9-13.

flProtect: Specifies the type of access protection applied to the allocated virtual memory. This parameter can be one value from Table 9-14.

Return Value

If the function succeeds, it returns a pointer to the base of the allocated memory region; otherwise it returns NIL. To get extended error information, call the GetLastError function.

See also

GlobalAlloc, HeapAlloc, VirtualFree, VirtualLock, VirtualProtect, VirtualQuery

Example

Listing 9-15: Allocating Virtual Memory

```
procedure TForm1.Button1Click(Sender: TObject);
type
  ArrayType = array[0..6000] of integer;
var
  Arrayptr: ^ArrayType;              // pointer to buffer
  iLoop: integer;                    // loop counter
  MemInfo: TMemoryBasicInformation;  // query structure
  OldProt: Integer;
begin
  {allocate memory from the virtual address space for this array}
  Arrayptr := VirtualAlloc(NIL,SizeOf(ArrayType),
                         MEM_RESERVE or MEM_COMMIT, PAGE_READONLY);

  {check for errors}
  if Arrayptr = nil then
  begin
    ShowMessage('Error allocating array');
    Exit;
  end;

  {Examine the memory attributes}
  VirtualQuery(Arrayptr, MemInfo, SizeOf(TMemoryBasicInformation));

  {display information on the memory region}
  ListBox1.Items.Add('Base Address: '+IntToHex(Longint(MemInfo.BaseAddress),8));
  ListBox1.Items.Add('Allocation Base: '+IntToHex(Longint(
                   MemInfo.AllocationBase),8));
  ListBox1.Items.Add('Region Size: '+IntToStr(MemInfo.RegionSize)+' bytes');
```

```
  ListBox1.Items.Add('Allocation Protection:');
  DisplayProtections(MemInfo.AllocationProtect);

  ListBox1.Items.Add('Access Protection:');
  DisplayProtections(MemInfo.Protect);

  case MemInfo.State of
    MEM_COMMIT:  ListBox1.Items.Add('State: MEM_COMMIT');
    MEM_FREE:    ListBox1.Items.Add('State: MEM_FREE');
    MEM_RESERVE: ListBox1.Items.Add('State: MEM_RESERVE');
  end;

  case MemInfo.Type_9 of
    MEM_IMAGE:   ListBox1.Items.Add('Type: MEM_IMAGE');
    MEM_MAPPED:  ListBox1.Items.Add('Type: MEM_MAPPED');
    MEM_PRIVATE: ListBox1.Items.Add('Type: MEM_PRIVATE');
  end;

  {Change the protection attributes on the memory block}
  if not VirtualProtect(Arrayptr,SizeOf(ArrayType),
                        PAGE_READWRITE,@OldProt)
      then ShowMessage('Error modifying protection');

  {Re-examine the memory attributes}
  VirtualQuery(Arrayptr, MemInfo, SizeOf(TMemoryBasicInformation));

  {display new access protection}
  ListBox1.Items.Add('New Access Protection:');
  DisplayProtections(MemInfo.Protect);

  {do something with the address space}
  for iLoop := 0 to 6000 do
  begin
    Arrayptr^[iLoop] := iLoop;
    StringGrid1.Cells[iLoop,0] := IntToStr(Arrayptr^[iLoop]);
  end;

  {decommit the memory and release the memory block}
  if not VirtualFree(Arrayptr, SizeOf(ArrayType), MEM_DECOMMIT)
    then ShowMessage('Error decommitting memory');

  if not VirtualFree(Arrayptr, 0, MEM_RELEASE)
    then ShowMessage('Error releasing memory');
end;

procedure DisplayProtections(ProtectFlag: DWORD);
begin
  case ProtectFlag of
    PAGE_READONLY:          Form1.ListBox1.Items.Add(' PAGE_READONLY');
    PAGE_READWRITE:         Form1.ListBox1.Items.Add(' PAGE_READWRITE');
    PAGE_WRITECOPY:         Form1.ListBox1.Items.Add(' PAGE_WRITECOPY');
    PAGE_EXECUTE:           Form1.ListBox1.Items.Add(' PAGE_EXECUTE');
    PAGE_EXECUTE_READ:      Form1.ListBox1.Items.Add(' PAGE_EXECUTE_READ');
    PAGE_EXECUTE_READWRITE: Form1.ListBox1.Items.Add(' PAGE_EXECUTE_READWRITE');
    PAGE_EXECUTE_WRITECOPY: Form1.ListBox1.Items.Add(' PAGE_EXECUTE_WRITECOPY');
```

```
      PAGE_GUARD:            Form1.ListBox1.Items.Add(' PAGE_GAURD');
      PAGE_NOACCESS:         Form1.ListBox1.Items.Add(' PAGE_NOACCESS');
      PAGE_NOCACHE:          Form1.ListBox1.Items.Add(' PAGE_NOCACHE');
    end;
  end;
```

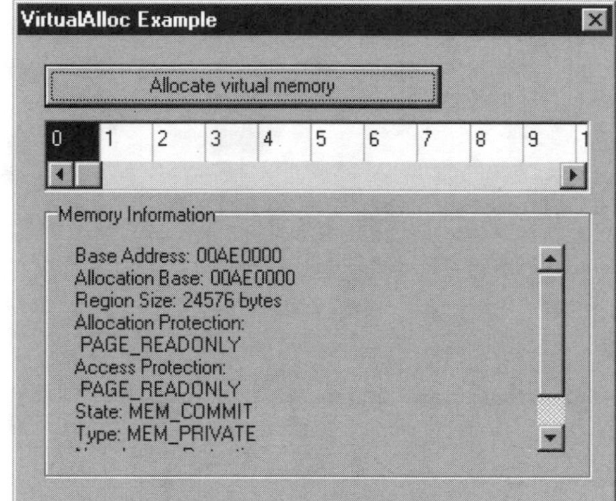

Figure 9-6: The allocated memory status.

Table 9-13: VirtualAlloc flAllocationType Values

Value	Description
MEM_COMMIT	Allocates the memory region to physical storage. This notifies the virtual memory manager that these pages are to be treated as active pages and should be swapped to disk if the memory space needs to be used for other purposes. A call to VirtualAlloc with this flag for a memory region that is already committed will not cause an error result.
MEM_RESERVE	Reserves the specified memory range so that calls to other memory allocation functions (such as GlobalAlloc, LocalAlloc, etc.) will not have access to that memory range.
MEM_TOP_DOWN	Windows NT only: Attempts to allocate memory at the highest possible address.

Table 9-14: VirtualAlloc flProtect Values

Value	Description
PAGE_EXECUTE	Specifies that the process may only execute code located in the memory region. Attempts to read or write to the committed region will result in an access violation.

Value	Description
PAGE_EXECUTE_READ	Specifies that execute and read access to the committed region of pages is allowed. Writing to the committed region will result in an access violation.
PAGE_EXECUTE_READWRITE	Specifies that execute, read, and write access to the committed region of pages is allowed.
PAGE_GUARD	Windows NT only: Specifies that pages in the region are guard pages. Reading from or writing to a guard page will cause the operating system to raise a STATUS_GUARD_PAGE exception and also turn off guard page status. This guard page status cannot be reset without freeing and recommitting the memory block. A violation is reported only once. PAGE_GUARD must be used in combination with at least one other flag except PAGE_NOACCESS. When the guard page becomes disabled due to an intrusion, the remaining page protection is still in effect with its normal error reporting.
PAGE_NOACCESS	All access to the page is prohibited. Any type of access will raise an access violation.
PAGE_NOCACHE	Specifies that the memory is not to be cached. This is not for general use, and is normally only applicable to device drivers or other system software requiring constant presence in memory. PAGE_NOCACHE must be used in combination with at least one other flag except PAGE_NOACCESS.
PAGE_READONLY	Specifies that the process can only read from the memory region. Attempts to write to this memory region will generate an access violation. Executing code within the read-only area on systems which differentiate code execution from memory reading will also generate an error.
PAGE_READWRITE	Specifies that both read and write access are allowed in the committed region of pages.

VirtualFree *Windows.Pas*

Syntax

```
VirtualFree(
lpAddress: Pointer;          {a pointer to the memory region}
dwSize: DWORD;               {the size of the memory region in bytes}
dwFreeType: DWORD            {option flags}
): BOOL;                     {returns TRUE or FALSE}
```

Description

This function releases memory previously allocated by VirtualAlloc back to the virtual address space of the calling process. This memory is available for use by any subsequent calls to memory allocation functions. VirtualFree can also decommit a region of memory, marking it as reserved until recommitted by a subsequent call to VirtualAlloc. The state of all pages in the region of memory to be freed must be compatible with the type of freeing operation specified by the dwFreeType parameter.

Parameters

lpAddress: A pointer to the memory region to be decommitted or released. If the dwFreeType parameter is set to MEM_RELEASE, this parameter must be set to the return value from the VirtualAlloc function call that initially reserved the memory region.

dwSize: The size of the region to be freed in bytes. The actual region of pages freed includes all pages containing one or more bytes in the memory range of lpAddress through lpAddress+dwSize. Thus, a two-byte range of memory crossing a 64k page boundary will cause both 64k pages to be freed. If the dwFreeType parameter is set to MEM_RELEASE, this parameter must be set to zero.

dwFreeType: Specifies the type of freeing operation to perform. This parameter can be one value from Table 9-15.

Return Value

If the function succeeds, it returns TRUE; otherwise it returns FALSE. To get extended error information, call the GetLastError function.

See also

GlobalAlloc, GlobalFree, VirtualAlloc

Example

Please see Listing 9-15 under VirtualAlloc, and the SwapTest.Exe program on the CD.

Table 9-15: VirtualFree dwFreeType Values

Value	Description
MEM_DECOMMIT	Decommits the specified region from physical storage, marking it as reserved. Decommitting a page that has already been decommitted will not cause a failure.
MEM_RELEASE	Specifies that the memory region is to be released back to the virtual address space of the calling process. The memory should be decommitted first if it has been committed to memory.

VirtualProtect Windows.Pas

Syntax

```
VirtualProtect(
lpAddress: Pointer;          {a pointer to the memory region}
dwSize: DWORD;               {the size of the region in bytes}
flNewProtect: DWORD          {the requested access protection}
lpflOldProtect: Pointer      {a pointer to a variable receiving the previous protection}
): BOOL;                     {returns TRUE or FALSE}
```

Description

VirtualProtect modifies the protection attributes on the specified memory region. The entire memory region must be committed to physical storage.

Parameters

lpAddress: A pointer to the base of the memory region whose access protection attributes are to be changed. Every page in this region must have been allocated from a single call to VirtualAlloc.

dwSize: Specifies the size of the region pointed to by the lpAddress parameter in bytes. The actual region of pages whose access protection attributes are modified includes all pages containing one or more bytes in the memory range of lpAddress through lpAddress+dwSize. Thus, a two-byte range of memory crossing a 64k page boundary will cause the access protection attributes of both 64k pages to be modified.

flNewProtect: Specifies the new type of access protection applied to the specified virtual memory region. This parameter can be one value from Table 9-16.

lpflOldProtect: A pointer to a variable that receives the previous access protection setting.

Return Value

If the function succeeds, it returns TRUE; otherwise it returns FALSE. To get extended error information, call the GetLastError function.

See also

VirtualAlloc

Example

Please see Listing 9-15 under VirtualAlloc.

Table 9-16: VirtualProtect flNewProtect Values

Value	Description
PAGE_EXECUTE	Specifies that the process may only execute code located in the memory region. Attempts to read or write to the committed region will result in an access violation.
PAGE_EXECUTE_READ	Specifies that execute and read access to the committed region of pages is allowed. Writing to the committed region will result in an access violation.
PAGE_EXECUTE_READWRITE	Specifies that execute, read, and write access to the committed region of pages is allowed.
PAGE_GUARD	Windows NT only: Specifies that pages in the region are guard pages. Reading from or writing to a guard page will cause the operating system to raise a STATUS_GUARD_PAGE exception and also turn off guard page status. This guard page status cannot be reset without freeing and recommitting the memory block. A violation is reported only once. PAGE_GUARD must be used in combination with at least one other flag except PAGE_NOACCESS. When the guard page becomes disabled due to an intrusion, the remaining page protection is still in effect with its normal error reporting.
PAGE_NOACCESS	All access to the page is prohibited. Any type of access will raise an access violation.
PAGE_NOCACHE	Specifies that the memory is not to be cached. This is not for general use, and is normally only applicable to device drivers or other system software requiring constant presence in memory. PAGE_NOCACHE must be used in combination with at least one other flag except PAGE_NOACCESS.
PAGE_READONLY	Specifies that the process can only read from the memory region. Attempts to write to this memory region will generate an access violation. Executing code within the read-only area on systems which differentiate code execution from memory reading will also generate an error.
PAGE_READWRITE	Specifies that both read and write access are allowed in the committed region of pages.

VirtualQuery Windows.Pas

Syntax

```
VirtualQuery(
lpAddress: Pointer;                     {a pointer to the memory region}
var lpBuffer: TMemoryBasicInformation;  {pointer to TMemoryBasicInformation}
dwLength: DWORD                         {the size of the information structure}
): DWORD;                               {returns the number of bytes in info structure}
```

Description

VirtualQuery provides information about a range of pages allocated from the virtual address space of the current process. VirtualQuery examines the first memory page specified by the lpAddress parameter, examining consecutive pages that have an exact match in attributes, until a page is encountered that does not have an exact attribute match or the end of the allocated memory range is encountered. It then reports the amount of consecutive memory found with the same attributes.

Parameters

lpAddress: A pointer to the base of the memory region from which to retrieve information. This value is rounded down to the next 64k page boundary.

lpBuffer: A pointer to a TMemoryBasicInformation structure which receives the information on the specified range of pages. The TMemoryBasicInformation data structure is defined as:

```
TMemoryBasicInformation = record
      BaseAddress : Pointer;          {a pointer to the memory region}
      AllocationBase : Pointer;       {pointer to base address of memory region}
      AllocationProtect : DWORD;      {initial access protection flags}
      RegionSize : DWORD;             {the size of the region}
      State : DWORD;                  {state flags}
      Protect : DWORD;                {access protection flags}
      Type_9 : DWORD;                 {page type flags}
end;
```

BaseAddress: A pointer to the region of pages being queried.

AllocationBase: A pointer to the base of the memory region as returned by the VirtualAlloc call that initially allocated the region. The address pointed to by the BaseAddress member will be contained within this region.

AllocationProtect: Specifies the access protection attributes of the region when it was initially defined. See the VirtualAlloc function for a list of possible access protection attributes.

RegionSize: Specifies the size, in bytes, of the region of pages having identical attributes, starting at the address specified by the BaseAddress member.

State: Specifies the state of the pages within the examined region, and can be one value from Table 9-17.

Protect: Specifies the current access protection attributes of the region. See the VirtualAlloc function for a list of possible access protection attributes.

Type_9: Specifies the type of pages within the examined region, and can be one value from Table 9-18.

dwLength: Specifies the size of the TMemoryBasicInformation data structure in bytes, and should be set to SizeOf(TMemoryBasicInformation).

Return Value

If the function succeeds, it returns the number of bytes copied to the TMemoryBasicInformation data structure; otherwise it returns zero.

See also

GetSystemInfo, VirtualAlloc, VirtualProtect

Example

Please see Listing 9-15 under VirtualAlloc.

Table 9-17: VirtualQuery lpBuffer.State Values

Value	Description
MEM_COMMIT	Specifies that the pages within the region have been committed to physical storage.
MEM_FREE	Specifies that the pages within the region are free and available for allocation. The AllocationBase, AllocationProtect, Protect, and Type_9 members are undefined.
MEM_RESERVE	Specifies that the pages within the region are reserved and are not consuming physical storage space. The Protect member is undefined.

Table 9-18: VirtualQuery lpBuffer.Type_9 Values

Value	Description
MEM_IMAGE	Specifies that the pages within the region are mapped into the view of an image section.
MEM_MAPPED	Specifies that the pages within the region are mapped into the view of a section.
MEM_PRIVATE	Specifies that the pages within the region are private, and are not shared with other processes.

ZeroMemory Windows.Pas

Syntax

ZeroMemory(
Destination: Pointer; {a pointer to a memory block}
Length: DWORD {the size of memory block}
); {this procedure does not return a value}

Description

ZeroMemory fills each byte in the specified memory block with the value zero.

Parameters

Destination: A pointer to the memory block whose values are to be set to zero.

Length: The size of the memory block pointed to by the Destination parameter.

See also

CopyMemory, FillMemory, MoveMemory

Example

Listing 9-16: Initializing a Memory Block

```
procedure TForm1.Button1Click(Sender: TObject);
var
  iLoop: integer;
begin
  {initialize the array with some random values}
  for iLoop :=0 to 200 do
  begin
    TheArray[iLoop] := iLoop;
    StringGrid1.Cells[iLoop,0] := IntToStr(TheArray[iLoop]);
  end;
  {toggle button states}
  Button1.Enabled := FALSE;
  Button2.Enabled := TRUE;
end;

procedure TForm1.Button2Click(Sender: TObject);
var
  iLoop: integer;
begin
  {zero the memory}
  ZeroMemory(@TheArray, SizeOf(TheArray));
  {display the zeroed values}
  for iLoop :=0 to 200 do
  begin
    StringGrid1.Cells[iLoop,0] := IntToStr(TheArray[iLoop]);
  end;
end;
```

Chapter 10

Clipboard Manipulation Functions

Sharing information between applications allows a Windows user to be more productive. Information could be prepared in one application, such as a graphical drawing program, and then copied and pasted into another application, such as a word processor. The ability to copy and paste information from one application to another is a standard expectation of Windows users, and the clipboard manipulation functions provide the means to implement this functionality.

Clipboard Internals

The clipboard is little more than a system hosted environment for data storage and retrieval. It can be thought of as a group of storage bins, with each bin holding a handle to information in a specific format. The clipboard supports a number of predefined formats for holding information of various types, such as graphics and text, but the application can also define its own formats. The predefined formats are listed under the GetClipboardData and SetClipboardData functions.

To place information on the clipboard, an application must first call the OpenClipboard function. It should then call the EmptyClipboard function, which deletes all information on the clipboard in every format, and assigns the ownership of the clipboard to the window passed in the hWndNewOwner parameter of the OpenClipboard function. Next, the application calls SetClipboardData, passing it a flag indicating the format associated with the type of data, and a handle to the data itself. The CloseClipboard function completes the operation. When an application wishes to retrieve data from the clipboard, it uses the GetClipboardData function, passing it a flag indicating the format for the requested data. If data exists on the clipboard in this format, a handle to the data is returned.

When an application places data on the clipboard, it should place the data in as many formats that make sense for the data as possible. This allows a broader range of applications to retrieve and make use of the information. For example, a word processor may place text on the clipboard in a proprietary clipboard format that it uses internally. Placing text on the clipboard in the CF_TEXT and CF_UNICODETEXT formats in addition to its proprietary format will allow other Windows applications, such as

Notepad, to retrieve the information in a format that it understands. If the text was placed on the clipboard in only the proprietary format, only the word processor would be able to retrieve the text.

Conversion Formats

Windows provides data conversions from one format to another for many of the predefined clipboard formats. This conversion is performed by the system on the fly, and is transparent to the application. When data is available on the clipboard in a format for which there exists a conversion, an application can simply request the data by calling the GetClipboardData function and passing it the desired format without any further processing. The following table lists the format conversions available by platform.

Table 10-1: Clipboard Format Conversions

Clipboard Formats	Conversion Format	Supported Platform
CF_BITMAP	CF_DIB	Windows 95, Windows NT
CF_DIB	CF_BITMAP	Windows 95, Windows NT
CF_DIB	CF_PALETTE	Windows 95, Windows NT
CF_METAFILEPICT	CF_ENHMETAFILE	Windows 95, Windows NT
CF_ENHMETAFILE	CF_METAFILEPICT	Windows 95, Windows NT
CF_OEMTEXT	CF_UNICODETEXT	Windows NT
CF_OEMTEXT	CF_TEXT	Windows 95, Windows NT
CF_TEXT	CF_OEMTEXT	Windows 95, Windows NT
CF_TEXT	CF_UNICODETEXT	Windows NT
CF_UNICODETEXT	CF_OEMTEXT	Windows NT
CF_UNICODETEXT	CF_TEXT	Windows NT

Delayed Rendering

Storing large amounts of data on the clipboard, such as multiple complex formats, GDI objects, or graphics, can take time and will eat away at resources. Fortunately, Windows allows an application to perform something called delayed rendering. To initiate delayed rendering, an application passes a zero in the hMem parameter to the SetClipboardData function. The clipboard will appear to have data in the specified format, but when an application requests this data, Windows will send the WM_RENDERFORMAT or WM_RENDERALLFORMATS message to the clipboard owner (the application that commenced the delayed rendering). Inside the handlers for these messages, the application must prepare the information and then call the SetClipboardData function, this time passing it the handle to the information. This technique is useful if the application supports many different formats of complex data, as it does not have to take the time to render every format to the clipboard. The following example demonstrates delayed rendering.

Listing 10-1: Delayed Rendering of Information

```
type
  TForm1 = class(TForm)
    Edit1: TEdit;
    Edit2: TEdit;
    Label1: TLabel;
    Label2: TLabel;
    Button1: TButton;
    Button2: TButton;
    procedure FormCreate(Sender: TObject);
    procedure Button1Click(Sender: TObject);
    procedure Button2Click(Sender: TObject);
  private
    { Private declarations }
  public
    { Public declarations }
    procedure WMDestroyClipboard(var Msg: TWMDestroyClipboard);
              message WM_DESTROYCLIPBOARD;
    procedure WMRenderFormat(var Msg: TWMRenderFormat);
              message WM_RENDERFORMAT;
  end;

  {our proprietary data format}
    ProprietaryData = record
    Number: Integer;
    Text: array[0..255] of char;
  end;

var
  Form1: TForm1;
  NewFormatID: UINT;      // holds the application defined clipboard format ID
  DataHandle: THandle;    // a handle to our data

implementation

{$R *.DFM}

procedure TForm1.FormCreate(Sender: TObject);
begin
  {register an application defined clipboard format}
  NewFormatID := RegisterClipboardFormat('New Format Example');
end;

procedure TForm1.Button1Click(Sender: TObject);
begin
  {Open the clipboard}
  OpenClipboard(Form1.Handle);

  {empty the clipboard contents. Note that it is important to call the
   OpenClipboard function passing it the form's handle, and then call
   EmptyClipboard so that the form will be set as the clipboard owner.
```

```
   Only the clipboard owner will recieve the WM_RENDERFORMAT message.}
  EmptyClipboard;

  {indicate that our proprietary clipboard format is available, but
   set the data for delayed rendering}
  SetClipboardData(NewFormatID, 0);

  {close the clipboard}
  CloseClipboard;
end;

procedure TForm1.WMRenderFormat(var Msg: TWMRenderFormat);
var
  DataPointer: ^ProprietaryData;  // a pointer to our data structure
begin
  if Msg.Format = NewFormatID then
  begin
    {allocate enough memory to hold our data structure}
    DataHandle := GlobalAlloc(GMEM_DDESHARE or GMEM_MOVEABLE,
                  SizeOf(ProprietaryData));

    {retrieve a pointer to the allocated memory}
    DataPointer := GlobalLock(DataHandle);

    {set the members of the structure with the supplied values}
    DataPointer^.Number := StrToInt(Edit1.Text);
    StrCopy(DataPointer^.Text, PChar(Edit2.Text));

    {unlock the handle to the data}
    GlobalUnlock(DataHandle);

    {copy our proprietary data to the clipboard}
    SetClipboardData(NewFormatID, DataHandle);

    {indicate that the message was handled}
    Msg.Result := 0;
  end
  else
    inherited;
end;

procedure TForm1.Button2Click(Sender: TObject);
var
  RetrievedData: THandle;         // a handle to data
  DataPointer: ^ProprietaryData;  // a pointer to our data type
begin
  {open the clipboard}
  OpenClipboard(Form1.Handle);

  {retrieve the data in our application defined format}
  RetrievedData := GetClipboardData(NewFormatID);

  {get a pointer to the data}
  DataPointer := GlobalLock(RetrievedData);
```

```
  {display the data values}
  Label1.Caption := IntToStr(DataPointer^.Number);
  Label2.Caption := string(DataPointer^.Text);

  {unlock the data handle}
  GlobalUnlock(RetrievedData);

  {close the clipboard}
  CloseClipboard;
end;

procedure TForm1.WMDestroyClipboard(var Msg: TWMDestroyClipboard);
begin
  {the clipboard is being emptied, so free our data}
  GlobalFree(DataHandle);
  inherited;
end;
```

Clipboard Viewers

A window can register itself with the system as a clipboard viewer by calling the SetClipboardViewer function. A clipboard viewer's function is to simply display the contents of the clipboard; it should never modify the clipboard in any way, nor should it leave the data it retrieves from the clipboard in a locked state. Windows maintains a list of clipboard viewers called the clipboard viewer chain, and when a window calls the SetClipboardViewer function, it is placed at the beginning of this clipboard viewer list. A clipboard viewer will receive the WM_DRAWCLIPBOARD message when the contents of the clipboard changes, and the WM_CHANGECBCHAIN message when a window has been added to or removed from the clipboard viewer chain. When the clipboard viewer receives one of these messages, it should pass the message on to the other clipboard viewers in the chain. See the SetClipboardViewer function for an example of registering a clipboard viewer.

Clipboard Manipulation Functions

The following clipboard manipulation functions are covered in this chapter:

Table 10-2: Clipboard Manipulation Functions

Function	Description
ChangeClipboardChain	Removes a window from the clipboard viewer chain.
CloseClipboard	Closes the clipboard.
CountClipboardFormats	Returns the number of formats for which there is data available on the clipboard.
EmptyClipboard	Empties the clipboard and assigns clipboard ownership.
EnumClipboardFormats	Returns the clipboard formats for which there is data available on the clipboard.

Function	Description
GetClipboardData	Retrieves clipboard data for the specified format.
GetClipboardFormatName	Retrieves the name of a user-defined clipboard format.
GetClipboardOwner	Retrieves a handle to the clipboard owner window.
GetClipboardViewer	Retrieves a handle to the first window in the clipboard viewer chain.
GetOpenClipboardWindow	Retrieves a handle to the window that currently has the clipboard opened.
GetPriorityClipboardFormat	Returns the first clipboard format from an array of clipboard formats for which there is data available on the clipboard.
IsClipboardFormatAvailable	Indicates if data is currently available in the specified format.
OpenClipboard	Opens the clipboard for modification.
RegisterClipboardFormat	Registers a user-defined clipboard format with the system.
SetClipboardData	Copies data onto the clipboard in the specified format.
SetClipboardViewer	Registers a window as a clipboard viewer and places it in the clipboard viewer chain.

ChangeClipboardChain   Windows.Pas

Syntax

```
ChangeClipboardChain(
hWndRemove: HWND;          {a handle to the window to remove}
hWndNewNext:HWND           {a handle to the next window}
): BOOL;                   {returns TRUE or FALSE}
```

Description

This function removes the window identified by the hWndRemove parameter from the chain of clipboard viewer windows. The window identified by the hWndNewNext parameter replaces the previous window's position in the viewer chain. The hWndNewNext parameter should be set to the value returned by the call to SetClipboardViewer that inserted the hWndRemove window into the chain. ChangeClipboardChain causes the WM_CHANGECBCHAIN message to be sent to the first window in the clipboard viewer chain.

Parameters

hWndRemove: A handle to the window being removed from the clipboard viewer chain.

hWndNewNext: A handle to the next window in the clipboard viewer chain.

Return Value

This function returns the result of processing the WM_CHANGECBCHAIN message by the subsequent windows in the clipboard viewer chain. Typically, these windows return FALSE when processing this message. This function will return TRUE if there is only one window in the clipboard viewer chain.

See also

SetClipboardViewer, WM_CHANGECBCHAIN

Example

Please see Listing 10-6 under SetClipboardViewer.

CloseClipboard Windows.Pas

Syntax

CloseClipboard: BOOL; {returns TRUE or FALSE}

Description

This function closes a clipboard after an application has opened it with the OpenClipboard function. The clipboard must be closed before other applications can access it.

Return Value

If the function succeeds, it returns TRUE; otherwise it returns FALSE. To get extended error information, call the GetLastError function.

See also

GetOpenClipboardWindow, OpenClipboard

Example

Please see Listing 10-5 under SetClipboardData and Listing 10-6 under SetClipboardViewer.

CountClipboardFormats Windows.Pas

Syntax

CountClipboardFormats: Integer; {returns the number of formats currently on the clipboard}

Description

This function returns the number of clipboard formats that are currently on the clipboard.

Return Value

If the function succeeds, it returns the number of clipboard formats that are currently on the clipboard; otherwise it returns zero. To get extended error information, call the GetLastError function.

See also

EnumClipboardFormats, RegisterClipboardFormat

Example

Please see Listing 10-2 under EnumClipboardFormats.

EmptyClipboard Windows.Pas

Syntax

```
EmptyClipboard: BOOL;            {returns TRUE or FALSE}
```

Description

This function empties the clipboard, freeing any data stored in the clipboard. The clipboard must first be opened by calling the OpenClipboard function. Once the clipboard is emptied, this function assigns clipboard ownership to the window passed in the OpenClipboard function. If the application passes zero as the window handle to the OpenClipboard function, this function will succeed but the clipboard will not be assigned an owner.

Return Value

If this function succeeds, it returns TRUE; otherwise it returns FALSE. To get extended error information, call the GetLastError function.

See also

OpenClipboard, SetClipboardData, WM_DESTROYCLIPBOARD

Example

Please see Listing 10-5 under SetClipboardData.

EnumClipboardFormats Windows.Pas

Syntax

```
EnumClipboardFormats(
format: UINT                {an available clipboard format ID}
): UINT;                    {returns the next available clipboard format ID}
```

Description

This function returns the clipboard data formats that are currently available on the clipboard. Clipboard formats are enumerated in the order in which they were placed on the clipboard. To begin enumeration, set the format parameter to zero and call the function. This will return the first available clipboard format. Then, call the EnumClipboardFormats function again, setting the format parameter to the value returned from the previous call. This should continue in a loop until EnumClipboardFormats returns zero. The clipboard must be opened with a call to the OpenClipboard function before enumeration can begin. For clipboard formats that have an automatic type conversion, the clipboard format will be enumerated, followed by the clipboard formats to which it can be converted.

Parameters

format: Specifies a clipboard format identifier. For a list of possible clipboard format identifiers, see the SetClipboardData function.

Return Value

If the function succeeds, it returns the next available clipboard format identifier; otherwise it returns zero. To get extended error information, call the GetLastError function. If there are no more clipboard format identifiers left to enumerate, the function will succeed but will return zero, in which case GetLastError will return ERROR_SUCCESS.

See also

CountClipboardFormats, GetClipboardData, OpenClipboard, RegisterClipboardFormat, SetClipboardData

Example

Listing 10-2: Enumerating Available Clipboard Formats

```
procedure TForm1.Button1Click(Sender: TObject);
const
  {an array defining all of the predefined clipboard format names}
  PredefinedClipboardNames: array[1..17] of string = ('CF_TEXT', 'CF_BITMAP',
                                    'CF_METAFILEPICT', 'CF_SYLK', 'CF_DIF',
                                    'CF_TIFF', 'CF_OEMTEXT', 'CF_DIB',
                                    'CF_PALETTE', 'CF_PENDATA', 'CF_RIFF',
                                    'CF_WAVE', 'CF_UNICODETEXT',
                                    'CF_ENHMETAFILE', 'CF_HDROP', 'CF_LOCALE',
                                    'CF_MAX');
var
  FormatID: UINT;                     // holds a clipboard format ID
  FormatName: array[0..255] of char;  // holds a clipboard format name
  Len: Integer;                       // the length of a clipboard format @program
= name
begin
  {clear out the list box}
```

10 Chapter

```
  ListBox1.Items.Clear;

  {display the number of formats on the clipboard}
  Label1.Caption := 'Total Formats Available: '+IntToStr(CountClipboardFormats);

  {open the clipboard}
  OpenClipboard(0);

  {retrieve the first available clipboard format}
  FormatID := EnumClipboardFormats(0);

  {retrieve all clipboard formats}
  while (FormatID <> 0 ) do
  begin
    {get the name of the clipboard format. Note that this will only
     return a format name if it is a registered format, not one
     of the predefined formats}
    Len := GetClipboardFormatName(FormatID,FormatName,255);

    {if len is equal to zero then it's a predefined format}
    if Len = 0 then
      ListBox1.Items.Add(PredefinedClipboardNames[FormatID]+' (Predefined)'+
                         ' [' + IntToStr(FormatID)+ ']')
    else
      {otherwise it contains a registered format name}
      ListBox1.Items.Add(FormatName+' [' + IntToStr(FormatID)+ ']');

    {retrieve the next available clipboard format}
    FormatID:=EnumclipboardFormats(FormatID);
  end;

  {we are done with the enumeration, so close the clipboard}
  CloseClipboard;
end;
```

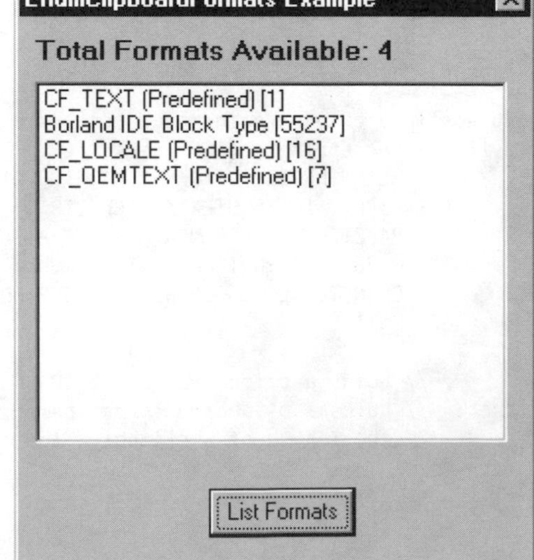

Figure 10-1: The clipboard formats available after copying text from Delphi's text editor.

GetClipboardData Windows.Pas

Syntax

```
GetClipboardData(
uFormat: UINT                {a clipboard format identifier}
): THandle;                  {a handle to the clipboard data}
```

Description

This function retrieves data from the clipboard in the format specified by the uFormat parameter. This data is retrieved in the form of a global memory handle. This handle belongs to the clipboard, and should not be freed or left locked by the application. Consequently, the application should make a copy of the data immediately upon receiving the handle. If there is data on the clipboard in a format for which the operating system provides a data conversion, this data can be retrieved in the alternative format, and the system converts it on the fly (i.e., CF_OEMTEXT data can be retrieved as CF_TEXT).

Parameters

uFormat: Specifies a clipboard format identifier. This can be one value from Table 10-3.

Return Value

If the function succeeds, it returns a handle to the data retrieved from the clipboard in the specified format; otherwise it returns zero. To get extended error information, call the GetLastError function.

See also

EnumClipboardFormats, SetClipboardData

Example

Please see Listing 10-5 under SetClipboardData.

Table 10-3: GetClipboardData uFormat Values

Value	Description
CF_BITMAP	A handle to a bitmap.
CF_DIB	A handle to a memory object containing a device-independent bitmap in the form of a TBitmapInfo data structure, followed by the bitmap image bits. Please see the CreateDIBSection function for a description of the TBitmapInfo data structure.
CF_DIF	Data in the form of Software Art's Data Interchange.
CF_DSPBITMAP	Bitmap data in a private format unique to the application.
CF_DSPENHMETAFILE	Enhanced metafile data in a private format unique to the application.

Value	Description
CF_DSPMETAFILEPICT	A handle to a memory object identifying a TMetafilePict data structure that contains a metafile in a private format unique to the application.
CF_DSPTEXT	A handle to text data in a private format unique to the application.
CF_ENHMETAFILE	A handle to an enhanced metafile
CF_GDIOBJFIRST through CF_GDIOBJLAST	A handle to an application-defined GDI object. This handle is not the actual handle to the GDI object but the handle returned from GlobalAlloc used to allocate memory for the object. The data identified by these values is not automatically freed when the clipboard is emptied; this is the responsibility of the clipboard owner.
CF_HDROP	A handle identifying files that have been dragged and dropped from the Windows Explorer.
CF_LOCALE	A handle to a locale identifier associated with the text on the clipboard. This can be used to determine the character set used when the text was copied to the clipboard. Windows NT only: Windows uses the code page associated with the CF_LOCALE handle to convert the text from the CF_TEXT format to the CF_UNICODE format.
CF_METAFILEPICT	A handle to a memory object identifying a TMetafilePict data structure that contains a metafile.
CF_OEMTEXT	Text containing characters from the OEM character set. Each line ends with a carriage return and line feed, and a null-terminating character identifies the end of the data.
CF_OWNERDISPLAY	Indicates that the clipboard owner must update and display the clipboard viewer window. The clipboard owner will receive the following messages: WM_ASKCBFORMAT-NAME, WM_HSCROLLCLIPBOARD, WM_PAINTCLIP-BOARD, WM_SIZE CLIPBOARD, and WM_VSCROLL-CLIPBOARD.
CF_PALETTE	Data in the form of a color palette. When an application places a bitmap on the clipboard, it should also place the bitmap's palette on the clipboard.
CF_PENDATA	Data used for Microsoft Pen Computing extensions.
CF_PRIVATEFIRST through CF_PRIVATELAST	Private clipboard format data. The value associated with this type of format is not freed by Windows; the clipboard owner must free these resources in response to the WM_DESTROYCLIPBOARD message.
CF_RIFF	Complex audio data.
CF_SYLK	Data in the Microsoft Symbolic Link format.
CF_TEXT	Regular ANSI text. Each line ends with a carriage return and line feed, and a null-terminating character identifies the end of the data.

Value	Description
CF_WAVE	Audio data in a standard Windows wave format.
CF_TIFF	An image in a tagged image file format.
CF_UNICODETEXT	Windows NT only: Text in Unicode format. Each line ends with a carriage return and line feed, and a null-terminating character identifies the end of the data.

The TMetafilePict data structure is defined as:

```
TMetafilePict = packed record
     mm: Longint;                 {the mapping mode}
     xExt: Longint;               {the width of the metafile}
     yExt: Longint;               {the height of the metafile}
     hMF: HMETAFILE;              {a handle to the metafile}
end;
```

For a description of this data structure, see the SetClipboardData function.

GetClipboardFormatName *Windows.Pas*

Syntax

```
GetClipboardFormatName(
format: UINT;                 {a clipboard format identifier}
lpszFormatName: PChar;        {a pointer to a buffer that receives the format name}
cchMaxCount: Integer          {the size of the lpszFormatName buffer}
): Integer;                   {returns the number of characters copied to the buffer}
```

Description

This function retrieves the name of a registered clipboard format, storing it in the buffer pointed to by the lpszFormatName parameter. This function only retrieves format names for clipboard formats registered with the RegisterClipboardFormat function, and returns a zero for any predefined clipboard formats.

Parameters

format: Specifies a user-defined clipboard format identifier returned from the RegisterClipboardFormat function.

lpszFormatName: A pointer to a buffer receiving the name of the registered clipboard format.

cchMaxCount: Specifies the maximum number of characters to copy to the buffer pointed to by the lpszFormatName parameter. Any characters over this specified limit will be truncated.

Return Value

If the function succeeds, it returns the number of characters copied to the buffer pointed to by the lpszFormatName parameter. If the function fails, or the specified format is one of the predefined clipboard formats, it returns zero. To get extended error information, call the GetLastError function.

See also

EnumClipboardFormats, RegisterClipboardFormat

Example

Please see Listing 10-2 under EnumClipboardFormats.

GetClipboardOwner   Windows.Pas

Syntax

GetClipboardOwner: HWND;   {returns the handle to a window}

Description

This function retrieves the handle to the window that owns the clipboard. The clipboard owner is generally the window that last placed data onto the clipboard. The EmptyClipboard function can reassign the clipboard owner to zero, indicating that the clipboard is not currently owned. The clipboard can contain data if it does not have an owner.

Return Value

If the function succeeds, it returns a handle to the window which currently owns the clipboard. If the function fails, or the clipboard does not have an owner, the function returns zero. To get extended error information, call the GetLastError function.

See also

EmptyClipboard, GetClipboardViewer

Example

Please see Listing 10-6 under SetClipboardViewer.

GetClipboardViewer   Windows.Pas

Syntax

GetClipboardViewer: HWND;   {returns a handle to a window}

Description

This function returns the handle to the first clipboard viewer window in the clipboard viewer chain.

Return Value

If this function succeeds, it returns the handle to the first window in the clipboard viewer chain. If the function fails, or there are no clipboard viewers, it returns zero. To get extended error information, call the GetLastError function.

See also

GetClipboardOwner, SetClipboardViewer

Example

Please see Listing 10-6 under SetClipboardViewer.

GetOpenClipboardWindow Windows.Pas

Syntax

GetOpenClipboardWindow: HWND; {returns a handle to a window}

Description

This function returns the handle of the window that has opened the clipboard but has not yet closed it.

Return Value

If this function succeeds, it returns the handle of the window which currently has the clipboard opened. If the function fails, the clipboard is not currently open, or the clipboard is open but not associated with any window, this function returns zero. To get extended error information, call the GetLastError function.

See also

GetClipboardOwner, GetClipboardViewer, OpenClipboard

Example

Listing 10-3: Retrieving the Window Opening the Clipboard

```
procedure TForm1.Button1Click(Sender: TObject);
var
 TheWindow: HWND;                      // holds the handle of the window
 WindowText: array[0..255] of char;   // holds the text of the window
begin
  {open the clipboard}
  OpenClipboard(Handle);
```

```
  {retrieve the handle of the window which currently
   has the clipboard open}
  TheWindow := GetOpenClipboardWindow;

  {get the caption of the window}
  GetWindowText(TheWindow, WindowText, 255);

  {display the caption}
  Button1.Caption := 'Currently, '+string(WindowText)+' has the clipboard open';

  {close the clipboard}
  CloseClipboard;
end;
```

GetPriorityClipboardFormat Windows.Pas

Syntax

GetPriorityClipboardFormat(	
var paFormatPriorityList;	{a pointer to an array of clipboard format identifiers}
cFormats: Integer	{the number of entries in the paFormatPriorityList array}
): Integer;	{returns the first clipboard format containing data}

Description

This function returns the clipboard format identifier for the first format in the array pointed to by the paFormatPriorityList parameter for which data is available on the clipboard. The values in the paFormatPriorityList array should be arranged in the order of importance.

Parameters

paFormatPriorityList: A pointer to an array of clipboard format identifiers. Please see the SetClipboardData function for a list of predefined clipboard format identifiers.

cFormats: Specifies the number of entries in the array pointed to by the paFormatPriorityList parameter.

Return Value

If the function succeeds, it returns the first clipboard format identifier in the list for which data is available on the clipboard. If the clipboard contains data but not in any format listed, the function returns –1. If the function fails or the clipboard is empty, it returns zero. To get extended error information, call the GetLastError function.

See also

CountClipboardFormats, EnumClipboardFormats, GetClipboardFormatName, IsClipboardFormatAvailable, RegisterClipboardFormat, SetClipboardData

Example

Please see Listing 10-4 under IsClipboardFormatAvailable.

IsClipboardFormatAvailable Windows.Pas

Syntax

```
IsClipboardFormatAvailable(
format: UINT                  {a clipboard format identifier}
): BOOL;                      {returns TRUE or FALSE }
```

Description

This function determines if the clipboard currently contains data in the format specified by the format parameter. If an application has a Paste menu item, then it can use this function to determine if the Paste menu should be disabled if the application supports only specific clipboard formats.

Parameters

format: Specifies a clipboard format identifier. For a list of possible clipboard format identifiers, see the SetClipboardData function.

Return Value

If the function succeeds and the clipboard contains data in the specified format, the function returns TRUE. If the function fails or the clipboard does not contain data in the specified format, it returns FALSE. To get extended error information, call the GetLastError function.

See also

CountClipboardFormats, EnumClipboardFormats, GetPriorityClipboardFormat, OpenClipboard, RegisterClipboardFormat, SetClipboardData

Example

Listing 10-4: Interrogating Clipboard Format Availability

```
procedure TForm1.ListBox1Click(Sender: TObject);
const
  {a list of predefined clipboard formats}
  ClipboardFormats: array[1..17] of integer = (CF_TEXT, CF_BITMAP,
                                    CF_METAFILEPICT, CF_SYLK, CF_DIF, CF_TIFF,
                                    CF_OEMTEXT, CF_DIB, CF_PALETTE, CF_PENDATA,
                                    CF_RIFF, CF_WAVE, CF_UNICODETEXT,
                                    CF_ENHMETAFILE, CF_HDROP, CF_LOCALE,
                                    CF_MAX);
begin
  {retrieve the format ID of the first available format}
  if GetPriorityClipboardFormat(ClipboardFormats, 22)>0 then
```

```
    Label4.Caption := 'The first format containing data: '+ListBox1.Items[
                      GetPriorityClipboardFormat(ClipboardFormats, 22)-1];;

  {determine if the selected clipboard format is available}
  if IsClipboardFormatAvailable(ClipboardFormats[ListBox1.ItemIndex+1]) then
    Label3.Caption := 'TRUE'
  else
    Label3.Caption := 'FALSE';
end;
```

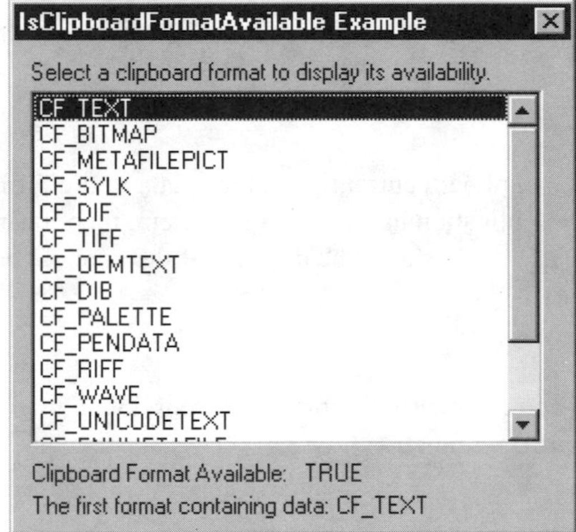

Figure 10-2: This clipboard format is available.

OpenClipboard Windows.Pas

Syntax

OpenClipboard(	
hWndNewOwner: HWND	{the handle of the window opening the clipboard}
): BOOL;	{returns TRUE or FALSE}

Description

This function opens the clipboard, preparing it for examination or modification. The clipboard can only be opened by one window at a time. The clipboard must be closed by calling the CloseClipboard function before another window can have access to it.

Parameters

hWndNewOwner: A handle to the window that will be associated with the opened clipboard. If this parameter is set to zero, the clipboard will be opened but will not be associated with a window.

Return Value

If the function succeeds, it returns TRUE; otherwise it returns FALSE. To get extended error information, call the GetLastError function.

See also

CloseClipboard, EmptyClipboard

Example

Please see Listing 10-5 under SetClipboardData and Listing 10-6 under SetClipboardViewer.

RegisterClipboardFormat Windows.Pas

Syntax

```
RegisterClipboardFormat(
lpszFormat: PChar                  {a pointer to a null-terminated string}
): UINT;                           {returns the new clipboard format identifier}
```

Description

This function registers an application-defined clipboard format, and returns a value in the range $C000 through $FFFF. This new format identifier can be used to place application specific data onto the clipboard. If the registered format already exists, this function simply returns the clipboard format identifier of the registered format, allowing two applications which registered the same format to share data through the clipboard.

Parameters

lpszFormat: A pointer to a null-terminated case-sensitive string containing the name of the new clipboard format.

Return Value

If the function succeeds, it returns a new clipboard format identifier; otherwise it returns zero. To get extended error information, call the GetLastError function.

See also

CountClipboardFormats, EnumClipboardFormats, GetClipboardFormatName

Example

Please see Listing 10-5 under SetClipboardData.

SetClipboardData Windows.Pas

Syntax

```
SetClipboardData(
uFormat: UINT;          {a clipboard format identifier}
hMem: THandle           {a handle to the data being copied to the clipboard}
): THandle;             {returns the handle to the data}
```

Description

This function copies the data identified by the hMem parameter onto the clipboard in the format specified by the uFormat parameter. The window copying the data must open the clipboard using the OpenClipboard function, and should empty the clipboard with the EmptyClipboard function before the SetClipboardData function is called. However, if the application is responding to a WM_RENDERFORMAT or WM_RENDERALLFORMATS message, it must not call the OpenClipboard function and can directly call SetClipboardData.

Parameters

uFormat: Specifies the clipboard format identifier for the format of the data being copied to the clipboard. This parameter can be either a user-defined clipboard format identifier as returned by the RegisterClipboardFormat function, or one of the predefined clipboard formats listed in Table 10-4.

hMem: A handle to the data being copied to the clipboard. If this handle identifies a memory object, the memory object must have been allocated by the GlobalAlloc function using the flags GMEM_MOVEABLE and GMEM_DDESHARE. If this parameter is set to zero, the clipboard will indicate that data of the specified format exists, although it has not been placed onto the clipboard. When an application tries to retrieve this data from the clipboard, the application that copied the data will receive either a WM_RENDERFORMAT or WM_RENDERALLFORMATS message. The application must process these messages, calling SetClipboardData with a real value in the hData parameter.

Return Value

If the function succeeds, it returns the handle of the data being copied to the clipboard; otherwise it returns zero. To get extended error information, call the GetLastError function.

See also

CloseClipboard, EmptyClipboard, GetClipboardData, GlobalAlloc, OpenClipboard, RegisterClipboardFormat, WM_RENDERFORMAT, WM_RENDERALLFORMATS

Example

Listing 10-5: Setting and Retrieving Clipboard Data

```
{our proprietary data format}
  ProprietaryData = record
    Number: Integer;
    Text: array[0..255] of char;
  end;

var
  Form1: TForm1;
  NewFormatID: UINT;       // holds the application defined clipboard format ID
  DataHandle: THandle;     // a handle to our data

implementation

procedure TForm1.FormCreate(Sender: TObject);
begin
  {register an application defined clipboard format}
  NewFormatID := RegisterClipboardFormat('New Format Example');
end;

procedure TForm1.Button1Click(Sender: TObject);
var
  DataPointer: ^ProprietaryData;  // a pointer to our data structure
begin
  {allocate enough memory to hold our data structure}
  DataHandle := GlobalAlloc(GMEM_DDESHARE or GMEM_MOVEABLE,
                SizeOf(ProprietaryData));

  {retrieve a pointer to the allocated memory}
  DataPointer := GlobalLock(DataHandle);

  {set the members of the structure with the supplied values}
  DataPointer^.Number := StrToInt(Edit1.Text);
  StrCopy(DataPointer^.Text, PChar(Edit2.Text));

  {unlock the handle to the data}
  GlobalUnlock(DataHandle);

  {Open the clipboard}
  OpenClipboard(Form1.Handle);

  {empty the clipboard contents and assign Form1 as the clipboard owner}
  EmptyClipboard;

  {copy our proprietary data to the clipboard}
  SetClipboardData(NewFormatID, DataHandle);

  {close the clipboard}
  CloseClipboard;
end;

procedure TForm1.WMDestroyClipboard(var Msg: TWMDestroyClipboard);
```

```
begin
  {the clipboard is being emptied, so free our data}
  GlobalFree(DataHandle);
  inherited;
end;

procedure TForm1.Button2Click(Sender: TObject);
var
  RetrievedData: THandle;         // a handle to data
  DataPointer: ^ProprietaryData;  // a pointer to our data type
begin
  {open the clipboard}
  OpenClipboard(Form1.Handle);

  {retrieve the data in our application defined format}
  RetrievedData := GetClipboardData(NewFormatID);

  {get a pointer to the data}
  DataPointer := GlobalLock(RetrievedData);

  {display the data values}
  Label1.Caption := IntToStr(DataPointer^.Number);
  Label2.Caption := string(DataPointer^.Text);

  {unlock the data handle}
  GlobalUnlock(RetrievedData);

  {close the clipboard}
  CloseClipboard;
end;
```

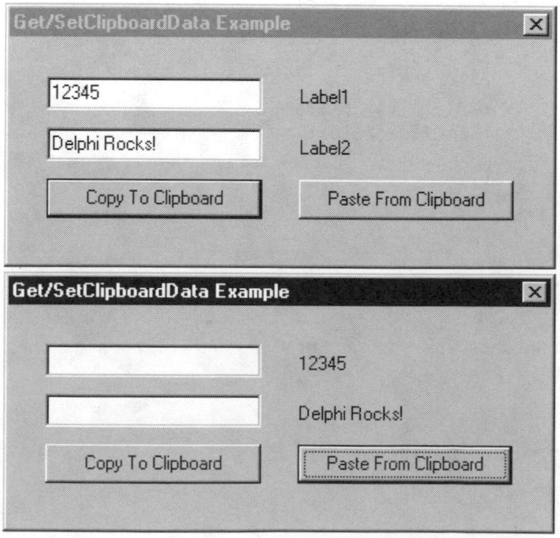

Figure 10-3: Sharing user-defined data between applications through the clipboard.

Table 10-4: SetClipboardData uFormat Values

Value	Description
CF_BITMAP	A handle to a bitmap.
CF_DIB	A handle to a memory object containing a device-independent bitmap in the form of a TBitmapInfo data structure, followed by the bitmap image bits.
CF_DIF	Data in the form of Software Art's Data Interchange.
CF_DSPBITMAP	Bitmap data in a private format unique to the application.
CF_DSPENHMETAFILE	Enhanced metafile data in a private format unique to the application.
CF_DSPMETAFILEPICT	A handle to a memory object identifying a TMetafilePict data structure that contains a metafile in a private format unique to the application.
CF_DSPTEXT	A handle to text data in a private format unique to the application.
CF_ENHMETAFILE	A handle to an enhanced metafile
CF_GDIOBJFIRST through CF_GDIOBJLAST	A handle to an application-defined GDI object. This handle is not the actual handle to the GDI object, but the handle returned from GlobalAlloc used to allocate memory for the object. The data identified by these values is not automatically freed when the clipboard is emptied; this is the responsibility of the clipboard owner.
CF_HDROP	A handle identifying files that have been dragged and dropped from the Windows Explorer.
CF_LOCALE	A handle to a locale identifier associated with the text on the clipboard. This can be used to determine the character set used when the text was copied to the clipboard. Windows NT only: Windows uses the code page associated with the CF_LOCALE handle to cover the text from the CF_TEXT format to the CF_UNICODE format.
CF_METAFILEPICT	A handle to a memory object identifying a TMetafilePict data structure that contains a metafile.
CF_OEMTEXT	Text containing characters from the OEM character set. Each line ends with a carriage return and line feed, and a null-terminating character identifies the end of the data.
CF_OWNERDISPLAY	Indicates that the clipboard owner must update and display the clipboard viewer window. The clipboard owner will receive the following messages: WM_ASKCBFORMATNAME, WM_HSCROLLCLIPBOARD, WM_PAINTCLIPBOARD, WM_SIZECLIPBOARD, and WM_VSCROLLCLIPBOARD.
CF_PALETTE	Data in the form of a color palette. When an application places a bitmap on the clipboard, it should also place the bitmap's palette on the clipboard.
CF_PENDATA	Data used for Microsoft Pen Computing extensions.

Value	Description
CF_PRIVATEFIRST through CF_PRIVATELAST	Private clipboard format data. The value associated with this type of format is not freed by Windows; the clipboard owner must free these resources in response to the WM_DESTROYCLIPBOARD message.
CF_RIFF	Complex audio data.
CF_SYLK	Data in the Microsoft Symbolic Link format.
CF_TEXT	Regular ANSI text. Each line ends with a carriage return and line feed, and a null-terminating character identifies the end of the data.
CF_WAVE	Audio data in a standard Windows wave format.
CF_TIFF	An image in a tagged image file format.
CF_UNICODETEXT	Windows NT only: Text in Unicode format. Each line ends with a carriage return and line feed, and a null-terminating character identifies the end of the data.

The TMetafilePict data structure is defined as:

```
TMetafilePict = packed record
    mm: Longint;            {the mapping mode}
    xExt: Longint;          {the width of the metafile}
    yExt: Longint;          {the height of the metafile}
    hMF: HMETAFILE;         {a handle to the metafile}
end;
```

mm: Specifies the mapping mode in which the metafile was originally drawn.

xExt: Specifies the width of the rectangle within which the metafile was drawn, in units corresponding to the specified mapping mode.

yExt: Specifies the height of the rectangle within which the metafile was drawn, in units corresponding to the specified mapping mode.

hMF: A handle to the memory based metafile.

SetClipboardViewer *Windows.Pas*

Syntax

```
SetClipboardViewer(
hWndNewViewer: HWND    {a handle to the new clipboard viewer window}
): HWND;               {returns a handle to the next viewer window in the chain}
```

Description

This function adds the window identified by the hWndNewViewer parameter to the chain of clipboard viewer windows. A clipboard viewer window receives the WM_DRAWCLIPBOARD message when the clipboard contents change, and the

WM_CHANGECBCHAIN message when another clipboard window is added to or removed from the clipboard viewer chain. These messages must be sent to the next window in the chain, identified by the value returned from the call to SetClipboard-Viewer, after they have been processed by the current clipboard viewer. When no longer needed, the clipboard viewer window must remove itself from the clipboard viewer chain by calling the ChangeClipboardChain function.

Parameters

hWndNewViewer: A handle to the new clipboard viewer window being added to the clipboard viewer chain.

Return Value

If the function succeeds, it returns the handle to the next window in the clipboard viewer chain. If the function fails, or there are no more windows in the clipboard viewer chain, the function returns zero. To get extended error information, call the Get-LastError function.

See also

ChangeClipboardChain, GetClipboardViewer, WM_CHANGECBCHAIN, WM_DRAWCLIPBOARD

Example

Listing 10-6: Viewing the Clipboard Contents

```
TForm1 = class(TForm)
    Memo1: TMemo;
    Panel1: TPanel;
    Image1: TImage;
    procedure FormCreate(Sender: TObject);
    procedure FormDestroy(Sender: TObject);
  private
    { Private declarations }
    procedure DisplayClipboard(var Msg: TWMDrawClipBoard); message
WM_DRAWCLIPBOARD;
  public
    { Public declarations }
  end;

var
  Form1: TForm1;
  hNextClipboardViewerWindow: HWND;  // holds the next window in the chain

implementation

procedure TForm1.DisplayClipboard(var Msg: TWMDrawClipBoard);
var
  hClipboardData: THandle;                   // a handle to clipboard data
  lpText: PChar;                             // a pointer to text
  ClassName: array[0..255] of char;          // holds a window class name
```

```
  OwnerWindow: HWND;                          // a handle to the clipboard owner
begin
  {this example can render data in the form of text or bitmaps. If
   this format is available on the clipboard, then continue}
  if IsClipboardFormatAvailable(CF_TEXT) or
  IsClipboardFormatAvailable(CF_BITMAP) then
  begin
    {bring the window into the foreground}
    SetForegroundWindow(Form1.Handle);

    {retrieve the class name of the window that put the data onto the clipboard}
    OwnerWindow := GetClipboardOwner;
    GetClassName(OwnerWindow, ClassName, 255);

    {display the window owner class name}
    Form1.Caption := 'Clipboard Viewer Example - Data Pasted From A '+
                     string(ClassName)+' Class Window';

    {open the clipboard for examination}
    OpenClipboard(Form1.Handle);

    {if the data placed on the clipboard was text...}
    if IsClipboardFormatAvailable(CF_TEXT)then
    begin
      {...retrieve a global handle to the text}
      hClipboardData := GetClipboardData(CF_TEXT);
      if hClipboardData = 0 then
        raise Exception.Create('Error getting clipboard data');

      {convert the global handle into a pointer}
      lpText := GlobalLock(hClipboardData);

      {hide the bitmap display surface, making the memo visible}
      Panel1.Visible := FALSE;

      {display the copied text}
      SetWindowText(Memo1.Handle, lpText);

      {unlock the global handle, as we do not own it}
      GlobalUnLock(hClipboardData);
    end;

    {if the data placed on the clipboard was a bitmap...}
    if IsClipboardFormatAvailable(CF_BITMAP) then
    begin
      {...retrieve the bitmap handle}
      hClipboardData:=GetClipboardData(CF_BITMAP);
      if (hClipboardData = 0)  then
        raise Exception.Create('Error getting clipboard data');

      {show the bitmap display surface, making the memo invisible}
      Panel1.Visible := TRUE;

      {assign the bitmap to the image}
      Image1.Picture.Bitmap.Handle := hClipboardData;
```

```
      {display the copied bitmap}
      Image1.Repaint;
    end;

    {close the clipboard}
    CloseClipboard;
  end;

  {send the message to the next clipboard viewer in the chain}
  SendMessage(hNextClipboardViewerWindow, WM_DRAWCLIPBOARD, 0, 0);
end;

procedure TForm1.FormCreate(Sender: TObject);
var
   PreviousViewer: HWND;               // a handle to the previous viewer
   WindowText: array[0..255] of char; // holds the window caption
begin
   {empty the entire clipboard contents}
   OpenClipboard(Form1.Handle);
   EmptyClipboard;
   CloseClipboard;

   {retrieve the clipboard viewer window, and display its caption}
   PreviousViewer := GetClipboardViewer;
   if PreviousViewer>0 then
   begin
      GetWindowText(PreviousViewer, WindowText, 255);
      ShowMessage('Previous clipboard viewer was: '+string(WindowText));
   end
   else
      ShowMessage('No previous clipboard viewer is installed.');

   {register this window as a clipboard viewer}
   hNextClipboardViewerWindow := SetClipboardViewer(Form1.Handle);
end;

procedure TForm1.FormDestroy(Sender: TObject);
begin
   {remove the application window from the chain of clipboard viewers}
   ChangeClipboardChain(Form1.Handle, hNextClipboardViewerWindow);
end;
```

Chapter 11

Input Functions

Windows has the responsibility of providing input services to an application from a variety of input devices including the keyboard, mouse, and joystick. The input resources are shared devices. Windows performs reasonably well in directing the inputs to the correct application in a multitasking environment. At the same time, an application can have some control in its own management of monitoring all system inputs from an input device such as the mouse.

The Keyboard

Windows can provide keyboard input functionality in the context of international character sets. The programmer can have an application load, unload, and select an active keyboard layout. There are API functions for getting keyboard characters translated in the context of the active keyboard layout into virtual keys. The keyboard state may be queried to see which key combination might have been pressed by the user. The keyboard state along with the virtual key codes give the programmer capabilities to deploy an internationally ready application. The underlying Windows operating system takes care of much of the low-level language translation work.

The keyboard can be emulated with the keybd_event API function. This function generates the same Windows messages that the system itself would generate from actual keypresses. Keyboard messages are normally sent to the window that has focus.

The Mouse

The mouse is another shared device that is monitored and managed by Windows. The mouse activity is normally reported to the window that is directly under the mouse cursor. However, an application can assign or "capture" the mouse activity and cause the mouse messages to go to a capture window. This behavior continues until the capture is released.

There are also API functions for restricting the motion of the mouse to a rectangular area. The ClipCursor function provides this capability. An application which assumes such a global control of a valuable system resource should take care that it releases the device when appropriate.

Mouse activity can be simulated just like the keyboard can. See the program example for the mouse_event function. The mouse motion, location, and button activity can all be synthesized using the mouse_event function. It may be easier to control the mouse programmatically using mouse_event rather than sending mouse messages to a target window.

The input functions which provide input simulation described in this chapter can be used for creating training or demo programs. By being able to simulate keystrokes and mouse activity, an application can demonstrate to the user how an application works. The value of seeing the mouse move on the screen under program control can have a big impact on training effectiveness. They can also be used to provide hints or other user interface services as the application needs dictate.

Input Functions

The following input functions are covered in this chapter:

Table 11-1: Input Functions

Function	Description
ActivateKeyboardLayout	Activates a specified keyboard layout.
ClipCursor	Confines the mouse cursor to a rectangular region.
DragDetect	Captures the mouse and tracks its movement.
GetAsyncKeyState	Determines if a specific key is up or down.
GetCapture	Retrieves the handle of the window with the mouse capture.
GetCaretBlinkTime	Retrieves the caret blink rate.
GetCaretPos	Retrieves the caret position.
GetClipCursor	Retrieves the mouse cursor confinement coordinates.
GetCursorPos	Retrieves the mouse cursor position relative to the screen.
GetDoubleClickTime	Retrieves the double-click interval.
GetInputState	Determines if there are mouse or keyboard messages in the message queue.
GetKeyboardLayout	Retrieves a keyboard layout.
GetKeyboardLayoutList	Retrieves a list of keyboard layouts for the current locale.
GetKeyboardLayoutName	Retrieves a keyboard layout name.
GetKeyboardState	Retrieves the up or down state of all 256 virtual key codes.
GetKeyboardType	Retrieves information about the keyboard.
GetKeyNameText	Retrieves a string representing the name of the key.
GetKeyState	Retrieves the up or down state of an individual virtual key.
keybd_event	Simulates keyboard activity.

Function	Description
joyGetDevCaps	Gets the capabilities of an installed joystick.
joyGetNumDevs	Retrieves the number of joysticks installed.
joyGetPos	Retrieves the position of the joystick.
joyGetPosEx	Retrieves additional information concerning the joystick position.
joyGetThreshold	Retrieves the joystick threshold value.
joyReleaseCapture	Releases joystick message capturing.
joySetCapture	Captures joystick messages.
joySetThreshold	Sets the joystick threshold value.
LoadKeyboardLayout	Loads a keyboard layout.
MapVirtualKey	Translates a virtual key code.
MapVirtualKeyEx	Translates a virtual key code according to the keyboard layout.
mouse_event	Simulates mouse activity.
OemKeyScan	Converts OEM ASCII codes.
ReleaseCapture	Releases mouse capture.
SetCapture	Captures mouse messages.
SetCaretBlinkTime	Sets the caret blink rate.
SetCaretPos	Sets the caret position.
SetCursorPos	Sets the mouse cursor position.
SetDoubleClickTime	Sets the double-click interval.
SetKeyboardState	Sets the state of all 256 virtual key codes.
SwapMouseButton	Swaps the logical mouse buttons.
UnloadKeyboardLayout	Unloads a loaded keyboard layout.
VkKeyScan	Translates a character into a virtual key code.
VkKeyScanEx	Translates a character into a virtual key code according to the keyboard layout.

ActivateKeyboardLayout *Windows.Pas*

Syntax

```
ActivateKeyboardLayout(
klh: HKL;                    {keyboard layout handle}
Flags: UINT                  {activation flag}
): HKL;                      {returns previous handle}
```

Description

The ActivateKeyboardLayout function activates the keyboard layout identified by the specified keyboard layout handle. In Windows 95, it takes effect for the current thread. In Windows NT, it affects all threads.

Parameters

klh: The keyboard layout handle. This handle can be obtained by calling LoadKeyboardLayout or GetKeyboardLayoutList. This parameter can also be set to HKL_NEXT or HKL_PREV which refer to the next or previous entries in the keyboard layout list.

Flags: Specifies keyboard layout options, and can be one value from Table 11-2.

Return Value

If the function succeeds, the return value is the keyboard layout handle of the previous keyboard layout. If the function fails, it returns zero, indicating no matching keyboard layout was found. To get extended error information, call the GetLastError function.

See also

GetKeyboardLayoutList, LoadKeyboardLayout, UnloadKeyboardLayout

Example

Please see Listing 11-6 under LoadKeyboardLayout.

Table 11-2: ActivateKeyboardLayout Flags Values.

Value	Description
0	Do not reorder.
KLF_REORDER	Reorder the keyboard handle list object by placing the specified layout at the head of the list. Without this flag, the list is rotated without any change in the keyboard layout order.
KLF_UNLOADPREVIOUS	Windows NT only: Unload the previous keyboard layout.

ClipCursor   Windows.Pas

Syntax

```
ClipCursor(
lpRect: PRect              {specifies the rectangular clipping region}
): BOOL;                   {returns TRUE or FALSE}
```

Description

The ClipCursor function limits the cursor movements to the rectangular region specified by the lpRect parameter. This affects all cursor movement in all applications until the original rectangular coordinates are restored. To save the original coordinates, call the GetClipCursor function. Once the cursor has been confined with ClipCursor, any call to the SetCursorPos function will be based on the specified clipping region coordinates.

Parameters

lpRect: Points to a TRect structure which specifies the coordinates for the clipping region. If this parameter is zero, the cursor is free to move anywhere.

Return Value

If the function succeeds it returns TRUE, otherwise it returns FALSE. To get extended error information, call GetLastError function.

See also

GetClipCursor

Example

Please see Listing 11-10 under SwapMouseButton.

DragDetect Windows.Pas

Syntax

```
DragDetect(
p1: HWND;                {handle of window receiving mouse input}
p2: TPoint               {initial mouse position}
): BOOL;                 {returns TRUE or FALSE}
```

Description

The DragDetect function captures mouse messages and receives the cursor coordinates until the left mouse button is released, the Esc key is pressed, or the cursor goes outside of the drag rectangle around the point specified by parameter p2. The specifications for the drag rectangle may be obtained with the GetSystemMetrics API function.

Parameters

p1: Handle of the window receiving the mouse input.

p2: Position of the mouse in coordinates relative to the screen.

Return Value

If the function succeeds, and if the mouse moves inside of the drag rectangle while holding the left mouse button down, the function returns TRUE; otherwise it returns FALSE.

See also

GetSystemMetrics

Example

Listing 11-1: Using DragDetect in a Graphics Paint Application

```
procedure TForm1.Panel1MouseDown(Sender: TObject; Button: TMouseButton;
  Shift: TShiftState; X, Y: Integer);
var
  XY_coordinates, UV_coordinates: TPoint;   // holds coordinates
begin
  {coordinates for the rectangle}
  XY_coordinates.X:= Panel1.Width;
  XY_coordinates.Y:= Panel1.Height;

  {detect mouse drags on the panel}
  while(DragDetect(Panel1.Handle,XY_coordinates)) do
  begin
    {retrieve the cursor position}
    GetCursorPos(UV_coordinates);
    Windows.ScreenToClient(Panel1.Handle, UV_coordinates);

    {display the mouse coordinates}
    Edit1.Text:= IntToStr(UV_coordinates.X);
    Edit2.Text:= IntToStr(UV_coordinates.Y);

    {draw a pixel at the mouse coordinates}
    SetPixel(GetDc(Panel1.Handle), UV_coordinates.x, UV_coordinates.Y,
             ColorGrid1.ForegroundColor);
  end
end;

procedure TForm1.ColorGrid1Change(Sender: TObject);
begin
  {erase the background}
  Panel1.Color:= ColorGrid1.BackgroundColor;
end;

procedure TForm1.Button1Click(Sender: TObject);
begin
  {redraw the panel}
  Panel1.Refresh;
end;
```

Figure 11-1: The detected drag coordinates.

GetAsyncKeyState

Syntax

```
GetAsyncKeyState(
vKey: Integer               {a virtual key code}
): SHORT;                   {key press state code}
```

Description

This function determines if the key indicated by the virtual key code specified in the vKey parameter is up or down at the time of the function call. It also determines if the key was pressed after a previous call to GetAsyncKeyState. This function will also work with mouse buttons, but it reports the state of the physical mouse buttons regardless of logical mouse button mapping.

Parameters

vKey: Specifies a virtual key code.

Return Value

If the function succeeds, and the most significant bit is set in the return value, the specified key is down at the time of the function call. If the least significant bit is set, the key was pressed after a previous call to the GetAsyncKeyState function. If the function fails, or a window in another thread has focus, it returns zero.

See also

GetKeyboardState, GetKeyState, GetSystemMetrics, MapVirtualKey, SetKeyboardState

Example

Please see Listing 11-7 under MapVirtualKey.

GetCapture Windows.Pas

Syntax

```
GetCapture: HWND;           {returns a handle to the window which has the capture}
```

Description

The GetCapture function determines which window has the mouse capture. Only one window may have mouse capture assigned to it, and that window will receive the mouse input regardless of where the mouse cursor is on the screen.

Return Value

If the function succeeds, and a window in the current thread has the mouse capture, it returns the handle to the window with the mouse capture; otherwise it returns zero.

See also

ReleaseCapture, SetCapture

Example

Please see Listing 11-10 under SwapMouseButton.

GetCaretBlinkTime Windows.Pas

Syntax

```
GetCaretBlinkTime: UINT;        {returns the blink time interval in milliseconds}
```

Description

The GetCaretBlinkTime function returns the blink time of the caret in milliseconds. The blink time is the time interval between the first appearance and the second appearance of the caret.

Return Value

If the function succeeds, it returns the caret blink time in milliseconds; otherwise it returns zero. To get extended error information, call the GetLastError function.

See also

SetCaretBlinkTime

Example

Please see Listing 11-9 under SetCaretBlinkTime.

GetCaretPos Windows.Pas

Syntax

```
GetCaretPos(
var lpPoint: TPoint             {points to caret coordinates}
): BOOL;                        {returns TRUE or FALSE}
```

Description

The GetCaretPos function retrieves the current position of the caret, in client coordinates.

Parameters

lpPoint: Points to TPoint structure which receives the coordinates of the caret. The coordinates are always given relative to the client area.

Return Value

If the function succeeds, it returns TRUE, otherwise it returns FALSE. To get extended error information, call GetLastError function.

See also

SetCursorPos

Example

Please see Listing 11-9 under SetCaretBlinkTime.

GetClipCursor Windows.Pas

Syntax

```
GetClipCursor(
var lpRect: TRect              {coordinates for the clipping region}
): BOOL;                       {returns TRUE or FALSE}
```

Description

The GetClipCursor function retrieves the coordinates of the current clipping region, defined as the rectangle where the mouse cursor is confined.

Parameters

lpRect: Points to a TRect structure that receives the coordinates for the clipping region. The TRect structure must be allocated by the caller.

Return Value

If the function succeeds, it returns TRUE; otherwise it returns FALSE. To get extended error information, call GetLastError function.

See also

ClipCursor, GetCursorPos

Example

Please see Listing 11-10 under SwapMouseButton.

GetCursorPos Windows.Pas

Syntax

```
GetCursorPos(
var lpPoint: TPoint            {receives coordinates of cursor}
): BOOL;                       {returns TRUE or FALSE}
```

Description

The GetCursorPos function retrieves the mouse cursor position relative to the screen.

Parameters

lpPoint: Points to TPoint structure which receives the current mouse cursor's position in screen coordinates. This structure must be allocated by the caller.

Return Value

If the function succeeds, it returns TRUE; otherwise it returns FALSE. To get extended error information, call the GetLastError function.

See also

ClipCursor, SetCursorPos, SetCaretPos

Example

Please see Listing 11-10 under SwapMouseButton.

GetDoubleClickTime Windows.Pas

Syntax

GetDoubleClickTime: UINT;	{returns time interval elapsed between two mouse clicks}

Description

The GetDoubleClickTime function gets the time interval in milliseconds that can elapse between the first and second mouse clicks. If the mouse moves or if the time interval between clicks is greater than this time interval, the system will not treat the event as a double mouse click. To change the double-click time, use the SetDouble-ClickTime function.

Return Value

If the function succeeds, it returns the double-click time in milliseconds. This function does not indicate an error upon failure.

See also

SetDoubleClickTime

Example

Please see Listing 11-10 under SwapMouseButton.

GetInputState Windows.Pas

Syntax

GetInputState: BOOL; {returns TRUE or FALSE}

Description

GetInputState examines the message queue for mouse, button, keyboard, or timer event messages. It returns a Boolean value reflecting the existence of these message types in the queue.

Return Value

This function returns TRUE if there are input messages in the queue, or FALSE if not. The function does not indicate an error upon failure.

See also

GetQueueStatus

Example

Please see Listing 11-2 under GetKeyboardType.

GetKeyboardLayout Windows.Pas

Syntax

```
GetKeyboardLayout(
dwLayout: DWORD                {thread being queried}
): HKL;                        {returns a keyboard layout handle}
```

Description

GetKeyboardLayout retrieves the handle for the active keyboard layout for the specified thread. To get the layout for current thread, set the dwLayout parameter to zero. Under Windows NT, GetKeyboardLayout returns the keyboard layout handle for the system.

Parameters

dwLayout: Specifies the handle for the thread that is being queried. This must be a valid handle for a thread.

Return Value

If the function succeeds, it returns the handle of the keyboard layout for the specified thread. The low-order word is the language identifier for the thread, and the high-order word is the device handle for the keyboard layout. If the function fails, it returns zero.

See also

LoadKeyboardLayout, GetKeyboardLayoutList, UnloadKeyboardLayout

Example

Please see Listing 11-11 under VkKeyScanEx.

GetKeyboardLayoutList Windows.Pas

Syntax

```
GetKeyboardLayoutList(
nBuff: Integer;                {number of keyboard layout handles}
var List                       {receives array of keyboard layout handles}
): UINT;                       {returns the number of handles}
```

Description

The GetKeyboardLayoutList function retrieves the list of loaded keyboard layout handles for the current system locale. It can be used to retrieve the actual list or the number of entries in the list.

Parameters

nBuff: Specifies the number of handles that the buffer can hold. If this parameter is set to zero, the function returns the number of entries in the list.

List: Points to an array which receives the keyboard layout handles. If the nBuff parameter is zero, this parameter is ignored.

Return Value

If nBuff is not zero and the function succeeds, it returns the number of handles placed in the buffer pointed to by the List parameter. If nBuff is zero, GetKeyboardLayoutList returns the number of keyboard layout handles. This function does not indicate an error upon failure.

See also

GetKeyboardLayout, LoadKeyboardLayout, UnloadKeyboardLayout

Example

Please see Listing 11-6 under LoadKeyboardLayout.

GetKeyboardLayoutName Windows.Pas

Syntax

```
GetKeyboardLayoutName(
pwszKLID: PChar                 {output buffer for keyboard layout name}
): BOOL;                        {returns TRUE or FALSE}
```

Description

The GetKeyboardLayoutName function retrieves the name of the active keyboard layout in the form of a string. The buffer pointed to by the pwszKLID parameter will receive a null-terminated string representation of a hexadecimal value composed of a primary language identifier and a sublanguage identifier. Under Windows 95, this function retrieves the active keyboard layout only for the calling thread. Under Windows NT, it retrieves the keyboard layout for the system.

Parameters

pwszKLID: A pointer to a null-terminated string which receives the name of the keyboard layout identifier.

Return Value

If the function succeeds, it returns TRUE; otherwise it returns FALSE. To get extended error information, call the GetLastError function.

See also

GetKeyboardLayoutList, LoadKeyboardLayout, UnloadKeyboardLayout

Example

Please see Listing 11-6 under LoadKeyboardLayout.

GetKeyboardState Windows.Pas

Syntax

```
GetKeyboardState(
var KeyState: TKeyboardState        {array to receive virtual key codes}
): BOOL;                            {returns TRUE or FALSE}
```

Description

The GetKeyboardState function retrieves the status of all 256 virtual keys into an array of 256 bytes. Use the virtual key codes as an index into this array to retrieve individual virtual key states (i.e., KeyState[VK_Shift]). The values in the array change as keyboard messages are removed from the queue, not when they are posted. To get the status of a single key, use the GetKeyState or GetAsyncKeyState functions.

Parameters

KeyState: Points to a TKeyboardState structure, which is an array of 256 bytes. This array receives the information about key states for all 256 virtual keys. If the high-order bit of an array value is 1, that key is pressed. If the low-order bit is 1, the key is toggled on, such as the Caps, Shift, or Alt keys. TKeyboardState is defined as follows:

```
TKeyboardState = array[0..255] of Byte;        {virtual key code states}
```

Return Value

If the function succeeds, it returns TRUE; otherwise it returns FALSE. To get extended error information, call the GetLastError function.

See also

GetAsyncKeyState, GetKeyNameText, MapVirtualKey

Example

Please see Listing 11-7 under MapVirtualKey.

GetKeyboardType Windows.Pas

Syntax

```
GetKeyboardType(
nTypeFlag: Integer              {type of information}
): Integer;                     {returns the specified information}
```

Description

The GetKeyboardType function retrieves information about the keyboard depending on what type data is requested. The type, subtype, and number of function keys may be obtained according to the state of the nTypeFlag parameter.

Parameters

nTypeFlag: Specifies the type of information to retrieve, such as keyboard type, subtype, or number of function keys. This parameter can be set to one value from Table 11-3. If the keyboard subtype is requested, the return value will be OEM specific with a meaning that is described in Table 11-4. If the number of function keys is requested, the return value is not the number of function keys but a code that is translated using Table 11-5.

Return Value

If the function succeeds, it returns the requested information about the keyboard; otherwise it returns zero.

See also

keybd_event

Example

Listing 11-2: Retrieving Information about the Keyboard

```
procedure TForm1.FormActivate(Sender: TObject);
begin
  {display the keyboard type}
  ComboBox1.ItemIndex := GetKeyboardType(0) - 1;

  {display the number of function keys}
  Edit1.Text := IntToStr(GetKeyboardType(2));
end;

procedure TForm1.Timer1Timer(Sender: TObject);
begin
  {check the state of the input queue}
  if (GetInputState = TRUE) then
    StatusBar1.SimpleText := 'Input messages in the queue'
  else
    StatusBar1.SimpleText := 'No input messages in the queue';
end;
```

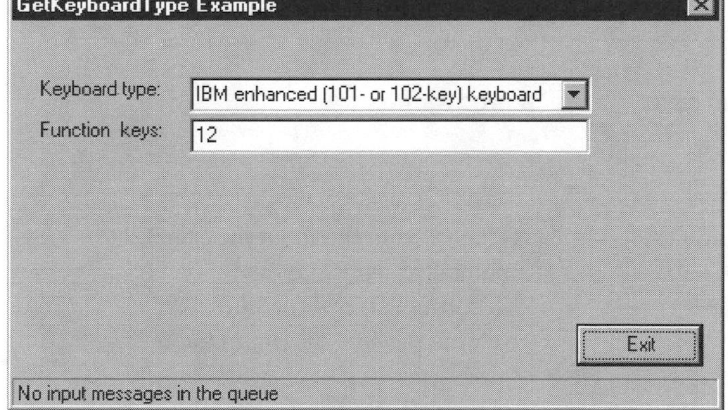

Figure 11-2: The current keyboard type.

Table 11-3: GetKeyboardType nTypeFlag Values

Value	Description
0	Requesting keyboard type.
1	Requesting keyboard subtype.
2	Requesting number of function keys.

Table 11-4: GetKeyboardType Subtype Return Values

Value	Description
1	IBM PC/XT or compatible keyboard (83 keys).
2	Olivetti "ICO" (102-key) keyboard.
3	IBM PC/AT (84-key) keyboard.
4	IBM enhanced (101- or 102-key) keyboard.
5	Nokia 1050 and similar keyboard.
6	Nokia 9140 and similar keyboard.
7	Japanese keyboard.

Table 11-5: GetKeyboardType Function Key Count Return Values

Value	Description
1	10
2	12 or 18
3	10
4	12
5	10
6	24
7	other (dependent on hardware and the OEM)

GetKeyNameText Windows.Pas

Syntax

```
GetKeyNameText(
lParam: Longint;            {lParam from the input message)
lpString: PChar;            {pointer to output buffer}
nSize: Integer              {maximum size of the buffer}
): Integer                  {returns the size of data in the buffer}
```

Description

The GetKeyNameText function retrieves the name of the specified key and stores it in the buffer pointed to by the lpString parameter. The format of the key name depends on the currently loaded keyboard layout. On some keyboards, key names are longer than one character. The name list for keys is maintained by the keyboard driver. Under Windows 95, the key name is translated according to the currently loaded keyboard layout for the current thread. Under Windows NT, the key name is translated according to the currently loaded keyboard layout for the system.

Parameters

lParam: Specifies the LParam parameter of a keyboard message. This parameter contains information on the keystroke whose key name is to be retrieved, and is interpreted as described in Table 11-6.

lpString: Points to the output buffer which will receive the name of the key.

nSize: Specifies size of the output buffer pointed to by the lpString parameter.

Return Value

If the function succeeds, it returns the size of the string copied to the output buffer in characters, not including the null terminator. This function does not indicate an error upon failure.

See also

GetKeyState

Example

Listing 11-3: Retrieving Keystroke Names

```
procedure TForm1.WndProc(var Msg: TMessage);
var
  lpString: PChar;   // holds the key name
begin
  {if the message was a keystroke message...}
  if Msg.Msg = WM_KEYDOWN then
  begin
    {retrieve the name of the key pressed}
    lpString := StrAlloc(100);
    GetKeyNameText(Msg.LParam, lpString, 100);
    StaticText1.Caption := lpString  + ' Key Was Pressed';
    StrDispose(lpString);

    {indicate if the Shift key was pressed}
    if HiByte(GetKeyState(VK_Shift)) <> 0 then
      StaticText4.Font.Color := clRed
    else
      StaticText4.Font.Color := clBlack;

    {indicate if the Ctrl key was pressed}
    if HiByte(GetKeyState(VK_CONTROL)) <> 0 then
      StaticText3.Font.Color := clRed
    else
      StaticText3.Font.Color := clBlack;

    {indicate if the Alt key was pressed}
    if HiByte(GetKeyState(VK_MENU)) <> 0 then
      StaticText2.Font.Color := clRed
    else
      StaticText2.Font.Color := clblack;
  end;
```

```
  {pass all messages to the window procedure}
  inherited WndProc(Msg);
end;

procedure TForm1.WMGetDlgCode(var Message: TWMGetDlgCode);
begin
  inherited;

  {this forces the system to send all keys to the form}
  Message.Result := Message.Result or DLGC_WANTALLKEYS or DLGC_WANTARROWS
    or DLGC_WANTTAB;
end;
```

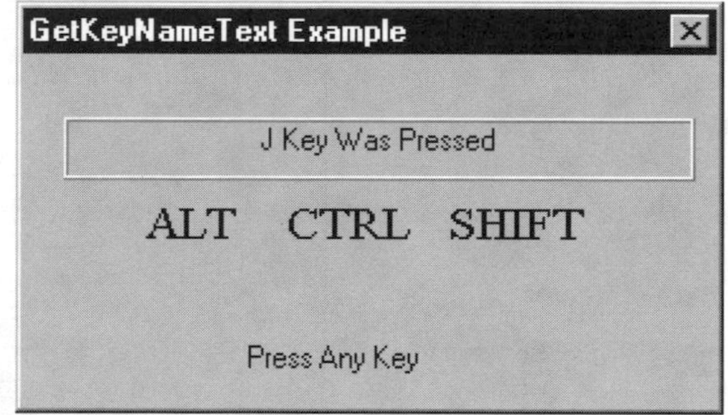

Figure 11-3: The keystroke name.

Table 11-6: GetKeyNameText lParam Values

Bits	Description
16-23	Specifies the key scan code.
24	Distinguishes extended key behavior on enhanced keyboard.
25	If this bit is set, the function does not differentiate between left and right Shift and Ctrl keys.

GetKeyState *Windows.Pas*

Syntax

```
GetKeyState (
nVirtKey: Integer        {virtual key code}
): SHORT;                {returns the state}
```

Description

The GetKeyState function retrieves the status of the key specified by the nVirtKey parameter. The key state can be up, down, or toggled (i.e., Caps, Shift, or Ctrl).

Parameters

nVirtKey: Specifies the virtual key code for which to retrieve the status. The virtual key code for keys between A to Z and 0 to 9 are the same as the ASCII value of the keys. See Table 11-7.

Return Value

If the function succeeds, it returns the state of the specified key. If the high-order bit is set, the key is pressed. If the low-order bit is set, the key is toggled to an on state. This function does not indicate an error upon failure.

See also

GetAsyncKeyState, GetKeyboardState, MapVirtualKey, SetKeyboardState

Example

Please see Listing 11-3 under GetKeyNameText.

Table 11-7: GetKeyState nVirtKey Values

Value	Description
VK_F1–VK_F12	Function keys F1–F12
VK_NUMPAD0–VK_NUMPAD9	Numeric keypad 0–9 with NUMLOCK on
VK_CANCEL	Ctrl-Break
VK_RETURN	Enter
VK_BACK	Backspace
VK_TAB	Tab
VK_CLEAR	Numeric keypad 5 with NUMLOCK off
VK_SHIFT	Shift
VK_CONTROL	Ctrl
VK_MENU	Alt
VK_PAUSE	Pause
VK_ESCAPE	Esc
VK_SPACE	Spacebar
VK_PRIOR	Page Up and PgUp
VK_NEXT	Page Down and PgDn
VK_END	End
VK_HOME	Home
VK_LEFT	Left arrow
VK_UP	Up arrow
VK_RIGHT	Right arrow
VK_DOWN	Down arrow
VK_SNAPSHOT	Print Screen
VK_INSERT	Insert and Ins

Value	Description
VK_DELETE	Delete and Del
VK_MULTIPLY	Numeric keypad *
VK_ADD	Numeric keypad +
VK_SUBTRACT	Numeric keypad –
VK_DECIMAL	Numeric keypad .
VK_DIVIDE	Numeric keypad /
VK_CAPITAL	Caps Lock
VK_NUMLOCK	Num Lock
VK_SCROLL	Scroll Lock

keybd_event *Windows.Pas*

Syntax

```
keybd_event(
bVk: Byte;                  {virtual key code}
bScan: Byte;                {scan code}
dwFlags: DWORD;             {option flags}
dwExtraInfo: DWORD          {additional information about the key}
);                          {this procedure does not return a value}
```

Description

The keybd_event function simulates a keystroke. The system generates a WM_KEYUP or WM_KEYDOWN message as if the key were pressed on the keyboard.

Parameters

bVk: The virtual key code in the range of 1-254. See GetKeyState for virtual keycode identifiers.

bScan: The hardware scan code for the key.

dwFlags: Flags identifying keystroke operations. This parameter can contain one or more values from Table 11-8.

dwExtraInfo: Specifies an additional 32-bit value associated with the keystroke.

See also

GetAsyncKeyState, GetKeyState, MapVirtualKey, SetKeyboardState

Example

Listing 11-4: Simulating the PRNTSCRN Key Using keybd_event

```
procedure TForm1.ButtonSnapShotClick(Sender: TObject);
var
```

```
  Bitmap: TBitmap;      // holds a bitmap
begin
  {see which radio button is checked}
  if ImageOptions.ItemIndex = 0 then
    keybd_event(VK_SNAPSHOT,1,0,0)     {desktop window snapshot}
  else
    keybd_event(VK_SNAPSHOT,0,0,0);    {client window snapshot}

  {check to see if there is a picture}
  if Clipboard.HasFormat(CF_BITMAP) then
  begin
    {Create a bitmap to hold the contents of the Clipboard}
    Bitmap := TBitmap.Create;

    {trap for clipboard bitmap errors}
    try
      {get the bitmap off the clipboard using Assign}
      Bitmap.Assign(Clipboard);

      {copy the bitmap to the Image}
      Image1.Canvas.Draw(0, 0, Bitmap);
    finally
      {the bitmap is no longer needed, so free it}
      Bitmap.Free;
    end;
  end;
end;
```

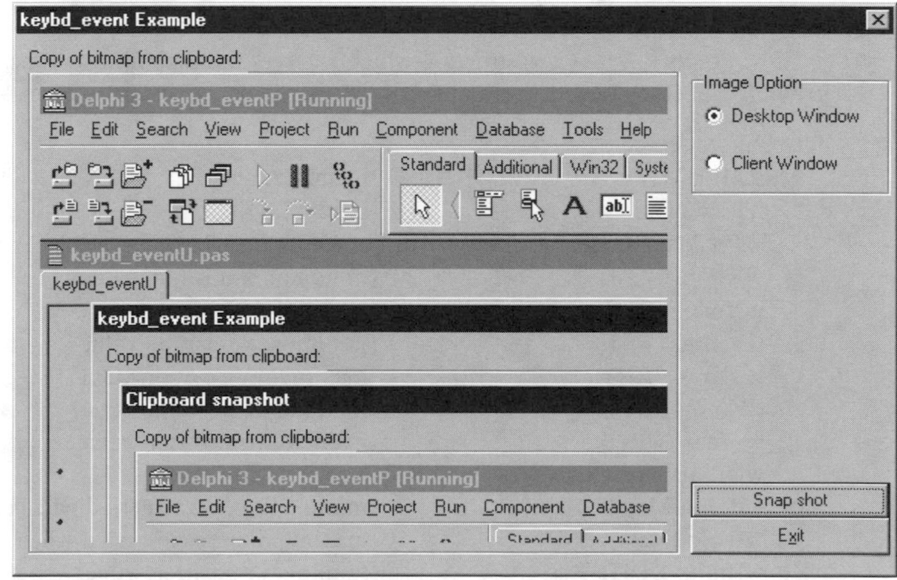

Figure 11-4: The simulated PRNTSCRN results.

Table 11-8: keybd_event dwFlags Values

Value	Description
KEYEVENTF_EXTENDEDKEY	If this flag is specified, then the scan code is prefixed with the byte value $E0 (224).
KEYEVENTF_KEYUP	If specified, the key is being released. If not, the key is being pressed.

joyGetDevCaps *Mmsystem.Pas*

Syntax

```
joyGetDevCaps (
uJoyID: UINT;              {joystick identifier}
lpCaps: PJoyCaps;          {points to TJoyCaps structure}
uSize: UINT                {size of the TJoyCaps structure}
): MMRESULT;               {returns an error condition}
```

Description

joyGetDevCaps retrieves the joystick capabilities into a TJoyCaps structure provided by the caller.

Parameters

uJoyID: A joystick identifier which can be JOYSTICKID1 or JOYSTICKID2.

lpCaps: Points to TJoyCaps structure which receives the capabilities of the specified joystick. The TJoyCaps data structure is defined as:

```
TJoyCaps = record
      wMid: Word;                        {manufacturer ID}
      wPid: Word;                        {product ID}
      szPname: array[0..MAXPNAMELEN-1] of AnsiChar;     {product name}
      wXmin: UINT;                       {minimum x position value}
      wXmax: UINT;                       {maximum x position value}
      wYmin: UINT;                       {minimum y position value}
      wYmax: UINT;                       {maximum y position value}
      wZmin: UINT;                       {minimum z position value}
      wZmax: UINT;                       {maximum z position value}
      wNumButtons: UINT;                 {number of buttons}
      wPeriodMin: UINT;                  {minimum message period when captured}
      wPeriodMax: UINT;                  {maximum message period when captured}
      wRmin: UINT;                       {minimum r position value}
      wRmax: UINT;                       {maximum r position value}
      wUmin: UINT;                       {minimum u (5th axis) position value}
      wUmax: UINT;                       {maximum u (5th axis) position value}
      wVmin: UINT;                       {minimum v (6th axis) position value}
```

```
        wVmax: UINT;                {maximum v (6th axis) position value}
        wCaps: UINT;                {joystick capabilities}
        wMaxAxes: UINT;             {maximum number of axes supported}
        wNumAxes: UINT;             {number of axes in use}
        wMaxButtons: UINT;          {maximum number of buttons supported}
        szRegKey: array[0..MAXPNAMELEN - 1] of AnsiChar;          {registry key}
        szOEMVxD: array[0..MAX_JOYSTICKOEMVXDNAME - 1] of AnsiChar;
                                                                  {OEM VxD}
end;
```

wMid: Manufacturer's identifier.

wPid: Product identifier.

szPname: Name of the joystick as a null-terminated string.

wXmin: Minimum value of the joystick's x coordinate.

wXmax: Maximum value of the joystick's x coordinate.

wYmin: Minimum value of the joystick's y coordinate.

wYmax: Maximum value of the joystick's y coordinate.

wZmin: Minimum value of the joystick's z coordinate.

wZmax: Maximum value of the joystick's z coordinate.

wNumButtons: Number of buttons on the joystick.

wPeriodMin: Smallest polling frequency supported with joySetCapture on.

wPeriodMax: Largest polling frequency supported with joySetCapture on.

wRmin: Minimum rudder value (4th axis).

wRmax: Maximum rudder value (4th axis).

wUmin: Minimum value of 5th axis.

wUmax: Maximum value of 5th axis.

wVmin: Minimum value of 6th axis.

wVmax: Maximum value of 6th axis.

wCaps: Joystick capabilities as shown in Table 11-9.

wMaxAxes: Maximum number of axes supported.

wNumAxes: Number of axes in current use.

wMaxButtons: Number of buttons supported.

szRegKey: Joystick registry key as a null-terminated string.

szOEMVxD: Name of the OEM driver as a null-terminated string.

uSize: Specifies the size, in bytes, of the TJoyCaps structure.

Return Value

The function will return a success or failure result code as shown in Table 11-10.

See also

joyGetPosEx, joyGetPos

Example

Please see Listing 11-5 under joySetCapture.

Table 11-9: joyGetDevCaps lpCaps.wCaps Values

Value	Description
JOYCaps_HASZ	Joystick has z-coordinate information.
JOYCaps_HASR	Joystick has 4th axis information.
JOYCaps_HASU	Joystick has 5th axis information.
JOYCaps_HASV	Joystick has 6th axis information.
JOYCaps_HASPOV	Joystick has point-of-view information.
JOYCaps_POV4DIR	Joystick point-of-view supports discrete values for centered, forward, backward, left, and right.
JOYCaps_POVCTS	Joystick point-of-view supports continuous degree bearings.

Table 11-10: joyGetDevCaps Return Values

Value	Description
JOYERR_NOERROR	The function succeeded.
MMSYSERR_NODRIVER	Joystick driver is not present.
MMSYSERR_INVALPARAM	Invalid parameter is passed.

joyGetNumDevs   *Mmsystem.Pas*

Syntax

joyGetNumDevs: UINT;   {returns the number of joysticks supported by the driver}

Description

The joyGetNumDevs retrieves the number of joysticks supported by the current joystick driver. Use joyGetPos to determine if a joystick is attached to the system.

Return Value

If the function succeeds, it returns the number of joysticks supported by the current joystick driver. If the function fails, or there is no joystick driver present, it returns zero.

See also

joyGetDevCaps

Example

Please see Listing 11-5 under joySetCapture.

joyGetPos Mmsystem.Pas

Syntax

```
joyGetPos(
uJoyID: UINT;               {joystick identifier}
lpInfo: PJoyInfo            {points to TJoyInfo structure}
): MMRESULT;                {returns an error condition}
```

Description

The joyGetPos function retrieves information about joystick position and button status for the joystick identified by the uJoyID parameter. Position and button status are stored in a TJoyInfo structure. This function can be used to determine if the joystick is currently attached to the system by checking the return value.

Parameters

uJoyID: The joystick identifier of the joystick whose position is to be checked. This parameter can be set to JOYSTICKID1 or JOYSTICKID2.

lpInfo: A pointer to a TJoyInfo structure that receives the joystick position information. The TJoyInfo data structure is defined as:

```
TJoyInfo = record
      wXpos: UINT;              {x position}
      wYpos: UINT;              {y position}
      wZpos: UINT;              {z position}
      wButtons: UINT;           {button states}
end;
```

wXpos: The current X position of the joystick.

wYpos: The current Y position of the joystick.

wZpos: The current Z position of the joystick.

wButtons: Status of the buttons as shown in Table 11-11.

Return Value

The function will return a success or failure result code as shown in Table 11-12.

See also

joyGetPosEx

Example

Please see Listing 11-5 under joySetCapture.

Table 11-11: joyGetPos lpInfo.wButtons Values

Value	Description
JOY_BUTTON1	1st joystick button is pressed.
JOY_BUTTON2	2nd joystick button is pressed.
JOY_BUTTON3	3rd joystick button is pressed.
JOY_BUTTON4	4th joystick button is pressed.

Table 11-12: joyGetPos Return Values

Value	Description
JOYERR_NOERROR	The function succeeded.
MMSYSERR_NODRIVER	Joystick driver not found.
MMSYSERR_INVALPARAM	Invalid parameter.
JOYERR_UNPLUGGED	Joystick is unplugged.

joyGetPosEx *Mmsystem.Pas*

Syntax

```
joyGetPosEx(
uJoyID: UINT;              {joystick identifier}
lpInfo: PJoyInfoEx         {points to TJoyInfoEx structure}
): MMRESULT;               {returns an error condition}
```

Description

The joyGetPosEx retrieves information about joystick position and button status for the joystick identified by the uJoyID parameter. Position and button status are stored in a TJoyInfoEx structure. This function provides more information about the joystick position than the joyGetPos function.

Parameters

uJoyID: The joystick identifier of the joystick whose position is to be checked. This parameter can be set to JOYSTICKID1 or JOYSTICKID2.

lpInfo: A pointer to a TJoyInfoEx structure that receives the joystick position information. The TJoyInfoEx data structure is defined as:

```
TJoyInfoEx = record
    dwSize: DWORD;           {size of structure}
    dwFlags: DWORD;          {flags indicating what to return}
```

```
        wXpos: UINT;                    {x (1st axis) position}
        wYpos: UINT;                    {y (2nd axis) position}
        wZpos: UINT;                    {z (3rd axis) position}
        dwRpos: DWORD;                  {4th axis position}
        dwUpos: DWORD;                  {5th axis position}
        dwVpos: DWORD;                  {6th axis position}
        wButtons: UINT;                 {button states}
        dwButtonNumber: DWORD;          {current button number pressed}
        dwPOV: DWORD;                   {point of view state}
        dwReserved1: DWORD;        {reserved for system comm. with joystick driver}
        dwReserved2: DWORD;        {reserved for future use}
end;
```

dwSize: The size of this structure in bytes. This member should be set to SizeOf(TJoyInfoEx).

dwFlags: Option specifying which data is requested as shown in Table 11-13.

wXpos: Current 1st axis coordinate.

wYpos: Current 2nd axis coordinate.

wZpos: Current 3rd axis coordinate.

dwRpos: Current 4th axis coordinate.

dwUpos: Current 5th axis coordinate.

dwVpos: Current 6th axis coordinate.

wButtons: The current state of all 32 buttons supported by the system. Each button has an identifier (JOY_BUTTON1 through JOY_BUTTON32) which is simply an identifier for the bit positions in the 32-bit wButtons value. If the specified bit is set, the button is pressed.

dwButtonNumber: The current button number that is pressed.

dwPOV: The current position of the point-of-view control in hundredths of degrees. This value can range from 0 to 35,900. When the JOY_RETURNPOV flag is set in the dwFlags entry, the value of dwPOV will be one of the values from Table 11-14. An application that supports only the point-of-view values shown in the table must have the JOY_RETURNPOV flag set. If the application can accept the variable degree information, it should set the JOY_RETURN-POVCTS flag, which also supports the JOY_POV constants in the dwPOV table below.

dwReserved1: Reserved for future use.

dwReserved2: Reserved for future use.

Return Value

The function will return a success or failure result code as shown in Table 11-15.

See also

joyGetPos, joyGetDevCaps

Example

Please see Listing 11-5 under joySetCapture.

Table 11-13: joyGetPosEx lpInfo.dwFlags Values

Value	Description
JOY_RETURNALL	Equivalent to setting all of the JOY_RETURN bits except for the JOY_RETURNRAWDATA bit.
JOY_RETURNBUTTONS	dwButtons contains information about each joystick button.
JOY_RETURNCENTERED	Centers the joystick neutral position to the central value of each axis.
JOY_RETURNPOV	The dwPOV member contains information about the point-of-view control, expressed in whole degrees.
JOY_RETURNPOVCTS	The dwPOV member contains valid information about the point-of-view control expressed in continuous, one-hundredth degree units.
JOY_RETURNR	The dwRpos member contains valid rudder pedal data for the 4th axis.
JOY_RETURNRAWDATA	Data stored in this structure contains uncalibrated joystick readings.
JOY_RETURNU	The dwUpos member contains valid data for a 5th axis.
JOY_RETURNV	The dwVpos member contains valid data for a 6th axis.
JOY_RETURNX	The dwXpos member contains valid data for the x-coordinate (1st axis) of the joystick.
JOY_RETURNY	The dwYpos member contains valid data for the y-coordinate (2nd axis) of the joystick.
JOY_RETURNZ	The dwZpos member contains valid data for the z-coordinate (3rd axis) of the joystick.
JOY_USEDEADZONE	Expands the range for the neutral position of the joystick as a dead zone. Coordinate information is the same for all positions in the dead zone.

Table 11-14: joyGetPosEx lpInfo.dwPOV Values

Value	Description
JOY_POVBACKWARD	Point-of-view hat is pressed backward. The value 18,000 represents 180.00 degrees (to the rear).
JOY_POVCENTERED	Point-of-view hat is in the neutral position. The value –1 means there is no angle to report.
JOY_POVFORWARD	Point-of-view hat is pressed forward. The value 0 represents 0.00 degrees (straight ahead).
JOY_POVLEFT	Point-of-view hat is pressed to the left. The value 27,000 represents 270.00 degrees (90.00 degrees to the left).
JOY_POVRIGHT	Point-of-view hat is pressed to the right. The value 9,000 represents 90.00 degrees (to the right).

Table 11-15: joyGetPosEx Return Values

Value	Description
JOYERR_NOERROR	The function succeeded.
MMSYSERR_NODRIVER	Joystick driver is not present.
MMSYSERR_INVALPARAM	Invalid parameter is passed.
MMSYSERR_BADDEVICEID	Joystick identifier is invalid.
JOYERR_UNPLUGGED	Joystick is unplugged.

joyGetThreshold *Mmsystem.Pas*

Syntax

```
joyGetThreshold(
uJoyID: UINT;                {joystick identifier}
lpuThreshold: PUINT          {points to joystick threshold value}
): MMRESULT;                 {returns an error code}
```

Description

The joyGetThreshold function retrieves the joystick movement threshold. The threshold is the distance that the joystick must be moved before the driver sends a WM_JOYMOVE message.

Parameters

uJoyID: The joystick identifier of the joystick whose threshold is to be retrieved. This parameter can be set to JOYSTICKID1 or JOYSTICKID2.

lpuThreshold: A pointer to an integer receiving the joystick threshold value.

Return Value

The function will return a success or failure result code as shown in Table 11-16.

See also

joySetThreshold

Example

Please see Listing 11-5 under joySetCapture.

Table 11-16: joyGetThreshold Return Values

Value	Description
JOYERR_NOERROR	The function succeeded.
MMSYSERR_NODRIVER	Joystick driver is not present.
MMSYSERR_INVALPARAM	Invalid parameter is passed.

joyReleaseCapture   Mmsystem.Pas

Syntax

```
joyReleaseCapture (
uJoyID: UINT                    {joystick identificr}
): MMRESULT;                    {returns an error code}
```

Description

The joyReleaseCapture function releases the captured joystick.

Parameters

uJoyID: The joystick identifier of the joystick to be released. This parameter can be set to JOYSTICKID1 or JOYSTICKID2.

Return Value

The function will return a success or failure result code as shown in Table 11-17.

See also

joySetCapture

Example

Please see Listing 11-5 under joySetCapture.

Table 11-17: joyReleaseCapture Return Values

Value	Description
JOYERR_NOERROR	The function succeeded.
MMSYSERR_NODRIVER	The joystick driver was not found.
JOYERR_PARMS	The specified joystick uJoyID is invalid.

joySetCapture   Mmsystem.Pas

Syntax

```
joySetCapture(
Handle: HWND;                   {identifies the window to be captured}
uJoyID: UINT;                   {joystick identifier}
uPeriod: UINT;                  {polling frequency}
bChanged: BOOL                  {change flag for message frequency}
): MMRESULT;                    {returns an error code}
```

Description

The joySetCapture function captures the messages generated by the joystick driver. Joystick messages will be sent to the window specified by the Handle parameter. The function fails if the joystick is already captured. joyReleaseCapture may be used to release the capture before calling joySetCapture. The joystick is automatically released if the capture window is destroyed.

Parameters

Handle: Identifies the window which receives the joystick messages.

uJoyID: The joystick identifier of the joystick to be captured. This parameter can be set to JOYSTICKID1 or JOYSTICKID2.

uPeriod: The polling frequency in milliseconds.

bChanged: Indicates when messages are to be sent to the capture window. If this parameter is set to TRUE, messages are to be sent to the capture window only when the unreported motion exceeds the threshold value. If this parameter is set to FALSE, the messages are to be sent to the capture window when the polling interval has passed.

Return Value

The function will return a success or failure result code as shown in Table 11-18.

See also

joyReleaseCapture

Example

Listing 11-5: Joystick Motion in Delphi

```
var
  Form1: TForm1;
  Threshold: Integer;         // holds the joystick threshold value

implementation

procedure TForm1.WndProc(var Msg: TMessage);
var
   Cpoint: TPoint;           // holds the joystick position coordinates
begin
  {if the joystick has moved...}
  if Msg.Msg = MM_JOY1MOVE then
  begin
    {retrieve the coordinates relative to the panel}
    Cpoint.X := Msg.LParamLo;
    Cpoint.Y := Msg.LParamHI;
    JoyToClient(Cpoint);

    {modify the Smiley picture based on the position of the joystick}
    if ((Cpoint.x >= 50) and (Cpoint.x <= 55)) and
       ((Cpoint.y >= 40) and (Cpoint.y <= 45)) then
      Image2.Picture.Bitmap.Canvas.CopyRect(Rect(0,0,105,85),
        Image4.Picture.Bitmap.Canvas, Rect(0,0,105,85))
    else
      Image2.Picture.Bitmap.Canvas.CopyRect(Rect(0,0,105,85),
```

```
        Image3.Picture.Bitmap.Canvas, Rect(0,0,105,85));

    {draw the crosshair}
    Image2.Picture.Bitmap.Canvas.Pen.Color := clRed;
    Image2.Picture.Bitmap.Canvas.Pen.Width := 2;
    Image2.Picture.Bitmap.Canvas.MoveTo(Cpoint.X - 8 ,Cpoint.Y);
    Image2.Picture.Bitmap.Canvas.LineTo(Cpoint.X + 8 ,Cpoint.Y);
    Image2.Picture.Bitmap.Canvas.MoveTo(Cpoint.X ,Cpoint.Y - 8);
    Image2.Picture.Bitmap.Canvas.LineTo(Cpoint.X ,Cpoint.Y + 8);
    Image2.Picture.Bitmap.Canvas.Ellipse(Cpoint.X - 4 ,Cpoint.Y -4,
      Cpoint.X + 4 ,Cpoint.Y +4);
  end;

  {if a joystick button was pressed...}
  if Msg.Msg = MM_JOY1BUTTONDOWN then
  begin
    {color in a shape depending on which button was pressed}
    if Boolean(Msg.WParam and JOY_BUTTON1) then
      Shape1.Brush.Color := clRed;
    if Boolean(Msg.WParam and JOY_BUTTON2) then
      Shape2.Brush.Color := clRed;
  end;

  {if a joystick button was released...}
  if Msg.Msg = MM_JOY1BUTTONUP then
  begin
    {refill the shape with its original color}
    if not Boolean(Msg.WParam and JOY_BUTTON1) then
      Shape1.Brush.Color := clMaroon;
    if not Boolean(Msg.WParam and JOY_BUTTON2) then
      Shape2.Brush.Color := clMaroon;
  end;

  {send the messages on to the default message handler}
  inherited WndProc(Msg);
end;

procedure TForm1.joyInit;
var
  lpjoyInfoEx: TJOYINFOEX;    // holds extended joystick information
  lpjoyInfo: TJOYINFO;        // holds joystick information
  NumOfDevs: Integer;         // holds the number of joystick devices
  Dev1: Integer;              // holds joystick position return values
begin
  {get joystick threshold}
  joyGetThreshold(JOYSTICKID1, @Threshold);

  {get number of joystick}
  NumofDevs := joyGetNumDevs;

  {if there are no joystick devices present, indicate an error}
  if  NumOfDevs = 0  then
  begin
    MessageBox(Form1.Handle, 'Joystick driver not present', 'Error',
               MB_OK or MB_ICONWARNING);
```

```
    Exit;
  end;

  {determine if there is a joystick present}
  Dev1 := joyGetPosEx(JOYSTICKID1, @lpjoyInfoEx);
  if Dev1 = MMSYSERR_BADDEVICEID then
    MessageBox(Form1.Handle,'Joystick 1 is not present', 'Error ', MB_OK);

  {determine if the joystick is unplugged}
  Dev1 := joyGetPos(JOYSTICKID1, @lpjoyInfo);
  if Dev1 = JOYERR_UNPLUGGED then
    MessageBox(Form1.Handle,'Joystick is unplugged', 'Error ', MB_OK);

  {set the joystick threshold}
  joySetThreshold(JOYSTICKID1, 125);
end;

procedure TForm1.FormActivate(Sender: TObject);
begin
  {capture joystick messages}
  if (joySetCapture(Form1.Handle, JOYSTICKID1, 0, TRUE) <> JOYERR_NOERROR ) then
  begin
    {indicate that there was a problem capturing the joystick}
    MessageBox(Form1.Handle,'Joystick is not captured', 'Error',
               MB_OK or MB_ICONWARNING);
    Close;
  end;
end;

{convert joystick coordinates to client coordinates}
procedure TForm1.joyToClient(var pptJoyPos: TPoint);
var
  JCaps: TJoyCaps;     // holds joystick device capabilities
  CRect: TRect;        // holds window coordinates
begin
  {get joystick capabilities}
  if (JoyGetDevCaps(JOYSTICKID1, @JCaps, SizeOf(TJOYCaps))<>JOYERR_NOERROR) then
    Exit;

  {set the joystick position relative to the panel}
  Windows.GetClientRect(Panel1.Handle, CRect);
  pptJoyPos.X := TRUNC((Panel1.Width - 1) * (pptJoyPos.X - JCaps.wXmin) /
    (JCaps.wXmax - JCaps.wXmin));
  pptJoyPos.Y := TRUNC((Panel1.Height - 1) * (pptJoyPos.Y - JCaps.wYmin) /
    (JCaps.wYmax - JCaps.wYmin));
end;

procedure TForm1.FormCreate(Sender: TObject);
begin
  {initialize joystick}
  Application.ProcessMessages;
  JoyInit;
end;

procedure TForm1.FormDestroy(Sender: TObject);
```

```
begin
  {release joystick capture}
  JoyReleaseCapture(JOYSTICKID1);
end;

procedure TForm1.BitBtn1Click2(Sender: TObject);
begin
  Close;
end;
```

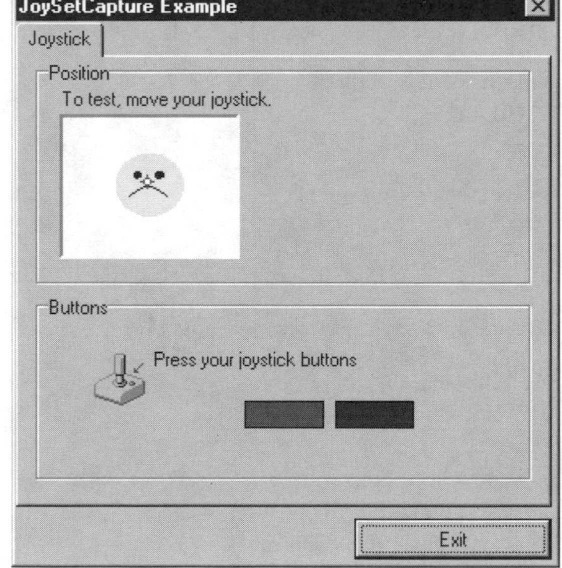

Figure 11-5: Smiley experiences Delphi's joystick capabilities.

Table 11-18: joySetCapture Return Values

Value	Description
JOYERR_NOERROR	The function succeeded.
JOYERR_NOCANDO	The capture cannot take place because of a system conflict, such as a timer not being available for polling.
JOYERR_UNPLUGGED	Joystick is unplugged.

joySetThreshold *Mmsystem.Pas*

Syntax

```
joySetThreshold (
uJoyID: UINT;                {joystick identifier}
uThreshold: UINT             {joystick threshold}
): MMRESULT;                 {returns an error code}
```

Description

The joySetThreshold function sets the movement threshold for the joystick. The joystick threshold is defined by the distance the joystick axis has to move before a WM_JOYMOVE message is generated.

Parameters

uJoyID: The joystick identifier of the joystick whose threshold is to be set. This parameter can be set to JOYSTICKID1 or JOYSTICKID2.

uThreshold: Specifies the new threshold movement value.

Return Value

The function will return a success or failure result code as shown in Table 11-19.

See also

joySetCapture

Example

Please see Listing 11-5 under joySetCapture.

Table 11-19: joySetThreshold Return Values

Value	Description
JOYERR_NOERROR	The function succeeded.
MMSYSERR_NODRIVER	Joystick driver is not present.
JOYERR_PARMS	Joystick identifier (uJoyID) is invalid.

LoadKeyboardLayout Windows.Pas

Syntax

```
LoadKeyboardLayout(
pwszKLID: PChar;          {keyboard layout identifier}
Flags: UINT               {layout options}
): HKL;                   {returns a keyboard layout handle}
```

Description

LoadKeyboardLayout loads the specified keyboard layout into the system. Several keyboard layouts may be loaded simultaneously, but only one will be active at a time.

Parameters

pwszKLID: A pointer to a null-terminated string containing the name of the keyboard layout. This null-terminated string is the hexadecimal value of the layout ID. See the example for how the primary language identifier and sublanguage identifier are combined for the language ID.

Flags: Specifies how the keyboard layout is to be loaded. This parameter can contain one value from Table 11-20.

Return Value

If the function succeeds, it returns the handle of the requested keyboard layout that was loaded. If the function failed, or if no matching keyboard layout was found, it returns zero. To get extended error information, call the GetLastError function.

See also

ActivateKeyboardLayout, GetKeyboardLayoutName, UnloadKeyboardLayout

Example

Listing 11-6: Loading a Keyboard Layout

```
var
  Form1: TForm1;
  List : array [0..MAX_HKL] of HKL;    // list of keyboard handles

implementation

{$R *.DFM}

procedure TForm1.Button1Click(Sender: TObject);
var
  MyLangID: WORD;  // holds a language identifier
begin
  {load the keyboard layout specified by language IDs}
  MyLangID:=MakeLangID(WORD(StrToInt(Edit1.Text)), WORD(StrToInt(Edit2.Text)));
  if LoadKeyBoardLayout(PChar('0000' + IntToHex(MyLangID,4)),KLF_ACTIVATE) = 0
  then ShowMessage('Error loading keyboard layout');
end;

procedure TForm1.Button2Click(Sender: TObject);
begin
  {activate the highlighted keyboard layout}
  if (ActivateKeyboardLayout(StrToInt(ListBox1.Items[Listbox1.Itemindex]),
      KLF_REORDER) = 0) then
    ShowMessage('Error activating the keyboard layout');

  {clear the keyboard layout list and repopulate it}
  ListBox1.Clear;
  FormCreate(Sender);
end;

procedure TForm1.FormCreate(Sender: TObject);
var
  pwszKLID: PChar;          // holds the name of a keyboard layout
  MyListIndex: Integer;     // specifies a list index
begin
  {get the keyboard layout lists}
  GetKeyboardLayoutList(MAX_HKL, List);
```

```
  {allocate a buffer for the keyboard layout name string}
  GetMem(pwszKLID, KL_NAMELENGTH);

  {retrieve the name string for active keyboard layout}
  GetKeyboardLayoutName(pwszKLID);
  ShowMessage('The active keyboard layout is '+pwszKLID);
  StatusBar1.SimpleText:= 'Active keyboard layout ' +  pwszKLID;

  {retrieve the code page identifier}
  StaticText1.Caption:=IntTostr(GetACP);

  {free the string memory}
  FreeMem(pwszKLID);

  {list all the keyboard layout in the list box}
  MyListIndex := 0;
  while (List[MyListIndex] <> 0) do
  begin
    ListBox1.Items.Add(IntToStr(List[MyListIndex]));
    Inc(MyListIndex);
  end;
end;

procedure TForm1.Button3Click(Sender: TObject);
begin
  {unload keyboard layout}
  if not UnloadKeyboardLayout(StrToInt(ListBox1.Items[Listbox1.ItemIndex])) then
    ShowMessage('Error Unloading Keyboard Layout');
end;

function MakeLangID(PrimLang, SubLang:WORD): WORD;
begin
  {make a language ID by combining the primary language ID and sublanguage ID}
  Result := (SubLang SHL 10) + PrimLang;
end;
```

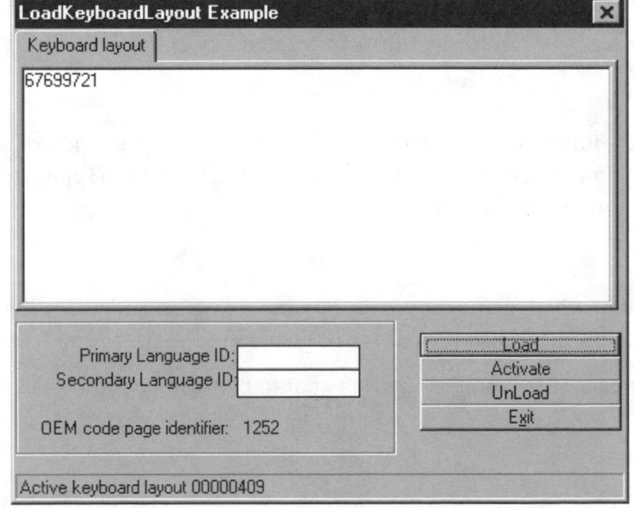

Figure 11-6: The keyboard layouts.

Table 11-20: LoadKeyboardLayout Flags Values

Value	Description
KLF_ACTIVATE	The function will load the layout if not already loaded and set it to the currently active layout. If it is already loaded and the KLF_REORDER flag is not specified, the function will rotate the keyboard layout list and set the next layout as the active layout.
KLF_NOTELLSHELL	Prevents a ShellProc hook from receiving an HSHELL_LANGUAGE message until the entire list of layouts is loaded.
KLF_REORDER	This will make the given layout the active layout by rotating the internal layout list when more than one keyboard layout is loaded.
KLF_REPLACELANG	Loads the new layout if it is the same language as the currently active keyboard layout. If this flag is not set and the requested layout has the same language as the active layout, the new keyboard layout is not loaded and the function returns zero.
KLF_SUBSTITUTE_OK	Specifies that the substitute layout is loaded from the system registry under the key HKEY_CURRENT_USER\Keyboard Layout\Substitutes. For example, if the key indicates the value name "00000409" with value "00010409," it loads the Dvorak U.S. English layout.

MapVirtualKey *Windows.Pas*

Syntax

```
MapVirtualKey(
uCode: UINT;                {key code, scan code, or virtual key}
uMapType: UINT              {flags for translation mode}
): UINT;                    {returns translated key code}
```

Description

The MapVirtualKey function converts a virtual key code to a scan code or character value, or it converts a scan code into a virtual key code. The uMapType parameter determines which conversion is performed.

Parameters

uCode: The key code which can be a virtual key code or scan code. How this value is interpreted depends on the translation mode flag specified in the uMapType parameter.

uMapType: Specifies a translation mode. This parameter can contain one value from Table 11-21.

Return Value

If the function succeeds, it returns a scan code, virtual key code, or character value depending on parameters. If the function fails, or there is no translation, it returns zero.

See also

GetAsyncKeyState, GetKeyboardState, GetKeyState, SetKeyboardState

Example

Listing 11-7: Using MapVirtualKey to Translate Keyboard Characters

```
var
  Form1: TForm1;
  Key_Value: Word;      // holds a virtual key code

implementation

{$R *.DFM}

procedure TForm1.FormKeyDown(Sender: TObject; var Key: Word;Shift: TShiftState);
begin
  {store the pressed virtual key value}
  Key_Value := Key;

  {display the OEM scan code}
  Panel1.Caption:=IntToStr(OemKeyScan(Key));

  {display the virtual key code for the lowercase form of the keystroke}
  Panel2.Caption:=IntToStr(MapVirtualKey(Key,2));

  {display the scan code of the pressed key}
  Panel3.Caption:=IntToStr(MapVirtualKey(VkKeyScan(Char(Key)),0));
end;

procedure TForm1.GetCapsKeyState(sender: TObject);
var
  KeyState: TKeyboardState;       // holds the keyboard state array
  Key_State: Word;                // holds the key pressed state
begin
  {retrieve the current state of the keyboard}
  GetKeyboardState(KeyState);

  {indicate if the caps lock key is on or off}
  if (KeyState[VK_CAPITAL] and $01) = $01 then
    StatusBar1.SimpleText := 'Caps LOCK / ON'
  else
    StatusBar1.SimpleText:= 'Caps LOCK / OFF';

  {indicate if a key is currently pressed}
  Key_State := GetAsyncKeyState(vkKeyScan(CHAR(Key_Value)));
  if Boolean(HiByte(Key_State)) then
    StaticText2.Caption := 'Key is pressed'
  else
```

```
    StaticText2.Caption := 'Key is not pressed';
end;

procedure TForm1.Timer2Timer(Sender: TObject);
var
  KeyState: TKeyboardState;      // holds the keyboard state array
begin
  {retrieve the current state of the keyboard}
  GetKeyboardState(KeyState);

  {toggle the CapsLOCK key}
  if (KeyState[VK_CAPITAL] and $01) = $01 then
    KeyState[VK_CAPITAL] := 0
  else
    KeyState[VK_CAPITAL] := $81;

  {set the new state of the keyboard}
  SetKeyboardState(KeyState);
end;
```

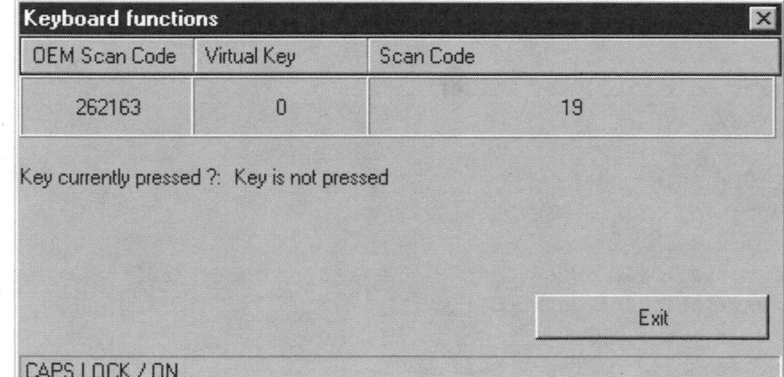

Figure 11-7: The translated keyboard characters.

Table 11-21: MapVirtualKey uMapType Values

Value	Description
0	uCode is a virtual key code to be translated to a scan code. The value returned does not differentiate between left and right Ctrl and Shift keys; it only returns values for the left-hand control keys.
1	uCode is a scan code to be translated to a virtual key code. The value returned does not differentiate between left and right Ctrl and Shift keys; it only returns values for the left-hand control keys.
2	uCode is a virtual key code to be translated to an unshifted character value.
3	uCode is a scan code to be translated to a virtual key code. The value returned does differentiate between left and right Ctrl and Shift keys.

MapVirtualKeyEx *Windows.Pas*

Syntax

```
MapVirtualKeyEx(
uCode: UINT;                  {key code, scan code, or virtual key}
uMapType: UINT;               {flags for translation mode}
dwhkl: HKL                    {keyboard layout handle}
): UINT;                      {returns a translated key code}
```

Description

MapVirtualKeyEx converts a virtual key code to a scan code or character value, or it converts scan code into a virtual key code. The uMapType parameter determines which conversion is performed.

The difference between the MapVirtualKeyEx and MapVirtualKey functions is that MapVirtualKeyEx translates the character using the language of the physical keyboard layout, as specified by the keyboard layout handle in the dwhkl parameter. MapVirtualKeyEx will not translate a virtual key code to a scan code and distinguish between left and right keys, such as VK_Shift, VK_CONTROL, or VK_MENU. An application can get the proper scan code which distinguishes between left and right keys by setting the uCode parameter to VK_LSHIFT, VK_RSHIFT, VK_LCONTROL, VK_RCONTROL, VK_LMENU, or VK_RMENU.

Parameters

uCode: The virtual key code or a scan code to be translated. How this value is interpreted depends on the translation mode flag in the uMapType parameter.

uMapType: Specifies the translation mode. This parameter can contain one value from Table 11-22.

dwhkl: Specifies the keyboard layout handle which is used to translate characters into their corresponding virtual key codes. The keyboard layout handle can be obtained by calling the GetKeyboardLayout or LoadKeyboardLayout functions.

Return Value

If the function succeeds, it returns a scan code, virtual key code, or character value depending on parameters. If the function fails or there is no translation, it returns zero.

See also

GetAsyncKeyState, GetKeyboardState, GetKeyState, SetKeyboardState, MapVirtualKey

Example

Please see Listing 11-11 under VkKeyScanEx.

Table 11-22: MapVirtualKeyEx uMapType Values

Value	Description
0	uCode is a virtual key code to be translated to a scan code. The value returned does not differentiate between left and right Ctrl and Shift keys; it only returns values for the left-hand control keys.
1	uCode is a scan code to be translated to a virtual key code. The value returned does not differentiate between left and right Ctrl and Shift keys; it only returns values for the left-hand control keys.
2	uCode is a virtual key code to be translated to an unshifted character value.
3	uCode is a scan code to be translated to a virtual key code. The value returned does differentiate between left and right Ctrl and Shift keys.

mouse_event *Windows.Pas*

Syntax

```
mouse_event(
dwFlags: DWORD;             {mouse activity codes}
dx: DWORD;                  {horizontal location or change}
dy: DWORD;                  {vertical location or change}
dwData: DWORD;              {wheel movement amount}
dwExtraInfo: DWORD          {application-defined data}
);                          {this procedure does not return a value}
```

Description

The mouse_event function simulates mouse activity. The system generates mouse messages as if the mouse was actually moved or a mouse button was actually pressed.

Parameters

dwFlags: Specifies which kind of mouse activity to simulate. This parameter can contain one or more values from Table 11-23.

dx: Specifies the horizontal location or change in location. If the dwFlags parameter contains the MOUSEEVENTF_ABSOLUTE flag, this parameter specifies a location. Otherwise, this parameter specifies the amount of mickeys (a measurement of mouse distance) to move.

dy: Specifies the vertical location or change in location. If the dwFlags parameter contains the MOUSEEVENTF_ABSOLUTE flag, this parameter specifies a location. Otherwise, this parameter specifies the amount of mickeys (a measurement of mouse distance) to move.

dwData: Specifies the amount of wheel movement if the dwFlags parameter contains the MOUSEEVENTF_WHEEL flag. A positive value indicates wheel movement away from the user; a negative value indicates wheel movement toward the user. This value is in terms of WHEEL_DELTA, approximately 120 mickeys. If the dwFlags parameter does not contain the MOUSEEVENTF_WHEEL flag, dwData should be set to zero.

dwExtraInfo: 32 bits of additional application-defined data. To retrieve this data, call the GetMessageExtraInfo function.

See also

GetMessageExtraInfo, SystemParametersInfo

Example

Listing 11-8: Using mouse_event to Control the Mouse Programmatically

```
var
  Form1: TForm1;
  MouseButtonIsDown: boolean;   // indicates if the mouse button is down

implementation

{$R *.DFM}

procedure TForm1.Image1MouseMove(Sender: TObject; Shift: TShiftState; X,
  Y: Integer);
begin
  {if the mouse button is down, draw a line}
  if MouseButtonIsDown then
    Image1.Canvas.LineTo(X,Y);
end;

procedure TForm1.Image1MouseDown(Sender: TObject; Button: TMouseButton;
  Shift: TShiftState; X, Y: Integer);
begin
  {if the mouse button is not down, move the initial drawing position}
  if not MouseButtonIsDown then
    Image1.Canvas.MoveTo(X,Y);

  {indicate that the mouse button is down so that drawing will occur}
  MouseButtonIsDown := TRUE;

  {if the right mouse button was clicked...}
  if Button = MBRight then
  begin
    {...while the mouse button is held down...}
    while MouseButtonIsDown = TRUE do
    begin
      {...simulate mouse movement by the specified amounts. The image
       continues to receive regular mouse messages as if the mouse was
       under user control}
      Mouse_Event(MOUSEEVENTF_MOVE,SpinEdit1.Value,SpinEdit2.Value,0,0);

      {update the screen and pause for a short amount of time}
      Application.ProcessMessages;
      Sleep(10);
```

```
    end;
  end;
end;

procedure TForm1.Image1MouseUp(Sender: TObject; Button: TMouseButton;
  Shift: TShiftState; X, Y: Integer);
begin
  {set the mouse button down variable to off}
  MouseButtonIsDown := FALSE;
end;

procedure TForm1.FormCreate(Sender: TObject);
begin
  {initialize the initial drawing position}
  Image1.Canvas.MoveTo(10,10);
end;

procedure TForm1.FormMouseMove(Sender: TObject; Shift: TShiftState; X,
  Y: Integer);
begin
  {initialize the mouse button down variable}
  MouseButtonIsDown := FALSE;
end;
```

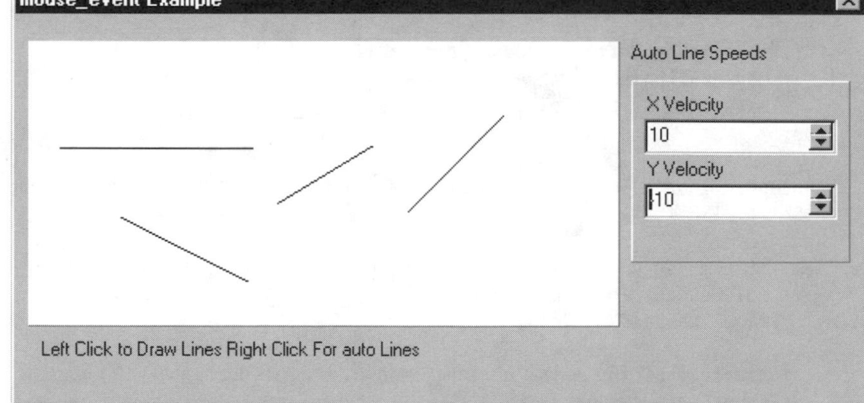

Figure 11-8: Drawing automatic lines with simulated mouse movement.

Table 11-23: mouse_event dwFlags Values

Value	Description
MOUSEEVENTF_ABSOLUTE	dx and dy contain normalized absolute coordinates. Otherwise, those parameters contain the change in position since the last reported position.
MOUSEEVENTF_MOVE	Movement occurred.
MOUSEEVENTF_LEFTDOWN	The left button changed to down.
MOUSEEVENTF_LEFTUP	The left button changed to up.

Value	Description
MOUSEEVENTF_RIGHTDOWN	The right button changed to down.
MOUSEEVENTF_RIGHTUP	The right button changed to up.
MOUSEEVENTF_MIDDLEDOWN	The middle button changed to down.
MOUSEEVENTF_MIDDLEUP	The middle button changed to up.
MOUSEEVENTF_WHEEL	Windows NT only: The wheel has been moved, if the mouse has a wheel. The amount of movement is provided in the dwData parameter.

OemKeyScan *Windows.Pas*

Syntax

```
OemKeyScan(
wOemChar: Word              {ASCII value of OEM character}
): DWORD;                   {returns scan code data}
```

Description

This function retrieves the OEM scan code for the OEM ASCII character value (between $00 and $FF) and state of the Shift, Ctrl, and Alt keys. OemKeyScan works only for characters that can be produced with a single keystroke.

Parameters

wOemChar: Specifies the OEM ASCII character value whose OEM scan code is to be retrieved.

Return Value

If the function succeeds, the low-order byte of the return value contains the OEM scan code, and the high-order byte contains the status of Shift, Ctrl, and Alt keys as shown in Table 11-24. If the function fails, it returns $FFFFFFFF.

See also

VkKeyScan, MapVirtualKey

Example

Please see Listing 11-7 under MapVirtualKey.

Table 11-24: OemKeyScan Return Values

Value	Description
1	The Shift key is pressed.
2	The Ctrl key is pressed.
4	The Alt key is pressed.

ReleaseCapture Windows.Pas

Syntax

```
ReleaseCapture: BOOL;            {returns TRUE or FALSE}
```

Description

The ReleaseCapture function releases mouse capture by a window. Normal flow of mouse messages to the underlying window is restored.

Return Value

If the function succeeds, it returns TRUE; otherwise it returns FALSE.

See also

GetCapture

Example

Please see Listing 11-10 under SwapMouseButton.

SetCapture Windows.Pas

Syntax

```
SetCapture(
hWnd: HWND                {handle of window capturing mouse messages}
): HWND;                  {returns the previous capture handle}
```

Description

The SetCapture function captures mouse input messages and sends them to the window specified by the hWnd parameter. If the mouse has been captured, all of the mouse input is directed to the capturing window, even when the cursor is outside the boundary of that window. When the window no longer requires the mouse input, it should call the ReleaseCapture function.

Parameters

hWnd: Specifies the handle of the window which is to capture the mouse input.

Return Value

If the function succeeds, it returns the handle of the window which previously had the mouse capture. If the function fails, or no window previously had the mouse capture, it returns zero.

See also

ReleaseCapture

Example

Please see Listing 11-10 under SwapMouseButton.

SetCaretBlinkTime Windows.Pas

Syntax

```
SetCaretBlinkTime(
uMSeconds: UINT                {caret blink time in milliseconds}
): BOOL;                       {returns TRUE or FALSE}
```

Description

SetCaretBlinkTime changes the cursor blink rate to the time specified in the uMSeconds parameter.

Parameters

uMSeconds: Specifies the new caret blink interval in milliseconds.

Return Value

If the function succeeds, it returns TRUE; otherwise it returns FALSE. To get extended error information, call the GetLastError function.

See also

GetCaretBlinkTime

Example

Listing 11-9: Modifying Caret Position and Blink Time

```
procedure TForm1.SpinEdit1Change(Sender: TObject);
begin
  {change the caret blink rate to the spinedit value.}
  SetCaretBlinkTime(SpinEdit1.Value);

  {set focus back to the memo to demonstrate the blink rate}
  Memo1.SetFocus;
end;

procedure TForm1.SpinEdit1MouseMove(Sender: TObject;
  Shift: TShiftState; X, Y: Integer);
begin
  {display the caret blink time in the spinedit box}
  SpinEdit1.Value := GetCaretBlinkTime;
end;

procedure TForm1.Button1Click(Sender: TObject);
var
  lpPoint: TPoint;      // holds the current caret position
begin
```

```
  {retrieve the caret position}
  GetCaretPos(lpPoint);

  {display the caret position}
  SpinEdit2.Value := lpPoint.X;
  SpinEdit3.Value := lpPoint.Y;

  {make sure the caret remains in the Memo box at the specified position}
  Memo1.SetFocus;
  SetCaretPos(lpPoint.X, lpPoint.Y);
end;

procedure TForm1.SpinEdit2Change(Sender: TObject);
begin
  {change the caret position in the memo}
  Memo1.SetFocus;
  SetCaretPos(SpinEdit2.Value, SpinEdit3.Value);
end;
```

Figure 11-9: The caret position and blink time.

SetCaretPos　　　Windows.Pas

Syntax

SetCaretPos(
X: Integer; {X coordinate for new caret position}
Y: Integer {Y coordinate for new caret position}
): BOOL; {returns TRUE or FALSE}

Description

The SetCaretPos function moves the caret to the coordinates specified by the X and Y parameters.

If the window's class style contains the CS_OWNDC style flag, the coordinates of the caret are mapped to the window's device context. This function will move the caret even if the cursor is hidden.

Parameters

X: Specifies the horizontal location of the new caret position.

Y: Specifies the vertical location of the new caret position.

Return Value

If the function succeeds, it returns TRUE; otherwise it returns FALSE. To get extended error information, call the GetLastError function.

See also

GetCaretPos

Example

Please see Listing 11-9 under SetCaretBlinkTime.

SetCursorPos Windows.Pas

Syntax

```
SetCursorPos(
X: Integer;                {X coordinate of the cursor}
Y: Integer                 {Y coordinate of the cursor}
): BOOL;                   {returns TRUE or FALSE}
```

Description

The SetCursorPos function relocates the mouse cursor to the location specified by the X and Y parameters in screen coordinates. If the cursor is confined to a rectangular region by calling the ClipCursor function, the system translates the coordinates to the appropriate coordinates within the rectangular region.

Parameters

X: Specifies the new x-coordinate for the cursor.

Y: Specifies the new y-coordinate for the cursor.

Return Value

If the function succeeds, it returns TRUE; otherwise it returns FALSE. To get extended error information, call the GetLastError function.

See also

ClipCursor, GetCursorPos, SetCaretPos

Example

Please see Listing 11-10 under SwapMouseButton.

SetDoubleClickTime Windows.Pas

Syntax

```
SetDoubleClickTime(
Interval: UINT                    {interval between clicks in milliscconds}
): BOOL;                          {returns TRUE or FALSE}
```

Description

The SetDoubleClickTime function changes the time interval between the first and second mouse click defining a double-click.

Parameters

Interval: Specifies the new time interval between clicks in milliseconds.

Return Value

If the function succeeds, it returns TRUE; otherwise it returns FALSE. To get extended error information, call the GetLastError function.

See also

GetDoubleClickTime

Example

Please see Listing 11-10 under SwapMouseButton.

SetKeyboardState Windows.Pas

Syntax

```
SetKeyboardState(
var KeyState: TKeyboardState          {array of the virtual key states}
): BOOL;                              {returns TRUE or FALSE}
```

Description

The SetKeyboardState function sets the status of all 256 virtual keys. The status of each virtual key is stored in an array of 256 bytes, identified by the KeyState parameter. Use the virtual key codes as an index into this array to specify individual virtual key states (i.e., KeyState[VK_Shift]).

Parameters

KeyState: Points to a TKeyboardState structure, which is an array of 256 bytes. Each index in the array should be set to a value indicating the state of individual virtual keys. If the high-order bit of an array value is 1, that key is pressed. If the low-order bit is 1, the key is toggled on, such as the Caps, Shift, or Alt keys. TKeyboardState is defined as follows:

TKeyboardState = array[0..255] of Byte; {virtual key code states}

Return Value

If the function succeeds, it returns TRUE; otherwise it returns FALSE. To get extended error information, call the GetLastError function.

See also

GetAsyncKeyState, GetKeyState, MapVirtualKey

Example

Please see Listing 11-7 under MapVirtualKey.

SwapMouseButton *Windows.Pas*

Syntax

SwapMouseButton(
fSwap: BOOL {reverse or restore mouse button's flag}
): BOOL; {returns TRUE or FALSE}

Description

The SwapMouseButton function exchanges or restores the mouse button messages generated by the mouse buttons. If the buttons are swapped, the left mouse button will generate right mouse button messages (i.e., WM_RBUTTONDOWN), and the right mouse button will generate left mouse button messages.

Parameters

fSwap: If this parameter is set to TRUE, the mouse buttons are interchanged left for right. If this parameter is set to FALSE, the mouse buttons are restored to their original configuration.

Return Value

If the function succeeds and the mouse buttons were reversed previously, it returns TRUE. If the function fails, or the mouse buttons were not reversed previously, it returns FALSE.

See also

SetDoubleClickTime

Example

Listing 11-10: Controlling Mouse Activity

```
var
  Form1: TForm1;
  SwapFlag: Boolean;        // tracks mouse button swapping
```

```
  glpRect: TRect;           // cursor coordinates

implementation

{$R *.DFM}

procedure TForm1.PanelClipRegionMouseMove(Sender: TObject; Shift: TShiftState; X,
  Y: Integer);
var
  lpWRect: TRect;       // holds window coordinates
  lpCPoint: TPoint;     // holds cursor coordinates
begin
  {retrieve the panel coordinates}
  GetWindowRect(PanelClipRegion.Handle, lpWRect);

  {retrieve the cursor position}
  GetCursorPos(lpCPoint);

  {display the cursor position in terms of the panel}
  Windows.ScreenToClient(PanelClipRegion.Handle,lpCPoint);
  EditXPos.Text:=IntToStr(lpCPoint.x);
  EditYPos.Text:=IntToStr(lpCPoint.y);

  {confine the cursor within the panel}
  ClipCursor(@lpWRect);
end;

procedure TForm1.ShapeMouseMouseDown(Sender: TObject; Button: TMouseButton;
  Shift: TShiftState; X, Y: Integer);
begin
  {fill in the appropriate rectangle for the mouse button pressed}
  if Button = mbLeft then
    Shape2.Brush.Color := clRed
  else
  if Button = mbRight then
    Shape3.Brush.Color := clRed;
end;

procedure TForm1.ShapeMouseMouseUp(Sender: TObject; Button: TMouseButton;
  Shift: TShiftState; X, Y: Integer);
begin
  {restore the rectangle's original color when the mouse button is released}
  Shape2.Brush.Color := clWhite;
  Shape3.Brush.Color := clWhite;
end;

procedure TForm1.ButtonSwapClick(Sender: TObject);
begin
  {toggle the mouse button swap flag}
  SwapFlag := not SwapFlag;

  {swap the mouse buttons}
  SwapMouseButton(SwapFlag);
end;
```

```
procedure TForm1.ButtonReleaseCursorClick(Sender: TObject);
var
  lpWRect: TPoint;         // holds mouse cursor coordinates
begin
  {set the mouse clipping region to the original region}
  ClipCursor(@glpRect);

  {move the mouse to the top left corner of the form}
  lpWRect.x:= Left;
  lpWRect.y:= Top;
  SetCursorPos(lpWRect.x,lpWRect.y);
end;

procedure TForm1.ButtonSetCursorPosClick(Sender: TObject);
begin
  {place the mouse cursor at the position indicated by the edit boxes.
   Note that this position will be relative to the screen}
  if not SetCursorPos(StrToInt(EditXPos.Text), StrToInt(EditYPos.Text)) then
    ShowMessage('Error setting cursor position');
end;

procedure TForm1.FormCreate(Sender: TObject);
begin
  {save the original cursor bounds}
  GetClipCursor(glpRect);

  {get the double click time}
  SpinEditClickTime.Value := GetDoubleClickTime;
end;

procedure TForm1.FormMouseDown(Sender: TObject; Button: TMouseButton;
  Shift: TShiftState; X, Y: Integer);
begin
  {indicate that the form received a mouse message (demonstrates mouse capture)}
  StatusBar1.SimpleText := 'The form received a mouse message';

  {bring the window to the top, if it lost focus}
  BringWindowToTop(Form1.Handle);
end;

procedure TForm1.ButtonMouseCaptureClick(Sender: TObject);
begin
  {make sure the mouse is not currently captured}
  ReleaseCapture;

  {capture the mouse and send all mouse messages to the form}
  if ((GetCapture = 0) and (SetCapture(Form1.Handle) <> 0))
    then ShowMessage('Error setting the mouse capture');
end;

procedure TForm1.BitBtnApplyClick(Sender: TObject);
begin
  {set the double-click interval}
  if not SetDoubleClickTime(SpinEditClickTime.Value) then
    ShowMessage('Error setting the double click time');
```

```
end;

procedure TForm1.ButtonReleaseCaptureClick(Sender: TObject);
begin
  {release the mouse capture}
  if not ReleaseCapture then
    ShowMessage('Error releasing mouse capture');
end;

procedure TForm1.BitBtnExitClick(Sender: TObject);
begin
   Close;
end;
```

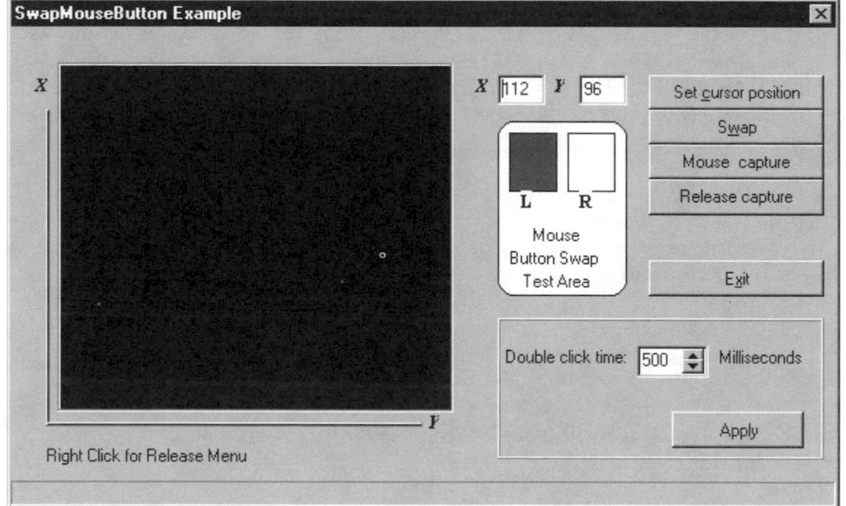

Figure 11-10: The mouse functions' testbed.

UnloadKeyboardLayout *Windows.Pas*

Syntax

UnloadKeyboardLayout(	
hkl: HKL	{keyboard layout handle}
): BOOL;	{returns TRUE or FALSE}

Description

UnloadKeyboardLayout removes the specified keyboard layout from the list of loaded keyboard layouts.

Parameters

hkl: Specifies the keyboard layout handle to unload.

Return Value

If the function succeeds, it returns TRUE; otherwise it returns FALSE. To get extended error information, call the GetLastError function.

See also

ActivateKeyboardLayout, GetKeyboardLayoutName, LoadKeyboardLayout

Example

Please see Listing 11-6 under LoadKeyboardLayout.

VkKeyScan Windows.Pas

Syntax

```
VkKeyScan(
ch: Char                    {ASCII character code}
): SHORT;                   {returns a translated code}
```

Description

The VkKeyScan function translates the specified character code to a virtual key code and returns the status of Shift, Ctrl, and Alt keys. Numeric keypad keys are not translated.

Parameters

ch: Specifies the character value of the key. This value is translated into a virtual key code.

Return Value

If the function succeeds, the low-order byte of the return value contains the virtual key code, and the high-order byte contains a code specifying the state of the Shift, Ctrl, and Alt keys. See Table 11-25 for the high-order byte codes. If the function fails, both the high- and low-order bytes contain –1.

See also

GetAsyncKeyState, GetKeyboardState, GetKeyNameText, MapVirtualKey, VkKeyScanEx

Example

Please see Listing 11-7 under MapVirtualKey.

Table 11-25: VkKeyScan Return Values

Value	Description
1	The Shift key is pressed.
2	The Ctrl key is pressed.
4	The Alt key is pressed.

VkKeyScanEx *Windows.Pas*

Syntax

```
VkKeyScanEx(
ch: Char;                {character value to translate}
dwhkl: HKL               {keyboard layout handle}
): SHORT;                {returns a translated code}
```

Description

The VkKeyScanEx function translates the specified character code to a virtual key code and returns the status of Shift, Ctrl, and Alt keys. Numeric keypad keys are not translated. The difference between the VkKeyScan and VkKeyScanEx functions is that the VkKeyScanEx function takes an extra parameter which specifies the keyboard layout handle. The translation will be performed in the context of that keyboard layout. The keyboard layout handle is obtained from the GetKeyboardLayout or LoadKeyboardLayout functions.

Parameters

ch: Specifies the character value of the key to be translated into a virtual key code.

dwhkl: Specifies the keyboard layout handle used to translate the character to its corresponding virtual key code.

Return Value

If the function succeeds, the low-order byte of the return value contains the virtual key code, and the high-order byte contains a code specifying the state of the Shift, Ctrl, and Alt keys. See Table 11-26 for these high-order byte codes. If the function fails, both the high- and low-order bytes contain –1.

See also

GetAsyncKeyState, GetKeyboardState, GetKeyNameText, MapVirtualKey, VkKeyScan

Example

Listing 11-11: Translating Scan Codes to ASCII Values

```
procedure TForm1.Button1Click(Sender: TObject);
```

```
var
  MyKeyboardHandle: HKL;    // holds a keyboard layout handle
  MyChar: Char;             // input character from user
  Mode: Integer;            // type of translation
  ScanString: string;       // result message
begin
  {initialize the displayed message}
  ScanString := 'Scan code is ';

  {if the edit box has text within it, retrieve the first character}
  if Boolean(Edit1.GetTextLen) then
      MyChar:= Edit1.Text[1];

  {if the character is an uppercase letter}
  if IsCharUpper(MyChar) then
  begin
    {retrieve the indicated translation mode}
    if RadioGroup1.ItemIndex = 0 then
      Mode := 0
    else
    begin
      Mode := 2;
      ScanString := 'ASCII character value is ';
    end;

    {retrieve the current keyboard layout}
    MyKeyboardHandle := GetKeyboardLayout(0);

    {display the translated character}
    StatusBar1.SimpleText := ScanString + IntToStr(MapVirtualKeyEx(
                             VKKeyScanEx(MyChar, MyKeyboardHandle), Mode,
                             MyKeyboardHandle));
  end;
end;

procedure TForm1.BitBtn1Click(Sender: TObject);
begin
   Close;
end;
```

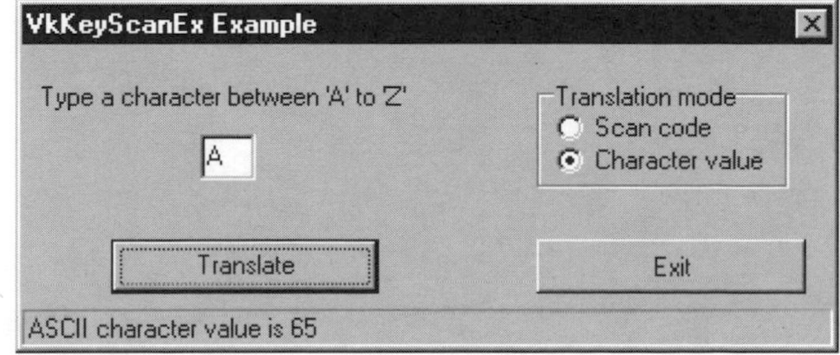

Figure 11-11: The translated character.

Table 11-26: VkKeyScanEx Return Values

Value	Description
1	The Shift key is pressed.
2	The Ctrl key is pressed.
4	The Alt key is pressed.

Chapter 12

File Input/Output Functions

File Creation

Windows handles file creation through the CreateFile function. This function can also open an existing file for modification or for simple data retrieval. When a file is opened or created, the system maintains a pointer into the file. This pointer changes location as data is read into or out of the file. An application can change this file pointer to different locations within the file by using the SetFilePointer function. This allows an application to randomly access information in a file if the file structure is known at runtime.

When a file is created or opened, a file handle is returned. This works similar to a window handle, as it identifies the file and allows other functions to manipulate the file. Any process that is started by the current process inherits all open file handles, if they were identified as inheritable. Although Windows will close any open files when the application terminates, information could be lost if an opened file is not explicitly closed by using the CloseHandle function.

Bear in mind that some of the file input/output functions covered in this chapter mention relative and qualified paths. A qualified path consists of the root drive followed by the directory name and each subdirectory name, including the filename (i.e., C:\Program Files\Borland\Delphi 3\Bin\Delphi32.exe). A relative path uses the relative path markers, such as "." and "..", to point to a directory using the current directory as the origin (i.e., ..\..\Database Desktop\Dbd32.exe).

File Times

Windows records file times in the Coordinated Universal Time (UTC) format. Coordinated Universal Time is defined as the current date and time in Greenwich, England. Specifically, the file times are stored as a TFileTime structure. The TFileTime structure is defined as:

```
TFileTime = record
    dwLowDateTime: DWORD;       {the low-order 32 bits of the file time}
    dwHighDateTime: DWORD;      {the high-order 32 bits of the file time}
end;
```

The TFileTime structure combines to make a 64-bit value that specifies the number of 100 nanosecond intervals that have elapsed since 12:00 a.m., January 1, 1601 (per Coordinated Universal Time).

The file time stored by the system when the file is written to disk is based on the system time, which is in UTC format. However, an application will usually want to display a file time in local time format. Typically, an application converts a file time to the user's local time zone by calling FileTimeToLocalFileTime, and passing the returned TFileTime structure to the FileTimeToSystemTime function. This function returns a data structure with the appropriate values for date and time in the local time zone. This is the method by which the Explorer displays file times in the local time zone format.

File Input/Output Functions

The following file input/output functions are covered in this chapter:

Table 12-1: File Input/Output Functions

Function	Description
CloseHandle	Closes an open handle.
CompareFileTime	Compares two TFileTime file times.
CopyFile	Copies a file to a new file.
CreateDirectory	Creates a new directory.
CreateDirectoryEx	Creates a directory with the attributes of a specified template directory.
CreateFile	Creates a new file or opens an existing one.
CreateFileMapping	Creates a file mapping object.
DeleteFile	Deletes a file.
DosDateTimeToFileTime	Converts a DOS-based date and time value into the system file time format.
FileTimeToDosDateTime	Converts a system file time value into the DOS date and time format.
FileTimeToLocalFileTime	Converts a UTC-based system file time value into a local file time value.
FileTimeToSystemTime	Converts a file time value into a TSystemTime data structure format.
FindClose	Closes a search handle.

Function	Description
FindCloseChangeNotification	Discontinues monitoring of a change notification handle.
FindFirstChangeNotification	Creates a change notification handle.
FindFirstFile	Searches a directory for a file or directory name.
FindNextChangeNotification	Restores a change notification handle for further monitoring.
FindNextFile	Continues a file search from a previous call to the FindFirstFile function.
FlushFileBuffers	Forces a file to be written to disk.
FlushViewOfFile	Forces a memory mapped file to be written to disk.
GetCurrentDirectory	Retrieves a path for the current directory.
GetFileAttributes	Retrieves attributes for the specified file.
GetFileInformationByHandle	Retrieves file information from an open file handle.
GetFileSize	Retrieves the specified file's size in bytes.
GetFileTime	Retrieves the specified file's creation, last access, and last write times.
GetFileType	Retrieves the specified file's type.
GetFileVersionInfo	Retrieves the specified file's version information resource.
GetFileVersionInfoSize	Retrieves the size of the specified file's version information resource.
GetFullPathName	Retrieves the full path and long filename of the specified file.
GetShortPathName	Retrieves short path (8.3 filename format) for the specified file.
GetTempFileName	Creates a temporary filename.
GetTempPath	Retrieves the environment defined path for temporary file storage.
LocalFileTimeToFileTime	Converts a local file time value to a system UTC-based file time.
LockFile	Locks a portion of a file.
MapViewOfFile	Maps the specified file into the address space of the calling process.
MoveFile	Moves a file from one directory to another.
OpenFileMapping	Opens an existing file mapping object.
ReadFile	Reads information from a file.
RemoveDirectory	Deletes the specified directory.
SearchPath	Searches for a filename on the environment defined path.
SetCurrentDirectory	Changes directories to the specified directory.
SetEndOfFile	Explicitly sets the end of the specified file.
SetFileAttributes	Sets file attributes.
SetFilePointer	Moves the file pointer within an open file.

Function	Description
SetFileTime	Sets the creation, last access, and last write times of the specified file.
SystemTimeToFileTime	Converts the system time information to the UTC-based system file time.
UnlockFile	Unlocks a previously locked file.
UnmapViewOfFile	Removes a mapped file from the calling process's address space.
VerQueryValue	Retrieves a value from the file's information resource.
WriteFile	Writes information to a file.

CloseHandle *Windows.Pas*

Syntax

```
CloseHandle (
hObject: THandle              {an object handle}
): BOOL;                      {returns TRUE or FALSE}
```

Description

The CloseHandle function closes an open device or object, and should be used to close handles for console input and output, event files, mapped files, mutexes, named pipes, processes, semaphores, threads, files created from a call to CreateFile, and tokens (Windows NT only). This function invalidates the specified handle and decrements the handle count of the object associated with the handle by one. Once the object's handle count reaches zero the object is removed from memory. Attempting to close an invalidated handle will raise an exception.

Parameters

hObject: Specifies an open handle.

Return Value

If the function succeeds, it returns TRUE; otherwise it returns FALSE. To get extended error information, call the GetLastError function.

See also

CreateFile, DeleteFile, FindClose, FindFirstFile

Example

Please see Listing 12-4 under CreateFile.

CompareFileTime Windows.Pas

Syntax

```
CompareFileTime(
const lpFileTime1: TFileTime;        {a pointer to a TFileTime record}
const lpFileTime2: TFileTime         {a pointer to a TFileTime record}
): Longint;                          {returns a file time equality indicator}
```

Description

This function compares lpFileTime1 to lpFileTime2 and returns the result indicating their difference. This function could be used with GetFileTime to determine if a file was written to when it was last accessed.

Parameters

lpFileTime1: A pointer to a TFileTime structure containing the 64-bit time of the first file to compare.

lpFileTime2: A pointer to a TFileTime structure containing the 64-bit time of the first file to compare.

Return Value

If the function succeeds, it returns a -1, indicating that the first file time is older than the second; a 0, indicating that the file times are equal; or a 1, indicating that the first file time is newer than the second. The function does not indicate an error upon failure.

See also

FileTimeToLocalFileTime, FileTimeToSystemTime, GetFileTime

Example

Listing 12-1: Comparing Two File Times

```
var
  Form1: TForm1;
  File1AccessTime: TFileTime;    // holds the file times to be compared
  File2AccessTime: TFileTime;

implementation

{converts the file time into the proper system time}
procedure TForm1.DisplayTime(TheTime: TFileTime; TheLabel: TLabel);
var
  SystemTime: TSystemTime;      // holds the system time information
  Intermediate: TFileTime;      // holds the local file time
  AMPM: string;                 // indicates morning or evening
begin
   {we must first convert the file time into the local file time,
    and then convert this into the system time to get the correct
    modification time}
```

```
    FileTimeToLocalFileTime(TheTime, Intermediate);
    FileTimeToSystemTime(Intermediate, SystemTime);

    {indicate morning or evening, and modify the time so we are
     not displaying military standard}
    if SystemTime.wHour>11 then AMPM := ' PM' else AMPM := ' AM';
    if SystemTime.wHour>12 then SystemTime.wHour := SystemTime.wHour-12;

    {display the time}
    TheLabel.Caption := IntToStr(SystemTime.wMonth)+'/'+
                        IntToStr(SystemTime.wDay)+
                        '/'+IntToStr(SystemTime.wYear)+'  '+
                        IntToStr(SystemTime.wHour)+':'+
                        IntToStr(SystemTime.wMinute)+':'+
                        IntToStr(SystemTime.wSecond)+AMPM;
end;

procedure TForm1.FileListBox1Click(Sender: TObject);
var
 Security: TSecurityAttributes;   // holds file security information
 hFile:THandle;                   // holds a handle to the file
begin
   {initialize the security attributes}
   Security.nLength:=SizeOf(TSecurityAttributes);
   Security.bInheritHandle:=FALSE;

   {open the file so we can retrieve a handle to it}
   hFile := CreateFile(PChar(TFileListBox(Sender).FileName), GENERIC_READ,
                       FILE_SHARE_READ, @Security, OPEN_EXISTING,
                       FILE_ATTRIBUTE_NORMAL, 0);
   if hFile = INVALID_HANDLE_VALUE then
   begin
     ShowMessage('Error Opening File');
     Exit;
   end;

   {retrieve the file time and display it}
   if Sender=FileListBox1 then
   begin
     GetFileTime(hFile, nil, nil, @File1AccessTime);
     DisplayTime(File1AccessTime, Label7);
   end
   else
   begin
     GetFileTime(hFile, nil, nil, @File2AccessTime);
     DisplayTime(File2AccessTime, Label2);
   end;
end;

procedure TForm1.Button1Click(Sender: TObject);
var
   lResult: Longint;  // holds the result of the time comparison
begin
   {compare the file times}
   lResult := CompareFileTime(File1AccessTime,FIle2AccessTime);
```

```
    {display the file comparison result}
    case lResult of
      -1: StatusBar1.SimpleText := 'First file is older than second file';
       0: StatusBar1.SimpleText := 'File times are equal';
       1: StatusBar1.SimpleText := 'First file is younger than second file';
    end;
end;
```

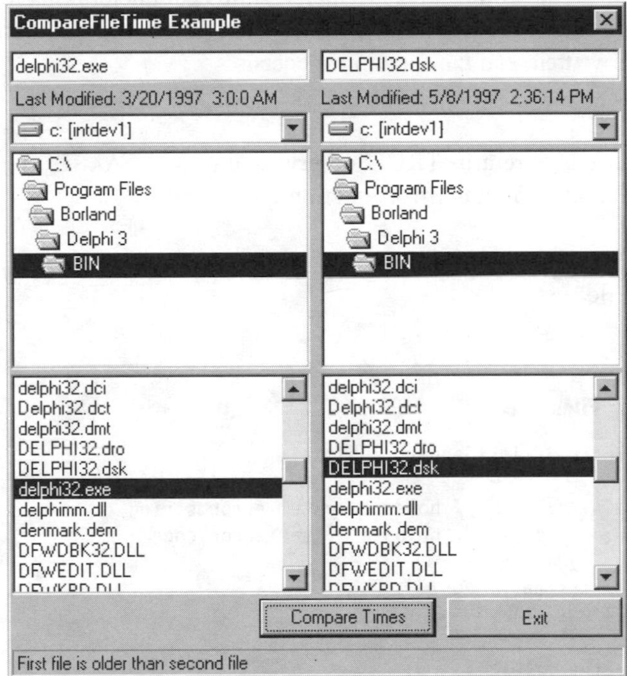

Figure 12-1: One file is older than the other.

CopyFile *Windows.Pas*

Syntax

CopyFile(	
lpExistingFileName: PChar;	{a pointer to an existing filename}
lpNewFileName: PChar;	{a pointer to a new filename}
bFailIfExists: BOOL	{existing file flags}
): BOOL;	{returns TRUE or FALSE}

Description

This function copies an existing file to a new file. The security attributes of a file are not copied, but the file attributes are (i.e., if the existing file is read only, the new file will also be read only).

Parameters

lpExistingFileName: A null-terminated string containing a pointer to the name of the file to be copied.

lpNewFileName: A null-terminated string containing a pointer to the name of the new file.

bFailIfExists: Determines how a file is copied if a file exists with the same name as that pointed to by the lpNewFileName parameter. If this parameter is set to TRUE and the new file already exists, the function will fail. If this parameter is set to FALSE, the existing file is overwritten, and the function succeeds.

Return Value

If the function succeeds, it returns TRUE; otherwise it returns FALSE. To get extended error information, call the GetLastError function.

See also

CreateFile, MoveFile

Example

Listing 12-2: Copying Files

```
procedure TForm1.Button1Click(Sender: TObject);
var
  ErrorMessage: Pointer;      // holds a system error string
  ErrorCode: DWORD;           // holds a system error code
begin
  {blank out the status bar}
  StatusBar1.SimpleText:='';

  {attempt to copy the file}
  if not CopyFile(PChar(Edit1.Text+'\'+ExtractFilename(FileListBox1.FileName)),
                  PChar(Edit2.Text+'\'+ExtractFilename(FileListBox1.FileName)),
                  not CheckBox1.Checked) then
  begin
    {if the file was not copied, display the error message}
    ErrorCode := GetLastError;
    FormatMessage(FORMAT_MESSAGE_ALLOCATE_BUFFER or FORMAT_MESSAGE_FROM_SYSTEM,
                  nil, ErrorCode, 0, @ErrorMessage, 0, nil);
    StatusBar1.SimpleText:='Error Copying File: '+string(PChar(ErrorMessage));
    LocalFree(hlocal(ErrorMessage));
  end;
end;
```

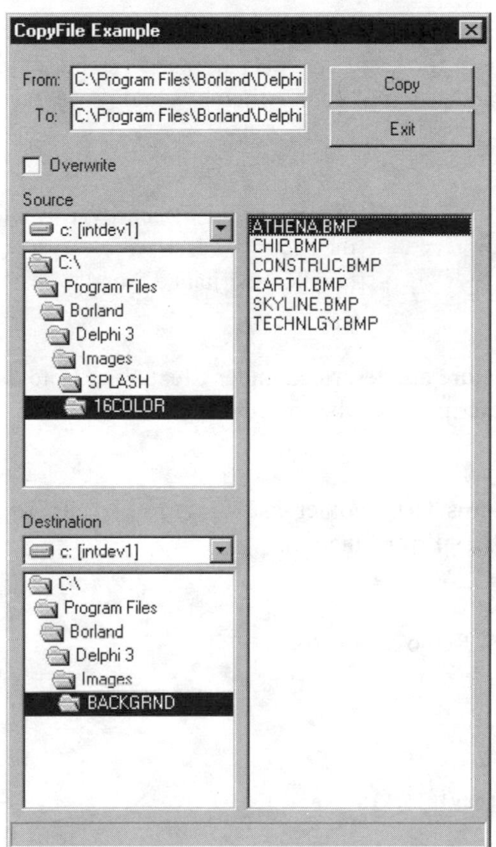

Figure 12-2: The file was copied.

CreateDirectory Windows.Pas

Syntax

```
CreateDirectory (
lpPathName: PChar;                              {the new directory path string}
lpSecurityAttributes: PSecurityAttributes       {pointer to directory security attributes}
): BOOL;                                        {returns TRUE or FALSE}
```

Description

This function creates a new directory as specified by the lpPathName parameter. Under Windows NT and other file systems that support individual file and directory compression, such as NTFS, a new directory inherits the compression attributes of its parent directory.

Parameters

lpPathName: A pointer to a null-terminated string containing the name of the new directory. This directory name must be less than MAX_PATH characters in size.

lpSecurityAttributes: A pointer to a TSecurityAttributes structure containing information about handle inheritance and file security. This parameter can be set to NIL, indicating that the directory handle cannot be inherited by child processes. The TSecurityAttributes data structure is defined as:

```
TSecurityAttributes = record
    nLength: DWORD;                    {the size of the TSecurityAttributes structure}
    lpSecurityDescriptor: Pointer;     {the security descriptor}
    bInheritHandle: BOOL;              {handle inheritance flags}
end;
```

The members of this data structure are described under CreateFile. Note that under Windows 95 the lpSecurityDescriptor member of this structure is ignored.

Return Value

If the function succeeds, it returns TRUE; otherwise it returns FALSE. To get extended error information, call the GetLastError function.

See also

CreateDirectoryEx, CreateFile, RemoveDirectory

Example

Listing 12-3: Creating a Directory

```
procedure TForm1.CreateDirectory1Click(Sender: TObject);
var
  ErrorMessage: Pointer;    // holds a system error message
  ErrorCode: DWORD;         // holds a system error code
begin
  {determine if a directory path has been specified}
  if DirName.GetTextLen = 0 then
  begin
    StatusBar1.SimpleText := 'Directory name not specified';
    Exit;
  end;

  {if so, then create the new directory under the current directory}
  if not CreateDirectory(PChar(DirectoryListBox1.Directory + '\' +
                         DirName.Text), nil) then
  begin
    {if there was an error creating the directory, display the error message}
    ErrorCode := GetLastError;
    FormatMessage(FORMAT_MESSAGE_ALLOCATE_BUFFER or FORMAT_MESSAGE_FROM_SYSTEM,
                  nil, ErrorCode, 0, @ErrorMessage, 0, nil);
    StatusBar1.SimpleText:='Error Copying File: '+string(PChar(ErrorMessage));
    LocalFree(hlocal(ErrorMessage));
  end;

  {update the directory listing to show the new directory}
  DirectoryListBox1.Update;
```

```
end;

procedure TForm1.CreateDirectoryFromTemplate1Click(Sender: TObject);
var
  ErrorMessage: Pointer;    // holds a system error message
  ErrorCode: DWORD;         // holds a system error code
begin
  {determine if a directory path has been specified}
  if DirName.GetTextLen = 0 then
  begin
    StatusBar1.SimpleText := 'Directory name not specified';
    Exit;
  end;

  {if so, then create the new directory under the current directory}
  if not CreateDirectoryEx(PChar(Template.Text),PChar(DirectoryListBox1.
                           Directory + '\' + DirName.Text), nil) then
  begin
    {if there was an error creating the directory, display the error message}
    ErrorCode := GetLastError;
    FormatMessage(FORMAT_MESSAGE_ALLOCATE_BUFFER or FORMAT_MESSAGE_FROM_SYSTEM,
                  nil, ErrorCode, 0, @ErrorMessage, 0, nil);
    StatusBar1.SimpleText:='Error Copying File: '+string(PChar(ErrorMessage));
    LocalFree(hlocal(ErrorMessage));
  end;

  {reset UI elements}
  Template.Text := '';
  CreateDirectoryFromTemplate1.Enabled := FALSE;
  CreateDirectory1.Enabled := TRUE;
  Template1.Enabled := TRUE;
  ClearTemplate1.Enabled := FALSE;

  {update the directory listing to show the new directory}
  DirectoryListBox1.Update;
end;
```

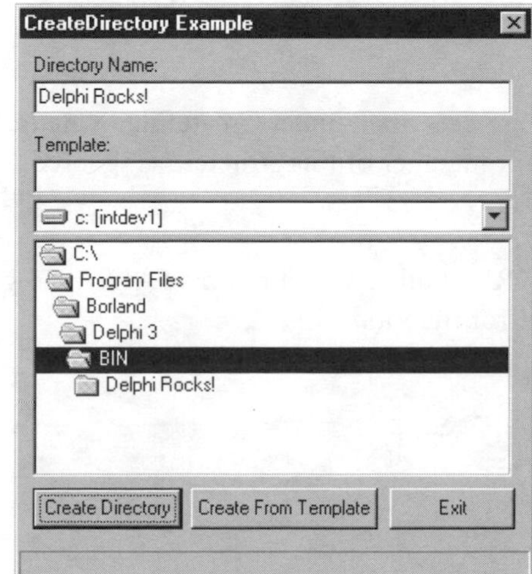

Figure 12-3: A new directory was created.

CreateDirectoryEx Windows.Pas

Syntax

```
CreateDirectoryEx (
lpTemplateDirectory: PChar;                 {the directory template string}
lpPathName: PChar;                          {the new directory path string}
lpSecurityAttributes: PSecurityAttributes   {pointer to directory security attributes}
): BOOL;                                    {returns TRUE or FALSE}
```

Description

This function creates a new directory as specified by the lpPathName parameter which receives the attributes of the template directory specified by the lpTemplateDirectory parameter. Under Windows NT and other file systems that support individual file and directory compression, such as NTFS, a new directory inherits the compression attributes of its parent directory.

Parameters

lpTemplateDirectory: A null-terminated string containing the name of an existing directory whose attributes are applied to the new directory being created.

lpPathName: A pointer to a null-terminated string containing the name of the new directory. This directory name must be less than MAX_PATH characters in size.

lpSecurityAttributes: A pointer to a TSecurityAttributes structure containing information about handle inheritance and file security. This parameter can be set to NIL, indicating that the directory handle cannot be inherited by child processes. The TSecurityAttributes data structure is defined as:

```
TSecurityAttributes = record
    nLength: DWORD;                   {the size of the TSecurityAttributes structure}
    lpSecurityDescriptor: Pointer;    {the security descriptor}
    bInheritHandle: BOOL;             {handle inheritance flags}
end;
```

The members of this data structure are described under CreateFile. Note that under Windows 95 the lpSecurityDescriptor member of this structure is ignored.

Return Value

If the function succeeds, it returns TRUE; otherwise it returns FALSE. To get extended error information, call the GetLastError function.

See also

CreateDirectory, CreateFile, RemoveDirectory

Example

Please see Listing 12-3 under CreateDirectory.

CreateFile Windows.Pas

Syntax

```
CreateFile(
lpFileName: PChar;                              {contains the filename to create or open}
dwDesiredAccess: Integer;                       {read/write access flags}
dwShareMode: Integer;                           {file sharing flags}
lpSecurityAttributes: PSecurityAttributes;      {a pointer to a TSecurityAttributes
                                                structure}
dwCreationDisposition: DWORD;                   {open or creation flags}
dwFlagsAndAttributes: DWORD;                    {file attribute and access flags}
hTemplateFile: THandle;                         {a handle to a template file}
): THandle;                                     {returns a handle to the opened file}
```

Description

This function opens or creates the file specified by the lpFileName parameter. Files can be opened for reading, writing, or both, and can be created with numerous file attributes and access options. If a file is being created, the function adds the FILE_ATTRIBUTE_ARCHIVE file attribute to those specified by the dwFlagsAndAttributes parameter, and the file length is initialized to zero bytes. When the application no longer needs the object, it should close the object's handle by calling the CloseHandle function.

Parameters

lpFileName: A pointer to a null-terminated string containing the name of the file to create or open. This string must not exceed MAX_PATH characters in length.

dwDesiredAccess: Specifies the type of access desired for the file. This parameter may contain one or more values from Table 12-2.

dwShareMode: Specifies how the file is to be shared between applications. If this parameter is set to zero, the file cannot be shared, and any subsequent open operations on the file will fail until the handle is closed. This parameter may contain one or more values from Table 12-3.

lpSecurityAttributes: A pointer to a TSecurityAttributes structure containing information about handle inheritance and file security. This parameter can be set to NIL, indicating that the handle cannot be inherited by child processes. The TSecurityAttributes data structure is defined as:

```
TSecurityAttributes = record
    nLength: DWORD;                     {the size of the TSecurityAttributes structure}
    lpSecurityDescriptor: Pointer;      {the security descriptor}
    bInheritHandle: BOOL;               {handle inheritance flags}
end;
```

nLength: Specifies the size of the TSecurityAttributes parameter, in bytes. This member should be set to SizeOf(TSecurityAttributes).

lpSecurityDescriptor: A pointer to a security descriptor for the object that controls the sharing of the file. If this member is set to NIL, the file is assigned the default security descriptor for the process. If CreateFile is opening a file, this parameter is ignored. Note that under Windows 95 this member is always ignored.

bInheritHandle: Indicates if the returned handle is inherited when a new process is created. A value of TRUE indicates that new processes inherit the returned file handle.

dwCreationDisposition: Specifies the function's behavior when a file does or does not exist. This parameter may contain one or more values from Table 12-4.

dwFlagsAndAttributes: Specifies the file attributes and access flags. This parameter may contain one or more values from Table 12-5. If CreateFile is opening a file, this parameter is ignored.

hTemplateFile: Specifies a handle to a file that was previously opened with the GENERIC_READ flag specified. The file being created gets its file attribute flags from the file specified by this parameter. Note that under Windows 95 this functionality is not supported and this parameter must be set to zero. If CreateFile is opening a file, this parameter is ignored.

Return Value

If the function succeeds, it returns a handle to the opened or created file. If the function fails, it returns INVALID_HANDLE_VALUE. To get extended error information, call the GetLastError function.

See also

CloseHandle, CreateDirectory, GetDiskFreeSpace, ReadFile, SetEndOfFile, SetFilePointer, VirtualAlloc, WriteFile

Example

Listing 12-4: Creating, Reading, and Writing to a New File

```
{the data structure for our information}
  Information = record
    Name: array[0..255] of char;
    Title: array[0..255] of char;
    Age: Integer;
  end;

var
  Form1: TForm1;

implementation

procedure TForm1.Button1Click(Sender: TObject);
```

```
var
  FileHandle: THandle;             // a handle to the opened file
  TheInfo: Information;            // holds our information
  NumBytesWritten: DWORD;          // variable to track bytes written
  Security: TSecurityAttributes;  // opened file security attributes
begin
  {copy the supplied information to the data structure}
  StrPCopy(TheInfo.Name, Edit1.Text);
  StrPCopy(TheInfo.Title, Edit2.Text);
  TheInfo.Age := StrToInt(Edit3.Text);

  {create a generic, binary file}
  Security.nLength := SizeOf(TSecurityAttributes);
  Security.bInheritHandle := FALSE;
  FileHandle := CreateFile('TempFile.nfo', GENERIC_WRITE, 0, @Security,
                           CREATE_ALWAYS, FILE_ATTRIBUTE_NORMAL or
                           FILE_FLAG_SEQUENTIAL_SCAN, 0);

  {write the data in the data structure directly to the file}
  WriteFile(FileHandle, TheInfo, SizeOf(Information), NumBytesWritten, nil);

  {implicitly set the end of the file.  This could be used to set
   the end of the file to somewhere in the middle}
  SetEndOfFile(FileHandle);

  {force any cached file buffers to write the file to disk}
  FlushFileBuffers(FileHandle);

  {close the file}
  CloseHandle(FileHandle);
end;

procedure TForm1.Button2Click(Sender: TObject);
var
  FileHandle: THandle;               // a handle to the opened file
  TheInfo: Information;              // holds our information
  NumBytesRead: DWORD;               // holds the number of bytes read
  Security: TSecurityAttributes;    // opened file security attributes
  TheTitle: array[0..255] of char; // holds a title string
begin
  {open the existing file for reading}
  Security.nLength := SizeOf(TSecurityAttributes);
  Security.bInheritHandle := FALSE;
  FileHandle := CreateFile('TempFile.nfo', GENERIC_READ, 0, @Security,
                           OPEN_EXISTING, FILE_ATTRIBUTE_NORMAL or
                           FILE_FLAG_SEQUENTIAL_SCAN, 0);
  {indicate an error if the file does not exist}
  if FileHandle=INVALID_HANDLE_VALUE then
  begin
    ShowMessage('No file exists yet.  Press the ''Write to file'' button to '+
                'create a file.');
    Exit;
  end;

  {lock the entire file so no other process may use it}
```

```
  LockFile(FileHandle, 0, 0, SizeOf(Information), 0);

  {read in a block of information and store it in our data structure}
  ReadFile(FileHandle, TheInfo, SizeOf(Information), NumBytesRead, nil);

  {display the information}
  Label7.Caption := TheInfo.Name;
  Label8.Caption := TheInfo.Title;
  Label9.Caption := IntToStr(TheInfo.Age);

  {the title is located 256 bytes into the file from the beginning (this is
   how long the Name string is), so reposition the file pointer for reading}
  SetFilePointer(FileHandle, SizeOf(TheInfo.Name), nil, FILE_BEGIN);

  {read one particular string from the file}
  ReadFile(FileHandle, TheTitle, SizeOf(TheTitle), NumBytesRead, nil);

  {display the string}
  Label11.Caption := TheTitle;

  {unlock and close the file}
  UnlockFile(FileHandle, 0, 0, SizeOf(Information), 0);
  CloseHandle(FileHandle);
end;
```

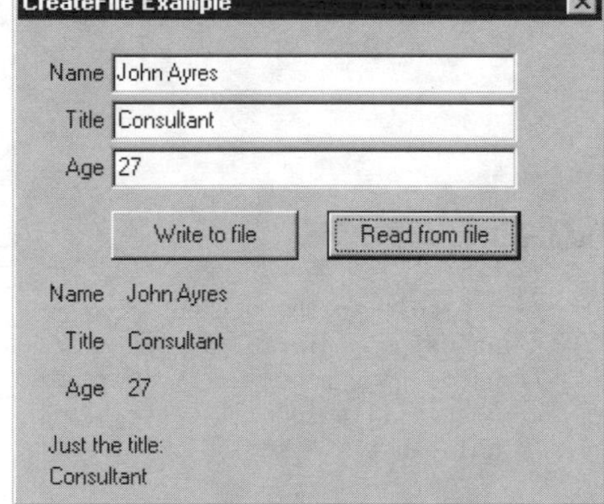

Figure 12-4: The file was created successfully.

Table 12-2: CreateFile dwDesiredAccess Values

Value	Description
0	Specifies query access to the file.
GENERIC_READ	Specifies read access to the file. Data can be retrieved from the file and the file pointer can be moved.
GENERIC_WRITE	Specifies write access to the file. Data can be written to the file and the file pointer can be moved.

Table 12-3: CreateFile dwShareMode Values

Value	Description
FILE_SHARE_DELETE	Windows NT only: Subsequent open operations on this file will succeed only if they specify the FILE_SHARE_DELETE flag.
FILE_SHARE_READ	Subsequent open operations on this file will succeed only if they specify the FILE_SHARE_READ flag.
FILE_SHARE_WRITE	Subsequent open operations on this file will succeed only if they specify the FILE_SHARE_WRITE flag.

Table 12-4: CreateFile dwCreationDisposition Values

Value	Description
CREATE_NEW	Creates a new file. The function will fail if the file already exists.
CREATE_ALWAYS	Always creates a new file, overwriting the file if it already exists.
OPEN_EXISTING	Opens an existing file. The function will fail if the file does not exist.
OPEN_ALWAYS	Always opens the file, creating one if it does not already exist.
TRUNCATE_EXISTING	Opens the specified file and truncates it to a size of zero bytes. The function fails if the file does not exist. The dwDesiredAccess parameter must contain the GENERIC_WRITE flag.

Table 12-5: CreateFile dwFlagsAndAttributes Values

Value	Description
FILE_ATTRIBUTE_ARCHIVE	Indicates an archive file or directory, and is used by applications to mark files and directories for removal or backup.
FILE_ATTRIBUTE_DIRECTORY	Indicates that the specified filename is a directory.
FILE_ATTRIBUTE_HIDDEN	Indicates that the specified file or directory is hidden, and will not appear in normal directory listings.
FILE_ATTRIBUTE_NORMAL	Indicates that the specified file or directory does not have any other file attributes set.
FILE_ATTRIBUTE_OFFLINE	Indicates that the specified file or directory is not immediately available, and that it has been physically moved to offline storage.
FILE_ATTRIBUTE_READONLY	Indicates that the specified file or directory is read only. Applications may read from the file or directory but may not write to it or delete it.
FILE_ATTRIBUTE_SYSTEM	Indicates that the specified file or directory is used by the system.

Value	Description
FILE_ATTRIBUTE_TEMPORARY	Indicates that the specified file or directory is temporary. The system will not automatically delete temporary files during shutdown.
FILE_FLAG_WRITE_THROUGH	Instructs the operating system to bypass any intermediate cache and write directly to disk.
FILE_FLAG_OVERLAPPED	Performs asynchronous reads and writes on the file. The ReadFile and WriteFile functions may return before the read or write operation has completed. The operating system will not maintain the file pointer when this flag is specified. Note that Windows 95 does not support asynchronous reads or writes to a disk-based file.
FILE_FLAG_NO_BUFFERING	The specified file is opened with no intermediate buffer or cache, which may provide performance increases in some situations. However, the application must conform to specific rules when opening files with this flag: 1 - File access must begin at the offsets that are a multiple of the volume's sector size. For example, if the sector size is 512, file access could begin at offset 0, 512, 1024, etc. 2 - Bytes can be read into a buffer only in increments equal to the volume's sector size. 3 – Buffer addresses for read and write operations must reside in memory at addresses that are a multiple of the volume's sector size. It is suggested that the developer use the VirtualAlloc function to allocate memory for the buffers, as VirtualAlloc automatically allocates memory at addresses that are a multiple of the volume's sector size. The application can retrieve the size of a volume's sector by calling the GetDiskFreeSpace function.
FILE_FLAG_RANDOM_ACCESS	Indicates that the file will be accessed randomly, allowing the system to optimize file caching for this method of access.
FILE_FLAG_SEQUENTIAL_SCAN	Indicates that the file will be accessed sequentially, allowing the system to optimize file caching for this method of access.
FILE_FLAG_DELETE_ON_CLOSE	Instructs the operating system to immediately delete the file after every open handle for the file is closed. Subsequent open requests for this file will fail unless the FILE_SHARE_DELETE flag is specified.
FILE_FLAG_BACKUP_SEMANTICS	Windows NT only: Indicates that the file is being opened or created for backup or restore purposes.

CreateFileMapping Windows.Pas

Syntax

```
CreateFileMapping(
hFile: THandle;                                {a handle to the file being mapped}
lpFileMappingAttributes: PSecurityAttributes;  {a pointer to a TSecurityAttributes
                                                structure}
flProtect: DWORD;                              {mapping object protection flags}
dwMaximumSizeHigh: DWORD;                      {high-order double word of maximum size}
dwMaximumSizeLow: DWORD;                       {low-order double word of maximum size}
lpName: PChar                                  {a pointer to the mapping object name}
): THandle;                                    {returns a handle to the file mapping object}
```

Description

This function creates a file mapping object based on the file identified by the hFile parameter. This file mapping object is a direct representation of the file in memory, and any changes to the file in memory affect the file on disk. If the specified size of the memory mapped file is larger than the file on disk, the disk-based file is increased to the specified size. However, if the size of the file on disk increases beyond the maximum size of the file mapping object, the file mapping object will not contain the extra information in the file. A memory mapped file can be shared between processes through the use of the OpenFileMapping function. Once a file mapping object is created, the application can obtain access to the file's contents by mapping a view of the file using the MapViewOfFile function. If two processes share the same mapped file object handle, they will see the same data. However, if two processes map the file individually (both of them call the CreateFileMapping function for the same file), changes made to the file by one process will not be seen by the other process. When the application has finished using the mapped file object, it should be closed by calling the UnmapViewOfFile function for every mapped view of the file and CloseHandle for the actual mapped file object handle.

Parameters

hFile: A handle to an open file from which the file mapping object is created. This file must be opened in an access mode compatible with the protection flags specified by the flProtect parameter. This parameter can be set to THandle($FFFFFFFF), which creates a file mapping object of the specified size in the Windows swap file instead of an actual disk-based file. In this case, the dwMaximumSizeHigh and dwMaximumSize-Low parameters must contain values.

lpFileMappingAttributes: A pointer to a TSecurityAttributes structure containing information about handle inheritance and file security. This parameter can be set to NIL, indicating that the handle cannot be inherited by child processes. The TSecurityAttributes data structure is defined as:

```
TSecurityAttributes = record
    nLength: DWORD;                    {the size of the TSecurityAttributes structure}
    lpSecurityDescriptor: Pointer;     {the security descriptor}
    bInheritHandle: BOOL;              {handle inheritance flags}
end;
```

Please see the CreateFile function for a description of this data structure.

flProtect: Specifies the access protection and attributes of the file mapping object. This parameter may be one value from Table 12-6, plus any combination of values from Table 12-7.

dwMaximumSizeHigh: Specifies the high-order double word of the maximum size for the file mapping object.

dwMaximumSizeLow: Specifies the low-order double word of the maximum size for the file mapping object. If this parameter and the dwMaximumSizeHigh parameter are set to zero, the file mapping object will be the same size as the file identified by the hFile parameter.

lpName: A pointer to a null-terminated string containing the name of the file mapping object. This string may contain any character except the backslash (\). If this parameter contains the name of an existing file mapping object, the function requests access to the existing object. This parameter may contain NIL to create an unnamed file mapping object.

Return Value

If the function succeeds, it returns a handle to the file mapping object, either a new one or an existing one if the lpName parameter points to the name of an existing file mapping object. In this case, GetLastError will return ERROR_ALREADY_EXISTS. If the function fails, it returns zero. To get extended error information, call the GetLastError function.

See also

CloseHandle, FlushViewOfFile, MapViewOfFile, OpenFileMapping, ReadFile, UnmapViewOfFile, VirtualAlloc, WriteFile

Example

Listing 12-5: Creating a Mapped File Object

```
var
  Form1: TForm1;
  Data: Pointer;              // holds a pointer to the memory mapped file
  hMapping: THandle;          // holds a handle to the memory mapped file object

implementation

function OpenMappedFile(FileName: string; var FileSize: DWORD): Boolean;
var
```

```
  hFile: THandle;       // a handle to the opened file
  HighSize: DWORD;      // the high order double word of the file size
begin
  {initialize the result of the function in case of errors}
  Result := FALSE;

  {if no filename was specified, exit}
  if Length(FileName)= 0 then Exit;

  {open the file for reading and writing. Indicate a
   sequential scan access for better optimization}
  hFile := CreateFile(PChar(FileName), GENERIC_READ or GENERIC_WRITE,
                      FILE_SHARE_READ, nil, OPEN_EXISTING,
                      FILE_FLAG_SEQUENTIAL_SCAN, 0);

  {if the file was not opened, exit;}
  if hFile = INVALID_HANDLE_VALUE then Exit;

  {retrieve the size of the file}
  FileSize := GetFileSize(hFile, @HighSize);

  {create a read/write mapping of the opened file}
  hMapping:=CreateFileMapping(hFile, nil, PAGE_READWRITE, 0, 0,
                              'Delphi File Mapping Example');

  {if the file mapping failed, exit}
  if (hMapping = 0) then
  begin
    CloseHandle(hFile);
    Exit;
  end;

  {close the file handle, as we no longer need it}
  CloseHandle(hFile);

  {map a view of the file}
  Data := MapViewOfFile(hMapping, FILE_MAP_WRITE, 0, 0, 0);

  {if a view of the file was not created, exit}
  if (Data=nil) then Exit;

  {to ensure that the file's data can be displayed directly as
   a string, set the very last byte in the file data to a null terminator}
  PChar(Data)[FileSize] := #0;

  {the file was successfully opened and mapped}
  Result := TRUE;
end;

function OpenPreviousMappedFile(var FileSize: Integer): Boolean;
begin
  {initialize the result of the function in case of errors}
  Result := FALSE;
```

```
  {open an existing file mapping}
  hMapping := OpenFileMapping(FILE_MAP_WRITE, FALSE,
                              'Delphi File Mapping Example');

  {if there was an error opening the existing file mapping, exit}
  if hMapping=0 then Exit;

  {map a view of the file}
  Data := MapViewOfFile(hMapping, FILE_MAP_WRITE, 0, 0, 0);

  {if a view of the file was not created, exit}
  if (Data=nil) then Exit;

  {retrieve the length of the data (which can be represented as a null-
   terminated string due to adding the null terminator to the end when
   the file was opened)}
  FileSize := StrLen(PChar(Data));

  {indicate that the file was successfully opened and mapped}
  Result := TRUE;
end;

procedure DisplayMappedFile(FileName: string; Size: Integer);
var
  Index: Integer;      // general loop counter
  DataPtr: PChar;      // a pointer to the mapped file data
  HexString: PChar;    // a pointer to a concatenated hexadecimal string
begin
  {display the name of the mapped file}
  Form1.StatusBar1.SimpleText := FileName;

  {allocate memory for the hexadecimal representation of the file,
   and initialize it to zeros}
  GetMem(HexString,Size * 3);
  ZeroMemory(HexString, Size*3);

  {set the pointer to the beginning of the mapped file data}
  DataPtr := Data;

  {begin looping through the data}
  Index:=0;
  while (Index < Size) do
  begin
    {display the value of each byte in the file as a hexadecimal number}
    StrCat(HexString, PChar(IntToHex(Byte(DataPtr[Index]),2)+ ' '));
    Inc(Index);
  end;

  {display the hexadecimal representation of the data and the ASCII
   representation of the data}
  SetWindowText(Form1.Memo1.Handle,HexString);
  SetWindowText(Form1.Memo2.Handle,PChar(Data));

  {free the memory for the hexadecimal string}
```

```
  FreeMem(HexString, Size * 3);
end;

procedure TForm1.Button1Click(Sender: TObject);
var
  Size: Integer;      // holds the size of the memory mapped file
begin
  {open an existing file...}
  if OpenDialog1.Execute then
  begin
    {...map the file...}
    OpenMappedFile(OpenDialog1.FileName, Size);

    {...and display the memory mapped file}
    DisplayMappedFile(OpenDialog1.FileName, Size);
  end;
end;

procedure TForm1.Button3Click(Sender: TObject);
var
  Size: Integer;      // holds the size of the memory mapped file
begin
  {open a previously mapped file...}
  if OpenPreviousMappedFile(Size) then
    {...and display it}
    DisplayMappedFile('Existing mapped file', Size);
end;

procedure TForm1.FormClose(Sender: TObject; var Action: TCloseAction);
begin
  {write any changes to the file}
  FlushViewOfFile(Data, 0);

  {unmap the view of the file}
  if not UnMapViewOfFile(Data) then ShowMessage('Cannot unmap file');

  {close the mapped file handle}
  if not CloseHandle(hMapping) then ShowMessage('Cannot Close File');
end;
```

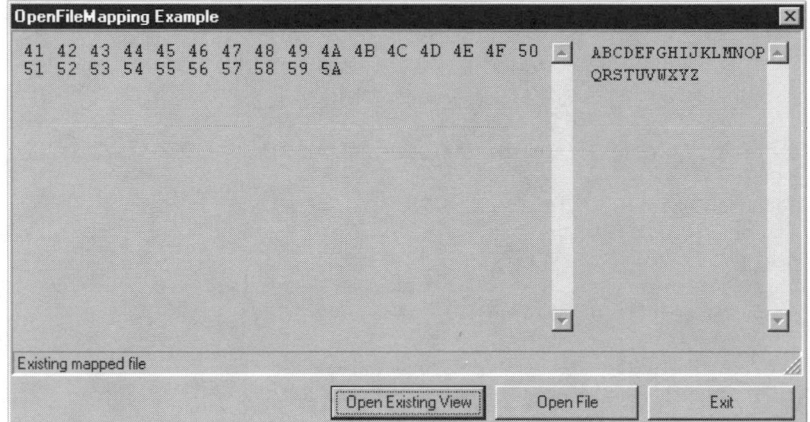

Figure 12-5: The mapped file.

Table 12-6: CreateFileMapping flProtect Protection Values

Value	Description
PAGE_READONLY	Specifies read-only access to the mapped file memory. Attempting to write to this area will cause an access violation. The file must be opened with the GENERIC_READ flag specified.
PAGE_READWRITE	Specifies read and write access to the mapped file memory. The file must be opened with the GENERIC_READ and GENERIC_WRITE flags specified.
PAGE_WRITECOPY	Specifies that any changes to the file will result in the memory mapped object containing a copy of the modified data, and the original file will remain unchanged. The file must be opened with the GENERIC_READ and GENERIC_WRITE flags specified.

Table 12-7: CreateFileMapping flProtect Section Attributes Values

Value	Description
SEC_COMMIT	Causes the function to allocate memory for the mapped file from physical storage or the paging file. This is the default behavior.
SEC_IMAGE	The specified file is an executable image. Mapping information and access protection are retrieved from the file. This flag cannot be combined with any other section attribute flags.
SEC_NOCACHE	The entire memory occupied by the memory mapped file object is not cached, and file changes are written directly to disk. This flag must be combined with either the SEC_COMMIT or SEC_RESERVE flags.

Value	Description
SEC_RESERVE	Causes the function to reserve memory for the mapped file without allocating physical storage. This reserved memory area cannot be accessed by other memory functions until it is released. The reserved memory area can be committed using the VirtualAlloc function. This flag is only valid when the hFile parameter is set to THandle($FFFFFFFF), indicating a memory mapped file residing in the Windows swap file.

DeleteFile Windows.Pas

Syntax

```
DeleteFile(
lpFileName: PAnsiChar            {the name of the file to delete}
): BOOL;                         {returns TRUE or FALSE}
```

Description

DeleteFile function deletes the file indicated by the lpFileName parameter. This function will fail if an application attempts to delete a nonexistent file. Under Windows NT, the function will fail if the application attempts to delete an opened file or a file that has been memory mapped. Under Windows 95, these operations will succeed.

Parameters

lpFileName: A null-terminated string containing the name of the file to delete.

Return Value

If the function succeeds, it returns TRUE; otherwise it returns FALSE. To get extended error information, call the GetLastError function.

See also

CloseHandle, CreateFile, RemoveDirectory

Example

Please see Listing 12-8 under FindFirstFile.

DosDateTimeToFileTime Windows.Pas

Syntax

```
DosDateTimeToFileTime(
wFatDate: WORD;                  {a 16-bit DOS date}
wFatTime: WORD;                  {a 16-bit DOS time}
var lpFileTime: TFileTime        {a pointer to a TFileTime structure}
```

): BOOL; {returns TRUE or FALSE}

Description

This function converts DOS 16-bit date and time values into a 64-bit TFileTime usable by the Windows 95/NT file system.

Parameters

wFatDate: Specifies the 16-bit DOS date value. This is a packed 16-bit value whose bits define the information as described in Table 12-8.

wFatTime: Specifies the 16-bit DOS time value. This is a packed 16-bit value whose bits define the information as described in Table 12-9.

lpFileTime: A pointer to a 64-bit TFileTime structure that receives the Windows 95/NT compatible date and time value based on the given DOS date and time values.

Return Value

If the function succeeds, it returns TRUE; otherwise it returns FALSE. To get extended error information, call the GetLastError function.

See also

FileTimeToDosDateTime, FileTimeToLocalFileTime, FileTimeToSystemTime, GetFileTime, LocalFileTimeToFileTime, SetFileTime, SystemTimeToFileTime

Example

Please see Listing 12-6 under FileTimeToSystemTime.

Table 12-8: DosDateTimeToFileTime wFatDate Values

Bit	Description
0-4	The day of the month (1-31).
5-8	The month number (1 = January).
9-15	The year offset from 1980 (add this value to 1980 to get the actual year).

Table 12-9: DosDateTimeToFileTime wFatTime Values

Bit	Description
0-4	The seconds, divided by two.
5-10	The minute (0-59).
11-15	The hour (0-23, military time).

FileTimeToDosDateTime Windows.Pas

Syntax

```
FileTimeToDosDateTime(
const lpFileTime: TFileTime;    {a pointer to a TFileTime structure}
var lpFatDate: WORD;            {pointer to a buffer receiving the 16-bit DOS date}
var lpFatTime: WORD             {pointer to a buffer receiving the 16-bit DOS time}
): BOOL;                        {returns TRUE or FALSE}
```

Description

This function converts a 64-bit Windows 95/NT date and time value into component DOS 16-bit date and time values. FileTimeToDosDateTime can only convert dates in the range of 1/1/1980 to 12/31/2107. The function will fail if the date pointed to by the lpFileTime parameter falls outside of this range.

Parameters

lpFileTime: A pointer to a 64-bit TFileTime structure containing the Windows 95/NT file time to convert.

lpFatDate: A variable receiving the 16-bit DOS date value. This is a packed 16-bit value whose bits define the information as described in Table 12-10.

lpFatTime: A variable receiving the 16-bit DOS time value. This is a packed 16-bit value whose bits define the information as described in Table 12-11.

Return Value

If the function succeeds, it returns TRUE; otherwise it returns FALSE. To get extended error information, call the GetLastError function.

See also

DosDateTimeToFileTime, FileTimeToLocalFileTime, FileTimeToSystemTime, GetFileTime, LocalFileTimeToFileTime, SetFileTime, SystemTimeToFileTime

Example

Please see Listing 12-6 under FileTimeToSystemTime.

Table 12-10: FileTimeToDosDateTime lpFatDate Values

Bit	Description
0-4	The day of the month (1-31).
5-8	The month number (1 = January).
9-15	The year offset from 1980 (add this value to 1980 to get the actual year).

Table 12-11: FileTimeToDosDateTime lpFatTime Values

Bit	Description
0-4	The seconds, divided by two.
5-10	The minute (0-59).
11-15	The hour (0-23, military time).

FileTimeToLocalFileTime *Windows.Pas*

Syntax

```
FileTimeToLocalFileTime(
const lpFileTime: TFileTime;          {a pointer to a TFileTime structure}
var lpLocalFileTime: TFileTime        {a pointer to a TFileTime structure}
): BOOL;                              {returns TRUE or FALSE}
```

Description

The FileTimeToLocalFileTime function converts the specified Coordinated Universal Time-based time pointed to by the lpFileTime parameter to the local file time.

Parameters

lpFileTime: A pointer to a TFileTime structure holding the 64-bit Coordinated Universal Time value to be converted.

lpLocalFileTime: A TFileTime variable that receives the converted local file time.

Return Value

If the function succeeds, it returns TRUE; otherwise it returns FALSE. To get extended error information, use the GetLastError function.

See also

DosDateTimeToFileTime, FileTimeToDosDateTime, FileTimeToSystemTime, GetFileTime, LocalFileTimeToFileTime, SetFileTime, SystemTimeToFileTime

Example

Please see Listing 12-6 under FileTimeToSystemTime.

FileTimeToSystemTime *Windows.Pas*

Syntax

```
FileTimeToSystemTime(
const lpFileTime: TFileTime;          {a pointer to a TFileTime structure}
var lpSystemTime: TSystemTime         {a pointer to a TSystemTime structure}
): BOOL;                              {returns TRUE or FALSE}
```

Description

This function converts the 64-bit file time pointed to by the lpFileTime parameter into a system time format, which is stored in the TSystemTime structure pointed to by the lpSystemTime parameter.

Parameters

lpFileTime: A pointer to a TFileTime structure holding the 64-bit file time value to convert.

lpSystemTime: A pointer to a TSystemTime structure that receives the converted file time. The TSystemTime data structure is defined as:

```
TSystemTime = record
      wYear: Word;               {the current year}
      wMonth: Word;              {the month number}
      wDayOfWeek: Word;          {the day of the week number}
      wDay: Word;                {the current day of the month}
      wHour: Word;               {the current hour}
      wMinute: Word;             {the current minute}
      wSecond: Word;             {the current second}
      wMilliseconds: Word;       {the current millisecond}
end;
```

wYear: Specifies the current calendar year.

wMonth: Specifies the month number, where 1 = January, 2 = February, etc.

wDayOfWeek: Specifies the day of the week, where 0 = Sunday, 1 = Monday, etc.

wDay: Specifies the day of the month in the range of 1 through 31.

wHour: Specifies the current hour in the range of 0 through 23 (military time).

wMinute: Specifies the current minute in the range of 0 through 59.

wSecond: Specifies the current second in the range of 0 through 59.

wMilliseconds: Specifies the current milliseconds in the range of 0 through 999.

Return Value

If the function succeeds, it returns TRUE; otherwise it returns FALSE. To get extended error information, use the GetLastError function.

See also

DosDateTimeToFileTime, FileTimeToDosDateTime, FileTimeToLocalFileTime, GetFileTime, LocalFileTimeToFileTime, SetFileTime, SystemTimeToFileTime

Example

Listing 12-6: Retrieving and Setting the File Time

```
{these record structures allow for easy manipulation of DOS
```

```
    date and time values}
  TDosTime=Record
    Hour      : Byte;
    Minutes   : Byte;
    seconds   : Byte;
  end;

  TDosDate = Record
    Year   : Word;
    Month  : Byte;
    Day    : Byte;
  end;

var
  Form1: TForm1;
  hFile: THandle;            // a handle to the opened file

implementation

{this function provides a convenient way to convert a
 DOS time into its component parts}
function ConvertDosTimeToSystemTime(FileDosTime: WORD): TDosTime;
var
  DosTime: TDosTime;
begin
  DosTime.Seconds := (FileDosTime and $1F) * 2;
  DosTime.Minutes := (FileDosTime and $7E0) shr 5;
  DosTime.Hour    := (FileDosTime and $F800) shr 11;
  Result          := DosTime;
end;

{this function provides a convenient way to convert a
 DOS date into its component parts}
function ConvertDosDateToSystemDate(FileDosDate: WORD): TDosDate;
var
  DosDate: TDosDate;
begin
  DosDate.Day   := FileDosDate and $1F;
  DosDate.Month := FileDosDate and $1E0 shr 5;
  DosDate.Year  := (FileDosDate and $FE00) shr 9 + 1980;
  Result        := DosDate;
end;

procedure TForm1.SpeedButton2Click(Sender: TObject);
var
  Security: TSecurityAttributes;        // attributes for the opened file
  FileName: PChar;                      // holds the filename
  WriteTime, LocalTime: TFILETIME;      // holds file times
  DosDate, DosTime: WORD;               // holds the DOS date and time
  infoDosTime: TDosTime;                // holds DOS time information
  infoDosDate: TDosDate;                // holds DOS date information
  SystemTime: TSystemTime;              // holds the last modification time
begin
  {set up the security attributes for the opened file}
  Security.nLength := SizeOf(TSecurityAttributes);
```

```
Security.lpSecurityDescriptor := nil;
Security.bInheritHandle := FALSE;

{display the open dialog box}
if OpenDialog1.Execute then
begin
  {display the selected filename...}
  FileName := PChar(OpenDialog1.FileName);
  StatusBar1.SimpleText := FileName;

  {...and open it}
  hFile := CreateFile(PChar(FileName),GENERIC_READ or GENERIC_WRITE,
                     FILE_SHARE_READ or FILE_SHARE_WRITE, @Security,
                     OPEN_ALWAYS, FILE_ATTRIBUTE_NORMAL, 0);

  {if there was an error, show a message}
  if hFile = INVALID_HANDLE_VALUE then
  begin
    ShowMessage('Error Opening File');
    Exit;
  end;
end;

{retrieve the last modification time}
GetFileTime(hFile, nil, nil, @WriteTime);

{convert the time to local file time}
FileTimeToLocalFileTime(WriteTime, LocalTime);

{finally, convert the time to the system time, so that it
 will match the file time displayed in the Explorer}
FileTimeToSystemTime(LocalTime, SystemTime);

{convert the file time into DOS date and time components...}
FileTimeToDosDateTime(LocalTime, DosDate, DosTime);

{...and convert it back}
if not DosDateTimeToFileTime(DosDate, DosTime, LocalTime) then
  ShowMessage ('An error occurred when converting DOS date and time back to'+
               ' file time.');

{break out the component parts of the DOS date and time for easy display}
infoDosTime := ConvertDosTimeToSystemTime(DosTime);
infoDosDate := ConvertDosDateToSystemDate(DosDate);

with infoDosTime do
  Edit1.Text := ComboBox1.Items[infoDosDate.Month - 1]+ ' ' +
                IntToStr(infoDosDate.Day) + ',' +
                IntToStr(infoDosDate.Year) + '  ' +
                IntToStr(Hour) + ':' +
                IntToStr(Minutes) + ':' +
                IntToStr(Seconds) ;

{indicate the time of day}
case SystemTime.WHour of
```

```
    12         : Label1.Caption := 'PM';
    13..24     : begin
                   Label1.Caption := 'PM';
                   SystemTime.wHour:=SystemTime.wHour - 12;
                 end;
    0          : SystemTime.wHour:= 12;
  else
    Label1.Caption := 'AM';
  end;

  {display the last modification time of the file}
  SpinEdit1.Value     := SystemTime.wYear;
  SpinEdit2.Value     := SystemTime.wHour;
  SpinEdit3.Value     := SystemTime.wMinute;
  SpinEdit4.Value     := SystemTime.wSecond;
  ComboBox1.ItemIndex := SystemTime.wMonth - 1;
  Calendar1.Month     := SystemTime.wMonth;
  Calendar1.Day       := SystemTime.wDay;
end;

procedure TForm1.SpeedButton3Click(Sender: TObject);
var
  FileTime, LocalFileTime: TFileTime;  // holds file times
  SystemTime: TSystemTime;             // holds system time information
begin
  {prepare the time information from the values set by the user}
  SystemTime.wHour   := SpinEdit2.Value;

  if (Label1.Caption = 'PM') and (SystemTime.wHour < 12)
  then
      SystemTime.wHour := SystemTime.wHour + 12;

  SystemTime.wMinute := SpinEdit3.Value;
  SystemTime.wSecond := SpinEdit4.Value;
  SystemTime.wYear   := SpinEdit1.Value;
  SystemTime.wMonth  := ComboBox1.ItemIndex + 1;
  SystemTime.wDay    := Calendar1.Day;

  {convert the system time to a local file time}
  SystemTimeToFileTime(SystemTime,LocalFileTime);

  {convert the local file time to a file time that the file system understands}
  LocalFileTimeToFileTime(LocalFileTime,FileTime);

  {use this time to set the last modification time which shows
   up in the Explorer}
  SetFileTime(hFile, nil, nil, @FileTime);
end;
```

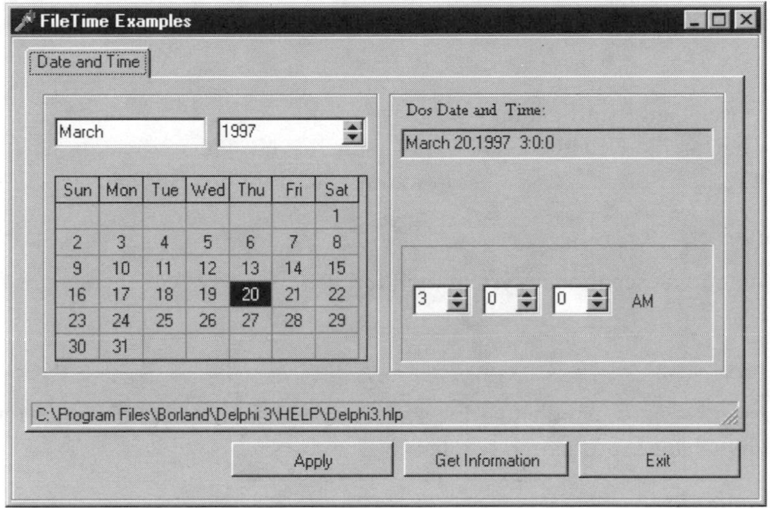

Figure 12-6: The selected file modification time.

FindClose   Windows.Pas

Syntax

```
FindClose(
hFindFile: THandle          {the search handle}
): BOOL;                    {returns TRUE or FALSE}
```

Description

This function closes a search handle as returned by the FindFirstFile and FindNextFile functions.

Parameters

hFindFile: The file search handle to close.

Return Value

If the function succeeds, it returns TRUE; otherwise it returns FALSE. To get extended error information, call the GetLastError function.

See also

FindFirstFile, FindNextFile

Example

Please see Listing 12-8 under FindFirstFile.

FindCloseChangeNotification Windows.Pas

Syntax

```
FindCloseChangeNotification (
hChangeHandlc: THandle          {a handle to a change notification object}
): BOOL;                        {returns TRUE or FALSE}
```

Description

This function discontinues system monitoring of a file system change notification handle.

Parameters

hChangeHandle: A handle to a file system change notification object as returned by the FindFirstChangeNotification function.

Return Value

If the function succeeds, it returns TRUE; otherwise it returns FALSE. To get extended error information, call the GetLastError function.

See also

FindFirstChangeNotification, FindNextChangeNotification

Example

Please see Listing 12-7 under FindFirstChangeNotification.

FindFirstChangeNotification Windows.Pas

Syntax

```
FindFirstChangeNotification(
lpPathName: PChar;              {a pointer to the name of the directory to monitor}
bWatchSubtree: BOOL;            {subtree monitor flag}
dwNotifyFilter: DWORD           {change condition flags}
): THandle;                     {returns a handle to a change notification object}
```

Description

This function creates a file system change notification object. It causes the system to monitor the specified directory or subdirectories for specific changes, such as file deletions or name changes. When the conditions specified by the dwNotifyFilter parameter have occurred, the system notifies the returned change notification object. The handle to this object is meant to be used with the WaitForSingleObject function, which causes the calling thread to be suspended until the indicated conditions have occurred. After the notification, the system can continue monitoring the specified directory by passing the returned handle to the FindNextChangeNotification function. When the notification object is no longer needed, it should be closed by calling the FindCloseChangeNotification function. Ideally, this function would be used in a multithreaded application with threads specifically dedicated to monitoring the change notification object.

Parameters

lpPathName: A pointer to a null-terminated string containing the name of the directory to monitor.

bWatchSubtree: Indicates if the system monitors just the specified directory. If this parameter is set to FALSE, only the specified directory is monitored; a value of TRUE indicates that both the directory and all of its subdirectories are monitored.

dwNotifyFilter: A series of bit flags indicating the conditions under which a change notification will be signaled. This parameter may contain one or more values from Table 12-12.

Return Value

If the function succeeds, it returns a handle to a file system change notification object; otherwise it returns INVALID_HANDLE_VALUE. To get extended error information, call the GetLastError function.

See also

FindCloseChangeNotification, FindNextChangeNotification

Example

Listing 12-7: Waiting for a Filename Change

```
var
  Form1: TForm1;
  NotificationHandle: THandle;    // holds the handle to the notification object

implementation

procedure TForm1.Button2Click(Sender: TObject);
begin
  {establish a notification for filename changes on the selected directory}
  NotificationHandle := FindFirstChangeNotification(PChar(DirectoryListBox1.
                                         Directory), FALSE,
                                         FILE_NOTIFY_CHANGE_FILE_NAME);

  {if the notification was set up correctly, modify some UI elements...}
  if (NotificationHandle <> INVALID_HANDLE_VALUE) then
  begin
    Button1.Enabled := TRUE;
    Button2.Enabled := FALSE;
  end
  else
  begin
    {...otherwise indicate that there was an error}
    ShowMessage('There was an error setting the notification');
```

```
    Exit;
  end;
end;

procedure TForm1.Button1Click(Sender: TObject);
var
  dwResult: DWORD;          // holds the result of waiting on the notification
  Waiting: Boolean;         // loop control variable
begin
  {set up the loop control for a continuous loop}
  Waiting := TRUE;

  {indicate that the application is waiting for the change notification to fire}
  Button1.Enabled := FALSE;
  StatusBar1.SimpleText := 'Now waiting for a filename change';
  Application.ProcessMessages;

  {enter the loop}
  while Waiting do
  begin
    {at this point, the application is suspended until the notification
     object is signaled that a filename change has occurred in the
     selected directory (this includes file deletions)}
    dwResult := WaitForSingleObject(NotificationHandle,INFINITE);
    if (dwResult = WAIT_OBJECT_0) then
    begin
      {indicate that the notification object was signaled}
      ShowMessage('The selected directory signaled a filename change');

      {query the user to see if they wish to continue monitoring this
       directory}
      if Application.MessageBox('Do you wish to continue monitoring this
                                directory?', 'Continue?', MB_ICONQUESTION or
                                MB_YESNO) = IDYES then
        {if the user wishes to continue monitoring the directory, reset
         the notification object and continue the loop...}
        FindNextChangeNotification(NotificationHandle)
      else
        {...otherwise break out of the loop}
        Waiting := FALSE;
    end;
  end;

  {close the notification object}
  FindCloseChangeNotification(NotificationHandle);

  {reset UI elements}
  Button1.Enabled := FALSE;
  Button2.Enabled := TRUE;
  StatusBar1.SimpleText := '';
  FileListBox1.Update;
end;
```

Table 12-12: FindFirstChangeNotification dwNotifyFilter Values

Value	Description
FILE_NOTIFY_CHANGE_ATTRIBUTES	The notification object is signaled when any file or directory attributes change.
FILE_NOTIFY_CHANGE_DIR_NAME	The notification object is signaled when any directory name changes, including deleting or creating a directory.
FILE_NOTIFY_CHANGE_FILE_NAME	The notification object is signaled when any filename change occurs, including renaming, deleting, or creating a file.
FILE_NOTIFY_CHANGE_LAST_WRITE	The notification object is signaled when the last write time of a file or directory is changed. This is detected only when the file is written to disk, and may not occur until the file cache is flushed.
FILE_NOTIFY_CHANGE_SECURITY	The notification object is signaled when the security descriptor of any file or directory changes.
FILE_NOTIFY_CHANGE_SIZE	The notification object is signaled when any file in the directory changes size. This is detected only when the file is written to disk, and may not occur until the file cache is flushed.

FindFirstFile *Windows.Pas*

Syntax

```
FindFirstFile(
lpFileName: PChar;                       {a pointer to a filename}
var lpFindFileData: TWin32FindData       {a pointer to a TWin32FindData structure}
): THandle;                              {returns a search handle}
```

Description

This function searches the current directory for the first file that matches the filename specified by the lpFileName parameter. This function will find both files and subdirectories, and the filename being searched for can contain wild cards.

Parameters

lpFileName: A pointer to a null-terminated string containing the path and filename for which to search. This filename may contain wild cards ("*" and "?").

lpFindFileData: A pointer to a TWin32FindData data structure containing information about the file or subdirectory that was found. The TWin32FindData data structure is defined as:

```
TWin32FindData = record
    dwFileAttributes: DWORD;                          {file attributes}
    ftCreationTime: TFileTime;                        {file creation time}
    ftLastAccessTime: TFileTime;                      {last file access time}
    ftLastWriteTime: TFileTime;                       {last file modification time}
    nFileSizeHigh: DWORD;                 {high-order double word of file size}
    nFileSizeLow: DWORD;                  {low-order double word of file size}
    dwReserved0: DWORD;                               {reserved for future use}
    dwReserved1: DWORD;                               {reserved for future use}
    cFileName: array[0..MAX_PATH - 1] of AnsiChar;    {long filename}
    cAlternateFileName: array[0..13] of AnsiChar;     {short filename}
end;
```

dwFileAttributes: Specifies the file attribute flags for the file. See the GetFileAttributes function for a list of possible file attribute flags.

ftCreationTime: Specifies the time that the file was created.

ftLastAccessTime: Specifies the time that the file was last accessed.

ftLastWriteTime: Specifies the time that the file was last modified.

nFileSizeHigh: Specifies the high-order double word of the file size.

nFileSizeLow: Specifies the low-order double word of the file size.

dwReserved0: This member is reserved for future use, and its value is undetermined.

dwReserved1: This member is reserved for future use, and its value is undetermined.

cFileName: A null-terminated string containing the long version of the filename.

cAlternateFileName: A null-terminated string containing the short (8.3) version of the filename.

Return Value

If the function succeeds, it returns a search handle that can be used in subsequent calls to FindNextFile. If the function fails, it returns INVALID_HANDLE_VALUE.

See also

FindClose, FindNextFile, SearchPath, SetCurrentDirectory

Example

Listing 12-8: Finding Files

```
var
  Form1: TForm1;
  ExistingFileName: PChar;    // used in renaming a file

implementation
```

```
procedure TForm1.Button1Click(Sender: TObject);
var
  strFileName: string;            // holds the name of the file to find
  FindFileData: TWin32FindData;   // holds file information
  SearchHandle: THandle;          // holds the search handle
begin
  {clear any listed files}
  ListView1.Items.Clear;

  {if there was no file specified, then specify all files}
  if Edit2.GetTextLen = 0 then Edit2.Text:= '*.*';

  {construct the filename string}
  strFileName:= DirectoryListBox2.Directory + '\' + Edit2.Text;

  {set the directory to the specified directory}
  SetCurrentDirectory(PChar(DirectoryListBox2.Directory));

  {begin the search}
  SearchHandle:=FindFirstFile(PChar(strFileName), FindFileData);

  {continue searching for all matching files in the current directory}
  if (SearchHandle <> INVALID_HANDLE_VALUE) then
  repeat
    ListView1.Items.Add.Caption:=FindFileData.cFileName;
  until (FindNextFile(SearchHandle,FindFileData) = FALSE);

  {all files have been found, so close the search handle}
  Windows.FindClose(SearchHandle);
end;

procedure TForm1.SpeedButton2Click(Sender: TObject);
var
  lpBuffer: PChar;       // receives a path and filename
  lpFilePart: PChar;     // points to the filename
begin
  {clear the listview}
  ListView1.Items.Clear;

  {allocate memory to hold a filename}
  GetMem(lpBuffer,MAX_PATH);

  {if a filename was specified, search for it}
  if Edit1.GetTextLen <> 0 then
  begin
    if (SearchPath(nil, PChar(Edit1.Text), nil, MAX_PATH, lpBuffer,
        lpFilePart) <> 0) then
        {if a file was found, add it to the listview}
        ListView1.Items.Add.Caption:=StrPas(lpBuffer)
    else
      MessageBox(0,'File was not found','Error ',MB_OK or MB_ICONWARNING);
  end;

  {free the filename buffer}
```

```
  FreeMem(lpBuffer);
end;

procedure TForm1.Delete1Click(Sender: TObject);
begin
  {verify file deletion}
  if (MessageBox (Form1.Handle, 'Are you sure you want to proceed?',
                  'Delete File or Folder', MB_OKCANCEL or
                  MB_ICONQUESTION) =ID_OK) then
  begin
    {delete the file...}
    if (DeleteFile(PChar(ListView1.Selected.Caption)) = FALSE) then
      {...or directory}
      if (RemoveDirectory(PChar(ListView1.Selected.Caption)) = FALSE) then
      begin
        {indicate an error}
        MessageBox(Form1.Handle, 'Error Deleting File or Folder',
                   'Delete File or Folder ',MB_ICONERROR or MB_OK);
        Exit;
      end;

    {delete the value from the list view}
    ListView1.Items.Delete(ListView1.Items.IndexOf(ListView1.Selected));
  end;
end;

procedure TForm1.ListView1Edited(Sender:TObject; Item:TListItem; var S:String);
var
  OldName,NewName: PChar;    // holds the old and new filenames
begin
  {allocate memory for the filename strings}
  GetMem(OldName,MAX_PATH);
  GetMem(NewName,MAX_PATH);

  {retrieve the existing filename}
  ExistingFileName := PChar(ListView1.Selected.Caption);

  {copy the new and old filenames, including path, to the string buffers}
  StrPCopy(NewName,DirectoryListBox2.Directory + '\' + S);
  StrPCopy(OldName,DirectoryListBox2.Directory + '\' + ExistingFileName);

  {rename the file}
  if not MoveFile(OldName,NewName) then
   ShowMessage('Error Renaming file');

  {free the string buffers}
  FreeMem(OldName);
  FreeMem(NewName);
end;
```

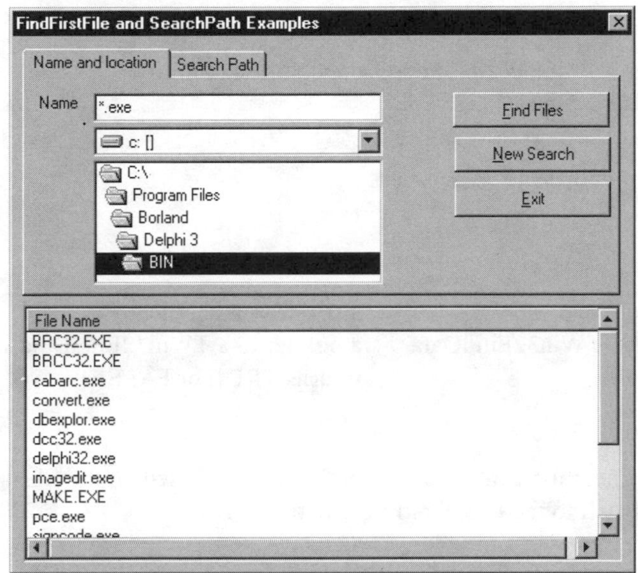

Figure 12-7: Some files were found.

FindNextChangeNotification Windows.Pas

Syntax

```
FindNextChangeNotification(
hChangeHandle: THandle          {a handle to a change notification object}
): BOOL;                        {returns TRUE or FALSE}
```

Description

This function instructs the system to monitor the specified file system change notification object for another change in its original notification conditions. The notification object is created by calling the FindFirstChangeNotification function. After the FindNextChangeNotification has reset the change notification object, it can be used with the WaitForSingleObject function to suspend the calling thread until the specified change conditions have occurred.

Parameters

hChangeHandle: A handle to a file system change notification object as returned by a call to the FindFirstChangeNotification function.

Return Value

If the function succeeds, it returns TRUE; otherwise it returns FALSE. To get extended information, call the GetLastError function.

See also

FindCloseChangeNotification, FindFirstChangeNotification

Example

Please see Listing 12-7 under FindFirstChangeNotification.

FindNextFile Windows.Pas

Syntax

```
FindNextFile(
hFindFile: THandle;                   {a file search handle}
var lpFindFileData: TWin32FindData    {a pointer to a TWin32FindData structure}
): BOOL;                              {returns TRUE or FALSE}
```

Description

The FindNextFile function continues to search for a file based on the filename specified by a previous call to the FindFirstFile function.

Parameters

hFindFile: A search handle as returned by a previous call to the FindFirstFile function.

lpFindFileData: A pointer to a TWin32FindData data structure containing information about the file or subdirectory that was found. The TWin32FindData data structure is defined as:

```
TWin32FindData = record
    dwFileAttributes: DWORD;                              {file attributes}
    ftCreationTime: TFileTime;                            {file creation time}
    ftLastAccessTime: TFileTime;                          {last file access time}
    ftLastWriteTime: TFileTime;                           {last file modification time}
    nFileSizeHigh: DWORD;                   {high-order double word of file size}
    nFileSizeLow: DWORD;                    {low-order double word of file size}
    dwReserved0: DWORD;                                   {reserved for future use}
    dwReserved1: DWORD;                                   {reserved for future use}
    cFileName: array[0..MAX_PATH - 1] of AnsiChar;        {long filename}
    cAlternateFileName: array[0..13] of AnsiChar;         {short filename}
end;
```

Please see the FindFirstFile function for a description of this data structure.

Return Value

If the function succeeds, it returns TRUE; otherwise it returns FALSE. To get extended error information, call the GetLastError function.

See also

FindClose, FindFirstFile, SearchPath

Example

Please see Listing 12-8 under FindFirstFile.

FlushFileBuffers Windows.Pas

Syntax

```
FlushFileBuffers(
hFile:THandle                  {a handle to an opened file}
): BOOL;                       {returns TRUE or FALSE}
```

Description

This function clears any file buffers for the file associated with the handle in the hFile parameter, causing any buffered data to be immediately written to disk.

Parameters

hFile: A handle to an open file that is to be written to disk. This file must have been opened with the GENERIC_WRITE flag specified.

Return Value

If the function succeeds, it returns TRUE; otherwise it returns FALSE. To get extended error information, call the GetLastError function.

See also

CreateFile, WriteFile, ReadFile

Example

Please see Listing 12-4 under CreateFile.

FlushViewOfFile Windows.Pas

Syntax

```
FlushViewOfFile(
const lpBaseAddress: Pointer;        {base address of mapped file data}
dwNumberOfBytesToFlush: DWORD        {the number of bytes to flush}
): BOOL;                             {returns TRUE or FALSE}
```

Description

This function forces the specified range of bytes within a memory mapped file to be immediately written to the disk-based representation of the file.

Parameters

lpBaseAddress: A pointer to the base address within the memory mapped file object data of the range of data to write to disk.

dwNumberOfBytesToFlush: Specifies the number of bytes to write to disk. If this parameter is set to zero, the entire memory mapped file object is written to disk.

Return Value

If the function succeeds, it returns TRUE; otherwise it returns FALSE. To get extended error information, call the GetLastError function.

See also

CreateFileMapping, MapViewOfFile, OpenFileMapping, UnmapViewOfFile

Example

Please see Listing 12-5 under CreateFileMapping.

GetCurrentDirectory Windows.Pas

Syntax

```
GetCurrentDirectory (
nBufferLength: DWORD;    {the size of lpBuffer in characters}
lpBuffer: PAnsiChar      {a pointer to a buffer receiving the directory name}
): DWORD;                {returns the number of characters copied to the buffer}
```

Description

This function returns the path of the current directory for the calling process. This directory is stored in the buffer pointed to by the lpBuffer parameter.

Parameters

nBufferLength: Specifies the size of the buffer pointed to by the lpBuffer parameter, in bytes, and must include the null terminator.

lpBuffer: A pointer to a buffer that receives the absolute path for the current directory of the calling process. If this parameter is set to NIL, the return value indicates the required size of the buffer to hold the directory path, including the null terminator.

Return Value

If the function succeeds, it returns the number of characters copied to the lpBuffer buffer, not including the null terminator. If the function fails, it returns zero. To get extended error information, call the GetLastError function.

See also

CreateDirectory, GetSystemDirectory, GetWindowsDirectory, RemoveDirectory, SetCurrentDirectory

Example

Please see Listing 12-11 under SetFileAttributes.

GetFileAttributes Windows.Pas

Syntax

```
GetFileAttributes(
lpFileName: PChar            {the filename whose attributes are retrieved}
): DWORD;                    {returns file attribute flags}
```

Description

This function returns the file attributes for the file or directory specified by the lpFileName parameter.

Parameters

lpFileName: A null-terminated string containing the name of the file or directory from which to retrieve file attributes. This string must not be longer than MAX_PATH characters.

Return Value

If the function succeeds, the return value contains one or more of the values from Table 12-13, indicating the current file attributes for the specified file or directory. If the function fails, it returns $FFFFFFFF. To get extended error information, call the GetLastError function.

See also

FindFirstFile, FindNextFile, SetFileAttributes

Example

Please see Listing 12-11 under SetFileAttributes.

Table 12-13: GetFileAttributes Return Values

Value	Description
FILE_ATTRIBUTE_ARCHIVE	Indicates an archive file or directory, and is used by applications to mark files and directories for removal or backup.
FILE_ATTRIBUTE_COMPRESSED	Indicates that the specified file or directory is compressed.

Value	Description
FILE_ATTRIBUTE_DIRECTORY	Indicates that the specified filename is a directory.
FILE_ATTRIBUTE_HIDDEN	Indicates that the specified file or directory is hidden, and will not appear in normal directory listings.
FILE_ATTRIBUTE_NORMAL	Indicates that the specified file or directory does not have any other file attributes set.
FILE_ATTRIBUTE_OFFLINE	Indicates that the specified file or directory is not immediately available, and that it has been physically moved to offline storage.
FILE_ATTRIBUTE_READONLY	Indicates that the specified file or directory is read only. Applications may read from the file or directory but may not write to it or delete it.
FILE_ATTRIBUTE_SYSTEM	Indicates that the specified file or directory is used by the system.
FILE_ATTRIBUTE_TEMPORARY	Indicates that the specified file or directory is temporary. The system will not automatically delete temporary files during shutdown.

GetFileInformationByHandle *Windows.Pas*

Syntax

```
GetFileInformationByHandle(
hFile: THandle;                                      {a handle to a file}
var lpFileInformation: TByHandleFileInformation      {a pointer to file information}
): BOOL;                                             {returns TRUE or FALSE}
```

Description

This function retrieves file information for the file associated with the handle identified by the hFile parameter. This handle cannot then be handle to a pipe. GetFileInformationByHandle is affected by the type of file system that the indicated file resides on, and may return partial information if certain information elements are not supported by the file system.

Parameters

hFile: The handle to the file for which information is retrieved.

lpFileInformation: A pointer to a TByHandleFileInformation data structure receiving information about the indicated file. The TByHandleFileInformation structure is defined as:

```
TByHandleFileInformation = record
      dwFileAttributes: DWORD;           {file attribute flags}
      ftCreationTime: TFileTime;         {file creation time}
      ftLastAccessTime: TFileTime;       {last file access time}
```

```
    ftLastWriteTime: TFileTime;         {last file modification time}
    dwVolumeSerialNumber: DWORD;        {volume serial number}
    nFileSizeHigh: DWORD;               {high-order order double word of file size}
    nFileSizeLow: DWORD;                {low-order order double word of file size}
    nNumberOfLinks: DWORD;              {number of links to the file}
    nFileIndexHigh: DWORD;              {high-order double word of unique identifier}
    nFileIndexLow: DWORD;               {low-order double word of unique identifier}
end;
```

dwFileAttributes: Specifies the file attribute flags for the file. See the GetFileAttributes function for a list of possible file attribute flags.

ftCreationTime: Specifies the time that the file was created

ftLastAccessTime: Specifies the time that the file was last accessed.

ftLastWriteTime: Specifies the time that the file was last modified.

dwVolumeSerialNumber: Specifies the serial number of the volume that contains the file.

nFileSizeHigh: Specifies the high-order double word of the file size.

nFileSizeLow: Specifies the low-order double word of the file size.

nNumberOfLinks: Specifies the number of links to the file. The FAT system always sets this member to one, but other file systems, such as NTFS, can set this member to a greater value.

nFileIndexHigh: Specifies the high-order double word of the file's unique identifier.

nFileIndexLow: Specifies the low-order double word of the file's unique identifier.

Return Value

If the function succeeds, it returns TRUE; otherwise it returns FALSE. To get extended error information, call the GetLastError function.

See also

CreateFile, GetFileAttributes, GetFileTime, GetFileSize

Example

Listing 12-9: Retrieving File Information from a Handle

```
procedure TForm1.FileListBox1Change(Sender: TObject);
var
  Security: TSecurityAttributes;         // security attributes for the file
  hFile: Integer;                        // holds the file handle
  FileInfo: TByHandleFileInformation;    // holds the file information
  Intermediate: TFileTime;               // holds a file time
  SystemTime: TSystemTime;               // holds the converted file time
  FileType: DWORD;                       // holds the file type
```

```
  AMPM: string;                          // morning/evening indicator
begin
  {clear the status bar}
  StatusBar1.SimpleText:= '';

  {initialize the security information}
  Security.nLength:=SizeOf(TSecurityAttributes);
  Security.bInheritHandle:=FALSE;

  {open the selected file for reading}
  hFile:=CreateFile(PChar(FileListBox1.FileName), GENERIC_READ, 0, @Security,
                  OPEN_EXISTING, FILE_ATTRIBUTE_NORMAL, 0);
  if (hFile <> INVALID_HANDLE_VALUE) then
  begin
    {retrieve the file information}
    GetFileInformationByHandle(hFile,FileInfo);

    {display the selected file's attributes}
    checkBox1.Checked := BOOLEAN(FileInfo.dwFileAttributes and
                                 FILE_ATTRIBUTE_ARCHIVE);
    CheckBox2.Checked := BOOLEAN(FileInfo.dwFileAttributes and
                                 FILE_ATTRIBUTE_DIRECTORY);
    CheckBox3.Checked := BOOLEAN(FileInfo.dwFileAttributes and
                                 FILE_ATTRIBUTE_HIDDEN);
    CheckBox4.Checked := BOOLEAN(FileInfo.dwFileAttributes and
                                 FILE_ATTRIBUTE_OFFLINE);
    CheckBox5.Checked := BOOLEAN(FileInfo.dwFileAttributes and
                                 FILE_ATTRIBUTE_READONLY);
    CheckBox6.Checked := BOOLEAN(FileInfo.dwFileAttributes and
                                 FILE_ATTRIBUTE_SYSTEM);
    CheckBox7.Checked := BOOLEAN(FileInfo.dwFileAttributes and
                                 FILE_ATTRIBUTE_NORMAL);
    CheckBox8.Checked := BOOLEAN(FileInfo.dwFileAttributes and
                                 FILE_ATTRIBUTE_TEMPORARY);

    {display the file name}
    Label1.Caption := ExtractFileName(FileListBox1.FileName);

   {we must first convert the file time into the local file time,
    and then convert this into the system time to get the correct
    modification time}
   FileTimeToLocalFileTime(FileInfo.ftLastWriteTime, Intermediate);
   FileTimeToSystemTime(Intermediate, SystemTime);

   {indicate morning or evening, and modify the time so we are
    not displaying military standard}
   if SystemTime.wHour>11 then AMPM := ' PM' else AMPM := ' AM';
   if SystemTime.wHour>12 then SystemTime.wHour := SystemTime.wHour-12;

   {display the time}
   Label2.Caption := IntToStr(SystemTime.wMonth)+'/'+
                     IntToStr(SystemTime.wDay)+'/'+
                     IntToStr(SystemTime.wYear)+'  '+
                     IntToStr(SystemTime.wHour)+':'+
                     IntToStr(SystemTime.wMinute)+':'+
```

```
                        IntToStr(SystemTime.wSecond)+AMPM;

    {display the volume serial number}
    Label8.Caption:=IntToStr(FileInfo.dwVolumeSerialNumber);

    {display the file size}
    Label4.Caption:=IntToStr(GetFileSize(hFile, nil))+ ' bytes';

    {display the file type}
    FileType:=GetFileType(hFile);
    case (FileType) of
      FILE_TYPE_UNKNOWN: Label6.Caption:='File is of unknown type';
      FILE_TYPE_DISK   : Label6.Caption:='File is disk based';
      FILE_TYPE_CHAR   : Label6.Caption:='File is a character file';
      FILE_TYPE_PIPE   : Label6.Caption:='File is a named or anonymous pipe';
    end;

    {we are through examining the file, so close the handle}
    CloseHandle(hFile);
  end
  else
    {if the file could not be opened, indicate that it is in use}
    StatusBar1.SimpleText:= 'File is in use';
end;
```

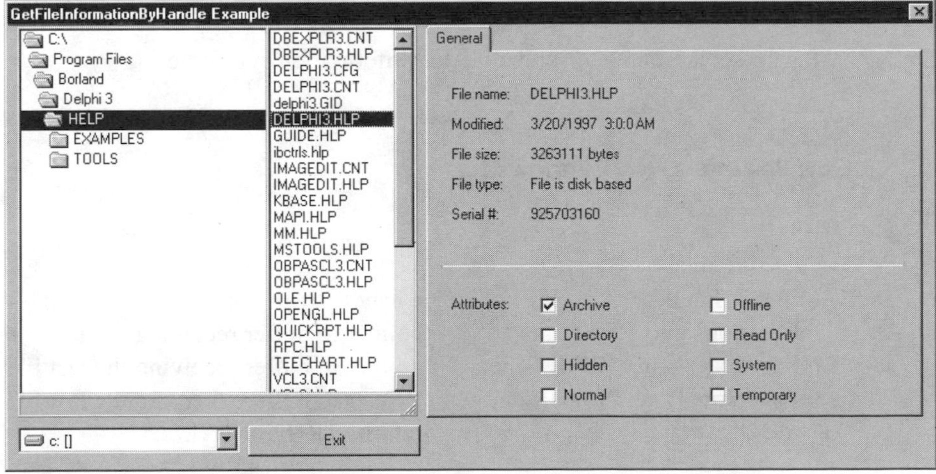

Figure 12-8: The file information.

GetFileSize   Windows.Pas

Syntax

```
GetFileSize(
hFile: THandle;              {the handle of a file}
lpFileSizeHigh: Pointer      {a pointer to the high-order double word of the file size}
): DWORD;                    {returns the low-order double word of the file size}
```

Description

This function returns the size, in bytes, of the file associated with the handle specified by the hFile parameter. This file handle must identify a disk-based file.

Parameters

hFile: A handle to the file from which the size is being retrieved. This file must be opened with the GENERIC_READ and GENERIC_WRITE flags.

lpFileSizeHigh: A pointer to a variable receiving the high-order double word of the file size, if the file is large. If the size of the file being queried will not exceed the capacity of the double word value returned by the function, this parameter can be set to NIL.

Return Value

If the function succeeds, it returns the low-order double word of the file size, and the high-order double word is stored in the variable pointed to by the lpFileSizeHigh parameter. If the function fails, it returns $FFFFFFFF. To get extended error information, call the GetLastError function.

See also

GetFileInformationByHandle, GetFileType

Example

Please see Listing 12-9 under GetFileInformationByHandle.

GetFileTime Windows.Pas

Syntax

```
GetFileTime(
hFile: THandle;                   {a handle to an opened file}
lpCreationTime: PFileTime;        {pointer to buffer receiving the file creation time}
lpLastAccessTime: PFileTime;      {pointer to buffer receiving the last file access time}
lpLastWriteTime: PFileTime        {pointer to buffer receiving the last file write time}
): BOOL;                          {returns TRUE or FALSE}
```

Description

This function retrieves the file creation time, last file access time, and last file write time of the opened file associated with the handle given in the hFile parameter.

Parameters

hFile: A handle to the opened file whose file times are to be retrieved. This file must have been opened with the GENERIC_READ access flag specified.

lpCreationTime: A pointer to a TFileTime data structure to receive the 64-bit file creation time. This parameter may be set to NIL if this time value is not required. Under Windows 95, this value is undefined.

lpLastAccessTime: A pointer to a TFileTime data structure to receive the 64-bit last file access time. This parameter may be set to NIL if this time value is not required. Under Windows 95, this value is undefined.

lpLastWriteTime: A pointer to a TFileTime data structure to receive the 64-bit last file modification time. This parameter may be set to NIL if this time value is not required. This time value is the time value displayed in the Explorer.

Return Value

If the function succeeds, it returns TRUE; otherwise it returns FALSE. To get extended error information, call the GetLastError function.

See also

FileTimeToLocalFileTime, FileTimeToSystemTime, SetFileTime

Example

Please see Listing 12-6 under FileTimeToSystemTime.

GetFileType Windows.Pas

Syntax

```
GetFileType(
hFile: THandle              {the handle of a file}
): DWORD;                   {returns a flag indicating the file type}
```

Description

This function retrieves the type file represented by the specified handle.

Parameters

hFile: The handle to the file whose type is being retrieved.

Return Value

If the function succeeds, it returns one value from Table 12-14; otherwise it returns zero.

See also

GetFileSize, GetFileTime

Example

Please see Listing 12-9 under GetFileInformationByHandle.

Table 12-14: GetFileType Return Values

Value	Description
FILE_TYPE_UNKNOWN	The file type is not known.
FILE_TYPE_DISK	The file is a disk-based file.
FILE_TYPE_CHAR	The file is a character stream, such as a console or LPT device.
FILE_TYPE_PIPE	The file is a named or anonymous pipe.

GetFileVersionInfo Windows.Pas

Syntax

```
GetFileVersionInfo(
lptstrFilename: PChar;      {a pointer to a filename}
dwHandle: DWORD;            {this parameter is ignored}
dwLen: DWORD;               {the size of the lpData buffer}
lpData: Pointer             {a pointer to a buffer receiving the version resource}
): BOOL;                    {returns TRUE or FALSE}
```

Description

This function retrieves the file version information resource from the specified file. It will only succeed on Win32 file images; 16-bit file images are not supported.

Parameters

lptstrFilename: A pointer to a null-terminated string containing the path and filename of the file for which the version information resource is retrieved.

dwHandle: This parameter is completely ignored and may contain any value.

dwLen: Specifies the size of the buffer pointed to by the lpData parameter, in bytes. This parameter should be set to the value returned by the GetFileVersionInfoSize function.

lpData: A pointer to a buffer that receives the file version information resource from the specified file. The pointer to this buffer is used in subsequent calls to VerQuery-Value to retrieve individual file version information values.

Return Value

If the function succeeds, it returns TRUE; otherwise it returns FALSE. To get extended error information, call GetLastError function.

See also

GetFileVersionInfoSize, LoadResource, VerQueryValue

Example

Please see Listing 12-12 under VerQueryValue.

GetFileVersionInfoSize   Windows.Pas

Syntax

```
GetFileVersionInfoSize(
lptstrFilename: PChar;          {a pointer to a filename}
var lpdwHandle: DWORD           {a variable that is set to zero}
): DWORD;                       {returns size of the version information resource}
```

Description

This function retrieves the size of the specified file's version information resource, in bytes, which is used in a subsequent call to GetFileVersionInfo. This function will only succeed on Win32 file images; 16-bit file images are not supported.

Parameters

lptstrFilename: A pointer to a null-terminated string containing the path and filename of the file for which the size of the version information resource is retrieved.

lpdwHandle: A variable that the function sets to zero.

Return Value

If the function succeeds, it returns the size of the specified file's version information resource, in bytes; otherwise it returns zero. To get extended error information, call GetLastError function.

See also

GetFileVersionInfo, LoadResource, VerQueryValue

Example

Please see Listing 12-12 under VerQueryValue.

GetFullPathName   Windows.Pas

Syntax

```
GetFullPathName(
lpFileName: PAnsiChar;          {the filename}
nBufferLength: DWORD;           {the size of lpBuffer, in characters}
lpBuffer: PAnsiChar;            {a pointer to a buffer receiving the path}
var lpFilePart: PAnsiChar       {a pointer to the filename part inside lpBuffer}
): DWORD;                       {returns the number of characters copied to the buffer}
```

Description

This function returns the full path and filename, including the drive, for the filename identified by the lpFileName parameter. The resulting filename and path is not checked for validity or that it points to an existing file. The returned filename will be in the long filename format.

Parameters

lpFileName: A null-terminated string containing the filename for which to retrieve a full path.

nBufferLength: Specifies the size of the buffer pointed to by the lpBuffer parameter, in characters, and must include the null terminator.

lpBuffer: A pointer to a buffer that receives the full path and filename. If this parameter is set to NIL, the return value indicates the required size of the lpBuffer to hold the full path and filename.

lpFilePart: A pointer to a variable that receives a pointer into the lpBuffer at the beginning of the filename in the full path.

Return Value

If the function succeeds, it returns the number of characters copied to the buffer pointed to by the lpBuffer parameter, including the null terminator. If the function fails, it returns zero. To get extended error information, call the GetLastError function.

See also

GetShortPathName, GetTempPath, SearchPath

Example

Please see Listing 12-11 under SetFileAttributes.

GetShortPathName   Windows.Pas

Syntax

```
GetShortPathName (
lpszLongPath: PChar;         {the long path name}
lpszShortPath: PChar;        {a pointer to a buffer that receives the short path name}
cchBuffer: DWORD             {the size of the lpszShortPath buffer, in characters}
): DWORD;                    {returns the number of characters copied to the buffer}
```

Description

This function extracts the short path version of the path specified by the lpszLongPath parameter (i.e., the resulting path is in the 8.3 filename form, and contains the "~" character to display long directory names). If the volume that the specified long path name resides on does not support the 8.3 filename format, this function will return ERROR_INVALID_PARAMETER if the specified path is longer than 67 characters.

Parameters

lpszLongPath: A null-terminated string containing the long path from which to extract the short path name. This does not necessarily have to be a fully qualified path.

lpszShortPath: A pointer to a buffer that receives the full path and filename. If this parameter is set to NIL, the return value indicates the required size of lpszShortPath buffer to hold the short path. This buffer can be the same buffer pointed to by the lpszLongPath parameter.

cchBuffer: Specifies the size of the buffer pointed to by the lpszShortPath parameter, and must include the null terminator.

Return Value

If the function succeeds, it returns the number of characters copied to the buffer pointed to by the lpszShortPath parameter, not including the null terminator. If the function fails, it returns zero. To get extended error information, call the GetLastError function.

See also

GetFullPathName, GetTempPath, FindFirstFile, SearchPath

Example

Please see Listing 12-11 under SetFileAttributes.

GetTempFileName   Windows.Pas

Syntax

```
GetTempFileName(
lpPathName: PChar;            {a pointer to a path}
lpPrefixString: PChar;        {a pointer to the filename prefix string}
uUnique: UINT;                {a unique number used in the filename}
lpTempFileName: PChar         {a pointer to a buffer receiving the temporary filename}
): UINT;                      {returns the unique number used in the filename}
```

Description

This function creates a temporary filename based on the given path, prefix string, and unique number. The filename created always has a .TMP extension. Temporary files created with this function are not automatically deleted when Windows shuts down.

Parameters

lpPathName: A pointer to a null-terminated string containing the path where the temporary file is stored. Typically, this value is the path returned from the GetTempPath function.

lpPrefixString: A pointer to a null-terminated string containing the prefix characters to be used in the filename. The first three letters in the temporary filename are set to the first three letters in the string pointed to by this parameter.

uUnique: An unsigned integer that is converted into a hexadecimal string that follows the prefix characters in the temporary filename. If this parameter is nonzero, the hexadecimal string formed from this parameter is appended to the prefix string obtained from the lpPrefixString parameter to create the temporary filename, but the file is not created and the function does not test the filename to see if it is unique. If this parameter is set to zero, the function uses a hexadecimal string derived from the current system time. The filename is assembled, and if it is unique, it is created in the target directory. If it is not unique, the hexadecimal number is incremented by one and the filename is tested again. This process continues until a unique filename is found.

lpTempFileName: A pointer to a null-terminated string buffer that receives the created temporary filename string.

Return Value

If the function succeeds, it returns the unique numeric value used in the temporary filename; otherwise it returns zero. To get extended error information, call the GetLastError function.

See also

CreateFile, GetTempPath

Example

Listing 12-10: Creating a Unique Filename

```
var
  Form1: TForm1;
  PathName: array[0..MAX_PATH] of char;  // holds the temporary file path

implementation

procedure TForm1.FormCreate(Sender: TObject);
begin
  {retrieve the path for temporary files}
  GetTempPath(MAX_PATH, @PathName);

  {change the listbox directory to this directory, and display it}
  FileListBox1.Directory := string(PathName);
  Label2.Caption := string(PathName);
end;

procedure TForm1.Button1Click(Sender: TObject);
var
  NewTempName: array[0..MAX_PATH] of char;  // holds a temporary filename
begin
  {create a temporary filename}
  GetTempFileName(PathName, 'WOW', 0, @NewTempName);
```

```
  {display the filename, and update the file listbox}
  Label4.Caption := ExtractFileName(string(NewTempName));
  FileListBox1.Update;
end;
```

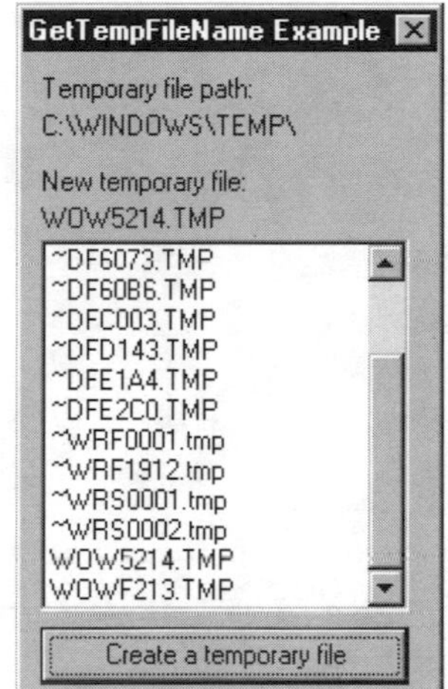

Figure 12-9: The temporary filename was created.

GetTempPath   Windows.Pas

Syntax

GetTempPath(	
nBufferLength: DWORD;	{the size of the lpBuffer buffer}
lpBuffer: PChar	{a pointer to a buffer receiving the temporary file path}
): DWORD;	{returns the number of characters copied to the buffer}

Description

This function retrieves the directory designated for storing temporary files. The directory is retrieved from the TMP environment variable, the TEMP environment variable if TMP is not defined, or the current directory if both the TMP and the TEMP environment variables are not defined.

Parameters

nBufferLength: Specifies the size of the buffer pointed to by the lpBuffer parameter. If this parameter is set to zero, the function returns the size required to store the temporary file path.

lpBuffer: A pointer to a null-terminated string buffer that receives the temporary file path.

Return Value

If this function succeeds, it returns the number of characters copied to the lpBuffer parameter, not including the null terminator character. If the function fails, it returns zero. To get extended error information, call the GetLastError function.

See also

GetTempFileName

Example

Please see Listing 12-10 under GetTempFileName.

LocalFileTimeToFileTime Windows.Pas

Syntax

```
LocalFileTimeToFileTime (
const lpLocalFileTime: TFileTime;      {a pointer to a TFileTime structure}
var lpFileTime: TFileTime              {a pointer to a TFileTime structure}
): BOOL;                               {returns TRUE or FALSE}
```

Description

The LocalFileTimeToFileTime function converts the specified local file time pointed to by the lpLocalFileTime parameter to a Coordinated Universal Time-based time value.

Parameters

lpLocalFileTime: A pointer to a TFileTime structure that contains the local file time to be converted.

lpFileTime: A TFileTime variable that receives the converted Coordinated Universal Time value.

Return Value

If the function succeeds, it returns TRUE; otherwise it returns FALSE. To get extended error information, use the GetLastError function.

See also

DosDateTimeToFileTime, FileTimeToDosDateTime, FileTimeToLocalFileTime, FileTimeToSystemTime, GetFileTime, SetFileTime, SystemTimeToFileTime

Example

Please see Listing 12-6 under FileTimeToSystemTime.

LockFile Windows.Pas

Syntax

```
LockFile(
hFile: THandle;                     {a handle to an open file}
dwFileOffsetLow: DWORD;             {low-order double word of lock region offset}
dwFileOffsetHigh: DWORD;            {high-order double word of lock region offset}
nNumberOfBytesToLockLow:            {low-order double word of lock region
      DWORD;                              length}
nNumberOfBytesToLockHigh:           {high-order double word of lock region
      DWORD                               length}
): BOOL;                            {returns TRUE or FALSE}
```

Description

This function reserves a region of an open file for exclusive access by the calling process. While the file is locked, no other process will have read or write access to the locked region. Although locked regions may not overlap, it does not cause an error to lock a region that goes beyond the end of the file. A locked region can be unlocked by calling the UnlockFile function. All locked regions on a file should be removed before the file is closed or the application is terminated. This function only succeeds on a FAT-based file system if Share.Exe is running.

Parameters

hFile: A handle to the open file which is to be locked. This file must have been created with either the GENERIC_READ or GENERIC_WRITE flags specified.

dwFileOffsetLow: Specifies the low-order word of the offset from the beginning of the file where the locked region should begin.

dwFileOffsetHigh: Specifies the high-order word of the offset from the beginning of the file where the locked region should begin.

nNumberOfBytesToLockLow: Specifies the low-order word of the length, in bytes, of the region to lock.

nNumberOfBytesToLockHigh: Specifies the high-order word of the length, in bytes, of the region to lock.

Return Value

If the function succeeds, it returns TRUE; otherwise it returns FALSE. To get extended error information, call GetLastError.

See also

CreateFile, UnlockFile

Example

Please see Listing 12-4 under CreateFile.

MapViewOfFile   Windows.Pas

Syntax

```
MapViewOfFile(
hFileMappingObject: THandle;         {a handle to a file mapping object}
dwDesiredAccess: DWORD;              {file view access flags}
dwFileOffsetHigh: DWORD;             {high-order double word of file offset}
dwFileOffsetLow: DWORD;              {low-order double word of file offset}
dwNumberOfBytesToMap: DWORD          {the number of bytes to map}
): Pointer;                          {returns a pointer to the mapped data}
```

Description

This function makes the indicated range of bytes in the memory mapped file specified by the hFileMappingObject parameter visible and accessible to the application. It returns a pointer to the beginning of the mapped memory, giving the application direct access to the file's data.

Parameters

hFileMappingObject: A handle to an open file mapping object as returned by the CreateFileMapping and OpenFileMapping functions.

dwDesiredAccess: Specifies the desired access to the memory occupied by the mapped file view. This parameter can be one value from Table 12-15.

dwFileOffsetHigh: Specifies the high-order double word of the offset from the beginning of the file from which to start the view mapping.

dwFileOffsetLow: Specifies the low-order double word of the offset from the beginning of the file from which to start the view mapping. The combined 64-bit offset from the beginning of the file must be a multiple of the system's memory allocation granularity. Memory allocation granularity can be retrieved by calling the GetSystemInfo function.

dwNumberOfBytesToMap: Specifies the number of bytes within the file to map. If this parameter is set to zero, the entire file is mapped into a view.

Return Value

If the function succeeds, it returns a pointer to the beginning of the mapped file's view. If the function fails, it returns NIL. To get extended error information, call the GetLastError function.

See also

CreateFileMapping, GetSystemInfo, OpenFileMapping, UnmapViewOfFile

Example

Please see Listing 12-5 under CreateFileMapping.

Table 12-15: MapViewOfFile dwDesiredAccess Values

Value	Description
FILE_MAP_WRITE	Specifies read/write access to the viewed memory range. The file mapping object must have been created with the PAGE_READWRITE flag specified.
FILE_MAP_READ	Specifies read-only access to the viewed memory range. The file mapping object must have been created with the PAGE_READWRITE or PAGE_READONLY flags specified.
FILE_MAP_COPY	Specifies copy on write access to the viewed memory range. Under Windows 95, the file mapping object must have been created with the PAGE_WRITECOPY flag specified. When the memory range for a mapped file is modified, the modifications are not written to the original disk file. If this memory mapped file is shared between processes by using the OpenFileMapping function, any changes to the memory mapped data will be seen by sharing processes under Windows 95, but will not be seen by other processes under Windows NT.

MoveFile *Windows.Pas*

Syntax

```
MoveFile(
lpExistingFileName: PAnsiChar;   {the name and path of the existing file}
lpNewFileName: PAnsiChar         {the name and path of the new file}
): BOOL;                         {returns TRUE or FALSE}
```

Description

This function renames the file or directory identified by the lpExistingFileName parameter to the new name identified by the lpNewFileName parameter. If a directory is moved (i.e., renamed), so are its child directories. However, this function will fail if the application attempts to move the directory across volumes.

Parameters

lpExistingFileName: A null-terminated string containing the name and path of the file or directory being renamed.

lpNewFileName: A null-terminated string containing the new name and path for the file or directory. The new file or directory name must not currently exist in the destination.

Return Value

If the function succeeds, it returns TRUE; otherwise it returns FALSE. To get extended error information, call the GetLastError function.

See also

CopyFile

Example

Please see Listing 12-8 under FindFirstFile.

OpenFileMapping Windows.Pas

Syntax

```
OpenFileMapping(
dwDesiredAccess: DWORD;        {memory mapped file access flags}
bInheritHandle: BOOL;          {handle inheritance flag}
lpName: PChar                  {a pointer to the name of the file mapping object}
): THandle;                    {returns a handle to a file mapping object}
```

Description

This function opens a named file mapping object that currently exists. This can be a file mapping object created by the current process or by another process.

Parameters

dwDesiredAccess: Specifies the desired access to the memory occupied by the mapped file view. This parameter can be one value from Table 12-16.

bInheritHandle: Indicates if the returned handle is inherited when a new process is created. A value of TRUE indicates that new processes inherit the returned file handle.

lpName: A pointer to a null-terminated string containing the name of a file mapping object previously created by the CreateFileMapping function, either within the current process or another process. If a file mapping object by this name is opened, and its memory access attributes do not conflict with those specified by the dwDesiredAccess parameter, the function succeeds.

Return Value

If the function succeeds, it returns a handle to the specified file mapping object; otherwise it returns zero. To get extended error information, call the GetLastError function.

See also

CreateFileMapping, MapViewOfFile, UnmapViewOfFile

Example

Please see Listing 12-5 under CreateFileMapping.

Table 12-16: OpenFileMapping dwDesiredAccess Values

Value	Description
FILE_MAP_WRITE	Specifies read/write access to the viewed memory range. The file mapping object must have been created with the PAGE_READWRITE flag specified.
FILE_MAP_READ	Specifies read-only access to the viewed memory range. The file mapping object must have been created with the PAGE_READWRITE or PAGE_READONLY flags specified.
FILE_MAP_COPY	Specifies copy on write access to the viewed memory range. Under Windows 95, the file mapping object must have been created with the PAGE_WRITECOPY flag specified. When the memory range for a mapped file is modified, the modifications are not written to the original disk file. If this memory mapped file is shared between processes by using the OpenFileMapping function, any changes to the memory mapped data will be seen by sharing processes under Windows 95, but will not be seen by other processes under Windows NT.

ReadFile *Windows.Pas*

Syntax

```
ReadFile(
hFile: THandle;                      {a handle to an open file}
var Buffer;                          {a pointer to the buffer receiving the retrieved data}
nNumberOfBytesToRead: DWORD;         {specifies number of bytes to read from file}
var lpNumberOfBytesRead: DWORD;      {receives the number of bytes actually read}
lpOverlapped: POverLapped            {a pointer to a TOverLapped structure}
): BOOL;                             {returns TRUE or FALSE}
```

Description

This function retrieves the number of bytes specified by the nNumberOfBytesToRead parameter from the file associated with the handle specified in the hFile parameter. These bytes are stored in the buffer pointed to by the Buffer parameter. The origin of the read operation within the file is dependent upon how the file was opened and the value of the lpOverlapped parameter. Typically, the lpOverlapped parameter contains NIL, and the read operation begins at the current file pointer. After the read operation has completed, the file pointer is incremented by the number of bytes read, unless the file was opened with the FILE_FLAG_OVERLAPPED flag specified. In this case, the file pointer is not incremented, and the application must move the file pointer explicitly. The read operation will fail if it attempts to read any part of a file that has been locked with the LockFile function. The application must not access the buffer pointed to by the Buffer parameter until the read operation has completed.

Parameters

hFile: A handle to the file being read. This file must have been opened with the GENERIC_READ flag specified. Note that Windows 95 does not support asynchronous reads on disk-based files.

Buffer: A pointer to a buffer receiving the information read from the file.

nNumberOfBytesToRead: Specifies the number of bytes to read from the file.

lpNumberOfBytesRead: A pointer to a double word receiving the number of bytes actually read from the file. This variable is initialized to zero before the function starts the read. This parameter must contain a pointer if the lpOverlapped parameter is set to NIL.

lpOverlapped: A pointer to a TOverlapped data structure. If the file identified by the hFile parameter was opened with the FILE_FLAG_OVERLAPPED flag specified, this parameter must contain a pointer. If the file was opened with the FILE_FLAG_OVERLAPPED flag specified, the read operation begins at the offset specified within the structure, and ReadFile may return before the read operation has completed. In this case, ReadFile will return FALSE, and GetLastError will return ERROR_IO_PENDING. The event specified in the TOverlapped structure will be signaled upon completing the read operation. If the file was not opened with the FILE_FLAG_OVERLAPPED flag specified and this parameter is not NIL, the read operation begins at the offset specified within the structure, and ReadFile does not return until the read operation is completed. If the file was not opened with the FILE_FLAG_OVERLAPPED flag specified and this parameter is NIL, the read operation begins at the current file pointer and does not return until the read operation is complete. The TOverlapped data structure is defined as:

```
TOverlapped = record
    Internal: DWORD;            {reserved for internal use}
    InternalHigh: DWORD;        {reserved for internal use}
    Offset: DWORD;              {specifies the file position from which to start}
    OffsetHigh: DWORD;          {the high-order double word of the starting offset}
    hEvent: THandle;            {a handle to an event object}
end;
```

Internal: This member is reserved for internal operating system use.

InternalHigh: This member is reserved for internal operating system use.

Offset: Specifies the low-order double word of the byte offset from the beginning of the file from which to start the operation.

OffsetHigh: Specifies the high-order double word of the byte offset from the beginning of the file from which to start the operation.

hEvent: A handle to an event object that is set to the signaled state when the operation has completed.

Return Value

If the function succeeds, it returns TRUE; otherwise it returns FALSE. To get extended error information, call the GetLastError function.

See also

CreateFile, LockFile, UnlockFile, WriteFile

Example

Please see Listing 12-4 under CreateFile.

RemoveDirectory Windows.Pas

Syntax

```
RemoveDirectory(
lpPathName: PAnsiChar          {the name of the directory to delete}
): BOOL;                       {returns TRUE or FALSE}
```

Description

This function deletes the directory specified by the lpPathName parameter. This directory must not contain any files, and the calling process must have delete access to the directory.

Parameters

lpPathName: A null-terminated string containing the path name of the directory to be deleted.

Return Value

If the function succeeds, it returns TRUE; otherwise it returns FALSE. To get extended error information, call the GetLastError function.

See also

CreateDirectory, CreateDirectoryEx

Example

Please see Listing 12-8 under FindFirstFile.

SearchPath Windows.Pas

Syntax

```
SearchPath(
lpPath: PChar;                {a pointer to a search path}
lpFileName: PChar;            {a pointer to a filename}
lpExtension: PChar;           {a pointer to a file extension}
nBufferLength: DWORD;         {the size of the lpBuffer buffer}
lpBuffer: PChar;              {a pointer to a buffer}
var lpFilePart: PChar         {a pointer to the filename}
): DWORD;                     {returns the number of characters copied to
                                  the buffer}
```

Description

The SearchPath function searches the path pointed to by the lpPath parameter for the filename pointed to by the lpFileName parameter.

Parameters

lpPath: A pointer to a null-terminated string containing the path in which to search for the specified filename. If this parameter is set to NIL, SearchPath will search the following directories in order:

1. The directory containing the application.
2. The current directory.
3. The Windows system directory as returned by the GetSystemDirectory function.
4. The Windows directory as returned by the GetWindowsDirectory function.
5. The directories listed in the PATH environment variable.

lpFileName: A pointer to a null-terminated string containing the file for which to search.

lpExtension: A pointer to a null-terminated string containing the file extension, including the period. If the file extension is not needed, or the filename pointed to by the lpFileName parameter contains an extension, this parameter can be set to NIL.

nBufferLength: Specifies the size of the buffer pointed to by the lpBuffer parameter, in characters. If this parameter is set to zero, the function returns the required size of the buffer to store the full path and filename.

lpBuffer: A pointer to a buffer which receives the path and filename of the file that was found.

lpFilePart: Receives a pointer into the lpBuffer buffer where the filename part of the returned path and filename begins, immediately following the final backslash of the path.

Return Value

If the function succeeds, it returns the number of characters copied to the buffer pointed to by the lpBuffer parameter. If the function fails, it returns zero. To get extended error information, call the GetLastError function.

See also

FindFirstFile, FindNextFile, GetSystemDirectory, GetWindowsDirectory, SetCurrentDirectory.

Example

Please see Listing 12-8 under FindFirstFile.

SetCurrentDirectory Windows.Pas

Syntax

```
SetCurrentDirectory(
lpPathName: PAnsiChar          {the name of the new current directory }
): BOOL;                       {returns TRUE or FALSE}
```

Description

This function changes the current directory of the calling process to the new directory identified by the lpPathName parameter.

Parameters

lpPathName: A null-terminated string containing the path to the new directory. This path can be either a fully qualified path or a relative path.

Return Value

If the function succeeds, it returns TRUE; otherwise it returns FALSE. To get extended error information, call the GetLastError function.

See also

GetCurrentDirectory

Example

Please see Listing 12-11 under SetFileAttributes.

SetEndOfFile Windows.Pas

Syntax

```
SetEndOfFile(
hFile: THandle                {a handle to an open file}
): BOOL;                      {returns TRUE or FALSE}
```

Description

This function sets the end of file to the current file pointer position, either extending or truncating the file. If the file is extended, the contents of the file between the old end of file position and the new one are undetermined. If the CreateFileMapping function has been used to create a file mapping object for the file associated with the handle in the hFile parameter, the application must call UnmapViewOfFile and CloseHandle to close the file mapping object before the SetEndOfFile function can be used.

Parameters

hFile: A handle to a file whose end of file position is to be moved. This file must have been opened with the GENERIC_WRITE flag specified.

Return Value

If the function succeeds, it returns TRUE; otherwise it returns FALSE. To get extended error information, call the GetLastError function.

See also

CloseHandle, CreateFile, CreateFileMapping, SetFilePointer, UnmapViewOfFile

Example

Please see Listing 12-4 under CreateFile.

SetFileAttributes Windows.Pas

Syntax

```
SetFileAttributes(
lpFileName: PChar;            {the filename}
dwFileAttributes: DWORD       {file attribute flags}
): BOOL;                      {returns TRUE or FALSE}
```

Description

This function sets the file attributes for the file or directory specified by the lpFileName parameter.

Parameters

lpFileName: A null-terminated string containing the name of the file or directory from which to retrieve file attributes. This string must not be longer than MAX_PATH.

dwFileAttributes: Specifies the attributes being set for the file. This parameter can contain one or more values from Table 12-17.

Return Value

If the function succeeds, it returns TRUE; otherwise it returns FALSE. To get extended error information, call the GetLastError function.

See also

GetFileAttributes

Example

Listing 12-11: Getting and Setting File Attributes

```
procedure TForm1.FileListBox1Change(Sender: TObject);
var
   PathBuffer: array[0..255] of char;    // holds path names
   FilePart: PChar;                      // a pointer to the filename
begin
  {if the file list box has an item selected, retrieve its information}
  if FileListBox1.ItemIndex>-1 then
  begin
    {unhook the checkbox OnClick methods, as accessing their Checked
     property fires the method}
    CheckBox1.OnClick := nil;
    CheckBox2.OnClick := nil;
    CheckBox3.OnClick := nil;
    CheckBox4.OnClick := nil;
    CheckBox5.OnClick := nil;
    CheckBox6.OnClick := nil;
    CheckBox7.OnClick := nil;
    CheckBox8.OnClick := nil;

    {retrieve and display the various file attributes for the selected file}
    CheckBox1.Checked := Boolean(GetFileAttributes(PChar(FileListBox1.FileName))
                                 and FILE_ATTRIBUTE_ARCHIVE);
    CheckBox2.Checked := Boolean(GetFileAttributes(PChar(FileListBox1.FileName))
                                 and FILE_ATTRIBUTE_DIRECTORY);
    CheckBox3.Checked := Boolean(GetFileAttributes(PChar(FileListBox1.FileName))
                                 and FILE_ATTRIBUTE_HIDDEN);
    CheckBox4.Checked := Boolean(GetFileAttributes(PChar(FileListBox1.FileName))
                                 and FILE_ATTRIBUTE_OFFLINE);
    CheckBox5.Checked := Boolean(GetFileAttributes(PChar(FileListBox1.FileName))
                                 and FILE_ATTRIBUTE_READONLY);
    CheckBox6.Checked := Boolean(GetFileAttributes(PChar(FileListBox1.FileName))
                                 and FILE_ATTRIBUTE_SYSTEM);
    CheckBox7.Checked := Boolean(GetFileAttributes(PChar(FileListBox1.FileName))
                                 and FILE_ATTRIBUTE_NORMAL);
    CheckBox8.Checked := Boolean(GetFileAttributes(PChar(FileListBox1.FileName))
                                 and FILE_ATTRIBUTE_TEMPORARY);

    {display the file's name}
    Label1.Caption := ExtractFileName(FileListBox1.FileName);
```

```
    {display the full, qualified path for the selected file}
    GetFullPathName(PChar(Label1.Caption), 255, PathBuffer, FilePart);
    Label10.Caption := string(PathBuffer);

    {display the short path form of the qualified path}
    GetShortPathName(PChar(DirectoryListBox1.Directory), PathBuffer, 255);
    Label11.Caption := string(PathBuffer);

    {display the current directory}
    GetCurrentDirectory(255, PathBuffer);
    Label12.Caption := string(PathBuffer);

    {rehook the checkbox OnClick methods}
    CheckBox1.OnClick := CheckBox1Click;
    CheckBox2.OnClick := CheckBox1Click;
    CheckBox3.OnClick := CheckBox1Click;
    CheckBox4.OnClick := CheckBox1Click;
    CheckBox5.OnClick := CheckBox1Click;
    CheckBox6.OnClick := CheckBox1Click;
    CheckBox7.OnClick := CheckBox1Click;
    CheckBox8.OnClick := CheckBox1Click;
  end;
end;

procedure TForm1.CheckBox1Click(Sender: TObject);
var
  FileAttributes: DWORD;      // holds collective file attributes
  ErrorMessage: Pointer;      // holds a system error string
  ErrorCode: DWORD;           // holds a system error code
begin
  {unhook the checkbox OnClick methods, as accessing their Checked
   property fires the method}
  CheckBox1.OnClick := nil;
  CheckBox2.OnClick := nil;
  CheckBox3.OnClick := nil;
  CheckBox4.OnClick := nil;
  CheckBox5.OnClick := nil;
  CheckBox6.OnClick := nil;
  CheckBox7.OnClick := nil;
  CheckBox8.OnClick := nil;

  {prepare to sum file attributes}
  FileAttributes := 0;

  {add all of the file attributes selected}
  if CheckBox1.Checked then
    FileAttributes := FileAttributes or FILE_ATTRIBUTE_ARCHIVE;
  if CheckBox2.Checked then
    FileAttributes := FileAttributes or FILE_ATTRIBUTE_DIRECTORY;
  if CheckBox3.Checked then
    FileAttributes := FileAttributes or FILE_ATTRIBUTE_HIDDEN;
  if CheckBox4.Checked then
    FileAttributes := FileAttributes or FILE_ATTRIBUTE_OFFLINE;
  if CheckBox5.Checked then
    FileAttributes := FileAttributes or FILE_ATTRIBUTE_READONLY;
```

```
  if CheckBox6.Checked then
    FileAttributes := FileAttributes or FILE_ATTRIBUTE_SYSTEM;
  if CheckBox7.Checked then
    FileAttributes := FileAttributes or FILE_ATTRIBUTE_NORMAL;
  if CheckBox8.Checked then
    FileAttributes := FileAttributes or FILE_ATTRIBUTE_TEMPORARY;

  {set the file attributes of the selected file}
  if not SetFileAttributes(PChar(FileListBox1.FileName), FileAttributes) then
  begin
    {if there was an error, display the error message}
    ErrorCode := GetLastError;
    FormatMessage(FORMAT_MESSAGE_ALLOCATE_BUFFER or FORMAT_MESSAGE_FROM_SYSTEM,
                  nil, ErrorCode, 0, @ErrorMessage, 0, nil);
    StatusBar1.SimpleText:='Error Copying File: '+string(PChar(ErrorMessage));
    LocalFree(hlocal(ErrorMessage));
  end;

  {rehook the checkbox OnClick methods}
  CheckBox1.OnClick := CheckBox1Click;
  CheckBox2.OnClick := CheckBox1Click;
  CheckBox3.OnClick := CheckBox1Click;
  CheckBox4.OnClick := CheckBox1Click;
  CheckBox5.OnClick := CheckBox1Click;
  CheckBox6.OnClick := CheckBox1Click;
  CheckBox7.OnClick := CheckBox1Click;
  CheckBox8.OnClick := CheckBox1Click;
end;

procedure TForm1.ComboBox1Change(Sender: TObject);
begin
  {set the current directory to the selected directory}
  SetCurrentDirectory(PChar(ComboBox1.Items[ComboBox1.ItemIndex]));

  {update the directory list box accordingly}
  DirectoryListBox1.Directory := ComboBox1.Items[ComboBox1.ItemIndex];
  DirectoryListBox1.Update;
end;
```

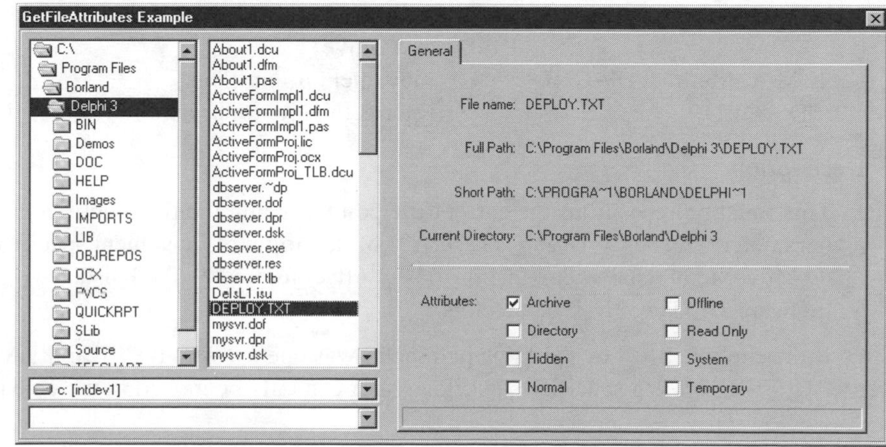

Figure 12-10: Viewing file attributes.

Table 12-17: SetFileAttributes dwFileAttributes Values

Value	Description
FILE_ATTRIBUTE_ARCHIVE	Indicates an archive file or directory, and is used by applications to mark files and directories for removal or backup.
FILE_ATTRIBUTE_DIRECTORY	Indicates that the specified filename is a directory.
FILE_ATTRIBUTE_HIDDEN	Indicates that the specified file or directory is hidden, and will not appear in normal directory listings.
FILE_ATTRIBUTE_NORMAL	Indicates that the specified file or directory does not have any other file attributes set.
FILE_ATTRIBUTE_OFFLINE	Indicates that the specified file or directory is not immediately available, and that it has been physically moved to offline storage.
FILE_ATTRIBUTE_READONLY	Indicates that the specified file or directory is read only. Applications may read from the file or directory, but may not write to it or delete it.
FILE_ATTRIBUTE_SYSTEM	Indicates that the specified file or directory is used by the system.
FILE_ATTRIBUTE_TEMPORARY	Indicates that the specified file or directory is temporary. The system will not automatically delete temporary files during shutdown.

SetFilePointer *Windows.Pas*

Syntax

```
SetFilePointer(
hFile: THandle;                    {a handle to an open file}
lDistanceToMove: Longint;          {the distance to move in bytes}
lpDistanceToMoveHigh: Pointer;     {points to high-order double word of distance to
                                       move}
dwMoveMethod: DWORD                {movement origin flags}
): DWORD;                          {returns the low-order double word of file pointer}
```

Description

This function repositions the current file pointer within the file identified by the hFile parameter. The new position is based off of the origin of movement specified by the dwMoveMethod parameter and the 64-bit offset formed by the lDistanceToMove and lpDistanceToMoveHigh parameters.

If the file identified by the hFile parameter was opened with the FILE_FLAG_NO_BUFFERING flag specified, the file pointer can only be moved in increments of the volume's sector size. A disk volume's sector size can be retrieved by calling the GetDiskFreeSpace function.

Parameters

hFile: A handle to the open file whose file pointer is to be repositioned. The file must have been opened with either the GENERIC_READ or GENERIC_WRITE flags specified.

lDistanceToMove: Specifies the low-order double word of the distance, in bytes, to move the file pointer. A positive value moves the file pointer forward in the file, and a negative value moves it backwards.

lpDistanceToMoveHigh: A pointer to the high-order double word of the distance, in bytes, to move the file pointer. This parameter can be set to NIL, in which case the file pointer can only be moved within a range of 2^32-2 bytes. If this parameter is not NIL, the file pointer can be moved within a range of 2^64-2 bytes, and the value pointed at by this parameter receives the new high-order double word of the file pointer when the function returns.

dwMoveMethod: Specifies the starting point of the file pointer for the movement. This parameter can be one value from Table 12-18.

Return Value

If the function succeeds, it returns the low-order double word of the new file pointer position. If the function fails, it returns $FFFFFFFF. To get extended error information, call the GetLastError function. If the lpDistanceToMoveHigh parameter is not NIL and the function failed, GetLastError will return NO_ERROR.

See also

CreateFile, GetDiskFreeSpace, ReadFile, SetEndOfFile, WriteFile

Example

Please see Listing 12-4 under CreateFile.

Table 12-18: SetFilePointer dwMoveMethod Values

Value	Description
FILE_BEGIN	The starting point for the movement begins at the beginning of the file.
FILE_CURRENT	The starting point for the movement begins at the current file pointer position.
FILE_END	The starting point for the movement begins at the end of the file.

SetFileTime Windows.Pas

Syntax

```
SetFileTime(
hFile: THandle;                    {a handle to an opened file}
lpCreationTime: PFileTime;         {pointer to buffer receiving the file creation time}
lpLastAccessTime: PFileTime;       {pointer to buffer receiving the last file access time}
lpLastWriteTime: PFileTime         {pointer to buffer receiving the last file write time}
): BOOL;                           {returns TRUE or FALSE}
```

Description

This function sets the file creation time, last file access time, and last file write time of the opened file associated with the handle given in the hFile parameter.

Parameters

hFile: A handle to the opened file whose file times are to be modified. This file must have been opened with the GENERIC_READ access flag specified.

lpCreationTime: A pointer to a TFileTime data structure containing the 64-bit time value with which to set the file's creation time. This parameter may be set to NIL if this time value does not need to be modified.

lpLastAccessTime: A pointer to a TFileTime data structure containing the 64-bit time value with which to set the file's last access time. This parameter may be set to NIL if this time value does not need to be modified.

lpLastWriteTime: A pointer to a TFileTime data structure containing the 64-bit time value with which to set the file's last modification time. This parameter may be set to NIL if this time value does not need to be modified. This time value is the time value displayed in the Explorer.

Return Value

If the function succeeds, it returns TRUE; otherwise it returns FALSE. To get extended error information, call the GetLastError function.

See also

FileTimeToLocalFileTime, FileTimeToSystemTime, GetFileTime

Example

Please see Listing 12-6 under FileTimeToSystemTime.

SystemTimeToFileTime *Windows.Pas*

Syntax

```
SystemTimeToFileTime(
const lpSystemTime: TSystemTime;      {a pointer to a TSystemTime structure}
var lpFileTime: TFileTime             {a pointer to a TFileTime structure}
): BOOL;                              {returns TRUE or FALSE}
```

Description

This function converts the values stored in the TSystemTime structure pointed to by the lpSystemTime parameter into a 64-bit file time.

Parameters

lpSystemTime: A pointer to a TSystemTime structure containing the system time information to be converted. The TSystemTime data structure is defined as:

```
TSystemTime = record
    wYear: Word;              {the current year}
    wMonth: Word;             {the month number}
    wDayOfWeek: Word;         {the day of the week number}
    wDay: Word;               {the current day of the month}
    wHour: Word;              {the current hour}
    wMinute: Word;            {the current minute}
    wSecond: Word;            {the current second}
    wMilliseconds: Word;      {the current millisecond}
end;
```

Please see the FileTimeToSystemTime function for a description of this data structure.

lpFileTime: A pointer to a TFileTime structure receiving the 64-bit converted file time.

Return Value

If the function succeeds, it returns TRUE; otherwise it returns FALSE. To get extended error information, use the GetLastError function.

See also

DosDateTimeToFileTime, FileTimeToDosDateTime, FileTimeToLocalFileTime, FileTimeToSystemTime, GetFileTime, LocalFileTimeToFileTime, SetFileTime

Example

Please see Listing 12-6 under FileTimeToSystemTime.

UnlockFile *Windows.Pas*

Syntax

```
UnlockFile(
hFile: THandle;                       {a handle to an open file}
dwFileOffsetLow: DWORD;               {low-order double word of lock region offset}
dwFileOffsetHigh: DWORD;              {high-order double word of lock region offset}
nNumberOfBytesToUnlockLow:            {low-order double word of lock region
      DWORD;                                length}
nNumberOfBytesToUnlockHigh:           {high-order double word of lock region
      DWORD;                                length}
): BOOL;                              {returns TRUE or FALSE}
```

Description

This function unlocks a previously locked region in a file, providing access to the region to other processes. The unlocked region must exactly match the locked region as determined by the previous call to LockFile. All locked regions on a file should be removed before the file is closed or the application is terminated.

Parameters

hFile: A handle to the open file which is to be unlocked. This file must have been created with either the GENERIC_READ or GENERIC_WRITE flags specified.

dwFileOffsetLow: Specifies the low-order word of the offset from the beginning of the file where the locked region begins.

dwFileOffsetHigh: Specifies the high-order word of the offset from the beginning of the file where the locked region begins.

nNumberOfBytesToUnlockLow: Specifies the low-order word of the length, in bytes, of the region to unlock.

nNumberOfBytesToUnlockHigh: Specifies the high-order word of the length, in bytes, of the region to unlock.

Return Value

If the function succeeds, it returns TRUE; otherwise it returns FALSE. To get extended error information, call GetLastError.

See also

CreateFile, LockFile

Example

Please see Listing 12-4 under CreateFile.

UnmapViewOfFile *Windows.Pas*

Syntax

```
UnmapViewOfFile(
lpBaseAddress: Pointer       {a pointer to the base address of the mapped view}
): BOOL;                     {returns TRUE or FALSE}
```

Description

This function removes a view of a file mapping object from the process's address space. A file that has been mapped to memory using the CreateFileMapping function is not closed until all views of the file have been closed by using UnmapViewOfFile.

Parameters

lpBaseAddress: A pointer to the base address of the mapped view of the file mapping object. This pointer must be the exact address location originally returned by the previous call to the MapViewOfFile function.

Return Value

If the function succeeds, it returns TRUE; otherwise it returns FALSE. To get extended error information, call GetLastError.

See also

CreateFileMapping, MapViewOfFile, OpenFileMapping

Example

Please see Listing 12-5 under CreateFileMapping.

VerQueryValue *Windows.Pas*

Syntax

```
VerQueryValue(
pBlock: Pointer;             {a pointer to the version resource}
lpSubBlock: PChar;           {a pointer to a version value string}
var lplpBuffer: Pointer;     {a pointer to a buffer receiving a pointer to the value}
var puLen: UINT              {a pointer to a buffer receiving the value length}
): BOOL;                     {returns TRUE or FALSE}
```

Description

This function retrieves a pointer to the file version information type specified by the lpSubBlock parameter from the file version resource identified by the pBlock parameter. The pointer to this information is stored in the buffer pointed to by the lplpBuffer parameter. This function will only succeed on Win32 file images; 16-bit file images are not supported. Use the GetFileVersionInfo to retrieve the file version resource for the pBlock parameter.

Parameters

pBlock: A pointer to a buffer containing the file version resource as returned by GetFileVersionInfo.

lpSubBlock: A pointer to a null-terminated string containing the type of file version information to retrieve. This string can contain one value from Table 12-19. The file version information retrieved can be either a data structure containing specific information, or the actual name of a version information type. In order to use names, the application must first use the \\VarFileInfo\\Translation value to retrieve the translation code. This translation code is used in all subsequent version name values. To use the version code to specify a version name, the version code must be inserted in the version name as a string of hexadecimal numbers consisting of the low word of the conversion code concatenated with the high word of the conversion code. See below for an example of using version name values.

lplpBuffer: A pointer to a buffer which receives a pointer to the requested file version information. The pointer received will point to a null-terminated string.

puLen: A pointer to a buffer which receives the length of the requested file version information in characters.

Return Value

If the function succeeds and the file version information resource contains the requested information type, it returns TRUE. If the function fails, or there is no file version information for the requested information type, it returns FALSE.

See also

GetFileVersionInfo, GetFileVersionInfoSize, LoadResource

Example

Listing 12-12: Retrieving File Version Information

```
procedure TForm1.FileListBox1Click(Sender: TObject);
var
  VerInfoSize: DWORD;          // holds the size of the version info resource
  GetInfoSizeJunk: DWORD;      // a junk variable, its value is ignored
  VersionInfo: Pointer;        // points to the version info resource
  Translation: Pointer;        // holds version info translation table
  InfoPointer: Pointer;        // a pointer to version information
  VersionInfoSize: UINT;       // holds the size of version information
  VersionValue: string;        // holds the version info request string
begin
  {retrieve the size of the version information resource, if one exists}
  VerInfoSize := 0;
  VerInfoSize := GetFileVersionInfoSize(PChar(FileListBox1.FileName),
                                        GetInfoSizeJunk);
```

```
{if there was a version information resource available...}
if VerInfoSize>0 then
begin
  {hide the 'not available' indicator}
  Label1.Visible := FALSE;

  {retrieve enough memory to hold the version resource}
  GetMem(VersionInfo, VerInfoSize);

  {retrieve the version resource for the selected file}
  GetFileVersionInfo(PChar(FileListBox1.FileName), 0,
                     VerInfoSize, VersionInfo);

  {retrieve a pointer to the translation table}
  VerQueryValue(VersionInfo, '\\VarFileInfo\\Translation',
                Translation, VersionInfoSize

  {initialize the version value request string}
  VersionValue :='\\StringFileInfo\\'+
                IntToHex(LoWord(LongInt(Translation^)),4)+
                IntToHex(HiWord(LongInt(Translation^)),4)+
                '\\';

  {retrieve and display the company name}
  VerQueryValue(VersionInfo, PChar(VersionValue+'CompanyName'),
                InfoPointer, VersionInfoSize);
  Label17.Caption := string(PChar(InfoPointer));

  {retrieve and display the file description}
  VerQueryValue(VersionInfo, PChar(VersionValue+'FileDescription'),
                InfoPointer, VersionInfoSize);
  Label16.Caption := string(PChar(InfoPointer));

  {retrieve and display the file version}
  VerQueryValue(VersionInfo, PChar(VersionValue+'FileVersion'), InfoPointer,
                VersionInfoSize);
  Label15.Caption := string(PChar(InfoPointer));

  {retrieve and display the internal filename}
  VerQueryValue(VersionInfo, PChar(VersionValue+'InternalName'), InfoPointer,
                VersionInfoSize);
  Label14.Caption := string(PChar(InfoPointer));

  {retrieve and display the legal copyright}
  VerQueryValue(VersionInfo, PChar(VersionValue+'LegalCopyright'),
                InfoPointer, VersionInfoSize);
  Label13.Caption := string(PChar(InfoPointer));

  {retrieve and display the legal trademarks}
  if VerQueryValue(VersionInfo, PChar(VersionValue+'LegalTrademarks'),
                   InfoPointer, VersionInfoSize) then
    Label19.Caption := string(PChar(InfoPointer))
  else
    Label19.Caption := '';
```

```
    {retrieve and display the original filename}
    VerQueryValue(VersionInfo, PChar(VersionValue+'OriginalFilename'),
                  InfoPointer, VersionInfoSize);
    Label12.Caption := string(PChar(InfoPointer));

    {retrieve and display the product name}
    VerQueryValue(VersionInfo, PChar(VersionValue+'ProductName'), InfoPointer,
                  VersionInfoSize);
    Label11.Caption := string(PChar(InfoPointer));

    {retrieve and display the product version}
    VerQueryValue(VersionInfo, PChar(VersionValue+'ProductVersion'),
                  InfoPointer, VersionInfoSize);
    Label10.Caption := string(PChar(InfoPointer));

    {retrieve and display the comments. Some version info resources may
     not have this information.}
    if VerQueryValue(VersionInfo, PChar(VersionValue+'Comments'), InfoPointer,
                     VersionInfoSize) then
      Label21.Caption := string(PChar(InfoPointer))
    else
      Label21.Caption := '';

    {retrieve and display file build flags}
    if VerQueryValue(VersionInfo, '\', InfoPointer, VersionInfoSize) then
    begin
      CheckBox1.Checked := BOOL(TVSFixedFileInfo(InfoPointer^).dwFileFlags and
                           VS_FF_DEBUG);
      CheckBox2.Checked := BOOL(TVSFixedFileInfo(InfoPointer^).dwFileFlags and
                           VS_FF_PRERELEASE);
      CheckBox3.Checked := BOOL(TVSFixedFileInfo(InfoPointer^).dwFileFlags and
                           VS_FF_PATCHED);
      CheckBox4.Checked := BOOL(TVSFixedFileInfo(InfoPointer^).dwFileFlags and
                           VS_FF_PRIVATEBUILD);
      CheckBox5.Checked := BOOL(TVSFixedFileInfo(InfoPointer^).dwFileFlags and
                           VS_FF_INFOINFERRED);
      CheckBox6.Checked := BOOL(TVSFixedFileInfo(InfoPointer^).dwFileFlags and
                           VS_FF_SPECIALBUILD);
    end
    else
    begin
      CheckBox1.Checked := FALSE;
      CheckBox2.Checked := FALSE;
      CheckBox3.Checked := FALSE;
      CheckBox4.Checked := FALSE;
      CheckBox5.Checked := FALSE;
      CheckBox6.Checked := FALSE;
    end;

    {free the version resource memory}
    FreeMem(VersionInfo, VerInfoSize);
  end
  else
  begin
```

```
    {otherwise, indicate that no version information is available}
    Label1.Visible := TRUE;

    {delete any previous version information}
    Label17.Caption := '';
    Label16.Caption := '';
    Label15.Caption := '';
    Label14.Caption := '';
    Label13.Caption := '';
    Label12.Caption := '';
    Label11.Caption := '';
    Label10.Caption := '';
    Label19.Caption := '';
    Label21.Caption := '';

    CheckBox1.Checked := FALSE;
    CheckBox2.Checked := FALSE;
    CheckBox3.Checked := FALSE;
    CheckBox4.Checked := FALSE;
    CheckBox5.Checked := FALSE;
    CheckBox6.Checked := FALSE;
  end;
end;
```

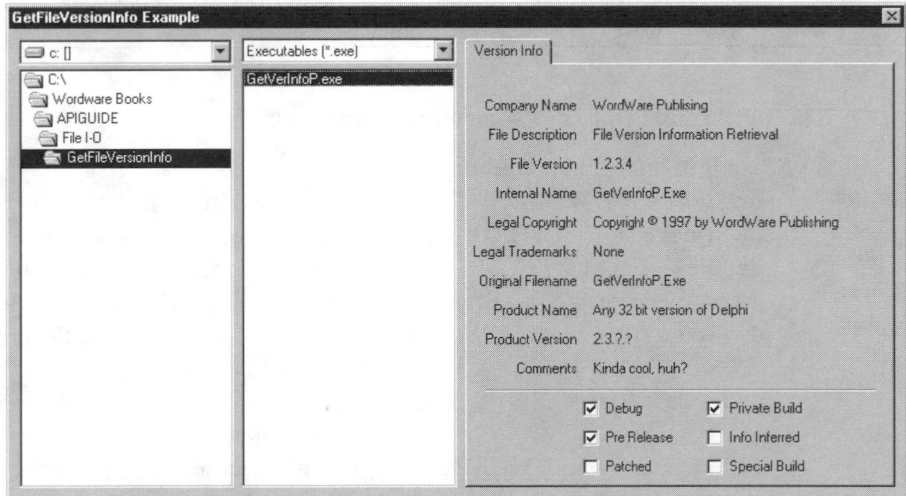

Figure 12-11: The file version information.

Table 12-19: VerQueryValue lpSubBlock Values

Value	Description
\	Stores a pointer to a TVSFixedFileInfo data structure in the buffer pointed to by the lplpBuffer parameter. The TVSFixedFileInfo structure contains specific file version information.
\\VarFileInfo\\Translation	Retrieves a pointer to a translation value. This translation value is needed for the following values.

Value	Description
\\StringFileInfo\\<*translation value*>\\CompanyName	Retrieves a pointer to a string containing the name of the company that created the file.
\\StringFileInfo\\<*translation value*>\\FileDescription	Retrieves a pointer to a string containing a description of the file.
\\StringFileInfo\\<*translation value*>\\FileVersion	Retrieves a pointer to a string containing the file version number.
\\StringFileInfo\\<*translation value*>\\InternalName	Retrieves a pointer to a string containing the internal name of the file.
\\StringFileInfo\\<*translation value*>\\LegalCopyright	Retrieves a pointer to a string containing the legal copyright of the company that created the file, if any.
\\StringFileInfo\\<*translation value*>\\LegalTrademarks	Retrieves a pointer to a string containing the legal trademarks of the company that created the file, if any.
\\StringFileInfo\\<*translation value*>\\OriginalFilename	Retrieves a pointer to a string containing the original name of the file.
\\StringFileInfo\\<*translation value*>\\ProductName	Retrieves a pointer to a string containing the name of the product to which the file belongs.
\\StringFileInfo\\<*translation value*>\\ProductVersion	Retrieves a pointer to a string containing the version of the product to which the file belongs.
\\StringFileInfo\\<*translation value*>\\Comments	Retrieves a pointer to a string containing any comments about the file.

The TVSFixedFileInfo data structure is defined as:

```
TVSFixedFileInfo = packed record
    dwSignature: DWORD;           {the data structure signature}
    dwStrucVersion: DWORD;        {the data structure version}
    dwFileVersionMS: DWORD;       {most significant 32 bits of the file version}
    dwFileVersionLS: DWORD;       {least significant 32 bits of the file version}
    dwProductVersionMS: DWORD;    {most significant 32 bits of the product
                                      version}
    dwProductVersionLS: DWORD;    {least significant 32 bits of the product
                                      version}
    dwFileFlagsMask: DWORD;       {bitmask representing valid version
                                      attributes}
    dwFileFlags: DWORD;           {version attribute flags}
    dwFileOS: DWORD;              {file operating system type}
    dwFileType: DWORD;            {file type flags}
    dwFileSubtype: DWORD;         {file subtype flags}
    dwFileDateMS: DWORD;          {most significant 32 bits of the file date}
    dwFileDateLS: DWORD;          {least significant 32 bits of the file date}
end;
```

dwSignature: Always contains the value $FEEF04BD.

dwStrucVersion: Specifies the version number of this structure, where the high-order word indicates the major version number and the low-order word indicates the minor version number.

dwFileVersionMS: Specifies the most significant 32 bits of the file's version number. This value can be combined with the value of the dwFileVersionLS member to obtain the full 64-bit file version number.

dwFileVersionLS: Specifies the least significant 32 bits of the file's version number. This value can be combined with the value of the dwFileVersionMS member to obtain the full 64-bit file version number.

dwProductVersionMS: Specifies the most significant 32 bits of the version number of the product to which this file belongs. This value can be combined with the value of the dwProductVersionLS member to obtain the full 64-bit product version number.

dwProductVersionLS: Specifies the least significant 32 bits of the version number of the product to which this file belongs. This value can be combined with the value of the dwProductVersionMS member to obtain the full 64-bit product version number.

dwFileFlagsMask: A bitmask indicating which bits of the dwFileFlags member are valid.

dwFileFlags: A series of bit flags indicating various attributes of the file. This member can contain one or more flags from Table 12-20.

dwFileOS: Specifies the operating system for which this file was designed to operate on. This member can be one value from Table 12-21.

dwFileType: Indicates the file type. This member can be one value from Table 12-22.

dwFileSubtype: Indicates the function of the file. This value is dependent on the value of the dwFileType member, and can be one value from Table 12-23. For any values of dwFileType not listed in the table, dwFileSubtype will contain zero. If the dwFileType parameter contains VFT_VXD, dwFileSubtype will contain the virtual device identifier.

dwFileDateMS: Specifies the most significant 32 bits of the file's date and time stamp.

dwFileDateLS: Specifies the least significant 32 bits of the file's date and time stamp.

Table 12-20: VerQueryValue TVSFixedFileInfo.dwFileFlags Values

Value	Description
VS_FF_DEBUG	The file contains debug information and was compiled with debug features enabled.
VS_FF_PRERELEASE	The file is a development version, and is not meant for public distribution.

Value	Description
VS_FF_PATCHED	The file has been modified and is not identical to the original shipping version.
VS_FF_PRIVATEBUILD	The file was not built using standard release procedures, and is intended for internal use only.
VS_FF_INFOINFERRED	The file's version information was created dynamically and some of the information in this structure may be incomplete or incorrect.
VS_FF_SPECIALBUILD	The file was built using standard release procedures, but it is a variation of the normal shipping version of the file.

Table 12-21: VerQueryValue TVSFixedFileInfo.dwFileOS Values

Value	Description
VOS_UNKNOWN	The file was designed for an unknown operating system.
VOS_NT	The file was designed for use under Windows NT.
VOS_WINDOWS32	The file was designed for use under the Win32 API.
VOS_DOS_WINDOWS32	The file was designed for use under the Win32 API running on MS-DOS.
VOS_NT_WINDOWS32	The file was designed for use under the Win32 API running on Windows NT.

Table 12-22: VerQueryValue TVSFixedFileInfo.dwFileType Values

Value	Description
VFT_UNKNOWN	The file type is unknown.
VFT_APP	The file is an application.
VFT_DLL	The file is a dynamic link library.
VFT_DRV	The file contains a device driver.
VFT_FONT	The file contains a font.
VFT_VXD	The file contains a virtual device driver.
VFT_STATIC_LIB	The file contains a static link library.

Table 12-23: VerQueryValue TVSFixedFileInfo.dwFileSubtype Values

Value of dwFileType	Value	Description
VFT_DRV	VFT2_UNKNOWN	The driver type is unknown.
VFT_DRV	VFT2_DRV_PRINTER	The file contains a printer driver.
VFT_DRV	VFT2_DRV_KEYBOARD	The file contains a keyboard driver.
VFT_DRV	VFT2_DRV_LANGUAGE	The file contains a language driver.
VFT_DRV	VFT2_DRV_DISPLAY	The file contains a display driver.
VFT_DRV	VFT2_DRV_MOUSE	The file contains a mouse driver.
VFT_DRV	VFT2_DRV_NETWORK	The file contains a network driver.

Value of dwFileType	Value	Description
VFT_DRV	VFT2_DRV_SYSTEM	The file contains a system driver.
VFT_DRV	VFT2_DRV_INSTALLABLE	The file contains an installable driver.
VFT_DRV	VFT2_DRV_SOUND	The file contains a sound driver.
VFT_FONT	VFT2_UNKNOWN	The font type is unknown.
VFT_FONT	VFT2_FONT_RASTER	The file contains a raster font.
VFT_FONT	VFT2_FONT_VECTOR	The file contains a vector font.
VFT_FONT	VFT2_FONT_TRUETYPE	The file contains a TrueType font.

WriteFile *Windows.Pas*

Syntax

```
WriteFile(
hFile: THandle;                       {a handle to an open file}
const Buffer;                         {the buffer containing the data to be written}
nNumberOfBytesToWrite: DWORD;         { the number of bytes to write to the file}
var lpNumberOfBytesWritten:           {receives the number of bytes actually
      DWORD;                                written}
lpOverlapped: POverlapped             {a pointer to a TOverLapped structure}
): BOOL;                              {returns TRUE or FALSE}
```

Description

This function writes the number of bytes specified by the nNumberOfBytesToWrite parameter to the file associated with the handle specified in the hFile parameter. These bytes come from the buffer pointed to by the Buffer parameter. The origin of the write operation within the file is dependent upon how the file was opened and the value of the lpOverlapped parameter. Typically, the lpOverlapped parameter contains NIL, and the write operation begins at the current file pointer. After the write operation has completed, the file pointer is incremented by the number of bytes written, unless the file was opened with the FILE_FLAG_OVERLAPPED flag specified. In this case, the file pointer is not incremented, and the application must move the file pointer explicitly. The write operation will fail if it attempts to write to any part of a file that has been locked with the LockFile function. The application must not access the buffer pointed to by the Buffer parameter until the write operation has completed.

Parameters

hFile: A handle to the file being read. This file must have been opened with the GENERIC_WRITE flag specified. Note that Windows 95 does not support asynchronous writes on disk-based files.

Buffer: A pointer to a buffer containing the information to be written to the specified file.

nNumberOfBytesToWrite: Specifies the number of bytes to be written to the file.

lpNumberOfBytesWritten: A pointer to a double word receiving the number of bytes actually written to the file. This variable is initialized to zero before the function starts the write. This parameter must contain a pointer if the lpOverlapped parameter is set to NIL.

lpOverlapped: A pointer to a TOverlapped data structure. If the file identified by the hFile parameter was opened with the FILE_FLAG_OVERLAPPED flag specified, this parameter must contain a pointer. If the file was opened with the FILE_FLAG_OVERLAPPED flag specified, the write operation begins at the offset specified within the structure, and WriteFile may return before the write operation has completed. In this case, WriteFile will return FALSE, and GetLastError will return ERROR_IO_PENDING. The event specified in the TOverlapped structure will be signaled upon completing the read operation. If the file was not opened with the FILE_FLAG_OVERLAPPED flag specified and this parameter is not NIL, the write operation begins at the offset specified within the structure, and WriteFile does not return until the write operation is completed. If the file was not opened with the FILE_FLAG_OVERLAPPED flag specified and this parameter is NIL, the write operation begins at the current file pointer and does not return until the write operation is complete. The TOverlapped data structure is defined as:

```
TOverlapped = record
    Internal: DWORD;          {reserved for internal use}
    InternalHigh: DWORD;      {reserved for internal use}
    Offset: DWORD;            {specifies the file position from which to start}
    OffsetHigh: DWORD;        {the high-order double word of the starting offset}
    hEvent: THandle;          {a handle to an event object}
end;
```

Please see the ReadFile function for a description of this data structure.

Return Value

If the function succeeds, it returns TRUE; otherwise it returns FALSE. To get extended error information, call the GetLastError function.

See also

CreateFile, LockFile, ReadFile, SetEndOfFile, UnlockFile

Example

Please see Listing 12-4 under CreateFile.

Chapter 13

String and Atom Functions

Although the Object Pascal runtime library provides a rich set of string manipulation and formatting routines, Windows provides a set of equivalent functions that are useful when dealing with internationalization. The Windows functions also give the application access to internal string tables used in reporting error messages. In addition, Windows provides a simple mechanism for sharing string information between processes.

Atom Tables

Windows applications can store strings of up to 255 characters in what is called an atom table. Each process has access to the global atom table and its own local atom table. The global atom table has a maximum of 37 entries and is shared with other processes. The local atom table is private to the process. The local atom has a default maximum size of 37 entries, but that maximum can be increased when it is created with the InitAtomTable function. The string is added to the atom table by using either the AddAtom or GlobalAddAtom functions, and deleted from the table with the Delete-Atom or GlobalDeleteAtom functions. When a string is added to the atom table, the returned value is an atom number that uniquely defines that string within the appropriate table.

Atom tables are normally used to store strings. However, they can also be used to store 16-bit integers. The same functions are used to store integers and strings, but the integer data for the atom table should be given as MakeIntAtom(integer value). MakeIntAtom is a Windows macro which produces a pointer to a null-terminated string that is compatible with the AddAtom and GlobalAddAtom functions. From there the data is treated as a string. The atom numbers for integer storage will be in the range 0 to 49151 ($0001 to $BFFF) while atom numbers for string storage will be in the range 49152 to 65535 ($C000 to $FFFF). The atom number zero is used as an error flag.

The most common use of the global atom table is for sharing string data in DDE applications. Rather than passing strings of data, the calling application stores the string in the global atom table and then passes only the 16-bit atom number. The DDE server can then look up the string in the global atom table using the atom number. This technique could also be used to share string data between regular applications by passing the atom number as a parameter inside a user-defined Windows message.

The local atom table exists for the duration of the process. When a process is terminated, the atom table is destroyed. The global atom table exists as long as Windows is running, and is not reset until Windows is restarted. Atoms in the global atom table remain there even after the process that stored it is terminated.

It is a good idea to always remove atoms from the atom tables when finished with them. This applies to both the global and the local atom tables. Since there are limits on the size of the global atom table and also by default for the local atom table (37 entries), it is wise to use the space sparingly and only as long as needed. There may be other applications with entries in the global atom table, so the limit for an application will often be less than 37.

Every atom in both atom tables is reference counted. If the AddAtom or GlobalAddAtom functions make an attempt to add a string to the atom table which is already there, a new entry in the table is not made. The reference count for the existing entry will be incremented and the existing string's unique atom number is returned as the result. When an atom is added that did not previously exist, a new entry is made and the reference count for the new atom is set to one. The DeleteAtom and GlobalDeleteAtom functions decrement the reference count by one, test it, and if it is found to be zero then the atom table entry is deleted. The sole exception to this rule is integer atoms. Integers stored in atom tables do not use reference counts. The deletion functions will delete the integer value from the atom table immediately. Unfortunately, there is no direct way to determine the reference count of an atom. In order to ensure that an atom was deleted from the atom table, the application should continually delete the atom using either the DeleteAtom or GlobalDeleteAtom functions until the function fails. An application should only delete atoms that it placed into the atom tables. Never delete an atom that was placed in the atom tables by other processes.

String Conversions

Several of the string functions involve converting characters to uppercase or lowercase. This processing is valid for either single-byte character structures (ANSI) or two-byte character formats (Unicode). For Windows 95 the case conversions and tests are made using the default locale set in the control panel. This could have been set at the time Windows was installed, or can be altered later. For Windows NT, the conversions and tests are made based on the language driver selected in the control panel or at Windows setup. If no language is selected, Windows NT makes the conversion based on the default mapping of the code page for the process locale.

String Formatting

GetDateFormat, GetTimeFormat, FormatMessage, and wvsprintf are functions which provide very powerful string formatting capabilities. They provide access to system data and message resources, and give output that is interpreted within the context of specified locales. These functions provide a rich mixture of options and capabilities. There is a significant overlap of functionality with the formatting functions in Delphi's Object Pascal and the VCL. However, knowledge of these functions will be useful when designing Delphi applications for international flexibility.

String and Atom Functions

The following string and atom functions are covered in this chapter:

Table 13-1: String and Atom Functions

Function	Description
AddAtom	Adds an atom to the local atom table.
CharLower	Converts characters to lowercase.
CharLowerBuff	Converts a range of characters to lowercase.
CharNext	Increments a pointer to the next character in the string.
CharPrev	Decrements a pointer to the previous character in the string.
CharToOem	Converts characters to the OEM character set.
CharToOemBuff	Converts a range of characters to the OEM character set.
CharUpper	Converts characters to uppercase.
CharUpperBuff	Converts a range of characters to uppercase.
CompareString	Compares two strings.
DeleteAtom	Deletes an atom from a local atom table.
EnumSystemCodePages	Lists available and installed system code pages.
EnumSystemLocales	Lists available system locales.
FindAtom	Finds an atom in the local atom table.
FormatMessage	Formats a string with arguments.
GetACP	Retrieves the current ANSI code page for the system.
GetAtomName	Retrieves an atom string from the local atom table.
GetCPInfo	Retrieves code page information.
GetDateFormat	Retrieves the date in the specified format.
GetOEMCP	Retrieves the current Original Equipment Manufacturer code page for the system.
GetTimeFormat	Retrieves the time in the specified format.
GlobalAddAtom	Adds an atom to the global atom table.
GlobalDeleteAtom	Deletes an atom from the global atom table.
GlobalFindAtom	Finds an atom in the global atom table.

Function	Description
GlobalGetAtomName	Retrieves an atom string from the global atom table.
InitAtomTable	Initializes the size of the local atom table.
IsCharAlpha	Determines if a character is an alphabetic character.
IsCharAlphaNumeric	Determines if a character is alphanumeric.
IsCharLower	Determines if a character is lowercase.
IsCharUpper	Determines if a character is uppercase.
lstrcat	Concatenates two null-terminated strings.
lstrcmp	Compares two null-terminated strings, case sensitive.
lstrcmpi	Compares two null-terminated strings, case insensitive.
lstrcpy	Copies one null-terminated string into another.
lstrlen	Retrieves the length of a null-terminated string.
MakeIntAtom	Creates an integer atom.
OemToChar	Converts a character from the OEM character set to ANSI.
OemToCharBuff	Converts a range of characters from the OEM character set to ANSI.
ToAscii	Translates a virtual key code into a Windows character.
wvsprintf	Formats a string with supplied arguments.

AddAtom *Windows.Pas*

Syntax

```
AddAtom(
lpString: PChar                {the string to add to atom table}
): ATOM;                       {returns the newly added atom}
```

Description

This function adds the specified string to the local atom table and returns the atom number. The string can be no longer than 255 characters. If the string already exists in the table, its reference count is incremented. This local atom table is local to the process only and is not shared with other processes.

Local atom tables have a default size of 37 entries. This maximum size can be increased when the local atom table is created. If the string has 255 or fewer characters and the AddAtom function still fails, the most likely cause would be that the table is full.

Parameters

lpString: A pointer to a null-terminated string to be added to the local atom table.

Return Value

If the function succeeds, it returns the atom number for the string that was added to the local atom table. The atom value is a 16-bit number in the range 49152 to 65535 ($C000 to $FFFF) for strings or in the range 1 to 49151 ($0001 to $BFFF) for integers. If the function fails, it returns zero. To get extended error information, call the GetLastError function.

See also

DeleteAtom, FindAtom, GetAtomName, GlobalAddAtom, GlobalDeleteAtom, GlobalFindAtom, GlobalGetAtomName, MakeIntAtom.

Example

Listing 13-1: Adding a String to the Local Atom Table

```
procedure TForm1.FormCreate(Sender: TObject);
begin
  {create an atom table for 200 possible atoms}
  InitAtomTable(200);
end;

procedure TForm1.Button1Click(Sender: TObject);
var
  MyAtom: Atom;          // the returned atom number
  TextTest: PChar;       // string for search result
  AtomTest: Atom;        // atom number from search results
begin
  {store string in local atom table}
  MyAtom := AddAtom(PChar(Edit1.Text));

  {search the table for atom number, given the string}
  AtomTest := FindAtom(PChar(Edit1.Text));
  Label1.Caption := 'Search by text, atom number: '+IntToStr(Atomtest);

  {search by atom number to get the string}
  TextTest := StrAlloc(256);
  GetAtomName(MyAtom,Texttest,256);
  Label2.Caption := 'Search by atom number, text: '+string(TextTest);

  {always clean up entries}
  DeleteAtom(MyAtom);
end;
```

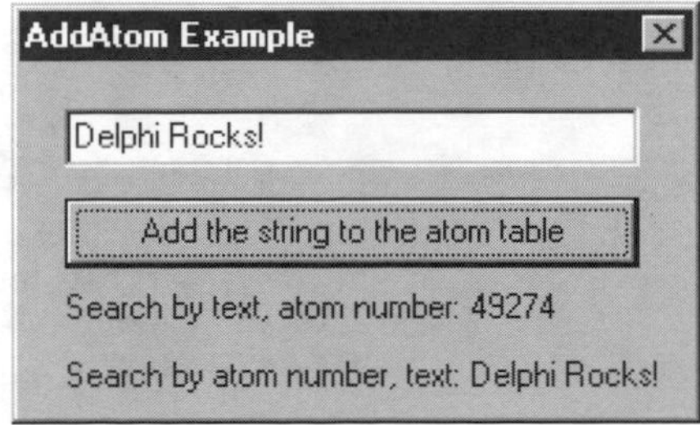

Figure 13-1: The atom.

CharLower Windows.Pas

Syntax

CharLower(
lpsz: PChar {a pointer to the character or string to convert}
): PChar; {returns a pointer to the converted character or string}

Description

This function converts a single character or every character in a null-terminated string to lowercase. Under Windows NT, the function uses the currently selected language driver for the conversion; under Windows 95, the conversion is based on the default locale.

Parameters

lpsz: A pointer to the null-terminated string to convert. For single-character conversion, load the character into the lower word of lpsz and set the upper 16 bits to zero. CharLower firsts tests the upper word of the lpsz parameter to determine whether the parameter should be interpreted as a character or as a pointer. In Delphi, the parameter can be typecast as an "array of char" with the single-byte character loaded into the first array element.

Return Value

This function returns either a single character in the lower word and the upper word is zero, or a pointer to the null-terminated string containing the converted string. This function does not indicate an error upon failure.

See also

CharLowerBuff, CharUpper, CharUpperBuff

Example

Listing 13-2: Converting Characters and Strings to Lowercase

```
procedure TForm1.Button1Click(Sender: TObject);
type
  CharArray= array[1..4] of char;
var
  MyString: Pchar;        // a pointer to the string
  StartLoc: Pchar;        // the start of the string
  NumChars: Integer;      // the number of characters in the string
  MyChar: Char;           // a single character
begin
  MyString := 'This is a STRING.';
  Label1.Caption := string(MyString);

  StartLoc := CharNext(MyString);          // do not convert first letter.
  StartLoc := CharLower(StartLoc);         // converts to lowercase.
  Label2.Caption := string(MyString);      //  Displays: This is a string.
```

```
  StartLoc := CharNext(StartLoc);            // skip another character
  NumChars := CharUpperBuff(StartLoc, 5);    // puts "is is" to uppercase.
  Label3.Caption := string(MyString);        // Displays:  ThIS IS a string.

  NumChars := strlen(MyString);
  NumChars := CharLowerBuff(MyString,NumChars);
  Label4.Caption := string(MyString);        // Displays:   this is a string.

  StartLoc := CharPrev(MyString, StartLoc);  // point to prev character
  StartLoc := CharPrev(MyString, StartLoc);  // points to start of string
  NumChars := CharUpperBuff(StartLoc, 4);    // converts  "this" to upper
  Label5.Caption := string(MyString);        // Displays:  THIS is a string.

  StartLoc := CharUpper(StartLoc);
  Label6.Caption := string(MyString);        // Displays:  THIS IS A STRING.

  MyChar := 'z';                             // assign as lowercase
  ZeroMemory(@StartLoc,4);                   // prepare variable with zeroes.
  CharArray(StartLoc)[1] := MyChar;          // load character
  StartLoc := CharUpper(StartLoc);           // convert character
  MyChar := CharArray(StartLoc)[1];          // put it back
  MoveMemory(MyString, @MyChar, 1);          // put it in the string.
  Label7.Caption := string(MyString);        // Displays:  ZHIS IS A STRING.

  StartLoc := CharLower(StartLoc);           // convert character
  MyChar := CharArray(StartLoc)[1];          // put it back again
  MoveMemory(MyString, @MyChar, 1);          // put it in the string.
  Label8.Caption := string(MyString);        // Displays: zHIS IS A STRING.
end;
```

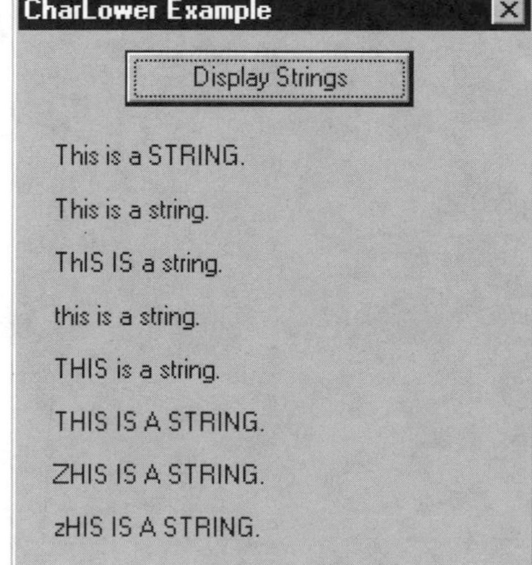

Figure 13-2: The lowercase converted strings.

CharLowerBuff Windows.Pas

Syntax

```
CharLowerBuff(
lpsz: PChar;                    {a pointer to the string to convert}
cchLength: DWORD                {the number of characters to convert}
): DWORD;                       {returns the number of characters processed}
```

Description

CharLowerBuff converts a specified number of characters in the string pointed to by the lpsz parameter to lowercase. Under Windows NT, the function uses the currently selected language driver for the conversion; under Windows 95, the conversion is based on the default locale. With this function it is possible to convert only a portion of a string by pointing the lpsz parameter to the starting position to convert, and giving the number of characters to convert in the cchLength parameter. The lpsz parameter does not have to point to the beginning of the string, and the cchLength parameter does not have to reflect the true length of the string.

Parameters

lpsz: A pointer to the null-terminated string that is to be converted to lowercase.

cchLength: Indicates the number of characters to convert. If the string is a Unicode string, then this count is the number of wide (two-byte) character positions. This function will travel past a null character if the cchLength value is larger than the length of the string.

Return Value

If this function succeeds, it returns the number of characters that were processed; otherwise it returns zero.

See also

CharLower, CharUpper, CharUpperBuff

Example

Please see Listing 13-2 under CharLower.

CharNext Windows.Pas

Syntax

```
CharNext(
lpsz: PChar                     {a pointer to the current character}
): PChar;                       {returns a pointer to the next character}
```

Description

This function increments the specified pointer to the next character in the string.

Parameters

lpsz: A pointer to the specified character in a null-terminated string.

Return Value

If the function succeeds, it returns a pointer to the next character in a string following the character pointed to by the lpsz parameter. The return value will point to the null terminator if lpsz is already at the end of the string. If the function fails, it returns the lpsz parameter.

See also

CharPrev

Example

Please see Listing 13-2 under CharLower.

CharPrev Windows.Pas

Syntax

```
CharPrev(
lpszStart: PChar;          {a pointer to the start of a string}
lpszCurrent: PChar         {a pointer to the current character}
): PChar;                  {returns a pointer to the previous character}
```

Description

This function returns a pointer to the previous character in the string pointed to by the lpszCurrent parameter.

Parameters

lpszStart: A pointer to the beginning of a string. This is provided so that CharPrev can tell if the lpszCurrent parameter is already at the beginning of the string.

lpszCurrent: A pointer to the current character.

Return Value

If this function succeeds, it returns a pointer to the character prior to the one pointed to by the lpszCurrent parameter. It will point to the beginning of the string if the lpszStart parameter is equal to lpszCurrent. If the function fails, it returns the lpszCurrent parameter.

See also

CharNext

Example

Please see Listing 13-2 under CharLower.

CharToOem Windows.Pas

Syntax

CharToOem(	
lpszSrc: PChar;	{a pointer to the string to translate}
lpszDst: PChar	{a pointer to the translated string}
): BOOL;	{always returns TRUE}

Description

CharToOem translates each character in the given string into the OEM-defined character set.

Parameters

lpszSrc: A pointer to the source string that is to be translated to an OEM character set string.

lpszDst: A pointer to the destination translated string. If the character set is ANSI (single-byte characters), then the source and destination strings can be the same string. In this case, the translation will be performed in place. If the character set is Unicode (double-byte characters), there must be a separate buffer for lpszDst.

Return Value

This function always returns TRUE.

See also

CharToOemBuff, OemToChar, OemToCharBuff

Example

Listing 13-3: Converting Characters to the OEM Character Set and Back

```
procedure TForm1.Button1Click(Sender: TObject);
var
  KeyedIn: PChar;                  // points to input string
  OEMstr: PChar;                   // OEM character set version
  ANSIstr: PChar;                  // ANSI character set version
  OEMbuff: array[1..100] of Char;  // string space
  ANSIbuff: array[1..100] of Char;
begin
  {point PChars to string space}
```

```
  OEMstr := @OEMbuff;
  ANSIstr := @ANSIbuff;
  KeyedIn := 'My String Data - ÀÊÎÕÜ';
  Label1.Caption := string(KeyedIn);

  {CharToOem converts string to OEM character set}
  CharToOem(KeyedIn, OEMstr);
  Label2.Caption := string(OEMstr);

  {CharToOemBff is the counted character version}
  CharToOemBuff(KeyedIn, OEMstr, StrLen(KeyedIn));
  Label3.Caption := string(OEMstr);

  {convert from OEM character set to ANSI characters}
  OemToChar(OemStr, ANSIstr);
  Label4.Caption := string(ANSIstr);

  {OemToCharBuff is the counted character version}
  OemToCharBuff(OemStr, ANSIStr, StrLen(OemStr));
  Label5.Caption := string(ANSIstr);
end;
```

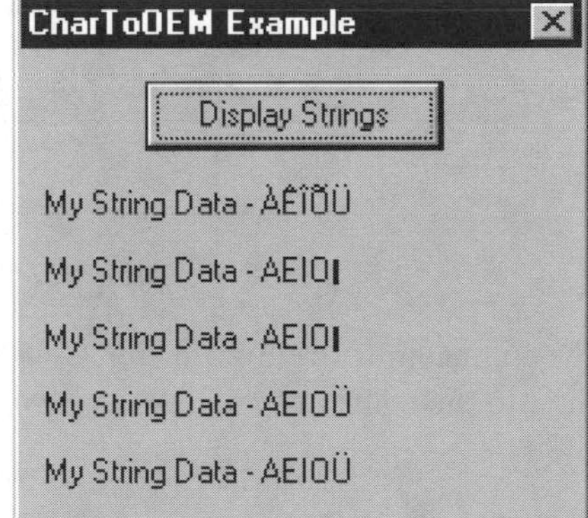

Figure 13-3: The converted characters.

CharToOemBuff   *Windows.Pas*

Syntax

CharToOemBuff(	
lpszSrc: PChar;	{a pointer to the string to translate}
lpszDst: Pchar;	{a pointer to the translated string}
cchDstLength: DWORD	{the number of characters to translate}
): BOOL;	{returns TRUE}

Description

CharToOemBuff translates the specified number of characters in the given string into the OEM-defined character set.

Parameters

lpszSrc: A pointer to the source string that is to be translated.

lpszDst: A pointer to the destination translated string. If the character set is ANSI (single-byte characters), then the source and destination strings can be the same string. In this case, the translation will be performed in place. If the character set is Unicode (double-byte characters), there must be a separate buffer for lpszDst.

cchDstLength: The number of characters to translate. If the character set is Unicode (double-byte characters), then this is the number of byte pairs (single characters) that will be translated in the destination string.

Return Value

This function always returns TRUE.

See also

CharToOem, OemToChar, OemToCharBuff

Example

Please see Listing 13-3 under CharToOem.

CharUpper Windows.Pas

Syntax

```
CharUpper(
lpsz: PChar          {a pointer to the character or string to convert}
): PChar;            {returns a pointer to the converted character or string}
```

Description

This function converts a single character or every character in a null-terminated string to uppercase. Under Windows NT, the function uses the currently selected language driver for the conversion; under Windows 95, the conversion is based on the default locale.

Parameters

lpsz: A pointer to the null-terminated string to convert. For single-character conversion, load the character into the lower word of lpsz and set the upper 16 bits to zero. Char-Upper first tests the upper word of the lpsz parameter to determine whether the parameter should be interpreted as a character or as a pointer. In Delphi, the parameter can be typecast as an "array of char" with the single-byte character loaded into the first array element.

Return Value

This function returns either a single character in the lower word and the upper word is zero, or a pointer to the null-terminated string containing the converted string. This function does not indicate an error upon failure.

See also

CharLower, CharLowerBuff, CharUpperBuff

Example

Please see Listing 13-2 under CharLower.

CharUpperBuff Windows.Pas

Syntax

```
CharUpperBuff(
lpsz: PChar;                {a pointer to the string to convert}
cchLength: DWORD            {the number of characters to convert}
): DWORD;                   {returns the number of characters processed}
```

Description

CharUpperBuff converts a specified number of characters in the string pointed to by the lpsz parameter to uppercase. Under Windows NT, the function uses the currently selected language driver for the conversion; under Windows 95, the conversion is based on the default locale. With this function it is possible to convert only a portion of a string by pointing the lpsz variable to the starting position to convert, and giving the number of characters to convert in the cchLength parameter. The lpsz parameter does not have to point to the beginning of the string, and the cchLength parameter does not have to reflect the true length of the string.

Parameters

lpsz: A pointer to the null-terminated string that is to be converted to uppercase.

cchLength: Indicates the number of characters to convert. If the string is a Unicode string, then this count is the number of wide (two-byte) character positions. This function will travel past a null character if the cchLength value is larger than the length of the string.

Return Value

If this function succeeds, it returns the number of characters that were processed; otherwise it returns zero.

See also

CharLower, CharLowerBuff, CharUpper

Example

Please see Listing 13-2 under CharLower.

CompareString Windows.Pas

Syntax

```
CompareString(
Locale: LCID;                    {the locale ID}
dwCmpFlags: DWORD;               {options for the comparison}
lpString1: Pchar;                {a pointer to the first string}
cchCount1: Integer;              {the size in characters of the first string}
lpString2: PChar;                {a pointer to the second string}
cchCount2: Integer               {the size in characters of the second string}
): Integer;                      {returns a comparison result code}
```

Description

CompareString performs a comparison of two strings based on the specified locale. The return value of 2 specifies that the two strings are equal in a lexical sense according to the specified flags even though it is possible for the strings to be different. If the strings are of different length but are compared as lexically equal up to the length of the shortest string, then the longer string will be specified as the greater in the comparison.

If the SORT_STRINGSORT flag is not specified in the dwCmpFlags parameter, the sort will ignore the hyphen and apostrophe characters. This means that "IT'S" will be equal to "ITS," and "DON'T" will be equal to "DONT." Some words might be spelled with an optional hyphen. This default behavior assures that the presence of the hyphen or apostrophe will not affect the ordering of strings in a list. For a stricter character-based sort, use the SORT_STRINGSORT flag. This flag treats the hyphen and apostrophe characters in their normal collating sequence.

In determining which sort function to use, note that CompareString has the availability of using the SORT_STRINGSORT option, where lstrcmp and lstrcmpi will always ignore hyphen and apostrophe characters when comparing strings.

In Arabic character sets, CompareString will ignore the Arabic Kashidas. This is equivalent to ignoring the hyphen and apostrophe characters if the SORT_STRINGSORT flag is not set. However, there is no option for determining whether or not the Arabic Kashidas will be ignored. They will always be ignored in Arabic character sets.

For fastest execution set the cchCount1 and cchCount2 parameters to –1 and set the dwCmpFlags parameter to either zero or to NORM_IGNORECASE.

Parameters

Locale: The locale identifier which provides the basis for the comparison. This parameter can be one value from Table 13-2.

dwCmpFlags: Flags which determine how the comparison will be made. This parameter can be set to zero to indicate default string comparison, or it can be set to any combination of values from Table 13-3.

lpString1: A pointer to the first string to compare.

cchCount1: Specifies the length of the first string in characters (single bytes for ANSI, double bytes for Unicode). If this value is –1 then CompareString will take the null terminator as the end of the string.

lpString2: A pointer to the second string to compare.

cchCount2: Specifies the length of the second string in characters (single bytes for ANSI, double bytes for Unicode). If this value is –1 then CompareString will take the null terminator as the end of the string.

Return Value

If the function succeeds, the return value will be one of the three comparison return codes in Table 13-4. If the function fails, it returns zero. To get extended error information, call the GetLastError function.

See also

GetSystemDefaultLCID, GetUserDefaultLCID, lstrcmp, lstrcmpi

Example

Listing 13-4: Using CompareString to Perform a Sort

```
procedure TForm1.Button1Click(Sender: TObject);
var
  L1: array[1..5] of PChar;  // data to sort
  Ltemp: PChar;              // temp for sort swapping
  Xsort,Xloop: Integer;      // loop counters for sort
  CompareResult: Integer;    // result of CompareString
  CompareFlags: DWORD;       // flags parameter
  CompareLocale: LCID;       // locale parameter
begin
  {define some data for sorting}
  L1[1] := 'abc-e';
  L1[2] := 'abcde';
  L1[3] := 'aBcd ';
  L1[4] := 'ab cd';
  L1[5] := 'a''bc ';

  {display the initial strings}
  for Xloop := 1 to 5 do
    ListBox1.Items.Add(string(L1[Xloop]));

  {pause}
  Application.ProcessMessages;
  Sleep(2000);

  {define flags to specify collation (sort) order}
```

```
  CompareFlags := NORM_IGNORECASE
              and SORT_STRINGSORT
              and NORM_IGNORENONSPACE;

  CompareLocale := LOCALE_USER_DEFAULT;

  {do a simplified bubblesort}
  for Xloop := 1 to 4 do
  for Xsort := 1 to 4 do begin
    CompareResult := CompareString(CompareLocale,
                     CompareFlags,
                     L1[Xsort],
                     -1,       // entire length of string
                     L1[Succ(Xsort)],
                     -1);      // entire length of string
    if CompareResult = 0 then begin    // error condition
      ShowMessage('CompareString error!');
      exit;
    end;
    if CompareResult = 3 then begin    // first > second
      {perform a swap}
      Ltemp := L1[xsort];
      L1[Xsort] := l1[Succ(Xsort)];
      L1[Succ(Xsort)] := Ltemp;
    end;
  end;

  {display the results}
  ListBox1.Clear;
  for Xloop := 1 to 5 do
    ListBox1.Items.Add(string(L1[Xloop]));

  // produces a list:
  // ab cd /  a'bc  /  aBcd  /  abcde  /  abc-e
  // these were interpreted with the above options as
  // ab cd /  abc   /  abcd  /  abcde  /  abce
  // spaces are interpreted as spaces
  // apostrophes and hyphens are deleted (ignored).
end;
```

Figure 13-4: The sorted strings.

Listing 13-5: Comparing Two Strings for Equality

```
procedure TForm1.Button1Click(Sender: TObject);
var
  MyResult: Integer;
begin
  {compare the strings}
  MyResult := CompareString(LOCALE_USER_DEFAULT,
                            NORM_IGNORECASE,
                            PChar(Edit1.Text),
                            -1,
                            PChar(Edit2.Text),
                            -1);
  if MyResult = 1 then
  begin   // first parameter is greater
    Label1.Caption := 'SMALLER';
    Label2.Caption := 'GREATER';
    Label3.Caption := '<';
  end;
  if MyResult = 2 then
  begin
    Label1.Caption := ' equal ';
    Label2.Caption := ' equal ';
    Label3.Caption := '=';
  end;
  if MyResult = 3 then
  begin
    Label1.Caption := 'GREATER';
    Label2.Caption := 'SMALLER';
    Label3.Caption := '>';
  end;
  if MyResult = 0 then
    ShowMessage('Error in CompareString');
end;
```

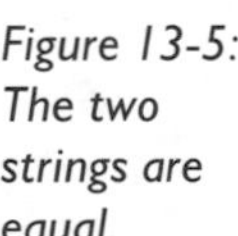
Figure 13-5: The two strings are equal.

Table 13-2: CompareString Locale Values

Value	Description
LOCALE_SYSTEM_DEFAULT	The system's default locale.
LOCALE_USER_DEFAULT	The user's default locale.

Table 13-3: CompareString dwCmpFlags Values

Value	Description
NORM_IGNORECASE	Ignore uppercase versus lowercase. They are treated as equal if this flag is set.
NORM_IGNOREKANATYPE	The Hiragana and the Katakana characters will be treated as equivalent character sets.
NORM_IGNORENONSPACE	Ignore nonspacing characters.
NORM_IGNORESYMBOLS	Ignore symbols.
NORM_IGNOREWIDTH	Character set width is ignored in the case of comparing an ANSI character string to a Unicode character string. The same character in the ANSI set and Unicode set are regarded as equal.
SORT_STRINGSORT	Punctuation characters are treated as symbols.

Table 13-4: CompareString Return Values

Value	Description
1	The first string is less in value than the second string in lexical comparison.
2	The two strings have equal lexical values according to the flags that are provided.
3	The first string is greater in value than the second string in lexical comparison.

DeleteAtom *Windows.Pas*

Syntax

```
DeleteAtom(
nAtom: ATOM              {the atom number to delete}
): ATOM;                 {returns zero or the nAtom value}
```

Description

DeleteAtom reduces the reference count for the specified atom in the local atom table by one. If the reference count for the specified atom is zero, the entry is deleted from the atom table. To make a deletion from the global atom table, use GlobalDeleteAtom.

Parameters

nAtom: The atom number to delete from the local atom table.

Return Value

If this function succeeds, it returns zero; otherwise it returns the atom number in the nAtom parameter. To get extended error information, call the GetLastError function.

See also

AddAtom, FindAtom, GlobalAddAtom, GlobalDeleteAtom

Example

Please see Listing 13-1 under AddAtom.

EnumSystemCodePages Windows.Pas

Syntax

```
EnumSystemCodePages(
lpCodePageEnumProc: TFNCodepageEnumProc;    {pointer to the callback function}
dwFlags: DWORD                              {code page selection options}
): BOOL;                                    {returns TRUE or FALSE}
```

Description

This function enumerates code pages that are installed or supported by the system. The callback function is called for each code page that is identified as meeting the selection criteria. The callback function receives each code page identifier and can store it programmatically according to the need of the calling routine. The process will continue until all code pages have been processed or the callback function returns zero.

Parameters

lpCodePageEnumProc: The address of the callback function provided by the caller of EnumSystemCodePages. The callback function receives a code page identifier for each installed or supported code page.

dwFlags: Determines which code pages to report to the callback function. This parameter can be one value from Table 13-5.

Return Value

If this function succeeds, it returns TRUE; otherwise it returns FALSE. To get extended error information, call the GetLastError function.

Callback Syntax

```
EnumSystemCodePagesProc(
AnotherCodePage: PChar      {a pointer to a string containing a code page identifier}
): Integer;                 {indicates if enumeration should continue}
```

Description

This callback function is called once for each code page identifier installed or supported by the system, and can perform any desired task.

Parameters

AnotherCodePage: A pointer to a null-terminated string containing a code page identifier.

Return Value

To continue enumeration, the callback function should return one; otherwise it should return zero.

See also

EnumSystemLocales

Example

Listing 13-6: Enumerating the System Code Pages

```
{the callback function prototype}
function EnumCodePageProc(AnotherCodePage: PChar): Integer; stdcall;

implementation

function EnumCodePageProc(AnotherCodePage: PChar):integer;
// callback function is called as many times as there are Code Pages.
// A single call to EnumSystemCodePages triggers the series of callbacks.
begin
  {display the code page}
  CodePages.Memo1.Lines.Add(string(AnotherCodePage));

  {continue enumeration}
  Result := 1;
end;

procedure TCodePages.ButtonExecuteClick(Sender: TObject);
var
  MyFlags: Integer; // parameter specified by Radio Buttons in this example.
begin
  {initialize for enumeration}
  Memo1.Clear;
  MyFlags := CP_SUPPORTED;  // set flags from radio buttons
  if RBinstalled.Checked then MyFlags := CP_INSTALLED;

  {enumerate code pages}
  if not EnumSystemCodePages(@EnumCodePageProc,MyFlags)
    then ShowMessage('Error getting system code pages');

  Label1.Caption := 'CodePages: '+IntToStr(Memo1.Lines.Count);
end;
```

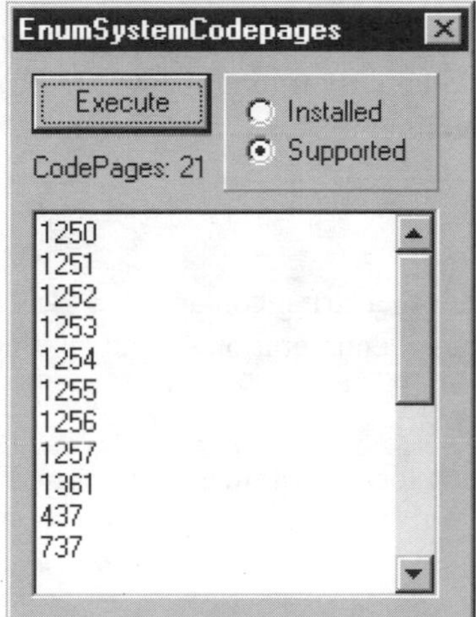

Figure 13-6: The system code page list.

Table 13-5: EnumSystemCodePages dwFlags Values

Value	Description
CP_INSTALLED	Report only code pages which are currently installed.
CP_SUPPORTED	Report all code pages which are supported by the system.

EnumSystemLocales *Windows.Pas*

Syntax

```
EnumSystemLocales(
lpLocaleEnumProc: TFNLocaleEnumProc;    {a pointer to the callback function}
dwFlags: DWORD                          {locale's selection options}
): BOOL;                                {returns TRUE or FALSE}
```

Description

This function enumerates locales that are installed or supported by the system. The callback function is called for each locale that is identified as meeting the selection criteria. The callback function receives each locale identifier and can store it programmatically according to the needs of the calling routine. The process will continue until all locales have been processed or the callback function returns zero.

Parameters

lpLocaleEnumProc: The address of the callback function provided by the caller of EnumSystemLocales. The callback function receives a locale code for each installed or supported locale.

dwFlags: Determine which locales to report to the callback function. This parameter can be one value from Table 13-6.

Return Value

If this function succeeds, it returns TRUE; otherwise it returns FALSE. To get extended error information, call the GetLastError function.

Callback Syntax

EnumSystemLocalesProc(	
AnotherLocale: PChar	{a pointer to a string containing a locale code}
): Integer;	{indicates if enumeration should continue}

Description

This callback function is called once for each locale installed or supported by the system, and can perform any desired task.

Parameters

AnotherLocale: A pointer to a null-terminated string containing a locale code.

Return Value

To continue enumeration, the callback function should return one; otherwise it should return zero.

See also

EnumSystemCodePages

Example

Listing 13-7: Enumerating System Locales

```
{the callback function prototype}
function EnumLocalesProc(AnotherLocale: PChar): Integer; stdcall;

implementation

function EnumLocalesProc(AnotherLocale: PChar): Integer;
// callback function is called for each locale.
// A single call to EnumSystemLocales
//    triggers the series of callbacks.
begin
  {display the locale}
  Locales.Memo1.Lines.Add(AnotherLocale);

  {continue enumeration}
  EnumLocalesProc := 1;
end;

procedure TLocales.ButtonExecuteClick(Sender: TObject);
var
  MyFlags: Integer;
begin
  {initialize for enumeration}
```

```
  Memo1.Clear;
  MyFlags := LCID_INSTALLED;
  if RBsupported.Checked then MyFlags := LCID_SUPPORTED;

  {enumerate the locales}
  if not EnumSystemLocales(@EnumLocalesProc,MyFlags)
    then ShowMessage('Error in getting locales.');

  Label1.Caption := 'Locales: '+IntToStr(Memo1.Lines.Count);
end;
```

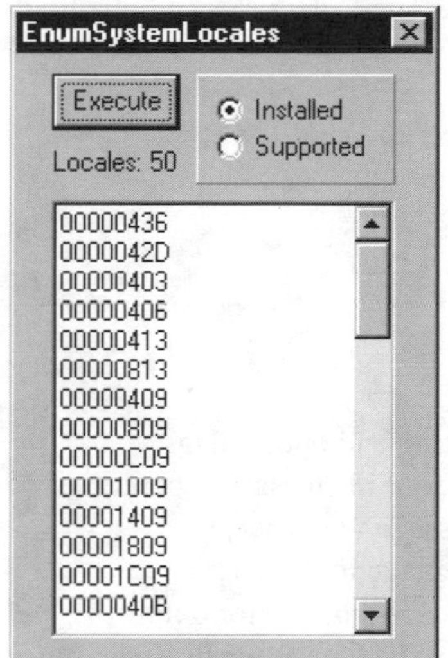

Figure 13-7: The system locales list.

Table 13-6: EnumSystemLocales dwFlags Values

Value	Description
LCID_INSTALLED	Report only locales which are currently installed.
LCID_SUPPORTED	Report all locales which are supported by the system.

FindAtom *Windows.Pas*

Syntax

FindAtom(
lpString: PChar {a pointer to the string to search for in the local atom table}
): ATOM; {returns the atom number for the string}

Description

FindAtom searches the local atom table for the string pointed to by the lpString parameter and returns the atom number if it is found. The string comparison is not case sensitive. To find an atom in the global atom table, use the GlobalFindAtom function.

Parameters

lpString: A pointer to the null-terminated string to search for in the local atom table.

Return Value

If the function succeeds, it returns the atom number for the specified string; otherwise it returns zero. To get extended error information, call the GetLastError function.

See also

AddAtom, DeleteAtom, GlobalAddAtom, GlobalDeleteAtom, GlobalFindAtom

Example

Please see Listing 13-1 under AddAtom.

FormatMessage Windows.Pas

Syntax

```
FormatMessage(
dwFlags: DWORD;                {formatting and option flags}
lpSource: Pointer;             {a pointer to the message source}
dwMessageId: DWORD;            {the message identifier}
dwLanguageId: DWORD;           {the language identifier}
lpBuffer: Pchar;               {a pointer to a buffer for output}
nSize: DWORD;                  {the size of the message buffer in bytes}
Arguments: Pointer             {a pointer to an array of message arguments}
): DWORD;                      {returns the number of bytes stored in the output buffer}
```

Description

FormatMessage prepares a message from a message identifier, a message table, selected language, and a variety of formatting options. It can be used for either system- or user-defined messages. FormatMessage will take the message identifier and search a message table for a suitable message that is available in the selected language. If no language is specified, it will search for a suitable language from a prioritized list of reasonable language alternatives. On finding a message string, it will process it according to the message arguments and copy the result to an output buffer.

If the dwFlags parameter contains the FORMAT_MESSAGE_FROM_STRING flag, the string pointed to by lpSource may contain special codes which designate where arguments are to be placed in the message and how they are to be formatted. The FormatMessage function reads the string, reads the corresponding arguments, and places the formatted result in the output buffer.

Parameters

dwFlags: A set of flags which determine how the FormatMessage function will operate and the meaning of the lpSource parameter. This parameter can contain one or more values from Table 13-7, combined with one value from Table 13-8 by using the Boolean OR operator. The low-order byte of the value of this parameter specifies how the FormatMessage function outputs line breaks, as well as the maximum width of an output line.

lpSource: A pointer to the source of the message. This will be either a module handle or a pointer to a null-terminated string, depending on the flags present in the dwFlags parameter. If neither the FORMAT_MESSAGE_FROM_HMODULE or FORMAT_MESSAGE_FROM_STRING flags are specified, the lpSource parameter is ignored. If the FORMAT_MESSAGE_FROM_STRING flag is specified in the dwFlags parameter, the string pointed to by the lpSource parameter will contain text and format specifiers as listed in Table 13-9.

dwMessageId: The 32-bit message identifier that is used to search a message table. This parameter is ignored if the dwFlags parameter contains the FORMAT_MESSAGE_FROM_STRING flag.

dwLanguageId: The 32-bit language identifier that specifies which language is used when retrieving the message definition from a message resource table. This parameter is ignored if the dwFlags parameter contains the FORMAT_MESSAGE_FROM_STRING flag. If no message is found in the specified language, then the function returns a value of ERROR_RESOURCE_LANG_NOT_FOUND. If this parameter contains zero and the FORMAT_MESSAGE_FROM_STRING flag is not set in the dwFlags parameter, then the function searches for a message definition for a language in the following order of priority.

1. Language neutral message definition, if present.
2. Thread LANGID. This is the language of the thread's locale.
3. User default LANGID. This is the language of the user's default locale.
4. System default LANGID. This is the language of the system's default locale.
5. U.S. English.
6. Any language.

lpBuffer: A pointer to a buffer for the output message. This buffer is prepared by the caller before FormatMessage is called unless the dwFlags parameter contains the FORMAT_MESSAGE_ALLOCATE_BUFFER flag. If this flag is set, then FormatMessage uses LocalAlloc to allocate the required amount of space, storing the buffer's address in the lpBuffer parameter. Note that the FORMAT_MESSAGE_ALLOCATE_BUFFER flag indicates that lpBuffer is a pointer to a pointer to a buffer.

nSize: If the FORMAT_MESSAGE_ALLOCATE_BUFFER flag is present in the dwFlags parameter, nSize specifies the minimum number of bytes to allocate for the output buffer. This allocation is carried out by FormatMessage and deallocated by the caller with LocalFree. If the FORMAT_MESSAGE_ALLOCATE_BUFFER flag is not set, then nSize indicates the maximum size of the output buffer.

Arguments: A pointer to an array of 32-bit arguments that are used to fill in the insertion points in the string pointed to by the lpSource parameter. If this string contains an argument insertion point code (the %n!C-style printf format string! value from Table 13-9), the number indicated by the argument insertion point code indicates which element in the array is used for that code. For example, if the argument insertion point code is "%1", the first element in the array is used; an argument insertion point code of "%2" uses the second element in the array, and so on. The output formatting of the argument will depend on additional codes in the string associated with that argument. If there are no additional formatting codes for an argument, the argument is treated as a PChar.

Return Value

If the function succeeds, it returns the number of bytes copied to the output buffer, excluding the null terminator character. If the function fails, it returns zero. To get extended error information, call the GetLastError function.

See also

LoadString, LocalFree

Example

Listing 13-8: Formatting Messages

```
{Whoops! Delphi does not automatically import this function, so
 we must do it manually}
function LocalHandle(Mem: Pointer): HLOCAL; stdcall;

implementation

{link in the function}
function LocalHandle; external kernel32 name 'LocalHandle';

procedure TForm1.Button1Click(Sender: TObject);
{ Examples of how to use FormatMessage.         }
{ allowed printf (c style) formatting options: }
{ x is unsigned hexadecimal format             }
{ u is unsigned integer                        }
{ d is decimal integer                         }
{ c is a character                             }
{ lu is accepted for unsigned long integer     }
{     but the l is not required.               }
{ o for octal is not supported                 }
{ e, f, F, g, and G formats are not supported. }
{ Use some other technique for floating point. }
const
  MyMessageSize = 200;
var
  MyMessageDefinition: Pchar;        // message format
```

```
  OutputMessage: PChar;              // holds a formatted message
  MyArguments: array[1..5] of PChar; // pointers to numeric arguments
  MyMessageID: Integer;              // holds a message identifier
  MyLanguageID: Integer;             // holds a language identifier
  MyMemoryHandle: HLOCAL;            // a handle to a formatted message
begin
  {Get space for output message}
  GetMem(OutputMessage,MyMessageSize);

  {format a message}
  MyMessageDefinition := 'Delphi %1.  I like %2.';
  MyArguments[1] := 'rocks';
  MyArguments[2] := 'Delphi 3';
  FormatMessage(FORMAT_MESSAGE_FROM_STRING or
                FORMAT_MESSAGE_ARGUMENT_ARRAY,
                MyMessageDefinition,0,0,
                OutputMessage,MyMessageSize,
                @MyArguments);
  MyArguments[1] := '';
  MyArguments[2] := '';

  {displays: Delphi rocks.  I like Delphi 3}
  Label1.Caption := string(OutputMessage);

  {examples of numeric substitution.  Arguments contain the data.
   This uses "C" style printf formatting}
  Integer(MyArguments[1]) := 54;
  Integer(MyArguments[2]) := 49;
  Integer(MyArguments[3]) := -100;
  Integer(MyArguments[4]) := -37;
  Integer(MyArguments[5]) := -37;

  {format the message}
  MyMessageDefinition :=
      'character:%1!c! decimal:%2!d! unsigned hexadecimal:%3!x!'
    + ' unsigned int:%4!u! or:%5!lu!';
  FormatMessage(FORMAT_MESSAGE_FROM_STRING or
                FORMAT_MESSAGE_ARGUMENT_ARRAY,
                MyMessageDefinition,0,0,
                OutputMessage,MyMessageSize,
                @MyArguments);
  Label2.Caption := string(OutputMessage);

  {format the message differently}
  MyMessageDefinition :=
      'unsigned hexadecimal:%3!x! character:%1!c! decimal:%2!d!'
    + ' unsigned int:%4!u! or:%5!lu!';
  FormatMessage(FORMAT_MESSAGE_FROM_STRING or
                FORMAT_MESSAGE_ARGUMENT_ARRAY,
                MyMessageDefinition,0,0,
                OutputMessage,MyMessageSize,
                @MyArguments);
  Label3.Caption := string(OutputMessage);

  {free output message space}
```

```
  Freemem(OutputMessage);

  {retrieve the system string for an error message}
  MyMessageID := ERROR_INVALID_FLAGS; // any system message ID
  MyLanguageID := 0;                  // default language

  {Use the option where FormatMessage allocates it's own message buffer.}
  FormatMessage(FORMAT_MESSAGE_FROM_SYSTEM or
                FORMAT_MESSAGE_ALLOCATE_BUFFER,nil,
                MyMessageID,MyLanguageID,
                @OutputMessage,0,nil);
  Label4.Caption := string(OutputMessage);

  {return message memory}
  MyMemoryHandle := LocalHandle(OutputMessage);
  if (LocalFree(MyMemoryHandle) <> 0) then
    ShowMessage('Error freeing memory');

end;
```

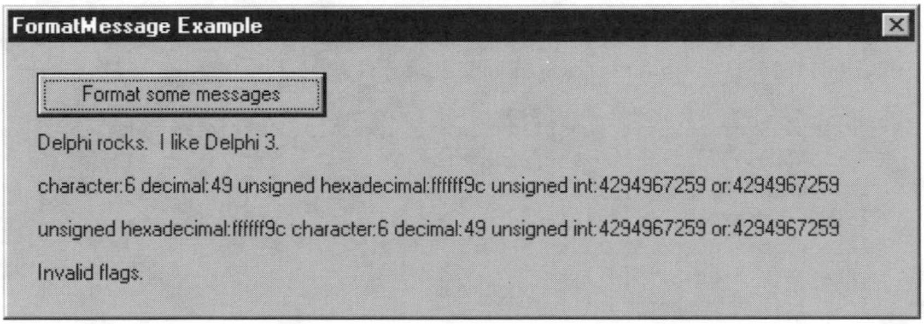

Figure 13-8: The formatted messages.

Table 13-7: FormatMessage dwFlags Values

Value	Description
FORMAT_MESSAGE_ALLOCATE_BUFFER	Indicates that the lpBuffer parameter is a pointer to a pointer for the output buffer. The output buffer has no memory allocation when FormatMessage is called. The function will use LocalAlloc to allocate enough memory to store the message. The nSize parameter specifies a minimum size to allocate for the buffer. FormatMessage then creates the buffer and places the address of the buffer at the address pointed to by the lpBuffer parameter. The application should declare a pointer for the output buffer and place the address of the pointer in the lpBuffer parameter. After the buffer is no longer needed, the caller should free the memory with a call to LocalFree.
FORMAT_MESSAGE_IGNORE_INSERTS	Specifies that FormatMessage will ignore the Arguments parameter, and pass the insert sequences to the output buffer without processing the values in the Arguments array.

Value	Description
FORMAT_MESSAGE_FROM_STRING	Indicates that lpSource is a pointer to a message string which may contain insert sequences. This flag cannot be combined with either FORMAT_MESSAGE_FROM_HMODULE or FORMAT_MESSAGE_FROM_SYSTEM.
FORMAT_MESSAGE_FROM_HMODULE	Indicates that lpSource is a handle to a message-table resource. If this option is set and lpSource is NIL, the resources in the current process will be searched. This flag cannot be used in combination with FORMAT_MESSAGE_FROM_STRING.
FORMAT_MESSAGE_FROM_SYSTEM	Indicates that FormatMessage should search the system's message table resources for the message definition. If this flag is specified in combination with FORMAT_MESSAGE_FROM_HMODULE, FormatMessage will search the message-table resources in the system and then in the module specified by lpSource. This flag cannot be used in combination with FORMAT_MESSAGE_FROM_STRING. This flag allows the application to pass the value returned from GetLastError to retrieve a system-defined error message string.
FORMAT_MESSAGE_ARGUMENT_ARRAY	Specifies that the Argument parameter is a pointer to an array of 32-bit values to be inserted into the message string.

Table 13-8: FormatMessage dwFlags Low-order Byte Values

Value	Description
0	There are no specifications for line breaks for the output buffer. FormatMessage will simply copy any line breaks in the message definition to the output buffer.
any nonzero value that is not FORMAT_MESSAGE_MAX_WIDTH_MASK	Indicates the maximum width of an output line. A line break will be used in the output buffer to send any remaining characters to the next line if it exceeds this value. Any line breaks that occur in the message definition will be ignored. FormatMessage will only break the line at a white space. Hardcoded line breaks in the message definition (%n) will be copied to the output buffer and a new line count begun for the next line.
FORMAT_MESSAGE_MAX_WIDTH_MASK	Regular line breaks in the message string will be ignored. Hardcoded line breaks will be copied to the output buffer. No other line breaks will be generated by FormatMessage regardless of line width.

Table 13-9: FormatMessage Arguments Formatting Code Values

Value	Description
%0 *(zero)*	Terminates the output message without a new-line character. Use this for a prompt or any situation where the cursor should remain at the end of the output without a carriage return/line feed being generated.
%n!*C-style printf format string*!	An argument insert point for the n-th argument. "%1" is the first argument, "%2" is the second argument, and so on up to a possible total of 99 arguments. The formatting instructions must include the exclamation points or it will simply be interpreted as part of the message. If no printf formatting is specified, !s! is used as a default, meaning that the corresponding argument is interpreted as a PChar variable pointing to a null-terminated string which is inserted in the message at that point in place of the "%n". If the printf format code is a numeric formatting code showing width and precision, then the "*" character can be given for either or both numbers. If a single "*" is given, then the next (%n+1) argument is used for the number. If two "*" characters are in the formatting code, then the next two arguments (%n+1 and %n+2) are used for the width and precision of the formatted number. The C-style formatting for floating point numbers using the o, e, E, f, g, and G options are not supported. However, x, d, c, u, and lu are supported. Formatting integers in octal format or real numbers in scientific notation should be formatted using other functions.
%%	Passes a single % symbol to the output buffer.
%n (the letter "n")	Places a hard line break in the output buffer. This is used when the message definition is determining the line width for a multiple line message.
%space	Forces a space in the output buffer. There can be several of these in sequence. This is useful for forcing spaces, including trailing spaces.
%. (period)	Forces a period to the output buffer regardless of position in the line. This can be used to place a period at the beginning of the line. A period without a percent sign would indicate the end of the message.
%!	Places an exclamation mark in the output buffer without being interpreted as a beginning or ending terminator for a formatting specification.

GetACP Windows.Pas

Syntax

GetACP: UINT; {returns an ANSI code page identifier}

Description

GetACP gets the current ANSI code page identifier for the system. If a code page is not defined, then the default code page identifier is returned.

Return Value

If the function succeeds, it returns a 32-bit ANSI code page identifier from Table 13-10; otherwise it returns zero.

See also

GetCPInfo, GetOEMCP

Example

Listing 13-9: Retrieving the Current ANSI Code Page

```
procedure TForm1.Button1Click(Sender: TObject);
var
  SystemCodePage: Integer;          // holds the system code page
  SystemCPInfo: TCPinfo;            // holds code page info
  Leadbytecount: Integer;           // indicates lead byte count
  LeadX: Integer;                   // loop counter
begin
  {retrieve the system code page}
  SystemCodePage := GetACP;
  case SystemCodePage of
    874:  Label1.Caption := 'The system code page is Thai';
    932:  Label1.Caption := 'The system code page is Japanese';
    936:  Label1.Caption := 'The system code page is Chinese (PRC, Singapore)';
    949:  Label1.Caption := 'The system code page is Korean';
    950:  Label1.Caption := 'The system code page is Chinese (Taiwan)';
    1200: Label1.Caption := 'The system code page is Unicode';
    1250: Label1.Caption := 'The system code page is Windows 3.1 East Europe';
    1251: Label1.Caption := 'The system code page is Windows 3.1 Cyrillic';
    1252: Label1.Caption := 'The system code page is Windows 3.1 Latin 1';
    1253: Label1.Caption := 'The system code page is Windows 3.1 Greek';
    1254: Label1.Caption := 'The system code page is Windows 3.1 Turkish';
    1255: Label1.Caption := 'The system code page is Hebrew';
    1256: Label1.Caption := 'The system code page is Arabic';
    1257: Label1.Caption := 'The system code page is Baltic';
  else
    Label1.Caption := 'The system code page is ' +IntToStr(SystemCodePage);
  end;

  {the TCPinfo parameter is a VAR parameter,
   just give the variable, not the address of the variable}
  if not GetCPInfo(SystemCodePage,SystemCPInfo)
```

```
    then Label2.Caption := 'Error in getting CP info.'
    else Label2.Caption := 'The default character for translation '
                + 'to this code page is: '
                + Char(SystemCPInfo.DefaultChar[0]);

  {display the character size}
  Label3.Caption := 'The max character size is '
                    + IntToStr(SystemCPInfo.MaxCharSize);

  {determine lead byte count}
  LeadByteCount := 0;
  for leadX := 5 downto 0 do
    if SystemCPInfo.LeadByte[2*leadx] = 0 then LeadByteCount := LeadX;

  Label4.Caption := 'There are '+IntToStr(LeadByteCount)+' lead byte ranges.';
end;
```

Table 13-10: GetACP Return Values

Value	Description
874	Thai
932	Japanese
936	Chinese (PRC, Singapore)
949	Korean
950	Chinese (Taiwan, Hong Kong)
1200	Unicode (BMP of ISO 10646)
1250	Windows 3.1 Eastern European
1251	Windows 3.1 Cyrillic
1252	Windows 3.1 Latin 1 (U.S., Western Europe)
1253	Windows 3.1 Greek
1254	Windows 3.1 Turkish
1255	Hebrew
1256	Arabic
1257	Baltic

GetAtomName *Windows.Pas*

Syntax

```
GetAtomName(
nAtom: ATOM;            {an atom number}
lpBuffer: PChar;        {a pointer to a buffer receiving the name}
nSize: Integer          {the length of the lpBuffer buffer}
): UINT;                {returns the number of characters copied to the buffer}
```

Description

This function finds the string associated with the specified atom number in the local atom table. If an integer value was stored, the value will be returned in a string format. For retrieving a string from an atom number from the global atom table, use the GlobalGetAtomName function.

Parameters

nAtom: The atom number whose string is to be retrieved.

lpBuffer: A pointer to a string buffer where the function will place the results of the search. The string buffer should be large enough to receive the string value plus the null terminator.

nSize: Specifies the size of the buffer pointed to by the lpBuffer parameter.

Return Value

If the function succeeds, the buffer pointed to by the lpBuffer parameter will contain the string associated with the specified atom number, and the function returns the number of characters copied to this buffer. If the function fails, it returns zero. To get extended error information, call the GetLastError function.

See also

AddAtom, DeleteAtom, FindAtom, GlobalAddAtom, GlobalDeleteAtom, GlobalFindAtom, GlobalGetAtomName

Example

Please see Listing 13-1 under AddAtom.

GetCPInfo Windows.Pas

Syntax

```
GetCPInfo(
CodePage: UINT;                {the code page identifier}
var lpCPInfo: TCPInfo          {a pointer to a TCPInfo structure}
): BOOL;                       {returns TRUE or FALSE}
```

Description

This function retrieves information about a specified code page and places the results in a TCPInfo structure.

Parameters

CodePage: The 32-bit code page identifier for which information is requested. This parameter can also be set to one value from Table 13-11.

lpCPInfo: A pointer to a TCPInfo structure that receives the code page information. The TCPInfo data structure is defined as:

```
TCPInfo = record
    MaxCharSize: UINT;                              {max length of a char in bytes}
    DefaultChar: array[0..MAX_DEFAULTCHAR - 1] of Byte;         {the default
                                                                 character}
    LeadByte: array[0..MAX_LEADBYTES - 1] of Byte;       {lead byte ranges}
end;
```

MaxCharSize: Specifies the default length, in bytes, of a character in this code page (1 for ANSI, 2 for Unicode).

DefaultChar: Specifies the default character used in character translations to this code page.

LeadByte: Specifies an array of lead byte ranges. Lead byte ranges are only used in double-byte character set code pages.

Return Value

If the function succeeds, it returns TRUE; otherwise it returns FALSE. To get extended error information, call the GetLastError function.

See also

GetACP, GetOemCP

Example

Please see Listing 13-9 under GetACP.

Table 13-11: GetCPInfo CodePage Values

Value	Description
CP_ACP	Uses the system default ANSI code page.
CP_MACCP	Uses the system default Macintosh code page.
CP_OEMCP	Uses the system default OEM code page.

GetDateFormat   Windows.Pas

Syntax

```
GetDateFormat(
Locale: LCID;               {the locale for specifying the date format}
dwFlags: DWORD;             {formatting options }
lpDate: PSystemTime;        {a pointer to the date to be formatted}
lpFormat: PChar;            {a pointer to the date format string}
lpDateStr: PChar;           {a pointer to a buffer for the formatted date}
```

```
cchDate: Integer            {the size of the output buffer}
): Integer;                 {returns the number of characters copied to the buffer}
```

Description

This function formats a given date according to a format string and specified options. A specific date or the system date can be used.

Parameters

Locale: The locale identifier to which the date is formatted. If the lpFormat parameter is NIL, the date is formatted according to the default date formatting for this locale. If the lpFormat parameter contains a formatting string, then the locale will only be used for formatting information not specified in the lpFormat string. This parameter can be set to one of the values from Table 13-12.

dwFlags: Indicates formatting options if the lpFormat parameter is set to NIL. If the lpFormat parameter is not set to NIL, then dwFlags must be zero. If the lpFormat parameter is NIL, the dwFlags parameter can be any combination of values from Table 13-13.

lpDate: A pointer to a TSystemTime structure that contains the date to format. If this parameter is set to NIL, the current system date will be used. The TSystemTime structure is defined as:

```
TSystemTime = record
      wYear: Word;              {indicates the year}
      wMonth: Word;             {indicates the month}
      wDayOfWeek: Word;         {indicates the day of the week}
      wDay: Word;               {indicates the day of the month}
      wHour: Word;              {indicates the hour}
      wMinute: Word;            {indicates the minute)
      wSecond: Word;            {indicates the seconds}
      wMilliseconds: Word;      {indicates the milliseconds}
end;
```

Please see the GetSystemTime function for a description of this data structure.

lpFormat: A pointer to a string containing the format picture. If this parameter is NIL, the default date format for the locale will be used. This string is a formatting picture containing formatting codes from Table 13-14. Spaces in the format will show in the output as they appear. Other than spaces, text or other literal characters may appear in single quotations.

lpDateStr: A pointer to the string buffer that receives the formatted date string.

cchDate: Indicates the size of the output buffer pointed to by the lpDateStr parameter, in characters. If this parameter is zero, the function returns the number of characters that would be required to hold the formatted output and the lpDateStr parameter is ignored.

Return Value

If the function succeeds, it returns the number of characters copied to the lpDateStr buffer; otherwise it returns zero. To get extended error information, call the GetLastError function.

See also

GetTimeFormat, SystemTime

Example

Listing 13-10: Formatting Dates

```
procedure TForm1.Button1Click(Sender: TObject);
var
  MyTime: PSystemTime;                      // pointer to TSystemTime structure
  MySystemTime: TSystemTime;                // TSystemTime structure in memory
  MyDate: PChar;                            // pointer to output buffer
  MyDateBuffer: array[1..40] of char;       // output buffer
  MyFormat: PChar;                          // format for formatting date
begin
  {initialize pointers}
  MyDate := @MyDateBuffer;
  MyTime := @MySystemTime;

  {display the system date}
  GetDateFormat(
      LOCALE_USER_DEFAULT,      // user locale
      DATE_LONGDATE,            // long date format
      nil,                      // get the system date
      nil,                      // use local formatting
      MyDate,                   // output buffer
      40);                      // size of output buffer
  Label1.Caption := 'The System Date is ' + MyDate;

  {initialize system time structure}
  FillChar(MyTime^,SizeOf(TSystemTime),0);
  MyTime^.wYear := 1981;                        // a special date
  MyTime^.wMonth :=   3;
  MyTime^.wDay :=     6;
  MyFormat := 'dddd, MMMM d, yyyy';

  GetDateFormat(LOCALE_USER_DEFAULT, 0, MyTime, MyFormat, MyDate, 40);
  Label2.Caption := 'I remember ' + MyDate;
end;
```

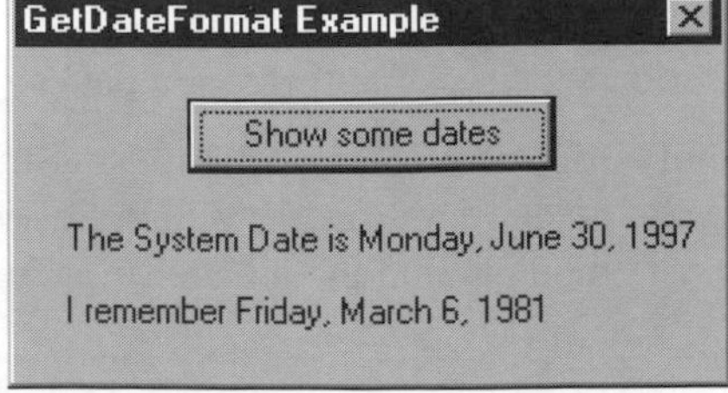

Figure 13-9: The formatted date output.

Table 13-12: GetDateFormat Locale Values

Value	Description
LOCALE_SYSTEM_DEFAULT	The system's default locale.
LOCALE_USER_DEFAULT	The user's default locale.

Table 13-13: GetDateFormat dwFlags Values

Value	Description
LOCALE_NOUSEROVERRIDE	Indicates that the default date format for the locale given in the Locale parameter will be used. Without this flag, any other formatting option will be used to override the locale default date format.
DATE_SHORTDATE	Uses the short date format as defined by the regional settings. This cannot be used in combination with DATE_LONGDATE.
DATE_LONGDATE	Uses the long date format as defined by the regional settings. This cannot be used in combination with DATE_SHORTDATE.
DATE_USE_ALT_CALENDAR	If an alternate calendar exists, use it to format the date string. The date format for the alternate calendar will be used instead of any other overriding specification. With this flag set, other formatting commands will be used only if there is no default date formatting defined for the alternate calendar.

Table 13-14: GetDateFormat lpFormat Values

Value	Description
d	Day of the month. Single-digit days will contain no leading zero.
dd	Day of the month. Single-digit days will contain a leading zero.
ddd	Day of the week abbreviated to three letters. The abbreviation is determined by the specified locale.
dddd	Day of the week, unabbreviated. The specified locale provides the unabbreviated day name.
M	Month with no leading zero for single-digit months.
MM	Month with a leading zero for single-digit months.
MMM	Month as a three-letter abbreviation. The abbreviation is determined by the specified locale.
MMMM	Month as its full unabbreviated name. The abbreviation is determined by the specified locale.
y	Last two digits of the year, with no leading zeroes for single-digit years.
yy	Last two digits of the year, with a leading zero for single-digit years.
yyyy	Year as a full four-digit number.

Value	Description
gg	Period/era as defined by the specified locale. This is ignored if the specified date does not have an associated era or period string.

GetOEMCP Windows.Pas

Syntax

GetOEMCP: UINT; {returns an OEM code page identifier}

Description

GetOEMCP gets the current OEM code page identifier for the system. If a code page is not defined, then the default code page identifier is returned.

Return Value

If the function succeeds, it returns a 32-bit OEM code page identifier from Table 13-15; otherwise it returns zero.

See also

GetCPInfo, GetACP

Example

Listing 13-11: Retrieving the Current OEM Code Page

```
procedure TForm1.Button1Click(Sender: TObject);
var
  SystemCodePage: Integer;         // holds the system code page
  SystemCPInfo: TCPinfo;           // holds code page info
  Leadbytecount: Integer;          // indicates lead byte count
  LeadX: Integer;                  // loop counter
begin
  {retrieve the system code page}
  SystemCodePage := GetOEMCP;
  case SystemCodePage of
    437:  Label1.Caption := 'MS-DOS United States';
    708:  Label1.Caption := 'Arabic (ASMO 708)';
    709:  Label1.Caption := 'Arabic (ASMO 449+, BCON V4)';
    710:  Label1.Caption := 'Arabic (Transparent Arabic)';
    720:  Label1.Caption := 'Arabic (Transparent ASMO)';
    737:  Label1.Caption := 'Greek (formerly 437G)';
    775:  Label1.Caption := 'Baltic';
    850:  Label1.Caption := 'MS-DOS Multilingual (Latin I)';
    852:  Label1.Caption := 'MS-DOS Slavic (Latin II)';
    855:  Label1.Caption := 'IBM Cyrillic (primarily Russian)';
    857:  Label1.Caption := 'IBM Turkish';
    860:  Label1.Caption := 'MS-DOS Portuguese';
    861:  Label1.Caption := 'MS-DOS Icelandic';
    862:  Label1.Caption := 'Hebrew';
```

```
    863:  Label1.Caption := 'MS-DOS Canadian-French';
    864:  Label1.Caption := 'Arabic';
    865:  Label1.Caption := 'MS-DOS Nordic';
    866:  Label1.Caption := 'MS-DOS Russian (former USSR)';
    869:  Label1.Caption := 'IBM Modern Greek';
    874:  Label1.Caption := 'Thai';
    932:  Label1.Caption := 'Japanese';
    936:  Label1.Caption := 'Chinese (PRC, Singapore)';
    949:  Label1.Caption := 'Korean';
    950:  Label1.Caption := 'Chinese (Taiwan, Hong Kong)';
    1361: Label1.Caption := 'Korean (Johab)';
  else
    Label1.Caption := 'The system code page is ' +IntToStr(SystemCodePage);
  end;

  {the TCPinfo parameter is a VAR parameter,
   just give the variable, not the address of the variable}
  if not GetCPinfo(SystemCodePage,SystemCPInfo)
    then Label2.Caption := 'Error in getting CP info.'
    else Label2.Caption := 'The default character for translation '
                + 'to this code page is: '
                + Char(SystemCPInfo.DefaultChar[0]);

  {display the character size}
  Label3.Caption := 'The max character size is '
                    + IntToStr(SystemCPInfo.MaxCharSize);

  {determine lead byte count}
  LeadByteCount := 0;
  for leadX := 5 downto 0 do
    if SystemCPInfo.LeadByte[2*leadx] = 0 then LeadByteCount := LeadX;

  Label4.Caption := 'There are '+IntToStr(LeadByteCount)+' lead byte ranges.';
end;
```

Table 13-15: GetOEMCP Return Values

Value	Description
437	MS-DOS United States
708	Arabic (ASMO 708)
709	Arabic (ASMO 449+, BCON V4)
710	Arabic (Transparent Arabic)
720	Arabic (Transparent ASMO)
737	Greek (formerly 437G)
775	Baltic
850	MS-DOS Multilingual (Latin I)
852	MS-DOS Slavic (Latin II)
855	IBM Cyrillic (primarily Russian)
857	IBM Turkish
860	MS-DOS Portuguese

Value	Description
861	MS-DOS Icelandic
862	Hebrew
863	MS-DOS Canadian-French
864	Arabic
865	MS-DOS Nordic
866	MS-DOS Russian (former USSR)
869	IBM Modern Greek
874	Thai
932	Japanese
936	Chinese (PRC, Singapore)
949	Korean
950	Chinese (Taiwan, Hong Kong)
1361	Korean (Johab)

GetTimeFormat   Windows.Pas

Syntax

```
GetTimeFormat(
Locale: LCID;               {the locale identifier}
dwFlags: DWORD;             {formatting options}
lpTime: PSystemTime;        {a pointer to the time to be formatted}
lpFormat: PChar;            {a pointer to the time format string}
lpTimeStr: PChar;           {a pointer to a buffer for the formatted time}
cchTime: Integer            {the size of the output buffer}
): Integer;                 {returns the number of characters copied to the buffer}
```

Description

This function formats a given time according to a format string and specified options. A specific time or the system time can be used.

Parameters

Locale: The locale identifier to which the time is formatted. If the lpFormat parameter is NIL, the time is formatted according to the default time formatting for this locale. If the lpFormat parameter contains a formatting string, then the locale will only be used for formatting information not specified in the lpFormat string. This parameter can be set to one of the values from Table 13-16.

dwFlags: Specifies the time formatting options. This parameter can be any combination of values from Table 13-17.

lpTime: A pointer to a TSystemTime structure that contains the time to format. If this parameter is set to NIL, the current system time will be used. The TSystemTime structure is defined as:

```
TSystemTime = record
    wYear: Word;            {indicates the year}
    wMonth: Word;           {indicates the month}
    wDayOfWeek: Word;       {indicates the day of the week}
    wDay: Word;             {indicates the day of the month}
    wHour: Word;            {indicates the hour}
    wMinute: Word;          {indicates the minutc)
    wSecond: Word;          {indicates the seconds}
    wMilliseconds: Word;    {indicates the milliseconds}
end;
```

Please see the GetSystemTime function for a description of this data structure.

lpFormat: A pointer to a string containing the format picture. If this parameter is NIL, the default date format for the locale will be used. This string is a formatting picture containing formatting codes from Table 13-18. The format codes are case sensitive. Any characters in a format string that are in single quotes will appear as is in the output string without being used as a format specifier. A typical time of "12:45 AM" could be formatted with an lpFormat parameter of "hh":"mm ss tt." If one of the time markers ("t" or "tt") is set and the TIME_NOTIMEMARKER flag is not set in the dwFlags parameter, the time marker information will be provided based on the specified locale.

lpTimeStr: A pointer to the string buffer that receives the formatted time string.

cchTime: Indicates the size of the output buffer pointed to by the lpTimeStr parameter, in characters. If this parameter is zero, the function returns the number of characters that would be required to hold the formatted output and the lpTimeStr parameter is ignored.

Return Value

If the function succeeds, it returns the number of characters copied to the lpDateStr buffer; otherwise it returns zero. To get extended error information, call the GetLast-Error function. No errors are returned for a bad format string. GetTimeFormat will simply use whatever it can and produce its best output using the format provided. If "hhh" or "ttt" are provided in the format string, the values of "hh" and "tt" will be used instead.

See also

GetDateFormat

Example

Listing 13-12: Retrieving a Formatted Time String

```
procedure TForm1.Button1Click(Sender: TObject);
var
  PMySystemTime: PSystemTime;          // pointer to a TSystemTime
  TMySystemTime: TSystemTime;          // TSystemTime structure in memory
  MyOutput: array[0..20] of Char;      // output buffer
  PMyOutput: PChar;                    // pointer to output
  OutputSize: Integer;                 // size of output buffer
  APIresult: Integer;                  // function result for error trapping
begin
  {initialize pointers}
  PMySystemTime := @TMySystemTime;
  PMyOutput := @MyOutput;
  OutputSize := SizeOf(MyOutput);      // find size of buffer

  {determine the requested time format}
  FillChar(TMySystemTime,SizeOf(TMySystemTime),0);
  if RadioButton1.Checked then PMySystemTime := nil;
  if RadioButton2.Checked then
  begin
    TMySystemTime.wHour   := StrToInt(Edit2.Text);
    TMySystemTime.wMinute := StrToInt(Edit3.Text);
    TMySystemTime.wSecond := StrToInt(Edit4.Text);
  end;

  {get the time for the specified format}
  APIresult := GetTimeFormat(LOCALE_SYSTEM_DEFAULT,
                             0, PMySystemTime,
                             PChar(Edit1.Text),
                             PMyOutput, OutputSize);
  if (APIresult = 0) and (GetLastError = ERROR_INVALID_PARAMETER) then
    ShowMessage('Invalid Parameter');

  {display the time}
  Label1.Caption := PMyOutput;
end;
```

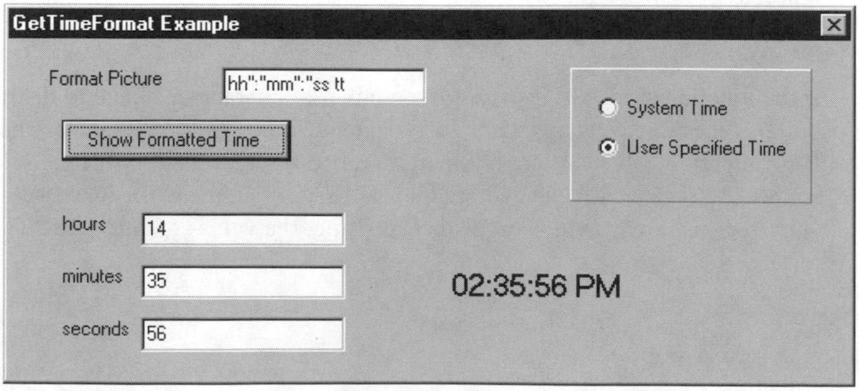

Figure 13-10: The formatted time output.

Table 13-16: GetTimeFormat Locale Values

Value	Description
LOCALE_SYSTEM_DEFAULT	The system's default locale.
LOCALE_USER_DEFAULT	The user's default locale.

Table 13-17: GetTimeFormat dwFlags Values

Value	Description
LOCALE_NOUSEROVERRIDE	When provided, this forces the function to use the system default time format for the specified locale. Otherwise, when not set, the function formats the output using any overrides in the locale's default time format. This flag can be used only if the lpFormat parameter is set to NIL.
TIME_NOMINUTESORSECONDS	Do not put minutes or seconds in the output.
TIME_NOSECONDS	Do not put seconds in the output.
TIME_NOTIMEMARKER	Do not use a time marker.
TIME_FORCE24HOURFORMAT	Use a 24-hour time format regardless of any locale settings.

Table 13-18: GetTimeFormat lpFormat Values

Value	Description
h	Hours with no leading zero in a 12-hour format.
hh	Hours with leading zeroes in a 12-hour format.
H	Hours with no leading zeroes in a 24-hour format.
HH	Hours with leading zeroes in a 24-hour format.
m	Minutes with no leading zeroes.
mm	Minutes with leading zeroes.
s	Seconds with no leading zeroes.
ss	Seconds with leading zeroes.
t	Single-character time marker, A for AM and P for PM.
tt	Multicharacter time marker, AM or PM.

GlobalAddAtom *Windows.Pas*

Syntax

```
GlobalAddAtom(
lpString: PChar              {the string to add to the atom table}
): ATOM;                     {returns the newly added atom}
```

Description

This function adds the specified string to the global atom table and returns the atom number. The string can be no longer than 255 characters. If the string already exists in the table, its reference count is incremented. This global atom table is shared system-wide with all other processes. Global atom tables have a set size of 37 entries.

Parameters

lpString: A pointer to a null-terminated string to be added to the global atom table.

Return Value

If the function succeeds, it returns the atom number for the string that was added to the global atom table. The atom value is a 16-bit number in the range 49152 to 65535 ($C000 to $FFFF) for strings or in the range 1 to 49151 ($0001 to $BFFF) for integers. If the function fails, it returns zero. To get extended error information, call the GetLastError function.

See also

AddAtom, DeleteAtom, FindAtom, GetAtomName, GlobalDeleteAtom, GlobalFindAtom, GlobalGetAtomName, MakeIntAtom

Example

Listing 13-13: Adding a String to the Global Atom Table

```
procedure TForm1.Button1Click(Sender: TObject);
var
  MyAtom: Atom;           // the returned atom
  AtomText: PChar;        // the string we will store
  TextTest: PChar;        // for testing search results
  AtomTest: Atom;         // for testing search results
begin
  {add the string to the global atom table}
  AtomText := 'This is my atom';
  Label1.Caption := 'The text: '+string(AtomText);

  MyAtom := GlobalAddAtom(AtomText);
  Label2.Caption := 'Atom Number: '+IntToStr(MyAtom);

  {search the table for atom number, given the string}
  AtomTest := GlobalFindAtom(AtomText);
  Label3.Caption := 'Atom number by string: '+IntToStr(AtomTest);

  {search by atom number to get the string}
  TextTest := StrAlloc(256);
  GlobalGetAtomName(MyAtom,Texttest,256);
  Label4.Caption := 'Text by atom number: '+string(TextTest);

  {clean up}
  GlobalDeleteAtom(MyAtom);
```

```
  StrDispose(texttest);
end;
```

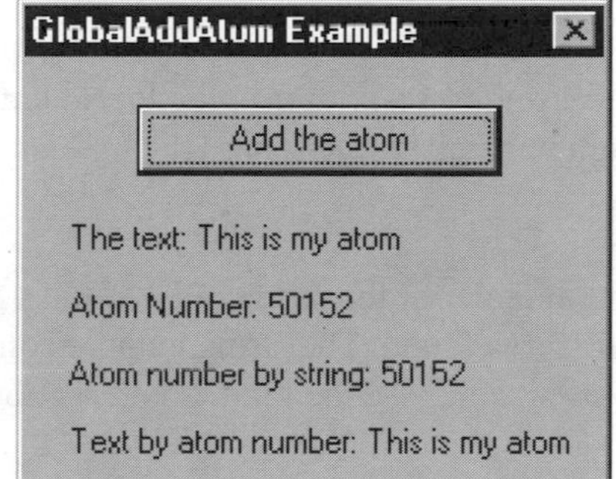

Figure 13-11: The atom was added.

GlobalDeleteAtom   Windows.Pas

Syntax

```
GlobalDeleteAtom(
nAtom: ATOM                {the atom number to delete}
): ATOM;                   {returns zero or the nAtom value}
```

Description

GlobalDeleteAtom reduces the reference count for the specified atom in the global atom table by one. If the reference count for the specified atom is zero, the entry is deleted from the atom table. To make a deletion from the local atom table, use DeleteAtom.

Parameters

nAtom: The atom number to delete from the global atom table.

Return Value

If this function succeeds, it returns zero; otherwise it returns the atom number in the nAtom parameter. To get extended error information, call the GetLastError function.

See also

AddAtom, FindAtom, DeleteAtom, GlobalAddAtom

Example

Please see Listing 13-13 under GlobalAddAtom.

GlobalFindAtom Windows.Pas

Syntax

```
GlobalFindAtom(
lpString: PChar          {a pointer to the string to search for in the local atom table}
): ATOM;                 {returns the atom number for the string}
```

Description

GlobalFindAtom searches the global atom table for the string pointed to by the lpString parameter and returns the atom number if it is found. The string comparison is not case sensitive. To find an atom in the local atom table, use the FindAtom function.

Parameters

lpString: A pointer to the null-terminated string to search for in the global atom table.

Return Value

If the function succeeds, it returns the atom number for the specified string; otherwise it returns zero. To get extended error information, call the GetLastError function.

See also

AddAtom, FindAtom, DeleteAtom, GlobalAddAtom, GlobalDeleteAtom

Example

Please see Listing 13-13 under GlobalAddAtom.

GlobalGetAtomName Windows.Pas

Syntax

```
GlobalGetAtomName(
nAtom: ATOM;             {an atom number}
lpBuffer: PChar;         {a pointer to a buffer receiving the name}
nSize: Integer           {the length of the lpBuffer buffer}
): UINT;                 {returns the number of characters copied to the buffer}
```

Description

This function finds the string associated with the specified atom number in the global atom table. If an integer value was stored, the value will be returned in a string format. For retrieving a string from an atom number from the local atom table, use the GetAtomName function.

Parameters

nAtom: The atom number whose string is to be retrieved.

lpBuffer: A pointer to a string buffer where the function will place the results of the search. The string buffer should be large enough to receive the string value plus the null terminator.

nSize: Specifies the size of the buffer pointed to by the lpBuffer parameter.

Return Value

If the function succeeds, the buffer pointed to by the lpBuffer parameter will contain the string associated with the specified atom number, and the function returns the number of characters copied to this buffer. If the function fails, it returns zero. To get extended error information, call the GetLastError function.

See also

AddAtom, DeleteAtom, FindAtom, GetAtomName, GlobalAddAtom, GlobalDeleteAtom, GlobalFindAtom

Example

Please see Listing 13-13 under GlobalAddAtom.

InitAtomTable   Windows.Pas

Syntax

```
InitAtomTable(
nSize: DWORD            {the desired number of entries in local atom table}
): BOOL;                {returns TRUE or FALSE}
```

Description

This function will initialize the local atom table to a specified number of entries. InitAtomTable does not need to be called before using any other local atom function. If InitAtomTable is not called, the local atom table defaults to a size of 37 entries. However, if the local atom table will be set to a larger size, InitAtomTable should be called before any other local atom function.

Parameters

nSize: The requested number of table entries. For optimal performance, this value should be a prime number.

Return Value

If the function succeeds, it returns TRUE; otherwise it returns FALSE.

See also

AddAtom, DeleteAtom, FindAtom, GetAtomName, GlobalAddAtom, GlobalDeleteAtom, GlobalFindAtom, GlobalGetAtomName

Example

Please see Listing 13-1 under AddAtom.

IsCharAlpha Windows.Pas

Syntax

IsCharAlpha(
ch: Char {the character to test}
): BOOL; {returns TRUE or FALSE}

Description

IsCharAlpha tests a character to see if it is an alphabetic character. The language that is selected at setup or in the Control Panel will determine how the test is performed.

Parameters

ch: The character to be tested.

Return Value

If the function succeeds and the character is an alphabetic character, it returns TRUE. If the function fails, or the character is not an alphabetic character, it returns FALSE.

See also

IsCharAlphaNumeric

Example

Listing 13-14: Testing Character Attributes

```
procedure TForm1.Button1Click(Sender: TObject);
var
  Mychar : Char;  // holds the character to test
begin
  {initialize the test variable}
  MyChar := 'A';
  Label1.Caption := 'The character: '+MyChar;

  {retrieve character information}
  if IsCharAlpha(MyChar)        then Label2.Caption := 'MyChar is alpha';
  if IsCharAlphaNumeric(MyChar) then Label3.Caption := 'MyChar is alphanumeric';
  if IsCharLower(MyChar)        then Label4.Caption := 'MyChar is lowercase';
  if IsCharUpper(MyChar)        then Label5.Caption := 'MyChar is uppercase';
end;
```

IsCharAlphaNumeric Windows.Pas

Syntax

```
IsCharAlphaNumeric(
ch: Char                        {the character to test}
): BOOL;                        {returns TRUE or FALSE}
```

Description

IsCharAlphaNumeric tests a character to see if it is an alphabetic or a numeric character. The language that is selected at setup or in the Control Panel will determine how the test is performed.

Parameters

ch: The character to be tested.

Return Value

If the function succeeds and the character is an alphanumeric character, it returns TRUE. If the function fails, or the character is not alphanumeric, it returns FALSE.

See also

IsCharAlpha

Example

Please see Listing 13-14 under IsCharAlpha.

IsCharLower Windows.Pas

Syntax

```
IsCharLower(
ch: Char                        {the character to test}
): BOOL;                        {returns TRUE or FALSE}
```

Description

IsCharLower tests the specified character to determine whether or not it is lowercase.

Parameters

ch: The character to be tested.

Return Value

If the function succeeds and the character is lowercase, it returns TRUE. If the function fails, or the character is not lowercase, it returns FALSE.

See also

IsCharUpper

Example

Please see Listing 13-14 under IsCharAlpha.

IsCharUpper Windows.Pas

Syntax

```
IsCharUpper(
ch: Char                    {the character to test}
): BOOL;                    {returns TRUE or FALSE}
```

Description

IsCharUpper tests the specified character to determine whether or not it is uppercase.

Parameters

ch: The character to be tested.

Return Value

If the function succeeds and the character is uppercase, it returns TRUE. If the function fails, or the character is not uppercase, it returns FALSE.

See also

IsCharLower

Example

Please see Listing 13-14 under IsCharAlpha.

lstrcat Windows.Pas

Syntax

```
lstrcat(
lpString1: PChar;           {the base string and destination address}
lpString2: PChar            {the string added to the base string}
): PChar;                   {returns a pointer to the concatenated string}
```

Description

lstrcat concatenates two null-terminated strings together, saving the concatenated string in the buffer pointed to by the lpString1 parameter. The resultant null-terminated string consists of the string pointed to by the lpString1 parameter followed by the string pointed to by the lpString2 parameter.

Parameters

lpString1: A pointer to a null-terminated string. This string must be large enough to contain both strings.

lpString2: A pointer to a null-terminated string. This string is added to the end of the string pointed to by the lpString1 parameter.

Return Value

If the function succeeds, it returns a pointer to the concatenated strings; otherwise it returns NIL. To get extended error information, call the GetLastError function.

See also

lstrcmp, lstrcmpi, lstrcpy, lstrlen

Example

Listing 13-15: Concatenating Two Strings

```
procedure TForm1.Button1Click(Sender: TObject);
var
  MyTotalString: PChar;      // holds the entire string
  MyStringToAppend: PChar;   // holds the string to append
begin
  {allocate memory for the entire string}
  MyTotalString := StrAlloc(255);

  {copy the text in edit1 to the full string}
  MyTotalString := lstrcpy(MyTotalString, PChar(Edit1.Text));

  {point the append string to the text in edit2}
  MyStringToAppend := PChar(Edit2.Text);

  {concatenate both strings}
  MyTotalString := lstrcat(MyTotalString, MyStringToAppend);

  {display the concatenated string}
  Label1.Caption := StrPas(MyTotalString);

  {dispose of allocated memory}
  StrDispose(MyTotalString);
end;
```

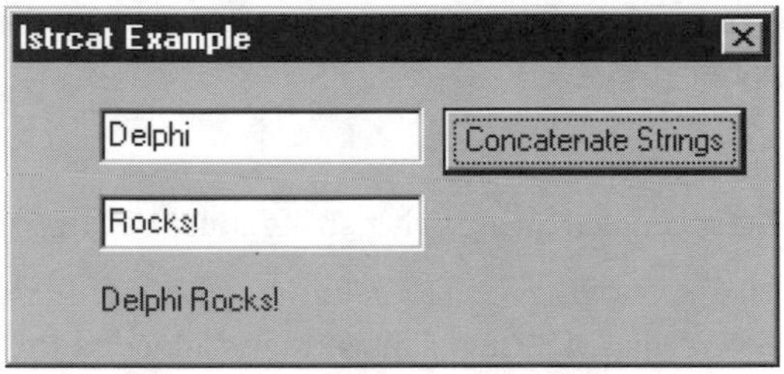

Figure 13-12: The concatenated strings.

lstrcmp Windows.Pas

Syntax

```
lstrcmp(
lpString1: PChar;              {a pointer to the first string to compare}
lpString2: PChar               {a pointer to the second string to compare}
): Integer;                    {returns the comparison results}
```

Description

lstrcmp is a simple string compare function. CompareString should be strongly considered instead of lstrcmp due to flexibility. lstrcmp has no options and is only interpreted in the context of the currently installed locale. If there was no locale installed at setup or selected in the Control Panel, then Windows will use a default locale. The two strings are compared using a word sort comparison, similar to the comparison that is used by the CompareString function without the SORT_STRINGSORT flag. If the strings are identical up to the end of the shorter string, then the shorter string is deemed smaller in value. This function has fewer options that CompareString but consequently is a little faster.

Parameters

lpString1: A pointer to the first null-terminated string in the comparison.

lpString2: A pointer to the second null-terminated string in the comparison.

Return Value

The function returns a number indicating the equality of the strings. This number will be one value from Table 13-19. This function does not indicate an error if it fails.

See also

CompareString, lstrcmpi, lstrcat, lstrcpy, lstrlen

Example

Listing 13-16: Comparing Two Strings

```
procedure TForm1.Button1Click(Sender: TObject);
var
```

```
  MyResult: Integer;   // holds the result of the string compare
begin
  MyResult := lstrcmp(PChar(Edit1.Text), PChar(Edit2.Text));
  if MyResult > 0 then
  begin   // first parameter is greater
    Label1.Caption := 'GREATER';
    Label2.Caption := 'SMALLER';
    Label3.Caption := '>';
  end;
  if MyResult < 0 then
  begin
    Label1.Caption := 'SMALLER';
    Label2.Caption := 'GREATER';
    Label3.Caption := '<';
  end;
  if MyResult = 0 then
  begin
    Label1.Caption := ' equal ';
    Label2.Caption := ' equal ';
    Label3.Caption := '=';
  end;
end;
```

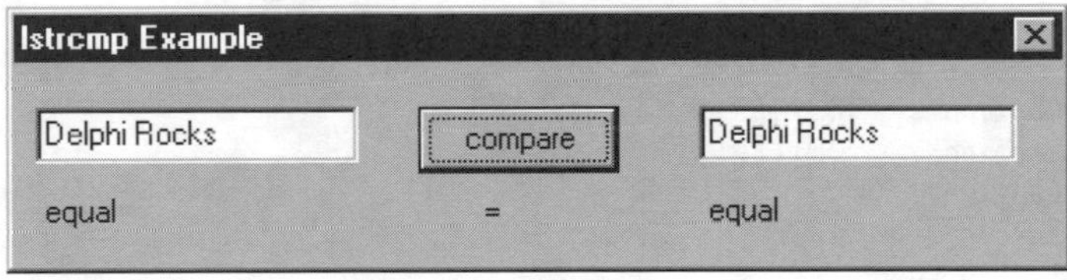

Figure 13-13: The two strings are equal.

Table 13-19: lstrcmp Return Values

Value	Description
negative numbers	lpString1 is less than lpString2.
zero	lpString1 and lpString2 are equal.
positive numbers	lpString1 is greater than lpString2.

lstrcmpi *Windows.Pas*

Syntax

```
lstrcmpi(
lpString1: PChar;          {a pointer to the first string to compare}
lpString2: PChar           {a pointer to the second string to compare}
): Integer;                {returns the comparison results}
```

Description

This function behaves exactly like lstrcmp except the string comparison is done on a case-insensitive basis.

Parameters

lpString1: A pointer to the first null-terminated string in the comparison.

lpString2: A pointer to the second null-terminated string in the comparison.

Return Value

The function returns a number indicating the equality of the strings. This number will be one value from Table 13-20. This function does not indicate an error if it fails.

See also

CompareString, lstrcmp, lstrcat, lstrcpy, lstrlen

Example

Listing 13-17: Comparing Two Strings

```
procedure TForm1.Button1Click(Sender: TObject);
var
  MyResult: Integer;     // holds the result of the comparison
begin
  MyResult := lstrcmpi(PChar(Edit1.Text), PChar(Edit2.Text));
  if MyResult > 0 then
  begin   // first parameter is greater
    Label1.Caption := 'GREATER';
    Label2.Caption := 'SMALLER';
    Label3.Caption := '>';
  end;
  if MyResult < 0 then
  begin
    Label1.Caption := 'SMALLER';
    Label2.Caption := 'GREATER';
    Label3.Caption := '<';
  end;
  if MyResult = 0 then
  begin
    Label1.Caption := ' equal ';
    Label2.Caption := ' equal ';
    Label3.Caption := '=';
  end;
end;
```

Figure 13-14: The strings are equal.

Table 13-20: lstrcmpi Return Values

Value	Description
negative numbers	lpString1 is less than lpString2.
zero	lpString1 and lpString2 are equal.
positive numbers	lpString1 is greater than lpString2.

lstrcpy *Windows.Pas*

Syntax

```
lstrcpy(
lpString1: PChar;        {a pointer to the destination buffer}
lpString2: PChar         {a pointer to the string to copy}
): PChar;                {returns a pointer to the destination buffer}
```

Description

lstrcpy copies the string pointed to by the lpString2 parameter to the buffer pointed to by the lpString1 parameter. It is a general purpose string copy routine that can be used for any null-terminated data structure regardless of length. The destination buffer must be allocated prior to calling lstrcpy.

Parameters

lpString1: A pointer to the destination string buffer. This buffer must be large enough to hold the entire string pointed to by the lpString2 parameter, including the null-terminating character.

lpString2: A pointer to the string being copied.

Return Value

If the function succeeds, it returns a pointer to the destination string buffer; otherwise it returns NIL. To get extended error information, call the GetLastError function.

See also

lstrcat, lstrcmp, lstrcmpi, lstrlen

Example

Please see Listing 13-15 under lstrcat.

lstrlen Windows.Pas

Syntax

lstrlen(
lpString: PChar {a pointer to a string}
): Integer; {returns the number of characters in the string}

Description

lstrlen finds the length in characters of the string pointed to by the parameter. The null terminator is not included in this count.

Parameters

lpString: A pointer to a string for which the length is returned.

Return Value

This function returns the number of characters in the string pointed to by the lpString parameter. This function does not indicate an error upon failure.

See also

lstrcmp, lstrcmpi, lstrcat, lstrcpy

Example

Listing 13-18: Finding the Length of a String

```
procedure TForm1.Button1Click(Sender: TObject);
var
  MyLength: Integer;   // holds the string length
begin
  MyLength := lstrlen(PChar(Edit1.Text));
  Label1.Caption := 'The length of the string is ' + IntToStr(MyLength);
end;
```

MakeIntAtom Windows.Pas

Syntax

MakeIntAtom(
wInteger: WORD {an integer value}
): PChar; {returns an integer atom}

Description

This function converts the integer identified by the wInteger value into an atom suitable for use with the AddAtom or GlobalAddAtom functions. DeleteAtom and GlobalDeleteAtom will always succeed for integer atoms, which are not reference counted like string atoms. GetAtomName and GlobalGetAtomName will return a null-terminated string with the first character as a pound (#) character; the remaining characters are the digits of the integer passed to MakeIntAtom.

Parameters

wInteger: A 16-bit value that is converted into an integer atom.

Return Value

If the function succeeds, it returns a pointer to a null-terminated string representing the integer that is suitable for use with the AddAtom and GlobalAddAtom functions. If the function fails, it returns NIL.

See also

AddAtom, DeleteAtom, GlobalAddAtom, GlobalDeleteAtom

Example

Listing 13-19: Adding an Integer Atom

```
procedure TForm1.Button1Click(Sender: TObject);
var
  My16: word;                // 16 bit value to put in local atom table
  MyAtom: Atom;              // Atom number in Local Atom Table
  MyString : Pchar;          // Resulting string in atom table
begin
  {make space for reading atom table}
  MyString := StrAlloc(256);

  {value to store in atom table}
  My16 := 42;

  {store the 16 bit atom}
  MyAtom := AddAtom(MakeIntAtom(My16));

  {display atom information}
  Label1.Caption := 'My Atom is ' + IntToStr(MyAtom);
  GetAtomName(MyAtom, MyString, 256);
  Label2.Caption := 'Atom Text is ' + MyString;

  {clean up}
  DeleteAtom(MyAtom);
  StrDispose(MyString);
end;
```

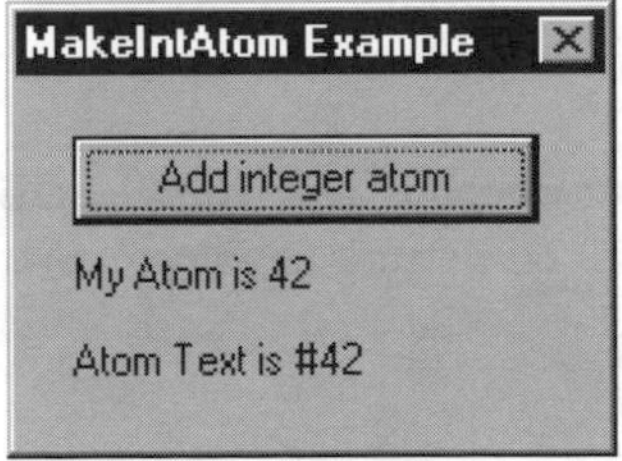

Figure 13-15: The integer atom.

OemToChar Windows.Pas

Syntax

```
OemToChar(
lpszSrc: PChar;            {a pointer to the string to translate}
lpszDst: PChar             {a pointer to the translated string}
): BOOL;                   {always returns TRUE}
```

Description

OemToChar translates the given string from the OEM character set to an ANSI or wide-character (Unicode) string.

Parameters

lpszSrc: A pointer to the string containing OEM characters.

lpszDst: A pointer to the translated string. If the destination character set is an ANSI set (single-byte characters), then the source and destination can be the same string. In this case, the translation will be performed in place. If the destination character set is a Unicode (double-byte) character set, there must be a separate buffer for lpszDst.

Return Value

This function always returns TRUE.

See also

CharToOem, CharToOemBuff, OemToCharBuff

Example

Please see Listing 13-3 under CharToOem.

OemToCharBuff Windows.Pas

Syntax

```
OemToCharBuff(
lpszSrc: PChar;            {a pointer to the string to translate}
lpszDst: PChar             {a pointer to the translated string}
cchDstLength: DWORD        {the number of characters to translate}
): BOOL;                   {always returns TRUE}
```

Description

OemToCharBuff translates the specified number of characters from the OEM source string to the destination string which can be an ANSI string (single-byte) or Unicode (double-byte) character set.

Parameters

lpszSrc: A pointer to the OEM source string that is to be translated.

lpszDst: A pointer to the destination string. If the destination character set is an ANSI set (single-byte characters), then the source and destination can be the same string. In this case, the translation will be performed in place. If the destination character set is a Unicode (double-byte) character set, there must be a separate buffer for lpszDst.

cchDstLength: Specifies the number of characters in the OEM source string to translate.

Return Value

This function always returns TRUE.

See also

CharToOem, CharToOemBuff, OemToChar

Example

Please see Listing 13-3 under CharToOem.

ToAscii Windows.Pas

Syntax

```
ToAscii(
uVirtKey: UINT;                     {a virtual key code to be translated}
uScanCode: UINT;                    {the hardware keyboard scan code}
const KeyState: TKeyboardState;     {the keyboard state}
lpChar: PChar;                      {a pointer to a buffer receiving the translated key}
uFlags: UINT;                       {menu active flags}
): Integer;                         {returns a conversion code}
```

Description

ToAscii translates a virtual key code and scan state into a Windows character, using the input language and the system keyboard layout.

Parameters

uVirtKey: The virtual key code to be translated to a Windows character.

uScanCode: The hardware scan code of the key to be translated. The high-order bit is set if the key is not pressed. The value of the uVirtKey parameter is the primary code used for translation. uScanCode is used to distinguish between a keypress and a key release and for translating Alt+*number key* combinations.

KeyState: A pointer to a 256-byte array indicating the current keyboard state. Each byte indicates the state for a single key. The most significant bit is set if the key is down. If the low bit is set, the Caps Lock key is toggled on. Scroll Lock and Num Lock are ignored.

lpChar: A pointer to a string buffer receiving the translated Windows character.

uFlags: Specifies if a menu is active. A value of 1 indicates that a menu is active; 0 indicates no menu is active.

Return Value

The function returns one value from Table 13-21. ToAscii does not indicate an error upon failure.

See also

ToAsciiEx, OemKeyScan, VkKeyScan

Example

Listing 13-20: Converting a Virtual Key Code

```
procedure TForm1.Button1Click(Sender: TObject);
var
  WindowsChar: array[0..1] of Char;  // translation will be put here
  VirtualKey: Integer;               // virtual key code to be translated
  ScanCode: Integer;                 // keyboard scan code, to detect keypress
  MyKeyState: TKeyboardState;        // array of key states for each key
  ReturnCode: Integer;               // API return code
begin
  VirtualKey :=  Ord('A');           // ascii char or a virtual key code
  ScanCode := $1E;                   // letter a or A on keyboard hardware

  {setting MyKeyState entries to $00 makes a lowercase a}
  Fillchar(MyKeyState,SizeOf(MyKeyState),$00);
  ReturnCode := ToAscii(VirtualKey, ScanCode, MyKeyState, @WindowsChar, 0);
  Label1.Caption := 'Return Code is '+IntToStr(ReturnCode);
  Label2.Caption := 'Translated Character is '+ WindowsChar;
end;
```

Table 13-21: ToAscii Return Values

Value	Description
negative	The specified key is a dead key (accent or diacritic key).
0	The specified key has no translation for the specified state of the keyboard.
1	One Windows character was produced by the translation and copied to the output buffer.
2	Two Windows characters were produced by the translation. This means an accent or diacritic key was required, and no Windows character was available for that combination.

wvsprintf *Windows.Pas*

Syntax

```
wvsprintf(
Output: PChar;          {a pointer to an output string buffer}
Format: PChar;          {a pointer to the format string}
arglist: va_list        {a pointer to a list of arguments}
): Integer;             {returns the number of characters copied to the
                              output buffer}
```

Description

This function places a string of formatted text into the buffer pointed to by the Output parameter, according to the format string and variables given as parameters. Values are placed into the argument list specified by the arglist parameter, and then processed by wvsprintf and inserted into the output according to what is specified in the format string.

Parameters

Output: A pointer to a string buffer receiving the formatted text. This buffer must be allocated by the calling process.

Format: A pointer to the format string that has the information on how the output is to be presented. It will generally contain one or more format specifiers, each of which will use a data element from the arglist parameter. Each format specifier will begin with a percent sign (%) followed by additional codes from Table 13-22. The general format for a format specifier is

%[-][#][0][width][.precision]type

The brackets indicate optional fields. The simplest specifier would be %s, which would take the string for the next PChar argument in the arglist parameter, and put it in place of the format specifier in the output buffer. If the % symbol is not followed by any of the codes listed below, the next character is generated as output. For example, %% would produce a single percent sign as output. Some of the specifiers are case sensitive. Those which are not case sensitive will have both representations shown in Table 13-23. The first table below shows the purpose of each of the fields in a format specifier that can exist in a format string. The second table shows all the possible entries in the "type" field, which is the last field in the specifier.

arglist: A pointer to the array of parameters for the format specifiers. Each format specifier in the Format parameter that uses a variable will use a parameter in the arglist. The size of the array will be whatever is needed to provide enough 4-byte elements to satisfy the format specifiers. Each array element can be a PChar or an integer value up to 4 bytes in length. See the FormatMessage function for more information and examples on using argument arrays.

Return Value

If the function succeeds, the returned value is the number of characters copied to the output buffer, not counting the final null termination character. If the function fails, it returns a number that is less than the size of the minimum expected output buffer. It is not adequate to check the result against the length of the format string, because it is possible that the final output is shorter than the format string. In the integer example the format string contains format specifications like "%1ld" which is four characters. The substituted value is only one character. Therefore the error check must compare against the length of the format string less six characters (two instances of three characters less). To get extended error information, call the GetLastError function.

See also

FormatMessage, GetDateFormat, GetTimeFormat

Example

Listing 13-21: Formatting an Array of Arguments

```
{Delphi does not link in LocalHandle, so we must do it explicitly}
function LocalHandle(Mem: Pointer): HLOCAL; stdcall;

implementation

{link in LocalHandle}
function LocalHandle; external kernel32 name 'LocalHandle';

procedure MyErrorHandler(ErrorNumber:integer);
var
  ErrorMessage: PChar;        // pointer to message area.
  MyMemoryHandle: HLOCAL;
begin
  {display the system error message if something went wrong}
  FormatMessage(FORMAT_MESSAGE_FROM_SYSTEM or
       FORMAT_MESSAGE_ALLOCATE_BUFFER,
       nil,
       ErrorNumber,    // ID of error message to fetch
       0,
       @ErrorMessage,  // points to PChar pointer
       0,
       nil);
  ShowMessage('wvsprintf error: ' + ErrorMessage);
  MyMemoryHandle := LocalHandle(ErrorMessage);
  if (LocalFree(MyMemoryHandle) <> 0) then
    ShowMessage('Error freeing memory');
end;

procedure TForm1.Button2Click(Sender: TObject);
var
  MyOutputPtr: PChar;                  // points to output buffer
  MyOutput: array[1..100] of Char;     // output buffer
  APIresult: Integer;                  // function result
```

```
  MyArguments: array[0..1] of Integer;  // list of arguments
  MyFormat: string;                     // format spec / template
begin
  {initialize the format string an parameters}
  MyOutputPtr := @MyOutput;
  MyFormat := 'There were %lld dogs and %lld birds in my house.';
  MyArguments[0] := 3;
  MyArguments[1] := 2;

  {display the formatted string}
  APIresult := wvsprintf(MyOutputPtr, PChar(MyFormat), @MyArguments);
  Label1.Caption := MyOutputPtr;

  {if there was a problem, display the error message}
  if APIresult < (length(MyFormat)-6) then
    MyErrorHandler(GetLastError);
end;

procedure TForm1.Button1Click(Sender: TObject);
var
  MyOutputPtr: PChar;                       // points to output buffer
  MyOutput: array[1..200] of Char;          // output buffer
  APIresult: Integer;                       // result of function call
  MyArguments: array[0..5] of PChar;        // argument array of strings
  MyStrings: array[0..5] of string;         // data space for strings
  MyFormatPtr: PChar;                       // points to format string
  FormatStr: string;                        // format string
begin
  {initialize the format string and format arguments}
  MyOutputPtr    := @MyOutput;
  FormatStr      := Edit1.Text;
  MyFormatPtr    := Pchar(FormatStr);
  MyStrings[0]   := Edit2.Text;
  MyArguments[0] := (PChar(MyStrings[0]));
  MyStrings[1]   := Edit3.Text;
  MyArguments[1] := (PChar(MyStrings[1]));
  MyStrings[2]   := Edit4.Text;
  MyArguments[2] := (PChar(MyStrings[2]));
  MyStrings[3]   := Edit5.Text;
  MyArguments[3] := (PChar(MyStrings[3]));
  MyStrings[4]   := Edit6.Text;
  MyArguments[4] := (PChar(MyStrings[4]));
  MyStrings[5]   := Edit7.Text;
  MyArguments[5] := (PChar(MyStrings[5]));

  {display the formatted string}
  APIresult := wvsprintf(MyOutputPtr, MyFormatPtr, @MyArguments);
  Label1.Caption := MyOutputPtr;

  {if there was a problem, display the error message}
  if APIresult < (strlen(MyFormatPtr)) then
    MyErrorHandler(GetLastError);
end;
```

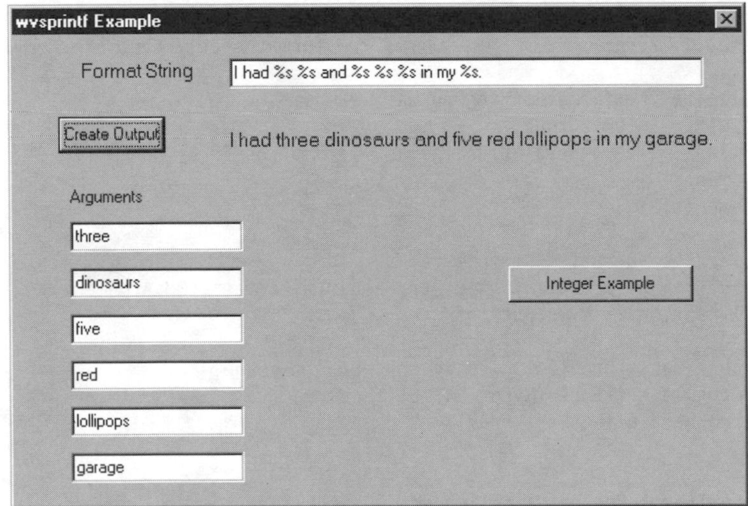

Figure 13-16: The formatted string.

Table 13-22: wvsprintf Format Fields

Value	Description
-	Pad the output to the right and justify to the left. If this is omitted, pad to the left and justify to the right.
#	Prefix hexadecimal output with 0x or 0X, uppercase or lowercase according to the specification of the "type" parameter.
0	Any padding is to be done with zeroes. If omitted, pad with spaces.
width	Total minimum width of the output. Padding will be performed according to the previous fields, but the output will never be truncated. If omitted, all output will be generated subject to the precision field.
.precision	Copy the specified digits to output for numerical specifications, or the number of characters for string specifications. The value is not truncated. This serves as a padding specification, not an absolute width specification. If this field is omitted, or given as a 0 or as a single period, the precision is 1.
type	Specification on how to format the output for strings, characters, or numbers. See Table 13-23 for possible field entries.

Table 13-23: wvsprintf Format Types

Type	Description
c	Single character. Values of zero are ignored. Wchar for Unicode programs and char otherwise.
C	Single character. Char for Unicode programs and Wchar otherwise. Consider using the c (lowercase) instead of C (uppercase) for general use.
d	Signed decimal integer. Same as i.

Type	Description
hc, hC	Single character. Always interpreted as a char, even in Unicode programs.
hs, hS	Null-terminated string (PChar), even in Unicode programs.
i	Signed decimal integer. Same as d.
lc, lC	Single character. Ignores zero values. Always treated as Wchar, regardless of whether or not the program is a Unicode program.
ld, li	Long signed decimal integer.
ls, lS, s	Wide null-terminated string (lpwstr), PChar to a wide string, even when not in a Unicode program.
lu	Interpreted as a long unsigned integer.
lx, lX	Long unsigned hexadecimal integer, in lowercase or uppercase.
S	Null-terminated string, always single-byte character width even in Unicode programs.
u	Interpreted as unsigned integer.
x, X	Unsigned hexadecimal integer, lowercase or uppercase.

Chapter 14

System Information Functions

At some point, certain applications will need to query the system to determine various aspects about the operating system it is running on, the machine hardware, etc. This chapter covers a broad range of information query and modification functions, such as retrieving the computer name, the current local time, startup information, the Windows version, and environment variables.

Accessibility Features

Just about any systemwide parameter a user can modify through a control panel applet is available to a Windows application. Everything from the size of a window border to the wallpaper selected for the desktop can be queried or modified by the System-ParametersInfo function. This function also makes a number of accessibility features available to the application. These accessibility features provide alternative forms of user interface communication to users who are physically challenged in one way or another. For example, Windows has an accessibility feature called SoundSentry. This feature allows the system to display a visual indicator when a sound has been generated, thus alerting a hearing impaired user that the application has emitted audible feedback. The following example demonstrates turning this accessibility feature on.

Listing 14-1: Using the Sound Sentry Accessibility Feature

```
procedure TForm1.Button1Click(Sender: TObject);
var
  SoundInfo: TSoundSentry;       // holds the sound sentry options
begin
  {initialize the sound sentry options}
  with SoundInfo do
  begin
    cbSize := SizeOf(TSoundSentry);
    dwFlags := SSF_SOUNDSENTRYON;
    iFSTextEffect := SSTF_BORDER;
    iFSTextEffectMSec := 500;
    iFSTextEffectColorBits := clRed;
    iFSGrafEffect := SSGF_DISPLAY;
    iFSGrafEffectMSec := 500;
    iFSGrafEffectColor := clRed;
```

```
    iWindowsEffect := SSWF_WINDOW;
    iWindowsEffectMSec := 500;
    lpszWindowsEffectDLL := NIL;
    iWindowsEffectOrdinal := 0
  end;

  {turn on the sound sentry for visual indication of sounds}
  if SystemParametersInfo(SPI_SETSOUNDSENTRY, SizeOf(TSoundSentry),
                          @SoundInfo, 0)
end;

procedure TForm1.Button2Click(Sender: TObject);
begin
  {output a sound through the internal speaker}
  MessageBeep(0);
end;
```

SystemParametersInfo could be used to create some very interesting utilities outside of the control panel. For example, the following application demonstrates how to change the desktop wallpaper.

Listing 14-2: Changing the Desktop Wallpaper

```
procedure TForm1.FileListBox1Click(Sender: TObject);
begin
  {display a preview of the selected image}
  Image1.Picture.LoadFromFile(FileListBox1.FileName);
end;

procedure TForm1.Button1Click(Sender: TObject);
begin
  {set the selected image as the desktop wallpaper.  this value
   will be written to the Win.ini file}
  if FileListBox1.ItemIndex>-1 then
    SystemParametersInfo(SPI_SETDESKWALLPAPER, 0, PChar(FileListBox1.FileName),
                         SPIF_SENDCHANGE);
end;
```

System Information Functions

The following system information functions are covered in this chapter:

Table 14-1: System Information Functions

Function	Description
ExpandEnvironmentStrings	Expands an environment variable string with its defined value.
FreeEnvironmentStrings	Frees an environment block returned from GetEnvironmentStrings.

Function	Description
GetCommandLine	Retrieves the command line used to launch the application.
GetComputerName	Retrieves the network computer name.
GetDiskFreeSpace	Retrieves information on free disk space.
GetDriveType	Retrieves a specified drive type, such as fixed or removable.
GetEnvironmentStrings	Retrieves a block of environment variable strings for the current process.
GetEnvironmentVariable	Retrieves the value of a single environment variable.
GetLocaleInfo	Retrieves information on the specified locale.
GetLocalTime	Retrieves the local time.
GetLogicalDrives	Retrieves the drives available to the machine.
GetLogicalDriveStrings	Retrieves the names of the drives available to the machine.
GetStartupInfo	Retrieves the startup information for the application's main window.
GetSystemDefaultLangID	Retrieves the system default language identifier.
GetSystemDefaultLCID	Retrieves the system default locale identifier.
GetSystemDirectory	Retrieves the Windows system directory.
GetSystemInfo	Retrieves system hardware information.
GetSystemTime	Retrieves the current system time.
GetSystemTimeAsFileTime	Retrieves the current system time in a file system time format.
GetTimeZoneInformation	Retrieves time zone information concerning standard and daylight savings time.
GetUserDefaultLangID	Retrieves the user-defined default language identifier.
GetUserDefaultLCID	Retrieves the user-defined default locale identifier.
GetUserName	Retrieves the logged on network user name.
GetVersionEx	Retrieves the Windows version.
GetVolumeInformation	Retrieves information on the specified volume.
GetWindowsDirectory	Retrieves the Windows directory.
SetComputerName	Sets the network computer name.
SetEnvironmentVariable	Sets the value of a single environment variable.
SetLocaleInfo	Sets the specified locale information.
SetLocalTime	Sets the local time.
SetSystemTime	Sets the system time.
SetVolumeLabel	Sets the specified volume's label.
SystemParametersInfo	Retrieves or modifies a number of systemwide parameters.
VerLanguageName	Retrieves the name of the specified language.

ExpandEnvironmentStrings Windows.Pas

Syntax

ExpandEnvironmentStrings(	
lpSrc: PChar;	{a string that contains the variable to expand}
lpDst: PChar;	{buffer to receive string}
nSize: DWORD	{the maximum size of buffer}
): DWORD;	{returns the number of bytes copied to the buffer}

Description

This function is used to expand an environment variable string. This function will also return the size of the new expanded string.

Parameters

lpSrc: A pointer to a null-terminated string containing the unexpanded environment variable. This string can contain one or more environment variable references. Each reference in the string is expanded and the resulting string is returned. These variable strings take the form of %*variable name*%, where the variable name is an environment variable.

lpDst: A pointer to a buffer that receives the new expanded string. If this parameter is set to NIL, the function returns the required size of the buffer to hold the expanded environment string.

nSize: The maximum size of the buffer. If the lpDst parameter is set to NIL, set this parameter to zero.

Return Value

If the function succeeds, it returns the number of characters copied to the buffer; otherwise it returns zero. To get extended error information, call the GetLastError function.

See also

GetEnvironmentStrings, GetEnvironmentVariable

Example

Listing 14-3: Expanding an Environment Variable

```
procedure TForm1.Button1Click(Sender:Tobject);
var
  ExpandedStr: array[0..255] of char;  // holds the expanded environment string
begin
  {expand the %TEMP% environment string}
  ExpandEnvironmentStrings('Temp directory is: %TEMP%',ExpandedStr,
                           SizeOf(ExpandedStr));

  {display the expanded string}
  Label1.Caption := StrPas(ExpandedStr);
end;
```

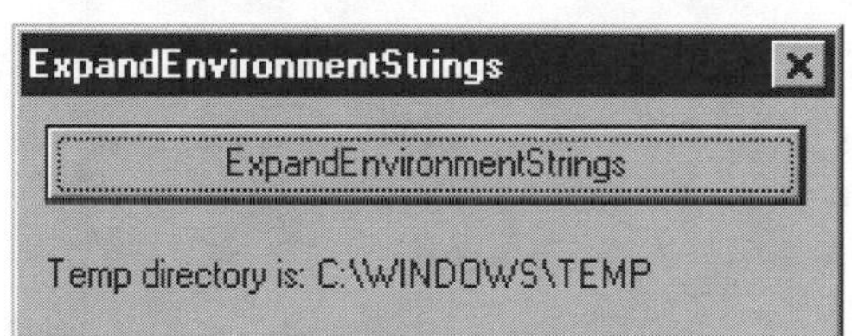

Figure 14-1: The expanded environment variable.

FreeEnvironmentStrings Windows.Pas

Syntax

```
FreeEnvironmentStrings(
p1: PChar                {a pointer to the environment strings block to free}
): BOOL;                 {returns TRUE or FALSE}
```

Description

This function frees a block of environment variable strings as returned by the GetEnvironmentStrings function.

Parameters

p1: A pointer to a block of environment variable strings as returned by the GetEnvironmentStrings function.

Return Value

If the function succeeds, it returns TRUE; otherwise it returns FALSE. To get extended error information, call the GetLastError function.

See also

GetEnvironmentStrings

Example

Please see Listing 14-7 under GetEnvironmentStrings.

GetCommandLine Windows.Pas

Syntax

```
GetCommandLine: PChar    {returns the command line string}
```

Description

The GetCommandLine function is used to get the command line that was used to start the program. This includes any command line parameters. The command line is returned in the form of a null-terminated string.

Return Value

If the function succeeds, it returns a pointer to the null-terminated command line string; otherwise it returns NIL.

See also

CreateProcess

Example

Listing 14-4: Retrieving the Command Line

```
procedure TForm1.Button1Click(Sender: TObject);
begin
  {retrieve the command line}
  Label1.Caption := StrPas(GetCommandLine);
end;
```

GetComputerName Windows.Pas

Syntax

GetComputerName(	
lpBuffer: PChar;	{a pointer to a buffer that receives the computer name}
var nSize: DWORD	{the size of the lpBuffer buffer}
): BOOL;	{returns TRUE or FALSE}

Description

This function retrieves the Windows networking computer name for the current system. The function also can retrieve the required size of the buffer to store the computer name. When the nSize parameter is set to zero and the lpBuffer parameter is set to NIL, the function will return the required size of the lpBuffer in the nSize parameter.

Parameters

lpBuffer: A pointer to a null-terminated string buffer receiving the computer name.

nSize: A variable that specifies the maximum length of the buffer pointed to by the lpBuffer parameter, in characters. This value should be at least MAX_COMPUTER-NAME_LENGTH in size.

Return Value

If the function succeeds, it returns TRUE and the variable pointed to by the nSize parameter receives the number of characters copied to the buffer. If the function fails, it returns FALSE. To get extended error information, call the GetLastError function.

See also

SetComputerName, GetUserName

Example

Please see Listing 14-20 under SetComputerName.

GetDiskFreeSpace Windows.Pas

Syntax

```
GetDiskFreeSpace(
lpRootPathName: PChar;                   {a pointer to the root path string}
var lpSectorsPerCluster: DWORD;          {the number of sectors per cluster}
var lpBytesPerSector: DWORD;             {the number of bytes per sector}
var lpNumberOfFreeClusters: DWORD;       {the number of free clusters}
var lpTotalNumberOfClusters: DWORD       {the total number of clusters on the drive}
): BOOL;                                 {returns TRUE or FALSE}
```

Description

The GetDiskFreeSpace function retrieves information about a drive partition. It returns all the information needed to calculate the available free space for a drive. Note that under Windows 95 prior to service release 2, this function will return incorrect values for volumes bigger than 2 gigabytes in size.

Parameters

lpRootPathName: A null-terminated string containing the root directory of the drive to query.

lpSectorsPerCluster: A variable receiving the number of sectors per cluster for the specified drive. A sector is a collection of bytes, a cluster is a collection of sectors.

lpBytesPerSector: A variable receiving the number of bytes in each sector of the drive.

lpNumberOfFreeClusters: A variable receiving the number of free clusters on the drive. Drives are used in full cluster increments. Storing a file that is smaller then one cluster will allocate the entire cluster. To get the amount of free drive space in bytes, take the number of free clusters multiplied by the number of sectors per cluster, multiplied by the number of bytes per sector as in the following formula:

FreeClusters * SectorsPerCluster * BytesPerSector = Free space in bytes

lpTotalNumberOfClusters: A variable receiving the total number of clusters on the drive. To find the total size of the drive in bytes, take the total number of clusters multiplied by the number of sectors per cluster, multiplied by the number of bytes per sector, as in the following formula:

TotalNumberOfClusters * SectorsPerCluster * BytesPerSector = Size of drive in bytes

Return Value

If the function succeeds, it returns TRUE; otherwise it returns FALSE. To get extended error information, call the GetLastError function.

See also

GetDriveType

Example

Listing 14-5: Retrieving the Free Disk Space

```
procedure TForm1.Button1Click(Sender: Tobject);
var
  SectorsPerCluster,  // holds the sectors per cluster
  BytesPerSector,     // holds the bytes per sector
  FreeClusters,       // holds the number of free clusters
  Clusters: DWORD;    // holds the total number of disk clusters
begin
  {retrieve the disk space information}
  if GetDiskFreeSpace('C:\',SectorsPerCluster,BytesPerSector,
                      FreeClusters,Clusters) then
  begin
    {display the disk space information}
    Panel2.Caption := IntToStr(SectorsPerCluster);
    Panel3.Caption := IntToStr(BytesPerSector);
    Panel4.Caption := IntToStr(FreeClusters);
    Panel5.Caption := IntToStr(Clusters);
    Panel6.Caption := IntToStr(FreeClusters*BytesPerSector*SectorsPerCluster);
    Panel7.Caption := IntToStr(Clusters*BytesPerSector*SectorsPerCluster);
  end;
end;
```

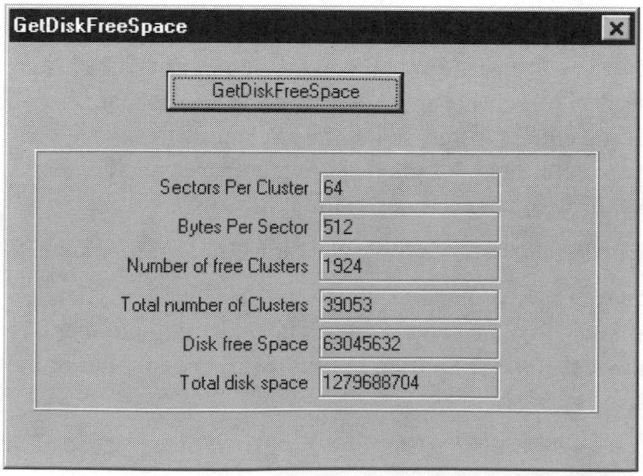

Figure 14-2: Free disk space.

GetDriveType Windows.Pas

Syntax

GetDriveType(
lpRootPathName: PChar {a pointer to the root path string}
): UINT; {returns a value based on the drive type}

Description

GetDriveType is used to determine the type of drive being accessed, and will indicate fixed, removable, or remote (network) drives.

Parameters

lpRootPathName: A null-terminated string containing the root directory of the drive to be queried. If this parameter is NIL, the function uses the root of the current directory.

Return Value

If the function is successful, it returns one value from Table 14-2; otherwise it returns DRIVE_UNKNOWN.

See also

GetDiskFreeSpace

Example

Listing 14-6: Retrieving Drive Types

```
procedure TForm1.DriveComboBox1Change(Sender: TObject);
var
  DrivePath: array[0..3] of char;     // holds the root directory to query
begin
  {assemble the name of the root path of the drive to query}
  StrPCopy(DrivePath, DriveComboBox1.Drive);
  StrCat(DrivePath, ':\');

  {retrieve the drive type and display it}
  case GetDriveType(DrivePath) of
    DRIVE_UNKNOWN:     Panel1.Caption := 'No Type Information';
    DRIVE_NO_ROOT_DIR: Label1.Caption := 'Root Directory does not exist';
    DRIVE_REMOVABLE:   Panel1.Caption := 'Removable';
    DRIVE_FIXED:       Panel1.Caption := 'Fixed';
    DRIVE_REMOTE:      Panel1.Caption := 'Remote';
    DRIVE_CDROM:       Panel1.Caption := 'CDROM';
    DRIVE_RAMDISK:     Panel1.Caption := 'RamDisk';
  end;
end;
```

Figure 14-3: This drive is a CD-ROM.

Table 14-2: GetDriveType Return Values

Value	Description
DRIVE_UNKNOWN	The drive type cannot be determined.
DRIVE_NO_ROOT_DIR	The root directory does not exist.
DRIVE_REMOVABLE	Indicates a removable disk drive.
DRIVE_FIXED	Indicates a nonremovable disk drive (hard drive).
DRIVE_REMOTE	Indicates a remote (network) drive.
DRIVE_CDROM	Indicates a CD-ROM drive.
DRIVE_RAMDISK	Indicates a RAM disk.

GetEnvironmentStrings Windows.Pas

Syntax

GetEnvironmentStrings: PChar {returns a pointer to the environment strings}

Description

The GetEnvironmentStrings function returns a pointer to the system environment variable strings. This includes environment variable settings such as the PATH, PROMPT, and LASTDRIVE environment variables. The return value from this parameter can be used to specify the environment address in a call to the CreateProcess function. When the environment strings block is no longer needed, it should be freed by calling the FreeEnvironmentStrings function.

Return Value

If the function succeeds, it returns a pointer to a null-terminated string buffer. This buffer is composed of each environment variable string separated by a null-terminating character. The buffer is ended with a double null-terminating character. If the function fails, it returns NIL.

See also

CreateProcess, GetEnvironmentVariable, SetEnvironmentVariable, FreeEnvironmentStrings

Example

Listing 14-7: Retrieving the Environment Strings

```
procedure TForm1.Button1Click(Sender: Tobject);
var
  MyPointer: PChar;        // holds the returned environment strings
begin
  {clear the memo}
  Memo1.Lines.Clear;

  {retrieve the environment strings}
  MyPointer := GetEnvironmentStrings;

  {begin displaying environment strings}
  if MyPointer <> nil then
    while MyPointer <> nil do
    begin
      {display an environment string}
      Memo1.Lines.Add(StrPas(MyPointer));

      {environment strings are separated by null terminators, so if we
       increment the pointer past the null terminator of the last string
       displayed, it will be at the beginning of the next string}
      Inc(MyPointer,StrLen(MyPointer)+1);

      {determine if we are at the end of the environment strings buffer}
      if (Byte(MyPointer[0]) = 0) then MyPointer := nil;
    end;

  {the environment strings are no longer needed, so free them}
  FreeEnvironmentStrings(MyPointer);
end;
```

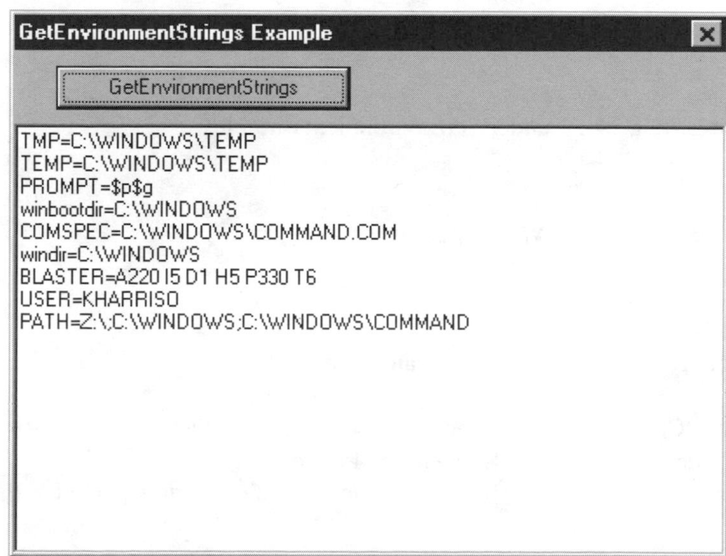

Figure 14-4: The returned environment strings.

GetEnvironmentVariable Windows.Pas

Syntax

```
GetEnvironmentVariable(
lpName: PChar;              {a pointer to the variable name string}
lpBuffer: PChar;            {a pointer to a string to receive the value}
nSize: DWORD                {the size of the lpBuffer}
): DWORD;                   {returns the number of bytes written to the buffer}
```

Description

The GetEnvironmentVariable function retrieves a given environment variable value. The function can also return the required size of buffer to hold the environment variable value.

Parameters

lpName: A null-terminated string containing the name of the environment variable to be retrieved.

lpBuffer: A pointer to a null-terminated string buffer that receives the environment variable's value. If this parameter is set to NIL, the function returns the size of buffer required to hold the environment variable's value.

nSize: Specifies the maximum size of the buffer in characters.

Return Value

If the function succeeds, it returns the number of characters copied to the buffer pointed to by the lpBuffer parameter; otherwise it returns zero.

See also

GetEnvironmentStrings, SetEnvironmentVariable

Example

Please see Listing 14-21 under SetEnvironmentVariable.

GetLocaleInfo Windows.Pas

Syntax

```
GetLocaleInfo(
Locale: LCID;               {the locale identifier}
LCType: LCTYPE;             {information type flag}
lpLCData: PChar;            {a pointer to an output buffer}
cchData: Integer            {the length of the output buffer}
): Integer;                 {returns the number of characters copied to the buffer}
```

Description

GetLocaleInfo retrieves specific information for a certain locale. A variety of information is available according to the flag specified in the LCType parameter. The function returns the locale information in the form of a string, stored in the buffer pointed to by the lpLCData parameter.

Parameters

Locale: The locale identifier from which information is requested. This can be a specific locale identifier or one value from Table 14-3.

LCType: A flag indicating the type of information requested. The constant LOCALE_NOUSEROVERRIDE may be combined with any one of the items from Table 14-4, which means user overrides are not considered and the system default value for the locale is returned.

lpLCData: A pointer to a string buffer that receives the requested locale information.

cchData: Specifies the size, in bytes, of the buffer pointed to by the lpLCData parameter. If this parameter is zero, the function returns the number of bytes required to hold the requested information, and the lpLCData parameter is ignored.

Return Value

If the function succeeds, it returns the number of bytes copied to the lpLCData buffer, and lpLCData will point to a string containing the requested information. If the function fails, it returns zero. To get extended error information, call the GetLastError function.

See also

GetSystemDefaultLCID, GetUserDefaultLCID, SetLocaleInfo

Example

Listing 14-8: Retrieving Locale Information

```
procedure TForm1.Button1Click(Sender: TObject);
var
  OutputBuffer: PChar;  // holds local info
  SelectedLCID: LCID;   // holds the selected LCID
begin
  {allocate memory for the string}
  OutputBuffer := StrAlloc(255);

  {get the native language}
  if RadioButton1.Checked then
    SelectedLCID := GetSystemDefaultLCID
  else
    SelectedLCID := GetUserDefaultLCID;

  GetLocaleInfo(SelectedLCID, LOCALE_SNATIVELANGNAME,
                OutputBuffer, 255);
```

```
  Label1.Caption :='Native language for user locale is ' + OutputBuffer;

  {get the measurement system}
  GetLocaleInfo(SelectedLCID, LOCALE_IMEASURE, OutputBuffer, 255);
  if OutputBuffer = '0' then
    Label2.Caption := 'This country uses metric measurements.';
  if OutputBuffer = '1' then     // pounds, ounces, quarts, miles, etc.
    Label2.Caption := 'This country uses British measurements.';

  {get the name of Sunday}
  GetLocaleInfo(SelectedLCID, LOCALE_SDAYNAME7, OutputBuffer, 255);
  Label3.Caption := 'This country calls Sunday ' + OutputBuffer;

  {dispose of the string memory}
  StrDispose(OutputBuffer);
end;
```

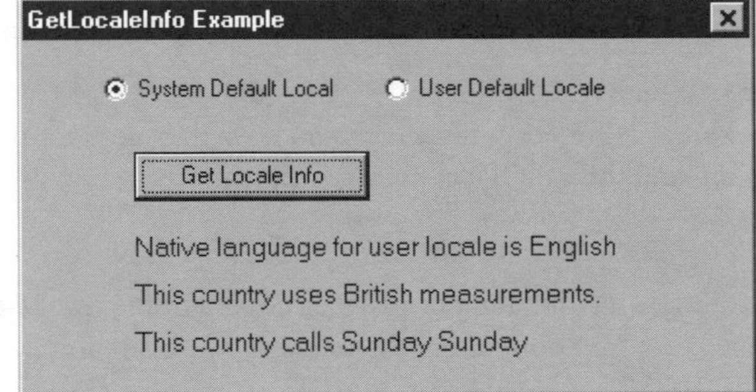

Figure 14-5: Default locale information.

Table 14-3: GetLocaleInfo Locale Values

Value	Description
LOCALE_SYSTEM_DEFAULT	The system's default locale.
LOCALE_USER_DEFAULT	The user's default locale.

Table 14-4: GetLocaleInfo LCType Values

Value	Description
LOCALE_ICENTURY	Specifier for four-digit century. The maximum number size of this string is 2. The specifier can be one of the following values: 0 = abbreviated two-digit century; 1 = four-digit century.
LOCALE_ICOUNTRY	Country code, given as an IBM country code (international phone code) with a maximum length of six characters.
LOCALE_ICURRDIGITS	Number of fractional digits for local monetary displays, with the maximum size of the returned output buffer being three characters.

Value	Description
LOCALE_ICURRENCY	Positive currency mode. Maximum output buffer is two characters. The mode values are given in Table 14-5.
LOCALE_IDATE	Short date format. The maximum size of this string is two. The specifier can be any of the values from Table 14-6.
LOCALE_IDAYLZERO	Specifier for leading zeroes in day fields. The maximum size of this string is two. The specifier can be one of the following values: 0 = no leading zeroes for days; 1 = leading zeroes for days.
LOCALE_IDEFAULTCODEPAGE	OEM code page for this country. This has a maximum size of six characters.
LOCALE_IDEFAULTCOUNTRY	Country code of the primary country of the locale. This has a maximum size of six characters.
LOCALE_IDEFAULTLANGUAGE	Language identifier of the primary language of the locale. This has a maximum size of five characters.
LOCALE_IDIGITS	This is the number of fractional digits. The maximum number of digits for this return value is three. That does not mean that the maximum number of fractional digits is three. It means the maximum number could possibly be 999, taking up three spaces in the returned output buffer.
LOCALE_IINTLCURRDIGITS	Number of fractional digits for international monetary displays, maximum size being three characters.
LOCALE_ILANGUAGE	Language of the locale. Maximum length is five.
LOCALE_ILDATE	Long date format. The maximum size of this string is two. The specifier can be any of the values from Table 14-6.
LOCALE_ILZERO	Specifies if leading zeroes exist for decimal fields. 0 = no leading zeroes, 1 = use leading zeroes. The maximum number of spaces returned for this field is two.
LOCALE_IMEASURE	System of measurement for the locale. 0 for metric (S.I.) and 1 for U.S. measurement system. The maximum size for this value is two characters.
LOCALE_IMONLZERO	Specifier for leading zeroes in month fields. The maximum size of this string is two. The specifier can be one of the following values: 0 = no leading zeroes for months; 1 = leading zeroes for months.
LOCALE_INEGCURR	Negative currency mode. Maximum size for this string is three. The mode can be any of the values in Table 14-7.

Value	Description
LOCALE_INEGSEPBYSPACE	Separation of monetary symbol in a negative monetary value. This value is 1 if the monetary symbol is separated by a space from the negative amount, 0 if it is not. The maximum size of this string is two.
LOCALE_INEGSIGNPOSN	Formatting index for negative values. The maximum size of this string is two. The index can be one of the values from Table 14-8.
LOCALE_INEGSYMPRECEDES	Position of monetary symbol in a negative monetary value. This value is 1 if the monetary symbol precedes the negative amount, 0 if it follows it. The maximum size of this string is two.
LOCALE_IPOSSEPBYSPACE	Separation of monetary symbol in a positive monetary value. This value is 1 if the monetary symbol is separated by a space from a positive amount, 0 if it is not. The maximum size of this string is two.
LOCALE_IPOSSIGNPOSN	Formatting index for positive values. The maximum size of this string is two. The index can be one of the values from Table 14-8.
LOCALE_IPOSSYMPRECEDES	Position of monetary symbol in a positive monetary value. This value is 1 if the monetary symbol precedes the positive amount, 0 if it follows it. The maximum size of this string is two.
LOCALE_ITIME	Time format specifier. The maximum size of this string is two. The specifier can be one of the following values: 0 = AM / PM 12-hour format; 1 = 24-hour format
LOCALE_ITLZERO	Specifier for leading zeroes in time fields. The maximum size of this string is 2. The specifier can be one of the following values: 0 = no leading zeroes for hours; 1 = leading zeroes for hours.
LOCALE_S1159	String for the AM designator.
LOCALE_S2359	String for the PM designator.
LOCALE_SABBREVCTRYNAME	ISO 3166 abbreviated country name.
LOCALE_SABBREVDAYNAME1	Native abbreviated name for Monday.
LOCALE_SABBREVDAYNAME2	Native abbreviated name for Tuesday.
LOCALE_SABBREVDAYNAME3	Native abbreviated name for Wednesday.
LOCALE_SABBREVDAYNAME4	Native abbreviated name for Thursday.
LOCALE_SABBREVDAYNAME5	Native abbreviated name for Friday.
LOCALE_SABBREVDAYNAME6	Native abbreviated name for Saturday.
LOCALE_SABBREVDAYNAME7	Native abbreviated name for Sunday.

Value	Description
LOCALE_SABBREVLANGNAME	Name of language, in abbreviated ISO 639 format, using the two-character abbreviation, with a possible third character to indicate a sublanguage.
LOCALE_SABBREVMONTHNAME1	Native abbreviated name for January.
LOCALE_SABBREVMONTHNAME2	Native abbreviated name for February.
LOCALE_SABBREVMONTHNAME3	Native abbreviated name for March.
LOCALE_SABBREVMONTHNAME4	Native abbreviated name for April.
LOCALE_SABBREVMONTHNAME5	Native abbreviated name for May.
LOCALE_SABBREVMONTHNAME6	Native abbreviated name for June.
LOCALE_SABBREVMONTHNAME7	Native abbreviated name for July.
LOCALE_SABBREVMONTHNAME8	Native abbreviated name for August.
LOCALE_SABBREVMONTHNAME9	Native abbreviated name for September.
LOCALE_SABBREVMONTHNAME10	Native abbreviated name for October.
LOCALE_SABBREVMONTHNAME11	Native abbreviated name for November.
LOCALE_SABBREVMONTHNAME12	Native abbreviated name for December.
LOCALE_SCOUNTRY	Unabbreviated localized name of the country.
LOCALE_SCURRENCY	Monetary symbol. ($ for the U.S.)
LOCALE_SDATE	Characters for the date separator.
LOCALE_SDAYNAME1	Native long name for Monday.
LOCALE_SDAYNAME2	Native long name for Tuesday.
LOCALE_SDAYNAME3	Native long name for Wednesday.
LOCALE_SDAYNAME4	Native long name for Thursday.
LOCALE_SDAYNAME5	Native long name for Friday.
LOCALE_SDAYNAME6	Native long name for Saturday.
LOCALE_SDAYNAME7	Native long name for Sunday.
LOCALE_SDECIMAL	Character that is used as a decimal separator (such as a period for U.S. floating point values).
LOCALE_SENGCOUNTRY	Unabbreviated English name of the country. This representation can always be shown in a 7-bit ASCII (127 character) character set.
LOCALE_SENGLANGUAGE	Full English name of the locale, in ISO Standard 639 format. This representation can always be shown in a 7-bit ASCII (127 character) character set.
LOCALE_SGROUPING	Number of decimal digits in each group to the left of the decimal character. This is a string with values separated by semicolons. The number in each group is given separately. If a number is common for all groups, specify the number followed by a zero group. In the U.S. this would be given by a string value 3;0; meaning that all the groups have three decimal digits.

Value	Description
LOCALE_SINTLSYMBOL	ISO 4217 international monetary symbol for the locale, given as three characters, followed by the character which separates the string from the amount display.
LOCALE_SLANGUAGE	Full unabbreviated localized language name for this locale.
LOCALE_SLIST	The character that is used as a list separator for the locale.
LOCALE_SLONGDATE	Long date formatting string for the current locale.
LOCALE_SMONDECIMALSEP	Characters used as the monetary decimal separator.
LOCALE_SMONGROUPING	Sizes for each group of decimal digits to the left of the decimal point. The number in each group is given separately. If a number is common for all groups, specify the number followed by a zero group. In the U.S. this would be given by a string value 3;0; meaning that all the groups have three decimal digits.
LOCALE_SMONTHNAME1	Native long name for January.
LOCALE_SMONTHNAME2	Native long name for February.
LOCALE_SMONTHNAME3	Native long name for March.
LOCALE_SMONTHNAME4	Native long name for April.
LOCALE_SMONTHNAME5	Native long name for May.
LOCALE_SMONTHNAME6	Native long name for June.
LOCALE_SMONTHNAME7	Native long name for July.
LOCALE_SMONTHNAME8	Native long name for August.
LOCALE_SMONTHNAME9	Native long name for September.
LOCALE_SMONTHNAME10	Native long name for October.
LOCALE_SMONTHNAME11	Native long name for November.
LOCALE_SMONTHNAME12	Native long name for December.
LOCALE_SMONTHOUSANDSEP	Characters used as monetary separators for groups of digits to the left of the decimal point.
LOCALE_SNATIVE DIGITS	The native digits for 0 through 9. This allows any characters in the locales character set to be used to represent numerical output regardless of their ASCII value mappings.
LOCALE_SNATIVECTRYNAME	Name of the country in the native language.
LOCALE_SNATIVELANGNAME	Name of the language in the native language.
LOCALE_SNEGATIVESIGN	String value for the negative sign.
LOCALE_SPOSITIVESIGN	String value for the positive sign.
LOCALE_SSHORTDATE	Short date formatting string for the current locale.

Value	Description
LOCALE_STHOUSAND	Character or characters used to separate digit groups on the left side of the decimal character (decimal point). This would be the comma for U.S. locales.
LOCALE_STIME	Characters for the time separator.
LOCALE_STIMEFORMAT	Time formatting strings for the current locale.

Table 14-5: LCType LOCALE_ICURRENCY Mode Values

Value	Description
0	Prefix with no separation.
1	Suffix with no separation.
2	Prefix with one character separation.
3	Suffix with one character separation.

Table 14-6: LCType LOCALE_IDATE and LOCALE_ILDATE Values

Value	Description
0	Month-Day-Year
1	Day-Month-Year
2	Year-Month-Day

Table 14-7: LCType LOCALE_INEGCURR Mode Values

Value	Description
0	($1.1)
1	-$1.1
2	$-1.1
3	$1.1-
4	(1.1$)
5	-1.1$
6	1.1-$
7	1.1$-
8	-1.1 $ (space before $)
9	-$ 1.1 (space after $)
10	1.1 $- (space before $)
11	$ 1.1- (space after $)
12	$ -1.1 (space after $)
13	1.1- $ (space before $)
14	($ 1.1) (space after $)
15	(1.1 $) (space before $)

Table 14-8: LCType LOCALE_INEGSIGNPOSN and LOCALE_IPOSSIGNPOSN Values

Value	Description
0	Parentheses surround the amount and the monetary symbol.
1	The sign string precedes the amount and the monetary symbol.
2	The sign string succeeds the amount and the monetary symbol.
3	The sign string immediately precedes the monetary symbol.
4	The sign string immediately succeeds the monetary symbol.

GetLocalTime *Windows.Pas*

Syntax

```
GetLocalTime(
var lpSystemTime: TSystemTime  {a pointer to a TSystemTime structure}
);                             {this procedure does not return a value}
```

Description

The GetLocalTime function retrieves the current local date and time.

Parameters

lpSystemTime: A pointer to a TSystemTime structure that receives the current local date and time. The TSystemTime data structure is defined as:

```
TSystemTime = record
      wYear: Word;              {the current year}
      wMonth: Word;             {the month number}
      wDayOfWeek: Word;         {the day of the week number}
      wDay: Word;               {the current day of the month}
      wHour: Word;              {the current hour}
      wMinute: Word;            {the current minute}
      wSecond: Word;            {the current second}
      wMilliseconds: Word;      {the current millisecond}
end;
```

Please see the FileTimeToSystemTime function for a description of this data structure.

See also

GetSystemTime, SetLocalTime

Example

Please see Listing 14-23 under SetLocalTime.

GetLogicalDrives Windows.Pas

Syntax

GetLogicalDrives: DWORD {returns a bitmask representing available drives}

Description

The GetLogicalDrives function retrieves a bitmask value, where each bit represents an available drive (bit 0 = drive A, bit 1 = drive B, etc.).

Return Value

If the function succeeds, it returns a bitmask value representing available drives; otherwise it returns zero.

See also

GetLogicalDriveStrings

Example

Listing 14-9: Retrieving a List of Available Drives

```
procedure TForm1.Button1Click(Sender: Tobject);
var
  AvailableDrives: DWord;            // holds the bitmask of available drives
  Counter: Integer;                  // general loop counter
  DrivePath: array[0..3] of Char;    // holds the drive name

  TheDriveStrings: array[0..4*26+2] of Char; // holds the drive strings
  StringPtr: PChar;                          // a pointer to the drive strings
begin
  {display column headings}
  StringGrid1.Cells[0,0] := 'Drive Letter';
  StringGrid1.Cells[1,0] := 'Status';
  StringGrid1.Cells[2,0] := 'Drive Type';

  {retrieve the available disk drives}
  AvailableDrives := GetLogicalDrives;

  {loop through all 26 possible drive letters}
  for Counter := 0 to 25 do
  begin
    {display the drive letter}
    StringGrid1.Cells[0,Counter+1] := Char(Ord('A')+Counter);

    {if this drive is available...}
    if LongBool(AvailableDrives and ($0001 shl Counter)) = True then
    begin
      {indicate that the drive is available}
      StringGrid1.Cells[1,Counter+1]:='Available';

      {prepare drive path for GetDriveType function}
      StrpCopy(DrivePath,Char(Ord('A')+Counter));
```

```
      StrCat(DrivePath,':\');

      {retrieve and display the drive type}
      case GetDriveType(DrivePath) of
        DRIVE_UNKNOWN:     StringGrid1.Cells[2,Counter+1]:= 'No Type Information';
        DRIVE_NO_ROOT_DIR: StringGrid1.Cells[2,Counter+1]:= 'Root does not exist';
        DRIVE_REMOVABLE:   StringGrid1.Cells[2,Counter+1]:= 'Removable';
        DRIVE_FIXED:       StringGrid1.Cells[2,Counter+1]:= 'Fixed';
        DRIVE_REMOTE:      StringGrid1.Cells[2,Counter+1]:= 'Remote';
        DRIVE_CDROM:       StringGrid1.Cells[2,Counter+1]:= 'CDROM';
        DRIVE_RAMDISK:     StringGrid1.Cells[2,Counter+1]:= 'RamDisk';
      end;
    end
    else
      {indicate that this drive is not available}
      StringGrid1.Cells[1,Counter+1]:='Not Available';
  end;

  {retrieve the logical drive strings}
  GetLogicalDriveStrings(SizeOf(TheDriveStrings), TheDriveStrings);

  {initialize the pointer to the beginning of the drive strings buffer}
  StringPtr := TheDriveStrings;

  {begin looping through the drive strings}
  while StringPtr<>nil do
  begin
    {add this string to the list box}
    ListBox1.Items.Add(StringPtr);

    {logical drive strings are seperated by null terminators, so if we
     increment the pointer past the null terminator of the last string
     displayed, it will be at the beginning of the next string}
    Inc(StringPtr,StrLen(StringPtr)+1);

    {determine if we are at the end of the logical drive strings buffer}
    if (Byte(StringPtr[0]) = 0) then StringPtr := nil;
  end;
end;
```

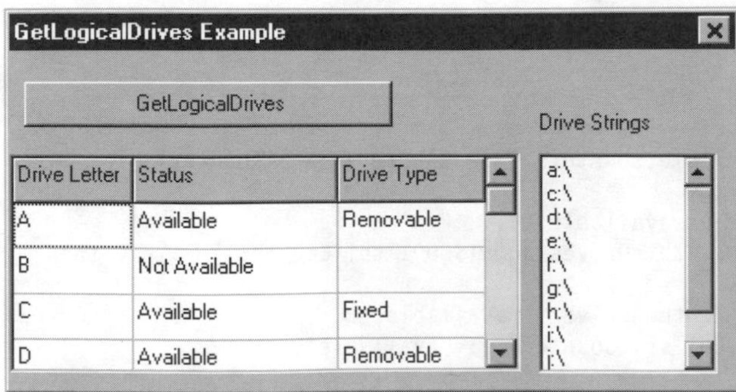

Figure 14-6: Available drives.

GetLogicalDriveStrings Windows.Pas

Syntax

```
GetLogicalDriveStrings(
nBufferLength: DWORD;        {the size of the buffer}
lpBuffer: PAnsiChar          {a pointer to a buffer receiving drive name strings}
): DWORD;                    {returns the number of characters copied to
                                  the buffer}
```

Description

This function retrieves the names of all logically defined drives, including mapped network drives, and stores them in the buffer pointed to by the lpBuffer parameter.

Parameters

nBufferLength: Specifies the size of the buffer pointed to by the lpBuffer parameter, excluding the null terminator.

lpBuffer: A pointer to a buffer that receives the names of the logical drives. Logical drive names are in the form of *driveletter*:\ (i.e., C:\). Each drive name in the string is separated by a null-terminating character, and the string is ended with two null-terminating characters. If this parameter is set to NIL, the function returns the size of the buffer required to hold the drive names.

Return Value

If the function succeeds, it returns the number of characters copied to the buffer, not counting the null terminator at the end. If the function fails, it returns zero. To get extended error information, call the GetLastError function.

See also

GetDriveType, GetDiskFreeSpace, GetLogicalDrives

Example

Please see Listing 14-9 under GetLogicalDrives.

GetStartupInfo Windows.Pas

Syntax

```
GetStartupInfo(
var lpStartupInfo: TStartupInfo     {record to receive startup info}
);                                  {this procedure does not return a value}
```

Description

The GetStartupInfo function retrieves information about the main window of the calling process when the process was created.

Parameters

lpStartupInfo: A pointer to a TStartupInfo structure that receives information about the main window of the calling process. The TStartupInfo structure is defined as:

```
TStartupInfo = record
      cb: DWORD;                          {the size of the TStartupInfo record}
      lpReserved: Pointer;                {reserved}
      lpDesktop: Pointer;                 {a pointer to the desktop}
      lpTitle: Pointer;                   {the title for console applications}
      dwX: DWORD;                         {the default column (left) position}
      dwY: DWORD;                         {the default row (top) position}
      dwXSize: DWORD;                     {the default width}
      dwYSize: DWORD;                     {the default height}
      dwXCountChars: DWORD;               {the screen width for a console app}
      dwYCountChars: DWORD;               {the screen height for a console app}
      dwFillAttribute: DWORD;             {color settings for a console app}
      dwFlags: DWORD;                     {flags to determine significant fields}
      wShowWindow: Word;                  {the default show window setting}
      cbReserved2: Word;                  {reserved}
      lpReserved2: PByte;                 {reserved}
      hStdInput: THandle;                 {the standard handle for input}
      hStdOutput: THandle;                {the standard handle for output}
      hStdError: THandle;                 {the standard handle for error output}
end;
```

Please see the CreateProcess function for a detailed description of this data structure.

See also

CreateProcess

Example

Listing 14-10: Retrieving the Startup Information

```
const
  {define the names of the ShowWindow constants}
  ShowConst: array[0..10] of string = ('SW_HIDE','SW_SHOWNORMAL',
                                       'SW_SHOWMINIMIZED', 'SW_SHOWMAXIMIZED',
                                       'SW_SHOWNOACTIVATE','SW_SHOW',
                                       'SW_MINIMIZE', 'SW_SHOWMINNOACTIVE',
                                       'SW_SHOWNA','SW_RESTORE',
                                       'SW_SHOWDEFAULT') ;

procedure TForm1.Button1Click(Sender: TObject);
var
  MyStartupInfo: TStartupInfo;    // holds window startup properties
begin
  {retrieve the startup properties}
```

```
  GetStartupInfo(MyStartupInfo);

  {display the startup properties}
  Panel_State.Caption  := ShowConst[MyStartupInfo.wShowWindow];
  Panel_Left.Caption   := IntToStr(MyStartupInfo.dwX);
  Panel_Top.Caption    := IntToStr(MyStartupInfo.dwY);
  Panel_Width.Caption  := IntToStr(MyStartupInfo.dwXSize);
  Panel_Height.Caption := IntToStr(MyStartupInfo.dwYSize);
end;
```

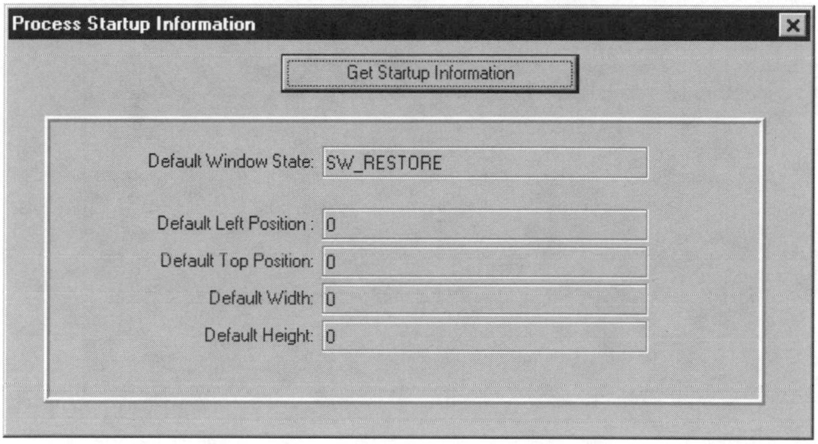

Process Startup Information

Get Startup Information

Default Window State: SW_RESTORE

Default Left Position : 0

Default Top Position: 0

Default Width: 0

Default Height: 0

Figure 14-7: The startup information.

GetSystemDefaultLangID   Windows.Pas

Syntax

GetSystemDefaultLangID: LANGID   {returns default system language identifier}

Description

This function returns the default language identifier for the system. Use the VerLanguageName function to get the name from the identifier.

Return Value

If the function succeeds, it returns the default numeric language identifier for the system; otherwise it returns zero.

See also

GetUserDefaultLangID, GetSystemDefaultLCID, VerLanguageName, GetLocaleInfo

Example

Listing 14-11: Retrieving the System Default Language Identifier

```
procedure TForm1.Button1Click(Sender: TObject);
var
```

```
  SDLName:array[0..255] of char;  // holds the name of the system language
  UDLName:array[0..255] of char;  // holds the name of the user language
begin
  {retrieve the names of the system and user default languages}
  VerLanguageName(GetSystemDefaultLangID,SDLName,255);
  VerLanguageName(GetUserDefaultLangID,UDLName,255);

  {display the names of the languages}
  Label_SD.caption := SDLName;
  Label_Ud.caption := UDLName;
end;
```

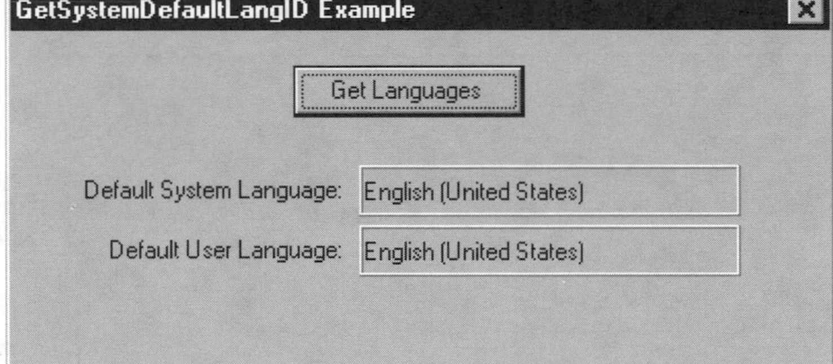

Figure 14-8: Language names for the system and user default languages.

GetSystemDefaultLCID Windows.Pas

Syntax

GetSystemDefaultLCID: LCID {returns the system default locale identifier}

Description

This function is used to retrieve the default locale identifier for the system.

Return Value

If the function succeeds, it returns the system default locale identifier. If the function fails, it returns zero.

See also

GetLocaleInfo, GetUserDefaultLCID

Example

Please see Listing 14-8 under GetLocaleInfo.

GetSystemDirectory Windows.Pas

Syntax

```
GetSystemDirectory(
lpBuffer: PChar;         {a pointer to a buffer receiving the directory string}
uSize: UINT              {the maximum size of the lpBuffer buffer}
): UINT;                 {returns the number of bytes written to the buffer}
```


Description

This function retrieves a string containing the path of the Windows system directory. Applications should not create files in this directory.

Parameters

lpBuffer: A pointer to a null-terminated string buffer receiving the Windows system directory path. If this parameter is set to NIL, the function returns the required size of the buffer to hold the Windows system directory path string.

uSize: Specifies the maximum size of the buffer pointed to by the lpBuffer parameter, in characters.

Return Value

If the function is successful, it returns the number of bytes written to the buffer pointed to by the lpBuffer parameter; otherwise it returns zero. To get extended error information, call the GetLastError function.

See also

GetCurrentDirectory, GetWindowsDirectory, SetCurrentDirectory

Example

Listing 14-12: Retrieving the Windows System Directory

```
procedure TForm1.Button1Click(Sender: TObject);
var
  SysDir: array[0..MAX_PATH] of Char;    // holds the system directory
begin
  {retrieve the system directory and display it}
  GetSystemDirectory(SysDir, MAX_PATH);
  Label1.Caption := StrPas(SysDir)
end;
```

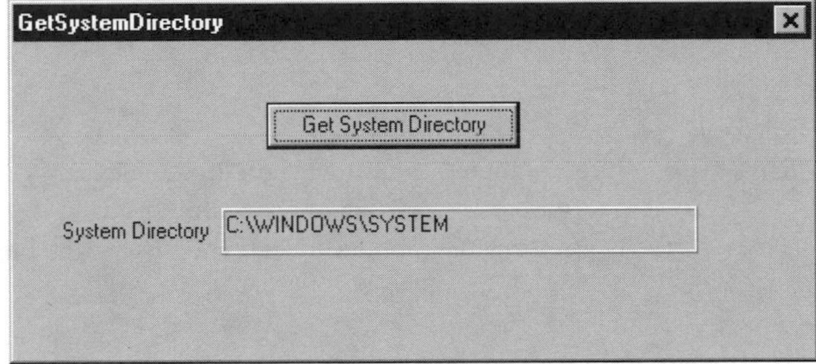

Figure 14-9: The Windows system directory.

GetSystemInfo　　　Windows.Pas

Syntax

```
GetSystemInfo(
var lpSystemInfo: TSystemInfo        {a pointer to a system information record}
);                                   {this procedure does not return a value}
```

Description

This function retrieves information about the type of system hardware in use.

Parameters

lpSystemInfo: A pointer to a TSystemInfo structure that receives information about the system and hardware upon which the process is running. The TSystemInfo data structure is defined as:

```
TSystemInfo = record
     case Integer of
     0: (
          dwOemId: DWORD)                        {specifies the ID of the OEM}
     1:(
          wProcessorArchitecture: Word           {the type of system processor}
          wReserved: Word                        {reserved}
          dwPageSize: DWORD                      {the page size for virtual memory}
          lpMinimumApplicationAddress: Pointer   {lowest memory access address}
          lpMaximumApplicationAddress: Pointer   {highest memory access address}
          dwActiveProcessorMask: DWORD           {a bit array of active processors}
          dwNumberOfProcessors: DWORD            {the number of processors}
          dwProcessorType: DWORD                 {the type of processor present}
          dwAllocationGranularity: DWORD         {granularity of virtual memory}
          wProcessorLevel: Word                  {system required processor level}
          wProcessorRevision: Word)              {system required processor revision}
     end;
```

dwOemId: This member is not used. Note that under Windows 95 this member will always be set to PROCESSOR_ARCHITECTURE_INTEL.

wProcessorArchitecture: Indicates the type of system specific processor architecture in the system, and can be one value from Table 14-9.

wReserved: This member is reserved for future use and is currently ignored.

dwPageSize: Indicates the page size of virtual memory. This value is used by the LocalAlloc function to allocate additional blocks of memory.

lpMinimumApplicationAddress: A pointer to the lowest memory address that is accessible by applications and DLLs.

lpMaximumApplicationAddress: A pointer to the highest memory address that is accessible by applications and DLLs.

dwActiveProcessorMask: An array of bits indicating which processors are present and active. Bit 0 indicates processor 0, bit 1 indicates processor 1, etc.

dwNumberOfProcessors: Indicates the total number of processors in the system.

dwProcessorType: Under Windows 95 and Windows NT prior to version 4, this member indicates the type of processor in the system. Under Windows NT version 4 and after, this member is ignored. This member can be one value from Table 14-10.

dwAllocationGranularity: Specifies the minimum amount of memory allocated each time virtual memory is used. In the past this has been hard coded to 64K, but it can vary for different processor architectures.

wProcessorLevel: This member is ignored under Windows 95. For windows NT 4.0 and later, this member indicates the level of the processor present, and can be one value from Table 14-11.

wProcessorRevision: This member is ignored under Windows 95. For windows NT 4.0 and later, this member indicates the revision of the processor present, and can be one value from Table 14-12.

See also

GetVersionEx

Example

Listing 14-13: Retrieving the System Information

```
const
  {Whoops!  These constants are used by the GetSystemInfo function,
   but they are not defined in the Delphi source code, so we must do it
   ourselves}
  PROCESSOR_INTEL_386 = 386;
  PROCESSOR_INTEL_486 = 486;
  PROCESSOR_INTEL_PENTIUM = 586;
  PROCESSOR_MIPS_R4000 = 4000;
  PROCESSOR_ALPHA_21064 = 21064;

  PROCESSOR_ARCHITECTURE_INTEL = 0;
```

```
  PROCESSOR_ARCHITECTURE_MIPS = 1;
  PROCESSOR_ARCHITECTURE_ALPHA = 2;
  PROCESSOR_ARCHITECTURE_PPC  = 3;
  PROCESSOR_ARCHITECTURE_UNKNOWN = $FFFF;

implementation

procedure TForm1.Button1Click(Sender: TObject);
var
  MySysInfo: TSystemInfo;   // holds the system information
begin
  {retrieve information about the system}
  GetSystemInfo(MySysInfo);

  {display the system's processor architecture}
  case MySysInfo.wProcessorArchitecture of
    PROCESSOR_ARCHITECTURE_INTEL: begin
      {dislay the processor architecture}
      Label_Arch.Caption := 'Intel Processor Architecture';

      {display the processor type}
      case MySysInfo.dwProcessorType of
        PROCESSOR_INTEL_386:     Label_Type.Caption := '80386';
        PROCESSOR_INTEL_486:     Label_Type.Caption := '80486';
        PROCESSOR_INTEL_PENTIUM: Label_Type.Caption := 'Pentium';
      end;
    end;
    PROCESSOR_ARCHITECTURE_MIPS:
      Label_Arch.Caption := 'MIPS Processor Architecture';
    PROCESSOR_ARCHITECTURE_ALPHA:
      Label_Arch.Caption := 'DEC ALPHA Processor Architecture';
    PROCESSOR_ARCHITECTURE_PPC:
      Label_Arch.Caption := 'PPC Processor Architecture';
    PROCESSOR_ARCHITECTURE_UNKNOWN:
      Label_Arch.Caption := 'Unknown Processor Architecture';
  end;
end;
```

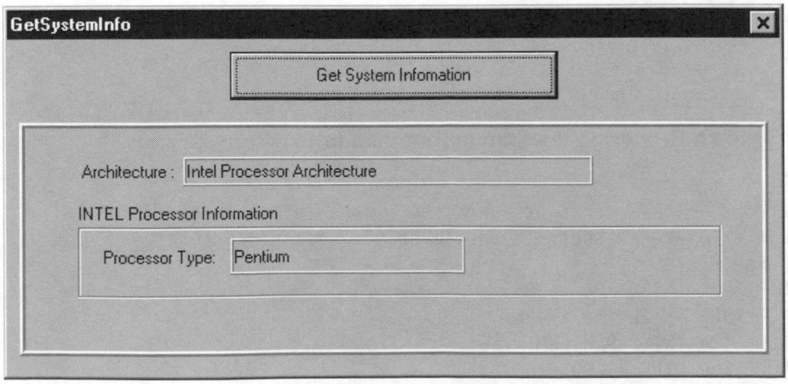

Figure 14-10: The processor architecture.

Table 14-9: lpSystemInfo wProcessorArchitecture Values

Name	Description
PROCESSOR_ARCHITECTURE_INTEL	Intel X86 processor architecture
PROCESSOR_ARCHITECTURE_MIPS	Windows NT only: MIPS processor architecture
PROCESSOR_ARCHITECTURE_ALPHA	Windows NT only: DEC ALPHI processor architecture
PROCESSOR_ARCHITECTURE_PPC	Windows NT only: PPC processor architecture
PROCESSOR_ARCHITECTURE_UNKNOWN	Windows NT only: Unknown processor architecture

Table 14-10: lpSystemInfo dwProcessorType Values

Name	Description
PROCESSOR_INTEL_386	Intel 386 processor.
PROCESSOR_INTEL_486	Intel 486 processor.
PROCESSOR_INTEL_PENTIUM	Intel Pentium processor.
PROCESSOR_MIPS_R4000	Windows NT only: R4000 processor
PROCESSOR_ALPHA_21064	Windows NT only: DEC ALPHA processor

Table 14-11: lpSystemInfo wProcessorLevel Values

wProcessorArchitecture Value	Value	Description
PROCESSOR_ARCHITECTURE_INTEL	1	Intel 80386
	2	Intel 80486
	3	Pentium
PROCESSOR_ARCHITECTURE_MIPS	4	MIPS R4000
PROCESSOR_ARCHITECTURE_ALPHA	21064	Alpha 21064
	21066	Alpha 21066
	21164	Alpha 21164
PROCESSOR_ARCHITECTURE_PPC	1	PPC 601
	3	PPC 603
	4	PPC 604
	6	PPC 603+
	9	PPC 604+
	20	PPC 620

Table 14-12: lpSystemInfo wProcessorRevision Values

Processor Type	Revision Breakdown
Intel 80386 or 80486	A value of the form xxyz. If xx = $FF then y - $A is the model number and z is the stepping identifier. For example, an Intel 80486-D0 will return a value of $FFD0. If xx < $FF then xx + "A" is the stepping letter and yz is the minor stepping.
Intel Pentium, Cyrix, or NextGen 586	A value of the form xxyy. xx = model number yy = stepping For example, a value of $0201 indicates Model 2, Stepping 1.
MIPS	A value of the form 00xx. xx = 8-bit revision number of the processor (the low-order 8 bits of the PRId register).
ALPHA	A value of the form xxyy. xx = model number yy = pass number For example, a value of $0201 indicates Model A02, Pass 01.
PPC	A value of the form xxyy. xx.yy = processor version register For example, a value of $0201 indicates Version 2.01.

GetSystemTime *Windows.Pas*

Syntax

```
GetSystemTime(
var SystemTime: TSystemTime          {a pointer to a system time structure}
)                                    {this procedure does not return a value}
```

Description

This function retrieves the current system date and time in Coordinated Universal Time (UTC) format.

Parameters

SystemTime: A pointer to a TSystemTime structure that receives the current system date and time. The TSystemTime data structure is defined as:

```
TSystemTime = record
    wYear: Word;                {the current year}
    wMonth: Word;               {the month number}
    wDayOfWeek: Word;           {the day of the week number}
    wDay: Word;                 {the current day of the month}
    wHour: Word;                {the current hour}
    wMinute: Word;              {the current minute}
    wSecond: Word;              {the current second}
    wMilliseconds: Word;        {the current millisecond}
end;
```


Please see the FileTimeToSystemTime function for a description of this data structure.

See also

GetLocalTime, SetSystemTime

Example

Please see Listing 14-24 under SetSystemTime.

GetSystemTimeAsFileTime Windows.Pas

Syntax

```
GetSystemTimeAsFileTime(
var lpSystemTimeAsFileTime: TFileTime      {returns system time as a TFileTime}
);                                         {this procedure does not return a value}
```

Description

This procedure is used to retrieve the current system date and time in the form of a file time variable. This value is expressed in Coordinated Universal Time (UTC).

Parameters

lpSystemTimeAsFileTime: A pointer to a TFileTime data structure that receives the current system time in Coordinated Universal Time (UTC) format. Please see the File Input/Output Functions chapter for more information about the Coordinated Universal Time (UTC) format and the TFileTime data structure.

See also

GetSystemTime, SystemTimeToFileTime

Example

Listing 14-14: Retrieving the System Time in 100-Nanosecond Intervals

```
procedure TForm1.Button1Click(Sender: TObject);
var
```

```
  MyFileTime: TFileTime;    // holds the system file time as a file time value
begin
  {retrieve the system time as a file time}
  GetSystemTimeAsFileTime(MyFileTime);

  {display the system time as a file time value}
  Panel1.Caption := IntToHex(MyFileTime.dwHighDateTime,8)+
                    IntToHex(MyFileTime.dwLowDateTime ,8) +
                    ' 100 Nanosecond intervals from January 1, 1601' ;
end;
```

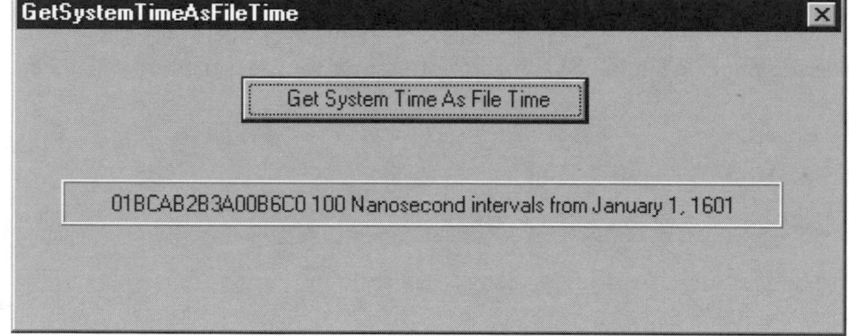

Figure 14-11: The current system time.

GetTimeZoneInformation   Windows.Pas

Syntax

GetTimeZoneInformation(
var lpTimeZoneInformation: TTimeZoneInformation   {a pointer to TTimeZoneInformation}
): DWORD;   {returns a time zone code}

Description

This function is used to retrieve the time zone information for the local system. The time zone information controls the translation between Coordinated Universal Time (UTC) and local time.

Parameters

lpTimeZoneInformation: A pointer to a TTimeZoneInformation data structure that receives the time zone information for the system. The TTimeZoneInformation data structure is defined as:

TTimeZoneInformation = record
    Bias: Longint   {Difference between times}
    StandardName: array[0..31] of WCHAR   {Name of time zone in Standard}
    StandardDate: TSystemTime   {Date of change to Standard time}
    StandardBias: Longint   {Standard time added to Bias}

```
    DaylightName: array[0..31] of WCHAR      {Name of time zone in Daylight}
    DaylightDate: TSystemTime                {Date of change to Daylight time}
    DaylightBias: Longint                    {Daylight time added to Bias}
end
```

Bias: Specifies the difference in local time and Coordinated Universal Time (UTC), in minutes. To find the translation between a UTC time format and local time, use the following formula:

Coördinated Universal Time = Local Time + Bias.

StandardName: Contains a null-terminated string describing the name of the time zone during Standard Daylight Time.

StandardDate: A TSystemTime structure that specifies the date that the system will change from Daylight Savings Time to Standard Time.

StandardBias: Additional difference in UTC and local time during Standard Time. This value is added to the Bias member when determining the difference in time during the Standard Time state, but most time zones value this to zero.

DaylightName: Contains a null-terminated string describing the name of the time zone during the Daylight Savings Time state.

DaylightDate: A TSystemTime structure that specifies the date that the system will change from Standard Time to Daylight Savings Time.

DaylightBias: Additional difference in UTC and local time during Daylight Savings Time. This valuc is added to the Bias member when determining the difference in time during the Daylight Savings Time state; most time zones value this to –60.

Return Value

If the function succeeds, it returns one time zone code from Table 14-13; otherwise it returns $FFFFFFFF. To get extended error information, call the GetLastError function.

See also

GetLocalTime, GetSystemTime

Example

Listing 14-15: Retrieving Time Zone Information

```
procedure TForm1.Button1Click(Sender: TObject);
var
  MyTimeZoneInformation: TTimeZoneInformation;  // holds time zone information
begin
  {retrieve the time zone information}
  GetTimeZoneInformation(MyTimeZoneInformation);

  {display the time zone information}
  Label_ST.Caption := WideCharToString(MyTimeZoneInformation.StandardName);
  Label_dt.Caption := WideCharToString(MyTimeZoneInformation.DaylightName);
```

```
  if MyTimeZoneInformation.StandardDate.wDay = 5 then
    Label_Startstandard.Caption := 'Last Sunday in '+
      LongMonthNames[MyTimeZoneInformation.StandardDate.wMonth]
  else
    Label_Startstandard.Caption :=
      IntToStr(MyTimeZoneInformation.StandardDate.wDay)+
      ' Sunday in '+ LongMonthNames[MyTimeZoneInformation.StandardDate.wMonth];
  if MyTimeZoneInformation.DaylightDate.wDay = 5 then
    Label_Startstandard.Caption := 'Last Sunday in '+
      LongMonthNames[MyTimeZoneInformation.DaylightDate.wMonth]
  else
    Label_Daylight.Caption := IntToStr(MyTimeZoneInformation.DaylightDate.wDay) +
      ' Sunday in '+ LongMonthNames[MyTimeZoneInformation.DaylightDate.wMonth];
end;
```

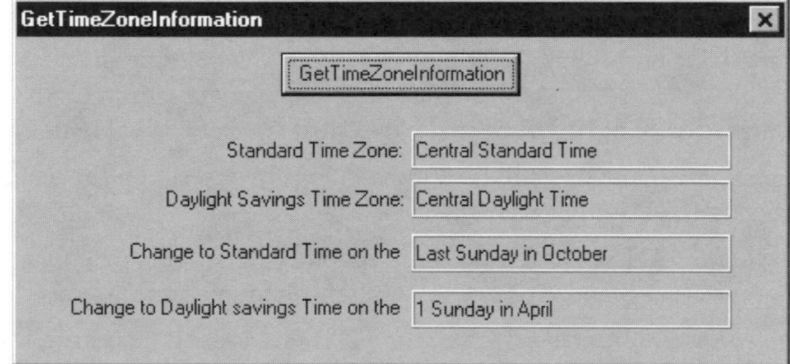

Figure 14-12: The time zone information.

Table 14-13: GetTimeZoneInformation Return Values

Value	Description
TIME_ZONE_ID_UNKNOWN	The system is in an unknown time zone.
TIME_ZONE_ID_STANDARD	The system is in Standard time state.
TIME_ZONE_ID_DAYLIGHT	The system is in Daylight Savings state.

GetUserDefaultLangID *Windows.Pas*

Syntax

GetUserDefaultLangID: LANGID {returns the default user language identifier}

Description

This function returns the default user identifier for the system. Use the VerLanguageName function to get the name from the identifier.

Return Value

If the function succeeds, it returns the default user numeric language identifier for the system; otherwise it returns zero.

See also

GetSystemDefaultLangID, GetUserDefaultLCID, VerLanguageName, GetLocaleInfo

Example

Please see Listing 14-11 under GetSystemDefaultLangID

GetUserDefaultLCID Windows.Pas

Syntax

```
GetUserDefaultLCID: LCID                {returns the user default locale identifier}
```

Description

This function is used to retrieve the default user locale identifier for the system.

Return Value

If the function succeeds, it returns the default user locale identifier. If the function fails, it returns zero.

See also

GetLocaleInfo, GetSystemDefaultLCID

Example

Please see Listing 14-8 under GetLocaleInfo.

GetUserName Windows.Pas

Syntax

```
GetUserName(
lpBuffer: PChar;              {a pointer to a buffer to receive the user name}
var nSize: DWORD              {the size of the buffer}
): BOOL;                      {returns TRUE or FALSE}
```

Description

This function is used to get the Windows networking user name for the current user logged onto the system.

Parameters

lpBuffer: A pointer to a null-terminated string receiving the user name. If this parameter is set to NIL, the variable identified by the nSize parameter will be set to the size of the buffer required to hold the user name string.

nSize: A variable containing the size of the buffer pointed to by the lpBuffer parameter, in characters. When the function returns, this variable will contain the number of characters copied to the lpBuffer buffer.

Return Value

If the function succeeds, it returns TRUE and the variable identified by the nSize parameter will contain the number of characters copied to the lpBuffer buffer. If the function fails, it returns FALSE. To get extended error information, call the GetLastError function.

See also

GetComputerName

Example

Listing 14-16: Retrieving the User Name

```
procedure TForm1.Button1Click(Sender: Tobject);
var
  UserName: PChar;     // holds the user name
  Count: Integer;      // holds the size of the user name
begin
  {retrieve the required size of the user name buffer}
  Count := 0;
  GetUserName(nil,Count);

  {allocate memory for the user name}
  Username := StrAlloc(Count);

  {retrieve the user name}
  if GetUserName(UserName,count) then
    Label1.Caption := StrPas(UserName)
  else ShowMessage('User Name Not Found');

  {dispose of allocated memory}
  StrDispose(UserName)
end;
```

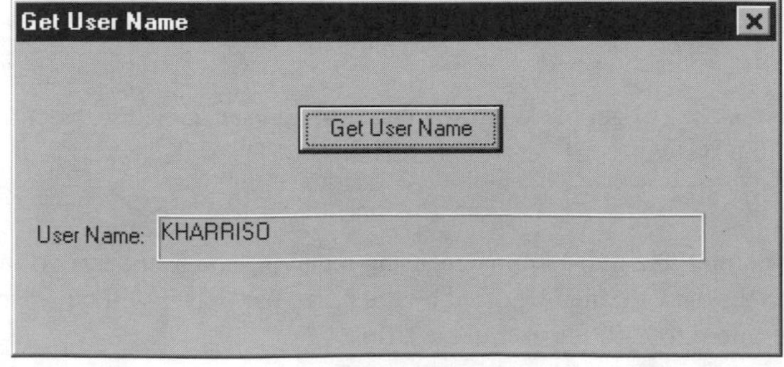

Figure 14-13: The user currently logged on.

GetVersionEx Windows.Pas

Syntax

```
GetVersionEx(
var lpVersionInformation: TOSVersionInfo     {pointer to a TOSVersionInfo structure}
): BOOL;                                      {returns TRUE or FALSE}
```

Description

This function retrieves information about the Windows version currently running on the system.

Parameters

lpVersionInformation: A pointer to a TOSVersionInfo data structure that receives information about the current version of Windows. The TOSVersionInfo data structure is defined as:

```
TOSVersionInfo = record
    dwOSVersionInfoSize: DWORD              {the size of TOSVersionInfo}
    dwMajorVersion: DWORD                   {the major version number}
    dwMinorVersion: DWORD                   {the minor version number}
    dwBuildNumber: DWORD                    {the build number}
    dwPlatformId: DWORD                     {operating system platform flags}
    szCSDVersion:array[0..127]of AnsiChar {additional O/S information}
end;
```

dwOSVersionInfoSize: Specifies the size of the TOSVersionInfo structure, in bytes. This member must be set to SizeOf(TOSVersionInfo).

dwMajorVersion: Specifies the major version number of the operating system.

dwMinorVersion: Specifies the minor version number of the operating system.

dwBuildNumber: Specifies the build number of the operating system. Under Windows 95, the high-order word of this value contains the major and minor version numbers.

dwPlatformId: A flag specifying the operating system platform. This member may contain one value from Table 14-14.

szCSDVersion: Contains a null-terminated string with additional information on the operating system.

Return Value

If the function succeeds, it returns TRUE; otherwise it returns FALSE. To get extended error information, call the GetLastError function.

See also

GetSystemInfo

Example

Listing 14-17: Retrieving Information about the Windows Version

```
procedure TForm1.Button1Click(Sender: TObject);
var
  MyVerInfo: TOSVersionInfo;    // holds version information
begin
  {set the size member of the TOSVersionInfo structure}
  MyVerInfo.dwOSVersionInfoSize := SizeOf(TOSVersionInfo);

  {retrieve the operating system version information}
  GetVersionEx(MyVerInfo);

  {display the operating system version information}
  Panel2.Caption := IntToStr(MyVerInfo.dwMajorVersion);
  Panel3.Caption := IntToStr(MyVerInfo.dwMinorVersion);
  Panel4.Caption := IntToStr(MyVerInfo.dwBuildNumber);
  case MyVerInfo.dwPlatformId of
    VER_PLATFORM_WIN32s:         Panel5.Caption := 'Win 32s under Windows 3.1';
    VER_PLATFORM_WIN32_WINDOWS: Panel5.Caption := 'Windows 95';
    VER_PLATFORM_WIN32_NT:       Panel5.Caption := 'Windows NT';
  end;
end;
```

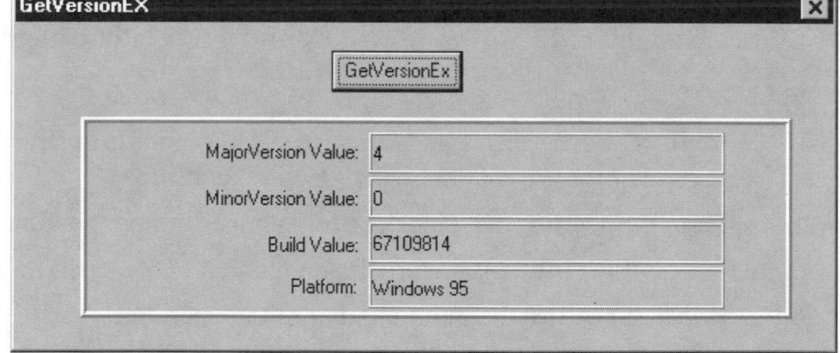

Figure 14-14: The current windows version.

Table 14-14: TOSVersionInfo dwPlatformId Values

Value	Description
VER_PLATFORM_WIN32s	Win32s on the 16-bit version of Windows
VER_PLATFORM_WIN32_WINDOWS	Windows 95
VER_PLATFORM_WIN32_NT	Windows NT

GetVolumeInformation Windows.Pas

Syntax

```
GetVolumeInformation(
lpRootPathName: PChar;                     {the path to the root directory}
lpVolumeNameBuffer: PChar;                 {the buffer receiving the volume name}
nVolumeNameSize: DWORD;                    {the maximum size of the buffer}
lpVolumeSerialNumber: PDWORD;              {a pointer to the volume serial number}
var lpMaximumComponentLength: DWORD;       {maximum file component name}
var lpFileSystemFlags: DWORD;              {file system flags}
lpFileSystemNameBuffer: PChar;             {the buffer receiving the file system name}
nFileSystemNameSize: DWORD                 {the maximum size of the file system name}
): BOOL;                                   {returns TRUE or FALSE}
```

Description

This function returns information about the file system and volume specified by the root directory path in the lpRootPathName parameter.

Parameters

lpRootPathName: A pointer to a null-terminated string containing the path of the root directory for the drive to query. If this parameter is set to NIL, the root directory of the current directory is used. For a UNC root directory path, add an additional backslash to the end (i.e., \\ServerName\ShareName\).

lpVolumeNameBuffer: A pointer to a null-terminated string buffer receiving the name of the volume.

lpVolumeNameSize: Specifies the maximum size of the lpVolumeNameBuffer buffer.

lpVolumeSerialNumber: A variable that receives the serial number of the volume.

lpMaximumComponentLength: A variable that receives the maximum size for filenames and directory names, in characters. Systems that support long filenames, such as the FAT system, will return a value of 255.

lpFileSystemFlags: A variable that receives a value indicating the type of file system in use. This variable can be set to any combination of values from Table 14-15.

lpFileSystemNameBuffer: A pointer to a null-terminated string buffer receiving the name of the file system, such as FAT or NTFS.

nFileSystemNameSize: Specifies the maximum size of the lpFileSystemNameBuffer buffer.

Return Value

If the function succeeds, it returns TRUE; otherwise it returns FALSE. To get extended error information, call the GetLastError function.

See also

GetFileAttributes, SetVolumeLabel

Example

Listing 14-18: Retrieving Volume Information

```
procedure TForm1.Button1Click(Sender: TObject);
var
  RootPath: array[0..20] of Char;     // holds the root directory name
  VolName: array[0..255] of Char;     // holds the volume name
  SerialNumber: DWORD;                // holds the serial number
  MaxCLength: DWORD;                  // holds the maximum file component length
  FileSysFlag: DWORD;                 // holds file system flags
  FileSysName: array[0..255] of Char; // holds the name of the file system
begin
  {indicate information is to be retrieved from the C drive}
  RootPath := 'C:\';

  {retrieve the volume information}
  GetVolumeInformation(RootPath, VolName, 255, @SerialNumber, MaxCLength,
     FileSysFlag, FileSysName, 255);

  {display the information}
  Panel2.Caption := VolName;
  Panel3.Caption := IntToHex(SerialNumber,8);
  Panel4.Caption := FileSysName;
end;
```

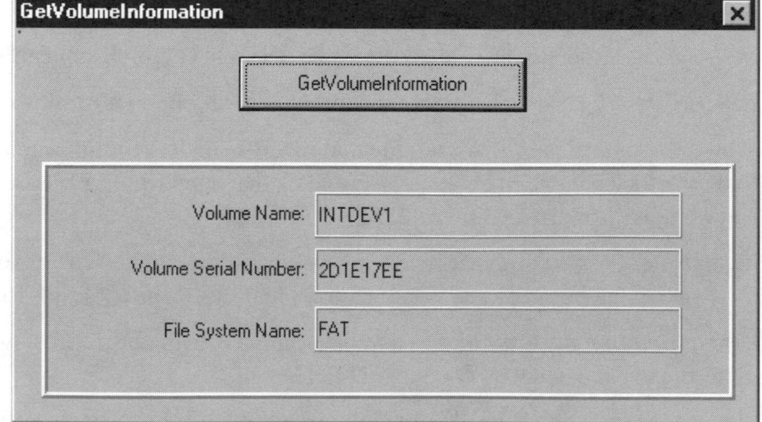

Figure 14-15: The current volume information.

Table 14-1:5 GetVolumeInformation lpFileSystemFlags Values

Value	Description
FS_CASE_IS_PRESERVED	Indicates that the case of the file or directory name is retained when it is stored to disk.

Value	Description
FS_CASE_SENSITIVE	Indicates that the file system supports case-sensitive filenames.
FS_UNICODE_STORED_ON_DISK	Indicates that the file system supports Unicode characters in filenames as they appear on disk.
FS_PERSISTENT_ACLS	Indicates that the file system preserves and enforces ACLs.
FS_FILE_COMPRESSION	Indicates that the file system supports file-based compression. This flag cannot be used with FS_VOL_IS_COMPRESSED.
FS_VOL_IS_COMPRESSED	Indicates that the specified volume is compressed. This flag cannot be used with FS_FILE_COMPRESSION.

GetWindowsDirectory   Windows.Pas

Syntax

```
GetWindowsDirectory(
lpBuffer: PChar;           {the buffer receiving Windows directory path}
uSize: UINT                {the maximum size of the buffer}
): UINT;                   {returns the number of bytes written to the buffer}
```

Description

This function retrieves the path for the Windows directory. Typically, this is the directory where applications should store initialization files and help files.

Parameters

lpBuffer: A pointer to a null-terminated string buffer receiving the Windows directory path. If this parameter is set to NIL, the function returns the required size of the buffer to hold the Windows directory path.

uSize: Specifies the maximum size of the buffer pointed to by the lpBuffer parameter, and should indicate a minimum size of MAX_PATH characters.

Return Value

If the function succeeds, it returns the number of characters copied to the buffer pointed to by the lpBuffer parameter, not including the null terminator. If the function fails, it returns zero. To get extended error information, call the GetLastError function.

See also

GetCurrentDirectory, GetSystemDirectory

Example

Listing 14-19: Retrieving the Windows Directory

```
procedure TForm1.Button1Click(Sender: TObject);
var
  WinDir: array[0..MAX_PATH] of char;   // holds the Windows directory
begin
  {retrieve the Windows directory...}
  GetWindowsDirectory(WinDir, MAX_PATH);

  {...and display it}
  Label1.Caption := StrPas(WinDir)
end;
```

SetComputerName Windows.Pas

Syntax

SetComputerName(
lpComputerName: PChar {a pointer to the new computer name}
): BOOL; {returns TRUE or FALSE}

Description

This function sets the computer name to the name specified by the lpComputerName parameter when the machine is rebooted.

Parameters

lpComputerName: A pointer to a null-terminated string containing the new name of the computer. This string cannot be longer than MAX_COMPUTERNAME_LENGTH characters.

Return Value

If the function succeeds, it returns TRUE; otherwise it returns FALSE. To get extended error information, call the GetLastError function.

See also

GetComputerName

Example

Listing 14-20: Setting and Retrieving the Computer Name

```
procedure TForm1.Button1Click(Sender: Tobject);
var
  ComputerName: array[0..MAX_COMPUTERNAME_LENGTH+1] of char;  // holds the name
  Size: Integer;                                               // holds the size
begin
  {initialize the computer name size variable}
```

```
  Size := MAX_COMPUTERNAME_LENGTH+1;

  {retrieve the computer name}
  if GetComputerName(ComputerName, Size) then
    Edit1.Text := StrPas(Computername)
  else Showmessage('Computer Name Not Found');
end;

procedure TForm1.Button2Click(Sender: TObject);
Var
  ComputerName: array[0..MAX_COMPUTERNAME_LENGTH+1] of char;  // holds the name
begin
  {copy the specified name to the ComputerName buffer}
  StrPCopy(ComputerName, Edit1.Text);

  {set the computer name}
  if SetComputerName(ComputerName) then
    ShowMessage('Computer Name Reset Setting will be used at next startup')
  else ShowMessage('Computer Name Not Reset');
end;
```


SetEnvironmentVariable Windows.Pas

Syntax

SetEnvironmentVariable(	
lpName: PChar;	{the name of the environment variable to change}
lpValue: PChar	{the new environment variable value}
): BOOL;	{returns TRUE or FALSE}

Description

This function sets an environment variable for the current process. This function can also add or delete the environment variable for the current process.

Parameters

lpName: A pointer to a null-terminated string containing the name of the environment variable to change. If the environment variable does not exist, the system will create it if the lpValue parameter does not contain NIL. If the environment variable exists and the lpValue parameter contains NIL, the system deletes the specified environment variable.

lpValue: A pointer to a null-terminated string containing the new value for the environment variable.

Return Value

If the function succeeds, it returns TRUE; otherwise it returns FALSE. To get extended error information, call the GetLastError function.

See also

GetEnvironmentVariable

Example

Listing 14-21: Setting and Retrieving Environment Variables

```
procedure TForm1.Button1Click(Sender: Tobject);
var
  ThePath: array[0..255] of char;        // holds the path environment variable
  Return: Integer;                       // holds the function return value
begin
  {retrieve the path environment variable}
  Return := GetEnvironmentVariable('Path', ThePath, SizeOf(ThePath));

  {indicate any errors retrieving the path variable}
  if Return = 0 then ShowMessage('Path variable not found')
  else if Return > 255 then ShowMessage('Path is greater than 255 characters')
  {otherwise, display the path environment variable}
  else Edit1.Text := ThePath;
end;

procedure TForm1.Button2Click(Sender: TObject);
var
  ThePath: array[0..255] of char;        // holds the path environment variable
begin
  {copy the specified path setting to the buffer}
  StrPCopy(ThePath, Edit1.Text);

  {set the path environment variable}
  if SetEnvironmentVariable('Path', ThePath) then
    ShowMessage('Variable has been Reset')
  else
    ShowMessage('Variable has not been set')
end;
```

Figure 14-16: The path environment variable.

SetLocaleInfo Windows.Pas

Syntax

SetLocaleInfo(
Locale: LCID; {the locale identifier}
LCType: LCTYPE; {locale data flag}
lpLCData: PChar {a pointer to the new data}
): BOOL; {returns TRUE or FALSE}

Description

This function sets specific information for the locale identified by the Locale parameter. However, only certain locale information can be modified with this function.

Parameters

Locale: The locale identifier for which the information will be set.

LCType: A flag indicating the type of locale information to change. This parameter can be set to one value from Table 14-16. Note that this table of values is a subset of the locale information flags available under the GetLocaleInfo function.

lpLCData: A pointer to a null-terminated string containing the locale information to be set.

Return Value

If the function succeeds, it returns TRUE; otherwise it returns FALSE. To get extended error information, call the GetLastError function.

See also

GetLocaleInfo

Example

Listing 14-22: Setting Locale Information

```
var
  Form1: TForm1;
  OriginalUnits: PChar;                     // holds original locale measurements
  OriginalUnitsBuff: array[0..1] of Char;

implementation

procedure TForm1.FormCreate(Sender: TObject);
begin
  {retrieve the original locale measurement units}
  OriginalUnits := @OriginalUnitsBuff;
  GetLocaleInfo(LOCALE_SYSTEM_DEFAULT, LOCALE_IMEASURE, OriginalUnits, 2);
end;

procedure TForm1.ButtonSetRadioClick(Sender: TObject);
var
```

```
  ChangeUnits: PChar;
  ChangeUnitsBuff: array[0..1] of Char;
begin
  {change the measurement units}
  ChangeUnits := @ChangeUnitsBuff;
  if RadioButtonBritish.Checked
    then ChangeUnits := '1'
    else ChangeUnits := '0';
  SetLocaleInfo(LOCALE_SYSTEM_DEFAULT, LOCALE_IMEASURE, ChangeUnits);

  {retrieve the set measurement units}
  GetLocaleInfo(LOCALE_SYSTEM_DEFAULT, LOCALE_IMEASURE, ChangeUnits, 2);
  if ChangeUnits = '0' then
    LabelMeasure.Caption := 'This country uses metric measurements.';
  if ChangeUnits = '1' then     // pounds, ounces, quarts, miles, etc.
    LabelMeasure.Caption := 'This country uses British measurements.';
end;

procedure TForm1.FormDestroy(Sender: TObject);
begin
  {restore original measurement units}
  SetLocaleInfo(LOCALE_SYSTEM_DEFAULT, LOCALE_IMEASURE, OriginalUnits);
end;
```

Table 14-16: SetLocaleInfo LCType Values

Value	Description
LOCALE_ICURRDIGITS	Number of fractional digits for local monetary displays, with the maximum size of the returned output buffer being three characters.
LOCALE_ICURRENCY	Positive currency mode. Maximum output buffer is two characters. The mode values are given in Table 14-17.
LOCALE_IDIGITS	This is the number of fractional digits. The maximum number of digits for this return value is three. That does not mean that the maximum number of fractional digits is three. It means the maximum number could possibly be 999, taking up three spaces in the returned output buffer.
LOCALE_ILZERO	Specifies if leading zeroes exist for decimal fields. 0 = no leading zeroes, 1 = use leading zeroes. The maximum number of spaces returned is two.
LOCALE_IMEASURE	System of measurement for the locale: 0 for metric (S.I.) and 1 for U.S. measurement system. The maximum size for this value is two characters.
LOCALE_INEGCURR	Negative currency mode. Maximum size for this string is three. The mode can be any of the values in Table 14-18.
LOCALE_ITIME	Time format specifier. The maximum size of this string is two. The specifier can be one of the following values: 0 = AM/PM 12-hour format; 1 = 24-hour format.

Value	Description
LOCALE_S1159	String for the AM designator.
LOCALE_S2359	String for the PM designator.
LOCALE_SCURRENCY	Monetary symbol. ($ for the U.S.)
LOCALE_SDATE	Characters for the date separator.
LOCALE_SDECIMAL	Character that is used as a decimal separator (such as a period for U.S. floating point values).
LOCALE_SGROUPING	Number of decimal digits in each group to the left of the decimal character. This is a string with values separated by semicolons. The number in each group is given separately. If a number is common for all groups, specify the number followed by a zero group. In the U.S. this would be given by a string value 3;0; meaning that all the groups have three decimal digits.
LOCALE_SLIST	The character that is used as a list separator for the locale.
LOCALE_SLONGDATE	Long date formatting string for the current locale.
LOCALE_SMONDECIMALSEP	Characters used as the monetary decimal separator.
LOCALE_SMONGROUPING	Sizes for each group of decimal digits to the left of the decimal point. The number in each group is given separately. If a number is common for all groups, specify the number followed by a zero group. In the U.S. this would be given by a string value 3;0; meaning that all the groups have three decimal digits.
LOCALE_SMONTHOUSANDSEP	Characters used as monetary separators for groups of digits to the left of the decimal point.
LOCALE_SNEGATIVESIGN	String value for the negative sign.
LOCALE_SPOSITIVESIGN	String value for the positive sign.
LOCALE_SSHORTDATE	Short date formatting string for the current locale.
LOCALE_STHOUSAND	Character or characters used to separate digit groups on the left side of the decimal character (decimal point). This would be the comma for U.S. locales.
LOCALE_STIME	Characters for the time separator.
LOCALE_STIMEFORMAT	Time formatting strings for the current locale.

Table 14-17: LCType LOCALE_ICURRENCY Mode Values

Value	Description
0	Prefix with no separation.
1	Suffix with no separation.
2	Prefix with one character separation.
3	Suffix with one character separation.

Table 14-18: LCType LOCALE_INEGCURR Mode Values

Value	Description
0	($1.1)
1	-$1.1
2	$-1.1
3	$1.1-
4	(1.1$)
5	-1.1$
6	1.1-$
7	1.1$-
8	-1.1 $ (space before $)
9	-$ 1.1 (space after $)
10	1.1 $- (space before $)
11	$ 1.1- (space after $)
12	$ -1.1 (space after $)
13	1.1- $ (space before $)
14	($ 1.1) (space after $)
15	(1.1 $) (space before $)

SetLocalTime *Windows.Pas*

Syntax

```
SetLocalTime(
const lpSystemTime: TSystemTime        {a pointer to a TSystemTime structure}
): BOOL;                               {returns TRUE or FALSE}
```

Description

This function sets the current local date and time. Under Windows NT, the calling process will need to have the SE_SYSTEMTIME_NAME security privilege or this function will fail.

Parameters

lpSystemTime: A pointer to a TSystemTime structure that contains the new current local date and time. The TSystemTime data structure is defined as:

```
TSystemTime = record
      wYear: Word;                {the current year}
      wMonth: Word;               {the month number}
      wDayOfWeek: Word;           {the day of the week number}
      wDay: Word;                 {the current day of the month}
      wHour: Word;                {the current hour}
```

```
    wMinute: Word;          {the current minute}
    wSecond: Word;          {the current second}
    wMilliseconds: Word;    {the current millisecond}
end;
```

Please see the FileTimeToSystemTime function for a description of this data structure.

Return Value

If the function succeeds, it returns TRUE; otherwise it returns FALSE. To get extended error information, call the GetLastError function.

See also

GetLocalTime, GetSystemTime, SetSystemTime

Example

Listing 14-23: Setting and Retrieving the Current Local Time

```
procedure TForm1.Button1Click(Sender: Tobject);
var
  CurrentTime : TSystemTime;                  // holds time information
begin
  {retrieve the local time}
  GetLocalTime(CurrentTime);

  {display the local time elements}
  Edit1.Text := IntToStr(CurrentTime.wMonth)+'/'+
                IntToStr(CurrentTime.wDay)+'/'+
                IntToStr(CurrentTime.wYear);
  Edit2.Text := IntToStr(CurrentTime.wDayOfWeek)+' Day of week';
  Edit3.Text := IntToStr(CurrentTime.wHour)+':'+
                IntToStr(CurrentTime.wMinute)+':'+
                IntToStr(CurrentTime.wSecond);
end;

procedure TForm1.Button2Click(Sender: TObject);
var
  CurrentTime : TSystemTime;                  // holds time information
begin
  {retrieve the current time to initialize members of the CurrentTime
   structure that are not initialized from UI elements}
  GetLocalTime(CurrentTime);
  try
    {set the date from the user supplied date}
    Decodedate(StrToDateTime(Edit1.Text),CurrentTime.wYear,CurrentTime.wMonth,
      CurrentTime.wDay);

    {set the time from the user supplied time}
    DecodeTime(StrToTime(Edit3.text),CurrentTime.wHour,CurrentTime.wMinute,
      CurrentTime.wSecond,CurrentTime.wMilliseconds);

    {set the local time}
```

```
    SetLocalTime(CurrentTime)
  except
    {display a message if an error occurred}
    on E:Exception do ShowMessage('Error setting local time');
  end;
end;
```

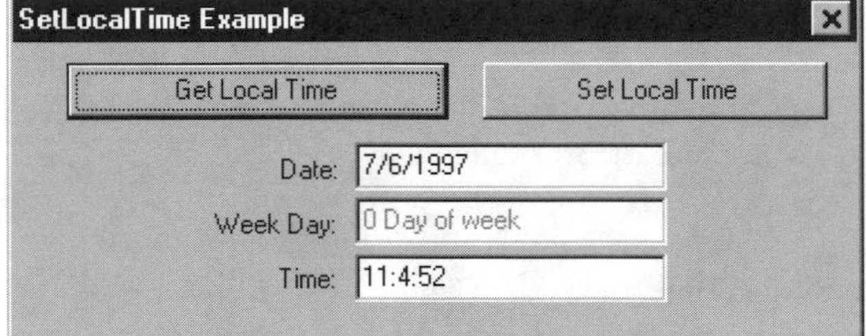

Figure 14-17: The current local time.

SetSystemTime Windows.Pas

Syntax

SetSystemTime(	
const lpSystemTime: TSystemTime	{a pointer to a TSystemTime structure}
): BOOL;	{returns TRUE or FALSE}

Description

This function sets the current system date and time. The system time is in Coordinated Universal Time (UTC) format. Under Windows NT, the calling process will need to have the SE_SYSTEMTIME_NAME security privilege or this function will fail.

Parameters

lpSystemTime: A pointer to a TSystemTime structure that contains the new current system date and time. The TSystemTime data structure is defined as:

TSystemTime = record	
wYear: Word;	{the current year}
wMonth: Word;	{the month number}
wDayOfWeek: Word;	{the day of the week number}
wDay: Word;	{the current day of the month}
wHour: Word;	{the current hour}
wMinute: Word;	{the current minute}
wSecond: Word;	{the current second}
wMilliseconds: Word;	{the current millisecond}
end;	

Note that the value of the wDayOfWeek member is ignored. Please see the FileTimeToSystemTime function for a description of this data structure.

Return Value

If the function succeeds, it returns TRUE; otherwise it returns FALSE. To get extended error information, call the GetLastError function.

See also

GetLocalTime, GetSystemTime, SetLocalTime

Example

Listing 14-24: Setting and Retrieving the System Time

```
procedure TForm1.Button1Click(Sender: Tobject);
var
  CurrentTime: TSystemTime;        // holds the system time
begin
  {retrieve the system time}
  GetSystemTime(CurrentTime);

  {display the system time}
  Edit1.Text := IntToStr(CurrentTime.wmonth)+'/'+
                IntToStr(CurrentTime.wDay)+'/'+
                IntToStr(CurrentTime.wYear);
  Edit2.Text := IntToStr(CurrentTime.wDayOfWeek)+' Day of week';
  Edit3.Text := IntToStr(CurrentTime.wHour)+':'+
                IntToStr(CurrentTime.wMinute)+':'+IntToStr(CurrentTime.wSecond);
end;

procedure TForm1.Button2Click(Sender: TObject);
var
  CurrentTime : TSystemTime;       // holds the system time
begin
  {retrieve the system time to initialize members of CurrentTime
   that are not supplied by the user}
  GetSystemTime(CurrentTime);
  try
    {set the date from the supplied date}
    DecodeDate(StrToDateTime(Edit1.Text),CurrentTime.wYear,CurrentTime.wMonth,
      CurrentTime.wDay);

    {set the time from the supplied time}
    DecodeTime(StrToTime(Edit3.Text),CurrentTime.wHour,CurrentTime.wMinute,
      CurrentTime.wSecond,CurrentTime.wMilliseconds);

    {set the system time}
    SetSystemTime(CurrentTime)
  except
    {indicate if there was an error}
    on E:Exception do ShowMessage('Error setting system time');
  end;
end;
```

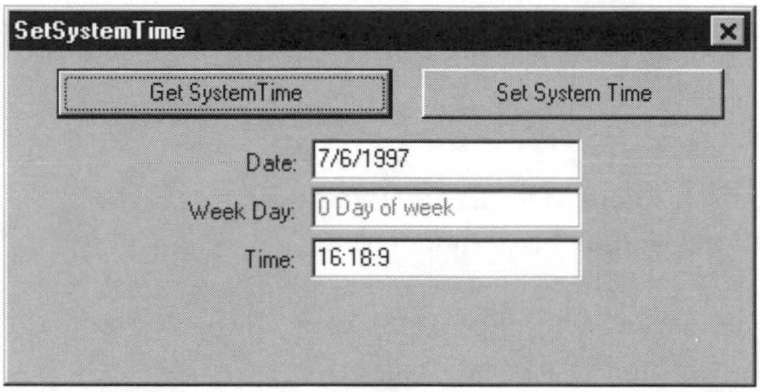

Figure 14-18: The current system time.

SetVolumeLabel Windows.Pas

Syntax

SetVolumeLabel(	
lpRootPathName: PChar;	{the root directory name of the volume to change}
lpVolumeName: PAnsiChar	{the new volume name}
): BOOL;	{returns TRUE or FALSE

Description

This function changes the volume name on the drive identified by the root path name contained in the lpRootPathName parameter.

Parameters

lpRootPathName: A pointer to a null-terminated string containing the path of the root directory on the drive whose volume name is to be changed. If this parameter is set to NIL, the volume containing the current directory is used.

lpVolumeName: A pointer to a null-terminated string containing the new name for the volume. If this parameter is set to NIL, the volume name is deleted.

Return Value

If the function succeeds, it returns TRUE; otherwise it returns FALSE. To get extended error information, call the GetLastError function.

See also

GetVolumeInformation

Example

Listing 14-25: Setting the Volume Name

```
procedure TForm1.Button2Click(Sender: TObject);
var
  VolName: array[0..50] of Char;    // holds the new volume label
begin
```

```
  {set the volume label for drive C}
  StrPCopy(VolName, Edit1.Text);
  SetVolumeLabel('C:\', VolName);
end;
```

SystemParametersInfo Windows.Pas

Syntax

```
SystemParametersInfo(
uiAction: UINT;         {the systemwide parameter to set or query}
uiParam: UINT;          {an integer dependent on uiAction}
pvParam: Pointer;       {a pointer to a structure dependent on uiAction}
fWinIni: UINT           {notification and save options}
): BOOL;                {returns TRUE or FALSE}
```


Description

This function can query or set a systemwide parameter, such as mouse trails or desktop wallpaper. Most of these parameters are available from various applets under the Control Panel.

Parameters

uiAction: Specifies which systemwide parameter to set or query, and can be one value from Table 14-19.

uiParam: An integer whose value is dependent on the value of the uiAction parameter. See Table 14-19 for a description of uiParam parameter values. Unless otherwise specified, this parameter should be set to zero.

pvParam: A pointer to a data structure. The type of data structure and its values are dependent on the value of the uiAction parameter. See Table 14-19 for a description of pvParam parameter structures. Unless otherwise specified, this parameter should be set to NIL.

fWinIni: Determines how the changes to the systemwide parameters are handled, and can be one value from Table 14-20.

Return Value

If the function succeeds, it returns TRUE; otherwise it returns FALSE. To get extended error information, call the GetLastError function.

See also

GetSystemMetrics

Example

Listing 14-26: Changing the Size of Nonclient Buttons

```
var
  MyNCM: TNonClientMetrics;                 // holds nonclient metric info
  OriginalWidth, OriginalHeight: Integer;  // holds original button sizes

procedure TForm1.Button1Click(Sender: TObject);
begin
  {initialize the size of the data structure}
  MyNCM.cbSize := SizeOf(TNonClientMetrics);

  {retrieve the settings for the nonclient button sizes}
  SystemParametersInfo(SPI_GetNonClientMetrics, SizeOf(TNonClientMetrics),
                       @MyNCM, 0);

  {double the size of nonclient buttons}
  MyNCM.iCaptionWidth  := MyNCM.iCaptionWidth * 2;
  MyNCM.iCaptionHeight := MyNCM.iCaptionHeight * 2;

  {set the size of nonclient buttons to the new size}
  SystemParametersInfo(SPI_SetNonClientMetrics,SizeOf(TNonClientMetrics),
                       @MyNCM,SPIF_SENDWININICHANGE);
end;

procedure TForm1.Button2Click(Sender: TObject);
begin
  {initialize the size of the data structure}
  MyNCM.cbSize := SizeOf(TNonClientMetrics);

  {retrieve the settings for the nonclient button sizes}
  SystemParametersInfo(SPI_GetNonClientMetrics, SizeOf(TNonClientMetrics),
                       @MyNCM, 0);

  {decrease the size of nonclient buttons}
  MyNCM.iCaptionWidth := MyNCM.iCaptionWidth div 2;
  MyNCM.iCaptionHeight := MyNCM.iCaptionHeight div 2;

  {set the size of nonclient buttons to the new size}
  SystemParametersInfo(SPI_SetNonClientMetrics,SizeOf(TNonClientMetrics),
                       @MyNCM,SPIF_SENDWININICHANGE);
end;

procedure TForm1.FormCreate(Sender: TObject);
begin
  {initialize the size of the data structure}
  MyNCM.cbSize := SizeOf(TNonClientMetrics);

  {retrieve the settings for the nonclient button sizes}
  SystemParametersInfo(SPI_GetNonClientMetrics, SizeOf(TNonClientMetrics),
                       @MyNCM, 0);

  {store the original settings for restoration when the application ends}
  OriginalWidth  := MyNCM.iCaptionWidth;
  OriginalHeight := MyNCM.iCaptionHeight;
end;

procedure TForm1.FormDestroy(Sender: TObject);
```

```
begin
  {initialize the size of the data structure}
  MyNCM.cbSize := SizeOf(TNonClientMetrics);

  {set the size of the buttons to the original size}
  MyNCM.iCaptionWidth  := OriginalWidth;
  MyNCM.iCaptionHeight := OriginalHeight;

  {change the size of the nonclient buttons}
  SystemParametersInfo(SPI_SetNonClientMetrics,SizeOf(TNonClientMetrics),
                       @MyNCM,SPIF_SENDWININICHANGE);
end;
```


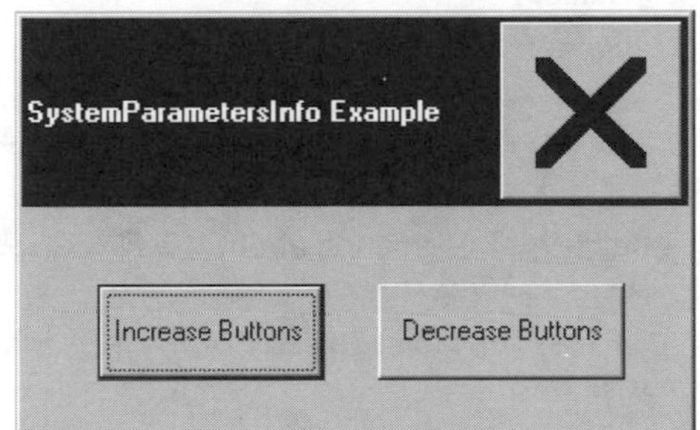

Figure 14-19: The modified nonclient buttons.

Table 14-19: SystemParametersInfo uiAction Values

Value	Description
SPI_GETACCESSTIMEOUT	Retrieves information about the timeout period for accessibility features. uiParam: Specifies the size of the TAccessTimeout structure. pvParam: Points to a TAccessTimeout structure that receives the timeout information.
SPI_GETANIMATION	Retrieves information about animation effects, such as animated window minimizing/restoring. uiParam: Specifies the size of the TAnimationInfo structure. pvParam: Points to a TAnimationInfo structure that receives the animation effects information.
SPI_GETBEEP	Indicates whether the warning beeper is on or off. uiParam: Not used. pvParam: Points to a Boolean value that receives TRUE if the beeper is on or FALSE if it is off.
SPI_GETBORDER	Retrieves the border multiplier that is used when determining the width of a window's sizing border. uiParam: Not used.

Value	Description
	pvParam: Points to an integer value that receives the border multiplier factor.
SPI_GETDEFAULTINPUTLANG	Retrieves the keyboard layout handle for the system default input language. uiParam: Not used. pvParam: Points to an integer value that receives the keyboard layout handle.
SPI_GETDRAGFULLWINDOWS	Indicates if full window dragging is enabled. This flag is supported under Windows 95 only if Windows Plus! is installed. uiParam: Not used. pvParam: Points to a Boolean value that receives TRUE if the full window dragging is enabled or FALSE if it is not.
SPI_GETFILTERKEYS	Retrieves information about the FilterKeys accessibility feature. uiParam: Specifies the size of the TFilterKeys structure. pvParam: Points to a TFilterKeys structure that receives information about the filter keys feature.
SPI_GETFONTSMOOTHING	Indicates whether anti-aliasing is used to make font curves appear smoother (known as font smoothing). This flag is supported under Windows 95 only if Windows Plus! is installed. uiParam: Not used. pvParam: Points to a Boolean value that receives TRUE if font anti-aliasing is used or FALSE if it is not.
SPI_GETGRIDGRANULARITY	Retrieves the granularity of the desktop sizing grid. uiParam: Not used. pvParam: Points to an integer value that receives the granularity value.
SPI_GETHIGHCONTRAST	Windows 95 only: Retrieves information about the HighContrast accessibility feature, which sets the color scheme and appearance of the user interface to provide for maximum visibility for visually impaired users. uiParam: Specifies the size of the THighContrast structure. pvParam: Points to a THighContrast structure that receives information about the high contrast feature.
SPI_GETICONMETRICS	Retrieves icon metric values, such as spacing and title wrap. uiParam: Specifies the size of the TIconMetrics structure.

Value	Description
	pvParam: Points to a TIconMetrics structure that receives information about icon metrics.
SPI_GETICONTITLELOGFONT	Retrieves the logical font for the current icon title font. uiParam: Specifies the size of the TLogFont structure. pvParam: Points to a TLogFont structure that receives the icon title logical font. Please see the CreateFontIndirect function for a description of the TLogFont data structure.
SPI_GETICONTITLEWRAP	Determines whether icon title wrapping is enabled. uiParam: Not used. pvParam: Points to a Boolean value that receives TRUE if icon title wrapping is enabled or FALSE if it is not.
SPI_GETKEYBOARDDELAY	Retrieves the keyboard repeat delay setting. uiParam: Not used. pvParam: Points to an integer value receiving the repeat delay setting.
SPI_GETKEYBOARDPREF	Retrieves user keyboard preference, indicating whether the user prefers the keyboard over the mouse and wants applications to display keyboard interfaces that would otherwise be hidden. uiParam: Not used. pvParam: Points to a Boolean value that receives TRUE if the user prefers the keyboard or FALSE if the user prefers the mouse.
SPI_GETKEYBOARDSPEED	Retrieves the keyboard repeat speed setting. uiParam: Not used. pvParam: Points to an integer value to receive the repeat speed setting.
SPI_GETMENUDROP-ALIGNMENT	Retrieves drop-down menu alignment, indicating whether drop-down menus are left or right aligned relative to the corresponding menu bar item. uiParam: Not used. pvParam: Points to a Boolean value that receives TRUE if drop-down menus are left aligned or FALSE if they are right aligned.
SPI_GETMINIMIZEDMETRICS	Retrieves the minimized window metrics, such as arrangement and width. UiParam: Specifies the size of the TMinimizedMetrics structure.

Value	Description
	PvParam: Pointer to a TMinimizedMetrics structure that receives the minimized window metric information.
SPI_GETMOUSE	Retrieves the two mouse speed threshold values and the mouse speed. uiParam: Not used. pvParam: Points to an array of the integer values to receive the mouse threshold values.
SPI_GETMOUSEHOVERHEIGHT	Windows NT only: Retrieves the height, in pixels, of the rectangle within which the mouse pointer has to stay for a WM_MOUSEHOVER message to be generated by the TrackMouseEvent function. uiParam: Not used. pvParam: Points to an integer value that will receive the height.
SPI_GETMOUSEHOVERTIME	Windows NT only: Retrieves the time, in milliseconds, that the mouse pointer has to stay in the hover rectangle for a WM_MOUSEHOVER message to be generated by the TrackMouseEvent function. uiParam: Not used. pvParam: Points to an integer value that will receive the time.
SPI_GETMOUSEHOVERWIDTH	Windows NT only: Retrieves the width, in pixels, of the rectangle within which the mouse pointer has to stay for a WM_MOUSEHOVER message to be generated by the TrackMouseEvent function. uiParam: Not used. pvParam: Points to an integer value that will receive the width.
SPI_GETMOUSEKEYS	Retrieves information about the MouseKeys accessibility feature. MouseKeys allow the mouse cursor to be controlled by the numeric keypad. The Num Lock key toggles between mouse control and normal operation. uiParam: Specifies the size of the TMouseKeys structure. pvParam: Points to a TMouseKeys structure that receives information about the mouse keys feature.
SPI_GETMOUSETRAILS	Windows 95 only: Indicates mouse trails are enabled. uiParam: Not used. pvParam: Pointer to an integer value. A value of 1 or 0 indicates mouse trails are disabled. A value greater then 1 indicates the number of mouse trails drawn to the screen.

Value	Description
SPI_GETNONCLIENTMETRICS	Retrieves metric values associated with the nonclient area of a window. uiParam: Specifies the size of the TNonClientMetrics structure. pvParam: Points to a TNonClientMetrics structure that receives the nonclient area metric values.
SPI_GETSCREENREADER	Windows 95 only: Indicates if a screen reviewer utility that directs textual information to an output device, such as a speech synthesizer or Braille display, is running. When this flag is set, an application should provide information in a textual format in situations where it would otherwise represent the information graphically. uiParam: Not used. pvParam: Points to a Boolean value that receives TRUE if a screen reviewer utility is running or FALSE if not.
SPI_GETSCREENSAVEACTIVE	Indicates if screen savers can activate. uiParam: Not used. pvParam: Points to a Boolean value that receives TRUE if screen savers are active, FALSE if not.
SPI_GETSCREENSAVETIMEOUT	Retrieves the screen saver timeout value, in seconds. uiParam: Not used. pvParam: Points to an integer value to receive the time out value.
SPI_GETSERIALKEYS	Windows 95 only: Retrieves information about the SerialKeys accessibility feature, which interprets data from a communication device attached to a serial port as keyboard and mouse input. uiParam: Specifies the size of the TSerialKeys structure. pvParam: Points to a TSerialKeys structure that receives information about the serial keys feature.
SPI_GETSHOWSOUNDS	Indicates if the ShowSounds accessibility feature is enabled. When this feature is enabled, applications should represent information visually when it would otherwise present it in an audible form. uiParam: Not used. pvParam: Points to a Boolean value that receives TRUE if the feature is enabled, FALSE if it is not.
SPI_GETSNAPTODEFBUTTON	Windows NT only: Indicates if the snap-to-default-button feature is enabled. If enabled, the mouse cursor automatically moves to the default button of a dialog box, such as "OK" or "Apply."

Value	Description
	uiParam: Not used. pvParam: Points to a Boolean value that receives TRUE if the feature is enabled, FALSE if it is not.
SPI_GETSOUNDSENTRY	Retrieves information about the SoundSentry accessibility feature. When the SoundSentry feature is on, the system displays a visual indicator when a sound is generated. Under Windows 95, the visual indicator is displayed only when a sound is generated through the internal PC speaker. Windows NT will display the visual indicator when a sound is generated through either the internal speaker or through a multimedia sound card. uiParam: Specifies the size of the TSoundSentry structure. pvParam: Points to a TSoundSentry structure that receives information about the sound sentry feature.
SPI_GETSTICKYKEYS	Retrieves information about the StickyKeys accessibility feature. The StickyKeys feature allows a user to press a modifier key, such as Shift, Ctrl, or Alt, and then a second key one at a time instead of simultaneously to produce uppercase letters or other key combinations. uiParam: Specifies the size of the TStickyKeys structure. pvParam: Points to a TStickyKeys structure that receives information about the sticky keys feature.
SPI_GETTOGGLEKEYS	Retrieves information about the ToggleKeys accessibility feature. When the ToggleKeys feature is enabled, Windows outputs a high-pitched tone when the user turns on the Caps Lock, Num Lock, or Scroll Lock keys, and a low-pitched tone when the user turns them off. uiParam: Specifies the size of the TToggleKeys structure. pvParam: Points to a TToggleKeys structure that receives information about the ToggleKeys feature.
SPI_GETWHEELSCROLLLINES	Windows NT only: Retrieves the number of lines scrolled when the mouse wheel is rotated for mice that come equipped with the mouse wheel. uiParam: Not used. pvParam: Points to an integer value that receives the number of lines scrolled.
SPI_GETWINDOWSEXTENSION	Windows 95 only: Indicates if Windows Plus! is installed. The function returns TRUE if Windows Plus! is installed, FALSE otherwise.

Value	Description
	uiParam: This parameter is always set to 1. pvParam: Not used.
SPI_GETWORKAREA	Retrieves the size of the desktop area not obscured by the taskbar. uiParam: Not used. pvParam: Points to a TRect that receives the dimensions of the work area.
SPI_ICONHORIZONTAL-SPACING	Sets the width of an icon cell for desktop spacing. uiParam: Specifies the width of the cell in pixels. pvParam: Not used.
SPI_ICONVERTICALSPACING	Sets the height of an icon cell for desktop spacing. uiParam: Specifies the height of the cell in pixels. pvParam: Not used.
SPI_SETACCESSTIMEOUT	Sets the timeout period associated with the accessibility features. uiParam: Specifies the size of the TAccessTimeout structure. pvParam: Points to a TAccessTimeout structure that contains the new timeout values.
SPI_SETANIMATION	Sets the animation effect values, such as window minimizing/restoring animation. uiParam: Specifies the size of a TAnimationInfo structure. pvParam: Points to a TAnimationInfo structure that contains the new animation effect values.
SPI_SETBEEP	Turns the warning beeper on or off. uiParam: Specifies zero to turn the option off, or nonzero to turn it on. pvParam: Not used.
SPI_SETBORDER	Sets the border multiplier that is used in determining the width of a window's sizing border. uiParam: Specifies the new border width multiplier. pvParam: Not used.
SPI_SETDEFAULTINPUTLANG	Sets the default input language for the system. The specified language must be displayable using the current character set. uiParam: Not used. pvParam: Points to a keyboard layout handle for the new default language.
SPI_SETDESKPATTERN	Sets the current desktop pattern. Windows retrieves this pattern from the Pattern setting in the WIN.INI file.

Value	Description
	uiParam: Not used. pvParam: Not used.
SPI_SETDESKWALLPAPER	Sets the desktop wallpaper. uiParam: Not used. pvParam: Points to a string that contains the name of the bitmap file to use for the wallpaper.
SPI_SETDOUBLECLICKTIME	Sets the maximum number of milliseconds that can occur between the first and second clicks of a double-click. uiParam: Specifies the new time in milliseconds. pvParam: Not used.
SPI_SETDOUBLECLKHEIGHT	Sets the height of the rectangle within which the mouse cursor must be located and the second click of a double-click must fall for it to be registered as a double-click. uiParam: Specifies the new height in pixels. pvParam: Not used.
SPI_SETDOUBLECLKWIDTH	Sets the width of the rectangle within which the mouse cursor must be located and the second click of a double-click must fall for it to be registered as a double-click. uiParam: Specifies new width in pixels. pvParam: Not used.
SPI_SETDRAGFULLWINDOWS	Sets full window dragging on or off. This flag is supported under Windows 95 only if Windows Plus! is installed. uiParam: Specifies 0 to disable full window dragging or nonzero to enable it. pvParam: Not used.
SPI_SETDRAGHEIGHT	Sets the height, in pixels, of the rectangle used to detect the start of a mouse drag operation. uiParam: Specifies the new rectangle height value. pvParam: Not used.
SPI_SETDRAGWIDTH	Sets the width, in pixels, of the rectangle used to detect the start of a mouse drag operation. uiParam: Specifies the new rectangle width value. pvParam: Not used.
SPI_SETFILTERKEYS	Sets the FilterKeys accessibility feature parameters. uiParam: Specifies the size of the TFilterKeys structure. pvParam: Points to a TFilterKeys structure that contains the new settings.

Value	Description
SPI_SETFONTSMOOTHING	Enables or disables anti-aliased font drawing, making font curves appear smoother. This flag is supported under Windows 95 only if Windows Plus! is installed. uiParam: Specifies 0 to disable anti-aliased font curve drawing or nonzero value to enable it. pvParam: Not used.
SPI_SETGRIDGRANULARITY	Sets the granularity of the desktop sizing grid. uiParam: Specifies the new granularity value. pvParam: Not used.
SPI_SETHIGHCONTRAST	Windows 95 only: Sets the HighContrast accessibility feature parameters. uiParam: Specifies the size of the THighContrast structure. pvParam: Points to the THighContrast structure that contains the new values.
SPI_SETICONMETRICS	Sets icon metrics, such as spacing and title wrap. uiParam: Specifies the size of the TIconMetrics structure. pvParam: Points to a TIconMetrics structure that contains the new values.
SPI_SETICONTITLELOGFONT	Sets the logical font used for icon titles. uiParam: Specifies the size of the TLogFont structure. pvParam: Points to a TLogFont structure that contains the new values.
SPI_SETICONTITLEWRAP	Turns icon title wrapping on or off. uiParam: Specifies zero to disable icon title wrapping or nonzero to enable. pvParam: Not used.
SPI_SETKEYBOARDDELAY	Sets the keyboard repeat delay setting. uiParam: Specifies the new repeat delay value in milliseconds. pvParam: Not used.
SPI_SETKEYBOARDPREF	Sets user keyboard preference, indicating whether the user prefers the keyboard over the mouse and wants applications to display keyboard interfaces that would otherwise be hidden. uiParam: Specifies zero to indicate a keyboard preference or nonzero to indicate a mouse preference. pvParam: Not used.

14 Chapter

Value	Description
SPI_SETKEYBOARDSPEED	Sets the keyboard repeat speed setting. uiParam: Specifies the new repeat speed value in milliseconds. pvParam: Not used.
SPI_SETLANGTOGGLE	Forces the system to read from the registry the hot key set for switching between input languages. uiParam: Not used. pvParam: Not used.
SPI_SETLOWPOWERACTIVE	Windows 95 only: Activates or deactivates the screen saver low-power phase. uiParam: Specifies 0 to deactivate the low-power phase or to 1 to activate it. pvParam: Not used.
SPI_SETLOWPOWERTIMEOUT	Windows 95 only: Sets the timeout value, in seconds, for the screen saver low-power phase. uiParam: Specifies the new value in seconds. pvParam: Not used.
SPI_SETMENUDROPALIGNMENT	Sets the alignment value of drop-down menus. uiParam: Specifies 0 for left alignment or 1 for right alignment. pvParam: Not used.
SPI_SETMINIMIZEDMETRICS	Sets minimized windows metrics. uiParam: Specifies the size of the TMinimizedMetrics structure. pvParam: Points to a TMinimizedMetrics structure that contains the new values.
SPI_SETMOUSE	Sets the two mouse speed threshold values and the mouse speed. uiParam: Not used. pvParam: Points to an array of three integers that contain the new values.
SPI_SETMOUSEBUTTONSWAP	Swaps or restores the left and right mouse buttons. uiParam: Specifies zero for standard mouse functionality, nonzero to swap the mouse buttons. pvParam: Not used.
SPI_SETMOUSEHOVERHEIGHT	Windows NT only: Sets the height, in pixels, of the rectangle within which the mouse pointer has to stay for a WM_MOUSEHOVER message to be generated by the TrackMouseEvent function. uiParam: Specifies the new height in pixels. pvParam: Not used.

Value	Description
SPI_SETMOUSEHOVERTIME	Windows NT only: Sets the time, in milliseconds, that the mouse pointer has to stay in the hover rectangle for a WM_MOUSEHOVER message to be generated by the TrackMouseEvent function. uiParam: Specifies the new time interval in milliseconds. pvParam: Not used.
SPI_SETMOUSEHOVERWIDTH	Sets the width, in pixels, of the rectangle within which the mouse pointer has to stay for TrackMouseEvent to generate a WM_MOUSEHOVER message. This value is only valid under Windows NT. uiParam: Specifies new width. pvParam: Not used.
SPI_SETMOUSEKEYS	Sets the MouseKeys accessibility feature parameters. uiParam: Specifies size of the TMouseKeys structure. pvParam: Points to a TMouseKeys structure that contains the new values.
SPI_SETMOUSETRAILS	Windows 95 only: Enables or disables mouse trails. uiParam: Specifies 0 or 1 to disable mouse trails; a value greater than one indicates the number of mouse trails to draw. pvParam: Not used.
SPI_SETNONCLIENTMETRICS	Sets the metrics values associated with the nonclient area of a window. uiParam: Specifies the size of the TNonClientMetrics structure. pvParam: Points to a TNonClientMetrics structure that contains the new values.
SPI_SETPENWINDOWS	Windows 95 only: Specifies that Window's pen extensions are being loaded or unloaded. uiParam: Specifies 0 to unload the pen extensions or nonzero to load pen extensions. pvParam: Not used.
SPI_SETPOWEROFFACTIVE	Windows 95 only: Activates or deactivates the screen saver power off phase. uiParam: Specifies 0 to deactivate or nonzero to activate. pvParam: Not used.
SPI_SETPOWEROFFTIMEOUT	Windows 95 only: Retrieves the timeout value, in seconds, for the screen saver power off phase. uiParam: Specifies the new value in seconds. pvParam: Not used.

Value	Description
SPI_SETSCREENREADER	Windows 95 only: Indicates if a screen reviewer utility is running. uiParam: Specifies zero to indicate no screen reader present or nonzero to indicate a screen reader is present. pvParam: Not used.
SPI_SETSCREENSAVEACTIVE	Enables or disables the screen saver. uiParam: Specifies 0 to disable the screen saver or 1 to enable it. When enabling the screen saver, the last screen saver selected will be used. pvParam: Not used.
SPI_SETSCREENSAVETIMEOUT	Sets the amount of time, in seconds, that the system must be idle before the screen saver activates. uiParam: Specifies the number of seconds to wait for the screen saver to activate. pvParam: Not used.
SPI_SETSERIALKEYS	Windows 95 only: Sets the SerialKeys accessibility feature parameters. uiParam: Specifies the size of the TSerialKeys structure. pvParam: Points to a TSerialKeys structure that contains the new values.
SPI_SETSHOWSOUNDS	Enables or disables the ShowSounds accessibility feature. uiParam: Specifies 0 to disable the ShowSounds feature or 1 to enable it. pvParam: Not used.
SPI_SETSNAPTODEFBUTTON	Windows NT only: Enables or disables the snap-to-default-button feature. uiParam: Specifies 0 to disable the snap-to-default-button feature or 1 to enable it. pvParam: Not used.
SPI_SETSOUNDSENTRY	Sets the SoundSentry accessibility feature parameters. uiParam: Specifies the size of the TSoundSentry structure. pvParam: Points to a TSoundSentry structure that contains the new values.
SPI_SETSTICKYKEYS	Sets the StickyKeys accessibility feature parameters. uiParam: Specifies the size of the TStickyKeys structure. pvParam: Points to a TStickyKeys structure that contains the new values.

Value	Description
SPI_SETTOGGLEKEYS	Sets the ToggleKeys accessibility feature parameters. uiParam: Specifies the size of the TToggleKeys structure. pvParam: Points to a TToggleKeys structure that contains the new values.
SPI_SETWHEELSCROLLLINES	Windows NT only: Sets the number of lines scrolled when the mouse wheel is rotated. uiParam: Specifies the number of lines to scroll. pvParam: Not used.
SPI_SETWORKAREA	Sets the size of the desktop area not obscured by the taskbar. uiParam: Not used. pvParam: Points to a TRect that contains the new work area size.

Table 14-20: SystemParametersInfo fWinIni Values

Value	Description
SPIF_UPDATEINIFILE	Update the system registry.
SPIF_SENDWININICHANGE	Update and broadcast the WM_SETTINGCHANGE message.

```
TAccessTimeout = packed record
    cbSize: UINT;              {the size of the TAccessTimeout structure}
    dwFlags: DWORD;            {timeout behavior properties}
    iTimeOutMSec: DWORD;       {the timeout value in milliseconds}
end;
```

cbSize: Indicates the size of the TAccessTimeout record. Set this member to SizeOf(TAccessTimeout).

dwFlags: Flags indicating the behavior of the timeout options. This member can contain one or more values from Table 14-21.

iTimeOutMSec: Indicates the length in milliseconds that must elapse without a keyboard or mouse action before the system will turn off the accessibility features.

Table 14-21: TAccessTimeout dwFlags Values

Value	Description
ATF_ONOFFFEEDBACK	The system will play a sound before the accessibility features are turned off.

Value	Description
ATF_AVAILABLE	Indicates that a user can set the timeout value but an application can only retrieve the value.
ATF_TIMEOUTON	The timeout interval has been set and the system will time-out at that interval. If this flag is not set the system will not time-out no matter what time interval is set.

```
TAnimationInfo = packed record
    cbSize: UINT;              {the size of the TAnimationInfo structure}
    iMinAnimate: Integer;      {enables or disables animation}
end;
```

cbSize: Specifies the size of the TAnimationInfo structure. This member should be set to SizeOf(TAnimationInfo).

iMinAnimate: Specifies if animation is enabled or disabled. A value of zero indicates that the animation is disabled; a nonzero value indicates that animation is enabled.

```
TFilterKeys = packed record
    cbSize: UINT;                {the size of the TFilterkeys structure}
    dwFlags: DWORD;              {sets behavior of filter keys}
    iWaitMSec: DWORD;            {acceptance delay}
    iDelayMSec: DWORD;           {repeat delay}
    iRepeatMSec: DWORD;          {repeat rate}
    iBounceMSec: DWORD;          {bounce time}
end;
```

cbSize: Specifies the size of the TFilterKeys record. This member should be set to SizeOf(TFilterKeys).

dwFlags: Indicates the behavior state of the filter keys options. This member can contain one or more values from Table 14-22.

iWaitMSec: Specifies the time in milliseconds that the user must hold down a key before the system will accept it. This is also referred to as slow keys.

iDelayMSec: Specifies the delay interval for the repeat rate. This is the amount of time in milliseconds the user must hold down a key before the system will start to repeat that key.

iRepeatMSec: Specifies the repeat rate. This is the amount of time in milliseconds the system will wait before it repeats the key stroke again.

iBounceMSec: Specifies the bounce time for key strokes. This is the amount of time that must pass before the system will accept another input from that key.

Table 14-22: TFilterKeys dwFlags Values

Value	Description
FKF_AVAILABLE	The filter keys feature is available.
FKF_CLICKON	The system will click when keys are pressed. When slow keys are used, another click will sound when the key is accepted.
FKF_CONFIRMHOTKEY	A dialog box will appear when enabling or disabling the filter keys options.
FKF_FILTERKEYSON	The filter keys feature is turned on.
FKF_HOTKEYACTIVE	The hot key is enabled for turning filter keys on or off. The hot key is the Shift key held down for 8 seconds.
FKF_HOTKEYSOUND	The system will play a sound when the filter keys feature is enabled or disabled.
FKF_INDICATOR	Windows will display an indicator when the hot keys option is turned on.


```
THighContrast = packed record
    cbSize: UINT;                        {the size of the THighContrast structure}
    dwFlags: DWORD;                      {sets the behavior of high contrast options}
    lpszDefaultScheme: PAnsiChar;        {the name of the standard scheme}
end;
```

cbSize: Specifies the size of the THighContrast structure. Set this member to SizeOf(THighContrast).

dwFlags: Indicates the behavior state of the High Contrast options. This member can contain one or more values from Table 14-23.

lpszDefaultScheme: A pointer to a null-terminated string that contains the name of the standard color scheme for the system.

Table 14-23: THighContrast dwFlags Values

Value	Description
HCF_AVAILABLE	The high contrast option is available.
HCF_CONFIRMHOTKEY	A dialog box will appear when enabling or disabling the high contrast options.
HCF_HIGHCONTRASTON	The high contrast mode is currently on.
HCF_HOTKEYACTIVE	The hot key for the high contrast mode is enabled. The hot key for turning the high contrast mode on and off is simultaneously pressing the left Alt, left Shift, and Print Screen keys.
HCF_HOTKEYAVAILABLE	Indicates if the hot key option is available on the system.

Value	Description
HCF_HOTKEYSOUND	The system will play a sound when the hot key is pressed to indicate that the high contrast option is enabled or disabled.
HCF_INDICATOR	Windows will display an indicator that the high contrast option is available.

```
TIconMetrics = packed record
      cbSize: UINT;                  {the size of the TIconMetrics structure}
      iHorzSpacing: Integer;         {horizontal spacing for icons}
      iVertSpacing: Integer;         {vertical spacing for icons}
      iTitleWrap: Integer;           {word wrap titles}
      lfFont: TLogFont;              {the font for desktop icons}
end;
```

cbSize: Specifies the size of the TIconMetrics structure. This member should be set to SizeOf(TIconMetrics).

iHorzSpacing: Specifies the horizontal spacing for icons on the desktop.

iVertSpacing: Specifies the vertical spacing for icons on the desktop.

iTitleWrap: Indicates if icon titles are word wrapped. A zero value indicates that icon titles will not be word wrapped; a nonzero value indicates that they will be wrapped.

lfFont: Indicates the font to be used when displaying the icon title.

```
TMinimizedMetrics = packed record
      cbSize: UINT;                  {the size of the TMinimizedMetrics structure}
      iWidth: Integer;               {the width of minimized windows}
      iHorzGap: Integer;             {the horizontal gap between minimized windows}
      iVertGap: Integer;             {the vertical gap between minimized windows}
      iArrange: Integer;             {minimized window arrangement}
end;
```

cbSize: Specifies the size of the TMinimizedMetrics structure. This member should be set to SizeOf(TMinimizedMetrics).

iWidth: Specifies the width of the minimized window.

iHorzGap: Specifies the horizontal space between each minimized window.

iVertGap: Specifies the vertical space between each minimized window.

iArrange: Specifies how the minimized windows are to be arranged. This member contains one value from Table 14-24 and one value from Table 14-25.

Table 14-24: TMinimizedMetrics iArrange Starting Position Values

Value	Description
ARW_BOTTOMLEFT	Start at the bottom left corner of the work area.
ARW_BOTTOMRIGHT	Start at the bottom right corner of the work area.
ARW_TOPLEFT	Start at the top left corner of the work area.
ARW_TOPRIGHT	Start at the top right corner of the work area.

Table 14-25: TMinimizedMetrics iArrange Direction Values

Value	Description
ARW_LEFT	Fill going to the left. Only valid with ARW_BOTTOMRIGHT and ARW_TOPRIGHT.
ARW_RIGHT	Fill going to the right. Only valid with ARW_BOTTOMLEFT and ARW_TOPLEFT.
ARW_UP	Fill going to the top. Only valid with ARW_BOTTOMRIGHT and ARW_BOTTOMLEFT.
ARW_DOWN	Fill going to the bottom. Only valid with ARW_TOPRIGHT and ARW_TOPLEFT.
ARW_HIDE	Tells the system to hide minimized windows. This is the default action for Windows 95.

```
TMouseKeys = packed record
    cbSize: UINT;                 {the size of the TMouseKeys structure}
    dwFlags: DWORD;               {sets behavior of mouse key options}
    iMaxSpeed: DWORD;             {maximum mouse speed}
    iTimeToMaxSpeed: DWORD;       {time delay to maximum speed}
    iCtrlSpeed: DWORD;            {control key multiplier}
    dwReserved1: DWORD;           {reserved for future use}
    dwReserved2: DWORD;           {reserved for future use}
end;
```

cbSize: Specifies the size of the TMouseKeys structure. This member should be set to SizeOf(TMouseKeys).

dwFlags: Indicates the behavior of the mouse keys options. This member can contain one or more values from Table 14-26.

iMaxSpeed: Specifies the maximum speed in pixels for the mouse. The value of this member may be in the range of 10 to 360. Under Windows 95, no range checking on this value is performed.

iTimeToMaxSpeed: Specifies the time delay in milliseconds before the maximum speed is achieved. The value of this member may be in the range of 1000 and 5000.

iCtrlSpeed: This member is used only under Windows 95. It indicates the multiplier to add to the speed if the control key is held down. This is only available if the dwFlags member contains the MKF_MODIFIERS flag.

dwReserved1: Reserved for future use.

dwReserved2: Reserved for future use.

Table 14-26: TMouseKeys dwFlags Values

Value	Description
MKF_AVAILABLE	The mouse key option is available.
MKF_CONFIRMHOTKEY	Windows 95 only: A dialog box will appear when enabling or disabling the mouse keys options.
MKF_HOTKEYACTIVE	The hot key for the mouse keys mode is enabled. The hot key for turning mouse keys on and off is Left Alt+Left Shift+Num Lock.
MKF_HOTKEYSOUND	The system will play a sound when the mouse keys are enabled or disabled by using the hot keys.
MKF_INDICATOR	Windows 95 only: Windows will display an indicator when mouse keys are turned on.
MKF_MOUSEKEYSON	The mouse keys are currently on.
MKF_MODIFIERS	Windows 95 only: Indicates if the Ctrl and Alt keys will affect the mouse movement.
MKF_REPLACENUMBERS	Windows 95 only: Indicates if the mouse will be moved if the Num Lock key is on or off. If this flag is not specified, the numeric keypad will move the mouse cursor when the Num Lock key is off.

```
TNonClientMetrics = packed record
    cbSize: UINT;                     {the size of TNonClientMetrics structure}
    iBorderWidth: Integer;            {sizing border width}
    iScrollWidth: Integer;            {standard scroll bar width}
    iScrollHeight: Integer;           {standard scroll bar height}
    iCaptionWidth: Integer;           {width of caption buttons}
    iCaptionHeight: Integer;          {height of caption buttons}
    lfCaptionFont: TLogFont;          {font to use in the caption bar}
    iSmCaptionWidth: Integer;         {width for tool bar buttons}
    iSmCaptionHeight: Integer;        {height for tool bar buttons}
    lfSmCaptionFont: TLogFont;        {font to use in the tool bar}
    iMenuWidth: Integer;              {menu bar button width}
    iMenuHeight: Integer;             {menu bar button height}
    lfMenuFont: TLogFont;             {font to use in menu bar}
    lfStatusFont: TLogFont;           {status bar font}
    lfMessageFont: TLogFont;          {message box font}
end;
```

cbSize: Specifies the size of the TNonClientMetrics structure. This member should be set to SizeOf(TNonClientMetrics).

iBorderWidth: Width of the window border for a sizable window.

iScrollWidth: Width of a standard vertical scroll bar.

iScrollHeight: Height of a standard horizontal scroll bar.

iCaptionWidth: Width of the caption bar buttons.

iCaptionHeight: Height of the caption bar buttons.

lfCaptionFont: Font to use in the caption bar.

iSmCaptionWidth: Width of the buttons in a tool bar window caption.

iSmCaptionHeight: Height of the buttons in a tool bar window caption.

lfSmCaptionFont: Font to use in a tool bar caption.

iMenuWidth: Width of buttons that appear in a menu bar.

iMenuHeight: Height of the buttons that appear in a menu bar.

lfMenuFont: Font to use in a menu bar.

lfStatusFont: Font to use in a status bar.

lfMessageFont: Font to use in a message dialog box.


```
TSoundSentry = packed record
    cbSize: UINT;                        {the size of the TSoundSentry structure}
    dwFlags: DWORD;                      {sets behavior of sound sentry option}
    iFSTextEffect: DWORD;                {text app sound effect}
    iFSTextEffectMSec: DWORD;            {length of text app sound effect}
    iFSTextEffectColorBits: DWORD;       {color of text app sound effect}
    iFSGrafEffect: DWORD;                {graphic app sound effect}
    iFSGrafEffectMSec: DWORD;            {length of graphic app sound effect}
    iFSGrafEffectColor: DWORD;           {color of graphic app sound effect}
    iWindowsEffect: DWORD;               {Windows app sound effect}
    iWindowsEffectMSec: DWORD;           {length of Windows app sound effect}
    lpszWindowsEffectDLL: PAnsiChar;     {DLL that contains special sound
                                              effect}
    iWindowsEffectOrdinal: DWORD;        {reserved for future use}
end;
```

cbSize: Specifies the size of the TSoundSentry structure. Set this member to SizeOf(TSoundSentry).

dwFlags: Indicates the behavior of the sound sentry options. This member can contain one value from Table 14-27.

iFSTextEffect: Indicates the behavior of the sound sentry options when a text-based application is running in a full screen window. This member may contain one value from Table 14-28. This member is not available under Windows NT and must be set to 0.

iFSTextEffectMSec: Specifies how long the text effect change will last, in milliseconds. This member is not available under Windows NT and must be set to 0.

iFSTextEffectColorBits: Specifies the color that will be used for the text change effect. This member is not available under Windows NT and must be set to 0.

iFSGrafEffect: Indicates the behavior of the sound sentry options when a graphic-based application is running in a full screen window. This member can contain one value from Table 14-29. This member is not available under Windows NT and must be set to 0.

iFSGrafEffectMSec: Specifies how long the graphic effect change will last, in milliseconds. This member is not available under Windows NT and must be set to 0.

iFSGrafEffectColor: Specifies the color that will be used for the graphic change effect. This member is not available under Windows NT and must be set to 0.

iWindowsEffect: Indicates the behavior of the sound sentry options when a Windows-based application is running. This member can contain one value from Table 14-30.

iWindowsEffectMSec: Specifies how long the Windows effect change will last, in milliseconds.

lpszWindowsEffectDLL: Specifies the name of the DLL that contains an exported SoundSentryProc callback function. This function will be called when a sound is generated. This member can be set to NIL if a DLL is not used.

iWindowsEffectOrdinal: Reserved for future use. This member must be set to zero.

Table 14-27: TSoundSentry dwFlags Values

Value	Description
SSF_AVAILABLE	Indicates that the SoundSentry feature is available.
SSF_SOUNDSENTRYON	Indicates that the SoundSentry feature is currently on.

Table 14-28: TSoundSentry iFSTextEffect Values

Value	Description
SSTF_BORDER	Flashes the screen border. This option is not available on all displays.
SSTF_CHARS	Flashes a character in the upper corner of the screen.
SSTF_DISPLAY	Flashes the entire display.
SSTF_NONE	No visual sound indicator.

Table 14-29: TSoundSentry iFSGrafEffect Values

Value	Description
SSGF_DISPLAY	Flashes the entire display.
SSGF_NONE	No visual sound signal.

Table 14-30: TSoundSentry iWindowsEffect Values

Value	Description
SSWF_CUSTOM	Calls the SoundSentryProc function exported by the DLL specified by the lpszWindowsEffectDLL member.
SSWF_DISPLAY	Flashes the entire display.
SSWF_NONE	No visual sound signal.
SSWF_TITLE	Flashes the title bar of the active window.
SSWF_WINDOW	Flashes the active window.


```
TStickyKeys = packed record
      cbSize: UINT;            {the size of the TStickyKeys structure}
      dwFlags: DWORD;          {sets the behavior of sticky keys options}
end;
```

cbSize: Specifies the size of the TStickyKeys structure. Set this member to SizeOf(TStickyKeys).

dwFlags: Indicates the behavior of the sticky keys options. This member can contain one or more values from Table 14-31.

Table 14-31: TStickyKeys dwFLags Values

Value	Description
SKF_AUDIBLEFEEDBACK	The system will play a sound any time the Ctrl, Alt, or Shift key is turned on.
SKF_AVAILABLE	Indicates that StickyKeys feature is available.
SKF_CONFIRMHOTKEY	Windows 95 only: A dialog box will appear when enabling or disabling the sticky keys options.
SKF_HOTKEYACTIVE	Enables or disables the StickyKeys feature hot key. The hot key is pressing the Shift key five times.
SKF_HOTKEYSOUND	The system will play a sound when the hot key is used to enable or disable sticky keys.
SKF_INDICATOR	Windows 95 only: Windows will display an indicator if sticky keys are on.
SKF_STICKYKEYSON	The sticky keys feature is turned on.
SKF_TRISTATE	Pressing a modifier key twice in a row locks that key until it is pressed a third time.

Value	Description
SKF_TWOKEYSOFF	Turns sticky keys off when releasing a modifier key that has been pressed in combination with any other key.

```
TToggleKeys = packed record
    cbSize: UINT;              {the size of the TToggleKeys structure}
    dwFlags: DWORD;            {sets the behavior of toggle keys options}
end;
```

cbSize: Specifies the size of the TToggleKeys structure. Set this member to SizeOf(TToggleKeys).

dwFlags: Indicates the behavior of the toggle keys options. This member can contain one or more values from Table 14-32.

Table 14-32: TToggleKeys dwFlags Values

Value	Description
TKF_AVAILABLE	Indicates that the ToggleKeys feature is available.
TKF_CONFIRMHOTKEY	Windows 95 only: A dialog box will appear when enabling or disabling the sticky keys options.
TKF_HOTKEYACTIVE	Enables or disables the ToggleKeys option hot key. The hot key is pressing the Num Lock key for eight seconds.
TKF_HOTKEYSOUND	The system will play a sound when the hot key is used to enable or disable the toggle keys option.
TKF_TOGGLEKEYSON	Indicates that the toggle keys feature is on.

```
TSerialKeys = packed record
    cbSize: UINT;                  {the size of the TSerialKeys structure}
    dwFlags: DWORD;                {sets behavior of serial keys option}
    lpszActivePort: PAnsiChar;     {name of active port}
    lpszPort: PAnsiChar;           {reserved}
    iBaudRate: UINT;               {port baud rate}
    iPortState: UINT;              {reaction state of port}
    iActive: UINT;                 {reserved}
end;
```

cbSize: Specifies the size of the TSerialKeys structure. This member should be set to SizeOf(TSerialKeys).

dwFlags: Indicates the behavior of the serial keys options. This member can contain one or more values from Table 14-33.

lpszActivePort: Indicates the name of the serial port to receive user input. This member can be set to "Auto" to instruct the system to monitor all unused serial ports.

lpszPort: This member is reserved and must be set to NIL.

iBaudRate: Specifies the current baud rate of the serial port identified by the lpszActivePort parameter. This member can contain one value from Table 14-34.

iPortState: Specifies the state of the serial port identified by the lpszActivePort parameter. This member can contain one value from Table 14-35.

iActive: Reserved for future use.

Table 14-33: TSerialKeys dwFlags Values

Value	Description
SERKF_ACTIVE	The SerialKeys option is currently receiving input on the serial port specified by lpszActivePort.
SERKF_AVAILABLE	Indicates that the SerialKeys feature is available.
SERKF_SERIALKEYSON	Indicates that the SerialKeys feature is on.

Table 14-34: TSerialKeys iBaudRate Values

Values	Description
CBR_110	110 Baud
CBR_300	300 Baud
CBR_600	600 Baud
CBR_1200	1200 Baud
CBR_2400	2400 Baud
CBR_4800	4800 Baud
CBR_9600	9600 Baud
CBR_14400	14,400 Baud
CBR_19200	19,200 Baud
CBR_38400	38,400 Baud
CBR_56000	56,000 Baud
CBR_57600	57,600 Baud
CBR_115200	115,200 Baud
CBR_128000	128,000 Baud
CBR_256000	256,000 Baud

Table 14-35: TSerialKeys iPortState Values

Value	Description
0	This port is ignored.
1	This port is watched for SerialKeys activation sequences when no other application has the port open.
2	All input on this port is treated as SerialKeys commands.

VerLanguageName Windows.Pas

Syntax

```
VerLanguageName(
wLang: DWORD;              {the language identifier}
szLang: PChar;             {the buffer receiving the language name}
nSize: DWORD               {the maximum size of the buffer}
): DWORD;                  {returns the number of bytes written to the buffer}
```

Description

This function retrieves a string describing the name of the language identified by the wLang parameter.

Parameters

wLang: Specifies the language identifier from which to retrieve the language name. This parameter can be set to the return value of GetSystemDefaultLangID, GetUser-DefaultLangID, or one value from Table 14-36.

szLang: A pointer to a null-terminated string buffer receiving the name of the language. If this parameter is set to NIL, the function returns the required size of the buffer to hold the name of the language.

nSize: Specifies the maximum size of the szLang buffer.

Return Value

If the function succeeds, it returns the number of characters copied to the szLang buffer, not including the null terminator; otherwise the function returns zero.

See also

GetSystemDefaultLangID, GetUserDefaultLangID, VerQueryValue

Example

Please see Listing 14-11 under GetSystemDefaultLangID.

Table 14-36: VerLanguageName wLang Values

Value	Description
$0000	Language neutral
$0400	The default process language
$0401	Arabic (Saudi Arabia)
$0801	Arabic (Iraq)
$0C01	Arabic (Egypt)
$1001	Arabic (Libya)
$1401	Arabic (Algeria)
$1801	Arabic (Morocco)

Value	Description
$1C01	Arabic (Tunisia)
$2001	Arabic (Oman)
$2401	Arabic (Yemen)
$2801	Arabic (Syria)
$2C01	Arabic (Jordan)
$3001	Arabic (Lebanon)
$3401	Arabic (Kuwait)
$3801	Arabic (U.A.E.)
$3C01	Arabic (Bahrain)
$4001	Arabic (Qatar)
$0402	Bulgarian
$0403	Catalan
$0404	Chinese (Taiwan)
$0804	Chinese (PRC)
$0C04	Chinese (Hong Kong)
$1004	Chinese (Singapore)
$0405	Czech
$0406	Danish
$0407	German (Standard)
$0807	German (Switzerland)
$0C07	German (Austria)
$1007	German (Luxembourg)
$1407	German (Liechtenstein)
$0408	Greek
$0409	English (United States)
$0809	English (United Kingdom)
$0C09	English (Australia)
$1009	English (Canada)
$1409	English (New Zealand)
$1809	English (Ireland)
$1C09	English (South Africa)
$2009	English (Jamaica)
$2409	English (Caribbean)
$2809	English (Belize)
$2C09	English (Trinidad)
$040A	Spanish (Traditional sort)
$080A	Spanish (Mexican)
$0C0A	Spanish (Modern sort)
$100A	Spanish (Guatemala)

Value	Description
$140A	Spanish (Costa Rica)
$180A	Spanish (Panama)
$1C0A	Spanish (Dominican Republic)
$200A	Spanish (Venezuela)
$240A	Spanish (Colombia)
$280A	Spanish (Peru)
$2C0A	Spanish (Argentina)
$300A	Spanish (Ecuador)
$340A	Spanish (Chile)
$380A	Spanish (Uruguay)
$3C0A	Spanish (Paraguay)
$400A	Spanish (Bolivia)
$440A	Spanish (El Salvador)
$480A	Spanish (Honduras)
$4C0A	Spanish (Nicaragua)
$500A	Spanish (Puerto Rico)
$040B	Finnish
$040C	French (Standard)
$080C	French (Belgium)
$0C0C	French (Canada)
$100C	French (Switzerland)
$140C	French (Luxembourg)
$040D	Hebrew
$040E	Hungarian
$040F	Icelandic
$0410	Italian (Standard)
$0810	Italian (Switzerland)
$0411	Japanese
$0412	Korean
$0812	Korean (Johab)
$0413	Dutch (Standard)
$0813	Dutch (Belgium)
$0414	Norwegian (Bokmal)
$0814	Norwegian (Nynorsk)
$0415	Polish
$0416	Portuguese (Brazil)
$0816	Portuguese (Standard)
$0418	Romanian
$0419	Russian

Value	Description
$041A	Croatian
$0C1A	Serbian
$041B	Slovak
$041C	Albanian
$041D	Swedish
$081D	Swedish (Finland)
$041E	Thai
$041F	Turkish
$0421	Indonesian
$0422	Ukrainian
$0423	Belarussian
$0424	Slovenian
$0425	Estonian
$0426	Latvian
$0427	Lithuanian
$081A	Serbian
$0429	Farsi
$042D	Basque
$0436	Afrikaans
$0438	Faeroese

Chapter 15

Timer Functions

Delphi's TTimer object provides an easy-to-use encapsulation of a Windows timer. However, the interval seems to have a limited resolution, and in general TTimer does not seem very reliable. The timeout value for a timer is only an approximation and is dependent on the system clock rate and how often the application retrieves messages from the message queue. The method by which Delphi encapsulates a Windows timer into an object tends to further reduce the reliability of the timeout interval.

Each TTimer object creates an invisible window. The window procedure for this window contains a message loop that calls the OnTimer event when it receives a WM_TIMER message. This method of encapsulation depletes from the maximum available window handles and from the maximum number of timers, making it slightly inefficient.

The API functions for creating and destroying a Windows timer are not complex. By using the SetTimer and KillTimer functions to create a standard Windows timer, the developer will save valuable sources. The other timer functions allow the developer to emulate a timer or perform precise timing measurements. A single application contains all of the code from the API function descriptions in this chapter.

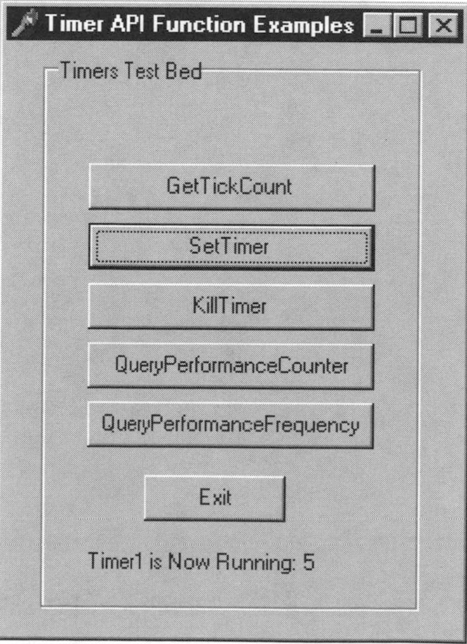

Figure 15-1: The Timer API Function Examples application.

Emulating a Timer

The maximum amount of timers an application can have is only limited by the system configuration. However, it is a finite number and each timer takes a certain amount of Windows resources to maintain. To circumvent consuming additional resources, a developer can emulate a timer by using GetTickCount inside of a loop. A variable is initialized with a starting time retrieved from GetTickCount. Through each iteration of the loop, this starting time is subtracted from the current value of GetTickCount. If the value is greater than the timeout value specified, then the application performs the desired actions and the process is started over. The following example demonstrates this technique.

Listing 15-1: Emulating a Timer

```
var
  Form1: TForm1;
  Running: Boolean;     // the loop control variable

implementation

{$R *.DFM}

procedure FlashLoop;
var
  StartTick: DWORD;     // holds the start time
begin
  {get the current tick count}
  StartTick := GetTickCount;

  {if the loop is still running...}
  while Running do
  begin
    {...check the elapsed time. If a second has passed...}
    if (GetTickCount-StartTick)>1000 then
    begin
      {...update the label on the form}
      Form1.Label1.Visible := not Form1.Label1.Visible;

      {reinitialize the start time for the next round}
      StartTick := GetTickCount;
    end;

    {this is required so the loop doesn't lock up the machine}
    Application.ProcessMessages;
  end;
end;

procedure TForm1.Button1Click(Sender: TObject);
begin
  {set the loop control variable...}
  Running := TRUE;

  {...and start the loop}
```

```
  FlashLoop;
end;

procedure TForm1.FormClose(Sender: TObject; var Action: TCloseAction);
begin
  {the loop control variable must be set to FALSE
   so the loop will exit and the program can close}
  Running := FALSE;
end;
.
```

A similar method can be used to provide a pause within a loop or function. This approach is convenient when a standard timer may be inappropriate or difficult to implement. The following example demonstrates this technique.

Listing 15-2: Pausing a Loop

```
var
  Form1: TForm1;
  Running: Boolean;     // the loop control variable

implementation

{$R *.DFM}

procedure FlashLoop;
var
  PacingCounter: DWORD;     // holds the reference start time
begin
  {if the loop is still running...}
  while Running do
  begin
    {...update the label on the form}
    Form1.Label1.Visible := not Form1.Label1.Visible;

    {pause the loop for one second}
    PacingCounter := GetTickCount;
    repeat
      {Let Windows process any pending messages}
      Application.ProcessMessages;
    until (GetTickCount-PacingCounter) > 1000;

  end;
end;

procedure TForm1.Button1Click(Sender: TObject);
begin
  {set the loop control variable...}
  Running := TRUE;

  {...and start the loop}
  FlashLoop;
end;

procedure TForm1.FormClose(Sender: TObject; var Action: TCloseAction);
```

```
begin
  {the loop control variable must be set to FALSE
   so the loop will exit and the program can close}
  Running := FALSE;
end;
```

Precise Timing

Most machines come equipped with a high-resolution timer. This timer fires several thousand times a second, making it very useful when precise timing information is required. This high-resolution timer is accessed with the QueryPerformanceCounter and QueryPerformanceFrequency functions. The QueryPerformanceCounter function returns the current value of the high-resolution timer, and the QueryPerformanceFrequency returns the number of times the high-resolution timer fires every second. This frequency will vary from machine to machine depending on the hardware configuration.

A useful application of these two functions is measuring the amount of time a particular function call takes to complete. This information is very important when optimizing an application, and using this technique in every function highlights those functions that consume a gross amount of processor time. Use QueryPerformanceCounter at the beginning and end of the function to retrieve the starting and ending time. The difference of these two values is then divided by the frequency of the high-resolution timer retrieved from QueryPerformanceFrequency to arrive at the total elapsed time. Use the following formula to measure the total function time in seconds:

(Starting Time – Ending Time) / High-Resolution Timer Frequency

The following example demonstrates this technique.

Listing 15-3: Measuring Function Time Using the High-Resolution Timer

```
procedure TForm1.Button1Click(Sender: TObject);
var
  Loop1, Loop2: Integer;        // general loop control counters
  StartCount,                   // this holds the start and stop time for
  EndCount: TLargeInteger;      // the function
  Frequency: TLargeInteger;     // the frequency of the high resolution timer
  ElapsedTime: Extended;        // holds the total elapsed time
begin
  {retrieve the frequency of the high resolution timer}
  QueryPerformanceFrequency(Frequency);

  {begin timing the function by retrieving the current
   value of the high resolution timer}
  QueryPerformanceCounter(StartCount);

  {perform some function. In this example, we fill a 100 X 100
   cell string grid with numbers.}
  for Loop1 := 0 to 99 do
```

```
    for Loop2 :=0 to 99 do
      StringGrid1.Cells[Loop2, Loop1] := IntToStr((Loop1*100)+Loop2);

  {the function is complete. Retrieve the current value
   of the high resolution counter as our end count}
  QueryPerformanceCounter(EndCount);

  {this formula computes the total amount of time the function
   took to complete}
  ElapsedTime := (EndCount.QuadPart-StartCount.QuadPart)/Frequency.QuadPart;

  {display the elapsed time, in seconds}
  Label1.Caption := 'Elapsed Time: '+FloatToStr(ElapsedTime)+' seconds.';
end;
```

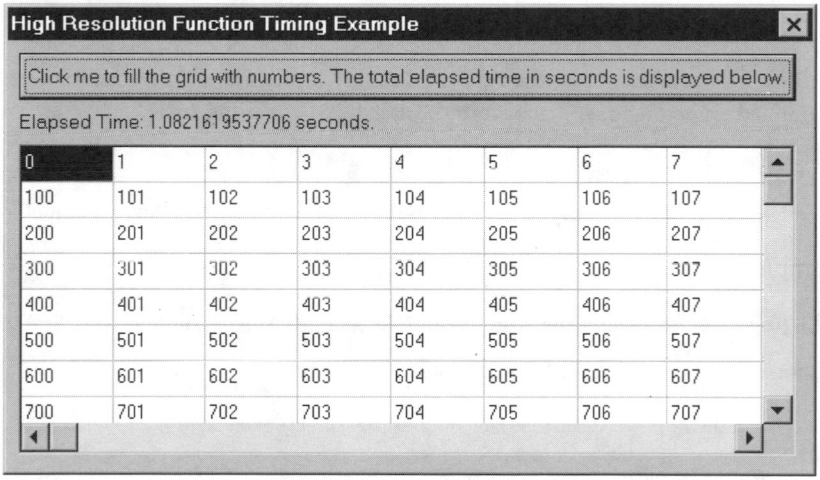

Figure 15-2: The result of timing the function.

Windows Timer Functions

The following timer functions are covered in this chapter:

Table 15-1: Windows Timer Functions

Function	Description
GetTickCount	Retrieves the number of milliseconds elapsed since Windows was started.
KillTimer	Deletes a timer.
QueryPerformanceCounter	Retrieves the current value of the high-resolution timer.
QueryPerformanceFrequency	Retrieves the frequency of the high-resolution timer.
SetTimer	Creates a timer.

GetTickCount Windows.Pas

Syntax

GetTickCount: DWORD; {returns a 32-bit number}

Description

This function returns the number of milliseconds that have elapsed since Windows was started. Since this time is stored in a DWORD, it will wrap to zero if Windows is left in operation for 49.7 days. Under Windows NT, the application can obtain the elapsed time since Windows was started by finding the System Up Time counter in performance data under the HKEY_PERFORMANCE_DATA registry key. This value will be an 8-byte number.

Return Values

If the function succeeds, the return value is the number of milliseconds that have elapsed since Windows was started; otherwise it returns zero.

See also

GetMessageTime, GetSystemTime, SetSystemTime, QueryPerformanceCounter

Example

Listing 15-4: Retrieving the Number of Milliseconds Since Windows was Started

```
procedure TForm1.Button1Click(Sender: TObject);
var
  Tick: DWORD;    // holds the number of milliseconds
begin
  {get the number of milliseconds since Windows was started}
  Tick:= GetTickCount;

  {display the number of milliseconds}
  Label1.Caption:= 'Number of Milliseconds: ' + IntToStr(Tick);
end;
```

KillTimer Windows.Pas

Syntax

```
KillTimer(
hWnd: HWND;          {a handle to the window that installed the timer}
uIDEvent: UINT       {the timer identifier}
): BOOL;             {returns TRUE or FALSE}
```

Description

The KillTimer function destroys the specified timer.

Parameters

hWnd: This is a handle to the window associated with the timer. This must be the same window handle that was passed to the SetTimer function that created the timer. If the hWnd parameter of SetTimer is zero, this parameter must be set to zero.

uIDEvent: This identifies the timer to be destroyed. This parameter must be the same as the uIDEvent value passed to SetTimer if the window handle passed to SetTimer is valid. Otherwise, if the application calls SetTimer with hWnd set to zero, this parameter must be the timer identifier returned by SetTimer.

Return Values

If the function succeeds, it returns TRUE; otherwise it returns FALSE. To get extended error information, call the GetLastError function.

See also

SetTimer, WM_TIMER

Example

Listing 15-5: Setting and Removing a Timer

```
{our timer callback prototype}
procedure TimerProc(hWnd: HWND; uMsg: UINT; idEvent: UINT; Time: DWORD);stdcall;

var
  Form1: TForm1;
  DemoCounter: Integer;    // a counter to demonstrate that a timer is running

const
  EXAMPLETIMER = 1;        // a timer identifier

implementation

procedure TForm1.Button2Click(Sender: TObject);
begin
  {reset our counter}
  DemoCounter:= 0;

  {create a timer to fire once per second}
  SetTimer(Form1.Handle,    // handle of window for timer messages
           EXAMPLETIMER,    // timer identifier
           1000,            // fire every 1000 milliseconds
           @TimerProc       // address of timer procedure
           );
end;

{this function is run every time EXAMPLETIMER fires}
procedure TimerProc(hWnd: HWND; uMsg: UINT; idEvent: UINT; Time: DWORD);
begin
  {display a message to show that the timer is running}
  Form1.Label1.Caption:= 'Timer1 is Now Running: ' + IntToStr(DemoCounter);
```

```
  {increment a counter to show that the timer is running}
  Inc(DemoCounter);
end;

procedure TForm1.Button3Click(Sender: TObject);
begin
  {remove our example timer}
  KillTimer(Form1.Handle,    // handle of window that installed timer
            EXAMPLETIMER     // timer identifier
            );

   {clear the caption}
   Label1.Caption:='';
end;
```

QueryPerformanceCounter Windows.Pas

Syntax

```
QueryPerformanceCounter(
var lpPerformanceCount: TLargeInteger      {points to the current counter value}
): BOOL;                                   {returns TRUE or FALSE}
```

Description

If the hardware supports a high-resolution performance timing counter, this function retrieves the current value of this counter.

Parameters

lpPerformanceCount: The address of a TLargeInteger structure that will be set to the current high-resolution performance counter value.

Return Values

If the function succeeds and the hardware supports a high-resolution performance counter, it returns TRUE. If the function fails, or the hardware does not support a high-resolution performance counter, it returns FALSE.

See also

GetTickCount, QueryPerformanceFrequency

Example

Listing 15-6: Retrieving the Current High-Resolution Performance Counter Value

```
procedure TForm1.Button4Click(Sender: TObject);
var
  PerformanceCount: TLargeInteger;
begin
  {if there is a high-resolution performance counter in the hardware...}
```

```
  if QueryPerformanceCounter(PerformanceCount) then
     begin
       {...display its current counter...}
       Label1.Caption:= 'Performance Counter Present';
       Label2.Caption:= FloatToStr(PerformanceCount.QuadPart);
     end
  else
    {...or display a message}
    Label1.Caption:= 'Performance Counter Not Present';
end;
```

QueryPerformanceFrequency Windows.Pas

Syntax

QueryPerformanceFrequency(	
var lpFrequency: TLargeInteger	{points to the current frequency value}
): BOOL;	{returns TRUE or FALSE}

Description

If the hardware supports a high-resolution performance timing counter, this function retrieves the frequency of this counter in counts per second.

Parameters

lpFrequency: The address of a TLargeInteger structure that will be set to the high-resolution performance counter frequency in counts per second.

Return Values

If the function succeeds and the hardware supports a high-resolution performance counter, it returns TRUE. If the function fails, or the hardware does not support a high-resolution performance counter, it returns FALSE.

See also

QueryPerformanceCounter

Example

Listing 15-7: Retrieving the High-Resolution Performance Counter Frequency

```
procedure TForm1.Button5Click(Sender: TObject);
var
  PerformanceFrequency: TLargeInteger;
begin
  {if there is a high resolution performance counter in the hardware...}
  if QueryPerformanceFrequency(PerformanceFrequency) then
     begin
       {...display its frequency...}
       Label1.Caption:= 'Performance Frequency Present';
       Label2.Caption:= FloatToStr(PerformanceFrequency.QuadPart);
```

```
      end
    else
      {...or display a message}
      Label1.Caption:= 'Performance Frequency Not Present';
  end;
```

SetTimer   Windows.Pas

Syntax

SetTimer(
hWnd: HWND; {a handle to the window receiving timer messages}
nIDEvent: UINT; {the timer identifier}
uElapse: UINT; {the timeout value, in milliseconds}
lpTimerFunc: TFNTimerProc {a pointer to the callback procedure}
): UINT; {returns an integer identifying the new timer}

Description

This function creates a timer that fires at the specified timeout. When the time-out is reached, either the window procedure for the specified window receives a WM_TIMER message, or the function pointed to by the lpTimerFunc parameter is called. If a WM_TIMER message is received, the wParam parameter of the message contains the value passed in the nIDEvent parameter.

Parameters

hWnd: This is a handle to the window associated with the timer, and must be owned by the calling thread. If this parameter is zero, the nIDEvent parameter is ignored and no window is associated with this timer.

nIDEvent: This is an integer that uniquely identifies this timer. If the hWnd parameter is set to zero, this parameter is ignored.

uElapse: Specifies the timeout value, in milliseconds.

lpTimerFunc: The address of the application-defined callback function. This function is called every time the timeout value is reached. If this parameter is set to NIL, the system posts a WM_TIMER message to the application queue, and the hWnd member of the message's MSG structure contains the value of the hWnd parameter passed into this function.

Return Value

If the function succeeds, it returns an integer identifying the new timer; otherwise it returns zero. The KillTimer function can use this value to remove the timer.

Callback Syntax

TimerProc(
hWnd: HWND; {a handle to the window associated with the timer}

```
uMsg: UINT;                {the WM_TIMER message}
idEvent: UINT;             {the timer identifier}
dwTime: DWORD              {the current system time}
);                         {this procedure does not return a value}
```

Description

This function is called every time the timeout value for the timer is reached, if the lpTimerFunc parameter is set. This callback function can perform any desired task.

Parameters

hWnd: A handle to the window associated with the timer.

uMsg: This identifies the WM_TIMER message.

idEvent: This is the timer's identifier.

dwTime: This is the number of milliseconds since Windows was started, and is the same value returned by the GetTickCount function.

See also

KillTimer, WM_TIMER

Example

Please see Listing 15-5 under KillTimer.

Chapter 16

Error Functions

Every Windows function returns a value from which the developer can determine if the function failed or succeeded. When some functions fail, they set a value in the thread local storage that gives more information on the cause of the failure. The developer can retrieve this information for assistance in debugging or to provide the user with a more detailed explanation of program failure.

It is very uncommon these days for a user to buy a machine that does not have some form of audio output device. Users now associate certain sounds with error messages, and the Control Panel allows users to set up their own sounds for certain events. Windows provides functions that allow the developer to use these familiar sounds to alert the user that an error has occurred.

Error Descriptions

When an API function fails, most only return a value of FALSE, which may not be very helpful in determining the cause of the failure. Some functions indicate that the developer can call the GetLastError function to retrieve more information about the failure. This function, coupled with the FormatMessage function, can be very helpful in debugging an application or giving the user a more detailed explanation of an operating system error message. The following example will try to launch a nonexistent application. The operating system will display a message, and then the GetLastError and FormatMessage functions are used to retrieve a description of why the function failed. There are literally hundreds of error messages that can be retrieved by GetLastError, and they are all listed in the Windows.Pas file.

Listing 16-1: Retrieving More Information about a Function Failure

```
procedure TForm1.Button1Click(Sender: TObject);
var
  ExecInfo: TShellExecuteInfo;     // required for ShellExecuteEx
  ErrorMessage: Pointer;           // a pointer to the error message text
  ErrorCode: DWORD;                // holds the last error code
begin
  {prepare the data structure for the ShellExecuteEx function. This
   function will attempt to open a nonexistent file. This causes
```

```
   an error code to be set.}
  ExecInfo.cbSize       := SizeOf(TShellExecuteInfo);
  ExecInfo.fMask        := SEE_MASK_NOCLOSEPROCESS;
  ExecInfo.Wnd          := Form1.Handle;
  ExecInfo.lpVerb       := 'open';
  ExecInfo.lpFile       := 'c:\I_Do_Not_Exist.exe';
  ExecInfo.lpParameters := '';
  ExecInfo.lpDirectory  := '';
  ExecInfo.nShow        := SW_SHOWNORMAL;

  {attempt to open and launch the nonexistent file}
  ShellExecuteEx(@ExecInfo);

  {get the last error code for the calling thread}
  ErrorCode := GetLastError;

  {retrieve the string describing this error code}
  FormatMessage(FORMAT_MESSAGE_ALLOCATE_BUFFER or FORMAT_MESSAGE_FROM_SYSTEM,
                nil, ErrorCode, 0, @ErrorMessage, 0, nil);

  {display the value of the last error code and its associated description}
  MessageDlg('GetLastError result: '+IntToStr(ErrorCode)+#13+
             'Error Description: '+string(PChar(ErrorMessage)),
             mtError, [mbOk], 0);

  {Windows allocated the memory for the description string,
   so we must free it.}
  LocalFree(hlocal(ErrorMessage));
end;
```

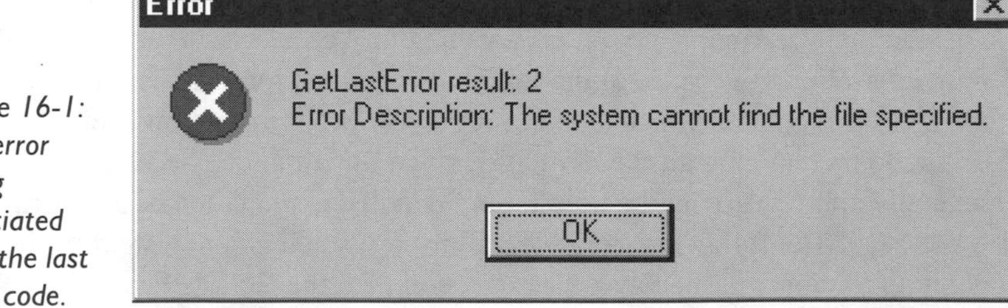

Figure 16-1: The error string associated with the last error code.

Audible Error Cues

The Sounds applet under the Control Panel allows users to associate sounds with certain events, including program or operating system errors such as the Exclamation or Asterisk events. The MessageBeep function allows a developer to alert the user of an error by playing the sounds they have associated for these events, as the following example demonstrates.

Listing 16-2: Alerting the User Through Sound

```
procedure TForm1.Button1Click(Sender: TObject);
begin
  {if the text in the edit boxes does not match...}
  if Edit1.Text<>Edit2.Text then
  begin
    {...play a sound and display a message alerting the user...}
    MessageBeep(MB_ICONEXCLAMATION);
    MessageDlg('The passwords did not match!', mtWarning, [mbOK], 0)
  end
  else
  begin
    {...or display a message alerting the user that
     the text in both edit boxes match}
    MessageDlg('Passwords matched.', mtInformation, [mbOK], 0)  end;
end;
```

Windows Error Functions

The following error functions are covered in this chapter:

Table 16-1: Windows Error Functions

Function	Description
Beep	Produces a standard beep.
ExitWindows	Closes all applications and logs off the user.
ExitWindowsEx	Shuts down the machine.
FatalAppExit	Forces the application to exit.
GetLastError	Retrieves the last error code.
MessageBeep	Plays specific sounds through the sound card.
SetLastError	Sets the error code.

Beep *Windows.Pas*

Syntax

```
Beep(
dwFreq: DWORD;              {the sound frequency}
dwDuration: DWORD           {the sound duration}
): BOOL;                    {returns TRUE or FALSE}
```

Description

This function plays simple tones through the PC speaker. It is synchronous, and will not return control to the application until the sound has finished. Under Windows 95, this function simply plays the default sound event on machines with a sound card, and the standard system beep on machines without one.

Parameters

dwFreq: The frequency of the sound, in hertz. This value must be between 37 and 32,767. Under Windows 95, this parameter is ignored.

dwDuration: The duration of the sound, in milliseconds. Under Windows 95, this parameter is ignored.

Return Value

If the function succeeds, it returns TRUE; otherwise it returns FALSE. To get extended error information, call the GetLastError function.

See also

MessageBeep

Example

Listing 16-3: Playing a Beep

```
procedure TForm1.Button1Click(Sender: TObject);
begin
  {under Windows 95, this plays the default beep sound}
  Windows.Beep(0,0)
end;
```

ExitWindows Windows.Pas

Syntax

```
ExitWindows(
dwReserved: DWORD;            {reserved}
Code: WORD                    {reserved}
): BOOL;                      {returns TRUE or FALSE}
```

Description

This function causes Windows to close all applications, log the current user off, and present the login dialog box. Under Windows NT, this function sends a WM_QUERYENDSESSION message to all running applications. Under Windows 95, this function sends a WM_QUERYENDSESSION message to all running applications except the one calling ExitWindows. Applications indicate they are shutting down by returning TRUE when receiving this message. If any application returns FALSE, the shutdown process is aborted. After the results of the WM_QUERYENDSESSION message have been processed, Windows sends a WM_ENDSESSION message to all running applications. The wParam parameter of the WM_ENDSESSION message is a nonzero value if the system is shutting down; otherwise it is zero. New applications cannot be launched during this process.

Parameters

dwReserved: This parameter is reserved and must be set to zero.

Code: This parameter is reserved and must be set to zero.

Return Value

If the function succeeds, it returns TRUE; otherwise it returns FALSE. To get extended error information, call the GetLastError function.

See also

ExitWindowsEx, WM_ENDSESSION, WM_QUERYENDSESSION

Example

Listing 16-4: Logging the User Off

```
procedure TForm1.Button1Click(Sender: TObject);
begin
  {then the button is pressed, Windows closes all
   applications and asks the user to log in}
  ExitWindows(0,0);
end;
```


ExitWindowsEx   Windows.Pas

Syntax

ExitWindowsEx(	
uFlags: UINT;	{a flag indicating the type of shutdown}
dwReserved: DWORD	{reserved}
): BOOL;	{returns TRUE or FALSE}

Description

This function can log a user off, power the system off, and reboot the system. Like the ExitWindows function, this function causes a series of WM_QUERYENDSESSION and WM_ENDSESSION messages to be sent to all processes, dependent upon the uFlags parameter. However, ExitWindowsEx returns immediately after the function is called and the shutdown process happens asynchronously, so the application cannot assume that all processes have been closed when the function returns. During this process, applications are given a specific amount of time to respond to the shutdown request. If the applications do not respond in this time period, a dialog box appears giving the user the options of forcing the application to close, retrying the shutdown, or canceling the shutdown request. If the EWX_FORCE flag is specified, this dialog box does not appear and all processes are forced to shut down. Under Windows NT, in order to shut down or restart the system the application must use the Windows NT API function AdjustTokenPrivileges to enable the SE_SHUTDOWN_NAME privilege.

Parameters

uFlags: A value indicating the type of shutdown. This flag can be one value from Table 16-2.

dwReserved: This parameter is reserved, and its value is ignored.

Return Value

If the function succeeds, it returns TRUE; otherwise it returns FALSE. To get extended error information, call the GetLastError function.

See also

ExitWindows, WM_ENDSESSION, WM_QUERYENDSESSION

Example

Listing 16-5: Shutting Down the System

```
procedure TForm1.Button1Click(Sender: TObject);
begin
  {when the button is clicked, Windows shuts the system down}
  ExitWindowsEx(EWX_SHUTDOWN, 0);
end;
```

Table 16-2: ExitWindowsEx uFlags Values

Value	Description
EWX_FORCE	Forces all processes to shut down. Windows does not send the WM_QUERYENDSESSION or WM_ENDSESSION messages to applications that are shut down. This can cause loss of data.
EWX_LOGOFF	Shuts down all running processes and logs off current user.
EWX_POWEROFF	Terminates all processes, logs the user off, shuts down the system, and turns off the power. The system must support the power off feature. Windows NT: The calling process must have the SE_SHUTDOWN_NAME privilege set.
EWX_REBOOT	Terminates all processes, logs the user off, shuts down the system, and reboots the machine. Windows NT: The calling process must have the SE_SHUTDOWN_NAME privilege set.
EWX_SHUTDOWN	Terminates all processes, logs the user off, and shuts down the system to the point where Windows displays the screen informing the user that it is safe to turn off the machine. Windows NT: The calling process must have the SE_SHUTDOWN_NAME privilege set.

FatalAppExit   Windows.Pas

Syntax

FatalAppExit(
uAction: UINT; {reserved}
lpMessageText: PChar {a pointer to a string}
); {this procedure does not return a value}

Description

This function displays a message box with the specified text, and terminates the application when the message box is closed. If a kernel debugger is running, the user can choose to cancel the message box and return to the application that called the FatalAppExit function. Use this function to terminate an application only when there is no other way to shut it down. FatalAppExit may not free memory or close files, and can cause a general failure of Windows.

Parameters

uAction: This parameter is reserved and must be set to zero.

lpMessageText: A pointer to a null-terminated string that is displayed in the message box. This message is displayed on a single line, and for low-resolution screens it should be no more than 35 characters long.

See also

ExitProcess, ExitThread, TerminateProcess, TerminateThread

Example

Listing 16-6: Terminating an Application

```
procedure TForm1.Button1Click(Sender: TObject);
begin
  {emergency termination of the application}
  FatalAppExit(0,'Terminating the application');
end;
```

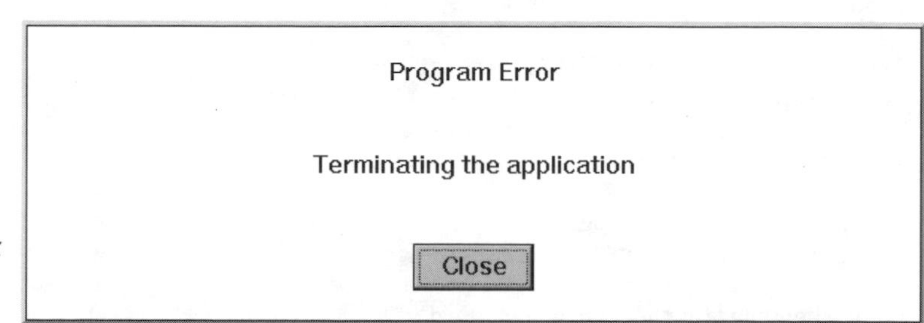

Figure 16-2: The dialog box presented by FatalAppExit.

GetLastError   Windows.Pas

Syntax

GetLastError: DWORD;   {returns the last error code}

Description

This function retrieves the last error code for the calling thread. This error code is set by calling the SetLastError function. The error code is a 32-bit value with the most significant bit as bit 31. Bit 29 is reserved for application-defined error codes, and will never be set by a Windows API function. If bit 29 is set, it indicates that the error code was defined by the calling application, and ensures that the error code does not conflict with any system-defined error codes. The developer should use GetLastError immediately when a function's return value indicates an error code is returned. Most API functions call SetLastError upon failure, but some call it upon success, setting the error code to zero and thus wiping out the error code from the function that last failed. Such cases are noted in the function reference. The error code is kept in thread local storage so multiple threads do not overwrite each other's error codes. The FormatMessage function can be used with the return value from GetLastError to retrieve a string describing the error for operating system error codes.

Return Value

If the function succeeds, it returns the last error code set by SetLastError. Individual function references list the conditions under which they use SetLastError to set the last error code. If the function fails, it returns zero.

See also

FormatMessage, SetLastError

Example

Listing 16-7: Setting and Retrieving the Last Error Code

```
procedure TForm1.Button1Click(Sender: TObject);
var
  ErrorCode: DWORD;   // holds our error code value
begin
  {set the last error code.  Bit 29 is set to indicate
   an application defined error code, and the low order
   word is set to a decimal value of 100}
  SetLastError($20000064);

  {retrieve the last error code}
  ErrorCode := GetLastError;

  {display the code in the low order word}
  Button1.Caption := 'User Defined Error Code: '+IntToStr(LoWord(ErrorCode));
end;
```

MessageBeep *Windows.Pas*

Syntax

```
MessageBeep(
uType: UINT                {the sound type}
): BOOL;                   {returns TRUE or FALSE}
```

Description

This function plays a wave through the sound card installed in the machine. This sound is played asynchronously, and control is immediately returned to the application. These sounds are assigned through the control panel, and are stored in the registry under the key HKEY_CURRENT_USER\AppEvents\Schemes\Apps\.Default. Individual sound events have their own key, and the current sound identified with the event is stored under its .Current key. If the specified sound could not be played, Windows attempts to play the system default sound. If the system default sound cannot be played, Windows outputs a standard beep sound through the PC speaker.

Parameters

uType: An integer identifying the sound to play. This parameter can be one value from Table 16-3.

Return Value

If the function succeeds, it returns TRUE; otherwise it returns FALSE. To get extended error information, call the GetLastError function.

See also

Beep

Example

Listing 16-8: Playing System Sounds

```
const
  {an array of sound constants}
  Sounds: array[0..5] of UINT = ($FFFFFFFF,MB_ICONASTERISK,MB_ICONEXCLAMATION,
                                 MB_ICONHAND,MB_ICONQUESTION,MB_OK);

implementation

procedure TForm1.Button1Click(Sender: TObject);
begin
  {play the selected sound}
  MessageBeep(Sounds[ComboBox1.ItemIndex]);
end;
```

Table 16-3: MessageBeep uType Values

Value	Description
$FFFFFFFF	A standard beep using the computer speaker.
MB_ICONASTERISK	The sound associated with the Asterisk event.
MB_ICONEXCLAMATION	The sound associated with the Exclamation event.
MB_ICONHAND	The sound associated with the Critical Stop event.
MB_ICONQUESTION	The sound associated with the Question event.
MB_OK	The sound associated with the Default Sound event.

SetLastError ***Windows.Pas***

Syntax

```
SetLastError(
dwErrCode: DWORD          {the error code}
);                        {this procedure does not return a value}
```

Description

This function sets the last error code for the calling thread. The error code is a 32-bit value with the most significant bit as bit 31. Bit 29 is reserved for application-defined error codes, and will never be set by a Windows API function. Setting this bit indicates that the error code was defined by the calling application, and ensures that the error code does not conflict with any system-defined error codes. Most API functions call SetLastError upon failure, but some call it upon success and such cases are noted in the function reference. The error code is kept in thread local storage so multiple threads do not overwrite each other's error codes. Use the GetLastError function to retrieve this value.

Parameters

dwErrCode: A value indicating the last error code for the calling thread.

See also

GetLastError

Example

Please see Listing 16-7 under GetLastError.

Appendix

Bibliography

There exists quite a large knowledge base on Windows programming in general and Delphi programming in particular. The information for this book is based in part on research and knowledge gleaned from the following books:

Miller, Powell, et. al., *Special Edition Using Delphi 3* [QUE, 1997]

Jarol, Haygood, and Coppola, *Delphi 2 Multimedia Adventure Set* [Coriolis Group Books, 1996]

Lischner, Ray, *Secrets of Delphi 2* [Waite Group Press, 1996]

Cooke and Telles, *Windows 95 How-To* [Waite Group Press, 1996]

Simon, Gouker, and Barnes, *Windows 95 Win32 Programming API Bible* [Waite Group Press, 1996]

Swan and Cogswell, *Delphi 32-Bit Programming Secrets* [IDG Books, 1996]

Pacheco and Teixeira, *Delphi 2 Developers Guide* [Sams Publishing, 1996]

Calvert, Charles, *Delphi 2 Unleashed* [Sams Publishing, 1996]

Wallace and Tendon, *Delphi 2 Developer's Solutions* [Waite Group Press, 1996]

Frerking, Wallace, and Niddery, *Borland Delphi How-To* [Waite Group Press, 1995]

Pietrek, Matt, *Windows 95 System Programming Secrets* [IDG Books, 1995]

Rector and Newcomer, *Win32 Programming* [Addison-Wesley Developers Press, 1997]

Petzold and Yao, *Programming Windows 95* [Microsoft Press, 1996]

Cluts, Nancy, *Programming The Windows 95 User Interface* [Microsoft Press, 1995]

Thorpe, Danny, *Delphi Component Design* [Addison-Wesley Developers Press, 1997]

Konopka, Ray, *Developing Custom Delphi 3 Components* [Coriolis Group Books, 1997]

Beveridge and Wiener, *Multithreading Applications in Win32*, [Addison-Wesley Developers Press, 1997]

Richter, Jeffrey, *Advanced Windows,* [Microsoft Press, 1997]

D

G

H

L

M

T

X

Z

The Tomes of Delphi 3: Win32 Core API CD Usage License Agreement

On the CD-ROM

The companion CD-ROM that accompanies this book is a multimedia experience containing all of the source code from the book, a complete Delphi syntax compliant help file, shareware, freeware, and an assortment of third-party development and evaluation tools. Using the CD browser you can navigate through the CD and choose which applications and chapter code to install with a single mouse click. Using the CD browser is simple; on a Windows 95 or Windows NT system, simply insert the CD and the browser will begin automatically.

Install Software allows you to install software included on the CD-ROM. Chapter Code allows you to install Delphi code included on the CD-ROM. API-Help Launch allows you to install the API Help file included on the CD-ROM. The help provides a nice companion to Delphi's help files, however, it is not a direct replacement for the Win32 SDK help file that ships with Delphi. In many cases, the Win32 help file will contain additional information that was impractical to include in the book or the help file.

NOTE: The CD browser requires a minimum of 256-color operation and a screen resolution of at least 640x480. Higher resolutions are recommended but not required for optimum viewing. Please review the system requirements for each individual application before installing the software. A description is provided along with system requirements for each application. All evaluation versions are capable of creating actual products, but in a limited form.